EUROPE

1450–1661

Derrick Murphy
Michael Tillbrook
Patrick Walsh-Atkins

Collins Educational

An Imprint of HarperCollinsPublishers

Published by Collins Educational
An imprint of HarperCollins *Publishers* Ltd
77–85 Fulham Palace Road
Hammersmith
London W6 8JB

www.**Collins**Education.com
On-line support for schools and colleges

ISBN 0 00 327130 7

Derrick Murphy, Michael Tillbrook and Patrick Walsh-Atkins assert the moral right to be identified as the authors of this work.

British Library Cataloguing in Publication Data
A catalogue record for this book is available from the British Library.

Edited by Steve Attmore
Design by Derek Lee
Cover design by Derek Lee
Map artwork by Tony Richardson
Picture research by Celia Dearing
Production by Kathryn Botterill
Printed and bound by Bath Press

Contents

ACKNOWLEDGEMENTS
Text extracts from the following titles are reprinted by permission of Addison Wesley Longman Ltd: *Spain 1469–1714: A Society in Conflict* (2nd edition, 1991); *The Emperor Charles V* by Martin Rady (Seminar Study, 1988); *Philip II* by Geoffrey Woodward (Seimanr Study, 1992); *The French Wars of Religion 1559–1598* by R. J. Knecht (1989); *Spain in the Seventeenth Century* by Graham Darby (Seminar Studies, 1994). Edward Arnold for extracts from *Imperial Spain 1469–1716* by J. H. Elliott (1963); *The Thirty Years' War and the Conflict for European Hegemony* by S. H. Steinberg (1966). Blackwell Publishers for extracts from *Spain under the Habsburgs 1516–1598* by John Lynch (2nd edition; Volume 1 of 'Empire and Absolutism', 1981); *Spain under the Habsburgs 1598–1700* by John Lynch (2nd edition, 1969); *The Hispanic World in Crisis and Change, 1598–1700* by John Lynch (1992). Cambridge University Press for permission to reproduce extracts from *The Ottoman Empire 1520–1566* by V. J. Parry (New Cambridge Modern History, 1962); *Rebels and Rulers 1600–1660* by Perez Zagorin (1982); *The French Wars of Religion 1562 to 1629* by Mack Holt (1995). HarperCollins Publishers Ltd for extracts from *The Rise and Fall of Renaissance France 1483–1610* by R. J. Knecht (1996); *The Rise and Fall of Great Powers 1500–2000* by Paul Kennedy (1988). Historical Association and Glyn Redworth for extract from *Government and Society in Late Medieval Spain*; and Koenrad Swart for extract from *William the Silent and the Revolt of the Netherlands* (1978). Hodder and Stoughton Educational Ltd for extracts from *Spain in the Reigns of Isabella and Ferdinand, 1474–1516* by Geoffrey Woodward (History in Depth, 1997). Macmillan Press Ltd for extracts from *A History of Sixteenth Century France 1483–1598* by Janine Garrison (1995); *The Birth of Absolutism. France 1598–1661* by Y-M Bercé (European Studies, 1996); *Early Modern Germany, 1477–1806* by Michael Hughes (1992). Oxford University Press for the extracts from *Early Habsburg Spain 1517–1598* by A. W. Lovett (1986); *Early Modern France* by Robin Briggs (1977). Pearson Education Ltd for extract from *Sixteenth Century Europe* by L. W. Cowie (Oliver & Boyd, 1977). Penguin Books Ltd for permission to reproduce approximately 85 words from *The Dutch Revolt* by Geoffrey Parker (Allen Lane 1977, revised edition 1985) © Geoffrey Parker (1977, 1985). Routledge for *The Thirty Years' War*, edited by Geoffrey Parker (2nd edition, 1997). Weidenfeld and Nicolson for extract from *The Golden Age of Spain 1516–1569* by Domiguez Ortiz (1971). Yale University Press as publisher for extracts from *Philip of Spain* by Henry Kamen (1997).

The publishers would like to thank the following for permission to reproduce pictures on these pages (T=Top, B=Bottom, L=Left, R=Right).

AKG London 64T, 68, Doge Palace, Venice 55, Galleria degli Uffizi, Florence 66, Bibliotheque Publique et Universitaire/Erich Lessing 80, Prado, Madrid 194; Bayerische Staatsbibliothek, Munich 368; **Bridgeman Art Library** 26, Galleria degli Uffizi, Florence 27, Palazzo Medici-Riccardi, Florence 28, National Gallery, London 29, Vatican Museums & Galleries 31, Pinacoteca di Brera, Milan 33, Private Collection 45, 100, 372, 378B, Kunsthistorisches Museum, Vienna 102, 378T, Alte Pinakothek, Munich 140, Monasterio de El Escorial Spain 184, Prado,Madrid 186, 298, Palazzo Pitti, Florence 191, Cheltenham Art Gallery & Museums 225, Victoria & Albert Museums, London 259, Royal Library, Stockholm 286, Musée des Beaux-Arts, Lille 313, Chateau de Versailles 317, Agnew & Sons 339L, Chateau de Versailles/Bulloz 339R; by permission of the **British Library** (146.i.10) 52, (3905 ccc 118) 96, (IC.9303)111, (C37 e.8) 136; **E.T. Archive** 156, 179, 201, 274, 315, 328, Koninklijke Museum Amberes Belgium 59; **Mary Evans Picture Library** 50, 60, 64B, 77, 79, 135, 150, 234, 263, Explorer 208; **Sonia Halliday Photographs** 49, 53; **Herzog August Bibliothek** Wolfenbüttel 359T(1H 210), 359B(1H 170); **Prentenkabinet**, University of Leiden 243.

Cover picture: English Ships and the Spanish Armada August 1588, English School. National Maritime Museum, London/Bridgeman Art Library.

Every effort has been made to contact the holders of copyright material, but if any have been inadvertently overlooked, the Publishers will be pleased to make the necessary arrangements at the first opportunity.

Study and examination skills

This chapter of the book is designed to aid Sixth Form students in their preparation for public examinations in History.

- Differences between GCSE and Sixth Form History
- Extended writing: the structured question and the essay
- How to handle sources in Sixth Form History
- Historical interpretation
- Progression in Sixth Form History
- Examination techniques

Differences between GCSE and Sixth Form History

- **The amount of factual knowledge required for answers to Sixth Form History** questions is more detailed than at GCSE. Factual knowledge in the Sixth Form is used as supporting evidence to help answer historical questions. Knowing the facts is important but not as important as knowing that factual knowledge supports historical analysis.

- **Extended writing is more important in Sixth Form History.** Students will be expected to answer either structured questions or essays.

Structured questions require students to answer more than one question on a given topic. For example:

1. In what ways did Ferdinand and Isabella increase the power of the monarchy in Castile and Aragon during their reigns?

2. To what extent did Ferdinand and Isabella establish a 'New Monarchy'?

Each part of the structured question demands a different approach.

Essay questions require students to produce one answer to a given question. For example:

To what extent did Spanish government under Charles I differ from government during the reign of the Catholic Monarchs (Ferdinand and Isabella)?

Similarities with GCSE

- Source analysis and evaluation

The skills in handling historical sources which were acquired at GCSE are developed in Sixth Form History. In the Sixth Form sources have to be analysed in their historical context, so a good factual knowledge of the subject is important.

● **Historical interpretations**

Skills in historical interpretation at GCSE are also developed in Sixth Form History. The ability to put forward different historical interpretations is important. Students will also be expected to explain why different historical interpretations have occurred.

Extended writing: the structured question and the essay

When faced with extended writing in Sixth Form History students can improve their performance by following a simple routine that attempts to ensure they achieve their best performance.

Answering the question

What are the command instructions?

Different questions require different types of response. For instance, 'In what ways' requires students to point out the various ways something took place in History; 'Why' questions expect students to deal with the causes or consequences of an historical question.

Are there key words or phrases that require definition or explanation?

It is important for students to show that they understand the meaning of the question. To do this, certain historical terms or words require explanation. For instance, if a question asked 'how far' a king or politician was an 'innovator', an explanation of the word 'innovator' would be required.

Does the question have specific dates or issues that require coverage?

If a question mentions specific dates, these must be adhered to. For instance, if you are asked to answer a question on the foreign policy of France it may state clear date limits such as 1498 to 1559. Also questions may mention a specific aspect such as 'domestic', 'religious', 'social' or 'economic'.

Planning your answer

Once you have decided on what the question requires, write a brief plan. For structured questions this may be brief. This is a useful procedure to make sure that you have ordered the information you require for your answer to make sure that you have ordered the information you require for your answer in the most effective way. For instance, in a balanced, analytical answer this may take the form of jotting down the main points for and against an historical issue raised in the question.

Writing the answer

Communication skills

The quality of written English is important in Sixth Form History. The way you present your ideas on paper can affect the quality of your answer. Since 1996 the Government have placed emphasis on the quality of written English in the Sixth Form. Therefore, punctuation, spelling and grammar, which were awarded marks at GCSE, require close attention. Use a dictionary if you are unsure of a word's meaning or spelling. Use the glossary of terms you will find in this book to help you.

The introduction

For structured questions you may wish to dispense with an introduction altogether and begin writing reasons to support an answer straight away.

However, essay answers should begin with an introduction. These should be both concise and precise. Introductions help 'concentrate the mind' on the question you are about to answer. Remember, do not try to write a conclusion as your opening sentence. Instead, outline briefly the areas you intend to discuss in your answer.

Balancing analysis with factual evidence
It is important to remember that factual knowledge should be used to support analysis. Merely 'telling the story' of an historical event is not enough. A structured question or essay should contain separate paragraphs, each addressing an analytical point that helps to answer the question. If, for example, the question asks for reasons why the Thirty Years' War began, each paragraph should provide a reason for the outbreak of war.

Seeing connections between reasons
In dealing with 'why'-type questions it is important to remember that the reasons for an historical event might be interconnected. Therefore, it is important to mention the connection between reasons. Also, it might be important to identify a hierarchy of reasons – that is, are some reasons more important than others in explaining an historical event?

Using quotations and statistical data
One aspect of supporting evidence that sustains analysis is the use of quotations. These can either be from an historian or a contemporary. However, unless these quotations are linked with analysis and supporting evidence, they tend to be of little value.

It can also be useful to support analysis with statistical data. In questions that deal with social and economic change, precise statistics which support your argument can be very persuasive.

Source analysis

Source analysis forms an integral part of the study of History. In Sixth Form History source analysis is identified as an important skill in Assessment Objective 3.

In dealing with sources you should be aware that historical sources must be used 'in historical context' in Sixth Form History. Therefore, in this book sources are used with the factual information in each chapter. Also, specific source analysis questions are included.

Assessment Objectives in Sixth Form History

1 knowledge and understanding of history

2 evaluation and analysis skills

3 a) source analysis in historical context

   b) historical interpretation

How to handle sources in Sixth Form History

In dealing with sources a number of basic hints will allow you to deal effectively with source-based questions, and to build on your knowledge and skill in using sources at GCSE.

Written sources

Attribution and date

It is important to identify who has written the source and when it was written. This information can be very important. If, for instance, a source was a private letter between Philip II and the Duke of Alba on the disturbances in the Netherlands in 1568, this information could be of considerable importance if you are asked about the usefulness (utility) or reliability of the source as evidence of Philip II's foreign policy.

It is important to note that just because a source is a primary source does not mean it is more useful or less reliable than a secondary source. Both primary and secondary sources need to be analysed to decide how useful and reliable they are. This can be determined by studying other issues.

Is the content factual or opinionated?

Once you have identified the author and date of the source it is important to study its content. The content may be factual, stating what has happened or what may happen. On the other hand, it may contain opinions that should be handled with caution. These may contain bias. Even if a source is mainly factual, there might be important and deliberate gaps in factual evidence that can make a source biased and unreliable. Usually, written sources contain elements of both opinion and factual evidence. It is important to judge the balance between these two parts.

Has the source been written for a particular audience?

To determine the reliability of a source it is important to identify to whom it is directed. For instance, a public speech may be made to achieve a particular purpose and may not contain the author's true beliefs or feelings. In contrast, a private diary entry may be much more reliable in this respect.

Corroborative evidence

To test whether or not a source is reliable, the use of other evidence to support or corroborate the information it contains is important. Cross-referencing with other sources is a way of achieving this; so is cross-referencing with historical information contained within a chapter.

Visual sources

Maps

Maps which appear in Sixth Form History are either contemporary or secondary sources. These are used to support factual coverage in the text by providing information in a different medium. Therefore, to assess whether or not information contained in maps is accurate or useful, reference should be made to other information. It is also important with line written sources to check the attribution and date. These could be significant.

Statistical data and graphs

It is important when dealing with this type of source to check carefully the nature of the information contained in date or in a graph. It might state the information in old forms of measurement such as pre-decimal currency: pounds, shillings and pence. One pound equalled 20 shillings, or 240 pence. It might also be stated in foreign currency, such as maravedis in Spain. Be careful to check if the information is in **index numbers**. These are a statistical device where a base year is chosen and given the figure 100. All other figures are based on a percentage difference from that base year. For instance, if 1500 is taken as base year for wool exports it is given a figure of 100. If the index number for 1505 is 117 it means that wool exports have risen 17% since 1500.

An important point to remember when dealing with data and graphs over a period of time is to identify trends and patterns in the information. Merely describing the information in written form is not enough.

Historical interpretation

An important feature of both GCSE and Sixth Form History is the issue of historical interpretation. In Sixth Form History it is important for students to be able to explain why historians differ, or have differed, in their interpretations of the past.

Availability of evidence

An important reason is the availability of evidence on which to base historical judgements. As new evidence comes to light, historians today may have more information on which to base their judgements than historians in the past. For instance, sources for early modern Europe include Philip II's state papers, including correspondence between the King and individuals such as Spanish ambassadors at other courts. Occasionally new evidence comes to light which may influence judgements about early modern European history.

Archaeological evidence is also important. The archaeological study of ships such as those used for the Spanish Armada, in 1558, has produced considerable evidence of naval warfare and weapons during the latter years of the 16th century.

'A philosophy of history?'

Many historians have a specific view of history that will affect the way they make their historical judgements. For instance, Marxist historians – who take the view from the writings of Karl Marx, the founder of modern socialism – believe that society has been made up of competing economic and social classes. They also place considerable importance on economic reasons in human decision making.

The role of the individual

Some historians have seen past history as being moulded by the acts of specific individuals who have changed history. Martin Luther, Suleiman the Magnificent, Charles V and Philip II are seen as individuals whose personalities and beliefs changed the course of 16th-century history. Other historians have tended to 'downplay' the role of individuals; instead, they highlight the importance of more general social, economic and political change. Rather than seeing Lorenzo de Medici, Jean Calvin or Ignatius Loyola as individuals who changed the course of history, these historians tend to see them as representing the views of wider social, religious or economic change.

Placing different emphasis on the same historical evidence

Even if historians do not possess different philosophies of history or place different emphasis on the role of the individual, it is still possible for them to disagree because they place different emphases on aspects of the same factual evidence. As a result, Sixth Form History should be seen as a subject that encourages debate about the past based on historical evidence.

Progression in Sixth Form History

The ability to achieve high standards in Sixth Form History involves the acquisition of a number of skills:

● Good written communication skills

● Acquiring a sound factual knowledge

● Evaluating factual evidence and making historical conclusions based on that evidence

● Source analysis

● Understanding the nature of historical interpretation

● Understanding the causes and consequences of historical events

● Understanding the themes in history which will involve a study of a specific topic over a long period of time

● Understanding the ideas of change and continuity associated with themes.

Students should be aware that the acquisition of these skills will take place gradually over the time spent in the Sixth Form. At the beginning of the course the main emphasis may be on the acquisition of factual knowledge, particularly when the body of knowledge studied at GCSE was different.

When dealing with causation students will have to build on their skills from GCSE. They will not only be expected to identify reasons for an historical event but also to provide a hierarchy of causes. They should identify the main causes and less important causes. They may also identify that causes may be interconnected and linked. Progression in Sixth Form History will come with answering the questions at the end of each sub-section in this book and practising the skills outlines through the use of the factual knowledge contained in the book.

Examination techniques

The ultimate challenge for any Sixth Form historian is the ability to produce quality work under examination conditions. Examinations will take the form of either modular examinations taken in January and June or in an 'end of course' set of examinations.

Here is some advice on how to improve your performance in an examination.

● **Read the whole examination paper thoroughly**
Make sure that the questions you choose are those for which you can produce a good answer. Don't rush – allow time to decide which questions to choose. It is probably too late to change your mind half way through answering a question.

● **Read the question very carefully**

Once you have made the decision to answer a specific question, read it very carefully. Make sure you understand the precise demands of the question. Think about what is required in your answer. It is much better to think about this before you start writing, rather than trying to steer your essay in a different direction half way through.

● **Make a brief plan**

Sketch out what you intend to include in your answer. Order the points you want to make. Examiners are not impressed with additional information included at the end of the essay, with indicators such as arrows or asterisks.

● **Pace yourself as you write**

Success in examinations has a lot to do with successful time management. If, for instance, you have to answer an essay question in approximately 45 minutes then you should be one-third of the way through after 15 minutes. With 30 minutes gone you should start writing the last third of your answer.

Where a question is divided into sub-questions make sure you look at the mark tariff for each question. If in a 20-mark question a sub-question is worth a maximum of 5 marks then you should spend approximately one-quarter of the time allocated for the whole question on this sub-question.

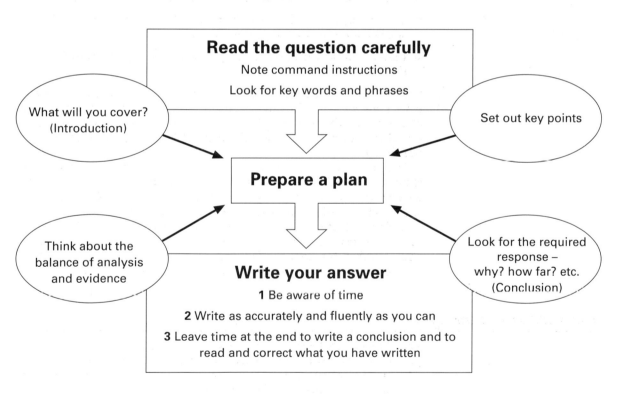

Europe 1450–1661: a synoptic assessment

Key Issues

● *In what ways did European international relations change between c.1450 and 1661?*

● *How significant were the social and religious changes that took place between c.1450 and 1661?*

● *How far did rulers increase their political power within their own states between c.1450 and 1661?*

1.1 What changes took place in international relations in Europe between c.1450 and 1661?

Perhaps the most significant change in international relations in this period was the rise in political power in Ottoman Turkey. As a relatively minor Middle European power the Ottoman Empire became the most powerful state in 16th-century Europe.

A significant date in the rise of Ottoman power was the capture of Constantinople in 1453. In the following century Ottoman power spread to include the Balkans, the Middle East and North Africa.

The Ottoman Turks were able to expand rapidly for a variety of reasons. The weakness and disunity of Christian states in Europe was important. For much of the period of Ottoman expansion France and the Habsburg lands were engaged in conflict. At the height of the conflict, in 1535, France even allied with the Turks against Charles V.

Ottoman strengths were also important. The Ottoman army was well organised and effectively led. The state was also fortunate in having a succession of very capable sultans: Mehmed II and Suleiman the Magnificent provided excellent leadership. It was only after Suleiman's death in 1566 that Ottoman expansion began to slow down. However, Ottoman power was still considerable. As late as 1683 the Ottomans were able to lay siege to Vienna.

What made the Ottomans such a formidable foe was the issue of religion. As an Islamic state, the conflict between Ottoman Turkey and Christian states took on the appearance of a Crusade or Jihad (Muslim Holy War).

The Ottoman impact on Europe was considerable. They occupied the Balkans and controlled the eastern Mediterranean. They also briefly threatened Italy and the Habsburg lands in Austria and western Hungary. Occasionally, the Ottomans and their allies were able to launch raids against the Spanish Mediterranean coast.

Another major change in international relations in the period was the creation of the union of Poland and Lithuania made at the Treaty of Lublin in 1569. This act created Europe's largest state, which dominated eastern Europe. Even the growth in power of Muscovy under Ivan III and Ivan IV had little impact on European international relations before 1661.

Towards the end of the period the most significant developments were the rise in power of Sweden and the United Provinces. Under Gustavus Vasa, the Swedish monarchy began to increase its power and wealth. However, it wasn't until the reign of Gustavus Adolphus, in the early 17th century, that Sweden began to have a major impact on the European stage. The entry of Sweden into the Thirty Years' War, in June 1630, was a turning point in that conflict. The Swedes prevented the victory of the Catholic-Habsburg forces and helped to ensure the survival of Protestantism in northern Germany. By the time of the Peace of Westphalia in 1648, Sweden had become the dominant power in the Baltic region.

The Dutch Revolt, from the 1560s, led to the creation of one of the 17th century's most dynamic states. Geographically centred at the mouth of a major river system and at the crossroad between the Mediterranean and Baltic seas, the United Provinces had become an important European power by the end of the Thirty Years' War.

Although economically wealthy, the individual Italian states remained politically weak. For virtually the whole period the Italian peninsula remained divided and under Spanish domination. From 1494 to 1559 it was the scene of a major conflict between France and the Habsburgs.

In western Europe the two most significant developments were the recovery of France and the rise and decline of Spain.

1.2 Why did French and Spanish influence on international affairs change during the period?

At the beginning of the period both France and Spain had limited influence in European affairs. France was still engaged in the 100 Years' War against England (1337–1453). Large areas of territory, technically part of France, were outside the control of the French king. These included lands held by England such as Calais, Burgundy and Brittany. By the mid 17th century France had become the dominant power in western Europe.

The recovery of France to a position of power in Europe began under Louis XI (1461–1483). He increased the financial power of the French monarchy and gained the Duchy of Burgundy in 1477. A major change in France's position in Europe came during the reign of Charles VIII. In 1494 he invaded Italy. His initial gain was to take over the Kingdom of Naples. The invasion, however, led to the long-term involvement of France in Italian affairs, which lasted until the Treaty of Câteau-Cambrésis in 1559.

The Italian wars became part of a wider conflict involving France. By 1519 Charles of Habsburg had become ruler of Spain and Holy Roman Emperor. From 1519 the Italian wars became part of the Habsburg–Valois wars. During these wars France attempted to maintain its position in Italy and also to break the encirclement of French territory by the Habsburgs (see map). The need to extend control on its eastern frontier in order to break Habsburg encirclement was a feature of French foreign policy into the late 17th century.

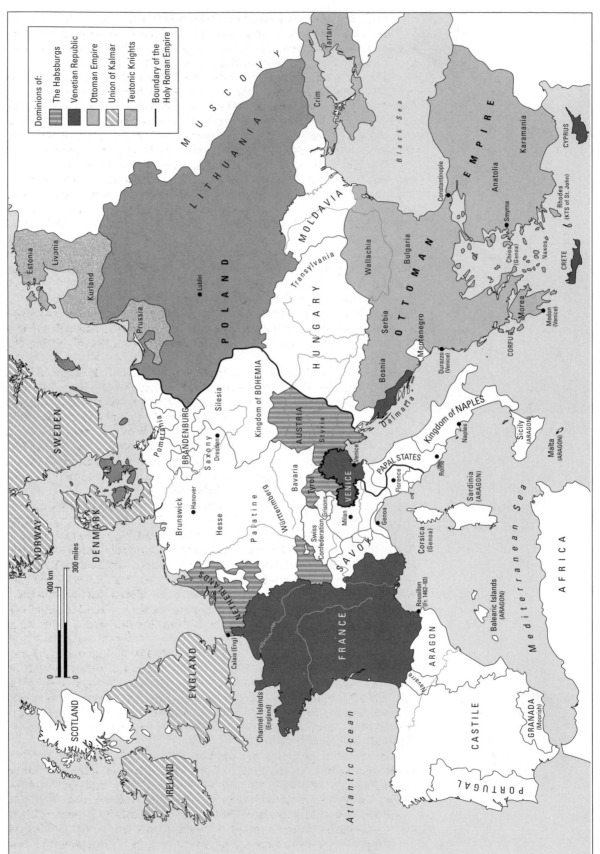

Europe in 1490

French influence in European affairs was not limited to Italy and the Habsburg–Valois wars. France also had influence, at various times, in Scotland. French influence reached a peak in 1558–59 when Mary of Guise and French army occupied and controlled central Scotland.

France was a major power in western European affairs for much of this period. However, the civil wars, known as the French Wars of Religion (1562–1598) greatly affected France's international position. Instead, France became an arena for foreign intervention. The English intervened in 1562–63 by briefly taking Le Havre. During the Wars of Religion, Protestant princes such as John Casimir of the Palatinate intervened.

The year 1598 stands out as an important turning point in French history. Not only did the Wars of Religion end, but also under Henry IV (1589–1610) France increased its influence in international affairs. It was not until the reign of Louis XIII (1610–1643) that France began to reassert itself as a major European power. Under the guidance of Cardinal Richelieu, France entered the Thirty Years' War in 1635. In 1643, at the Battle of Rocroi, the French heavily defeated the Spanish army. By the Treaty of the Pyrenees of 1659 with Spain, France had established itself as western Europe's major power.

Spain's international fortunes followed a different course. The period 1450–1659 could be regarded as witnessing the rise and decline of Spain as a great power in Europe. However, some historians note that Spain remained a major European power until the end of the War of the Spanish Succession (1713).

The rise of Spain was due to a mixture of effective leadership and luck. Until the middle of the 15th century the Iberian peninsula was divided into a number of states: Portugal, Aragon, Castile, Navarre and Granada (see map). Between 1469 and 1504 Castile and Aragon were united under the same monarchs. Both Navarre and Granada became part of Castile. In addition, Spain had territories in Italy (Sardinia and Naples) as well as new lands in the Americas. The clever diplomacy of Ferdinand of Aragon and the effectiveness of Spanish troops meant that Spain became a major power in the western and central Mediterranean.

Spain's transformation into western Europe's most powerful state began with the death of Ferdinand of Aragon in 1516. He was succeeded by Charles of Habsburg. In the period 1516–1519 Charles became King of Spain, ruler of the Netherlands and Austria, and Holy Roman Emperor. From 1519 until his abdication in 1556 Charles V dominated European affairs. He was almost continuously at war with France. He also faced conflict with Protestant princes in the Holy Roman Empire and the Ottoman Turks. In addition, he was ruler of a vast empire in the Americas. The New World territories provided Charles V and his successors with large amounts of gold and silver bullion.

It was during the reign of Philip II (1556–1598) that Spanish power reached its greatest extent. This was due, in part, to factors outside Philip II's control. From 1562 France was affected by the Wars of Religion. Also, after 1578, the Turks became less of a threat as they became involved in a war against Persia (Iran). Philip II was able to control Italy and the western Mediterranean. From 1580, he also acquired Portugal and the Portuguese overseas empire.

Nevertheless, Spanish power was not unlimited. From the 1560s, Spain faced a major internal rebellion in the northern Netherlands – the Dutch Revolt. From 1585, Spain became involved in a war with England that proved inconclusive. Then in 1584, Spain intervened in France.

Under Philip II's successor, Philip III (1598–1621), Spain continued to be western Europe's major power. However, under Philip IV (1621–1665) Spanish influence declined. In 1648 Spain was forced to recognise the independence of the United Provinces (see page 220). In 1659 France overtook Spain's position in western Europe. Since the 17th century, historians have attempted to explain why Spanish power declined. Henry Kamen goes so far as to say that Spanish power did not decline because it never possessed the economic and financial power to be a great power in the first place. Once France had recovered from the Wars of Religion, Spain's position was bound to be threatened.

1.3 To what extent did Europe experience social and economic change between c.1450 and 1661?

Europe in the period under review went through a time of profound social and economic change. So much so that, traditionally, this period is regarded as the beginning of early modern history and the end of medieval Europe.

A major influence on the social changes was the Renaissance, which began in Italy and subsequently, affected most of western and central Europe. The new ideas associated with a rediscovery of classical writing of ancient Greece and Rome altered people's perception of the role of the human race. New developments in art, architecture and learning re-established the study of human behaviour, in its widest sense. The artistic work of Leonardo da Vinci and the religious writings of Desiderius Erasmus can be seen as part of this intellectual and cultural change.

The development of printing was of critical importance in the development and spread of new ideas. By 1661 a large proportion of the upper classes across Europe had become literate. Books and pamphlets had become widely available. As a result, the control of knowledge, once the preserve of the Church, now became widely available. By the mid 17th century the astronomical discoveries of Copernicus and Galileo had transformed the view of humankind's place in the Universe.

The voyages of exploration and the discovery of new lands also changed the western European view of the world radically. By 1661 countries on the edge of Europe, such as Spain and Portugal, had acquired large overseas empires across the globe. The discovery of the Americas meant that countries on the western edge of Europe, such as England, France, Portugal and Spain, now began to dominate trade. The Holy Roman Empire went into a period of relative economic decline. The most dramatic example of a change in economic and trading power is that of the United Provinces. By 1661 they had come to dominate trade in the Baltic and around north-west Europe. From the beginning of the 17th century they had begun to make major inroads into trade in the East Indies (Indonesia) and South America.

The social and economic impact of the discovery of New Lands was not always beneficial. The influx of Spanish silver into the European economy in the second half of the 17th century helped to fuel a rise in prices (inflation). This had a detrimental effect on the cost of living of the lower classes. It also had an impact on the wealth of the landowning classes.

The period between c.1450 and 1661 is also characterised by a general rise in population. The 14th century had seen the devastating effects of the Black Death which was responsible for the death of around a third of Europe's population. From the mid 15th century to the end of the 16th century, European population increased. This was due to a number of factors. Not only was the incidence of plague reduced, but also child mortality fell. The average age of marriage also fell. Nevertheless, Europe was still affected by the adverse effects of poor harvests, disease and warfare. The 1590s were a period when these problems created severe problems for western European states, such as France, England and Spain. By the first half of the 17th century social and economic problems became so acute that historians have written about the 'general crisis of the 17th century'.

1.4 What impact did the Reformation have on European affairs?

Papacy: The position, power and authority of the Pope, including the length of time that a particular person holds this position.

The Reformation, which took place in Europe in the 16th and 17th centuries, involved two interlocking developments. Firstly, there was the Catholic Reformation. This involved the reform of the Catholic Church. In the 14th century the western Christian Church had been affected by a 'great schism' (division or split) in the **Papacy**. From 1378 to 1417 two popes resided over the Catholic Church, one in Rome and one in Avignon, France. At the start of the 15th century the reunification of the Church took place under Pope Martin. From the 15th century onwards attempts were made to reform religious orders, to found new orders and to end corruption within the Church.

Following the outbreak of the Protestant Reformation, the Catholic reform movement also involved attempts to win back to the Catholic Church lands lost to Protestantism. This phase of the Catholic Reformation has been called the Counter Reformation. The central policy-making body of the Counter Reformation was the Council of Trent (1545–1563). This General Council of the Catholic Church reformed the Church as an institution and produced a standard set of rules covering religious practices. In addition, a new religious order, the Society of Jesus (founded in 1540), led the campaign to win back lands lost to Protestantism. Jesuits not only worked in Europe, where the reconversion of Poland-Lithuania was their major achievement, but also in the New World and Far East. Jesuits helped to bring Catholicism to Japan and China under the leadership of St Francis Xavier.

Another important institution in defending Catholicism was the Holy Inquisition. This operated in Italy and, most notably, in Spain. The organisation attempted to identify non-Catholics and forced them either to return to Catholicism or face death.

As a result of the Catholic and Counter Reformations, the Catholic Church was stronger and more unified by 1661 than it had been in 1450.

The Protestant Reformation must stand as the most important social and religious development of the period. Beginning with the Lutheran Reformation in Germany and Scandinavia, Protestantism took on many forms. In England, a unique brand – the Church of England – contained elements of Lutheranism, Catholicism and Calvinism. It was the latter version of Protestantism which had a profound impact across western and central Europe. Founded in 1541 by Jean Calvin, Calvinism spread from Switzerland across the Netherlands, France and Scotland. Calvinism also had an important impact on England and on the Holy Roman Empire. The Thirty Years' War (1618–1648) can be seen, in part, as a conflict between the Catholic Habsburgs and their Protestant opponents. By the Treaty of Westphalia, which ended the war, Protestantism was firmly entrenched in Scandinavia, the United Provinces and the northern Holy Roman Empire (see map on page 18).

The Protestant Reformation not only affected religious belief it was also closely linked to political developments. By claiming authority over the Church within its own lands, the Protestant Princes of the Holy Roman Empire extended their own political power at the expense of both Catholic Church and Holy Roman Emperor. In England, control over the Church increased the Tudor Monarchy's political power and financial wealth. At the other extreme, Calvinism in France was seen as a 'state within a state' undermining the authority of the French King.

Europe in 1648, after the Treaty of Westphalia

1.5 How far were New Monarchies created in Europe between c.1450 and 1661?

1. What do you regard as the most important developments in European history between c.1450 and 1661 in

a) political affairs

b) religious affairs

c) social and economic affairs?

2. How far did European politics and society change between c.1450 and 1661?

One of the main differences between medieval and early modern Europe is supposed to be the rise of new types of political state. Known in the past as 'New Monarchies', these states had similar characteristics. The monarch increased his or her political power. This was done at the expense of the Church, the landowning classes (the **aristocracy**) and representative bodies such as local assemblies and national parliaments. At part of this development a new class of advisers and assistants aided monarchs. These were university-trained lawyers from the middle classes. In the 1533 Act of Supremacy Henry VIII declared England to be 'an empire'. This meant England was a completely independent state free from foreign interference.

Clearly, several of these characteristics can be found in England, France and Spain. In England, historians have referred to the creation of a 'Tudor Despotism (dictatorship)' beginning with the reign of Henry VIII. Later, in the 17th century, Charles I was accused of ruling as a tyrant during the years 1629 to 1640, without parliaments. Historians have stated that during the reigns of Francis I (1515–1547) and Henry II (1547–1559) France moved towards an 'absolute monarchy'. In Spain the Catholic monarchs, Ferdinand and Isabella (1479–1516), increased the power of the monarchy over both the Church and the nobility.

Although it is clear that monarchic power did increase in these states during the late 15th and 16th centuries, it did not mean that representative institutions and the aristocracy lost all political power. Within France the *parlement* retained the power to register royal edicts. Spain was a *monarquia* rather than a unified state. Throughout the period it was divided into Castile, Aragon and territories in the Netherlands and Italy. Each part was separate but owed allegiance to the same monarch. In England, France and Spain opposition to either centralisation or the growth of monarchic power led to a backlash. In England between 1642 and 1649 it led to civil war. In France in 1648 it resulted in the Frondes. Finally, in Spain it resulted in the revolt of Catalonia and Portugal in 1640.

An area that also saw a rise in the power of individual rulers was the Holy Roman Empire. From the late 15th century individual princes and rulers were increasing their own political power at the expense of the Holy Roman Emperor. This process was speeded up during the Reformation. By the Peace of Augsburg, 1555, the Holy Roman Emperor's power was greatly reduced. Individual Protestant princes now had power over both politics and religion within their own state. The Thirty Years' War saw the completion of this process. By 1661 the position of the Holy Roman Emperor had become a title of honour only, lacking any real political power.

The period 1450 to 1661 saw the collapse of the last remnants of the unity of western Christendom, which was meant to be a feature of medieval Europe. To many historians this period saw the emergence of completely independent 'nation states'.

The Italian Renaissance and voyages of discovery

Key Issues

● *How much continuity was there between medieval and Renaissance culture?*

● *To what extent did the Italian Renaissance represent a revival of interest in the classical past?*

● *How important were the voyages of discovery?*

Framework of Events

1397	Chrysoloras arrives in Florence to teach Greek
1401	Ghiberti begins work on the Baptistery doors in Florence
1414	Poggio Bracciolini discovers lost texts of Cicero, Lucretius, Quintilian and Vitruvius
1418–19	Work begins on Brunelleschi's great buildings, the Ospedale degli Innocenti and the Duomo in Florence
1434	Cosimo de' Medici assumes power in Florence
1436	Fra Angelico works on frescoes in the Priory of San Marco in Florence
1440	Federigo da Montefeltro becomes Duke of Urbino
1444	Building of Palazzo Ducale in Urbino begins
1450	Tempio Malatestino in Rimini, designed by Alberti
1456	John Argyropoulos is appointed Professor of Greek in Florence
1459	Frescoes in Medici Chapel painted by Benozzo Gozzoli
1468	Cardinal Bessarion presents his collection of Greek books to Venice
1469	Lorenzo de' Medici ('il Magnifico') assumes power in Florence
1478	Pazzi Conspiracy in Florence. Botticelli paints 'Primavera'
1485	Botticelli paints 'The Birth of Venus'. Ficino translates Plato
1490	Aldine Press set up in Venice by Manutius (publishing Greek authors by 1502)
1492	Death of Lorenzo de' Medici
1498	Execution of Savonarola in Florence
1506	Bramante begins work on new St Peter's in Rome
1508	Michelangelo begins painting the ceiling of the Sistine Chapel
	Raphael begins painting the 'Stanza della Segnatura', including 'The School at Athens', in the Vatican Palace
1512	Collapse of Florentine republic
1527	Sack of Rome
1532	Machiavelli's *Prince* is published.

Overview

THE term 'Renaissance' literally means 're-birth'. Scholars such as Ficino and Bruni were conscious they were living through a period of 're-birth'. Amongst historians, however, the term was not popularised until the middle of the 19th century. The French historian Jules Michelet, writing in 1855, used the term 'Renaissance' to describe the history of Europe during the 15th and 16th centuries. Shortly afterwards, the Swiss historian Jakob Burckhardt declared that the Renaissance marked the point at which the modern world emerged from the **Gothic barbarism** of the Middle Ages, an interpretation of cultural change that few current historians would accept.

Gothic barbarism: The term 'Gothic' was originally coined as a term of abuse, because it implied that the main features of Gothic art and architecture were associated with the tribes of barbarians who had overthrown the civilisation of the Roman Empire. In turn, 'Gothic barbarism' was overthrown by the civilising values of the Renaissance.

What can be accepted about the Italian Renaissance is that it was a period of immense cultural achievement – in the visual arts, literature and music – in the 15th and early 16th centuries.

The Renaissance began in Italy, primarily because Italy benefited from three advantages.

● Its Roman ruins still dominated the landscape and thereby demonstrated in a clear form the perceived greatness of classical civilisation. Many architects, for example Leon Alberti and Donato Bramante, were inspired by the buildings of ancient Rome.

● Northern Italy enjoyed immense wealth from trade and manufacturing.

● Its political culture, like that of ancient Greece, was based on the city state.

Map of Italy in 16th century showing the percentage of art commissioned 1280–1550

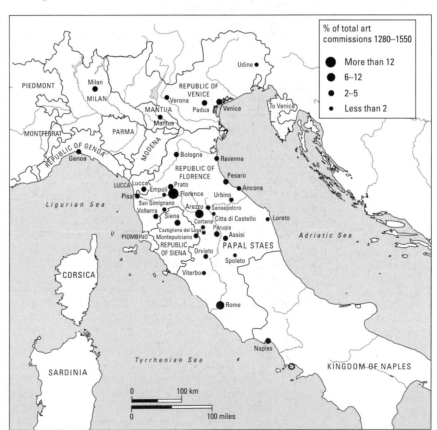

Patronage: This term relates to the willingness of wealthy or powerful sponsors to commission works from creative artists or to encourage writers and thinkers to develop their ideas.

This encouraged the celebration of local pride, the belief that living in a city was the most civilised form of existence, and the celebration of local and civic pride by means of cultural **patronage**.

As John Hale argued in *The Civilisation of Europe in the Renaissance*, the values of the Italian Renaissance spread from Italy and interacted with other cultures to produce a clear and coherent European culture which at an élite level, and despite many religious and political differences, was common to much of Europe.

This process was made easier by a fundamental change in Italian culture. From being primarily civic – that is, based on independent city states – it increasingly became princely. By the early 16th century artists and scholars were more likely to be in the service of the pope or of a duke than of a city council. This therefore made their work more intelligible to northern societies which were culturally dominated by aristocratic values. Once Renaissance values moved north of the Alps, they interacted with traditional cultures to produce new styles in art and literature.

2.1 *What were the origins and nature of the Italian Renaissance?*
A CASE STUDY IN HISTORICAL INTERPRETATION

Humanist/humanism: The 'humanista' was a student who educated himself in the politics of the day. He studied art, architecture, language and literature. The humanities were viewed as the essence of civilisation and enabled the student to discover the significant differences between classical and later cultures. The study of Plato and Homer, for instance, suggested that humans were not governed by destiny but could determine their own fate.

Giorgio Vasari (1511–1574)
A painter from Arezzo, Vasari gained greater fame as a writer. His *Lives of the Artists*, begun in 1543, was the first critical history of art. Vasari shared the contemporary assumption that maybe the careers of the great ought to be studied for encouragement and inspiration. He argued that art was reborn around 1250 and that it grew to maturity in three stages. The heroes of the first two stages were Giotto and Masaccio. In the third period, artists such as Leonardo da Vinci, Michelangelo and Raphael triumphed over nature.

The idea that 15th-century Italy experienced a cultural rebirth can be traced back to contemporary writers, though they did not necessarily agree either about precisely what was being reborn or about the processes by which it was coming about.

In his *Lives of Dante and Petrarch*, written in 1436, the Florentine **humanist** Leonardo Bruni argued that the Latin language reached its peak at the time of Cicero (106–43 BC), and then went into decline with the ending of the Roman Republic. It revived only 'when the Italian people recovered their liberty' in the 12th century.

Bruni's younger contemporary and friend, Matteo Palmieri, came up with a similar interpretation based on evidence drawn from the visual arts as well as literature. Painting was revived by Giotto at the end of the 13th century. Sculpture and architecture 'had been producing stupid monstrosities' but had been revived 'in our own time' by masters such as Donatello, Ghiberti and Brunelleschi.

A century later Giorgio Vasari, the first art historian, claimed that the visual arts had steadily declined during the Roman Empire. They were revived by a gradual process which began with the building of the church of San Miniato al Monte in Florence in the 11th century. From these modest beginnings sprang the great revival in art which Vasari linked with Giotto in the second half of the 13th century. The language of revival also led to a condemnation of the period before the revival began, which was seen as 'dark', 'barbaric' or 'gothic', a habit begun by Petrarch in the 14th century.

Amongst historians, however, the term 'Renaissance' was not popularised until the middle of the 19th century. Vasari had used the term *rinascita* (rebirth) to describe what had happened to the arts, and until the 19th century the term was also used to describe specific contexts. It was only in 1855 that the French historian Jules Michelet used the term 'Renaissance' to describe the history of Europe as a whole during the 15th and 16th centuries. He also publicised the concepts of 'the discovery of the world' and 'the discovery of man' which he saw as central to the period.

These concepts were further popularised by the Swiss historian Jakob Burckhardt in *The Civilization of the Renaissance in Italy*, published in 1860. For Burckhardt the Renaissance marked the point at which the modern world emerged from the Gothic barbarism of the Middle Ages.

Romantic: A term commonly used to describe the literature and art of the late 18th and early 19th centuries. Many writers and painters of that time, particularly from northern Europe, were heavily influenced by an imaginative approach to Italian culture.

This was an interpretation of cultural change few current historians would accept. Burckhardt's interpretation certainly sprang out of a view of Italy which was very influential amongst northern Europeans during the **Romantic** era. Burckhardt's opinion of the Renaissance was undoubtedly élitist. He was a 19th-century liberal who both valued intellectual freedom and feared the consequences of the growth of democracy, which would place a higher priority on the vulgar activities of the majority than on the refined tastes of the educated élite. Burckhardt saw Renaissance Italy, and especially republican Florence, as ideal societies which combined a free spirit with the enhancement of educated values. Moreover, the spirit of the age was most fully expressed in 'Renaissance men', such as Alberti, Leonard da Vinci and Michelangelo, who could express their 'many-sided' genius in a variety of ways.

Burckhardt's interpretation was also a product of its time in that he saw the Renaissance as 'not the revival of antiquity alone, but its union with the genius of the Italian people, which achieved the conquest of the western world'. He emphasised the 'national spirit' which had brought this about. Clearly, Burckhardt's conception of Italy was a reflection of the *Risorgimento* movement – the movement for Italian political unification, which was particularly influential at the time at which he was writing.

Burckhardt's ideas were firmly rooted in the politics and culture of his own time. Nevertheless, his interpretation remained unchallenged for two generations. Indeed, it was reinforced by such works as the multi-volume *The Renaissance in Italy* by the late 19th-century English liberal writer, John Addington Symonds.

After about 1920 a reaction set in against Burckhardt's writings. They were attacked by historians specialising in the medieval period who felt that he had been condescending and over-critical in his attitudes to the Middle Ages. They pointed out several fundamental flaws in Burckhardt's arguments.

- The rediscovery of classical thought was as much a product of writers in the 12th and 13th centuries as of the humanists of 15th-century Italy.

- Much Renaissance architecture was influenced as much by the style of **Tuscan Romanesque** as it was by classical architecture.

- The individualism which Burckhardt saw as characteristic of 15th-century Italy was arguably apparent in earlier societies.

- Many allegedly 'Renaissance men' had values and assumptions which were still essentially 'medieval'.

- Renaissance humanists, they argued, did little to bring about the scientific discoveries characteristic of a more modern world.

Tuscan Romanesque: A variation of the Romanesque style of architecture found in Tuscany and neighbouring parts of Italy from the 11th to the early 13th centuries. Buildings in this style included the church of San Miniato al Monte and the Baptistery in Florence, as well as the cathedral at Pisa. Tuscan Romanesque was arguably more influential in the development of Renaissance architecture than the emulation of classical models.

Michelangelo Buonarroti (1475–1564)
With Leonardo the presiding genius of the High Renaissance, he saw himself primarily as a sculptor, although patrons, especially the Papacy, preferred to employ him as a painter and architect. He divided his working life between his native Florence and Rome. His greatest work in the former city is 'David'; his greatest works in the latter are the ceiling of the Sistine Chapel and the design of the new St Peter's. In many respects a moody and difficult man, he, nevertheless, did a huge amount to expand the scale and conception of art.

Leonardo da Vinci (1452–1519)
Along with Michelangelo, he was one of the two all-round geniuses who came to personify the concept of the 'Renaissance man'. He was outstanding in numerous fields, including painting, drawing, various forms of engineering, optics, astronomy and zoology. He divided the Italian phase of his career between Florence and Milan, before ending his career in France. In the words of John White, 'he ushered in the modern age of the individual, socially mobile, entrepreneurial artist, free to prosper or to starve. He also epitomised the artist's new role, not only as a manual worker, but as a thinker and a theorist.'

Marxist influence: This refers to historians who have written under the influence of the ideas of the 19th-century political theorist, Karl Marx.

Anachronistic: This literally means 'out of time' and refers to incorrect application of circumstances or values to a particular historical period to which these could not possibly apply.

1. **What was new about the interpretations of the Renaissance put forward by Michelet and Burckhardt?**

2. **On what grounds have 20th-century historians disagreed with the interpretations of Michelet and Burckhardt?**

As Burckhardt's conception of the Renaissance was élitist, it was natural that his arguments should have been modified by historians writing under **Marxist influence**. In his *Sociology of the Renaissance* (1932), Alfred von Martin stressed in Marxist terms that the Renaissance represented a bourgeois revolution, but he accepted some of Burckhardt's assumptions by emphasising the modernising tendency of this revolution.

Another Marxist historian, Frederick Antal, in his *Florentine Painting and its Social Background* (1948) differentiated between the rational and progressive views of the Florentine upper middle classes, who patronised forward-looking artists like Masaccio, and the more conventional views of the feudal, land-holding classes. However, in putting forward these arguments both von Martin and Antal projected arguably **anachronistic** values on to the social groups which they were studying. This certainly limited the validity of their arguments. Nevertheless, it should be noted that even these historians of the political Left continued to accept Burckhardt's assumptions about the relationship between the Renaissance and the dawn of modernity.

From this point it was only a short step from attacking Burckhardt's arguments to questioning the fundamental concept of 'Renaissance'. The American historian, Wallace K. Ferguson, began this process in *The Renaissance in Historical Thought* (1948). It has been continued by British historians such as Denys Hay in *The Italian Renaissance in its Historical Background* (second edition 1977) and Peter Burke in *The Renaissance* (1987). This has involved, in Burke's words, an attempt 'to situate what was happening in 14th-century Florence, 15th-century Italy and 16th-century Europe in a sequence of connected changes between 1000 (or thereabouts) and 1800'. Little of Burckhardt's construction could have survived such an onslaught.

Two recent attacks on Burckhardt have concentrated on making explicit the links between cultural developments in 15th-century Italy with its medieval past. The American historian Lauro Martines, in *Power and Imagination: City-States in Renaissance Italy* (1980), has stressed the indebtedness of Italian cultural brilliance, which extended from the beginning of the 14th century to the late 15th century, to the political culture, society and economy of the city states of the 12th and 13th centuries. Most importantly, it was in this earlier period that the *civic* ideals emerged which made possible the humanism of the 15th century. The British historian George Holmes, in *Florence, Rome and the Origins of the Renaissance* (1986), suggests that Renaissance culture emerged out of the economic, cultural and religious life of Tuscany and its relationship with the Papacy during the late 13th and early 14th centuries. This was the context in which Dante and Giotto produced their masterpieces in the early 14th century, thereby providing the basis for what would become the achievements of the Renaissance. Though their interpretations are far removed from those of Burckhardt, it is important to note that both Martines and Holmes do accept the basic validity of 'Renaissance' as a concept.

2.2 Why did the Renaissance originate in Florence?

The cultural developments of the Renaissance could not have taken place had it not been for the flourishing nature of society in many cities in central and northern Italy. Without the fortunes made from commerce and industry there could have been no patronage. Without patronage it would have been impossible to produce great art on such a considerable scale.

It was no surprise that Florence was the cradle of Renaissance culture. Florentine banking had earned an international reputation long before the creation of the Medici Bank in 1397. By the start of the 15th century

Guilds: In the Middle Ages city-dwellers who followed a particular skilled occupation or profession grouped themselves together for mutual protection and to support good causes.

Filippo Brunelleschi (1377–1446)
A Florentine architect, he was assumed to have restored the Roman manner of building in works such as the cupola of Florence Cathedral, the Innocenti Hospital, the churches of San Lorenzo and Santo Spirito and the Pazzi Chapel of the church of Santa Croce.

Cosimo de' Medici (1389–1464)
From 1434 Cosimo had a dominant, though unofficial, role in Florentine government, secured as a result of the vast wealth generated by the family's banking, commercial and industrial interests. His role as a patron of the arts and learning was immense. Among those who benefited from his support were Argyropoulos, Ficino, Donatello and Michelozzo.

Byzantine: Byzantium (later Constantinople) became the capital of the Roman Empire in the East when the Empire was divided. The term 'Byzantine' usually refers to the culture associated with, and spread by, the city of Byzantium.

Despotic: This refers to states that were ruled by individuals whose powers were not limited by reference to a constitution.

1. What factors encouraged the emergence of Renaissance culture in Florence?

2. In what respects did Florentine culture in the first half of the 15th century reflect the concept of civic humanism?

Florence had the basis for a luxury economy. The strength of Florentine banking was complemented by a powerful manufacturing base. Much of this was concerned with the production of luxury goods, which generated significant profits in relation to investment and which underpinned the patronage of the **guilds**, which was crucial to the development of Florence's culture in the early 15th century. Thus, it was the Cloth Merchants who staged a competition to find the best design for the doors of the baptistery in Florence in 1401–1402, and it was their rivals the Silk Merchants who commissioned Brunelleschi to build the Foundling Hospital (Ospedale degli Innocenti) in 1418. At the same time, a number of guilds competed to pay for statues in the niches of Orsanmichele.

Individuals as well, such as Giovanni Rucellai and Cosimo de' Medici, adopted a competitive approach to artistic patronage. Florence was, by the standards of the time, an 'open society'. The emphasis on trade encouraged travel and the spread of ideas. The republican structure of government further encouraged a civic pride which had in any case been strong for two centuries and was further encouraged by Florence's takeover of other Tuscan cities, such as Arezzo (1387) and Pisa (1406). The city had had a flourishing cultural tradition since the end of the 13th century.

In addition, it was to Florence that the **Byzantine** scholar Manuel Chrysoloras came to teach Greek in 1397. This was no coincidence. Chrysoloras was invited to Florence by the city's chancellor, Coluccio Salutati, a humanist scholar who had been inspired by the classical enthusiasms of his friend, the poet Petrarch, and who secured public funding for Chrysoloras' appointment. Chrysoloras clearly influenced many of the next generation of Florentine humanists. Thus, Leonardo Bruni, for example, was able to become expert in Greek as well as in Latin. He translated works by Aristotle and Plato from the former into the latter, thereby making them accessible to a wider though, by definition, highly educated readership. Bruni also demonstrated his characteristic civic pride by writing *Praise of the City of Florence*, which celebrated Florentine republicanism and the city's cultural tradition, and a *History of the Florentine People*. Such civic pride and republican liberty were crucial to the concept of civic humanism which Hans Baron, in *The Crisis of the Early Italian Renaissance* (1955), saw as being *politically* essential to the emergence of the Renaissance. Florentines became collectively aware of this identification with the great republican cities of Athens and Rome, argued Baron, when the city and its liberty appeared under threat from Giangaleazzo Visconti, the ruler of Milan, at the end of the 14th century.

During the first third, at least, of the 15th century Florence remained culturally predominant. This predominance was aided by a range of factors.

- Florence's rival republics, such as Siena, Pisa and Lucca, were declining and could no longer sustain the level of cultural production which had existed in earlier centuries.

- Venice, though hugely wealthy, would not emerge as a great centre of painting until much later in the century.

- Rome had not yet recovered financially and politically from the Papacy's removal to Avignon.

- The courtly cultures associated with small **despotic** states such as Urbino and Mantua were yet to emerge.

- Civic patronage expressed through the guilds was substantially superseded by the patronage of hugely wealthy individuals such as Palla Strozzi and Cosimo de' Medici.

2.3 How important was the role of patrons in the development of the Renaissance?

In what respects does the Duomo demonstrate classical influences?

The Duomo in Florence

One of the great myths of the Renaissance was that artists of the period were free to create masterpieces which then would be eagerly acquired by patrons who combined their good taste with great wealth. In the words of Mary Hollingsworth, in *Patronage in Renaissance Italy: from 1400 to the early Sixteenth Century* (1994), this myth 'disguises the fact that it was the patron who was the real initiator of the architecture, sculpture and painting of the period'. Patrons were 'active consumers' rather than 'passive connoisseurs'. In making this comment Mary Hollingsworth was following a number of historians, most importantly Martin Wackernagel and Michael Baxandall, who had challenged Burckhardt's assumptions about individual genius. Instead, they had paid particular reference to the importance of the patron in determining the form and content of art.

Florence

At the start of the 15th century patronage in Florence was exercised largely by members of the city's merchant élite within a framework in which the city's authorities had considerable influence. The city had controlled the construction of the two great buildings begun in the 1290s: the Duomo (Cathedral) and the Palazzo della Signoria, now known as the Palazzo Vecchio (town hall). This control was extended to many other churches and public buildings. The city's government exercised its control by transferring responsibility to individual guilds. During the early 15th century it was the individual guilds which competed to exercise the most lavish patronage at a time when, following Florence's victory over Milan, the city's confidence and civic pride was at its height. The three most important guilds in Florence in terms of their patronage were the wool merchants, cloth merchants and silk merchants.

Wool merchants

The Wool Merchants guild had responsibility for the upkeep of the Duomo and the Piazza della Signoria. It was the wool merchants who commissioned Brunelleschi to design the dome of the cathedral. Brunelleschi's conceptions came either from a study of Roman models, which is what the Florentine humanists preferred to believe, or, more likely, from Byzantine models in Ravenna.

Cloth merchants

Gothic: For most of the Middle Ages Gothic was the dominant form of architecture. It was particularly associated with church architecture and was characterised by such features as pointed and decorated windows, pointed arches and flying buttresses.

The Cloth Merchants guild had responsibility for the upkeep of three of the city's leading buildings: the Baptistery, the Franciscan church of Santa Croce and the Benedictine church of San Miniato al Monte. They established a competition to decide who should decorate the Baptistery doors. At this stage the guild showed that its taste was conservative in awarding the contract to Ghiberti, whose original concept was **Gothic** in character. It might also have been significant that Ghiberti's concept was less expensive than those of some of his competitors.

Silk merchants

The major responsibilities of the Silk Merchants guild were the rebuilding of Orsanmichele and the building of the Foundling Hospital (Ospedale degli Innocenti). They had begun the rebuilding of Orsanmichele in 1337. Two years later, the city authorities approved their scheme to allow individual guilds to decorate part of the building. By 1406 only six guilds had done so, but over the next few years the other guilds responded positively. According to Mary Hollingsworth, Orsanmichele 'offered a unique site for a direct comparison of the status, power and prestige of both major and minor guilds'. This posed a particular threat to the wool merchants who, in their own words, 'always sought to be the master and the superior of the other guilds'. In response, they commissioned a bronze statue from Ghiberti 'so that this tabernacle will exceed, or at least equal, in beauty and decoration the more beautiful ones'.

The silk merchants showed their openness to new styles by approving Brunelleschi's designs for the Foundling Hospital in 1419. This differed hugely in style from the Gothic forms that were common in most public architecture. It did, however, recall the once-popular style of Tuscan Romanesque.

Individual patrons

Several wealthy patrons became heavily involved in artistic patronage in Florence during the first third of the 15th century. To some extent this patronage reflected the city's political and commercial rivalries. Rival patrons favoured contrasting styles. Thus, Palla Strozzi, for example, paid for the rebuilding and decoration of his local church, Santa Trinità, in the International Gothic style associated at that time with the rulers of Europe.

The redecoration of Santa Trinità included the altarpiece 'The Adoration of the Magi' by Gentile da Fabriano. This painting is colourful, full of detailed and natural observation and richly decorated. It is, arguably, the greatest single masterpiece associated with the International Gothic style. As such, it should be contrasted with the paintings of Masaccio who was active at the same time.

Detail from Benozzo Gozzoli's 'Procession of the Magus Caspar'. The two figures riding immediately behind the King are Cosimo and Piero de' Medici.

What political messages are conveyed by their depiction in the painting?

On the other hand, Strozzi's rival, Giovanni di Bicci de' Medici, founder of the Medici family fortunes, favoured a contrasting and more 'Florentine' form of architecture deriving ultimately from Tuscan Romanesque. It was probably Giovanni di Bicci who persuaded the silk merchants to adopt Brunelleschi's designs for the Foundling Hospital. This political contrast between Gothic and 'Florentine' forms should not be pushed too far. It was, for example, a close associate of Strozzi, Felice Brancacci, who sponsored Masaccio's decoration of the Brancacci Chapel whose frescoes were hugely influential in developing perspective.

Florence itself became politically very turbulent in the 1430s. The Medicis were exiled in 1433. However, they were able to avenge themselves on their Strozzi enemies in the following year. Both Palla Strozzi and Felipe Brancacci were permanently exiled from the city as a result. Some artistic works with which they had been associated were either destroyed or abandoned as a result. On the other hand, the beginning of Medici control, however harmful to notions of republican liberty, was to result in a flowering of patronage unprecedented even by Florentine standards.

Cosimo de' Medici, although theoretically only a private citizen, controlled Florence politically from 1434 until his death 30 years later. Medici power was symbolised by the Medici Palace designed by Michelozzo in 1444. Cosimo's money also ensured the completion of the church of San Lorenzo, designed by Brunelleschi, and of the Dominican monastery of San Marco, decorated by a large number of frescoes on simple religious themes by Fra Angelico. He made many other donations to churches and public buildings, not only in Florence but also in several other cities. By lavishing such generosity on the Church, Cosimo was undoubtedly fulfilling his Christian duty as he saw it. However, he was engaging in massive self-promotion, with motives that were largely political. This self-promotion was most strongly marked in Benozzo Gozzoli's 1459 fresco cycle 'The Procession of the Magi', which was commissioned to decorate the walls of the Medici Palace. In this work, according to Mary

Lorenzo de' Medici (1449–1492)

The grandson of Cosimo, Lorenzo achieved political leadership in Florence in 1469. As a patron of the arts he was responsible for what John Hale has called 'the last great phase of Florentine cultural leadership'. The artists he patronised included Botticelli, Ghirlandaio and Benozzo Gozzoli, and he did much to encourage the flourishing of neo-Platonist scholarship.

Sandro Botticelli (1445–1510)

One of the key figures in the development of Florentine art, Botticelli's greatest achievements were the neo-Platonist and allegorical paintings, 'Primavera' and 'The Birth of Venus', which he produced for Lorenzo de' Medici. Botticelli was therefore at the centre of the movement that attempted to synthesise Christian and classical elements in painting.

Neo-Platonists: Neo-Platonism was a synthesis of the philosophy of Plato and other Greek writers with the basic principles of Christianity. This was very important in legitimating the concerns of the humanists in the eyes of the Catholic Church.

In what ways does this painting represent the religious and social values of Savonarola and his followers?

Hollingsworth, Cosimo and his son Piero ensured that the artist produced a 'traditional and courtly image', demonstrating their aspirations to princely prestige and openly showing their willingness to undermine Florence's republican ideals.

The pattern of patronage adopted by Cosimo's grandson, Lorenzo de' Medici ('il Magnifico'), differed considerably. On one level he played a vitally important role as the key patron of **neo-Platonists**, such as Ficino and Poliziano, who dominated the intellectual life of Florence. At another level, his artistic patronage was much more private than that of his grandfather. Instead of making the objects of his patronage visible in public places such as churches, he preferred either using artists to decorate his own private properties, such as his country villa at Poggia a Caiano, or acting as an intermediary. He arranged patronage on behalf of others by recommending favoured artists and architects to rulers such as the kings of Naples and Hungary.

More visible public patronage was demonstrated by a number of Lorenzo's Florentine contemporaries. Thus, Giovanni Tornabuoni and Francesco Sassetti, both senior figures within the Medici Bank, commissioned frescoes from Domenico Ghirlandaio which decorated respectively the churches of Santa Maria Novella and Santa Trinità. Giovanni Rucellai, who defined the purpose of patronage as the service of God, the city and himself, used Leon Battista Alberti to design his palace in Florence. He also paid for the façade of Santa Maria Novella. Filippo Strozzi paid for the decoration of a chapel in Santa Maria Novella, this time painted by Filippino Lippi. It is easy to discern an element of competition among the Florentine élite at such a range of artistic patronage within a single church.

A reaction in Florence against lavish artistic patronage took place with the collapse of Medici rule in 1494. This had been brought about by the Dominican preacher Girolamo Savonarola (see also Chapter 9). He preached against excessive materialism and Medici abuse of power and called for a return to a more republican constitution. Part of his attack on the Medicis related to what he saw as their pornographic misuse of art, the worst offence being the depiction of the Virgin Mary as a whore. Savonarola instigated what he termed a 'bonfire of the vanities', destroying some of the most offensive images. This caused some artists, most notably Sandro Botticelli, to rethink their whole approach. Giving up the obviously sexual connotations of paintings such as 'Venus and Mars', Botticelli then started producing works like the 'Mystic Nativity', which much more clearly represented Savonarola's sexual and artistic prudity.

Botticelli's 'Mystic Nativity', 1500/1501

The Florentine Republic

After Savonarola's fall in 1498 and the creation of a formal republic under Piero Soderini in 1502, artistic patronage in Florence once again came to reflect republican and civic virtues. The most famous artistic expression of such attitudes was Michelangelo's 'David'. This was commissioned by the civic authorities and the statue symbolised the republic's struggle against foreign (i.e. French) and native (i.e. Medici) oppression.

Venice

Venice, though as wealthy and commercially significant as Florence, proved more conservative in its artistic tastes throughout much of the 15th century. Byzantine influences remained strong and the Doge's Palace was International Gothic in its conception. It was not until the second half of the 15th century that a distinctive Venetian Renaissance style began to emerge which, whilst rejecting Gothic forms, placed far more emphasis on Byzantine rather than Roman influences. This style was evident in a number of public buildings, for example the entrance to the Arsenale and the late 15th-century additions to the Doge's Palace.

There was also a strong Byzantine influence on painting. For example, Gentile Bellini had visited Constantinople in 1479. By this time the Venetian state was recognising the contribution made by painters. Both Gentile and Giovanni Bellini were granted a state income for life. In return, they assisted with the decoration of the Doge's Palace.

One of the most characteristic features of Venetian patronage was the *scuole*. Moreover, their civic links were further emphasised by the fact that they needed the approval of the Council of Ten to undertake their artistic projects. According to Mary Hollingsworth they made a 'major contribution' to the appearance of Venice. Among the most famous Venetian paintings commissioned by the *scuole* were Vittore Carpaccio's 'St Augustine' and the cycle depicting Venetian miracles produced for the Scuola di San Giovanni Evangelista by seven painters. The Bellinis and Carpaccio specialised in the 'eye-witness' style, which emphasised strong narrative and contained much anecdotal detail.

Another significant difference between the motives of Florence and Venice was that self-glorification was much more restrained in the latter city. Far more important was the desire of Venetians, in Mary Hollingsworth's words, to 'give visual expression to their religious piety'. As well as the *scuole*, this was marked by the huge amount of state-controlled church building and rebuilding which occurred in the second half of the 15th century. Interior decoration was often undertaken by executors of wills in response to bequests. The most impressive work to be commissioned in this way was Giovanni Bellini's 'Virgin and Child with Saints' in the Frari church.

It was only in the last quarter of the 15th century that classical influences established themselves firmly in Venice. The influence of classical mythology was shown in the monument to **Doge** Pietro Mocenigo in the church of Santi Giovanni e Paolo, which was decorated by a depiction of Hercules in conflict with the Hydra. That there was now a market for Greek learning in Venice was shown by the publication of Greek classics by Aldo Manuzio (Manutius) from 1495. Moreover, by the beginning of the 16th century classical imagery had become prominent in Venetian art, particularly in 'Three Philosophers' and 'Sleeping Venus' by Giorgione.

It was not until after the Sack of Rome in 1527 that classical forms became the norm in Venetian architecture. This reflected a move from Byzantine to Roman influences urged by the Doge Andrea Gritti, who led the pro-Roman faction in Venice. The classical style in architecture became the principal visual way in which this political attitude, which

Scuole: Guilds who had a duty to exercise charity but which also in Venice had an important civic role, for example through their participation in many of the great civic rituals.

Doge: Chief magistrate in the republics of Venice and Genoa.

was aristocratic rather than commercial in character, could be expressed, not only in Venice but also in the mainland cities controlled by Venice, such as Verona and Padua. This programme was entrusted principally to two architects, Michele Sanmicheli and Jacopo Sansovino. Sanmicheli specialised in fortifications, including the fortress of San Andrea and the city gates of his native Verona. Sansovino designed such public buildings in Venice as the Logetta beneath the bell-tower of St Mark's, the Library and the Mint. The new style was also evident in the private buildings commissioned by the pro-Roman élite, the most notable example being the Palazzo Corner designed by Sansovino.

Painters, such as Titian and Veronese, abandoned the older 'eye-witness' style of the Bellinis and Carpaccio. Instead, they emphasised the new fashion in Venice for classical allegory. Many key political and mercantile figures of Venice, for example Doge Andrea Gritti, also employed Titian to paint their portrait

There was a renewed emphasis also on church decoration after Venice's recovery from defeat at the Battle of Agnadello in 1509. The most notable example was Titian's 'Assumption of the Virgin', commissioned in 1516.

Rome

Through much of the Middle Ages Rome was a political and cultural back-water. The Popes had moved to Avignon, and the city failed to generate the commercial wealth associated with many other Italian cities. This had an important side-effect: surviving classical ruins were not completely van-dalised for their building stone, thereby ensuring that they could act as an inspiration to artists and scholars. Rome's revival as a cultural centre can be traced to Pope Martin V (1417–1431) who began the restoration of St Peter's and other churches and invited artists such as Masaccio and Gentile da Fabriano to work for him. This work was continued under his successors such as Nicholas V (1447–1455) and Sixtus IV (1471–1484).

In what specific ways does this painting demonstrate the importance of classical influences during the Renaissance?

Detail from Raphael's 'The School of Athens' – a pictorial expression of the influence of classical learning in that Raphael depicts various key figures in classical learning in the guise of great figures of his own time. For example, the central figure of Plato, pointing upwards to stress the transcendental nature of his philosophy, is Leonardo da Vinci. Next to him, Aristotle is more concerned with earthly reality. Heraclitus, the solitary figure writing on a block of stone, is Michelangelo, characteristically failing to communicate with his colleagues. The mathematician Euclid, demonstrating the principles of his geometry to a group of youths, is the architect Bramante.

However, it was not until the 'High Renaissance' Popes, Julius II (1503–1513) and Leo X (1513–1521), that Rome achieved real cultural prominence. For example, it was Julius who first employed Donato Bramante to rebuild St Peter's. He also commissioned Michelangelo to design his tomb. Most importantly, however, Julius II commissioned two of the key works of the High Renaissance for the Vatican: Raphael's decoration of the Stanze della Segnatura and Michelangelo's decoration of the ceiling of the Sistine Chapel. The former included 'The School at Athens', which defined the contemporary view of the nature of classical cultural influences on the art and intellectual life of the time.

Leo X, a son of Lorenzo de' Medici, saw himself consciously reviving the traditions and greatness of ancient Rome. He continued his predecessor's patronage of Raphael who worked on several more rooms in the Vatican, including the Stanza d'Eliodoro which glorified Leo X by featuring episodes from the lives of Leo III and Leo IV, both of whom were depicted as Leo X.

Papal artistic patronage understandably was reduced after the Sack of Rome in 1527. Pope Clement VII's main priority was the rebuilding of those areas of the city which had been destroyed and, in any case, he was too heavily in debt to consider further artistic patronage. That tradition was, however, revived by his successor Paul III, who was responsible for bringing Michelangelo back to Rome to complete the painting of the Sistine Chapel with 'The Last Judgement' and the design of the new St Peter's by adding its dome.

The small Italian states

Mantua

Mantua was a small state in northern Italy. Ludovico Gonzaga, duke from 1444 to 1478, transformed Mantua into a leading cultural centre. He extensively renovated the Ducal Palace. His original decorations were in the International Gothic style. However, round about 1450 his tastes began to change, and he adopted the classical forms which had become fashionable in Florence. In 1457 he began to employ Andrea Mantegna as his court painter. Mantegna was an enthusiast for ancient Rome. The emphasis on Roman traditions was given its fullest display in the huge 'Triumphs of Caesar', commissioned by Ludovico's grandson, Francesco. Francesco's wife, Isabella d'Este, was a patron and collector on a huge scale who was very conscious of her image as a patron. Her tastes in painting were heavily humanistic and she was highly influenced by **allegorical** themes.

Urbino

Urbino was a tiny city which was part of the Papal States, a group of territories in central Italy which owed political allegiance to the Pope. Under the leadership of Federigo da Montefeltro, who, according to Marsilio Ficino, combined 'wisdom with eloquence and prudence with the military art', Urbino gained a cultural prominence out of all proportion to its tiny size. Federigo spent lavishly on the Ducal Palace, designed by Luciano Laurana and Francesco di Giorgio Martini, to emphasise his military prowess. He commissioned a well-known Flemish weaver, Jean Grenier, to produce large-scale tapestries of the Trojan War. He employed as his court painter Piero della Francesca. Piero produced two portraits of Federigo, one with his wife, Battista Sforza, and the other showing him kneeling in front of the Virgin, Child and various saints. Federigo also commissioned the most puzzling of all of Piero paintings, the 'Flagellation', which was clearly influenced by the painter's application of mathematical rules and understanding of perspective.

Allegorical: In the style of an allegory; a painting or story in which the literal presentation is intended to be interpreted as having another parallel meaning.

1. What were the distinctive features of patronage in Florence in the first half of the 15th century?

2. In what ways, and why, did the pattern of cultural patronage change during the period of the Renaissance?

In what respects does this painting glorify the role of the patron who commissioned it?

Piero della Francesca's 'Madonna and Child enthroned with angels and saints, with Federigo da Montefeltro', 1472

2.4 What was the importance of humanism in the Renaissance?

Humanism was a term coined in the 19th century to define what was taught by th*e umanista*, the teacher of the *studia humanitatis*. The study of the humanities had come to include Latin and sometimes Greek texts dealing with grammar, rhetoric, history, poetry and moral philosophy.

What was distinctive about humanist study was the attempt to study such texts on their own terms, in what was to become known as philology, rather than interpreting them through medieval Christianity. What was important was the 'new learning' of humanist scholarship rather than the 'old learning' of medieval scholasticism. Such approaches can be found in cities like Padua and Verona as far back as the early 14th century, but it was the poet Petrarch later in the century who was largely responsible for developing a humanist approach more fully, especially with his enthusiasm for classical texts.

After Petrarch's death many of his books were acquired by the chancellor of the Florentine republic, Coluccio Salutati, who built up a library of over 600 books, which he freely loaned to friends and scholars. The hunger for hunting manuscripts was continued by Poggio Bracciolini and Niccolò Niccoli, the latter being largely responsible for the creation of the concept of the public library.

The emphasis on 'new learning' was reinforced in humanist educational practice. This was especially evident in the schools established at Ferrara and Mantua by Florentine humanists such as Ficino and Poliziano. Humanists placed a strong emphasis on textual study. Thus, they searched out previously unknown manuscripts and purged known works of what they considered to be textual corruptions. In the process, for example, the Roman humanist Lorenzo Valla was able to prove that the text of the *Donation of Constantine*, on which the Papacy based its claims to political power, was forged.

The emphasis on the rediscovery of Greek texts led to the revival of interest in the philosophical ideas of Plato (428–348 BC) and an attempt to reconcile his philosophical ideas with the central principles of the Christian faith. Many of Plato's themes tied in neatly with the concerns of 15th-century humanists, especially his emphasis on the proper education of rulers. Moreover, scholars such as Marsilio Ficino, who translated many of Plato's works from Greek into Latin, and Giovanni Pico della Mirandola created out of the work of Plato and other writers a philosophical system which became known as neo-Platonism. Not only did this successfully synthesise Platonist philosophy and Christianity, it also provided a basis for many of the most complex allegorical paintings of the period with its emphasis on the ethical significance of beauty and love. Such ideas were spread at the Platonist academy which Ficino founded under the patronage of Lorenzo de' Medici.

One of the most important results of the humanist emphasis on philology concerned its impact on the study of the Bible, in particular the New Testament. Biblical scholars, such as Erasmus, could apply the same methodological tools to the Greek New Testament that Ficino had applied to classical Greek texts, in the process undermining the authority of the Catholic Church and smoothing the path of the Protestant reformers.

1. What were the main features of the studia humanitatis *(humanist study)?*

2. To what extent was humanism a concern only of the most powerful and influential people of the time?

2.5 In what ways and with what consequences did the Renaissance spread beyond Italy?

In the mid 15th century northern European culture was Gothic. This was demonstrated in a variety of ways.

Perpendicular: This refers to the final stage of medieval architecture in England. The term describes the characteristic form of windows whose design was based mainly on upright panels.

● The courts of northern Europe had flourishing cultures based on the medieval concept of chivalry. The best example of such a court was that of the dukes of Burgundy.

● The **perpendicular** style of Gothic architecture flourished in England; for example, the chapel of King's College, Cambridge.The flamboyant style flourished in France and Flanders; for example, the cloth hall at Ypres.

● Gothic styles, which combined realistic depictions of figures with an intense religious devotion, dominated in sculpture and were best exemplified in the work of Claus Sluter, whose finest works were produced for Philip the Bold, Duke of Burgundy.

● Northern European painting was dominated by the great Flemish masters Jan van Eyck, Robert Campin and Roger van der Weyden. The chief characteristics of their painting were the emphasis on detail and the mastery of oil as a medium. The intensity of their religious paintings was later developed by such northern European artists as the Dutchman Hieronymus Bosch and the German Matthias Grünewald.

- Much northern European literature was still written in the form of chivalric romances.

- Flemish music, associated with composers such as Josquin des Prés and Johannes Ockeghem, was recognised as the finest in Europe.

The century after 1450 witnessed a transformation in northern European culture, often deriving from its interaction with Italian culture. Royal courts, such as those of England and France, increasingly looked to Italy for their models of behaviour. Baldassare Castiglione's *The Book of the Courtier*, based on his descriptions of behaviour at the Court of Urbino, became the model on which courtly behaviour was based.

By the second half of the 16th century Italianate styles were being adopted in many northern European cities. Italian architects were working in countries as far away as Poland and Hungary. The city of Krakow, for example, was substantially rebuilt under Italian influences. Italianate influences were also apparent in French royal chateaux (large country houses) in the Loire valley, such as Amboise and Chambord.

The realism of northern painting and the use of oil as a medium were successfully passed on to Italian painters, and there was a fruitful interaction between the German artist Albrecht Dürer and the great figures of Venetian art. Meanwhile, northern painters became increasingly keen to adopt the Italian Renaissance emphasis on idealism and classicism. This can be seen, for example, in some of the painting which took place at, or about, the Court of Queen Elizabeth I in England. Painters such as Hans Eworth used classical themes, and classical imagery and idealism can be found in the work of the miniaturist painter, Nicholas Hilliard.

The influence of Italian writers – for example Petrarch, who popularised the use of the sonnet, and Boccaccio – became much stronger. Italian influences on writers such as Rabelais, Montaigne and Shakespeare can be seen in both French and English literature. Most of Shakespeare's poetry was written in the sonnet form. Many of his plays were derived from Italian sources or, like *Romeo and Juliet* and *The Taming of the Shrew*, were set in Italy. Contemporaries of Shakespeare, such as the poets Sir Philip Sydney and Edmund Spenser, were also subjected to Italian influences.

Italian music became increasingly influenced by Flemish composers such as Ockeghem. In return, secular music in northern Europe became more influenced by Italian models. The madrigal, for example, which was particularly popular in Elizabethan England, was first developed in the Courts of northern Italy, especially Mantua.

The interactions between Italy and other parts of Europe were two-way. Italian culture benefited from the influence of northern Europe, especially in painting and music. Northern European countries assimilated the culture of the Italian Renaissance to differing degrees and with varying results. However, it is possible to discern, as John Hale argues in *The Civilization of Europe in the Renaissance* (1993), that a distinctive European culture emerged during this period.

1. In what ways was the culture of northern Europe transformed by the influence of the Italian Renaissance?

2. In what respects was Italian culture affected by northern influences?

Source-based questions: the importance of patronage during the Renaissance in Florence

SOURCE A

At that moment my friends wrote to me that the Board of Works of [the Baptistery] was sending for experienced masters, of whom they wanted to see a test piece. A great many well-qualified masters came from all over Italy to put themselves to this test and competition ... . To each was given four bronze plates. The test set by the Board of Works was that everyone would do a scene for the doors; the one they chose was the sacrifice of Isaac and they wanted each of the contestants to do the same scene .... To me was conceded the palm of victory by all of the experts and by my fellow competitors. Universally they conceded to me the glory, without exception. Everyone felt I had surpassed the others in that time.

From The Commentaries *by Lorenzo Ghiberti*

SOURCE B

The above-mentioned consuls, assembled together in the palace of the [Wool] Guild ... have diligently considered the law approved by the captains of the Society of the Blessed Virgin Mary of Orsanmichele. This law decreed, in effect, that for the ornamentation of that oratory, each of the twenty-one guilds of the city of Florence ... in a place assigned to each of them by the captains of the Society, should construct ... a tabernacle, properly and carefully decorated for the honour of the city and the beautification of the oratory. The consuls have considered that all of the guilds have finished their tabernacles, and that those constructed by the Cloth and Banking Guilds, and by other guilds, surpass in beauty and ornamentation that of the Wool Guild ....

For the splendour and honour of the Guild, the lord consuls desire to provide a remedy for this .... They decree that ... the existing lord consuls ... are to construct, fabricate and remake a tabernacle and a statue of the blessed Stephen ... by whatever ways and means they choose, which will most honourably contribute to the splendour of the Guild, so that this tabernacle will exceed, or at least equal, in beauty and decoration the more beautiful ones.

Deliberations of the Consuls of the Wool Guild, 1425

SOURCE C

Having attended to the temporal affairs of the city – which inevitably burdened his conscience, as they are bound to burden all those who govern states and want to play the leading role – Cosimo became increasingly aware of the fact that if he wanted God to have mercy on him and conserve him in the possession of his temporal goods, he had to turn to pious ways, otherwise he knew he would lose them. So – although I can't say where it came from – his conscience pricked him about some money which he had come by not quite cleanly. Wanting to lift this weight from his shoulders, he went to talk to Pope Eugenius who was then in Florence. Pope Eugenius ... told Cosimo what he was thinking of, that to satisfy himself and to unburden his conscience he should spend ten thousand florins on building [the convent of San Marco]. Having spent then thousand florins without completing what was necessary, Cosimo finished the job by spending in all more than forty thousand florins – not only on the building but on the provision of everything necessary to live there.

From The Life of Vespasiano da Bisticci
(The author was a bookseller in Florence whose shop was often a meeting place for humanist scholars.)

SOURCE D

I have already spent a great deal of money on my house and on the façade of the church of Santa Maria Novella and on the chapel with the tomb I had made in the church of San Pancrazio, and also on the gold brocade vestments for the said church, which cost me more than a thousand ducats, and on the loggia opposite my house and garden of my place at Quaracchi and at Poggia a Caiano. All of the above-mentioned things have given and give me the greatest satisfaction and pleasure, because in part they serve the honour of God as well as the honour of the city and the commemoration of myself.

Giovanni Rucellai, writing in 1473

1. Study Source A.

What does Source A reveal about the character of Lorenzo Ghiberti?

2. Study Source B.

From the evidence of Source B and the information contained within this chapter, explain the importance of the role of the guilds in artistic patronage in 15th-century Florence.

3. Study Source C.

How reliable is Source C as evidence of the motives of Cosimo de' Medici in paying for the rebuilding of the Convent of San Marco?

4. Using all the sources and the information within this chapter, comment on the acceptability of the view that the primary motive for artistic patronage in Renaissance was selfishness.

2.6 Why did Europe widen its geographical horizons during this period?

Framework of Events

1445	Portuguese explorers reached the Azores and Cape Verde Islands. Portuguese begin establishing west African colonies
1486	Bartolomeu Dias rounds the Cape of Good Hope in southern Africa
1492	Christopher Columbus lands in the Bahamas on his first expedition
1493	Columbus' second expedition reaches the Caribbean
1494	Treaty of Tordesillas: the Pope divides newly-discovered territories between Spain and Portugal
1498	Vasco da Gama crosses the Arabian Sea and reaches southern India Columbus' third expedition reaches Trinidad and Venezuela
1499	Expedition led by Alonso de Ojeda explores much of the coastline of South America
1500	Discovery of coast of Brazil on behalf of Portugal by Pero Alvarez Cabral
1502	Sea-borne spices sold on the European market by the Portuguese
1509	Beginning of Spanish settlement in Colombia
1513	Balboa reaches the Pacific Ocean by crossing the American continent at its narrowest point, the isthmus of Panama
1517	Francisco Fernández de Córdoba begins to explore Mexico
1519	Cortés begins the systematic conquest of the lands of the Aztecs in Mexico A fleet under the command of Magellan begins the voyage that will circumnavigate the world.

How can the Renaissance be linked to the voyages of discovery?

Many historians have assumed that there was a clear link between the Renaissance and the voyages of discovery that took place during the 14th and 15th centuries. Both Michelet and Burckhardt believed that 'the discovery of the world of man' was part of the process of Renaissance. Proving the existence of links between the two is more difficult. The impetus for exploration came about in Portugal and Spain and was far distant from the centres of Renaissance culture. The explorers were practical and often crude and uneducated men, far removed from Renaissance ideals embodying education, sophistication and civility. Nevertheless, some connections can be detected. For example, geographical knowledge had been improved by the revival of interest in the texts of Ptolemy and Strabo, whose work was known to the Florentine humanist, Paolo Toscanelli, who certainly influenced Columbus.

What technical improvements enabled voyages of discovery to take place?

At the start of the 15th century, though Europe maintained substantial trading links with Asia, most educated Europeans had little knowledge of other lands and cultures. By the end of the 16th century, however, much of America had been located and colonies had begun to be established there, contacts with Africa and Asia had increased, and map-making and printing had developed hugely.

In order to explain why this situation came about it is necessary to examine both the means that enabled it to take place and the range of motives that encouraged the activities of exploration and colonisation to take place.

A range of technical and infrastructural improvements took place during the 15th century to enable exploration to take place.

● The Portuguese nobleman, Prince Henry the Navigator (1394–1460), offered extensive patronage. He formed a committee to organise Portuguese trade with Africa, acquired a large collection of charts and books on exploration and personally sponsored voyages of exploration.

● Developments in marine technology assisted the process. The caravel (or carrack) was a more efficient craft than its predecessors. Though small, it was more easily manoeuvrable than earlier craft and required only a relatively small crew. It was, therefore, both a more efficient and a more cost-effective craft.

● There had been an improvement in navigational techniques. The astrolabe could be used, at least in calm waters, for measuring latitude. By 1462 the Pole Star was in use as a navigational aid and in 1484 a group of astronomers advised King John II of Portugal that a ship's latitude might most easily be calculated by reference to the height of the midday sun.

● There was an improvement in geographical knowledge. Ptolemy's *Astronomy* had been translated into Latin in the 12th century and his *Geography* had been translated into Latin in 1406. Though Ptolemy's works contained many errors and false assumptions, they did make it clear that the Earth was spherical and not flat. A number of other writers had also asserted, since the 13th century, that Asia could be reached by crossing the Atlantic. Columbus, in particular, was well acquainted with the writings of Paolo Toscanelli, an astronomer from Florence, who, inspired by the ancient Greek geographer Strabo, had argued that case as recently as 1474.

What were the motives of the explorers?

Naturally enough, a variety of economic, political and religious motives had persuaded Europeans to mount the dangerous and expensive voyages that helped to bring this about.

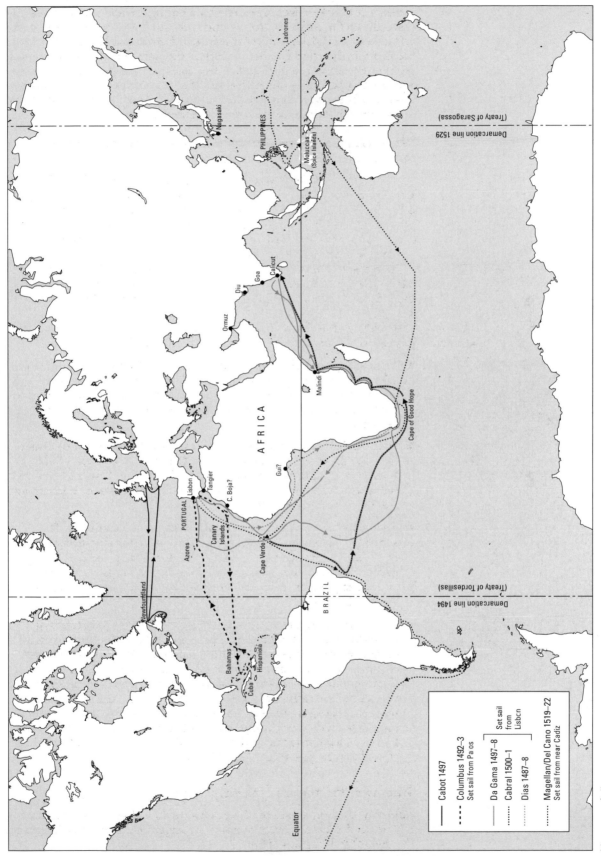

Voyages of discovery

Firstly, there was widespread resentment in Europe at the increasing costs incurred in importing spices by land from Asia into Europe. There was also widespread hostility towards the virtual control of this trade held by Venetian and Genoese merchants. There was therefore a strong economic motive to reduce the cost of the spice trade and end Venetian and Genoese control, and, therefore, find a sea route to the sources of the spices and other luxury goods in the East. This financial motive was reinforced by the fear of the Ottoman Turks whose increasing power posed a potential threat to the trade.

Secondly, there was a shortage in Europe of gold, most of which was obtained from West Africa, transported across the Sahara Desert and sold to Italian and Spanish merchants in North Africa. The Portuguese, in particular, sought to exploit these sources of gold more directly by reaching them by sea. Later, it became an obsession among explorers employed by the Spanish Crown that vast quantities of gold were obtainable from the lands they hoped to find.

The Portuguese, in particular, looked upon Africa as a source of slaves. Also, Portuguese explorers along the African coast were looking for Christian communities. They were motivated by the desire to secure Christian allies for further crusades against **Islam**. Columbus wished to find sufficient gold to be able to wage a crusade against the Turks in order to regain control for Christian Europe of the Holy Land. Later, the Spanish occupation of much of the Americas prompted the need to convert the native peoples to Catholicism.

Once the existence of areas like America had become firmly established, this opened up opportunities to those starved of wealth and position in Europe to achieve power, wealth and status in America.

The monarchs of Portugal and Castile were competing to reach the Indies in order to control the spice trade. The Portuguese developed a flourishing sea empire as a result, but had relatively little political or cultural impact on the areas which they reached. The Spanish 'discovery' of the Americas was an accidental by-product of this process, which then concentrated Spanish minds on exploiting this success.

Islam: the religious faith of the Ottomans.

1. **What factors enabled voyages of discovery to take place?**

2. **How justified is the claim that the explorers were motivated mainly by greed?**

2.7 What were the short-term consequences of European expansion?

The East Indies

The Portuguese, having reached the southern tip of Africa in 1488, were worried by Columbus' claim that he had reached the Indies by sailing west. Within a few years, however, they convinced themselves that Columbus' claim was bogus. Therefore in 1497 King Manuel I sponsored an expedition, led by Vasco da Gama, whose objective was to reach India. With the help of the Asian navigator, Ahmed ibn Majid, da Gama was able to reach the port of Calicut in India in May 1498. Arriving back in Lisbon in September 1499, da Gama confidently asserted that the trading prospects were huge. In 1501 Pero Alvarez Cabral was able to trade with Calicut's rival port, Cochin, and on da Gama's second expedition in 1502 he was able not only to crush a hostile Arab fleet, but also to return with a substantial cargo of spices. From that point on, the Portuguese were able to develop a network of trading posts, forts and colonies to assist the conduct of trade. Their position was always precarious, and their relative weakness in terms of resources contributed eventually to their loss of influence to the Dutch.

The Americas

The Spanish conquest of the New World was an uncertain affair. This was partly because, at first, Columbus insisted that he found the Indies. Once it became apparent that he had found a 'New World', attempts at colonisation and exploitation could take place. An early colonial settlement was set up on the island of Hispaniola. Diego Velázquez established a settlement on the island of Cuba and Vasco Nuñez de Balboa established a settlement in what is now Panama and in 1513 he became the first European to encounter the Pacific Ocean.

The second stage in the development of the Spanish Empire came with the conquest of Mexico. The first Spanish incursion into Mexico came when Francisco Fernández de Cordoba began exploring there in 1517. Two years later Hernán Cortés entered the territory of the powerful Aztec tribe with a handful of followers. By 1521 they had destroyed the Aztec Empire owing to a combination of luck, assistance from local enemies of the Aztecs, superior weapons and the ability to use their horses to good strategic effect. Between 1521 and 1524 Cortés added to the Mexican territory under his control as Governor of New Spain, a position from which he was to be removed by Charles I.

In succeeding years the Spanish made piecemeal additions to their overseas empire, establishing control over much of Central America during the 1520s. However, the most spectacular increase in the size of the Spanish Empire came with the conquest of the Inca Empire in Peru. After a failure in 1530, Francisco Pizarro set off on a second expedition to conquer Peru in 1532. Emulating Cortés both in operating with a small force and making alliances with local tribes opposed to Inca domination, Pizarro acted with complete ruthlessness in murdering the Inca ruler, Atahualpa, and by capturing the Inca capital of Cuzco. The Spanish colonisers immediately fell out among themselves, but by this stage the Incas were too weakened to be able to take advantage of their quarrels.

The main objective of the Spanish colonists was to find gold. Unfortunately for the *conquistadores*, gold proved to be a largely elusive commodity. The search for *El Dorado* always ended in failure. Silver proved to be a different matter. Plentiful quantities were found, and a huge silver mine was created at Potosí in Peru in 1545 which was to employ some 13,000 labourers.

In the end, however, Spanish colonisers were far more concerned with agriculture than with mining. Large landed estates known as *encomiendas* were created. In return for offering military service to the Spanish Crown, the estate holders were given the right in effect to enslave local labour. Huge flocks of sheep and cattle were kept, and a variety of crops were grown, including sugar, olives and a range of grains. Shipbuilding and textiles were important growth industries. The wealth generated by and for the Spanish colonisers enabled them to create a number of impressive new cities, such as Lima, Mexico City and Santiago as well as create an effective bureaucratic structure for the administration of the territories. The price for such affluence was paid largely by the native Americans, who suffered enslavement and huge rates of mortality due to their inability to resist European diseases.

The Ottoman Empire

3.1 What were the main reasons for the rapid growth of the Ottoman Empire in the late 15th and early 16th centuries?

3.2 Why was Suleiman the Magnificent able to expand on his superb inheritance of 1520?

3.3 What were the main reasons for the remarkable success of the Ottomans?

3.4 Historical interpretation: To what extent and why did the Ottoman Empire decline in the period after the death of Suleiman?

Key Issues

● *What were the main reasons for the expansion of the Turkish Empire in the 16th century?*

● *What was the impact of the Ottoman Turks on the rest of Europe in the 16th century?*

● *How important was the work of Suleiman the Magnificent both inside and outside the Ottoman Empire?*

Framework of Events

1451	Accession of Mehmed II
1453	Capture of Constantinople
1481	Accession of Bayezid II
1499	War with Venice
1512	Accession of Selim I
1514	Great victory over Shi'ites – Battle of Lake Van in Persia
1517	Capture of Jerusalem
1520	Accession of Suleiman the Magnificent
1521	Capture of Belgrade
1522	Capture of Rhodes
1526	Battle of Mohácz in Hungary
1529	Turks failure to capture Vienna
1534	Capture of Tunis and Baghdad
1535	Formal Treaty of Alliance with France
1538	Barbarossa defeats Papal/Spanish/Venetian navy
1551	Capture of Tripoli
1566	Death of Suleiman the Magnificent. Accession of Selim II
1569	Expedition to Russia fails. Persian Campaign fails
1570	Cyprus taken
1571	Battle of Lepanto
1574	Accession of Murad III

Overview

O N the fringes of what, today, we see as Europe lay a remarkable new Empire which grew up in this period. In its own way this empire, known as the Ottoman Empire, had a strong impact on events in 'mainland' Europe. Because of the growing threat this new empire represented to central

Europe and to Spain, Charles V, the Holy Roman Emperor and master of much of central Europe, was unable to pay the full attention he wished to the problems of Martin Luther and his heresy (see Chapter 4). France looked for friendship from the Turks, as an ally against a growing Hapsburg encirclement of France. Spain found itself distracted from expansion to the West and in North Africa by a threat from the other end of the Mediterranean. Spain was also unable to put its full might into suppressing its rebels in breakaway Holland. Therefore Dutch independence owes something to the amazing military advances and successes of the Turks. The Papacy was also threatened, both in the attacks on Italy itself and by the expansion of militant Islam. The Turks were committed **evangelists** as well as **imperialists**, so the Papacy was unable to pay full attention to the growing threat in the North from Luther and the other Protestants. As a distraction alone the Turks were to play a major part in the history of Europe in the 16th century.

At the same time it was a period of remarkable expansion for the Turks. They grew from a small unit in what is now a part of Turkey called Anatolia and expanded consistently until the late 16th century. They were to end up with an empire which not only covered most of what is modern Turkey, but also large parts of Europe, North Africa and the Middle East. That Empire remained a major force in world politics, as well as European politics, until the 20th century. It lasted until the major peace treaties which brought the First World War to an end. The reasons for this remarkable expansion need to be examined with care. We need to see whether it was the work of two remarkable rulers, or the society which produced them. There is also debate as to whether the rise of this Empire is more to do with the division, weakness and distraction of its opponents rather than with the skills of its rulers or soldiers. It was a remarkable achievement to found the greatest empire of its day and in a very short space of time. Given the huge distances between the 'base' in Constantinople (modern Istanbul) and the far-flung corners of the Empire, it is an even more outstanding achievement. Few empires have grown so rapidly, covered such a vast area, and survived for so long.

Evangelists: People determined to spread their faith (Islam).

Imperialists: Supporters of the Holy Roman Emperor (as opposed to religious leaders) who wanted Ottoman rule to expand by acquiring extra territory.

3.1 What were the reasons for the growth of the Ottoman Empire in the late 15th and early 16th centuries?

The main reasons for the rapid growth of the Ottoman Empire lie in the talents of two rulers, Mehmed II (1451–1481) and Selim (1512–1520), as well as the remarkable society of which they were a product. Many of the foremost Ottomans were not those born in what we now know as Turkey. The élite of Turkish society, the Ottomans, was often European born and educated. Many of them were former slaves who had been taken as part of the booty of raids into Europe. By the late 14th and the early 15th centuries what became the Turkish Empire was spreading across the Bosphorus (see map on page 44) from Turkey in Asia into modern Greece by 1400. The colonial rule established by the Ottomans was competent, and not dissimilar to that used by the Romans in their heyday. They tolerated local religions and practices (provided Ottoman **sovereignty** was accepted, necessary taxes paid and soldiers provided for the army). In many cases the rule of the Ottomans was preferable to that of the former masters of these Eastern European peoples.

Sovereignty: The political power that a country possesses to govern itself or another country or state.

Mehmed's first great success was the capture of Constantinople in 1453. This is seen as an event of great significance as Constantinople was the capital of the Christian Church in the East and the centre of the

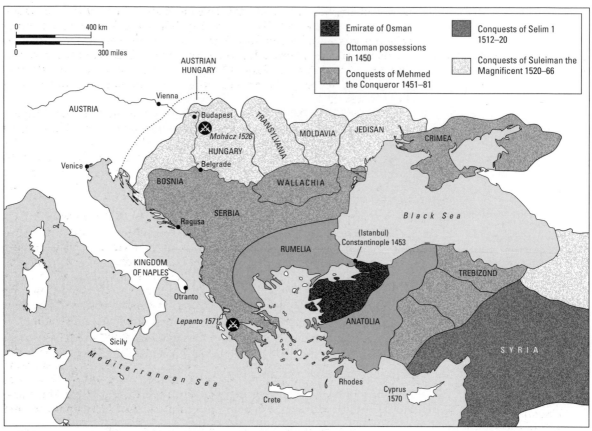

The growth of the Ottoman Empire 1450–1566

Galley: A low, single-decked vessel powered by wind and by oars. It was similar to the old Roman galleys.

former great Byzantine Empire. Tremors of fear were sent across Europe that an Islamic invader was coming. It also brought real prestige to its Ottoman captors. What is more, it also gave the Ottomans a superb base and a capital of strategic, commercial and political influence. From there they could dominate the whole of the Middle East and Eastern Mediterranean, as well as Eastern Europe and North Africa. Under the last Byzantine Emperors the city of Constantinople had decayed and had become largely depopulated. Under the dynamic leadership of the Ottomans, it became the largest, wealthiest and most densely populated of cities (over 100,000) in the known world at the time.

With Constantinople as his base, Mehmed – a brilliant fighter and natural aggressor – started to expand outwards in all directions from that base. He was to make Constantinople into the centre of a huge, constantly growing empire. By the time of his death he had created a large empire by any standards, covering most of what is modern Turkey, Greece, Bulgaria and Romania and much of what was to become Bosnia, Serbia and Albania. He also took the Crimean peninsula in the south of modern Russia. Using the Crimea as a base, he expanded the empire into mainland Russia. Mehmed also started to build a large **galley** fleet. He had important naval victories over the then dominant Mediterranean naval power, Venice, and by 1480 the Ottomans had defeated the Venetian fleet at Otranto and become the naval masters of the Eastern Mediterranean.

The military reasons for Mehmed's success will be detailed later, as his even more expansionist successors – Selim and Suleiman the Magnificent – used the same military traditions and practices. What provided much of the dynamism for this and the following reigns was the motivation of the Ottomans. The Ottomans felt strongly that they had a divine claim to universal empire. They had been given a mission by God to bring Islam to the rest of the world. To them a Holy War (Jihad) to stamp out other religions was a God-given duty. The chance of revenge on the Christians for their centuries of **crusades** to recapture the Christian holy places was also appealing. With the duty of holy war and the guarantee of salvation to those who fell in it, there was a strong motivational force for conquest and expansion.

Mehmed II can be seen as the real founder of the Ottoman Empire. He brought together so many differing strands of Ottoman life. He gave it a purpose and harnessed the fighting qualities of his peoples. He demonstrated the potential of his people and what could be achieved. In overthrowing the Byzantine Empire and taking the city of Constantinople for his capital, he signalled to the rest of the world that his was a people on the rise.

The reign of the next Sultan, Bayezid II (1481–1512) was more a period of consolidation. The reign had a difficult start, as there were two possible claimants to the throne. This caused divided loyalties among his subjects. It was normally the custom on the death of the Sultan for the successful claimant to kill all possible rivals (and that included the wives of the former Sultan who might be pregnant just in case they were carrying a rival). This was done in order to avoid the sort of situation which faced Henry VII when he took the throne of England from Richard III where dissidents could gather around other claimants.

In spite of these political difficulties, it was an important period of consolidation, as well as expansion, for the Ottoman Empire. There were further victories against the Venetians at sea, when considerable harm was done to Venetian merchant shipping. With the defeats of the Venetians, Ottoman commerce could start to dominate the Mediterranean and

Crusades: Attempts by Christians to drive out Islam from Jerusalem.

1. What does this show about the nature of Mediterranean naval warfare in the late 15th century?

2. How does it differ from the contemporary plan on page 50 and the painting by Vincentino (page 55)?

A contemporary woodcut of a naval clash between the Ottomans and the Venetians. The Venetian ships have the lion flag of Venice, the Ottoman ships fly a crescent flag.

produce real wealth for the Sultans and their peoples. Both the Ottoman army and the navy were modernised – the former in the way in which it fought and was led, and the latter in its leadership, number of ships and in its tactics. Shipyards were built and a large galley fleet was created. The Eastern Mediterranean had become Ottoman controlled. That navy was also able to dominate much of the central Mediterranean. The Ottoman fleet started to work with those of Naples and Milan, two of the independent Italian city states, against both France and Venice.

The Turkish Empire was becoming more and more of a power to be reckoned with in both European and Mediterranean affairs. Others were anxious to have the Turks as allies in their local conflicts. Naturally this division between Italian states and between other European powers enabled the Turks to gain footholds and contacts further west, and there was no sign of any concerted Christian attempt to block the future advance of the Ottomans. Selim's Christian opponents were too concerned with their own religious and dynastic affairs to see the encroaching Islamic menace.

Primogeniture: The rule that the first-born son should succeed his father.

Under Selim I, another period of rapid expansion was to come about. Selim deposed his father and basically killed his way to the top. The normal rules of **primogeniture** never applied to the Ottomans. They believed in survival of the fittest, and looking at some of the monarchs who were to play a part in the history of Europe in the 16th century, the Turks had a point. Selim was also favoured by the **Janissaries** as being appropriately warlike and more likely to meet the expectations of this warrior class of men who dominated this society geared so much for war.

Janissaries: The core of the Turkish army: the military élite, often as many as 10,000 first-rate soldiers, who also acted as the Sultan's personal bodyguard.

The Ottoman Empire underwent yet another period of remarkable expansion under Selim I. Selim saw himself as a new Alexander the Great (the great Macedonian emperor and empire builder), whose empire had stretched throughout much the Mediterranean and the Middle East, and who attempted to add India to his conquests. Selim was an educated monarch who had read some of the great classical writers and had learned of the great Greek warrior-king, Alexander. With his first great success in defeating a rival Muslim leader, Shah Ismail of Iran at Lake Van in 1514. Shah Ismail was leader of the **Shi'ite Muslims**. This led to the expansion of the Ottoman Empire into what are now Iraq and Syria. The absence of any clear geographical boundaries to the south-east made this a difficult area to conquer and hold, and Selim was perhaps unwise to start to take on such an area and to take on enemies who were difficult to defeat. Unlike much of Europe, Iraq and Syria were barren and unproductive. There was little loot to be gained there and Selim's army could not really survive in such a barren area. Not all of Selim's successors thanked him for that legacy, as it was always difficult to hold on to.

Shi'ite Muslims: The Shi'ite/Sunnite Muslim split had its origins in a dispute about the successor to the great Muslim prophet Mohammed. The Ottomans were Sunni Muslims.

Selim also attacked north towards the Caucasus Mountains; another dangerous area to move into as it stretched his supply lines. The fact that he and his successors were able to hold on to regions such as this, as well as down the valleys of the Tigris and Euphrates (modern Iraq) is a tribute to Ottoman skills as fighters, administrators and suppliers. Again geographical factors, with the absence of any natural barrier, made it difficult to defend and even more difficult to attack. Selim also destroyed the Mamluk Empire, a dynasty that dominated what is now modern Egypt. He took Jerusalem and Damascus by 1517 and soon worked his way around the Mediterranean coast to take Cairo. Here he started to lay the basis of a North African Empire. With the Muslim Holy cities of Mecca and Medina also in his possession by the end of the reign, Selim was in effect the master of the whole Arab and Muslim world. He was now the foremost Muslim leader in the world and had played an important role in bringing peace to his part of Europe and the Middle East when he wished. Selim accumulated considerable wealth and developed the process of self-funding conquest that was to grow throughout the 16th century. This meant that the territories he captured had to pay him for the privilege of being conquered by him.

Selim was also very careful to open new trade routes to the East in the wake of his conquests – to generate more income for himself and to the benefit of his subjects. Ottoman traders were moving rapidly down the Red Sea and into the Gulf of Arabia and were heading towards India and the spice trade of the East. All in all, it was a remarkable achievement for one man.

A mixture of brilliant leadership, great opportunism, an efficient army and navy and weak and divided opponents all played an important part, between 1451 and 1520, in the rapid growth and establishment of a major empire centred on Constantinople. Religious motivation and a great sense of mission were also important to both Sultans and the way in which they managed their newly-acquired empire and its diverse subjects. They were fortunate in not discovering the major limits which geography and logistics can impose on expanding empires. Their successors were to do that, but the way in which they harnessed the potential of their resources, added to those resources, and took every opportunity to achieve what they felt was their divine mission was remarkable. There were to be few imitators in modern history.

1. What were the main reasons for the expansion of the Ottoman Empire before 1520?

2. To what extent were the two Sultans, Mehmed and Selim, the most important factor in Ottoman expansion?

3.2 Why was Suleiman the Magnificent able to expand on his superb inheritance of 1520?

There are three main reasons why Suleiman was able to develop his father's legacy into an even greater empire:

1 His own ability as a leader and warrior. He was also able to harness the enormous energy and skills of his many subjects.

2 He inherited a system of government and logistics (movement of people and equipment) which was designed to wage war and expand territory.

3 Suleiman was fortunate in that for much of the first part of his reign the other powers most able to oppose him were locked in conflict elsewhere. He had a free hand in the Mediterranean as well as in the other areas into which he wished to expand.

The initial reaction of both Turk and foreigner to the death of Selim and the succession of his supposedly shy and retiring son, Suleiman, was one of relief. They all hoped the reign of terror coming into south-eastern Europe would now be over, peace would come and that central Europe would no longer be menaced by this Islamic invader. They were wrong, completely wrong. Within months, Suleiman had moved an army into the Balkans and laid siege to Belgrade and invaded Hungary at the same time. As well as this he started to lay siege to the island of Rhodes which he saw as an obstacle to his domination of the Eastern Mediterranean. It was an essential base if he wished to expand further West. He could not have his galleys and merchants ships threatened from the rear.

Suleiman personally led the attack on Belgrade and the campaign was a major success mainly through his leadership. The great fortress and city of Belgrade fell to him in 1521. His tactics were ingenious and very successful: several columns of lightly armed and highly mobile cavalry attacked as diversions to both the North and to the West. These distracted his opponents and cut off any chance of relief supplies or columns getting through to Belgrade. Suleiman made very effective use

Siege artillery: Large, powerful guns which are transported on wheels. They were very useful in attacking a city under attack.

of large **siege artillery**. It had been a massive task to get the guns there from his new foundries near Constantinople. Suleiman organised the building of massive engineering works to get the guns in close enough to the walls of Belgrade. He also made clever use of his naval forces on the river Danube to isolate his enemy and to bring up supplies. This led to a remarkable personal success, which had been denied to Mehmed in 1456.

Encouraged by his success in Belgrade, Suleiman then moved north and invaded Hungary. His main aim seems to have been to capture Vienna; he was nothing if ambitious. He destroyed the Hungarian army at Moház in 1526. This was quite an achievement in that it was only one of several campaigns he was involved in at the time. The flexibility of the Ottoman troops, as well as their clever use of artillery, was vital to the Ottoman success. Also important was the poor leadership of the Hungarians. Their king, Lewis, and most of his nobility were killed, and Suleiman moved on to take the towns of Buda and Pest. This defeat of a 'European' power aroused interest and fear in the West, not only as King Lewis had married the sister of Charles V, the Holy Roman Emperor, but also because Lewis was childless. This gave Charles V's brother Ferdinand a claim to the throne of Hungary. Now the Ottomans were to have a more formidable foe in the Emperor and his family than the weaker Hungarians had proved.

Suleiman moved west to try to take Vienna, which forced the Habsburgs into rapid action. This attempt was driven back in 1529. The capture of Vienna was to remain an ambition for both Suleiman and his successors for some time to come.

Suleiman was able to leave Hungary divided between the Habsburgs and his own supporter/nominee, Zápolyai, while he turned his attention elsewhere. He had made major advances and expanded his Empire into more of the Balkan region and he had served notice on the Western European powers that he was a force to be reckoned with. The Turkish threat from the East was to be a major factor in the thinking of Charles V, and a major influence on his policies and those of his son, Philip II of Spain, in the second part of the 16th century.

Suleiman abandoned his attempt on Vienna reluctantly, but time and distance from Constantinople were major factors. The Habsburgs could not normally count on much help from the German princes, unless the Turks came too close to home. Faced with Charles V defending the heart of his Empire in Vienna, backed with substantial numbers of experienced German solders, Suleiman knew the merits of strategic withdrawal. However, he left a weakened and divided Hungary behind, which was no threat to him and could be brushed aside when he had the resources to do it.

Knights of St John: These were an old crusading order, originally founded to lead the assault on the Muslim possession of Jerusalem. At the time of Suleiman the Magnificent they may have numbered only a few thousand, but they were determined fighters and effective pirates.

Suleiman turned his attention to the Mediterranean island of Rhodes, owned by the Christian **Knights of St John**. Rhodes was an important naval base in the age of the galley. It was also an important link in the East–West and North–South Mediterranean trade routes. The fact that the Knights of St John were a militant Christian order was also a factor which encouraged their suppression. They were effective pirates when it came to capturing Muslim shipping. The Knights held out at first, but Suleiman managed to raise a fleet of around 200 ships and nearly 100,000 men. With no help forthcoming from Christian Europe, the Knights had to surrender in 1522. Tenacity and clever engineering were vital factors in the fall of Rhodes, as well as the personal leadership of Suleiman. In only two years there had been further expansion led by the supposedly quiet 'nonentity', Suleiman. It looked as if he was going to be worse, from Western Christian Europe's viewpoint, than his terrible father.

Barbary pirates: Superb seaman, based in Algiers in northern Africa, who tended to make their living from piracy.

Corsairs: These were pirates who attacked shipping. The Barbary corsairs operated in the Mediterranean from their bases along the Barbary coast in the western part of north Africa. 'Corsair' came from the Latin *cursus* which means 'to make inroads'.

Fearing that militant Christian Spain, which was known to be hostile to its own Muslim population, would try to drive Islam out of North Africa, Suleiman employed the leader of the **Barbary pirates**, Barbarossa, as his naval commander. They moved west across the North African mainland and shore. By 1534 Tunis had fallen to the Ottomans. Barbarossa brought with him highly-skilled naval captains, of which Suleiman had a shortage. Barbarossa was more than a match for the Genoese naval commander, Andrea Doria. Egypt was integrated fully into the Ottoman Empire. Charles V expelled the Ottomans from Tunis a year later, but they were soon to return and recapture it.

In 1538 Barbarossa's galley fleet, financed largely by Suleiman, had managed to destroy the combined fleets of Venice, Spain and the Papacy (see page 50) in the Adriatic Sea. Barbarossa was raiding both sides of the Italian coast by 1540. The fight was on to gain both the central and the western Mediterranean and to dominate the entire sea. Barbarossa's **corsairs** and the Ottoman fleet wintered in the French port of Toulon in 1540–41 with the encouragement of the French King, who was anxious to encourage anything which would damage his Habsburg opponents. Such support was an asset to Suleiman, as it meant that his sailors did not have the exhausting row back to his bases in the eastern Mediterranean and the equally tiring return journey in the spring. Another major Christian fleet was smashed off Djerba in 1560 and it looked as if the dream of an Ottoman Empire in the Mediterranean was coming true.

However, just before Suleiman's death in 1566, he failed to take the vital base of Malta, now occupied by the Knights of St John. Philip II of Spain, the Italian States and the Papacy all realised that if the Ottomans got Malta, they would command the whole central Mediterranean. They would then be able not only to attack Italy with ease, but also destroy much of the trade which was so important to the wealth of Italy. For once the major powers, Spain in particular, got themselves organised to destroy the westward Ottoman advance. They hoped to drive the galley fleets of Barbarossa and the Ottomans back into the eastern Mediterranean in 1565. The Spanish and Habsburg counter-offensive against the Ottomans continued. The great Ottoman fleet, the key to so much success in the Mediterranean, was virtually destroyed in 1571 at Lepanto off the coast of Greece.

In addition to the expansion in virtually every other direction, Suleiman tried to continue his father's expansionary work to the East and South-East of his empire. In the 1530s and 1540s he attacked towards what are now modern Iran and Iraq. Baghdad was taken in 1534 and in 1535 he obtained a sort of settled frontier, but with such huge distances involved it was never possible to end the conflict there. Possession of Egypt led inevitably to expansion down into the Red Sea, and Ottoman rule extended by the end of Suleiman's reign to both what is now Yemen and Aden. In addition, his sailors and merchants were challenging the Portuguese monopoly of trade to India and beyond.

How useful is this Ottoman painting of the siege to a historian writing about warfare in the early 16th century?

Manuscript page showing the siege of Vienna, 1529, by the army of Suleiman the Magnificent

A contemporary plan (top) of the Battle of Lepanto. The Venetian galleys are in the centre, surrounded by Islamic/Ottoman forces. (Bottom) a contemporary engraving of the Battle of Lepanto

1. What information does the plan provide for a historian writing about naval tactics in the Mediterranean in the late 16th century?

2. Of what value is the artist's impression to historians writing about the importance of the Battle of Lepanto to Christian Europe?

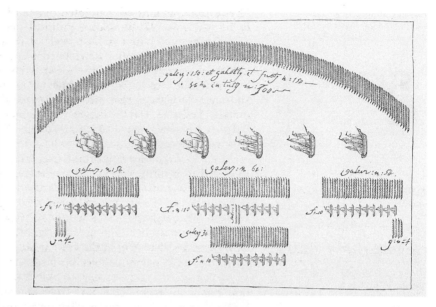

1. Explain how the Ottoman Empire expanded during the reign of Suleiman.

2. Assess the nature and extent of the achievements of Suleiman the Magnificent.

By Suleiman's death in 1566 a large empire had been built. Large parts of it remained in being until the 20th century and it was not seriously dismantled until after the First World War. It was a huge achievement.

3.3 *What were the main reasons for the remarkable success of Ottoman expansion?*

In 1560 the Austrian ambassador to Suleiman's court in Constantinople wrote:

'On their side are the resources of a mighty empire, they have experience and practice in fighting, are accustomed to victory, endurance of toil, unity, order, discipline frugality and watchfulness. On our side is public poverty, private luxury, broken spirit, lack of endurance and training … can we doubt what the result will be?'

The Austrian ambassador pointed out to his master, Emperor Ferdinand, in Vienna that all the social, political and military institutions of the country he was based in were geared to war and conquest. With the system based on personal slaves both in the army and in government, and with an able man at the helm, they were an unstoppable force.

The main reason for the remarkable success during the reign of Suleiman and his predecessors was the quality of the leadership and the driving ambition of the three great emperors – Mehmed, Selim and Suleiman – between 1451 and 1566. The one intervening sultan, Bayezid, who ruled between 1481 and 1512, was by no means incompetent. He allowed an important breathing space for the conquests of Mehmed to be absorbed and consolidated upon. The fact that it was an **autocracy** was also important. There was no aristocracy, such as in France (see Chapter 7), demanding the right to lead both armies and society and to share power with the King. Those who were delegated power to administer regions or ministries tended to be former slaves who owed loyalty only to the monarch and not to any **caste**. There was no concern about noble 'privileges'. The rulers of the Ottoman Empire always worked on the simple system of promoting by merit alone, regardless of origin. This was very unusual in the 16th century, but highly effective. The custom of training the sons of the monarch in the skills of government, and the law of fratricide (killing of brothers), ensured the brutal survival of the fittest. This custom also involved the killing of all possible rivals or bearers of rivals, so there were no rivals for the affections and loyalty of their subjects. It may not have been a pleasant system, but it led to efficiency.

While the focus was on overseas expansion – and the whole Ottoman Empire seemed to be built around the idea of permanent conquest and absorption of new territories – domestic factors were not neglected. The decaying Constantinople was made into an outstanding capital city after 1453. It became both an administrative base and a growing commercial centre which began to attract merchants from Holland, England and Portugal as the 16th century progressed. Constantinople increasingly became the trade centre for the whole of the Middle East, with links and trade routes going up into Russia and down towards the Indian Ocean and the Red Sea.

There was always a stress on the necessary roads and communications, and the need to educate the future leaders of both the administration and the army was recognised. There was always a sense that they were looking to the future. The importance placed on getting good men in the right position and developing ways of keeping them loyal was vital to Ottoman success. Suleiman recognised the need for a uniform and comprehensible legal system, which not only made it clear who was the ruler, but also adapted to the different needs and customs of the peoples of his hugely diverse empire. The Ottomans had to spend remarkably little time and few resources in repressing and containing the conquered peoples in their Empire. This meant that their troops could be used for expansionary purposes and not guarding lines of communication and **garrisoning** subject peoples. Suleiman created a quality civil service and a competent legal system. These provided intelligent rule of subject nations and also led to an efficient system of raising taxes and organising armies. As with other successful commanders, Suleiman realised that the key lay in an efficient system of supply and pay. Paid and fed soldiers fight well.

Another key reason for their success was the real quality of the Ottoman army and its leaders, and in the quality of the civil service which backed up the army and administered the conquered territories. The Ottoman method

Autocracy: Government of a country or empire by one person who has complete power. Any dissent is usually dealt with harshly.

Caste: Social class or system that is based on dividing people into groups according to their family, rank, wealth, profession etc.

Garrisoning: The placing of soldiers in a town to protect it.

of recruiting its army was unusual. In the territories under their control one of the main forms of taxation was to hand over a set number of young boys, mainly from the captured Christian areas in the Balkans. These were removed from their families, often as young as three, and were taken away into the heart of the Empire to be trained. This process was known as the 'Devshirme'. Some selection took place at the point of collection, so the handicapped and less physically robust were eliminated.

Further selection took place away from the point of collection. The more intellectually able were set aside to become commanders and civil servants, and trained accordingly. Conversion to Islam was part of the process. The training process could take up to seven years. This was not dissimilar in many respects to that given to their equally fanatical opponents the Jesuits, although they waged a different war in a different way. On the whole they were well treated and lived in better conditions than in their Balkan village. Once 'qualified', they were paid and promoted according to merit. It was quite possible for one of the boys to rise to the status of Grand Vizier (the equivalent of Prime Minister), and great wealth and status were possible. They also had the advantage of being completely loyal to the Sultan alone, and were easily removable. They were not allowed to marry, so that their loyalty would be to the Sultan totally.

The less able of these 'recruits' became the Sultan's standing army, known as the Janissaries. It was normal for them to be sent in their teens to work as

> *How useful are these woodcuts to a historian writing about the Ottoman Army?*

These are woodcuts from a book by Melchior Lorich, ambassador of the Holy Roman Emperor to Ottoman Turkey. They were made between 1554 and 1562. The aim of the book was to awaken Christian troops to the danger of Ottoman attack. The Ottoman Janissary (left) is bearing a shield, and is armed with a sword, a long spear and a mace. The Ottoman cavalrymen (see right) were free landowners, receiving land grants from the state on condition of providing military service when summoned.

A manuscript illustration showing Suleiman the Magnificent with his Army at the Battle of Mohácz. It was produced in the Ottoman Empire.

What information does this painting provide a historian about the Ottoman Army in the reign of Suleiman the Magnificient?

agricultural labourers to toughen them up and ensure their conversion to Islam. They were then sent to Constantinople to be trained further in the arts of war. They formed a core of about 14,000 men, probably the largest standing army in existence at the time. The Janissaries were superbly trained, both on horse and on foot, and could use the traditional weaponry as well as the musket and the cannon. They could also fight at sea, as galley warfare often consisted of little more than ramming and boarding.

With the Janissaries as the shock troops – a highly mobile and flexible force as the core of the army – further troops could be raised according to need through the system of land tenure (known as the Timar), which existed both in the original empire and in the conquered territories. The system was not dissimilar to the old feudal system brought into England by the Normans after the conquest. Land was granted to loyal supporters of the Sultan in the form of a tenancy; in return the holder had to provide a certain numbers of soldiers from the profits of that land, and to ensure that they were paid and equipped. What was important was that when the owner of the land died, it was not passed on to a son, but reverted to the

Sultan. This way no aristocracy could be built up which might challenge the authority of the Sultan. With a system of permanent conquest, it is easy to see how the Sultans could raise huge armies at minimal cost to themselves. The problems started to arise when conquest stopped and those who the Sultan intended to hold the land on a temporary basis saw it more as a permanent possession.

It could be argued that it was the weakness of the opponents that enabled the Ottomans to expand so rapidly into so many areas. Without the Habsburg–Valois conflict a more resolute defence could have been maintained by the joint efforts of the Spanish and Austrian rulers. If they had been backed up by the experienced and wealthy naval forces of cities like Venice, defeat of the Ottomans could have been possible. With the growing Lutheran threat in Germany dividing their Christian opponents, and constant warfare among some the great Italian trading city states (such as Venice and Genoa who took pleasure out of seeing their opponents' ships sunk and crews enslaved), the Ottomans had an easy time. The Popes tended to get on badly with the Emperors, and it must have given great encouragement to Suleiman to see the armies of his military rival, Charles V, sack the capital of his great spiritual rival, the Pope, in 1527. The growing civil and religious war in Germany in the 1540s made Suleiman's task of expanding in the Mediterranean much easier. The quality of his army, opposed to the undisciplined and frequently unpaid troops of his opponents, was also a major factor. All three great Ottoman leaders took care never to fight a major war on two fronts. A look at the Framework of Events for this chapter (page 42) will show a major focus on one area at a time.

1. How important were the Ottoman army and navy to the success of Suleiman the Magnificent?

2. To what extent was it the weaknesses and divisions of their opponents that led to the huge success of the Ottomans?

3.4 To what extent did the Turkish Empire decline in the period after the death of Suleiman the Magnificent?
A CASE STUDY IN HISTORICAL INTERPRETATION

It is often easy to see the seeds of decline as the empire itself expands. The Ottoman Empire, while it did not expand much more in the 16th century after the death of Suleiman in 1566 (and not for the want of trying), did not show serious signs of declining until well into the 17th century. Even then, as mentioned before, it was still a major force until well into the 20th century.

Certainly contemporaries – and several are quoted in Andrina Stiles' *The Ottoman Empire 1450–1700* (1989) – in the later part of the 16th century were conscious of a decline, particularly as the Empire had now reached such an enormous size that it was simply not possible for it to continue to expand. One contemporary, quoted by J.H. Parry in the *New Cambridge Modern History*, writing in 1596–97, stated that:

'justice was becoming ill administered in the empire, that incapable men untested in long years of service rose to the highest offices of state and that the Ottoman armies had lost much of the obedience and discipline, the courage and skill of former times; the sultans had fallen into a life of ease and self indulgence, viziers intrigued against each other, the influence of the harem and women was growing, and that Sultans stopped leading their troops into battle or lead affairs themselves.'

The faction fighting grew at court as the early principle of promotion and tenure of office by merit alone disappeared. The weakness that comes with divided authority at the centre spread. A system which was based entirely on conquest and gave it its *raison d'être* (reason for being) ground to a halt, and it had real problems in adapting to a period without growth.

The Battle of Lepanto by Vincentino, a contemporary Italian artist

Holy League: Anti-Ottoman forces organised by the Pope, usually with Italian and Spanish forces.

None of the three rulers who followed Suleiman the Magnificent between 1566 and 1603 – Selim II, Murad III or Mehmed III – had the determination and leadership skills of Suleiman, but there were successes. Expansion continued into Iraq and up into the Caucasus Mountains in the North. In 1571 the island of Cyprus was captured, ensuring Ottoman control of the Eastern Mediterranean. Tunis and the surrounding territory was taken in 1570, and held off the furious attacks of the Habsburgs led by the victor of Lepanto, Don Juan of Austria. The final battle near Tunis took place in 1574 and the Ottomans remained in control of North Africa. Philip II of Spain had to abandon his imperial ambitions there. Crete was to be taken in the latter part of the 17th century, after years of fighting. The great drive for expansion did not stop.

Elsewhere, however, the successes under the three leaders did not continue. Attempts to expand further into Russia failed in 1569, as did another campaign to take over all of modern Persia in 1570. In both cases weather, distance and the huge logistical problems were too great, and the old rule of placing all your eggs in one military basket at a time was weakening. Heavy fighting in Hungary throughout the last 15 years of the century achieved no real gain and only served to blunt the impetus of other offensives. Also damaging in terms of prestige was the first major naval defeat that the Turks suffered, at Lepanto in 1571. It was part of a determined effort by the Christian forces to save Cyprus. While it did not save Cyprus, it did destroy a large Ottoman naval force, which severely damaged its prestige. It showed that the Turks could be beaten at sea, and this was bound to encourage more resistance. But it was not followed up by Don Juan, and another major naval battle the following year off Southern Greece was a draw. It demonstrated the capacity of the Turks to recoup and rebuild, and the **Holy League** never seriously threatened Ottoman rule in the Eastern Mediterranean again. That situation remained until at least the 1660s.

Certainly some worrying features can be seen in the first part of the 17th century, ranging from rapidly rising food prices to a lower quality of sultan. An example of this came in 1589: the Janissaries rose in rebellion when government wished to pay them in a new, debased coinage. None of those rulers in the first part of the 17th century matched in quality any of the three great conquerors of the late 15th and 16th centuries. The military tactics which had caused so much devastation in Europe and in North Africa were now being matched and bettered by countries such as

Tercios: A new system of infantry fighting in heavily armed columns.

Spain with its **tercios** and modern warships with new and heavier guns. Success bred a casual attitude towards the efficient maintenance of the system of producing and paying for soldiers. The wish to expand further meant greater problems of supplying and paying for troops as inevitably they had to expand further and further away from home. Once conquest was gone, then the system of reward lagged as well. A growing population, with fixed or declining resources of food, led to price increases and a growth in internal looting and fighting.

Historians Helmut Koenigsberger and G. Mosse, in *Europe in the 16th Century* (1968), argue that fundamental weaknesses start to appear within the Ottoman system during the reign of Suleiman, that is before the 1560s. They argue that by giving preference to one particular wife, Roxolana, and her son, who was to become the incompetent Selim II, Suleiman was ending the system whereby only the able rose to rule the Ottoman Empire. They also mention the degree of corruption that had begun to set in in the administrative system. They quote one of Suleiman's chief ministers in 1540 writing: 'Bribes to officials are an incurable disease – oh God save us from bribes.' They also point out the increasing problems that Suleiman was having in raising sufficient troops to take on the large number of enemies he had. The failure to take Malta in 1565, in spite of huge efforts, is an indication that the Ottomans were reaching the end of their resources.

Historian V. J. Parry, in the *New Cambridge Modern History*, places the roots of decline more in the second part of the 16th century, after the death of Suleiman. He argues that it was the toughness of the opposition to the Ottomans, in areas such as Hungary and Persia, that caused major problems to the Turks. The Ottoman military system was built on conquest and expansion and now it could no longer conquer or expand. Parry also stresses the damage done by **inflation** to the Ottoman empire which made paying and feeding armies progressively more difficult. He also stresses that with an increasingly incompetent and corrupt administration the conquered territories were no longer producing the conscripts needed to sustain the Ottoman military machine. Like Koenigsberger and Mosse, Parry also stresses that the system depended on a quality leader, and that was not present after Suleiman's death.

Inflation: A general increase in the prices of goods and services in a country.

Andrina Stiles, in *The Ottoman Empire 1450–1700*, has a detailed study of the decline and its **historiography**. She looks at the views of contemporaries, who felt that the causes of decline lay in the fact that sultans after Suleiman changed the social system adversely. They ignored external factors, such as more determined enemies. Stiles places more emphasis on events in the latter part of the 16th century. She mentions the declining quality of the Sultans, inflation and a population explosion, which placed a strain on limited resources. The deep conservatism of the Ottomans meant they were finding it increasingly difficult to face up to the new weaponry of their enemies in Europe. Stiles also places a lot of emphasis on the failure of the Ottoman nobility to adapt to a time when there was simply no more conquest.

Historiography: The different ways in which historians of all periods have looked at a problem.

The Turks had aroused a great fear in the 16th century and their ability to weaken the Habsburgs in the fight against both Protestantism and France inevitably played an important part in the history of Europe in the 16th century. However, after Lepanto and their increasingly obvious inability to advance beyond the frontiers left at the time of the death of Suleiman the Magnificent, the Ottomans became less of a threat to Europe in the 17th century. Nevertheless, the capacity of the Ottomans to make their presence felt was still there, as they arrived in force outside the gates of Vienna in the second part of the 17th century. As Sir Thomas Roe, the English ambassador, wrote about the Empire in the 1620s: 'that the Ottoman Empire might stand, but never rise again'.

1. In what ways have historians differed in their views about why the Ottoman Empire declined?

2. Why have historians differed in their interpretation of Ottoman decline?

Source-based questions: The reasons for Turkish supremacy in the Mediterranean in the 16th century

SOURCE A

On their side are the resources of a mighty empire ... they have experience and practice in fighting and are accustomed to victory, endurance of toil, unity, order, discipline, frugality and watchfulness. On our side is public poverty, private luxury, broken spirit, lack of endurance and training. Can we doubt what the result of conflict with them will be?

G de Busbecq, Austrian Ambassador to Turkey, 1560

SOURCE B

In the Sultan's view, there should only be on empire, only one faith and only one sovereign in the whole world. No place did more deserve than Istanbul for the creation of this unity in the world. The Sultan believed that, thanks to this city, he could extend his rule over the whole world.

A Turkish writer, writing in the late 15th century

SOURCE C

The reign of Suleiman owed it splendour to far more than great campaigns of conquest. Administrators and statesman of exceptional skill...flourished at the time. The Sultan devoted large revenues to frontier defence, as in the repair of the fortress at Rhodes, Belgrade and Buda...he also built mosques, bridges, aqueducts and other public utilities. Above all he strove to embellish his capital on the Golden Horn his people. Suleiman became known as Kanuni, the law maker...men of his time emphasised his zeal for justice and the Venetian Navagero paid him high tribute indeed when he wrote that Suleiman, provided he were well informed, did wrong to no one.

From The Ottoman Empire, 1520–1566, in New Cambridge Modern History by V J Parry, 1962

---

1. With reference to Sources A, B and C, and to information contained within this chapter, explain the meaning of the three terms highlighted in the sources:

a) 'the resources of a mighty empire' (Source A)

b) 'only one faith' (Source B)

c) 'the fortress at Rhodes' (Source C).

2. Study Sources A, B and C. How far do these sources agree on the reasons for the success of the Ottoman Turks in the 16th century?

3. How useful are these sources to a historian writing about the rise of the Turkish Empire in the 16th century?

4. Study all three sources and use the information contained within this chapter.

'The skill of the Sultan was the primary reason for the growth and consolidation of the huge and successful Ottoman Empire.'

Assess the validity of this statement.

The Reformation

Key Issues

● Why did a religious reformation occur in early 16th-century Europe?

● Why and how did it spread with such speed and permanence?

● What was the impact of this religious upheaval, not only in terms of religion, but also in political, economic and social terms?

Framework of Events

1483	Birth of Martin Luther
1505	Luther becomes a monk
1507	Luther becomes a priest
1509	Erasmus publishes 'In Praise of Folly'
1517	Luther nails his 95 theses on church door at Wittenberg
1519	Debate between Luther, Karlstadt and Eck
	Erasmus publishes New Testament in Latin
1520	Luther publishes 'Address to the Christian Nobility of the German Nation' and other pamphlets
	Luther is excommunicated
1521	Luther placed under 'Ban of the Empire'
1522	Zwingli starts reformation process in Zurich
1522	Luther publishes New Testament in German
1523	First evidence of Anabaptism seen in Switzerland
1524	Peasants revolt in Germany
1526	League of Torgau is formed by German princes to prevent Worms edicts being implemented
	Diet of Speyer
1527	Schleitheim meeting of Anabaptists
1529	Diet of Speyer. 'Protestantism' used for first time.
	Colloquy of Marburg. Attempt by Zwingli and Luther to find common ground fails
1530	Confession of Augsburg
1531	Schmalkaldic League is formed for armed defence of Protestantism
	Zwingli killed at Battle of Kappel
1534	Anabaptists take control of Münster
1536	Calvin publishes his 'Institutes' (first edition)
1537	Calvin is expelled from Geneva
1541	Calvin returns to Geneva and publishes *Ecclesiastical Ordinances*
1559	Geneva Academy for training missionaries opens in Geneva.

Overview

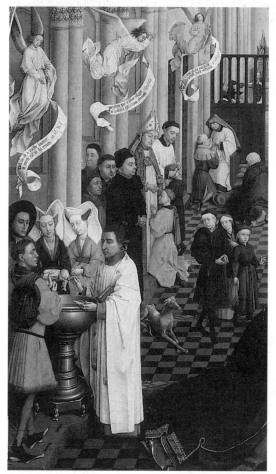

The Catholic sacraments – baptism, confirmation and confession – from an altarpiece by Roger van der Weyden, c.1453–1455

Pulpit: Place in church from where the priest preached.

Monopoly: Having total control and therefore no competition. The Hanse had a shipping monopoly at the time, as there were no serious challengers to the Baltic area. The clergy had a virtual 'monopoly' of education in Europe at the time as they were the only ones doing the teaching.

T HE religious events that were to dominate European history for most of the 16th century are known as the Reformation. The Roman Catholic Church had been the single most important influence on European society for well over a thousand years. It dominated education, laid down moral values, and the values of society generally. To a large extent it had complete control over all 'thought', as literacy was mainly the preserve of the clergy. Without the use of the printing press, the clergy wrote and published, and kept in its own libraries, almost every book written. Through the **pulpit** it controlled perhaps the most important means of communicating with the vast mass of most populations. Through its **monopoly** of education, the clergy provided monarchs with a literate and educated civil service. Bishops were great landowners and often warriors, and the Church was frequently asked to aid bankrupt monarchs.

An elected Pope, resident in Rome and usually an Italian, controlled the Roman Church. Increasingly, the Papacy had become a political and wealthy organisation. It seemed to forget its fundamental role of assisting people to search for the truth and helping them towards eternal salvation. It resented challenges and criticism.

The clergy's monopoly came under challenge in the late 15th century when the spread of humanist ideas (see Chapter 2) and a growth of learning and literacy encouraged men to rethink some of the ideas and values on which the Church had been based. This led to challenges on its Biblical basis for this self-imposed monopoly of the truth and real knowledge. Normally those who challenged, such as Jan Huss in Bohemia or John Wycliffe in England were thrown out of the Church.

Jan Huss (c.1373–1415)

Christian church reformer from Bohemia, who was excommunicated for attacks on church abuses. He was summoned before the Council of Constance in 1414, where he defended the English reformer, John Wycliffe, and rejected the Pope's authority. He was burned at the stake in 1415. His followers were called Hussites.

John Wycliffe (c.1320–1384)

English religious reformer who was educated at Oxford University. He became Master of Balliol College, Oxford, from where he sent out bands of travelling preachers. He attacked abuses in the church, maintaining that the Bible rather than the church was the supreme authority. He criticised such fundamental doctrines as priestly absolution, confession and indulgences (see page 60). His disciples translated the Bible into English. Although he was denounced as a heretic (see page 68), he did not suffer the same fate as Huss, but died peacefully at Lutterworth.

In 1517 a challenge to the Roman Church was made initially by a single monk on a single point of theology (religious belief). The challenge came from the dissatisfaction that many felt towards the Catholic Church's behaviour and values and its arrogant abuse of its monopoly of power. What is more, the challenge received support from rulers, social élites, priests and peasants. These all merged into a 'force for change', which the Roman Catholic Church was unable to resist.

The flame started in Germany under Martin Luther, a German monk, and his princely supporters, but spread rapidly into Switzerland and then into Scandinavia. By 1540 it had become a major force and had split the vast Catholic Church. Wars were to be fought as ruler after ruler was not prepared to see another religion exist in their country. They were prepared to use force to stamp out what they felt was not the religious truth. Religious change was linked in with emerging **nationalism**. Also, social and economic changes, as well as artistic, literary and scientific turmoil, brought major changes in most European countries. This 'reformation' was the most dramatic and significant change to affect the history of Europe since the collapse of the Roman Empire over a thousand years before.

Nationalism: The growth and spread of loyalty towards a nation, rather than to an organisation such as the Church.

4.1 *What were the causes of the Reformation?*
A CASE STUDY IN HISTORICAL INTERPRETATION

This is one of the most complex topics that can be studied for A/S or A2 level, as there are perhaps as many views as there are historians. It involves an analysis of a wide range of issues, ranging from how much impact a single individual can have on the course of history to analysing the degree to which social, economic, nationalistic and political factors affect what appears to be a religious issue. There has also to be a grasp of both intellectual (the study of the development of ideas) history and theology, and a serious attempt by you to understand the important role played by religion in society and politics in 16th-century Europe.

The traditional view taught to sixth-form students up until the 1970s (e.g. V. H. H. Green's *Renaissance and Reformation,* 1952) was that in 1517 a complex and intellectual German monk, Martin Luther, raised doubts about

Tetzel selling indulgences, c.1517

What message is this woodcut trying to make about the selling of indulgences?

Indulgences: A person could gain partial remission of the time spent in **purgatory** by paying money to the Church for indulgences. These worked in a similar way to 'good works' such as going on pilgrimages and acts of charity.

Purgatory: Believed to be a half-way house between life on Earth and Heaven – an unpleasant place where someone received punishment for sins committed during their life.

a process used by an agent of the Papacy, the Dominican monk Johannes Tetzel, to raise money in Germany. The method Tetzel used for raising money was known as selling **indulgences**. An individual could shorten the amount of time they might have to spend in **purgatory** after death, and therefore attain eternal salvation more quickly.

Although Luther initially intended raising this 'doubt' as a debating issue, it was a challenge to the authority of the Pope. It was the normal practice at the time for a cleric such as Luther to argue the merits and demerits of the case with other Catholic academics/clerics in an academic way. However, it was soon to escalate, as the Catholic Church felt it was a challenge to its authority. This reaction by the Church, together with the stubbornness and intellectual prowess of Luther, led to an epic confrontation between the two. Secular princes and ordinary people aided Luther, and it grew into one of the greatest challenges the Catholic Church had ever faced.

This attack by Luther led to the clear division of Europe into two rival camps: one supporting the new religious ideas of Luther, and the other supporting the Catholic Church. Civil wars were fought in Scotland, France, Germany and the Low Countries (Netherlands). It was not until the early 18th century, nearly 200 years later, that religious stability and a degree of religious tolerance came to Europe.

This interpretation has been seen as simplistic. Although Luther's role is still seen as important, the role of two other key 'Protestant' reformers – Ulrich Zwingli and Jean Calvin – have also been considered. Many other factors were important, such as:

● the condition of the Catholic Church at the time

● the attitude of many towards the Church

● the impact of ideas coming out of the Renaissance

● the rise of new nationalistic ideas

● and the evolution of new social and economic forces.

These should be looked at as well.

The first challenge to the traditional interpretation came in the late 1960s when historian B. Moeller, in *The German Reformation* (1996), argued that there was far too much focus on Luther himself. One individual could not achieve so much in such a short space of time. Moeller argued that if it were not for the intellectual forces already at work as part of the Renaissance, then Luther would have been just another rebellious monk who would soon have been forgotten.

Although challenging the central role of Luther alone, Moeller did not really replace the traditional view with another clearly explained view. In recent years there has been an outpouring of serious scholarship in English – such as R.W. Scribner's *The German Reformation* (1986), B. Reardon's *Religious Thought in the Reformation* (1995), and E. Cameron's *The European Reformation* (1991) – and naturally more in German. These historians have developed the ideas and it is now possible to review why the ideas of a single monk between 1517 and 1522 could have had such a huge impact.

The Roman Catholic Church on the eve of the Reformation

One major reason for the religious change known as the Reformation was the state of the Roman Catholic Church in 1517. This led it to manage the attack on one aspect (and a comparatively minor one at that) of its work so badly. It also helps to explain why the ideas of one individual could be accepted so quickly by so many Roman Catholics.

The main beliefs of the Roman Catholic Church

- Supremacy of the Pope in all matters of religion.

- Beliefs based on Old and New Testament of the Bible.

- The Church was the sole interpreter of the Bible.

- Early commentators on the Bible also influential on matters of belief.

- Main beliefs in Ten Commandments – Thou shall not kill etc.

- Monotheistic – believed in one God.

- The Trinity of God the Father, the son and the Holy Spirit.

- Resurrection after death.

- Belief in purgatory (see page 61) – a state after death in which the souls of the dead Catholics were cleansed of their sins on earth, prior to entering heaven. The period spent in purgatory could be shortened by indulgences.

- A belief in eternal damnation in Hell for those who broke the rules of the Church.

- Good works would help towards the salvation of the individual.

- Important role for the Virgin Mary in worship.

- Worship also of Saints and relics – both of these were thought to help the individual towards eternal salvation.

- Route to eternal salvation lay through the Church.

- The Eucharist – the Communion service – was vital for salvation. During the service the bread and wine taken by the communicants were believed actually to become the body and blood of Christ.

- Priesthood had high status and had to be obeyed in order to understand the truth. Priests did not marry.

- Monasteries important part of Church life – where individuals committed themselves to permanent isolation from the world in search of the truth and salvation.

- Belief in seven sacraments, which were religious events in which it was important to participate, or as a means to achieve salvation, or a sign that you were marked out for salvation. They were as follows.

  1 Baptism – when the new born child was admitted into the Church
  2 Confirmation – when adolescents were formally admitted into the Church
  3 Communion
  4 Penance – where after confessing one's sins to a priest, a Catholic had to pay a penalty, usually prayer or charitable work, in order to ensure salvation
  5 Marriage – by a priest in a church
  6 Holy Orders – being a priest, monk or nun
  7 Extreme Unction – or the Last Rites – administered to the dying to ensure a shorter stay in purgatory.

Schism: Literally, to split into two separate sections. There was a schism within the Catholic Church: in the late 14th and early 15th centuries there were two Popes – one in Avignon and the other in Rome. Both claimed to be the true Pope.

The Roman Church in Europe had become wealthy and lax. Traditional interpretations of the causes of the Reformation have placed an emphasis on the serious flaws in the Church and its management. The Popes, the Church's spiritual guiders, had often set a poor example as religious leaders. Certainly, the personal failings of the Papacy must be seen as a central reason why the work of Martin Luther spread so quickly. It had never quite recovered from the **schism** of the previous century when they had been two Popes and virtual warfare between the two of them. Most of the Popes were Italian, seeing themselves as Italian princes, and they tended to neglect their role as spiritual leaders of the Roman Catholic Church throughout the whole of Europe. A few Italian families, such as the Medicis, tended to dominate the Papacy in the later 15th and early 16th centuries. They placed more of a focus on promoting their own families' interests, playing Italian politics, and appearing as supporters of art and new architecture, than on providing a proper leadership for the Christian movement. Some Popes, like Alexander VI (1492–1503), had reputations for immorality and for encouraging extremely low standards of moral behaviour both within the Curia (the Papal Court and administrative centre of the Roman Catholic Church) and in Rome itself.

Julius II (1503–1513) became known as the 'Warrior Pope' because of his active involvement in the Italian wars. He saw himself as a military and political leader, and neglected his work as the spiritual leader of millions of Catholics around Europe. The next Pope, Leo X (1513–1521), appeared to have a greater interest in the building of the great Renaissance masterpiece, St Peter's in Rome, than in the serious attack on his authority which was beginning to grow in Germany from 1517 onwards. The Popes failed to adapt to new ideas, failed to recognise the sensible ambitions of secular rulers, and failed as leaders of the Christian Church. The historian B. Reardon, in *Religious Thought in the Reformation* (1995), argues strongly that the Papacy was the real problem and must be seen as the major cause of the Reformation by failing to provide the moral and spiritual leadership when a major challenge came. The Papacy allowed incompetence and corruption to occur, which made the Church more open to attack and less able to resist it.

Why was the Church in need of reform in the early 16th century?

One conventional view of the causes of the Reformation centres around the poor state of the Church in the early 16th century. Not only was the Papacy corrupt and too concerned with making money, but also many senior and junior clergy were similar in their approach to their spiritual duties. Some Bishops regularly failed to attend to their duties in their **sees**. This was known as absenteeism. Some Bishops were reluctant to fulfil their pastoral duties in the monitoring of their clergy. There were concerns at the time about the poor quality education of many of the parish priests. Too many were illiterate and unable to provide the appropriate spiritual leadership to their flocks. Nepotism (giving jobs to relatives even though they were not qualified) was rife within the Church – the Popes were often the worst offenders. Clergy, in many cases, were not living up to their vows of poverty, chastity and obedience. The Church had a corrupt and money-seeking leadership, which seemed to have forgotten what its primary purpose was.

Sees: A see is the area in which a Bishop has responsibility for the spiritual life of all who live in it; also known as diocese or bishopric.

The Papacy did not set a good example of spiritual leadership. Some bishops were appointed at a very young age; in their early teens was not unknown. Very often they were not suited to the task. Many of the parish priests were badly educated and again not suited to their tasks. Many monks had lost the true sense of vocation (willingness to follow the strict rules of poverty, chastity and obedience to their religious leaders). They were more concerned with gaining a good life, and less in fulfilling the intentions of those who had set up monastic orders many centuries before.

Some clergymen held several different posts, collected the salaries from all of them and performed the duties of none. Cardinal Thomas Wolsey of England is a prime example. He drew many salaries from numerous posts as bishop and abbot, while working full time for the King as Chancellor. Wolsey seldom, if ever, visited his dioceses or abbeys to see if his subordinates were performing their duties properly. Also, several of his relatives were promoted to senior positions in the Church.

Certainly these abuses were quite important as causes of the Reformation process. The challenges that were to come from reformers such as Martin Luther needed intelligent and perceptive management, and the Church was not really in a position to provide that until much later in the 16th century. In addition, the poor example of behaviour set by many ranks of the clergy caused resentment among lay people, who disliked having to pay for what they saw as excesses on the part of the clergy. It led many lay people to examine the ideas of those who challenged the Roman Catholic Church with more sympathy and interest than they might otherwise have done. Historians like E. Cameron argue that dislike of the Roman Catholic Church and some of its members and practices did not cause this upheaval in the Church. However, it was to be an important factor in the rapid spread of Luther's new ideas, and of the willing acceptance of them by so many people from so many different ranks of society.

These woodcuts support Luther's attack on the Pope and the Catholic Church. What evidence is there in both woodcuts to support this view?

Coloured woodcut by Lucas Cranach the Elder, c.1545, contrasting Protestant and Catholic Christianity

A woodcut, early 16th century, contrasting the poverty of Christ (in the stable) with the wealth of the Pope – set up on high

What was the impact of the Renaissance on the Roman Catholic Church?

Perhaps more important as a major cause of the Reformation in Europe was the refusal of the Papacy and the Roman Catholic Church to adapt to many of the new ideas that were the product of the Renaissance. It is not the intention here to examine the Renaissance (see Chapter 2) but it is important to realise quite what an impact this intellectual ferment had on the religious life of Europe.

It is evident that the new religious leaders who emerged, such as Luther, Ximenez, Zwingli and Calvin, were profoundly influenced by this re-examination of ideas and beliefs, which had been accepted as the norm for many centuries. It was inevitable that religious belief would be influenced by this complete review of all thought.

There were many writers who contributed to the Renaissance, but it is worth looking at three who were particularly important. The first is Johann Reuchlin (1455–1522), a Greek and Hebrew scholar who analysed the Old Testament part of the Bible in great detail, placing emphasis on the original text and not on the commentaries by later writers. Not only did Reuchlin place real emphasis on a study of the original document by all believers, but he was also a strong critic of the Church's narrow attitudes to biblical interpretation. He was particularly important in encouraging literate men to study the original text of the Bible and to make up their own minds about how its meaning should be interpreted. Reuchlin wrote clearly and well. With the invention of the printing press, those ideas could spread easily.

Another German writer of the Renaissance period who was known to have influenced Luther is Ulrich von Hutten (1488–1523), a poet, soldier, German nationalist and strong critic of the Church. Like Reuchlin, he was a fine scholar. He insisted on being able to study the Bible in its original language. As a result, he too had an important influence in helping to break up the Roman Catholic Church's monopoly of biblical study and interpretation. The Renaissance produced men who were prepared to challenge basic beliefs and the medieval attitude of the Church in wishing to control thought and debate.

Many see Desiderius Erasmus as not only a vital influence on Luther, but also perhaps more than any other as the man who prepared the way for Luther in Germany. It was he who translated the New Testament into Greek in 1516 and into Latin in 1519. These were the translations which became the basis for further translations into languages such as a German or English. Up until then the Bible was not really available to the **laity**. It was a Latin edition that was normally used. This was of little use to most of those who were not clergy, as the few who did read did not necessarily understand Latin.

Erasmus placed much greater emphasis on the study of the Bible itself, and not on the interpretations provided by the Roman Church. He also placed great emphasis on personal freedom. Like Luther after him, he tended to see the Bible itself as the main authority for religious belief (and not the Church). He also felt lay people should be able to read it. Erasmus' views were seen by many as a challenge to the authority of the Pope. He encouraged debate, and he encouraged a new look at religious belief and practice. He put much stress on charity and inner belief. Erasmus was not that concerned with ritual and public observation of religious practices, which he felt took up too large a part of the life of the Church.

His main writings – 'In Praise of Folly' (1509) and 'The Handbook of a Christian Soldier' – were widely read. The printing press was to make a huge impact on the Reformation process. 'In Praise of Folly' was a clever

Laity: Ordinary members of the Church who were not priests, monks or nuns.

Desiderius Erasmus (1467–1536)

Born in Rotterdam, in what is now Holland, Erasmus was the illegitimate son of a priest. He was educated mainly at the University of Paris. Like Luther, he entered a priory where he discovered that 'this kind of life was good for neither mind nor body'. In 1493 Erasmus visited Oxford where he befriended Thomas More and John Colet. He was a fine biblical scholar and an outstanding student of Greek and Latin. After lecturing at Oxford Cambridge and Louvain, Erasmus moved to Switzerland in 1521, where he tied to escape from the controversy surrounding Luther and Zwingli. He died in Basle 15 years later.

satire, which poked fun at the Papacy and its failings. Erasmus was not anti-papal; he felt that the Church needed a leader, but he did criticise the contemporary Papacy. Erasmus wanted reform but not revolution. He did a great deal to criticise and therefore undermine the rather narrow theological debates that tended to dominate Roman Catholic life. He also did much to discredit superstition rather than religious practice within the Church. Erasmus was clearly hostile to the **monastic system** which seemed so out of place in the light of the new Renaissance ideas.

Monastic system: Where men cut themselves off from the world, and devoted their lives to prayer and meditation in monasteries.

What Erasmus was advocating was a return to a purer and simpler religion with a greater focus on the Bible itself. He wanted to remove much of what he saw as the excess religious baggage which had accumulated over the centuries. He hoped to provide a clear set of religious beliefs which could be understood by lay people and which placed less reliance on an increasingly worldly clergy to interpret their truth for them.

Erasmus and the other humanists cannot be seen as causes of the Reformation on their own, but if the Papacy had responded to Erasmus and the thinking of the other humanist writers, then Luther would have remained an obscure German monk. The ideas of Erasmus spread widely as the new printing presses helped to generate debate about contemporary religion and the Church's attitude towards new and old ideas. Luther, Zwingli and Calvin read the ideas of Erasmus and were influenced by his study of the Bible and his willingness to challenge ideas, institutions and the men who led the Church. Erasmus is sometimes seen as 'the man who laid the egg which Luther later hatched'. In fact, he later repudiated Luther's ideas but many contemporaries saw them as being similar in their thinking, at least until 1524. Erasmus' influence was of profound importance. He stimulated a debate which was later to reach conclusions he personally was appalled by. While others left the Church he had grown up in, he remained a Roman Catholic to his death. It is worth noting that when the Roman Catholic Church started its counter-attacks on the new Protestant faiths, one of the first authors they banned was Erasmus.

1. In what ways have historians disagreed about the causes of the Reformation?

2. What influence did Erasmus and the Renaissance have on the causes of the Reformation?

4.2 Why and how did Luther start the Reformation process in Germany?

Martin Luther was born in 1483 to a peasant family in Saxony in Germany. He had a harsh childhood. It was intended that Luther should be a lawyer, but he defied his father and became a monk. He later became a university lecturer at the University of Wittenberg in Saxony.

Luther proved be an extremely able academic and lecturer, and of course had plenty of time to research, read and think. He began to develop serious doubts about the possibility of his eternal salvation and it was in the course of his agonising that his superior, Johann von Staupitz, recommended a course of reading. Part of this reading included what were to be the most vital words for Luther, 'the just shall be saved by faith'. To Luther

Martin Luther (1483–1546)
Born the son of a silver miner, Martin Luther entered a priory in 1505 in search of the path to salvation. He left to join the newly established university of Wittenberg, where he became professor of biblical studies. While studying St Paul's *Epistle* he was struck by the phrase 'The righteous shall live by faith'. It led Luther to the belief that God could grant salvation through the gift of faith. This meant that the Catholic practices of penance, indulgences and good works were not needed; indeed they were harmful. The only sacrament that counted, as far as Luther was concerned, was the Eucharist (mass). Luther went on to become a leading part of the Reformation movement in Europe.

this meant it would be the actual personal beliefs of an individual, which would lead to eternal salvation. This view was against the beliefs of the Roman Catholic Church. The Church argued that good works (charity), the payment of indulgences, pilgrimages, worshipping the relics of long dead saints, or even leaving large sums of money for masses to be said after your death, could lead to the eternal salvation of the individual.

By 1517 it was clear that Luther believed firmly that it was only his own faith in Christ that mattered and that his eternal salvation was dependent on this. By then he was an academic and a preacher. He was known to have visited Rome in 1510. The traditional story was that he was disgusted by what he saw in terms of corruption and immorality within the Church, but there is not much evidence for this and the story emerges later as part of his personal propaganda drive against the Papacy. He became known in Wittenberg as an academic radical, but he does not appear to have been particularly anti-papal or anti-clerical before 1517. Certainly, he was placing more and more emphasis on the Bible as the basis of belief.

Why did Luther attack indulgences?

By 1517 Luther had established a strong local reputation in Wittenberg as a preacher and academic. He was not seen as anything other than part of a general movement which was questioning some of the ideas and beliefs of the Roman Catholic Church. What suddenly rocketed Luther to fame both inside and outside Germany was the arrival in a neighbouring area of Johann Tetzel, a monk who was running at eight-year long programme of selling indulgences. Tetzel had been banned from Saxony but the people of Wittenberg went outside the territory to visit him to purchase their 'tickets' to salvation. Tetzel was anxious to sell indulgences and had been commissioned to do so in order to raise substantial sums of money. The Pope benefited from the cash raised by the sale of indulgences because the money could be used to complete his great Church of St Peter's in Rome. The Archbishop of Mainz was also anxious to raise money to repay a debt to the Fuggers, the great bankers of Augsburg. He had borrowed large sums in order to raise the necessary bribes to become Archbishop in the first place. The third interested party were the Fuggers themselves who were anxious to get their own debts repaid.

Whether Luther would have reacted in the way he did if the motives of Tetzel and his employers had not been so blatant is a matter for debate. However, Luther's reaction was allegedly to pin his criticisms on a church door at Wittenberg. There is some debate about whether or not he did actually pin them on the Church door, but certainly by October 1517 the famous 95 theses were printed, and the challenge to Tetzel and his dubious practices was spreading across Germany.

Main points of the 95 Theses

- Criticism of the practice of selling indulgences
- Felt innocent and simple people were being misled by Tetzel
- Criticism of papal taxation
- Implicit criticism of the Pope for allowing indulgences
- Debating points about human salvation

Luther saw his 95 theses as discussion points. He felt the question of indulgences was still open for discussion. He questioned whether people 'pardoned' for their sins could be reconciled to God. Luther argued that a truly repentant Christian had already gained remission for his sins, and would gain salvation; money did not need to change hands.

This was seen as an attack on papal methods of raising money and was highly popular in Germany in 1517. There was a growing resentment at the Italian domination of the Roman Catholic Church. There was also growing resentment at the constant drain of cash from Germany to Italy in order to support papal extravagances. Inevitably, some of the points Luther made in his 95 theses were seen as a challenge to papal power. The monastic order, the **Dominicans**, of which Tetzel was a member, saw it as such, particularly as they knew the theological basis of indulgences was very dubious. They preferred to get at Luther by arguing that he was attacking the Pope.

The theses were inspired by genuine doubts on Luther's part about the appropriate way to salvation. The language Luther used was quite restrained. He was respectful towards the Papacy and to his spiritual leader locally, the Archbishop of Mainz.

Dominicans: An order of Catholic monks founded by St Dominic.

Martin Luther allegedly nailed his 95 Theses to the door of the castle church in Wittenberg in Saxony in 1517. This engraving by an unknown artist shows him writing on the door with an enormous pen, after receiving a ray of light from God. Right: Luther is being sheltered by Elector Frederick of Saxony.

What message is the engraving trying to give about the importance of Luther's 95 Theses? Give reasons for your answer.

Why did the indulgence controversy develop into a major confrontation with the Papacy?

The events that followed over the next three years, 1517–1520, were decisive and changed the history of Europe for centuries to come. The initial reaction by many of the Church's hierarchy was that this row over indulgences was no more than an academic squabble between two religious orders. Such squabbles were not new. Luther was an Augustian monk, while Tetzel was a Dominican. The leader of the Augustinians was asked to silence Luther. He declined.

In 1518, the Dominicans, furious that one of their number had been publicly attacked, started a campaign to persuade the Pope that Luther was a dangerous **heretic**. Initially, the Pope proved reluctant to act because of a complex political situation which was developing in Germany, over the possible election of a new Holy Roman Emperor. He was reluctant to offend Frederick of Saxony, who was Luther's ruler. Although Frederick was known to be a devout Catholic, he was also known to be very proud of his university of Wittenberg and one of its greatest lecturers, Martin Luther.

Heretic: One who no longer believed in the main Roman Catholic beliefs. The normal fate of heretics was to be burned at the stake as they were seen as such a terrible threat to believers and the true faith.

The fact that one of Luther's great friends and supporters, Spalatin, was chaplain and secretary to Frederick also helped to secure Luther's position.

The situation was not helped by some of Luther's students publicly burning the Dominican response to Luther's theses. Nor did Luther's reply in 1518 to a group of Augustinians, which not only challenged the whole principle of indulgences but also papal authority.

The whole issue was growing from what was a minor challenge to a not very important part of Catholic theology to a major confrontation about papal power and the core beliefs of Roman Catholicism. The whole issue of eternal salvation was naturally a fundamental aspect of Christian belief.

Events moved rapidly. In October 1518 a series of meetings were held between Cardinal Cajetan and Martin Luther. Cajetan attempted to get Luther to retract his views on the irrelevance of indulgences to salvation, and to accept papal authority. These meetings took place at Augsburg, to where Luther had been granted a safe conduct. Luther expected to be arrested and to suffer the normal fate of heretics. But in the end no disciplinary action was taken against him because all were frightened of offending his ruler, Frederick of Saxony. Frederick's vote might well be needed in the forthcoming Imperial elections. The Papacy did not wish to upset him into voting against their chosen candidate. Not for the last time were the intricacies of German politics to play an important role in the development of Lutheranism.

Luther's challenge to indulgences and papal power itself was put on hold until the Imperial elections could be sorted out. There is evidence that Luther was prepared to compromise at this stage, and to remain within the Roman Catholic Church. His opponents, and Cajetan in particular, were not inclined to compromise. They wanted Luther's blood and wanted to push the matter to a clear victory on their part. This brought Martin Luther's ability as a debater in public argument to the fore, and he made it clear that he was not prepared to withdraw his views unless he was presented with clear evidence from the Bible. More astute opponents might have begun to realise that they had a formidable opponent on their hands. The fact that Luther had powerful protectors and sympathisers both within the Church and outside might also have counselled caution to his opponents, but they pressed on in an attempt to destroy him.

Further attempts in early 1519 to silence Luther failed, so in a summer of 1519 a major disputation (public debate) took place in Leipzig, in Germany, between Johann Eck (for the Papacy) and Martin Luther. A more radical supporter, Karlstadt, also backed Luther. It was in Luther's preparation for this meeting and the treatment he got at the meeting itself that the decisive break between Roman Catholicism and what was to be called Protestantism took place. The ideas that had been maturing in Luther's mind for many years, the way he was treated and the nature of the debate led to the formal breach. The printing press and the whole nature of the debate, and the publicity accorded to it, ensured that the views expressed were known throughout the Christian world.

The debate at Leipzig proved to be decisive in a variety of ways. Eck managed to push Martin Luther into an admission that Huss, the Bohemian heretic, might have been correct in some ways. Huss had been condemned not only by the Church and the Pope, but also by a Church Council at Constance. This led to the view that Luther would not accept the authority of the Church as a whole.

The Leipzig debate widened the breach between Luther and the Church and almost certainly made a return to the Church impossible for Luther. Although still enjoying the protection of his ruler, Luther started to write furiously to justify and expand on his ideas. The publicity that had been created ensured that the quarrel, not only over indulgences but also over papal authority, began to spread and attract international attention. While Eck retired to Rome to gather strength and to get Luther excommunicated (expelled from the Church), Luther took advantage of the leisurely approach of the Papacy towards him to write three of his most important works.

What were Luther's key religious writings?

The first important text was 'Address to the Christian Nobility of the German Nation' (1520), which was a direct appeal to the secular leaders of the German people. Luther urged them to reform their churches, as the Church was incapable of doing it. It was a clear plan of how a ruler could reform the Church in his own lands. The fact that some of the wealth and influence of the Church might well fall into their hands and increase their own power was a logical conclusion to be drawn from Luther's writings. The chance to reduce papal influence and lower the drain of cash to Rome inevitably had an appeal to some of the rulers of Germany.

Priesthood of all believers: Individuals should be able to determine their own salvation and not rely on the Church in this respect.

There was a strong attack on the Papacy in this writing. The idea of the **priesthood of all believers** was beginning to be argued in a clear form. Certainly, the Papacy's right to dominate theology was challenged, as was the view that the Papacy had the right to call a church council to reform the Church. There was also an attack on the Papacy as an institution, and on the way in which it had become an increasingly secular and materialistic body. Much of the writing was nationalistic, arguing that it was the duty of the German nobility to overthrow established Papal power in Germany. It was well written and powerfully argued, and as it built on the ideas of others, it had considerable impact.

The second pamphlet, 'The Babylonian Captivity of the Church' (1520), was central to Luther's beliefs at the time and warrants careful study. It was, theologically, a radical document. Central to it was the idea of the priesthood of all believers. The Roman Catholic Church saw this as the preserve only of the clergy. Luther argued that the true Church was invisible and its members known to God alone. This second pamphlet was an attack on the whole purpose of the Catholic Church. Luther argued that the power and role of the Church should be limited. He also argued that its role should be quite separate from the secular authorities. Luther suggested reducing the number of sacraments (see page 62) from seven to three – Baptism, Communion and Penance – which was also very radical. In addition, he put forward new ideas on the communion service, separating it into two distinct parts – the taking of bread and the taking of wine. This was also a clear move away from normal Roman Catholic practice.

Transubstantiation: This is the belief that the bread and wine actually change into the flesh and blood of Christ during the course of the service.

Luther also attacked the idea of **transubstantiation**. He argued that the sacrificial aspect of the mass was wrong and that the Eucharist was part of the last will and testament of Christ. What was implicit in Luther's writing was that the Bible was the basis of all belief and he rejected the idea of the Church as the only interpreter of the 'truth'.

This pamphlet was a direct attack not only on some of the most basic parts of Roman Catholicism but also on the Church hierarchy, which had always felt itself to be the sole upholder of belief. Luther felt that he was still a true Catholic, and all he was wishing to do was to purify the Church from abuses that had grown up over the centuries. In fact, he saw himself as a conservative, wishing to return the Church to its proper ways of the past. The Papacy, however, saw it as a dangerous and possibly heretical attack.

There was no way in which the Roman Catholic Church and the Papacy, as they were then constituted, could accept these ideas, however much Luther may have felt that they were a basis for discussion and an opportunity to reform the Church. Luther did not see himself as a heretic, he saw himself as a purifier.

The third key writing of 1520, 'The Freedom of the Christian Man', was also important theologically. The main theme in it was the denial of the importance of good works when it came to assessing a person's chances for salvation. Salvation came by a person's faith and the mercy of God. It was not an attack on good works. Luther felt a right-thinking Christian would still practise them, but they were not part of the vital process for eternal salvation so important to the minds of many in the 16th century. The pamphlet, for good measure, encouraged disobedience to Canon Law (the law of the Roman Catholic Church).

How did Luther's ideas spread?

With these three documents the fundamental nature of Luther's ideas became clear. These ideas were popular in Germany for many reasons. Those who were literate and had been influenced by earlier humanist writers liked the focus on the individual and the individual's own reading and interpretation of the Bible. The attack on the worldliness and intellectual arrogance of the old Church which wanted to assume a monopoly of what went on in people's minds was also very much in line with Renaissance thinking. The medieval thinking of Roman Catholicism, with its focus on relic worship – which many saw as little more than superstition – was critically challenged by a powerful and effective writer and debater.

It was Luther's ability to get his points over, both orally and on paper, that was vital to the spread of his ideas. There was a receptive audience among the literate for his clear and powerfully expressed message. A man with his communication skills found it easy to get established. Secular rulers and the lay people of Germany had their own reasons for finding the message of Luther appealing. These ranged from sheer greed aroused from considering the wealth of the Church, to resentment at paying taxes, to a stirring German nationalism. Luther was writing not only in Latin, which was the language of the educated, but also in German, and this was vital in the spread of Lutheran ideas. The fact that the Papacy was inefficient and ineffective, and failed to analyse the nature of the Lutheran threat properly gave time for the ideas to spread. German politics played a decisive part in allowing Lutheranism to get established, to survive and to spread. With the printing press pouring out his pamphlets and with sympathisers putting forward his views from the pulpit, by 1522 Luther's views were spreading rapidly across Germany and in to other countries.

It was not until 1521 that the new young Holy Roman Emperor, Charles V, called a meeting of all the major rulers of Germany. This was known as the Diet of Worms. Charles approached the whole issue of Lutheranism with extreme caution. He was conservative, and conscious that he had made serious mistakes already as a ruler in Spain (see Chapter 5). He was also well aware of the German support for Luther, but had no illusions about what was expected of himself as the Holy Roman Emperor and supposed supporter of Roman Catholicism. It is also important to note that at this stage there was no indication whatever on the part of the Roman Catholic Church that Luther might be right. The Church was simply handing over to Charles the responsibility of dealing with, what they saw, as a heretic. Charles was not expected to negotiate with Luther, but to repress him.

Given what Luther had already debated and written, it could be argued that the meeting at Worms was doomed to failure. Certainly from Charles' point of view it was. Both in the public debates and in the private discussions he had with Luther it was clear there was no chance of Luther recanting (publicly admitting that he was wrong and that

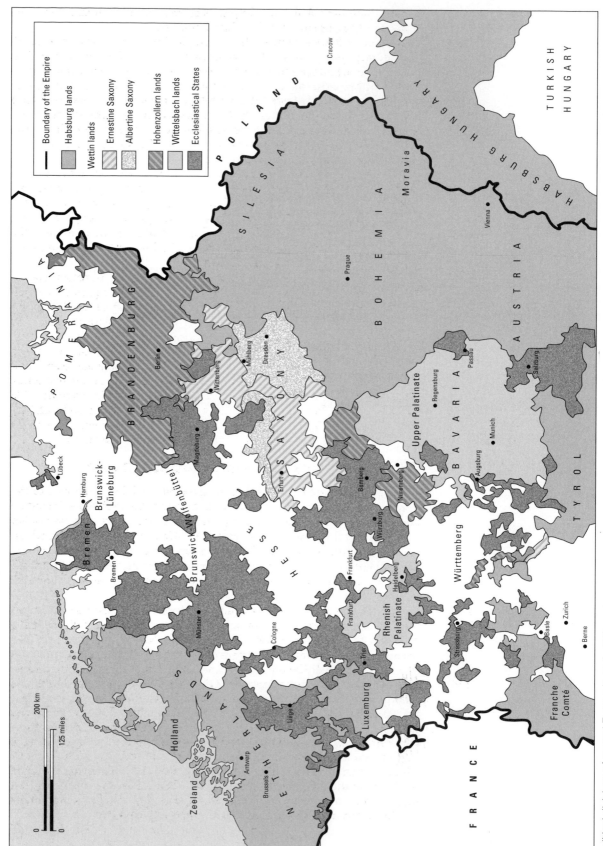

Political divisions of central Europe in early 16th century

Roman Catholicism and its old practices were right), which is what the leaders of the Roman Catholic Church wanted.

Emperor Charles argued that 'a single friar who goes counter all Christianity for a thousand years must be wrong'; Luther argued that, 'unless I am convinced by scripture and plain reason … My conscience is captive to the word of God. I cannot and will not recant.' It is then suggested that Luther followed this with the famous words, 'Here I stand. I can do no other.' He would not be moved. There is some debate about whether he actually said these words, but he certainly meant them. The outcome of this meeting at Worms was that Charles outlawed him and wished him expelled from the Empire.

Without strong secular support this would have been the end of Luther. However, on his way out of Worms he was kidnapped by his own ruler, and under the pseudonym of 'Junker Georg', was taken and hidden in Frederick's castle at Wartburg. There he remained for nearly a year. Still theoretically a Catholic, Frederick had no intention of handing over the most remarkable man in his kingdom to be burned. Local pride took precedence over support for the Church.

The period after 1522 was important for the development of Lutheranism in a number of ways. First, because it was a period in which Luther clarified and developed his ideas. Luther's first great work after the epic confrontations of Leipzig and Worms was to translate both the Old and the New Testament into German. These are seen as works of real genius because of the clarity of the translation and the use of modern German. Advocating that the Bible was to be the fundamental basis of all belief, it was vital that those who could read should have access to a document in a language which they understood. For those who were not able to read, they could listen in a language that they could comprehend. The Church was no longer to be the sole interpreter and guardian of the truth. Individuals now had the means to work out their own salvation.

What were the main features of the Lutheran Church?

In many writings and in his preaching Luther redefined the role of the Church. He saw it has not as a large and distant hierarchy dominated by a single individual, but as a group of people sharing a common belief who were to be treated as equals. The Church had to be based on scripture. Luther's study of the Bible saw no real role for either a large hierarchy, with lots of bishops and Cardinals, or monasteries. So he felt that they should be abolished along with the other abuses, such as indulgences.

Evangelise: To convert others to Lutheranism and to enthuse those who had doubts about it.

Luther felt the role of the Church was to preach, to **evangelise** and to administer the sacraments. Authority in his Church should lie with the members and not with a Pope. He rejected many of the Roman Catholic ideas about the sacraments, seeing them as 'signs and testaments of the will of God towards us'. The old Roman Catholic Church had seven sacraments (baptism, the Eucharist, penance, confirmation, Holy orders, marriage, and the last rites). Luther reduced the sacraments to either two or three. First was baptism, the second was the Eucharist and the third, possibly, was penance. The first two only appeared in the New Testament, and that was important to Luther. To him the most important aspect of religion was the faith of the individual. Other keys to individual salvation lay in the absolute faith of that individual in the message of Christ. The way to this salvation lay in the individual's prayer and personal reading of the Bible. A priest might be a useful guide in this process, and possibly a good example of how to achieve salvation, but it was not a vital part of the process.

How did Lutheranism become fully established in Germany?

Catechism: A statement of belief; all the main points of Luther's new faith such as justification by faith alone (see page 178) were stated simply in it.

Luther communicated his message with tremendous force and clarity. He and his followers gave Church services in German to German people. There was much greater focus on the evangelical role of the priest and in communicating the message powerfully through a sermon. There was now a German **catechism**. There were some extremely effective and powerful hymns in German.

This was quite a contrast to the way in which the Roman Catholic Church communicated to the lay people. With the real focus on individuals deciding for themselves and taking more responsibility for their own salvation, these straightforward and appealing ideas spread with remarkable speed. By the end of the decade, the message of Martin Luther was well established in many parts of northern Germany. Also the ideas were beginning to spread into Scandinavia and as far away as England.

In addition to the simplicity and clarity of the message, there were many other reasons why the ideas of this one man spread and became established so quickly in Germany. A major reason was the degree of support he received not only from his own ruler, Frederick the Wise of Saxony, but also from other German princes such as Philip of Hesse. There are various reasons why the German princes accepted Luther's ideas so enthusiastically. There was the attraction in gaining complete control of not only the right to appoint senior posts in the Church but also to control Church finance. Once the first prince had in effect nationalised monastic lands – and the monasteries were great landowners – then others soon followed. With land came status and more power. A German prince not only constrained by allegiance to Rome but also constrained by allegiance to the Holy Roman Emperor would naturally like a situation where he gained greater **autonomy** and wealth. Given the tremendous popular support that Luther gained from many of the laity, rulers who wished to maintain peace and unity within their kingdoms were naturally inclined to be sympathetic to the Lutheran cause.

Autonomy: Control or government of a country by itself rather than by others.

Other German rulers were very impressed by the quality of the evangelism of Luther and his supporters. Luther preached obedience to the secular ruler. They also liked the way in which he criticised his more radical supporters, but supported princely authority in the **Peasants Revolt** of 1525.

Peasants Revolt, 1525: A major revolt of the poor, caused mainly by social and economic reasons. The revolt had different causes in different areas of Germany. In some cases it was led not by peasants but by radical Protestant preachers or even minor nobility. Some of the peasants wanted just to retain their existing rights against greedy landlords, but others preached a more radical message, such as the equality of all men. Regardless of the causes, Luther attacked them all. This naturally improved his relations with the Princes who were also appalled by radical ideas of equality.

The first grouping of princes sympathetic to Luther came in Torgau in 1526. Their aim was to prevent the implementation of the decisions taken at the Diet of Worms to ban Luther and his ideas. Luther's strong criticism of the Anabaptists (see page 78) who were seen by many of the rulers as a dangerous and anarchic force, also encouraged princely rulers to endorse Luther's ideas. It was important for Lutheranism to be seen as a conservative force, which supported the role of secular leaders. The fact that Charles V was deeply distracted by a whole range of other problems, particularly his confrontation with France in northern Italy and the threatening Turks, enabled the German princes to operate as independent rulers until Charles felt able to return to Germany.

The 1529 Diet of Speyer (a meeting of all the principal rulers of Germany), re-affirmed the decisions taken at Worms, and demanded that there be no tolerance of Luther's ideas. It was far too late. Lutheranism was too deeply embedded in Germany for a halt to be called. It was at this meeting that a group of Lutheran Princes entered a written protest against the attempt to ban Lutheranism from the Empire into the record of the meeting. This led to the word 'Protestant' being used.

It was not until 1530 that Charles V finally returned to Germany, and at the great meeting at Augsburg attempted to deal with the issue of Martin

Philip Melanchthon (1497–1560
A theologian and great advocate of reform. Melanchthon was a vital figure in the spread of Lutheranism in Germany and Scandinavia. He did much to help Luther write out his beliefs.

Schmalkaldic League: Formed in 1531, it was a defensive alliance between princes and some German cities to defend themselves and their faith against Charles V and Roman Catholicism.

Artisans: People whose work requires skill with their hands, such as painters and sculptors, carpenters and engravers.

Merchants: People who buy and sell goods in large quantities, especially those who import and export them.

Entrepreneurial classes: Entrepreneurs are people who set up business deals to make a profit; so the entrepreneurial classes were that group of people who made a living from business.

Luther again. Although Luther himself did not attend this meeting, Philip Melanchthon attended on his behalf. There was no chance of any reconciliation. It was perhaps foolish of Charles V even to try it, as the chances of reconciliation between the Roman Catholic Church and Lutheranism had probably gone.

The following year several of the German princes formed together in the **Schmalkaldic League**, which looked like an armed group, designed to protect 'protesters'. A religious war between Protestant and Catholic did not actually occur for some years yet. This was partly out of respect for Charles V, but also because of the growing fear of a Turkish invasion. Vienna was under threat from the Turks. A temporary truce between the warring factions was negotiated at Nuremberg in 1532.

The longer it took to gather forces to crush Lutheranism, the more deeply embedded Luther's ideas became. The Roman Catholic Church was still managing to ignore any serious consideration of reform. It was looking to Charles V to do their work for them and this is another reason why Lutheranism spread.

What were the key reasons for Luther's success?

It was not only the support of the princes and the inability of Charles V to assess and manage the Lutheran threat effectively that led to the rapid spread and establishment of Lutheranism in Germany. Luther's ideas spread rapidly among the urban élites, particularly in the largely self-governing cities. There was a tradition of anti-clericalism (dislike of the clergy) in some of the cities, particularly in the northern German ports such as Hamburg. The status of the laity was raised in Luther's Church, and it had great appeal for the educated and the literate. In some cities preaching to the working classes had been effective, and this had forced the rulers to accept Lutheranism. There is also plenty of evidence that Lutheranism spread during the 1520s to the **artisans** and the merchant classes. The most mobile of these classes was naturally the **merchants**, and Lutheranism spread quickly along both the internal and the external trade routes. The Roman Catholic Church's disapproval of money lending encouraged the growth of Lutheranism among the **entrepreneurial classes**.

With Luther's message focused on the 'Common Man', Lutheranism rapidly became a mass movement. It had tremendous appeal to those with secular power, the princes – especially with Luther stressing the power of the secular authority.

Not all credit for this rapid religious transformation ought to go to Luther though. Certainly, he was a creative genius and a powerful communicator. However, he was not a great organiser. A great deal of important theological work was done by his friend and colleague, Melanchthon, who had been Professor of Greek at the University of Wittenberg. Melanchthon was a great scholar and thinker. He played an important part in the counter-attack against Eck. Although he was not a priest, he played a large part in helping Luther clarify his ideas on the authority of scripture and justification by faith alone. It has been argued that it was Melanchthon, and not Luther, who wrote the first pure work of Protestantism in 1521. This was known as the 'Theological Topics'. It contained important sections which were later to be seen as the central ideas of Protestantism. They included sections on:

● the nature of sin

● free will (the ability of people to choose between good and evil)

● Canon Law

● the role of the Bible

- the importance of good works in insuring salvation

- the mass

- and the relationship between Church and State.

Much of what Luther had felt and argued was contained in this writing. While Luther was absent in Wartburg Castle, Melanchthon had done much to contain Luther's more radical supporters, and prevent them from alienating vital princely support. It was also Melanchthon who had played a central role at the Diet of Speyer in 1529 with the Elector of Saxony, and had been shocked at its outcome. He was also one of the key figures at the Colloquy (Debate) of Marburg, when he tried to reconcile the differences between Luther and Zwingli (see page 78).

It was perhaps at Augsburg in 1530 that Melanchthon played his most important role. Charles V wanted unity in Germany. He was faced with a serious Turkish threat coming in from the East through Hungary. The Princes were divided, and so was Protestantism, between Luther and Zwingli. With Charles V still attempting religious peace and compromise, it fell to Melanchthon to draw up a list of Protestant ideas (at Charles' request). This Melanchthon did. He based them on ideas that had been evolving over the previous decade and had been clarified at the debate with Zwingli the previous year. As Luther was unable to attend Augsburg because of his Ban, it was Melanchthon who drew up what was seen as the defining statement of Protestantism, the Confession of Augsburg, in June 1530.

It was agreed by seven of the Protestant princes there and contains the main statements of Protestantism. The Confession of Augsburg makes clear the differences between Protestantism and Catholicism. The main points in it were:

- justification by faith

- the new role of the ministry and the Church as a whole

- the sacraments

- the relationship between Church and State

- hostility to Anabaptists

- attitudes towards the saints and saint worship.

It was a fairly mild document in the eyes of some. Melanchthon had intended it to be the basis for a compromise with Rome, if that were possible. Charles V, influenced strongly by Johann Eck, rejected it. The Protestants were given time in which to conform, but seven princes and 14 imperial cities declined. The rulers of Saxony and Hesse moved to form the Protestant Schmalkaldic League to protect their new faith. The battlelines were now drawn.

1. In what ways did Lutheranism differ from Roman Catholicism?

2. Why was Lutheranism able to establish itself so quickly in Germany?

After the publication of the Confession of Augsburg, Luther was to maintain a backroom role while the destiny of Protestantism was decided in the struggles between Charles V and the German princes. The initiative in the further spread of Protestantism passed to others. Luther continued to write, preach and debate. There was no great evangelical drive on his part, and the success of his creed depended more on political and military factors. If he had been more willing to compromise with Zwingli then perhaps Protestantism might have expanded more rapidly. However, if Luther had been prepared to compromise in the first place then there would have been no Protestantism.

4.3 Why did a second Reformation break out in Switzerland?

Another key figure in the Reformation process was Ulrich Zwingli. There is a debate among historians about how much he was influenced by Luther – his 'supporters' claiming that he was an original thinker, while others argue that he was merely an echo of Luther. Zwingli himself always acknowledged his debt to Luther's ideas but stressed he came to his conclusions independently.

Unlike Luther, Zwingli was probably more influenced by Huss and his ideas on the authority of the Bible. He always claimed that this fundamental part of his belief was his and his alone. In 1518 he was invited to be preacher at the Great Minster at Zurich, the capital of an important **canton.**

Canton: A region of Switzerland that was largely self-governing. The cantons were a group of small states ruled almost entirely by small merchant élites. They were traditionally left alone by the Popes and other surrounding rulers as they relied much on one of the Swiss' main exports, high-quality **mercenary soldiers**, for their wars.

Mercenary soldiers: Professional soldiers who sold their services to the highest bidder. They were therefore not motivated by any sense of loyalty to the cause they were fighting for.

Tithes: A tax which had to be paid by laymen to the Church.

Zwingli tended to preach directly from the Bible, which was unusual for those times. It 1522 Zwingli's ideas were publicly debated before the Council which ruled Zurich to decide whether to remain with the old Church or adapt the new ideas that were then sweeping Germany. Zwingli certainly placed a focus on indulgences and what he felt was wrong with them. He also stressed issues concerning the Roman Catholic Church which were more important to the Swiss – for example, the power of the Church courts over the lives of ordinary citizens and the high cost of **tithes**. Resentment at some of the practices of the Roman Catholic Church again made many prepared to listen to alternatives. Anti-clericalism was an important reason for reform gaining a receptive ear in Switzerland, as well as in Germany. By 1523 the ruling Council had opted out of the Roman Catholic Church, rejecting not only the authority of the Pope, but also many of the traditional practices such as fasting, celibacy for priests, and the cult of saints. They had also accepted the main emphases of the new Protestant belief, with the Bible as the basis of all authority. The sermon became the most important aspect of the work of the priest and the dominant part of the church service.

Zwingli provided energy and quality leadership but he could not write as powerfully as Luther. He was a sophisticated organiser and politician. Luther depended much on the support of the German princes, while Zwingli needed to work more for himself for his own salvation in the difficult waters of local Swiss politics.

Zwingli's main publication, produced in 1525, was entitled 'On the True and False Religion'. It was an appeal to the particular circumstances of Zurich, and contained a strong attack on the Papacy. It maintained the supremacy of the Bible but it was clear Zwingli viewed the Bible in a different way from Luther. He saw it more as an ancient text warranting serious study. It was a more traditional view than Luther's. Zwingli was never really one to analyse his beliefs in the same way that Luther did, as he was simply too busy preaching and dealing with the political problems of survival.

Ulrich Zwingli (1484–1531)

Zwingli, the son of a wealthy farmer, studied Latin and theology at Vienna and Basel universities. In 1506 he was appointed parish priest of Glarus, where he stayed for 10 years. He was influenced by the humanist debate of his youth and particularly by the writings of Erasmus. He agreed with Erasmus that the scriptures must be the basis of faith. Zwingli twice accompanied Swiss troops to Italy, but his experiences at the Battle of Marignano in 1515 led him to renounce warfare. Not surprisingly, his views were denounced and he was moved on from his parish, ending up in Zurich. He married in 1522, while still a priest. What was a surprise was that Zwingli died at the age of 47 in a battle!

There are, however, many similarities between Zwingli and Luther. Zwingli felt the role of the Church and its priests was to administer the sacraments, to preach and to evangelise (try to convert people to Christianity). They also had to discipline those who disagreed with their views. Zwingli spent a lot of time involved in religious controversy, perhaps too much. He argued at great length in the 1520s with Konrad Grebel and Simon Stumpf, known as 'the Swiss brethren', over whether the Church consisted of true believers only or whether it was possible to include some non-believers in the Church. These two also argued that there should be no relationship at all between Church and State. Additionally, Zwingli became involved in controversies with the **Anabaptists** over whether infant baptism should take place. Zwingli ensured that one of these dissidents, Manz, was drowned in 1525. It is suggested that Zwingli spent too long on debate and too little on ensuring the firm establishment of his ideas and the spreading of them.

Anabaptists: A religious group who did not believe in baptising children. Baptism had to wait until they were adult and capable of making such a decision for themselves. Anabaptism emerged as a significant religious force during the German Reformation, though its influence in Germany subsided after the disastrous failure of the 'Münster Experiment'. It remained a significant, though highly persecuted, minority faith in the Netherlands.

Key elements of Zwinglianism

- Hostile to papal power
- Hostile to saint and relic worship
- Hostile to monasticism
- Disliked idea of purgatory
- Disliked all images in church
- Disliked Bishops and any hierarchy in religious matters
- The Gospel was the source of all truth
- In favour of clerical marriage
- The **mass** was purely symbolic (disagreed with Luther on this).

Mass: The Roman Catholic Eucharist service (usually called Holy Communion by the Church of England). The proceedings were in Latin. It is the most important act of devotion that can be offered to God.

What attempts were made to unite Luther and Zwingli?

In 1529 the ruler of Hesse attempted to unite the two emerging strands of Protestantism. Luther and Zwingli met and debated at Marburg. This became known as the Colloquy of Marburg. There was some initial hostility towards Luther by Zwingli. Both men felt they should have priority over the other, both were extremely independent and both placed different degrees of emphasis on the Bible and other religious works. There was a natural rivalry. Each wished to assume the leadership of the Reformation process and there was some nationalistic antagonism between the German and the Swiss.

Both men were well aware that to survive and progress, Protestantism needed to unite. In the four-day debate they agreed on almost all the central issues. On any of the key areas – such as the trinity, original sin (whether man was born sinful or not), baptism, the role of the Bible, attitudes towards the Roman Catholic Church and the Papacy – they were in full agreement. However, on one key issue they disagreed. This was on the important issue of the Last Supper. Zwingli argued that no sacrament could alter the status of those who were already 'saved'. He felt that taking part in the Communion Service was simply a sign of allegiance to a set of beliefs – in other words, it was symbolic. Luther disagreed and the debate degenerated into personal abuse. Luther argued that the mass was a sacrifice and although he rejected transubstantiation (see page 70), he felt that Christ was actually present in the Eucharist, which means that individuals are needed to convey it. He felt that Christ was present during the service, although not actually in the elements of the bread and wine as Catholics believed.

The breach between the two, and their failure to agree, caused harm to the development of Protestantism. There were faults on both sides: Martin Luther would not compromise, but then he never did; Zwingli was not only long-winded but also tended to put forward poor explanations of his ideas.

Zwingli returned to Zurich to consolidate his brand of Protestantism in Switzerland. He was soon to die at the Battle of Kappel in a war between two of the rival cantons of Switzerland. Henry Bullinger, a fine writer and preacher, took over the leadership in Zurich. He continued to try for agreement with Luther over the Eucharist in 1534 and 1536. Luther remained hostile and critical, and there was to be no unity between these two groups.

Zwingli is important in that, regardless of whether he was a 'secret' Lutheran or not, he illustrated that the dissatisfaction with the Roman Church was not confined to Germany. The new faith could spread to other areas with different traditions. With his followers, Zwingli shows the impact of humanistic ideas. He was influenced more by the learning of Erasmus than of Luther. He also saw the need to ensure support from secular authorities. However, Zwingli was soon to be overshadowed by a far more dynamic force coming from another canton in Switzerland, Geneva.

Why did a third Reformation break out in Geneva, and how important was Calvin to it?

The third, and some would argue, the greatest, of the three men responsible for creating Protestantism in Europe was Jean Calvin. He was a great debater and a fine writer. He had the ability to write well in French. Calvin was certainly aware of the Lutheran heresies of the 1520s, but it is not known quite how he became converted to Protestantism. By 1530, however, it is clear that he had ceased to be a practising Roman Catholic. An intellectual conversion seems to have taken place by then. He fled from Paris, always a centre of Roman Catholic orthodoxy, in 1534, and certainly at one stage came under the influence of Martin Bucer, in Strasbourg.

Bucer placed an emphasis on the supremacy of the Bible as the basis of all faith and the need to open up the Bible and its message to all. He viewed the relationship between the Church and State differently from Martin Luther. He disliked the subordination of the Church to the State, which he saw in Lutheranism. Bucer was clearly moving towards ideas such as **predestination**, as well as new ideas on sacraments, the role of the Church, and church discipline. Many of these ideas were to find maturity in the writings of Calvin.

Martin Bucer (1491–1551)
A scholar and priest who was strongly influenced by both Erasmus and Luther. Bucer had defeated the Anabaptists by 1527. He advocated predestination and set out many ideas on discipline and Church and State relationships which Calvin was to put into practice in Geneva. Bucer was a great organiser and leader.

Predestination: The belief that God decided who should and should not be 'saved' at an early stage in life – therefore such things as 'good works' were irrelevant to salvation.

Jean Calvin (1509–1564)

Born in France, Calvin was educated at the University of Paris, studying theology at the Sorbonne before changing to law at Orleans and Bourges universities. As a student of law he learnt clarity, precision and caution. Calvin studied many of the great humanist writers and many of the old Greek scholars as well. Convinced that he was 'chosen by God to proclaim the truth', it is probable that Calvin composed the Protestant address in 1534 delivered by his friend, Nicholas Cop, the new rector of the Sorbonne. Both men were forced to leave France. Calvin travelled to various cities before reaching Geneva. He was persuaded to stay there for a while to help implement a reformation. However, his strict code of conduct, compulsory confession of faith and insistence that the city council submit to clerical control proved unpopular; Calvin was expelled from the city in 1538. For three years he lived in Strasbourg, where he befriended Martin Bucer. He was tempted back to Geneva in 1541 where he remained until his death.

Calvin came to Geneva almost by accident in 1536. Geneva was an independent state, although theoretically under the jurisdiction of the ruler of Savoy. It had about 10,000 inhabitants and was clearly following the example of other Swiss cantons, such as Zurich, in breaking away from the Roman Catholic Church. It was largely French speaking and was looking to William Farel for spiritual leadership. Farel had arrived in Geneva in 1532 and the canton had gradually become Protestant, after much debate and some violence.

Farel was no administrator, nor was he a charismatic leader or organiser. He looked to Calvin to provide much of what Geneva needed to consolidate the hold that Protestantism had, and to ensure its survival.

It was a brave decision on Calvin's part to stay. There were many different factions in Geneva, and although there had been a rejection of Roman Catholicism, there was as yet no clear move in a different direction. The penalty for being in the wrong group could be fatal.

One of the key reasons why Farel was anxious for Calvin to stay in Geneva was the fact that one of Calvin's major pieces of writing, 'The Institutes of the Christian Religion', was the basis of Calvinist beliefs. They were to be frequently modified. Certainly the first edition, in French, which was published in 1541, showed the influence of Bucer's thinking. Some have argued that Calvin was not a very original thinker. He did differ from both Luther and Zwingli in that he placed importance on the Old Testament as well as the New Testament of the Bible. There is some disagreement as to whether Calvin placed as much emphasis as the earlier reformers on the role of Christ and the Holy Spirit in helping toward salvation.

In his 'Institutes', Calvin wanted a clear statement of his beliefs. Its sub-title was 'the basic teaching of the Christian religion comprising almost the whole sum of godliness'. He was going to provide Christians with a clear statement of belief – the answer to all questions. To Calvin the Bible was the basis of all belief. He had no time for other sources. To him, the Bible was simply the word of God. He argued that some interpretation of

Calvinist Churches were plain, bare rooms centred not on the altar but on the pulpit (a sign that the sermon had replaced the mass as the heart of the service).

How does the Calvinist method of worship differ from the Roman catholic method of worship?

the Bible might be necessary by leaders such as himself. His interpretation was the truth. The Bible was the only way God communicated with humanity. His God was all-knowing, all-powerful and just. It would appear that Calvin's God was less loving and more severe, but this was because he placed more emphasis on the Old Testament's God of wrath and less on the loving, forgiving God of the New Testament. To Calvin, God was Master, man was the slave and the purpose of human life was to serve and to glorify God.

As well as predestination, Calvin believed in free will, that is the ability of man to choose between good and evil, but not to the extent that Luther did. Luther believed in single predestination; that is, God knows what an individual would do and could predict salvation or damnation. Luther did believe that the individual had a role in deciding whether they would be saved or damned. Calvin, however, believed in double predestination – God knew not only who would be saved but also those he would condemn to eternal damnation. There was nothing an individual could do about it.

Many disagreed with Calvin on this, preferring to see God as forgiving. They also felt that the essential New Testament role for Christ as the redeemer and saviour was being played down. Calvin saw his Church as central to belief. It was the only route to true life, the only way to learn about God and to serve God. He felt there were two vital sacraments: Communion (Eucharist) and Baptism. He rejected transubstantiation but, unlike Luther and Zwingli, he was not too concerned about the arguments over the real presence of Christ at Communion. Nor was he keen on the symbolic views of Zwingli.

Calvin's 'Institutes' was a model of clarity. It was a clearly stated set of beliefs encompassing much of what his predecessors had created. With these ideas, he was persuaded to stay in Geneva in 1536 to put them into practice. It was a turbulent time in Geneva. By 1537 Calvin had a clear programme for putting these ideas into practice. The Council, the ruling body of Geneva, agreed to attempt to impose them on the rival group of Protestants known as the Libertines. The Libertines fought back, resenting many of Calvin's ideas about marriage, education, singing in public worship and the Lord's Supper. Calvin was banished and returned to Germany.

Calvin was invited back in 1541 to build up a Christian state. This he proceeded to do, demonstrating his skill as an organiser. The relationship between Church and State had to be clarified, as what he was attempting was not just to impose a set of religious beliefs on a people, but also to change the whole nature and structure of society in Geneva. If he was going to create this system whereby God's Kingdom on earth could be seen, then there had to be a political and social structure in place that would make this possible.

In 1541 Calvin published his 'Ecclesiastical Ordinances', which created a civil and social structure that would enable him to put his beliefs into practice. There was to be a clearly established hierarchy of individuals who had a mixture of social and theological duties. In Calvin's mind there was no real difference between the two types of duty. There were to be pastors, doctors, elders, deacons; all with clear roles dealing with social and theological discipline, care of the poor, the teaching of the young and the vital role of evangelism and the study of religion.

Other sections of the 'Ordinances' dealt with the form of worship, the sacraments and when they should be administered, the role of the clergy, the marriage ceremony, the care of sick and dying people, and even the treatment of prisoners. There was also to be set up an organisation called the Consistory, which was a mixture of pastors who had a theological role and elders who were lay people who had a responsibility to regulate and investigate the personal lives of the citizens of Geneva. Initially, the Consistory had no power over the ordinary people of Geneva, but by the time Calvin died, in 1564, it was controlling the lives of the local citizens. The two elements of Church and State became inseparable. The Church preached and administered the sacraments; the State administered law and order. However, both were seen to be subordinate to implementing the will of God in their different ways. This state was called a theocracy, where the needs of theology dominated all, but Calvin didn't quite achieve what he wanted, as the city authorities never backed him fully. However, he did maintain a firm discipline throughout his time in Geneva. Over 58 dissenters are known to have been executed because of their disagreement with the views of Calvin. This included an epic struggle over the nature of the Trinity with Michael Servetus (1511–1553). Not only was religious uniformity imposed with an iron will, but also a particularly moral code of behaviour was enforced for all citizens and those who did not conform were informed on and disciplined.

Key elements of Calvinist beliefs

- Scripture the only source of faith

- Denial of free will

- Justification by faith alone

- Good works were irrelevant to salvation

- Inadmissibility of grace

- Certainly of salvation

- Absolute predestination

How great an impact did Calvin have on the Reformation?

Jean Calvin probably had an enormous impact on the whole course of the Reformation. The move towards Protestantism had begun to falter by the end of the 1530s, and it was Calvin who re-created it and ensured its survival.

Although Calvin may have used the ideas of others, he was a great leader with practical ability and he turned Geneva into a powerhouse for the Reformation process. Calvin was able to make Geneva into the centre of Protestantism, not just in Switzerland, but throughout Europe. It was because of Calvin's work that Scotland, Holland and parts of France became and remained Protestant. Unlike Lutheranism, which seemed suitable solely to the particular circumstances of Germany, Calvinism could travel. It was able to adapt itself to different countries with different social and political traditions. Calvin also had an influence on the survival and development of Protestantism in both Germany and Scandinavia. Whereas Luther has to be seen as the founder of Protestantism, Calvin must lay claim to being vital in its survival and spread throughout Europe. It was a remarkable achievement for a single man.

1. What were the main differences between Lutheranism and Calvinism?

2. Assess the nature of Calvin's achievement.

4.4 What were the causes and impact of the radical Reformation?

Even more radical ideas and movements spread during the 1520s. These movements have been lumped together as the Anabaptist movement but this is an over-simplification. Following the example of Luther and Zwingli in the 1520s, and responding to a large number of socio-economic and political pressures, other religious leaders emerged with ideas seen by the Roman Catholic Church as just as radical and horrifying as those of Luther, Zwingli and Calvin.

What makes these movements different from the 'mainstream' reformers already described was that they were opposed passionately not only by the Roman Catholic Church, but also by secular leaders and by the 'established' reformers.

The Anabaptist movement does not deserve the title of 'movement'. There is an element of historical convenience in this term, as there was no leader, no coherency, no agreed set of beliefs, and certainly no organisation. It was more of a spontaneous outburst of religious ideas, which in the 16th century had strong social and political implications, as they were all inseparable aspects of life at that time.

Just as the Socialists in the 20th century splintered into a large number of conflicting and sometimes warring groups, once Luther and Zwingli had broken through the barriers of the old authority, then others followed. Many of these men came from different backgrounds to Luther, who moved in university and princely circles. They were closer to, and had a greater degree of support from, the peasants and urban artisans. They were more responsive to the practical economic and social wishes of these groups.

It was as early as 1523, when both Luther's and Zwingli's movements were still in the embryonic stage, that more radical aspects of the Reformation emerged. The first really radical movement, sometimes known as the 'Swiss Brethren', emerged in Zurich in the early 1520s. It was a serious threat to Zwingli's attempt to convince the Zurich authorities that he was a serious and stable alternative to Roman Catholicism. Naturally, Zwingli was bound to dislike what he saw as extremists who might be seen by the respectable middle-class citizens who ruled Zurich as a real threat to the established social and political order. It was Balthaser Hubmaier (1485–1528) who was one of the first real radical reformers. He was a parish priest who had been a student of Eck. Another radical was Felix Mantz (1500–1527), a scholar-priest. A key layman was Konrad Grebel.

There was an economic aspect to their protest. Opposition to tithes was a major feature, but the main area of conflict was adult baptism. The city authorities backed Zwingli and expelled these 'radicals' in 1525. When Mantz returned in 1527 and refused to give up his views, he was drowned by order of Zwingli and the city authorities. Others who fled from Zurich were persecuted with equal vigour in areas which were Roman Catholic, and burned for their beliefs.

Luther, too, had his problems with dissidents – the key one being Thomas Muntzer (1490–1525). He had become a convert to Lutheran ideas while a parish priest. Like so many others, he had been strongly influenced by the humanists. He soon adopted more extreme ideas, in particular a belief in revelation (where the truth is shown through dreams and visions), and the way in which the Holy Spirit would communicate directly with the 'elect'. He felt that these 'elect', who in his eyes seemed to be primarily urban artisans, should turn on the ungodly with violence and wage a holy war against them. Luther, with his conservative social ideas and firm view of the role of the prince in society, turned against Muntzer.

Free city: A city that had a large degree of local control.

Egalitarian: All people are equal, and should have the same rights and responsibilities.

Anarchy: The situation where there is no government or law.

So did the princes of Germany. Why? Muntzer's bitter anti-clericalism and violent social message explains the loathing felt by many towards him.

Muntzer appeared in the **free city** of Muhlhausen in 1524, where the radical Protestant preacher Heinrich Pfeiffer was developing a popular urban reformation along Lutheran lines, but with radical political undertones. This linked up a wider social protest, known as the Peasants' War. This began because of social and economic factors such as the abolition of serfdom and feudal dues. Two key princes who supported Luther, Philip of Hesse and Duke Georg of Saxony, savagely repressed this movement in 1525. Muntzer was executed with over 50 others.

Few of Muntzer's radical supporters survived, but the action of the Zurich magistrates in expelling the radical opponents of Zwingli ensured that these ideas spread. The nearest the Anabaptist movement came to a meeting was in 1527 when they published 'The Seven Articles of Schleitheim'. Although not all those who were seen as more radical than Luther or Zwingli supported these ideas, they give a fair indication why the new Protestant reformers disliked them, and why there was uniformity of opposition to them. The 'Articles' stated that they wished the local community to select their own priests, and had firm views as to the **egalitarian** relationship between the priest and those who chose him. There was a strong dislike of those who would not accept their version of the 'truth'; 'sinners' had to be excluded from the community. Inevitably this was seen as a disruptive social force. No oaths were to be taken by anyone, and this included those of loyalty to civil and military leaders. This again was seen as leading to **anarchy**. Many of the Anabaptists believed in non-violence. If taken logically to its conclusion, then the pacifism implicit in the 'Articles' would make the task of the ruler seeking soldiers impossible. Baptism should only be gone through by adults, fully aware of what they were doing and why.

Whether this document was looked at by a German or a Catholic prince, a Catholic priest or by Luther himself, it was seen as a blueprint for anarchy and its supporters had to be destroyed. They were.

The movement spread largely among peasant communities in the Netherlands, north Germany and Moravia (part of the present Czech republic). Other leaders like Melchior Hoffman (1495–1543) spread these ideas into modern Belgium and Holland with a fair degree of success. Hoffman had quarrelled with Zwingli, but had gained some support form Luther who had encouraged him to preach and evangelise in Scandinavia. The seeds that Hoffman planted in the Netherlands soon spread. The secular authorities stamped them out with ferocity and thousands were killed in 1533 and 1534. Many fled into Germany, in particular to Münster.

A group of radical preachers in Münster, encouraged by a reforming Town Council, began to move towards adult baptism. They also began to advocate radical social and economic ideas such as common ownership of property among Christians. Joined by more radicals on the run from secular and religious authorities throughout Europe, such as Jan Matthys and John of Leyden, they defended the city of Münster from external attack for some months.

A semi-democratic state was set up, communal sharing of property was enforced and polygamy (being able to marry legally several husbands or wives) was practised. To what extent this 'communism' was part of the basic beliefs of the Anabaptists, or whether it was a necessity in a city under siege, is debatable. Whether the polygamy was part of the beliefs of Anabaptists or a result of a situation where there were some 1,700 men in the city and four times as many women, is also debatable. Certainly, it provided propaganda for the opponents of Anabaptism. All authorities, be they Protestant or Catholic, continued the persecution with renewed vigour. It is estimated that at least 30,000 Anabaptists were killed in the Netherlands in the decade after the fall of Münster, in 1535. Persecution of them was as vigorous by Calvin as it was by the dreaded Inquisition (see Chapter 6).

The movement survived in small pockets in the Netherlands but had died out as a major force by 1540. The Anabaptists were important in several ways. Many of their leaders had had a similar education to Luther and Zwingli, and they demonstrate that Luther was part of a wider movement of religious change. They have been called the 'Fourth Reformation', after those of Luther, Zwingli and Calvin, and they show how important it was for any reformation to have the support of the secular authorities. Many of their ideas were to reappear among Protestant non-conformist groups in later centuries when a greater degree of tolerance became possible. They were more fanatical and more enthusiastic than most Protestants. Anabaptists saw the Church as a more democratic and responsive organisation than Luther and Zwingli. Their focus on brotherhood, love and pacifism had its appeal. The working-class origin of many of its supporters gave it a democratic appeal to social groups feeling oppressed by a decaying feudal system. They may have been exterminated, but like the radicals whom Oliver Cromwell destroyed after the death of the King of England in 1649, their ideas lived on and reappeared as major influences in later centuries.

Conclusion

1. In what ways did the Anabaptists and other radicals differ from the main reforming groups?

2. Why were the Anabaptists seen as such a threat by so many?

By 1560 Europe had changed fundamentally. The Renaissance had not only had a huge effect on the way in which men thought, but also in what they believed. The Reformation was a logical continuation and result of that great intellectual turmoil. Luther had, in a way, been a catalyst for vast changes. Although his achievement must not be underestimated, without the support of countless priests, laymen and Princes, and the work of Calvin, he could have remained a footnote in history. Luther and his fellow Protestants not only provoked reform of the Roman Catholic Church, but also created new groups of religions, each with their own values. They started a process that redrew the map of Europe and led to the rise and fall of great nations. The Reformation was perhaps the event that had the greatest impact on European history for centuries passed, and centuries to come.

? Source-based questions: the causes of the Reformation in Germany

SOURCE A

But now the whole of Germany is in full revolt: nine-tenths raise the war-cry 'Luther!', while the watchword of the other tenth who are indifferent to Luther is: 'Death to the Roman Curia!' ... The bull [document issued by the Pope] accrediting giving, and me power to name representatives, should be sent and money for my expenses and for agents. Even if they are all much exasperated *against* us, a handful of gold will make them dance to our pipe, though even thus it is hard to win them, and impossible in any other way ....

Luther's picture was offered for sale here, and all the copies were disposed of in a trice before I could get one. Yesterday I saw on the same page Luther with a book and Hutten with a sword. Over them was printed ... 'To the Champions of Christian Freedom' .... So far has the world gone that the Germans in blind adoration press around these two scoundrels, and adore the men who were bold enough to cause a schism.

Papal Nuncio, Alexander, to Cardinal de' Medici, 8 February 1521

Source-based questions: the causes of the Reformation in Germany

SOURCE B

O God, Luther's books they burn.
Thy godly truth is slain in turn.
Pardon in advance is sold,
And heaven marketed for gold.
The German is bled white
And is not asked to be contrite.
To Martin Luther wrong is done
O God, be thou our champion

Ulrich Von Hutten, c. November 1520

SOURCE C

There are now at Nuremberg, Augsburg, Ulm and in Switzerland and in Saxony wives, maidens and maids, students, handworkers, tailors, shoemakers, bakers knights, nobles and princes such as the Elector of Saxony, who know more about the Bible than all the schools of Paris and Cologne and all the Papists in the world.

Comment of a pamphleteer c.1525

SOURCE D

Here then, is something fundamentally necessary for a Christian: to know that God foresees and purposes and does all things by his immutable, eternal and infallible will. Here is a thunderbolt by which free choice is completely prostrated and shattered. I established this point by my own argument and the authority of scripture. My dear Erasmus, I beg you to do at last as you promised; for you promised you would willingly yield to anyone who taught you better. I

recognise that you are a great man. Unlike the rest you have tackled the real issue and have not wearied me with irrelevancies about the papacy, purgatory, indulgences and such lie trifle, for which I sincerely thank you. But God has not yet willed or granted that you be equal to the matter at present at issue between us.

Martin Luther, 'On the Bondage of the Will', 1525

---

1. With reference to Sources A, B and D, and the information contained in this chapter, explain the meaning of the three terms highlighted in the context of the causes of the Lutheran Reformation.

a) 'to cause a schism' (Source A)

b) 'Pardon in advance is sold' (Source B)

c) 'authority of scripture' (Source D)

2. Study Source A. What is revealed in this source about the attitude of the Roman Catholic Church towards Luther?

3. Comment on the value of all four sources to a historian of the Reformation.

4. Study all four sources and use the information contained in this chapter to answer the question below.

To what extent was the Reformation in Germany simply a reaction against the Roman Catholic Church's wish to make money out of Germany?

5 The Holy Roman Empire under Maximilian I and Charles V, 1493–1556

5.1 How was the Holy Roman Empire governed?

5.2 What was the relationship between the Holy Roman Empire and the idea of Germany?

5.3 Why did attempts to reform the Empire fail during the reign of Maximilian I?

5.4 How justified is the claim that Maximilian I was the true founder of the Habsburg dynasty?

5.5 How great were the problems faced by Charles on his election?

5.6 In what ways was imperial government affected by the Lutheran revolt, 1521–1529?

5.7 To what extent was Charles' power limited by the increasing desire of the princes for self-government?

5.8 Historical interpretation: How successful were Maximilian I and Charles V as Holy Roman Emperors?

Key Issues

● *How did the government of the Holy Roman Empire change during the reigns of Maximilian I and Charles V?*

● *To what extent were the weaknesses of Imperial government caused by the shortcomings of the Emperors themselves?*

● *How important was the role of the territorial princes in weakening Imperial rule?*

Framework of Events

1356	Golden Bull establishes the Imperial constitution
1477	Marriage of Maximilian von Habsburg and Mary, daughter of the recently killed Charles, Duke of Burgundy
1486	Maximilian von Habsburg elected 'King of the Romans'
1488	Swabian League is formed
1489	Free Imperial Cities included in the Diet for first time
1491	Maximilian acquires substantial Austrian lands
1493	Maximilian I succeeds his father Frederick III as Holy Roman Emperor
1495	Diet of Worms
1499	The Swiss Confederation rises up and defeats the Swabian League
1500	Diet of Augsburg suggests a professional Imperial Army
1504	Swabian League defeats the Wittelsbach family in War of the Bavarian Succession (or Landshut War)
1505	Maximilian sells 'investiture' of Duchy of Milan to Louis XII of France
1506	Maximilian invades Hungary
1508	Maximilian formally frees Swiss Confederation from jurisdiction of the Imperial courts
1509	Maximilian participates in Holy League against France
1513	Swiss mercenaries defeat French attempt to recapture Milan
1514	Peasant uprising in Hungary
1515	Congress of Vienna confirms union between Habsburg and Jagiellon dynasties
1519	Death of Maximilian. Election of Maximilian's grandson, Charles
1520	Duchy of Württemberg sold to Charles V by the Swabian League
1521	Luther outlawed within the Empire. Charles creates separate Austrian inheritance for brother Ferdinand
1523	The Knights' War

1524	Outbreak of Peasants' War
1525	Peasants crushed. Imperial army is victorious at the Battle of Pavia
1526	Ottoman Turks win Battle of Mohácz; Louis II is killed in the battle
1527	Imperial troops sack Rome. Pope Clement VII becomes a prisoner of Charles V. Ferdinand is crowned King of Hungary
1529	Ottoman Turks recapture Buda and besiege Vienna. Protest of Speyer. Charles V's domination in Italy confirmed by Peace of Cambrai
1530	Charles V crowned Emperor by the Pope. Confession of Augsburg
1531	Schmalkaldic League is formed. Ferdinand elected King of the Romans
1532	Ottoman Turks invade Hungary again
1533	Ottoman–Habsburg truce in Hungary
1536	Imperial army invades Provence
1538	Truce between Emperor and King of France
1539	Revolt of Ghent against Charles V
1540	Ferdinand occupies Pest and besieges Buda
1541	Ottoman Turks invade Hungary and annex Buda
1542	Renewal of war between Emperor and King of France. Schmalkaldic League attacks Duchy of Brunswick-Wolfenbüttel
1544	Anglo-Imperial invasion of France. Peace of Crépy
1545	Truce between Emperor and Turks
1546	Death of Luther. Outbreak of the War of the League of Schmalkalden
1547	Ferdinand forced to pay 'tribute' to Turks for possession of part of Hungary. Charles defeats League of Schmalkalden at Battle of Mühlberg
1548	Charles attempts to impose religious settlement, the Augsburg Interim
1551	Lutherans form League of Torgau
1552	Ferdinand and Turks at war in Transylvania. Lutheran princes rebel successfully against Charles; Maurice and Ferdinand reach a settlement in the Treaty of Passau
1553	Failure of siege of Metz
1555	Religious issue settled with the Peace of Augsburg
1556	Charles abdicates as Emperor.

Overview

I N the insulting words of the 18th-century French writer Voltaire, the Holy Roman Empire was 'neither holy, nor Roman, nor an Empire'. To historians brought up to regard the **nation state** as the normal and accepted form of political organisation, it seems something of an oddity.

Though predominantly German, the Holy Roman Empire was not entirely so. It was a loose collection of over 300 states, each of which enjoyed largely independent control over its own affairs whilst owing a limited and, in some cases, grudging allegiance to the Emperor. Most significantly, perhaps, this loose confederation had become even more disunited and impotent during the 15th and 16th centuries when Germany's main rivals in northern Europe, England and France, were developing as powerful unified states.

Nation state: In the 19th century it became the conventional belief among many politicians and writers that the most 'normal' form of political organisation should be the 'nation state'. In other words, it was assumed that the German people were entitled to be part of a single state. The same thinking assumed that multi-national states were inappropriate political organisations. The Holy Roman Empire was a multi-national state which was bound to be inefficient. Maximilian and Charles were therefore criticised by 19th-century upholders of the nation state for trying to place the interests of the Empire above the interests of Germany.

Maximilian I (1459–1519)
Maximilian succeeded Frederick III as Holy Roman Emperor in 1493. He had united the Habsburgs with the House of Burgundy through his marriage with Mary of Burgundy in 1477, connected the Habsburgs with the ruling houses of Spain through the marriage of his son Philip with Joanna of Castile, and secured dynastic alliances in Bohemia and Hungary. In many respects, he was an able and charismatic emperor. Nevertheless, he presided over the loss of Switzerland from the Holy Roman Empire and antagonised many of those who favoured reform of the Empire. His military adventures in Italy proved to be extremely costly.

In 1493, when the Habsburg Maximilian I succeeded to the Imperial throne to which he had been elected seven years earlier, the Holy Roman Empire was in a weak state. The Empire as an institution had suffered from the lengthy reign but weak rule of Maximilian's father, Frederick III. At the same time, many of the leading princes of the Empire were asserting their own distinctive political positions using **particularism**.

Particularism: This describes the process by which princely territories within the Empire increased their independent power at the expense of the Emperor.

This situation created much dissatisfaction. On the one hand, Maximilian, supported by some of the smaller states within the Empire, sought to resolve matters by increasing the personal powers of the Emperor. He was trying to ensure that the Emperor emerged as a secure and unchallenged national ruler, in the mould of the kings of England and France. Maximilian had the opportunity to bring this about in 1505, but the chance was missed – just as his grandson was to miss a similar opportunity in 1547.

On the other hand, imperial reformers, led by Berthold von Henneberg (Archbishop of Mainz), sought to curb the powers of the Emperor still further by establishing strong institutions that would be dominated by the major princes.

In the end, the issue remained unresolved in Maximilian's reign. Maximilian built up an extremely successful set of dynastic alliances, which culminated in the succession of his grandson Charles not only to the Imperial crown but also to the Spanish thrones. This enabled Charles to build up a huge personal monarchy. It also established the Habsburg dominance of central Europe which was to come to an end only in 1918.

The tensions that were evident in Maximilian's reign were made worse by the emergence, right at the start of Charles' reign, of the Lutheran revolt against the Roman Catholic Church (see Chapter 4). This complicated relations between the Emperor and those princes who allied themselves with the Lutheran cause. Charles, who took the medieval conception of the Emperor as the secular head of Catholic Christendom seriously, sought to destroy the Lutheran threat. In doing so he had to tread carefully in view of the opposition to him of many of the princes, and because of the popular enthusiasm for religious reform which was evident in many parts of Germany. Charles had the opportunity to settle matters once and for all in favour of both Catholic Christianity and his own power following his triumph at the Battle of Mühlberg in 1547. However, the speed with which his triumph unravelled convinced Charles that his vision could not succeed. In quick succession, he accepted the establishment of Lutheranism in many parts of the Empire at the Peace of Augsburg in 1555 and abdicated from the Imperial throne in the following year.

5.1 How was the Holy Roman Empire governed?

What was the Holy Roman Empire?

Christendom: All the Christian peoples in the world. By Charles V's reign this was a concept that stressed the common values of a united and Christian Europe.

Over the centuries there had been several attempts to restore the title of emperor and, with it, the concept of a political institution exercising authority of much of western **Christendom**. Charlemagne had been crowned Emperor by the Pope on Christmas Day 800, but he saw his title in personal terms and divided his territories among his three sons on his death in 814. The concept was revived between the 10th and 13th centuries under the

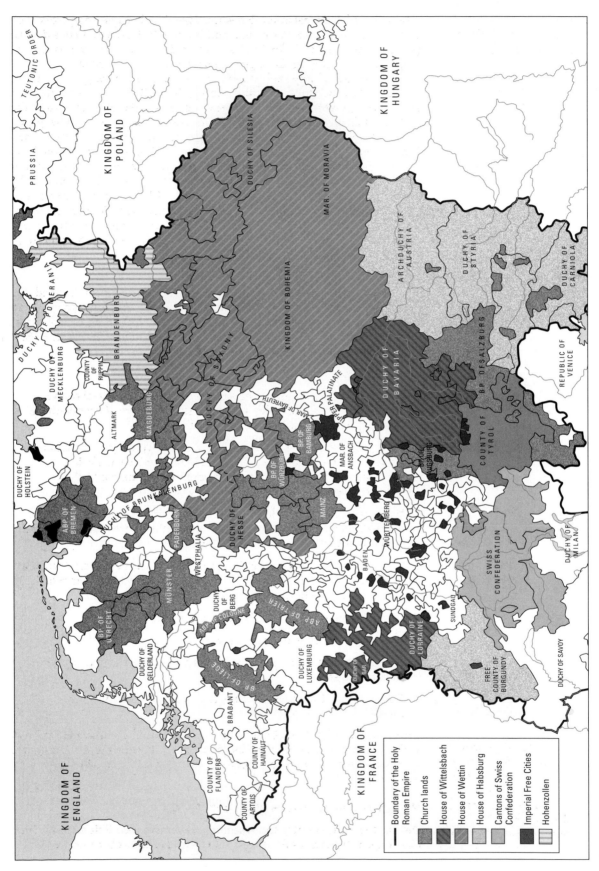

Central Europe, c. 1500

TEUTONIC ORDER

PRUSSIA

KINGDOM OF POLAND

KINGDOM OF HUNGARY

DUCHY OF POMERANIA

DUCHY OF MECKLENBURG

COUNTY OF RUPPIN

BRANDENBURG

DUCHY OF SILESIA

MAR. OF MORAVIA

ARCHDUCHY OF AUSTRIA

DUCHY OF STYRIA

DUCHY OF CARNIOLA

ALTMARK

MAGDEBURG

DUCHY OF SAXONY

KINGDOM OF BOHEMIA

DUCHY OF BAVARIA

BP. OF SALZBURG

REPUBLIC OF VENICE

DUCHY OF HOLSTEIN

MAR. OF BAYREUTH

UPPER PALATINATE

COUNTY OF TYROL

ABP. OF BREMEN

DUCHY OF BRUNSWICK-LÜNEBURG

BP. OF WÜRZBURG

BP. OF BAMBERG

MAR. OF ANSBACH

BP. OF AUGSBURG

MAINZ

NÜRNBERG

PADERBORN

DUCHY OF HESSE

DUCHY OF MILAN

MÜNSTER

WESTPHALIA

WÜRTTEMBERG

SWISS CONFEDERATION

BP. OF UTRECHT

DUCHY OF BERG

ABP. OF COLOGNE

ABP. OF TRIER

BADEN

SUNDGAU

DUCHY OF GELDERLAND

BP. OF LIÈGE

DUCHY OF LUXEMBURG

DUCHY OF LORRAINE

DUCHY OF BAR

FREE COUNTY OF BURGUNDY

DUCHY OF SAVOY

BRABANT

COUNTY OF FLANDERS

COUNTY OF HAINAUT

COUNTY OF ARTOIS

KINGDOM OF FRANCE

KINGDOM OF ENGLAND

Boundary of the Holy Roman Empire

Church lands

House of Wittelsbach

House of Wettin

House of Habsburg

Cantons of Swiss Confederation

Imperial Free Cities

Hohenzollern

Ottonian: The Ottonians were the first distinctively German dynasty (rulers who belong to the same family) to hold the Imperial Crown.

Hohenstaufen: A medieval dynasty under whose control German power reached its height.

Ottonian and **Hohenstaufen** dynasties. Like Charlemagne, emperors such as Henry IV, Frederick Barbarossa and Frederick II exercised considerable political power. After Frederick II's death in 1250, however, the concept of empire declined during the reigns of a succession of weak rulers.

This period of imperial weakness was reversed during the reign of Charles IV of the House of Luxemburg (1346–1378). Charles built up a substantial power base in his kingdom of Bohemia. He also issued the Golden Bull of 1356 to regulate future Imperial elections. The provisions set out in this document remained in force until the Holy Roman Empire met its end in 1806. In practice, the Golden Bull accepted the relative weakness of the Imperial title and attempted to limit the amount of political confusion which might occur at the death of an emperor by laying down on a permanent basis who should possess electoral power in the future. In the process, according to historian Geoffrey Dickens, the Golden Bull 'did much to protect Germany from the intermittent chaos which might so easily have followed the death of each Emperor'.

What was the Golden Bull of 1356?

The most important aspect of the Golden Bull was that it fixed the arrangements for the election of the Holy Roman Emperor. Before 1356 these arrangements had been uncertain. It was not clear, for example, which nobles had a clear right to participate in elections. The Golden Bull laid down the following rules for election.

● There should be *seven* electors.

● *Four* of the electors should be secular (outside the control of the Church) princes, the Duke of Saxony, the Margrave of Brandenburg, the King of Bohemia and the Count Palatine.

● *Three* of the electors should be ecclesiastical (relating to the Church) princes, the archbishops of Cologne, Mainz and Trier. Their appointment was an appropriate recognition of the political significance of the Church in Germany.

● It was recognised that the lands of the four lay electors could not be divided, thereby attempting to ensure that their power and influence would be sustained over the centuries.

● Each elector was given specific ceremonial functions to carry out at an Emperor's coronation – an important consideration in an era which placed great significance on symbols and ritual.

● It was deemed treason to rebel against an Elector.

● Electors could issue their own coins.

● Electors could make legal judgements without recourse to appeal to Imperial courts.

● The subjects of the Electors were not allowed to become citizens of towns.

Clearly, the Golden Bull conferred privileges on some of the great princes at the expense of others – such as the Duke of Bavaria and the Landgrave of Hesse – who might have considered themselves the equal of those who were chosen.

What were the functions of the Reichstag?

During the 15th century the Imperial parliament, the Reichstag or Diet, met frequently. As a result, its procedures and customs became settled.

Study the facing map carefully. What can be inferred from the map about the political structure of the Holy Roman Empire?

The Reichstag had three chambers:

1 The first chamber was the College of Electors.

2 The second chamber, the College of Princes represented all non-electoral princes of the Empire, both lay and ecclesiastical. It included rulers whose power, wealth and prestige varied enormously, with the opinions of the greater princes being accorded more weight than those of minor rulers.

3 From 1489 the Free Imperial Cities, about 65 in number – ranging from wealthy and influential Augsburg, Nuremberg and Strasbourg to minor places which were in no position to pursue independent policies – had their own Chamber.

The decisions of a Reichstag, known as the *Reichsabschied*, were theoretically binding, though the structures of the Empire were often incapable of imposing such decisions on reluctant princes or cities.

How significant was the role of the Emperor?

The role of the Emperor was varied.

● Charles V, in particular, saw his role as being that of the secular head of Christendom, using his political powers to defend the interests of the Roman Catholic Church.

● Both Maximilian I and Charles V also saw themselves as members of the Habsburg dynasty with a duty to enhance the dynastic interests of their family.

● Both Maximilian and Charles were territorial rulers in their own right.

● The Imperial Crown was important in that it conferred upon Maximilian and Charles, whether they liked it or not, a symbolic role as Emperor of the German people.

The nature of Imperial power was limited in a number of ways.

● The need for election meant that a candidate for the Imperial Crown might, like Charles V in 1519, have to make political concessions to electors or bribe them in order to secure election.

● Not only the Electors but also many of the princes had, in effect, acquired sovereign authority in their own territories. They, therefore, had a desire to avoid imperial interference in their own territories.

● The princes dominated the Reichstag and could use that domination to frustrate the Emperor's will, especially if the arch-chancellor of Germany could control Reichstag business in a way that might frustrate the Emperor.

● Noble power was often enhanced by the domination of senior offices in the Church by members of noble families.

● The Emperor did not possess a standing army.

● There was no effective system of Imperial taxation.

● Nobles were sometimes powerful enough to control previously self-governing towns.

On the other hand, there were some factors that helped to enhance the exercise of imperial power.

● The larger towns, which generated most of Germany's wealth, tended to support the Emperor.

Charles V (1500–1558)
King of Spain from 1516, he was elected Holy Roman Emperor in 1519, succeeding his grandfather Maximilian. A committed defender of the Roman Catholic faith, he sought unsuccessfully to remove heresy from the Empire and was forced to compromise with the Peace of Augsburg in 1555. He abdicated in 1556, considering himself a failure.

Swabian League: An alliance of lay and ecclesiastical princes, knights and towns in a grouping of cities and mainly small states in the south-west of Germany. The League lasted from 1488 to 1534. Fearful of the larger states in the region, the League usually looked to support the Emperor and often did so successfully, for example in the War of the Bavarian Succession in 1504.

- The **Swabian League**, which brought together in 1488 a group of lay and ecclesiastical princes and towns in the south-west of Germany, possessed an effective armed force which was used to enhance imperial authority.

- At the time of his accession in 1493, Maximilian enjoyed considerable personal prestige, especially as a result of his success as a military commander.

- Both Maximilian I and Charles V could boost their authority through their possession of vast amounts of territory. Maximilian, for example, had inherited the wealthy mining area of the Tyrol from his uncle.

- The Emperor was in a position to negotiate with the Reichstag over its final decisions.

- The Emperor was recognised as the supreme judge in legal matters within the Empire.

These powers and limitations suggest that the Emperor's relationship with the Electors was that of *primus inter pares* ('first among equals').

How important was the role of the major princes?

The powers and influence of the Electors had been confirmed in the Golden Bull of 1356. However, many other princes aspired to exercise similar levels of political power. Undoubtedly, in the case of such territorial magnates as the Duke of Bavaria and the Landgrave of Hesse, they were able to do so. During the reign of Frederick III, the greater princes tended to increase their power and authority. There were several reasons for this.

- The long reign and weak rule of Frederick III gave scope to the greater princes to develop their particularist ambitions.

- Some of the greater princes were developing the trappings of monarchy through the exercise of sovereign authority within their territories and the development of extensive courts in which artists and writers were offered patronage. The artist Lucas Cranach the Elder, for example, was employed at the court of the Elector of Saxony.

- Some princes were able to enhance their power through the consolidation of their territories by exchanging lands. This happened, for example, in Württemberg in 1482.

Berthold von Henneberg (d.1504)
A member of a long-standing noble family, Henneberg was Archbishop-Elector of Mainz and Imperial Chancellor. He had been influenced by the views of his teacher, Nicholas of Kues, who had favoured the devolution of power within the Empire. Henneberg led that group of reformers which hoped to secure better government by limiting the powers of the Emperor and by reforming the structures of the Empire to give effective authority to institutions which were answerable to the electors and to the Reichstag.

Estates: These were parliaments that existed within the lands of individual German princes. In the later 15th century, many Estates were increasing their power and influence.

1. **What limitations did the Imperial constitution place upon the activities and power of Maximilian I and Charles V?**

2. **In what ways did the Imperial constitution assist the German princes to resist the power of the Emperors?**

As a response to these trends, some princes argued that the individual states had been separate sovereign entities which had voluntarily subjected themselves to imperial control whilst retaining their princely liberties. This propagandist claim could then be used to justify particularist attitudes and policies; it could also be used to justify opposition to any attempt to restore a more centralised form of imperial government. Though these attitudes were explicitly anti-imperialist, this did not stop Maximilian accepting the logic of the claims when he was forced to negotiate as a virtual equal with the princes when he was desperate for support to upset the reforming proposals of Berthold von Henneberg.

On the other hand, many princes were short of money. Their traditional sources of income were in decline and, in many cases, this made them dependent on the support of the parliamentary **Estates**. Moreover, the power of rulers was sometimes dependent on the Estates. In 1498, for example, the Landtag of Württemberg had asserted the right to decide on the legality of participation in wars, and in 1504 it was the Estates of the three divided Bavarian duchies which originally proclaimed their reunification.

5.2 What was the relationship between the Holy Roman Empire and the idea of Germany?

Towards the end of the 15th century the Holy Roman Empire was changing in two ways: it was entering a period of political, economic, social and, eventually, religious unrest; and it was becoming less international and more German in character.

What was the condition of Germany in the late 15th century?

In the late 15th century Germany was becoming very unstable. This was partly a consequence of the spread of millenarian attitudes (the widely-held belief that the end of the world was near at hand). This was reflected in serious social divisions, growing violence, increasing **anti-Semitism** and a greater commitment to religion. The impact of these problems was made worse by the absence of a strong central political authority in Germany and by economic weaknesses.

Anti-Semitism: To be against Jews or the Jewish religion (Judaism).

The century and a quarter following the Black Death (1346–1349) had been one of considerable economic prosperity for Germany. The **Hanseatic League** dominated the trade of the Baltic and northern Europe. Cities such as Nuremberg, Augsburg and Frankfurt were not only key manufacturing centres, but also were increasingly important commercially. The Augsburg families of Fugger and Welser dominated European banking. Germany's central position within Europe, assisted by navigable waterways like the Rhine and the Danube, helped it to dominate European trade. German mining, particularly of silver, generated much wealth.

Hanseatic League: This was a league of north German ports, including Hamburg, Bremen and Lübeck, which had dominated northern European trade during the medieval period. It retained some influence during the late 15th and early 16th centuries, though its power and influence were declining.

Towards the end of the 15th century, however, this rosy picture began to fade. Hanseatic domination of northern European trade was increasingly challenged by the English and Dutch, and the economic primacy of Mediterranean and Baltic, which Germany could exploit due to its central position, was challenged by the rise of the 'Atlantic economy'. But despite the increasing pressures, particularly on farmers, there were many opportunities for the generation of wealth offered in the 4,000 towns and cities of Germany.

Germany certainly experienced much social and geographical mobility. The existence of opportunities for the enterprising needs to be balanced by trends such as the widening gulf between rich and poor, the resentment created by the displays of luxury of the newly rich and by an increasing rate of inflation which resulted in a fall in real incomes for the majority of Germans. In particular, peasants in western parts of Germany was beginning to suffer. Land-hunger led to increasing rents, old obligations of feudal tenure were becoming an increasing burden, many farms were divided with the resulting plots being unable to support the tenants, and yields were low. As a result, only a minority of wealthier and more enterprising peasants were able to benefit from the increasing market opportunities which were available. Such pressures contributed not only to the **Bundschuh** risings of the late 15th and early 16th centuries but also to the Peasants' War of 1524–25.

Bundschuh: This means 'the league of the boot', which became a symbol of peasant resistance to landlords and political authority in late 15th- and early 16th-century Germany.

Peasants were not the only ones to suffer. The economic and social status of the Imperial Knights was also being undermined. Claiming to owe allegiance only to the Emperor and freed from obligations to the local lord in return for military service, their position was being undermined by military changes, which was making their service less useful. Moreover, many of them were losing their autonomy to the territorial states. The more adaptable knights were able to secure employment in the imperial or princely courts. Many of them, the **Raubsritter**, turned to organised crime, thereby contributing significantly to the problem of law and order,

Raubsritter: Literally means 'robber knights'. The Raubsritter were often Imperial Knights whose weakening financial situation forced them to prey on others.

**Ulrich von Hutten
(1488–1523)**
An Imperial Knight, he was one
of the leaders of the knights
during the Knights' War. A
humanist and poet, he was an
early supporter of Luther,
whom he saw as a true
example of the German
national spirit.

**Franz von Sickingen
(1481–1523)**
An Imperial Knight, he assisted
Charles V in the election of 1519
and was rewarded with the post
of Imperial Chancellor. He broke
with Charles over religion, and
led those knights who sparked
off the Knights' War in 1522 by
attacking the lands of the
Archbishop-Elector of Trier.

Proletariat: The class of people in a
country who are paid wages for work
they do with their hands, and who
do not own much of the country's
wealth.

which was evident at the time. The knights' resentments came to a head in
1522. Led by Ulrich von Hutten and Franz von Sickingen, who had both
adopted the new Lutheran faith, they attacked the lands of the
Archbishop-Elector of Trier, with the intention of confiscating his land.
They tried to popularise their revolt by appealing to resentment against
the Roman Catholic Church's alleged plundering of German treasure. This
did them little good, and the knights were finally defeated in 1523 by an
army largely recruited from areas that were soon to turn Lutheran.

The towns were also experiencing growing tensions. There was
increasing polarisation in many towns between the urban élites and the
proletariat. This was often a consequence of economic problems, but it
sometimes reflected attempts by dominant élite groups to maintain their
local control by preventing the widening of rights of citizenship.

Political tensions appeared in many states. This was sometimes caused
by the attempts of rulers to give themselves the trappings of statehood;
for example by building up standing armies or by developing trained
bureaucracies. States such as Trier, Bohemia and Württemberg were
prominently involved in these processes. Government was becoming
more bureaucratic. This meant that the demand for trained bureaucrats
increased, stimulating the rise of a new class of legally trained graduate
bureaucrats who were products of the extensive German university
system. In the words of historian Michael Hughes, in *Early Modern
Germany, 1477–1806* (1992), 'the rise of the expert lawyer and administrator was seen as part of a general assault on traditional structures'.
Moreover, it was accompanied by significant changes in legal practice.
Roman law was gradually introduced into German practice, which not
only undermined traditional unwritten customary law but also made it
easier for rulers to enhance their power by strengthening the legal
powers of the state. This was reflected in the written law codes produced
for Nuremberg (1484) and Bavaria (1485–1495) and in the publication
of imperial laws in 1501 and 1531. Administrators and rulers saw such
developments as 'a means of improving efficiency and achieving standardisation'. A wider perception was that legal developments, as Michael
Hughes puts it, were also seen 'as a cause of problems: in contrast to the
good old days when there was only one law and everyone was happy,
there were now dozens of laws and thousands of lawyers and everyone
was miserable'.

How and why did a distinctive German national identity develop?

The emergence of a German national identity was speeded up by developments within the Holy Roman Empire.

- Imperial control over the Italian parts of the Empire had long since
  disappeared.

- In 1410, after the Battle of Tannenberg, the Order of Teutonic Knights
  was forced to give up sovereignty over Prussia to the Polish Crown.

- In 1466 the Order was forced to give the bulk of its territories to Poland.

- Anti-Bohemian sentiment had been fuelled by the war against the
  Hussites in the 1420s, and in 1491 Bohemia became temporarily
  detached from the Empire when the kingdom passed into the hands of
  the Polish royal house.

- In 1460 Schleswig had passed to Denmark.

- The Burgundian lands and the Netherlands drifted away from the
  Empire.

● The Swiss Confederation did not attend the Diet from 1471, and in 1495 they claimed exemption from the jurisdiction of the Imperial courts. This claim was accepted in practice in 1499 and by 1508 it was confirmed legally.

(See the map and accompanying question on pages 90 and 91.)

In effect, the Empire was acquiring clearer boundaries and becoming more German in character. This process was reflected in 1486 when the Empire's title was changed to the 'Holy Roman Empire of the German Nation'. This raises the question of how the 'German Nation' saw itself in the late 15th century.

According to Robin Du Boulay, the German language played a vital role in helping to form a German national identity from a society that was subject to so many political divisions. German was the language of business. Increasingly, it was also becoming the language of law and administration.

Title page to Hutten's *Gesprach Büchlein*, published in 1522. The illustrations make it clear that it is to be the Pope and his clergy who are to be conquered. Destroying them will end Germany's problems.

In what ways does this illustration depict German national feelings?

The spread of Renaissance ideas encouraged a new interest in German history. National heroes, such as Hermann, who had triumphed over the forces of the Roman Emperor Augustus, were rediscovered. In 1497 a German translation of *Germania* by the Roman author Tacitus was published. Maximilian supported humanist writers like Konrad Celtis and Sebastian Brant.

The symbols of Empire were given greater emphasis. The idea began to take root that the Holy Roman Empire represented the true descendant of the Roman Empire. The symbols of the Empire, such as eagles and the imperial crown, were widely used. Declining groups, such as the Imperial Knights, poorer peasants and the urban poor, looked to the revival of imperial power which would protect them from such oppressors as territorial princes, the corrupt clergy and the urban élites. The propaganda of Maximilian I and Charles V stressed that they were new leaders bringing about a rebirth of the German nation.

On the other hand, German nationalism took on a negative side. The essential honesty of Germans was compared with the deviousness of southern Europeans in general and Italians in particular. It was easy to translate such attitudes into anti-papal feeling, given the extent to which Germans had become convinced that they were being systematically robbed by the Papacy.

> **?** *What factors promoted the emergence of a distinct German identity during the late 15th and early 16th centuries?*

5.3 Why did attempts to reform the Empire fail during the reign of Maximilian I?

By the time of Maximilian I's accession in 1493 there were obvious weaknesses in the structure of the Empire. The Holy Roman Empire had experienced territorial losses, and there were persistent problems concerning law and order, often resolved by private armies or by courts whose jurisdiction was questionable. There was no system of imperial coinage, there was no imperial army and the Empire's legal structures were haphazard.

It was widely accepted, both by Maximilian and by many of the leading princes, that the situation needed to be reformed so that the Empire could acquire some of those features of an effective state which it clearly lacked. However, there were fundamental differences between the two conceptions of reform which were put forward at the time.

● Maximilian wanted to see the creation of a state which would have him firmly in charge. He would be guaranteed regular taxation and control of a standing army. A new supreme court would make the princes dependent on him. In other words, the reform of the Empire would take place at the expense of the particularist ambitions of the princes.

● Maximilian's opponents, led by Berthold von Henneberg, felt that coherence could be achieved through implementing reforms which would, in effect, neutralise the power of the Emperor. This would be brought about by a number of measures.

1　A **Reichsregiment** would be set up. This would be a standing committee comprising representatives of the Emperor and the Electors, which would be dominated by the latter. This was intended to develop into a permanent body to administer the Empire.

2　An imperial court, the **Reichskammergericht**, would be set up as a permanent body based in Frankfurt, well away from the Emperor's power base in Austria. Most of its judges would be appointed by the

Reichsregiment: A proposed governing council of the Empire, which was established in 1500. It was envisaged that this would become the permanent governing body of the Empire. It was opposed by Maximilian, who saw that his power would be further reduced. In the end, it was the reluctance of the princes to pay for the Reichsregiment that ensured its rapid downfall in 1502.

Reichskammergericht: The centrepiece of the attempts by the reformers, led by Henneberg, to re-organise the institutions of the Holy Roman Empire. Set up in Frankfurt, its role was to deal with legal disputes arising within the Empire. It was the first German central institution independent of the Crown. As such, it incurred Maximilian's hostility and he consistently tried to undermine its authority.

Common Penny: A tax to be imposed on all territories within the Empire. It was to be collected by the clergy and paid into a fund administered in Augsburg by the Imperial Treasurer who was subject to the control of the Reichstag. It was intended that the Common Penny should fund the **Reichskammergericht**. The tax met with widespread popular resistance in Switzerland and prompted the Swiss departure from the Empire. It was also perceived as a threat by some of the powerful princes. In 1505 Maximilian was able to secure its replacement by the **Reichsmatrikel**.

Reichkreise: Imperial 'circles of defence', i.e. groupings of states in which defence of the Empire was passed down to key princely figures. The first six circles were established in 1495. Four further circles were added in 1512.

Reichsmatrikel: The traditional and inefficient form of Imperial taxation. Each princely territory's financial obligations were laid down according to size, and it was the responsibility of the state governments to collect the taxes. Frequently they failed to do so. Moreover, the nobility was exempt from the tax, in contrast with the **Common Penny**.

Wittelsbachs: The main rivals to the Habsburgs in the south of Germany. Traditionally allied to the Kings of France, they were not only dukes of Bavaria but also electors of the Rhineland Palatinate. Their power was temporarily crushed by Maximilian's victory in the Landshut War of 1504–1505. With the onset of the Reformation the Bavarian Wittelsbachs remained Catholic and, often reluctantly, they became more supportive of their Habsburg co-religionists. Maximilian I was consolidating his power through his wise and popular rule in the Austrian lands, through the expansion of his influence by a series of marriage alliances, by his exploitation of patronage which increased the influence of his supporters among both ecclesiastical and lay princes, and by shrewd exploitation of his personal image, which emphasised his fighting qualities, generosity and concern for German interests.

princes. Its principal task would be to sit in judgement on disputes between territorial rulers.

3 An imperial tax, the **Common Penny**, was set up to finance the Reichskammergericht. It was to be collected by the clergy and administered by an imperial treasurer in Augsburg who would be responsible to the Reichstag.

4 A system of imperial Circles of Defence (**Reichskreise**) was established in 1500 and extended in 1512. Originally linked to the Reichsregiment, these were regional unions designed to maintain internal order and external defence. The Kreise covered the whole of the central part of the Empire, though, significantly, the kingdom of Bohemia was not part of the system. The rulers within each Circle were supposed to organise defence within their areas. Little, however, was done.

In 1495, Henneberg and his supporters renewed their pressure for the establishment of a Reichsregiment. Maximilian was able to block this temporarily, but only at the expense of accepting annual meetings of the Diet, which was to become the supreme legislative authority of the Empire. By the time of the Diet of Augsburg in 1500, Maximilian, weakened by the Swiss revolt, had also been forced to accept the Reichsregiment. It seemed as if Germany was about to become a constitutional monarchy.

Had these reforms succeeded, a very different Empire would have emerged. The Emperor would have been completely lacking in power, except that which he could exercise as a territorial ruler. Greater power within the Empire would have been exercised by some of the princes. Why was Maximilian able to prevent this from happening?

Maximilian recovered quickly from the revolt of the Swiss Confederation. He was sensible enough to realise that there was little he could do to prevent the Swiss from going their own way. As he was heavily dependent upon Swiss mercenaries to fight his foreign wars, he quickly made peace with the Swiss and accepted their demands.

The success of the reform movement depended upon the willingness of the territorial rulers to pay for reform by means of the Common Penny. This not only sparked off the Swiss Revolt, it was also avoided by members of the nobility who were expected to pay it, whereas hitherto they had been exempted from imperial taxation. Unsurprisingly, perhaps, the princes were unwilling to pay a financial sacrifice for the implementation of better government. This enabled Maximilian to secure the removal of the Reichsregiment in 1502.

Maximilian himself recovered from the political weakness that he had experienced from 1495 to 1500. In this he was strongly supported by the Swabian League, which, fearful of the growing power of the Swiss and the **Wittelsbachs**, was anxious to boost imperial power at the expense of their local rivals. Maximilian's defeat of the Bavarians in the Landshut War of 1504 owed much to the League.

What is more, the reform movement lost much of its drive and coherence with the death of Henneberg in 1504.

As a result, when the Diet met in Cologne in 1505, Maximilian had the outright support of five of the seven electors and had just crushed a sixth, the Elector Palatine. The Venetian Ambassador reported that 'his imperial majesty is now a true emperor of the empire and ruler of Germany'.

Maximilian now had *his* chance to impose his vision of reform upon the Empire.

- Germany should have a strong monarchy.

- There should be a Reichsregiment of 12 members drawn from the six Kreise.

- The Emperor would have the right to call the Reichsregiment, which would be accountable to him for its actions.

- The Reichskammergericht was reinstated, but had little practical significance.

Such proposals foundered partly on the rock of princely particularism. 'The princes would not accept the status of subjects to a state however constitutional; (Maximilian) would not sink to the level of a president of a federal republic.' In the end, Maximilian was unable to press the point because he needed noble support to re-assert the Habsburg claim to the throne of Hungary. Payments for the invasion of Hungary would be made through the revival of the Reichsmatrikel rather than the Common Penny, much to the delight of the nobility, who were exempt from the former tax.

However, they also fell victim to the fact that Maximilian's ambitions in Italy assumed a higher priority than reform of the Empire. By 1508 Maximilian had become expensively entangled in the Italian Wars, mainly in opposition to the Republic of Venice, which upset the trading interests of the south German towns. Moreover, his Italian adventures in 1508 and 1509 were marked by failure. Consequently, when Maximilian asked the Diet of Augsburg in 1510 to support another scheme for the reorganisation of defence, the response was hostile and the Diet buried the proposal. The continued failure of his ambitions in Italy reduced Maximilian's popularity and by the time of his death in 1519 the Empire was in a weak state. He had failed to arrange properly for the succession of his grandson, the Imperial Treasury was bankrupt, little territory had been gained in Italy, and law and order had broken down in the Rhineland. Even without the consequences of the Lutheran revolt, which began in 1517, Maximilian's legacy was to be significantly flawed.

1. What were the imperial reformers trying to achieve during the reign of Maximilian?

2. Why did attempts at Imperial reform fail during Maximilian's reign?

5.4 How justified is the claim that Maximilian I was the true founder of the Habsburg dynasty?

Let us start by looking at Maximilian the person. He was a noted patron of artists and musicians. The greatest German artist of the period Albrecht Dürer produced a set of woodcuts, 'The Triumphal Arch for Maximilian I' (see page 100), which emphasised his military and diplomatic triumphs. (The propaganda message was reinforced because woodcuts could be reproduced in large numbers and could therefore be seen by far more people than could see court paintings.)

Other court artists, such as Bernhard Strigel and Hans Burgkmair, also depicted Maximilian in a particularly heroic light. The propaganda was reinforced when he was often compared favourably with emperors from ancient Rome.

Maximilian was a great patron of musicians. Some of these were Flemish musicians whom he had first encountered in the Burgundian court. One of these was Henrik Isaak, who composed 'Imperii proceres' in 1507–1508. The text of this work praised Maximilian in lavish terms.

Nobles of the Empire, glory of the Roman rule,
You the electors and all priests,
Together with the whole order of the Church and leaders of arms,
You company of powerful noblemen of great repute

And you peoples, whom treaties unite in one Empire,
Take counsel together for the sake of all.
Give succour in times of weariness,
And support the Holy Church,
Let concord bind us together in holy bond
And be present in each man's affairs!
Hear me sing praises to pious Maximilian!
Let good fortune favour us.
Father of fathers, give your orders
And drive out rebellious murmurings;
Grant, O God, that any rival shall fall
To the just arms of the Empire!
Let us here send you devout thanks
In song, and let victorious Germany
Celebrate your praises.

1. What are the propaganda messages being conveyed by both the illustration and the song?

2. How successful were they likely to have been in getting their message across during the last decade of Maximilian's reign?

Albrecht Dürer's 'Triumphal Arch of Maximilian I', 1515, assembled from 174 individual printed sheets.

Maximilian's record as Holy Roman Emperor might have had its weaknesses. However, he enjoyed great success in two other key areas: he can be seen not only as the founder of the Austrian state, but also as the ruler who established the Habsburgs as one of the great European dynasties.

In Austria his original power base lay in the Tyrol, whose capital, Innsbruck, became the centre of his administration as early as 1490. After his father's death in 1493 Maximilian extended his direct control to include Lower Austria. Though he was sometimes opposed by the local

Ferdinand I (1503–1564)
Younger brother of Charles V, Ferdinand administered the Empire for long periods on his brother's behalf. Originally chosen to succeed his brother, he only managed to do so by forcing Charles to drop his change of plan, which would have involved Charles' son Philip succeeding to the Imperial Crown. Having succeeded Charles, he was able to bring about some reforms to the administrative structure of the Empire, and was able to complete the union of Austria with Hungary and Bohemia, which lasted until 1918.

estates, he was able to establish an effective central administration over Austria which was developed subsequently by his younger grandson, Ferdinand.

One of Maximilian's key dynastic objectives was to expand Habsburg power in Hungary and Bohemia. During the reign of Frederick III, Habsburg power in central Europe had been overshadowed by the King of Hungary, Mátyás Corvinus, whose territories spread from Brandenburg to Serbia. However, the death of Mátyás without a male heir in 1490 gave Maximilian his opportunity. He recovered Austrian land that had been lost to the Hungarians and asserted his claim to the Hungarian throne. Unfortunately for Maximilian, the Hungarian monarch was elected by the nobility, who had no wish to submit to Habsburg power. Instead, they elected the King of Bohemia, Ladislas Jagiellon, to the throne. Ladislas was the son of the King of Poland, which opened up the possibility of the emergence of a huge central European monarchy under Polish leadership. This would have destroyed Maximilian's dynastic ambitions at a stroke. Maximilian needed to act quickly to prevent this possibility. He invaded Hungary in 1491 and was able to force the Hungarians and Bohemians to accept, at the Treaty of Pressburg, that Maximilian and his heirs had the right of succession to the Hungarian and Bohemian thrones.

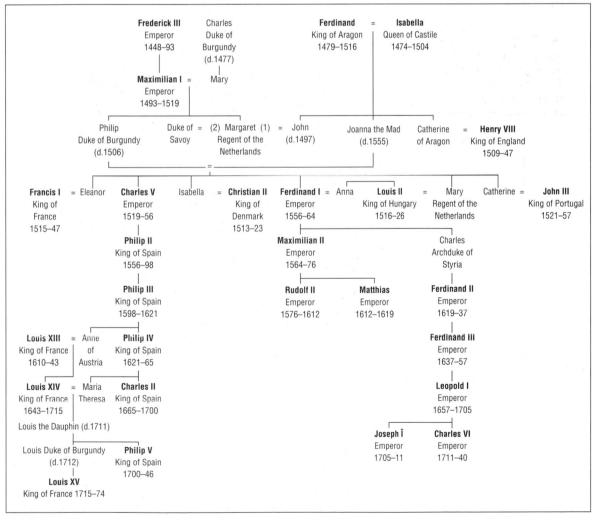

The House of Habsburg

Portrait of the Habsburgs by Bernhard Strigel (1460–1528). This is a portrait of Maximilian I and his family. It shows Maximilian with his late wife Mary of Burgundy and late son Philip of Burgundy, the father of Charles V. Charles is portrayed also, along with his brother Ferdinand and his sister Mary.

What is the political message of this painting?

John Zápolyai (1487–1540)
A powerful Hungarian noble, he was Governor of Transylvania 1511–1526 and regent for King Louis II during his minority. He made an accommodation with the Turks after their triumph in 1526 and, thereafter, ruled in Hungary as their 'puppet', though his power was frequently challenged by Ferdinand.

Thereafter, relations between Maximilian and Ladislas were good. However, many Hungarian nobles were opposed to Habsburg influence, and in October 1505 they forced the Hungarian Diet to declare that they would not accept a foreigner as successor to Ladislas. Maximilian, at the height of his power and influence, was able to counter this by using military pressure to force Ladislas to agree that his daughter Anne should marry a grandson of Maximilian and that his expected child, if a boy, should marry a granddaughter of Maximilian. Many Hungarian nobles continued to object to what they saw as Habsburg control and Maximilian was forced to invade Hungary to impose his will. Even so, some Hungarian nobles continued to resist the Habsburg claims and in 1512 they sought to revive the Polish alliance through the marriage of the sister of their leader, John Zápolyai, to King Sigismund of Poland. Nevertheless, Maximilian was able to secure confirmation of the succession agreements in 1515. He was himself conditionally betrothed to Anne of Hungary, but passed on that marriage promise to his grandson Ferdinand, who duly completed the marriage. Ladislas' son, Prince Louis, was betrothed to marry Maximilian's granddaughter Mary, and was also adopted by Maximilian as his own son.

1. What problems did Maximilian face in his relationships with the Hungarians and the Bohemians?

2. How skilful was Maximilian in pursuing his dynastic objectives?

These complicated alliances were intended to bring about Habsburg control in Hungary and Bohemia. Ferdinand was duly proclaimed as King of Bohemia by the Bohemian Diet. However, the situation in Hungary was more complicated. Many Hungarian nobles continued to be reluctant to accept Habsburg control. Moreover, the crushing victory of the Turks over the Hungarians at Mohácz in 1526 was to mean that much Hungarian territory fell into Turkish hands and Transylvania remained under the control of Zápolyai. Habsburg control of central Europe was thus never as complete, at least in the first half of the 16th century, as Maximilian had envisaged. It was undoubtedly Maximilian who had proved himself the father of the dynasty which would dominate that region down to 1918.

5.5 How great were the problems faced by Charles on his election?

Why did Charles experience such difficulty in being elected?

One of Maximilian's major shortcomings as Emperor was his failure to secure the Imperial succession for his grandson, Charles. When Charles' great rival, Francis I of France, declared himself a contender for the Imperial Crown, Charles was faced with a contested election, the result of which was by no means a foregone conclusion. The seven Electors were suspicious of Habsburg power and pretensions. Two of their number – the Wittelsbach Elector Palatine and the Archbishop of Trier – were particularly noted for their anti-Habsburg beliefs, and would definitely have preferred a French succession. To have supported a French candidacy openly at a time when German national sentiment was increasing would, however, have been politically difficult for them. For a time it looked as if the most senior Elector, the highly respected Frederick the Wise of Saxony, might have stood as a reluctant compromise candidate. In the end, however, a combination of bribery (Charles paid out 850,000 florins to the Electors) and fear of increasing French power led the electors to accept Charles' candidacy, and he was duly elected on 28 June 1519. In the words of historian Geoffrey Elton: 'the election gave him some further access of power; above all, it made him, in his own mind, the secular head of Christendom'.

What limitations were placed on Charles at his election?

There were limitations to the power that Charles could exercise. As part of the price of election, Charles had to agree to the Wahlkapitulation. This required him to make a number of concessions to the princes.

- He was to respect the rights and privileges of the princes.
- He agreed not to appoint foreigners to imperial offices.
- He was required not to bring any foreign troops into the Empire.
- He was not to declare war without the consent of the Electors.
- He was obliged to consult the Electors and the Reichstag on all imperial matters.

Clearly, this agreement not only reflected Charles' relative dependence on the Electors, it was also a clear demonstration of the Electors' fear that Charles might be tempted to drag the Empire into foreign wars.

What was the condition of the Empire at Charles' election?

By the time of Charles' election, the German lands were experiencing some prosperity. Bankers such as the Fuggers and Welsers were flourishing. The mining industry was growing rapidly. Peasants in the southern parts of the Empire were often quite prosperous. Many cities, particularly Nuremberg and Augsburg, were becoming wealthier. Also, many aspects of German intellectual and cultural life were impressive.

However, all was not well. Many peasants in central and eastern parts of Germany were suffering economically. More prosperous peasants were becoming dissatisfied with a political system that denied them the influence to match their increasing wealth.

The Imperial Knights were not only declining but also posed an extensive threat to law and order. The Church was increasingly perceived as being corrupt. Charles was financially weak because of his need to repay the loans that had secured his election. (He had borrowed 543,000 florins from the Augsburg bankers, the Fuggers.) The eastern part of the Empire was vulnerable to the Turkish threat, especially once the Turks' capture of Belgrade (1521) had opened the way to the Hungarian plain.

In what ways was the government of the Empire affected by Charles' personality and his view of Empire?

Charles lacked intellectual distinction and was rather shy. Nevertheless, he was a far from negligible ruler. He had a powerful sense of duty. This was shown especially in two respects: his loyalty to the principles of chivalry which he had inherited from his Burgundian ancestors; and his dedication to the interests, as he saw them, of the universal Church.

Charles was a courageous ruler and, by the political standards of the time, he was undoubtedly an honourable, dedicated and purposeful ruler. It is important to remember that Charles had a notion of empire, or *monarquia*, which far exceeded that of the Holy Roman Empire. Most of all, Charles saw himself as the secular head of a united Christendom, working hand in hand with the Pope, whose spiritual role he had a duty to defend. (Unfortunately for Charles, this was not an idea that was widely held by most of the popes of the time.)

It is also important to remember that the scale of Charles' possessions ensured that it was rarely possible for him to devote his attentions single-mindedly to the needs of the Holy Roman Empire. It was fortunate for him that his brother Ferdinand was a capable deputy. Most particularly, Charles always felt the need to tackle the Turkish threat head on. This was necessary for three reasons.

- As the inheritor of the Aragonese commercial empire, Charles had to combat the Turkish threat in the Mediterranean.
- As the Holy Roman Emperor and head of the Habsburgs, he had to withstand the Turkish incursions in Hungary.
- As the secular head of Christendom, he felt obliged to oppose the Turks on religious grounds.

As a result, war was always a central feature of his reign and his resources would always be stretched in attempting to deal with the Turkish threat, not to mention the threats posed by other enemies such as the French and the Lutherans.

1. What does the imperial election tell us about the power of the electors?

2. What limitations were placed on Charles' role as emperor as a result of the election?

5.6 In what ways was Imperial government affected by the Lutheran revolt, 1521–1529?

What Charles V persistently faced was the interaction between two key factors: princely particularism and the religious threat posed by Martin Luther.

He first became conscious of the threat posed by Luther at the Diet of Worms in 1521 (see Chapter 4). There was nothing new about princely particularism, but the heady atmosphere of 1521 made the situation more difficult for Charles. There were three main reasons for this.

- Luther had achieved the support of his territorial prince, the Elector Frederick the Wise of Saxony.

- Charles was reluctant publicly to oppose Frederick, who had been instrumental in bringing about Charles' election.

- Luther was able to exploit feelings of German nationalism which had been very strong at the time and which secured for him the support of powerful Imperial Knights such as Franz von Sickingen and Ulrich von Hutten.

The situation was made worse for Charles when the Knights' War broke out in 1523. This had been provoked by the attack by Sickingen and Hutten on the territories of the Archbishop-Elector of Trier. The archbishop was no friend of Charles and had opposed his election. However, Charles was forced to throw his support behind the remnants of the Swabian League. Although the League defeated Sickingen and Hutten it was significantly weakened as a political force in the process, thereby reducing the Emperor's ability to force his will on disobedient princes.

In the aftermath of the Peasants' War of 1524–25 (see Chapter 4), an increasing number of princes threw in their support with Luther and formed the first League of Torgau in March 1526 to withstand the Edict of Worms which had outlawed Luther in 1521. In opposition to this, the League of Regensburg was established, pledging itself to uphold the Edict of Worms. The irony of this was that Charles' brother Ferdinand, in cobbling together the League of Regensburg, was forced to do a deal with the hated rivals of the Habsburgs, the Wittelsbachs of Bavaria. In the meantime, the emerging Lutheran princes were able to exploit the Turkish threat at the Diet of Speyer. In the Recess of Speyer they secured for them the right to control religion within their territories, answerable only to 'God and his Imperial majesty'.

This triumph was short-lived. Charles' power and prestige were increased by his triumphs in Italy (see Chapter 2). Moreover, by the time of the 1529 Diet of Speyer the Lutherans had become divided among themselves. Charles was thus, temporarily, successful. The 1526 The Recess was rescinded and the need to enforce the Edict of Worms was once more enforced on all rulers. In reply, six Lutheran princes and 14 cities signed the Protest of Speyer (from which is derived the term 'Protestant'). Even the situation in eastern Europe had temporarily become relatively stable. Ferdinand had secured Bohemia, though in Hungary he was involved in a continuing struggle with John Zápolyai.

1. In what ways did the Lutheran princes and cities challenge the authority of the Emperor?

2. How effective was Charles' response to the Lutheran challenge?

5.7 To what extent was Charles' power limited by the increasing desire of the princes for self-government?

Unfortunately for Charles, this favourable situation lasted only a very short time. Once again the Turkish threat was becoming evident.

Charles needed the princes' support to withstand the possible Turkish threat. Moreover, he was anxious both to secure Ferdinand's election as King of the Romans and to secure an end to the schism (split) in the Church. In the circumstances, he was prepared late in 1530 to reach a deal with the Lutherans. For their part, the Lutherans put forward a moderate declaration of faith, the Confession of Augsburg, which they hoped could form the basis for a compromise. Though the Confession failed to bring about the desired compromise, Ferdinand was elected King of the Romans.

The more extreme Lutherans, led by Landgrave Philip of Hesse, were alienated by the failure to achieve religious compromise and by the Diet's decision to re-affirm the Edict of Worms. As a result, eight princes and 11 cities came together to form the League of Schmalkalden, the members of which agreed to help each other should they be attacked 'on account of the Word of God and the doctrine of the Gospel'. For the first time, a group of princes and cities appeared to be offering open defiance of the Emperor. To make matters worse, Charles was faced by a renewed Turkish threat in 1532, which he was able to limit only by agreeing to a treaty that left Zápolyai controlling most of Hungary under Turkish 'protection'.

Charles' power was further reduced in 1534 when the League of Schmalkalden, with the consent of the Wittelsbach Duke of Bavaria, were able to restore Duke Ulrich to his Duchy of Württemberg. Charles and Ferdinand were forced to accept this by suspending Reichskammergericht proceedings and agreeing to the Duke's restoration. This proved a great triumph for Philip of Hesse and the League. Many more princes and states now joined the organisation.

Bigamist: Someone who married twice, at the same time.

Philip remained dominant until 1540, when his position was weakened as a result of revelations about his private life. Not only was he exposed as a **bigamist**, but reformers such as Luther, Melanchthon and Bucer all suffered blows to their credibility when it was revealed that they had supported Philip in his offence. To make matters worse for Philip, bigamy was technically an offence punishable by death under the new legal code for the Empire, the **Carolina**, issued in 1532. Fearful for his life as well as his political future, Philip was forced to seek an Imperial pardon. Charles granted this in June 1541, in the process neutralising Philip as an anti-Imperial political force.

Carolina: This was the common criminal code of the Empire, and was adopted by the Diet of Regensburg in 1532.

Unfortunately for Charles, this success was to prove extremely short-lived, as once again his position was undermined by the threat from the Turks. Zápolyai had died in 1540 and his widow, contesting Ferdinand's claim to the Hungarian succession, appealed to Suleiman on behalf of her infant son. Once again, the Turks invaded Hungary, captured Buda and replaced their policy of having a client kingdom by direct occupation. Charles' attempt to seek a solution to Imperial problems through religious compromise at the Diet of Regensburg was thus destroyed.

Charles had genuinely hoped to be able to bury his differences with the Protestant princes and cities by compromise, mainly through establishing a General Council of the Church which he hoped would attempt to end the religious schism. Though his hopes were genuine, events after 1541 showed that they were unachievable.

- The threat from the Turks, now in alliance with the French, was worse than ever.

- Ferdinand had control of only a tiny piece of Hungary.

- The Schmalkaldic League recovered its nerve sufficiently to expel the last remaining Catholic secular prince in the north, Duke Henry of Brunswick-Wolfenbüttel, from his duchy.

- Even the archbishopric of Cologne seemed on the point of moving into the Lutheran camp.

Charles, in desperation, realised that he had to break the League of Schmalkalden. He was willing to break the terms of the Wahlkapitulation to do so. Charles was able to exploit divisions among the Protestant princes to achieve his ends, attracting to his side three Lutheran princes – Maurice Duke of Saxony, Albert Alcibiades the Margrave of Brandenburg-Kulmbach and John the Margrave of Brandenburg-Küstrin – who each had a motive for distrusting the League. Of these, Maurice was by far the most important. He fiercely hated his cousin, John Frederick, the Elector of Saxony. With these allies on his side, Charles proceeded to isolate the League, went to war with it in 1546 and defeated it at the Battle of Mühlberg in 1547.

Charles was, temporarily, triumphant. Even the Turks, more anxious now to advance east into Persia, wanted to make peace. His old adversaries, Francis I and Henry VIII, had both recently died. Charles enjoyed his triumph by imprisoning Philip of Hesse and John Frederick of Saxony. The latter lost his lands to his cousin Maurice. It looked as if Charles was on the point of being able simultaneously to restore the authority of the Emperor and re-establish the control of the Roman Catholic Church.

Charles had won the war. However, he proved dismally unable to win the peace. Within a few months his dominant position had been lost. There were several reasons for this.

- His newly captured territories failed to reconvert to Catholicism.

- He was running short of money and the Fuggers were refusing to guarantee further loans.

- His plan for a standing army and a general Imperial league was foiled by his Bavarian enemies.

- His plan to reassert Catholicism through the Augsburg Interim failed. The Interim tried to accommodate the Lutherans by accepting that there could be no return of church property confiscated by the Lutherans. However, the Lutheran princes, even including those who had been imprisoned by Charles, refused to give up their faith, and a new Protestant league was set up in 1551–52 to challenge Charles' authority.

1. Why did Charles fail to achieve a compromise peace in 1530–31?

2. To what extent was his power within the Empire reduced between 1531 and 1542?

3. What factors prevented Charles from exploiting his triumph at Mühlberg effectively?

However, the most important reason for Charles' failure was the scale of the dispute over the Imperial succession. Charles had decided that weaknesses in the way in which the Empire was financed would mean that the Imperial structure would be insupportable if the plan for him to be succeeded by Ferdinand went ahead. Accordingly, he tried to set aside this long-standing plan and attempted to ensure the succession of his son Philip to all of his territories. Ferdinand, who had served his brother loyally, was outraged. Moreover, the crucial figure of Maurice of Saxony soon realised what was going on. With a mixture of motives, some personal and some principled, Maurice ditched the Emperor and made an alliance with Henry II of France. Meanwhile, the Turks were once again advancing into Hungary. Thus, the set of advantages which Charles had enjoyed in 1546 were almost all destroyed; now the odds were stacked against him. After several years of war, Charles was forced both to reinstate Ferdinand and to acknowledge the triumph of the princely particularism which he had had been on the point of destroying in 1547. Thus the scene was set for Charles' abdication and, with it, his profound sense that he had failed as Holy Roman Emperor.

Spain 1450–1556

Key Issues

- *How far did Spain become a unified state in this period?*

- *To what extent did the government of Spain change between 1450 and 1556?*

- *How successful was Spain in foreign and imperial affairs?*

Framework of Events

1454	Henry IV becomes King of Castile
1458	John II becomes King of Aragon
1462	Start of a decade of civil war in Aragon
1464	Start of civil war in Castile
1469	Ferdinand marries Isabella
1474	Isabella becomes Queen of Castile
1474–79	War of Succession in Castile
1476	Ferdinand defeats the Portuguese at Battle of Toro
1478	Inquisition is established in Castile
1479	Ferdinand becomes King of Aragon
1480	Cortes of Toledo
1482	War against Granada begins
1492	Granada defeated
	Jews expelled from Castile
	Columbus discovers the New World
1493	Treaty of Barcelona with France; Aragon recovers Roussillon and Cerdagne
1495	Military intervention in the Italian Wars begins
1497	Death of Prince John, the only son of Ferdinand and Isabella
1499	Mudejar Revolt in Granada
1500	Birth of the future Charles I to Joanna the Mad and Philip the Fair
1504	Death of Isabella. She is succeeded by Joanna the Mad
1506	Ferdinand marries Germaine de Foix
1505–10	Capture of North African ports, including Algiers and Tripoli
1512	Kingdom of Navarre becomes part of Aragon; given to Castile in 1515
1516	Ferdiand dies. Charles I proclaimed King of Aragon and Castile jointly with his mother, Joanna the Mad
1519	Charles I elected Holy Roman Emperor, taking the title Charles V
	Cortés begins conquest of Aztec Empire in Mexico
1519–24	Germanias Revolt in Aragon
1520–21	Revolt of the Communeros in Castile
1521	French invade Navarre

1521–56	Charles involved in intermittent warfare with France
1522	Council of War is established in Castile
1523	Council of Finance is established in Castile
1525	French King Francis I is captured at Battle of Pavia in north Italy
1526	Charles I marries Isabella, sister of the King of Portugal
1527	Birth of future Philip II
1531	Francisco Pizarro begins conquest of Inca Empire in Peru
1535	Military expedition to Tunis
1541	Military expedition to Algiers
1542	New Laws of the Indies
1551	Muslims take Tripoli
1555	(24 October) Charles I abdicates. He leaves Philip II as ruler of Spain, the New World, Franche Comté, the Netherlands and Habsburg possessions in Italy
1556	(March) Philip II is proclaimed King of Spain.

Overview

Early map of Spain, 1482

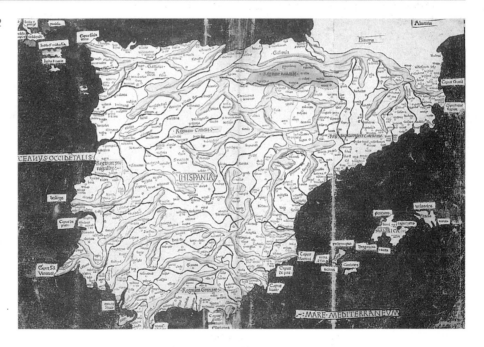

I N 1450 Spain was nothing more than a geographical expression, such as 'Germany' or 'Italy'. It was divided into a number of states (see map). The largest state was the Kingdom of Castile. There was also the Kingdom of Aragon, which itself was divided into three distinct kingdoms, each with its own Cortes (parliament) and laws: the Kingdom of Aragon, the Kingdom of Catalonia and the Kingdom of Valencia.

Outside Spain the Kingdom of Aragon controlled the Balearics, Sardinia and Sicily. Aragon also had claims to the Kingdom of Naples. To the north of Aragon lay the Kingdom of Navarre. In southern Spain was the Emirate of Granada. Unlike the others this was an Islamic state. Throughout the Middle Ages, Christian Spain had reconquered most of the Iberian **peninsula** from the Muslims (Moors) who had overrun much of the area since the 8th century. Granada was the last of these Muslim states. Finally, in the west, was the Kingdom of Portugal.

Peninsula: A body of land surrounded on three sides by water.

By 1556 Spain had been united under one monarch, Philip II. During his reign (1556–1598) Spain became the dominant western European state. As the American historian W. H. Prescott noted in 1837: 'the nation emerging from … a barbarous age, seemed to prepare like a giant to run its course'. A century later, in 1937, the English historian R. Trevor Davies described the period 1500 to 1621 as 'The Golden Century of Spain'.

	Square km	% of total area of peninsula	Inhabitants	% of total population	Inhabitants per square km
Crown of Castile	378,000	65.2	8,304,000	73.2	22.0
Crown of Aragon	100,000	17.2	1,358,000	12.0	13.6
Kingdom of Portugal	90,000	15.5	1,500,000	13.2	16.7
Kingdom of Navarre	12,000	2.1	185,000	1.6	15.4

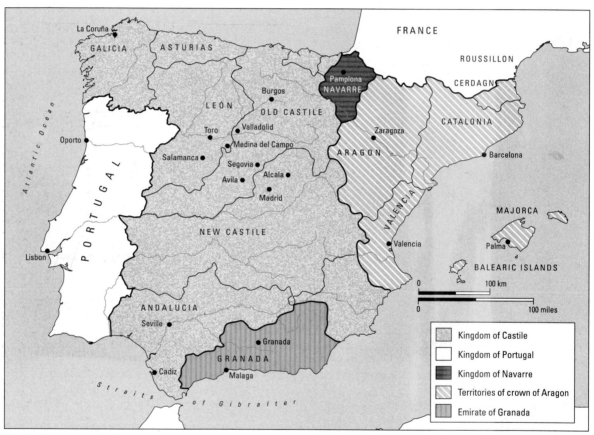

The Iberian peninsula at the beginning of the 16th century: the four states in relation each other

How did Spain rise to become a major western European power by 1556?

The reigns of Ferdinand of Aragon and Isabella of Castile mark an important stage in this process. Both members of the Trastámara family, they were proclaimed 'The Catholic Monarchs' by Pope Alexander VI in 1494. As joint monarchs, Ferdinand and Isabella helped restore law and order in their two kingdoms after a long period of political chaos. Their joint rule began with a period of civil war. Having overcome civil war, Ferdinand and Isabella helped to strengthen the power and position of the monarchy. The Catholic Monarchs also completed the *Reconquista* with the capture of Granada in 1492. In 1512, after Isabella's death, Ferdinand organised the takeover of the Kingdom of Navarre. By the accession of Charles I in 1516, the Iberian peninsula, apart from Portugal, was under one monarch. Outside the peninsula, Ferdinand extended Spanish influence to the North African coast and in southern Italy with the acquisition of the Kingdom of Naples.

Although regarded as relatively insignificant at the time, the discovery of the New World by Christopher Columbus in 1492 laid the foundations for a vast Spanish empire in the Americas. This new empire not only brought political prestige it also supplied large amounts of silver which acted as a major source of revenue to Spanish monarchs from the 1540s.

An important aspect of the territorial expansion was the fact that Navarre, Granada and the New World became possessions of Castile, not Castile and Aragon. By the time of the Ferdinand's death in 1516, it was clear that Castile was the dominant partner. During the reign of Charles I, Castile became the centre of his *monarquia* (monarchy). It provided large sums of revenue and soldiers for Charles' wars against France, the Turks and German Protestants. Unfortunately, by the time of Charles' abdication in 1555 his financial and military demands had created major economic problems.

The House of Trastámara

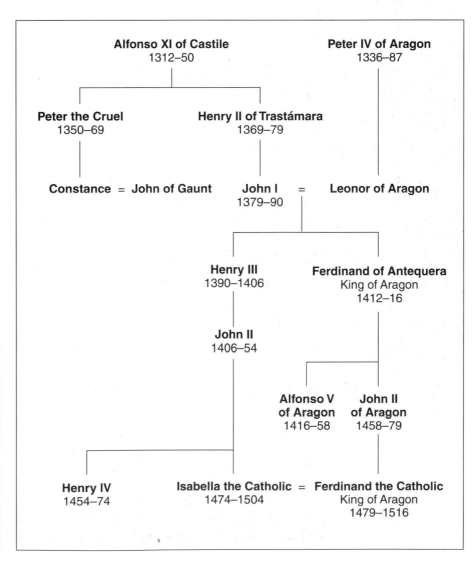

1. *How closely related were Isabella and Ferdinand before they married?*

2. *Why do you think they required the Pope's permission to marry?*

In 1516 Charles I and his mother were jointly proclaimed rulers of Castile and Aragon. In 1556 his son Philip II was proclaimed King of Spain. During the period 1450–1556 there had been major steps towards unifying Spain. Not only had the various Spanish territories fallen under the control of one monarch, but also attempts were made to centralise the administration. Beginning with the Catholic Monarchs, and continuing under Charles I, a conciliar system of government was developed (see page 139). However, the degree of unity within Spain, by the time of Charles' abdication, has been an important issue of debate among historians.

One distinct feature of Medieval Spain was the *conviviencia*. This involved considerable religious and cultural tolerance between three groups: the Christians, Jews and Muslims. Ferdinand III of Castile, who ruled during the first part of the 13th century, referred to himself as 'King of Three Religions'. The *conviviencia* came to an end under the Catholic Monarchs.

In 1478, one of the most distinctive features of 16th-century Spain was established: the Inquisition. It was initially designed to uncover among Jews who had converted to Christianity (*conversos*) those who still practised the Jewish religion. Later in its development, the Inquisition helped to uncover any group that did not accept the Catholic religion.

Spanish governments also adopted more extreme policies. In 1492, the Jews were expelled from Castile, and shortly afterwards from Aragon. In 1499, policies banning Muslim costume and the use of the Arabic language led to revolts by **Mudejars** in Granada. Throughout the following reign of Charles I, not only Mudejars but also Muslims who had converted to Christianity (Moriscos) were regarded with suspicion by the authorities. By Philip II's accession, in 1556, Spain had become a land noted for its religious intolerance.

Spain's rise in political importance was not matched by a similar growth in social and economic affairs. Throughout the period Spain was an overwhelmingly agricultural country with approximately 95% of the population living as peasants. Although a relatively large state by western European standards, mountains covered a considerable portion of the country. The availability of arable land for crop growing was made worse by the activity of the **Mesta**. The Mesta were given support by the monarchy. As a result of these factors, Spain became a net importer of grain during the first half of the 16th century.

The Spanish economy was also affected by other government policies. The decision to expel the Jews, in 1492, removed a social and religious group that was an important part of the commercial life of Spain. Commerce and industry were damaged further by government regulation. Finally, the tax demands of government, in particular Charles I, meant that the Spanish population became the most heavily taxed in Europe. Charles required the money to fight wars against the French, Turks and German Protestants. Shortly after Charles' abdication the financial problems of the government became so great that the country was effectively bankrupt.

In one area of economic activity there was noticeable improvement: trade. The export of wool by the Mesta encouraged trade links with the Netherlands, another part of Charles' possessions. Also, the creation of a large Spanish empire in the Americas led to the rapid expansion of transatlantic trade, particularly in silver.

Mudejars: Muslims living under Christian rule.

Mesta: This was an organisation, dominated by the aristocracy, which controlled sheep farming in Castile.

1. What were the major changes that affected Spain in the period 1450–1556?

You might consider the following issues.

a) Political changes

b) Religious changes

c) Changes in foreign affairs

d) Social and economic changes.

2. Explain which of the issues mentioned above involved the greatest amount of change. Give reasons to support your answer.

6.1 How far did Ferdinand and Isabella create a 'New Monarchy' in Spain?
A CASE STUDY IN HISTORICAL INTERPRETATION

Why did Isabella marry Ferdinand in 1469?

On 14 October 1469 Isabella of Castile married her cousin Ferdinand of Aragon. There is some dispute among historians over who arranged the marriage. John Lynch and A. W. Lovett believe Isabella made the decision to marry Ferdinand rather than other suitors, such as Alfonso of Portugal. Henry Kamen and J. N. Hillgarth take the view that the marriage was arranged by Alfonso Carillo (Archbishop of Toledo) and King John II of Aragon. Either way, the marriage, which was to have such a profound effect on the future history of Spain, was made for short-term political gain in a period of political instability in both states.

In the 15th century Castile and Aragon were states where the monarchy was weak. In Castile the monarchy was faced by a powerful aristocracy, which possessed considerable political and economic power. In order to survive as an independent force Castilian monarchs had attempted to ally themselves with either a powerful faction of the aristocracy or the cities. Cities in Castile had a considerable degree of self-government. The 17 most important cities had the right to send two representatives (*procuradores*) each to the Cortes.

The reign of Isabella's predecessor, Henry IV (1454–1474) was badly affected by rivalry between powerful groups of aristocrats. On one side was a group who supported the King's chief minister, Beltran de la Cueva. These were opposed by a group dominated by the Mendoza family. Henry IV had tried to increase royal authority by appointing *corregidores* (royal governors) to city councils. However, in 1464 civil war broke out when the Enriquez and Manrique family, supported by Archbishop Carillo of Toledo, attempted to replace Henry with his half-brother Alfonso. Unfortunately, Alfonso died of the plague in 1468. This placed Isabella, Henry's half-sister, in a conflict with Henry's daughter, Joanna, for succession to the throne. To strengthen her claim Isabella married her cousin Ferdinand. The marriage was initially beset by problems. It was technically against church law to marry a cousin. It was not until 1471 that Pope Sixtus IV gave his permission.

Secondly, Henry IV disowned Isabella in 1470 on hearing of the marriage. The marriage did have advantages for Ferdinand and his father King John II of Aragon. Like Castile, Aragon faced civil war, which had broken out in Catalonia in 1462. In the following year, Aragon was forced to hand over Roussillon and Cerdagne to Louis XI of France. Beset by these major problems, John II hoped his son's marriage to Isabella would strengthen his own position.

At face value the marriage seemed to favour Isabella. According to the marriage contract, Ferdinand had to live in Castile and acknowledge Isabella as the dominant partner. He had to supply Isabella with 100,000 gold florins and 4,000 troops if she required them. However, Juan (John) II staked everything on this marriage. As the historian A. R. Lovett remarks in *Early Habsburg Spain*:

'For the beleaguered house of Aragon the match was nothing short of a triumph. It held out the promise that once Isabella asserted her right to the Castillian throne she would co-operate in the task of restoring the authority of the crown in Aragon. The parties to the marriage contract thought in terms of their own pressing needs not a permanent union of the Iberian kingdoms and a united Spain.'

> **Differences between Castile and Aragon**
>
> ● Castile was four times larger in size.
>
> ● In 1500 Castile had approximately 5 million population, compared to 1 million in Aragon.
>
> ● Castile had one government and one Cortes (parliament); Aragon was divided into three Kingdoms – Aragon, Catalonia and Valencia – each with its own government and own Cortes.

Did Ferdinand and Isabella create a 'New Monarchy' in Castile and Aragon?

Five years after the marriage, on the death of Henry IV, Isabella declared herself queen. The action sparked off a war of succession with Joanna which lasted until the Treaty of Alcacovas in September 1479. Like the Wars of the Roses in England, the War of Succession in Castile was fought between rival groups of aristocrats. Isabella had the added advantage of being supported by most of the cities. Joanna, who had been born in 1462, was engaged to the ageing King Alfonso of Portugal who offered the most effective military aid. The turning point of the war came with the Battle of Toro in 1476 when Ferdinand defeated the Portuguese.

It was not until 1479 that Ferdinand became King of Aragon, on the death of John II. At the Concord of Segovia on 15 January 1475 he had already received powers in Castile equal with Isabella. In 1481, Isabella was given similar powers in Aragon.

Having won effective control of both their states, and with co-equal powers, the two monarchs were able to re-establish law and order and to create the conditions which enabled Spain to become a major western European power in the 16th century. Roger Merriman, in *The Rise of the Spanish Empire* (1918), claimed that the Catholic Monarchs reorganised government along lines similar to Henry VII in England and French Kings like Louis XI and Francis I.

> **Features of a new monarchy**
>
> (a) The political power of the aristocracy was reduced.
>
> (b) The monarchy became financially independent.
>
> (c) Government was centralised.
>
> (d) Lawyers played an important role in government.

Did Ferdinand and Isabella establish a 'New Monarchy' in their kingdoms?

Holy Brotherhood (Santa Hermandad)
At the height of the War of Succession, Ferdinand and Isabella revived the medieval organisation of the Hermandad. Initially regarded as a temporary measure, the Holy Brotherhood helped to re-establish law and order in Castile. In 1476 the Cortes of Madrigal set up a league of brotherhoods involving every village or town with over 50 inhabitants. With the authority to act as judge and jury, the Hermandades had the task of bringing peace to Castile. The crimes they could deal with included murder, rape, theft, rebellion and wilful damage. To aid them in their task the Brotherhoods had armed men, usually mounted on horses. According to the contemporary Lopez de Villalobos, Brotherhood justice 'was so severe that it appeared to be cruelty. There was much butchery, with the cutting off of feet, hands and heads.'

Nevertheless, the Holy Brotherhood was an important element in restoring law and order. Not only did the Brotherhoods extend royal control across Castile, they also helped to bring the towns together. Each brotherhood sent representatives to a national body called the Junta General. In the war against Granada (1482–1492) the Holy Brotherhood was an important source of men and material for the army. In the Kingdom of Catalonia, the *Sometent* provided a similar role in bringing order.

The Holy Brotherhood did act as an effective way to extend royal power. However, in 1495 the Cortes suppressed it.

The royal governors (corregidores)

Isabella also revived the use of another official to increase royal control of towns, the *corregidore*. Ferdinand attempted to extend the idea to Aragon but without success. In the Cortes of Toledo of 1480 royal governors were to be sent to all the towns where they did not already exist. Although corregidores gave the monarchy a voice in local affairs, it did not act as an agent for more central control. By 1494 there were corregidores in 54 places, rising to 64 by 1516.

According to historian Henry Kamen there were two types of judicial officials: lawyers and military men. Their effectiveness is open to question. Many towns such as Segovia and Burgos refused to accept their royal governor in 1483. They were also a target for the Communeros when they revolted against Charles I in 1520. However, as John Lynch notes in *Spain under the Habsburgs* (1981), because of the existence of the *corregidores* 'the towns were the more ready to acquiesce in royal policy as they benefited from the improvement of administration'.

Improvement in the justice system

According to historian Henry Kamen: 'The main achievement of Ferdinand and Isabella was to bring peace and order to Spain. The basic ingredient in pacification … was the firm use of direct personal authority.' With no fixed capital city, the Catholic Monarchs, and in particular Isabella, made a point of visiting the cities of Castile ensuring that the monarchy was seen as personal and public. They became the most travelled rulers in the history of Spain (see map on page 118). During her visits, Isabella dispensed justice.

The Royal Council met twice a week as the highest court of appeal in Castile. From 1489 a permanent court of appeal was established. At local level, justice was provided by local judges (*alcaldes*) who worked with royal governors (*corregidores*) and local mayors.

For much of their joint reign Ferdinand stayed in Castile. Therefore, he delegated power in Aragon to a number of **viceroys** who acted on his behalf. Catalonia received a viceroy in 1479, Aragon in 1482 and Valencia in 1496.

Viceroy: A person acting as governor of a country or province in the name, and by the authority of, the supreme ruler.

Conciliar government

In *Government and Society in Late Medieval Spain,* Glyn Redworth states:

> 'Ferdinand and Isabella [were] not launching pads for Spain's imperial greatness in the 16th and 17th centuries, but … medieval rulers who coped in largely traditional ways with problems that had long been familiar to their forebears.'

This is shown clearly with the organisation of national government, where the Catholic Monarchs inherited and then developed a system based on councils. The Royal Council was the centrepiece of their administration. It had dated from 1389 but had been reformed by Isabella's predecessor, Henry IV in 1459. To emphasise the personal form of monarchy, it met daily with Ferdinand or Isabella present. It was divided into five separate units dealing with justice, finance, foreign policy, the Holy Brotherhood (until it was dissolved in 1498) and Aragon (from 1494). Many of these units later developed into councils under Charles I.

However, the Catholic Monarchs also developed their own councils, such as a council for the Spanish Inquisition (1483) and the Military

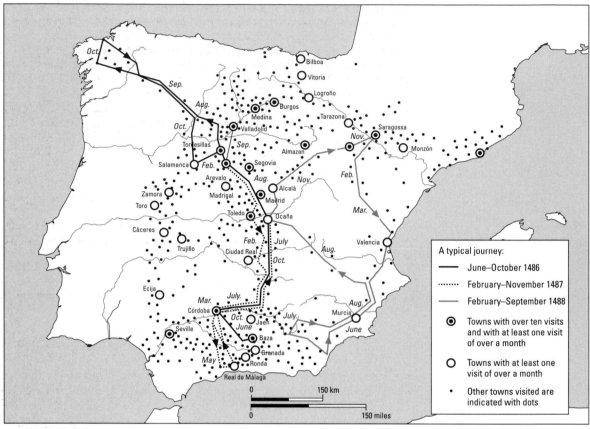

Spanish towns visited by
Ferdinand and Isabella

Orders (1489). By the time of Isabella's death, in 1504, the councils of
Castile, Aragon and the Inquisition were the most important. They were
not subject to other authority except the monarchs.

Although the Royal Council and its sub-units contained members of
the clergy and aristocrats the most important element were lawyers
(*letrados*). These were university educated and usually came from
towns. After 1493, all councillors with voting rights had to be *letrados*.
In this sense the administrations of Castile and Aragon did resemble
new developments elsewhere in western Europe. This point is made in
the *New Cambridge Modern History* where J. M. Batista i Roca claims that
the inclusion of *letrados* was a radical departure from previous practice.
It is possible that *letrados* had been used in Castile throughout the 15th
century. At local level, the administration still remained in the hands of
the aristocracy.

The aristocracy

A key feature of a 'New Monarchy' was the ability of the monarch to limit
the political power of the aristocracy. By the 15th century the Castillian
aristocracy was the most powerful social group. In some ways the reigns
of Ferdinand and Isabella did limit aristocratic power: the increased use of
letrados in administration was one; another was the royal control over the
Military Orders. These Orders were an important element in the
Reconquista and had grown powerful during the late medieval period.
Disputes between them were a cause of political instability. By the 15th
century they comprised the orders of Santiago (St James), Calatrava and
Alcántara in Castile and Montesa and St John in Aragon. From 1476 to
1494 the mastership of the Castillian orders became vacant. In each case

Ferdinand was elected master for life. From 1489 a council of state was established to oversee their operation. By the time of Ferdinand's death the Aragonese orders remained outside royal control.

At the Cortes of Toledo, in 1480, it was decided that all royal lands given to the aristocracy before 1464 should be returned to the Crown. However, the lands recovered were modest in size. Most royal lands had been given away at the beginning of Henry IV's reign. For much of the reigns of Ferdinand and Isabella, the power of the nobility, in particular in Castile, remained largely unaffected. Following Isabella's death, the aristocracy still posed a threat. In Andalucia the Duke of Medina Sidonia, the Marquis of Priego and the Count of Cabra caused instability. As Geoffrey Woodward notes in his reassessment of the reigns of the Catholic Monarchs: 'Political anarchy and domestic strife had not been suppressed, and public confidence in the Castillian government appears to have been justifiably low.'

The Catholic Monarchs may not have reduced the power of the aristocracy. What they did achieve was to provide a minimum level of law and order to pass on to their successor Charles I.

Finance

Currency in Spain

The Catholic Monarchs inherited different types of currency within their kingdoms. In Aragon the units of currency were pounds, shillings and pence.

> £1 = 20 shillings.
> 1 shilling = 12 pence

This is similar to Britain before the introduction of decimal currency in 1971. One Aragonese pound was equivalent to one Castillian ducat.

In Castile, from 1497 the main gold coin was the ducat and the main silver coin was the real. There was also a coin made from copper and silver called the blanca.

The value of goods and wealth in Castile was measured in maravedis.

> 1 ducat = 11 reals or 375 maravedis

Rising prices (inflation) makes it very difficult to give a modern-day equivalent for these coins. In 1937 the historian R. Trevor Davies claimed that 375 maravedis were equivalent to around 50p. However, by the year 2000 this would be equivalent to approximately £50.

The financial administration of Castile and Aragon under the Catholic Monarchs was not new. The head of the government's finances in Castile was Gonzalo Chacon who had worked with Isabella even before her accession to the throne.

The main sources of revenue were also traditional. The most important was the Sales Tax (*alcabala*), a form of VAT which provided 90% of their ordinary revenue. In addition, they received profits from mining salt and iron, and from customs duties. The clergy were exempt from paying the *alcabala*. The aristocracy were the main collectors in their own regions. As a result, at the start of Isabella's reign, in 1474, of the 73 million maravedis due from these sources of revenue; the Queen received only 11 million.

Government revenue in Castile	
	(in maravedis)
1474	11 million
1481	150 million
1504	315 million
1510	320 million

Cruzada: A tax granted to the Kings of Spain by the Pope initially to help finance a crusade against the Muslims.

Juros: Credit bonds paid annually to Crown bankers. These increased the Crown's debts.

According to historian J. N. Hillgarth the major innovation of the Catholic Monarchs was their ability to acquire revenue from extraordinary sources. For instance, grants from the Pope (known as the **cruzada**) and loans helped finance the war with Granada (1482–1492). The Cortes also voted large sums of money. In 1476, at Madrigal, it granted 162 million and at Toledo, in 1480, 104 million. The Monarchs also received revenue from the Holy Brotherhood: between 1480 and 1498 the average amount raised this way was 18 million. In 1500 the Military Orders of Santiago and Calatrava provided 26 million maravedis.

In all, the Catholic Monarchs increased these extraordinary sources of revenue by two-thirds, compared to their predecessors. Unfortunately, these large increases in income were used to finance the war against Granada and Ferdinand's wars in Italy after 1502. Large sums were used to establish a network of ambassadors. Between 1494 and 1504, 75 million maravedis were spent for this purpose alone.

According to Geoffrey Woodward, in *Spain in the Reigns of Ferdinand and Isabella, 1474–1516* (1997), 'the monarchs had no long-term plan for financing their governments but relied on short-term solutions'.

To bridge the gap between revenue and expenditure, the Monarchs paid off their debts at high rates of interest (10%). They sold this debt in the form of **juros**. This policy of non-tax revenue raising was followed by Charles I and Philip II with serious consequences for the financial stability of Spain.

The Cortes

An important national institution in Spain was the Cortes. Castile had one, while there were separate Cortes for Aragon, Catalonia and Valencia. Each of these could meet together, in the same city. This was called the *Cortes generales*.

Long before parliaments developed elsewhere in western Europe the Cortes had become established in the Spanish kingdoms. In Castile it contained three estates: the clergy, the aristocracy and the cities. The Cortes represented 17 cities (extended to 18 with the inclusion of Granada after 1492). The Cortes did not meet in a specific place as Castile did not have a fixed capital city. By the accession of Isabella, Segovia acted as an important base. The monarch possesses the right to summon a Cortes.

In both Aragon and Castile the Cortes had similar functions. Perhaps the most important was to raise revenue for the monarch. The Cortes also offered advice to the monarch, passed laws that the monarch required and acted as a place to put forward grievances to the monarch. In Castile the Cortes of Madrigal (1476) and Toledo (1480) were important for giving money and returning land to the monarchy. During the reigns of the Catholic Monarchs the Castillian Cortes met 16 times, mainly between 1498 and 1506. In Aragon the Cortes met seven times, in Valencia once and in Catalonia six times. There were also three *Cortes generales*. Although similar in many ways, the Cortes in Aragon had more power.

At no time during their reign did the Catholic Monarchs show any inclination to reduce the power of the Cortes. Given their limited financial resources and the need to establish law and order, it would have been very difficult for them to do so. Also, the Catholic Monarchs, in particular in Aragon, needed the support of the cities to counter-balance the power of the aristocracy.

Conclusion

Is there sufficient evidence to suggest that the Catholic Monarchs developed a new type of government in their kingdoms? Part of the problem lies with the propaganda surrounding their reigns. In 1626 Fernandez Navarrette declared that they 'began the greatness of this immense monarchy'. Some historians have seen the period as the foundation of Spain's Golden Age;

Government and administration under the Catholic Monarchs, 1474–1516

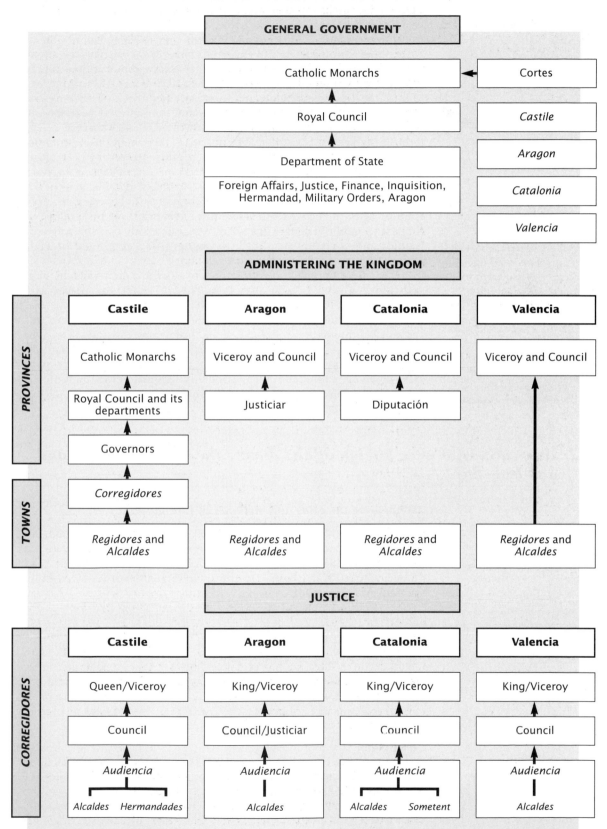

Don Menendez Pidal states that the reign of the Catholic Monarchs 'represents a happy golden age remembered nostalgically as incomparable by one and all'.

However, when Ferdinand and Isabella married they had no intention of creating a united Spain. If Ferdinand's son, by his marriage to Germaine de Foix, had survived, Aragon would have returned to complete independence on Ferdinand's death in 1516. Instead accident of birth meant the end of the Trastámara family and its replacement by the Habsburg family in the person of Charles I. Charles became the first person to be jointly king of Castile and Aragon.

It also seems clear that Ferdinand and Isabella used traditional methods of government to achieve their aims. However, the reigns did represent a new departure in some ways. In *Government and Society in Late Medieval Spain* (1993), Glyn Redworth states that what was new was 'the sheer energy the royal partners brought to government. In the middle ages, the best way to assert royal authority was for a monarch to appear in public. The fact that there were effectively two sovereigns who could hold court independently throughout the length and breadth of their dominions was an enormous advantage.'

What were the major achievements of the Catholic Monarchs in government? It would seem that they did not limit the power of the aristocracy in either kingdom. Nor did they reduce the power of the Cortes or establish financial independence. What they did achieve was to establish a minimum level of peace and order. Some historians have been more generous. John Lynch, in *Spain under the Habsburgs*, contends that: 'In giving Spain its state apparatus the Catholic Monarchs, operating from Castile and accepting the constitutional limitations of the union they had forged, liquidated the past and provided a basis on which their successors could build a national state.'

1. *Explain what is meant by the term 'New Monarchy'.*

2. *Why do you think some historians believe that Spain under the Catholic Monarchs was not a 'New Monarchy'?*

3. *How successfully did Ferdinand and Isabella extend their authority over Castile and Aragon?*

4. *To what extent were the reigns of the Catholic Monarchs a turning point in the history of Spain?*

6.2 How successful were foreign affairs during the reigns of Ferdinand and Isabella?

What were the aims and methods of foreign policy?

Later in the 16th century Philip II was supposed to have to said, when he stopped in front of a painting of Ferdinand, 'To him we owe it all'. Throughout their reigns, Isabella played a secondary role to her husband in foreign affairs. During their reigns Spain followed policies which contained traditional and new aims:

● The *Reconquista* was completed with the conquest of Granada by Castile in 1492 (see map). The war against Islam was then continued on the North African coast where Ferdinand launched expeditions against several seaports such as Algiers.

● Ferdinand also followed traditional Aragonese policy. This involved opposition to France. This would involve the attempt to recover Roussillon and Cerdagne, lost to Louis XI in 1462. It also involved Spanish intervention in the Italian Wars in defence of Naples.

● A minor aspect of foreign policy, which was to have a major impact on Spain in the 16th century, was the financing of voyages of discovery. Beginning with Columbus in 1492, Ferdinand laid the foundations for a Spanish Empire in the Americas.

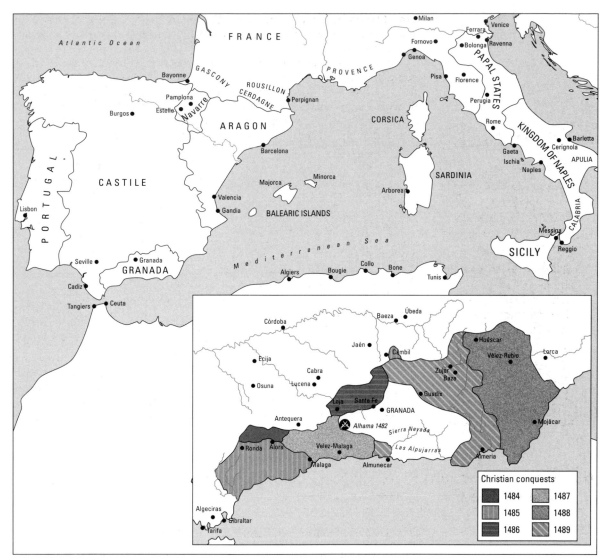

The foreign policy of the Catholic Monarchs; (inset) the conquest of Granada

To achieve these aims new and old methods of policy were used.

● Military intervention formed the backbone of policy towards Granada, Naples and North Africa.

● Ferdinand also used marriage alliances to further his interests, in particular, against France.

● In addition, he could be seen as one of the founders of 16th-century diplomacy, with the negotiations of military alliances during his campaign against Navarre and in the Italian Wars.

● Another new development was the creation of embassies in the major capitals of western Europe. These acted as intelligence-gathering centres and bases for the formation of military and marriage alliances.

Views of Ferdinand's aims and methods have varied. His Italian contemporary, Niccolo Machiavelli, in *The Prince*, was supposedly speaking of Ferdinand when he stated that he 'never preaches anything except peace and good faith, and he is an enemy of both one and the other'. On the other hand, the Spanish historian J. Doussinague was more generous. In

1944, in *La politica internacional de Fernando el Catolico* ('The foreign policy of Ferdinand the Catholic'), he saw Ferdinand's aims as waging a crusade against the Muslims and, after 1512, bringing peace to the Christians. Which of these two assessments of Ferdinand is the more accurate?

How did relations with Portugal develop?

The marriage of Ferdinand and Isabella had brought a union of crowns between Castile and Aragon. However, if circumstances had been slightly different, there might have been a union of crowns between Castile and Portugal. At one stage, Henry IV of Castile had tried to arrange a marriage between Isabella and King Alfonso of Portugal. Following Isabella's marriage to Ferdinand, Alfonso had become engaged to the young Castillian princess, Joanna – the daughter of Henry IV.

An important turning point in relations between Castile and Portugal came with the War of Succession following Isabella's decision to declare herself Queen, at Segovia, in 1474. Alfonso invaded Castile with a Portuguese army. The turning point of the war came at Toro, in 1476, when Ferdinand led an army that defeated the Portuguese. He also repelled a further Portuguese invasion in 1478. In the Treaty of Alcacovas, in 1479, Alfonso was forced to give up his claim to the throne of Castile, thereby removing an important threat to the union of the crowns of Castile and Aragon.

Also at Alcacovas, the Portuguese gave up their claim to the Canary Islands, off the coast of modern-day Morocco. Between 1482 and 1493 the islands were conquered and colonised by Castile. They become an important staging post to link Spain and its New World possessions. In 1492, Columbus' last port of call before setting off westward was the island of La Gomera in the Canaries. The main church in San Sebastian on La Gomera contains the inscription: 'From here water was taken which was the first used to baptise America.'

A common feature of international diplomacy during the reign of the Catholic Monarchs was the use of marriage to create better relations with other states. In 1490, as part of this process, the eldest daughter of Ferdinand and Isabella, also called Isabella, married Prince Alfonso, the heir to the Portuguese throne. In the following year, Alfonso became king. Partly as a result of this marriage, Spanish–Portuguese relations improved considerably for the rest of their reigns. Ultimately, in 1580, Philip II was able to use this dynastic link to claim the Portuguese throne and to unite the whole Iberian peninsula under one monarch for the first time.

How important was the Conquest of Granada in the foreign affairs of the Catholic Monarchs?

The conquest of Granada, between 1482 and 1492, brought to an end the *Reconquista*, which had been one of the most important aspects of the history of Medieval Spain. The war saw the establishment of the military reputation of Gonzalo de Cordoba, the Gran Capitan. It also saw the creation of a Spanish army that was to fight so effectively in the Italian Wars.

Although once a powerful state, Granada had declined in importance by 1480. It had been badly affected by political rivalry. Eventually, divisions within Granada were an important reason why it was conquered.

The war began with the Christian capture of Alhama, in February 1482, following an attack by the Muslim forces of Abu'l-Hasan on the Christian town of Zahara in December of the previous year.

To many chroniclers of the time, such as Fernando del Pulgar, the war was a crusade against Islam. This aspect of the war is supported by the evidence that religious imagery was used deliberately by Isabella to gain support for the war. The Pope also gave Ferdinand and Isabella grants (the *cruzada*) to fight the war. In 1494, Pope Alexander VI gave them the title Los Reyes Catolicos ('The Catholic Monarchs') in recognition of their achievement. On the tomb of the Catholic Monarchs, in Granada cathedral, only two of their many achievements are mentioned – one being 'the destruction of the Islamic sect'.

Unlike previous wars between Christian and Moor in Spain, the Granada war saw the rise in importance of artillery. The war was, in essence, a series of sieges; the final being the siege of the city of Granada which fell in January 1492. It was the Christian dominance in artillery that was one of the deciding factors in their victory. They were also aided by major divisions on the Muslim side. In 1485 Abu'l-Hasan was dethroned, resulting in a split over the succession between Boabdil and al-Zagal. From 1485 to 1492 the Christians were able to exploit this split. Initially, Fedinand used Boabdil to help defeat the Muslims. Between 1485 and 1489 Boabdil helped Ferdinand gain the upper hand in the war. An example of this was the fall of Loja, to the Christians, in 1489.

The war placed a major financial strain on Castile and Aragon. The total cost of the war has been estimated at 800 million maravedis. (Compare this sum with the revenue raised by Ferdinand and Isabella on page 119.) According to Professor Ladero, in *Castilla y la conquista* ('Castile and the Conquest'), a considerable amount was provided by the Catholic Church, in particular by Pope Sixtus IV and Pope Innocent VIII.

Emirate: A Muslim state ruled by an emir.

The war had a devastating effect on the population of the **Emirate** of Granada. Of the original 500,000 population, approximately 100,000 died in the war and a further 200,000 decided to emigrate. However, the initial terms of surrender put forward by Ferdinand and Isabella seemed to offer considerable hope to the 200,000 that remained. The citizens of the city of Granada were allowed to keep their arms. Converts from Christianity to Islam before 1492 were not to be persecuted. This policy of reconciliation was mainly due to Archbishop Talavera.

Unfortunately, the policy did not last. The declaration on arms affecting Granada lasted only a month. During the 1490s some 40,000 Christian peasants from Andalucia were allowed to settle in the former emirate. Finally, in 1499, Archbishop Cisneros reversed the policy of reconciliation. Forced conversions of Mudejars began. Also, the Inquisition was extended to Granada. The result was a major revolt by the Mudejars that was savagely suppressed. By 1501 it was declared that Granada had become a land of Moriscos (Muslims who had converted to Christianity).

The Granada war brought Ferdinand and Isabella considerable prestige both within their kingdoms and throughout Europe. Granada became part of the Kingdom of Castile, adding an extra 200,000 population. The new territory included important cities such as Malaga and Almeria, as well as Granada.

Why did the Catholic Monarchs acquire territory in North Africa?

To many the military expeditions to North Africa seemed to be a logical extension of the *Reconquista*. In 1494 Pope Alexander VI granted the Catholic Monarchs the right to lead a crusade against the Muslim kingdom of Fez (in modern-day Morocco). During the military expedition against the North African coast, between 1505 and 1515, Archbishop Cisneros played an important role in planning and organisation.

Apart from the religious dimension, the expeditions against the North African coast had an important effect on trade. Muslim pirates had been a major problem for seaborne trade in the western Mediterranean before the conquest of Granada.

Finally, there was rivalry between Portugal and the Catholic Monarchs for territory in the eastern Atlantic and Africa. The Treaty of Alcacovas of 1479 had given the islands of Cape Verde and Madeira to Portugal and the Canary Islands to Castile. By 1471 the Portuguese had already established themselves on the North African coast with a string of victories which had brought them Ceuta, Seghir and Tangier.

In 1505 Mers-el-Kebir was captured, in 1508 Penon de Velez and, by 1510, Bougie and Tripoli. Ferdinand did have plans to conquer Tunis for the Kingdom of Aragon, but an expedition to Djerba in 1510 failed. Part of the problem was Ferdinand's preoccupation with involvement in the Italian Wars.

How did Aragon recover Roussillon and Cerdagne?

The Union of Crowns brought several advantages to the Kingdom of Aragon. Firstly, it brought peace and security to Aragon's western border with Castile. Secondly, it gave Ferdinand the opportunity to use the military resources of his more powerful neighbour, Castile, in Aragon's traditional rivalry with France.

In 1462, at the height of the civil war in Catalonia, the French king Louis XI had taken over the Aragonese provinces of Roussillon and Cerdagne, which are located just north of the Pyrenees Mountains. However, rather than use military force to recover these territories, Ferdinand used diplomacy. Louis XI's successor, Charles VIII, wished to acquire the Kingdom of Naples, in southern Italy. To prevent any possible diversion he made agreements with Henry VII of England and the Holy Roman Emperor Maximilian, in the Netherlands. Ferdinand was able to exploit Charles VIII's position with the Treaty of Barcelona, signed on 19 January 1493. In return for Ferdinand's support for Charles VIII's claim to Naples, the French returned Roussillon and Cerdagne to Aragon.

Why did Ferdinand become involved in the Italian Wars?

Ferdinand's support of France proved short-lived. The most successful aspect of Ferdinand's foreign policy was Spain's involvement in the Italian Wars. By the time of Ferdinand's death in 1516 Spain had become a major European power whose influence went far beyond the Iberian peninsula (see map).

However, during the Middle Ages, the Kingdom of Aragon had acquired territories in the western Mediterranean and Italy. They controlled the Balearic Islands, Sardinia and Sicily. Until 1458, King Alsonso the Magnanimous of Aragon also ruled Naples.

One of the major turning points in the history of early modern Europe was France's military intervention in Italy from 1494. In that year a French army entered Italy in order to support Charles VIII's claim to the crown of Naples, held by King Ferrante I. The Italian Wars which followed eventually became a major western European conflict between Valois France and the Habsburgs, including Spain.

The French Army entered Naples on 22 February 1495. This prompted Ferdinand to defend the links between Aragon and Naples and he made a counter-claim to the throne of Naples.

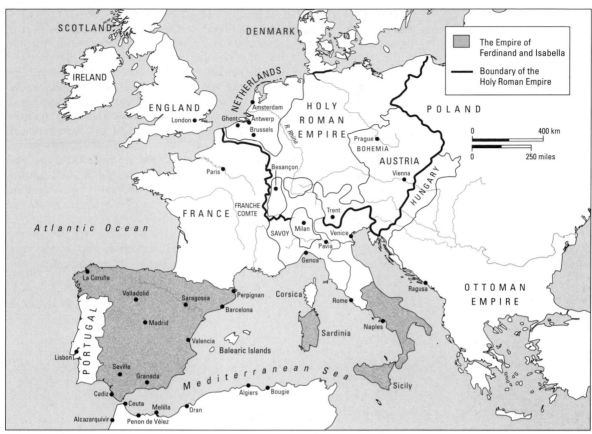

The Empire of Spain at the death
of Ferdinand, 1516

How successful was Ferdinand in Italy?

Ferdinand was able to force the French out of Naples by using a variety of
tactics. The most successful was his role in the formation of the Holy
League at the end of March 1495. It involved Pope Alexander VI (a
Spaniard from Valencia), Milan, Venice, Spain and Maximilian of Austria.
This agreement reversed the agreement with France made at the Treaty of
Barcelona in 1493. Troops from Milan and Venice helped defeat the
French at Fournovo, in north Italy. This was decisive in forcing the
French to withdraw.

To protect his interests in Italy, Ferdinand provided troops. Under the Gran Capitan, Gonzalo
Fernandez de Cordoba, a force of 2,000 infantry and 300 cavalry played
an important part in the military campaign in Naples in 1495–96. Perhaps
of greater importance for the withdrawal of the French was a revolt
against them in the city of Naples. This was followed by a truce between
Ferdinand and France in February 1497.

To protect his interests in Italy, Ferdinand arranged dynastic marriages
with other potential enemies of France, Maximilian of Austria and
Henry VII of England. In 1496 Maximilian's heir, Philip, married Joanna
of Castile. Their son would become Charles I of Spain. In the following
year, Philip's sister Margaret married Prince Juan, heir to the thrones of
Aragon and Castile. Unfortunately, Juan died shortly after the marriage. In
1501 another marriage alliance was made when Prince Arthur of England
married Catherine of Aragon.

At the Treaty of Granada in 1500, Ferdinand agreed to divide Naples
between Aragon and France. However, Spanish military intervention in

Naples resumed in 1501, this time with an army of 5,000. Under the leadership of the Gran Capitan, the Spanish struck a decisive blow with a victory at the Battle of Cerignola on 28 April 1503, which decided the fate of the Kingdom of Naples. By 1504 the French accepted a truce and the loss of Naples to Ferdinand. Spanish victory was followed by another dynastic marriage, this time with France. In the Treaty of Blois, 1505, Ferdinand married Germaine de Foix, the niece of the French king.

Unfortunately, Naples formed a base for the political ambitions of the Gran Capitan. Cordoba was removed by Ferdinand in 1507 and replaced by a viceroy.

To further Aragon's control of Naples, Ferdinand joined the League of Cambrai, formed in 1508 between the Pope, Spain, Maximilian, France and Milan against Venice. In the military campaign that followed, although Spain did not take part in the fighting, Ferdinand was able to take over from Venice control of seaports in the Apulia region of Naples.

Throughout Ferdinand's involvement in Italy he made temporary alliances with other states in order to achieve his aims. The Holy League of 1495 and the League of Cambrai of 1508 were followed by a new Holy League against France by 1511. This alliance involved Spain, the Pope, England, Venice and Maximilian. The aim was to remove the French from Milan. Although this was achieved in 1513, following a military campaign involving Spanish troops in 1515, under the new French King Francis I, Milan returned to French control.

In 1514 Ferdinand stated: 'For over 700 years the Crown of Spain has not been as great or resplendent as it is now, and all, after God, by my own work and labour.' Through the use of military power, dynastic marriages and temporary international alliances, Ferdinand had established Spain as a major Italian and western Mediterranean power.

Why was Ferdinand able to conquer Spanish Navarre?

The acquisition of the Kingdom of Navarre involved two central features of Ferdinand's: foreign policy diplomacy and the use of military force. The continued independence of the small Christian kingdom that straddled the Pyrenees was in question once Ferdinand had married the French princess Germaine de Foix, in 1506. This marriage provided him with a claim to Navarre, which he exploited when Gaston de Foix (Germaine's father) died in 1512. Using troops under the leadership of the Duke of Alba, Navarre was occupied. At the same time, France was distracted by an English attack on northern France by Henry VIII.

How important were the voyages of discovery during the reign of the Catholic Monarchs?

The most important long-term development in foreign affairs during the reigns of the Catholic Monarchs was the voyages of discovery to the New World. By the time of Ferdinand's death, in 1516, Spanish rule had been established on several Caribbean islands including Hispaniola, Cuba, Puerto Rico and Trinidad.

Although of significance later in the century, neither Ferdinand nor Isabella regarded this aspect of their policy very highly. However, within ten years of Columbus' discovery of the West Indies, in 1492, almost 6,000 Spanish colonists had arrived in the New World. The pattern of Spanish settlement for the rest of the century had become established. The *encomienda* system allowed settlers to acquire land in return for their protection of the native inhabitants. However, most settlers treated the natives as slaves.

1. What were Ferdinand's aims in foreign policy?

2. What methods did he use to achieve his aims?

3. To what extent had Spain extended its influence in foreign affairs by the death of Ferdinand in 1516?

6.3 How far did religious policy change between 1450 and 1556?

During the Middle Ages Spain had the reputation of being an area of religious tolerance. It was an area in which three religious and cultural traditions flourished: Christianity, Judaism and Islam. By the accession of Philip II this position had changed dramatically. Spain had become a land of religious intolerance where strict religious conformity to the Roman Catholic Church was official state policy.

Was late Medieval Spain a land of religious tolerance?

The idea of religious tolerance (*conviviencia*) had already begun to break down towards the end of the 14th century. In 1391 massacres of Jews had taken place in Toledo. By 1449 Jews were again attacked in Avila and Toledo.

Following attacks on Jews at the end of the 14th century, large numbers converted to Christianity. These *conversos* or New Christians gained important posts in government and commerce – so much so, that by the middle of the 15th century there was considerable tension between these *conversos* and traditional Christians, known as Old Christians.

Also, although Muslims (known as Mudejars) were allowed to follow their own religion under Christian rule, there was a strong Spanish tradition of the *Reconquista*. The Christian states of Portugal, Castile and Aragon had been involved in the process of conquering land ruled by Muslims. By 1450 the Emirate of Granada was the last surviving Islamic state on the Iberian peninsula. Therefore, by the accession of Isabella to the throne of Castile, considerable religious tension had built up.

Why was the Inquisition established?

The Inquisition was a special court for the detection, trial and punishment of heretics. Such a court had existed in Aragon since the 13th century but had become inactive by the time of the Catholic Monarchs. There had never been an Inquisition in Castile. In 1478 Pope Sixtus IV gave Ferdinand and Isabella permission to set up a new Inquisition in Castile. It was extended to Aragon in 1483.

What was different about this Inquisition was the fact that it was directly under the control of the monarchy, rather than the Catholic Church. Spanish monarchs could appoint personnel and control its finances. This gave the Spanish monarchy considerable influence in religious affairs. The Spanish Inquisition took on the form of a council of state called the Council of the Supreme and General Inquisition (*La Suprema*). The first Royal Inquisitor-General was the Dominican friar Tomas de Torquemada, appointed in 1481.

There are a number of views about why the Inquisition was established. According to another Dominican friar, Alonso de Hojeda, many Jews who had converted to Christianity (*conversos*) were secretly still practising Judaism. Throughout late medieval Spain there had been tension between Old Christians and conversos (known as New Christians). In Toledo in 1467 and Cordoba in 1473 this tension led to bloodshed between the two groups. As a result, the Inquisition can be seen as part of the rise of anti-Semitism in Spain. Attacks on conversos could lead directly to attacks on the Jews themselves.

An alternative view places emphasis on financial rather than religious reasons. Both Ferdinand and Isabella faced major financial problems during their reigns. The attack on conversos usually led to the confiscation of converso property, which was taken over by the Crown.

How effective was the Inquisition in dealing with heresy between 1478 and 1556?

According to historian Henry Kamen, the attack on the conversos 'amounted to a veritable holocaust'. He cites Andres Bernaldez who estimated that in Seville alone 'more than 700 persons were burnt and 5,000 punished' from 1480 to 1488. At national level, between 1483 and 1498 about 2,000 were put to death. However, the majority of persons accused did not suffer death but were punished or had property confiscated.

Although initially established to deal with the converso issue, the Spanish Inquisition extended its activities to include all forms of heresy. This included investigation of the Moriscos, followers of Erasmus and Protestants.

Illuminists: A mystical movement within the Spanish Catholic Church. Also called *alumbrados*. They were followers of the views of Erasmus and were affected by the new ideas of Humanism which arose during the Renaissance.

During the early part of the reign of Charles I the Inquisition investigated the **Illuminists (Los Alumbrados)**. This Christian group came under suspicion in 1519 but it was not until the arrival of Lutheranism that they were persecuted. Also during Charles I's reign the views and writings of Erasmus became the target of the Inquisition. This attack reached its height in 1529 when the Erasmian book *Dialogue of Christian Doctrine* was denounced and several Spanish Erasmians were arrested.

Unlike the rest of western Europe Spain did not possess its own Protestant movement. Therefore, Protestant ideas entered Spain through seaports such as Seville. As early as 1521 Adrian of Utrecht, the Inquisitor-General, banned Lutheran books. Throughout the reign of Charles I the **auto de fe** was used to deal with suspected Protestants. However, it was not until the early years of the reign of Philip II – between 1557 and 1562 – that Spanish Protestantism was persecuted virtually out of existence.

Auto de fe: A Catholic religious ceremony/festival. The term means, literally, 'act of faith'. People accused of heresy or Judaism were brought before the Inquisition, in public, to renounce any wrongdoing against the Church, before receiving punishment. If they refused to renounce their views they were burnt at the stake.

In many ways the Inquisition saved Spain from the religious conflicts that affected much of western Europe in the 16th century. Also only rarely did auto de fe involve execution. They became great social and religious occasions which were used as a means for expressing support for the Church. At no time did the Inquisition persecute Jews or Muslims for following their respective religions.

Why were the Jews expelled in 1492?

On 31 March 1492 the Catholic Monarchs issued a decree that required all Jews, to become Christians, within four months, or to leave the country. This was the culmination of anti-Semitic policies which had begun with attacks on the conversos. In 1480 the Cortes of Toledo had required Jews to wear distinctive badges. While two years later there was a partial expulsion of Jews from towns and parts of Andalucia.

There is some dispute among historians about the size of the Jewish population in 1492. Henry Kamen believed there were 70,000 Jews in Castile and 10,000 in Aragon. John Lynch believes the numbers for both states was 200,000. However, what is clear is that a significant number of Jews chose expulsion in 1492, although many later returned to accept conversion to Christianity.

Some historians have seen the anti-Semitic policy coming from pressure from below. There is evidence of widespread anti-Semitic feeling across Spain. However, the belief that conversos wanted to see the expulsion of the Jews in order to protect their own position seems unlikely.

Financial motives for expulsion have also been put forward. It is difficult to see the expulsion of the Jews as primarily due to the thirst for money on the part of the Monarchs. They were well aware of the economic damage done to the major cities by the persecution of the conversos, with the consequent decline in royal revenue.

It would seem the main motive was religious rather than political or financial. However, the attempt to enforce religious conformity was not successful. Many of the Jews who 'converted' in 1492 continued to practise Judaism secretly.

The expulsion also had serious economic and social effects on Spain. Many Jews were important traders and businessmen. Their loss damaged the development of the Spanish economy during the 16th century. Henry Kamen has quoted the Ottoman Turkish sultan who 'marvelled greatly at the expelling of the Jews from Spain, since this was to expel its wealth'.

How were Mudejars and Moriscos treated in Spain 1450–1556?

The treatment of converted Muslims (Moriscos) and Muslims living under Christian rule (Mudejars) changed considerable in this period. In Castile the numbers of Moriscos was very small. However, in Aragon, the Mudejars comprised around 30% of the population in Valencia and 20% in the Kingdom of Aragon.

The turning point in their treatment came with the conquest of Granada between 1482 and 1492. As a result, an additional 500,000 Mudejars were added to the population of Castile. Initially, under the influence of Archbishop Talavera, treatment of the Mudejars was lenient. However, by 1499, under the influence of Archbishop Cisneros, forced conversions of Granada's Mudejars had begun. This led to revolts in the city of Granada, in 1499, and in the Alpujarras region in 1502. From the turn of the 16th century the option facing the Mudejars was either emigration or conversion.

Throughout the first half of the 16th century, when Spain was intermittently at war with the Turks and North African Muslim states, the Moriscos were seen as a potential ally of Spain's Muslim enemies.

How successfully was the Catholic Church reformed 1450–1556?

Although Cardinal Ximenez de Cisneros is associated with religious intolerance against the Jews and Mudejars, he did begin a major reform of the Catholic Church within Spain. As part of a process which became known as the 'Catholic Reformation', religious orders were reformed. In 1493 Pope Alexander VI gave the Catholic Monarchs authority to carry out a major reorganistion of religious orders. Orders such as the Dominicans and Franciscans, as well as orders of nuns, received **visitations**. As a result of this process new rules on conduct were enforced and abuses of existing rules were brought to an end. With the discovery of the New World the religious orders had the opportunity to engage in extensive missionary work.

Attempts were also made to improve religious education. In 1484 Cardinal Mendoza founded the College of Santa Cruz for the improvement of the educational standards of priests. In 1504 Cardinal Cisneros founded the University of Alcala to promote theological studies. Biblical studies were enhanced with the publication, in 1522, of a polyglot Bible where the text was written in Latin, Greek and Hebrew, side by side. The religious reforms under the Catholic Monarchs, combined with the Inquisition, meant that Protestant ideas made little headway in Spain.

Of equal significance was the changing relationship between Spain and the Papacy. During this period the Papacy was in need of foreign assistance to protect its independence in Italian politics. In return for support, Popes gave Spanish monarchs considerable control over the Catholic

Visitations: The name given to the tour of a diocese by a bishop to check on religious practices.

1. What is meant by the term 'conviviencia' as it applied to Spain in the 15th century?

2. In what ways were Spanish monarchs able to increase their control over the Catholic Church between 1474 and 1556?

3. How far had Spain become a land of one religion by 1556?

Church in Spain. In 1486 Innocent VIII gave Ferdinand and Isabella the right to appoint all church offices in newly-conquered lands. This enabled them to appoint all senior church appointments in Granada.

In 1493, Alexander VI extended this right to include the New World. By 1508 Julius II gave the Spanish monarchs the right of Patronato which, in effect, gave them complete control of the Catholic Church in their New World possessions. The Patronato did not extend to Spain. However, in 1523, Charles I received permission from Pope Adrian VI to appoint all bishops within Spain.

By 1556 the Spanish Monarchy had gained considerable control over the Church. This was achieved through the Patronato and the Inquisition. The Monarchy also obtained financial support from the Church through loans and taxes. Religious reform started by Cisneros was continued by other individuals such as St Teresa of Avila and St John of the Cross. As a result of these developments Spain was not affected by the Church/State conflicts which affected England, Sweden and the Holy Roman Empire.

6.4 What problems did Spain face when dealing with its empire in the Americas between 1492 and 1556?

In 1492 Granada was conquered, the Jews were expelled from Spain and Columbus discovered the New World. Of these three events the last was seen as the least significant by the Catholic Monarchs. However, by 1556 Spain had acquired a large overseas empire. In *The World Encompassed*, historian G. V. Scammell states that 'no empire was more extensive or more swiftly established'.

The Spanish empire in the Americas

Hernán Cortés (1485–1547)

Born in Extremadura (a province of Castile), his parents were Hidalgos (members of the lower nobility). Cortés first visited the New World when he landed on Hispaniola in 1504. In 1511 he took part in the conquest of Cuba. He was named by Velásquez, Governor of Cuba, as leader of an expedition to conquer lands on the mainland of the Americas in 1518.

The expedition began a year later when Cortés landed at Vera Cruz with 600 men and 19 horses.

Cortés disobeyed Velasquez's orders, burned his boats and marched inland towards the valley of Mexico. He had been informed of the Aztec Empire by coastal Indians. Cortés expected to find gold and other precious metals. Between 1519 and 1521 he was able to conquer the Aztec Empire, due to a number of reasons: Cortés' own abilities, the support of other Indian tribes such as the Tlaxcalans but also because many Aztecs believed Cortés was a reincarnation of the serpent god Quetzlcoatl.

In 1520 the Spanish and their allies successfully conquered the Axtec capital, Tenochtitlan, after a 93-day siege. The Emperor of the Aztecs, Montezuma, was killed and Cortés became absolute ruler of central Mexico. In 1522 King Charles I made Cortés the first governor of New Mexico. After various quarrels with Spanish viceroys, Cortés retired to Spain in 1539.

Francisco Pizarro (c.1475–1541)

Born in Extremadura, the illegitimate son of an infantry officer. In 1502 he went to Hispaniola. In 1513 he was part of Balboa's expedition which crossed the Isthmus of Panama to the Pacific coast of the New World. In 1529 he was granted by the Council of the Indies the title of Captain-General and governor of any new lands he conquered in south America. Pizarro expected to find an empire of gold. In 1531 he set off for Peru with 180 men and 27 horses.

From 1532 to 1535, Pizarro conquered the Inca Empire. He had considerable good fortune. He arrived at a time when the Incas were split between two rival claimants to the throne. With considerable courage, Pizarro was able to exploit this split. The Inca Emperor, Atahualpa, completely underestimated Pizarro. Atahualpa accepted an invitation to visit Pizarro, who captured him and slaughtered the Inca nobility who had accompanied the Inca Emperor. Like Cortés, Pizarro used horses, ferocious dogs, firearms and small cannons to great effect against the Indians. He also exploited Indian superstition.

Later, Pizarro had quarrels with his supporters. In 1541, in Lima (Peru), he was killed by members of the Almagro family.

1. In what ways were the conquests of the Aztecs and Incas similar?

2. How far was the conquest of the Aztec and Inca empires due to the weaknesses of Spain's Indian opponents?

During that period Spanish conquistadores had conquered two large empires in the Americas. In the 1520s Hernán Cortés destroyed the Aztec Empire in Mexico. A decade later, Francisco Pizarro overthrew the Inca Empire in Peru, in south America. When Philip II became King of Spain in 1556 the Spanish controlled most of the Americas, from the present United States of America to Cape Horn. By the Treaty of Tordesillas of 1493 Portugal was given control of Brazil. Outside the Americas the Spanish also controlled the Philipine Islands in south-east Asia.

The acquisition of such a large empire brought many challenges and benefits to Spain. The Spanish monarchy had to provide effective government of a large new area many thousands of miles from Europe. It had to deal with issues such as keeping control over Spanish settlers and handling relations between Spanish settlers and the native Indian population. The empire in the New World also offered a great challenge to the Spanish Catholic Church. It had the opportunity to spread Christianity to a new and largely unknown Indian population.

The Americas provided Spain with new products such as chocolate, potatoes, maize and turkeys. However, by far the most important was the discovery of gold and silver. Gold and particularly silver gave the Spanish monarchy considerable wealth. It helped to finance the wars of Charles I and gave his successor, Philip II, a major source of revenue (see Chapter 9). Unfortunately, the arrival of large amounts of silver from the New World also had the effect of causing inflation in Spain in the second half of the 16th century.

How was the Spanish Empire governed?

As a result of the discoveries in the New World a special department known as the Casa de la Contratacion (House of Trade) was established in 1503. It was located in Seville. This Andalucian city became the centre for all trade with the New World. According to historian G. V. Scammell, the House of Trade controlled civil and criminal law in maritime and commercial matters, ran a navigation school and updated maps.

As with other aspects of Spanish government, the administration of the New World was placed under a Council. Between 1511 and 1519 a Council of the Indies was a committee of the Council of Castile. This reflected the fact that all the new territories discovered overseas became controlled by Castile, not Castile *and* Aragon. In 1524 a separate Council of the Indies was created. It acted as a supreme court for all matters relating to the Americas. In addition, it appointed colonial officials and passed laws affecting the Empire. In its early years, the Empire's administration and procedure was flexible. However, in 1542, its activities were to be governed by the New Laws.

Within the Americas, Spanish rule was organised into two viceroyalties. In 1535 New Spain was established, centred on Mexico. In 1543 New Castile was created centred on Peru. The office of viceroy had been widely used in Spanish history, in particular by Aragon. Viceroys were appointed by the monarch and were usually members of the military aristocracy. They usually held office for six years. Given the great distance from Spain the colonial viceroys possessed considerable power. They could appoint local officials and create their own law. They had control over local church appointments and had the power to raise armies to repel invasion.

Mexico and the West Indies under Spanish rule

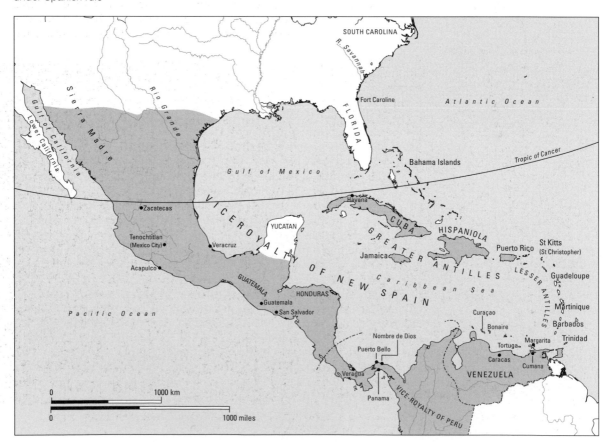

Spanish colonial rule possessed its own checks and balances. Vice-regal rule was limited by local *audiencia*. These were local councils that acted as courts of appeal and administrative committees. The Viceroy was expected to work with the *audienca*. In a dispute, either side could appeal to the Spanish monarch. Political power was divided further through the existence of town and city councils. Mayors (*alcaldes*) and assemblies (*cabildos*) possessed considerable administrative authority over their own town or city. However, each town council was under the leadership of a royal official.

In matters of taxation each viceroyalty had its own treasury. The taxes which were raised included the *alcabala* (sales tax), the *almojarifazo* (import tax), the *cruzada* (religious tax) and *la quinta* (the royal fifth), a tax on silver. Usually the collection of these taxed was '**farmed out**'. In turn, the tax and treasury officials were directly responsible to the accounts department of the Council of the Indies.

Farmed out: Allowing someone to collect the taxes for you in return for a commission on the amount that was collected.

What impact did Spanish settlers have on the Americas?

When the first Spanish settlers arrived in the islands of the Caribbean they established the *encomienda* system. Land was given to settlers. In return, they were meant to look after the interests of the Indians on their land. These grants of land were meant to be for a limited period of time. The landowners were also meant to be under the jurisdiction of the Spanish monarch. These *encomiendas* could be very large.

According to historian G. V. Scammell, in *The World Encompassed,* in the valley of central Mexico Cortes distributed 180,000 Indians between 30 encomiendas. By 1550, in Peru, 500 encomienderos controlled 5,000 Indians.

Unfortunately, little thought was given to the welfare of the native Indian population by the encomienderos. Large numbers of Indians were enslaved and poorly treated. However, the biggest catastrophe

How useful are these engravings to a historian writing about Spanish rule in the Americas in the first half of the 16th century?

Contemporary woodcuts, c.1550, of Indians working on Spanish estates in the Caribbean. (Left) gold mining; (right) a sugar-mill – having exhausted gold, they turned to sugar cultivation.

facing the native Indian population was the introduction of disease by the Spanish. Smallpox, typhus and influenza killed large numbers. By the end of the 16th century almost 90% of the native Indian population had been wiped out.

To replace the lost Indian population the Spanish settlers began importing black slaves from west Africa. By 1556 most of the West Indies encomienda possessed African slaves. In addition, there was considerable inter-breeding between races. The offspring of Spanish settlers and Indian women produced a large *mestizo* population. The children of White settlers and African women were known as *mulattos*, while the children of African slaves and Indian women were *zambos*. These developments gave the Spanish Empire, particularly in the Caribbean, a strong racial mix.

How successful were the Spanish in introducing Christianity to the Americas?

From the beginning of Spanish rule in the Americas the mission to convert the Indians to Christianity was a important issue. In the Papal Bull of 1493 the Catholic Monarchs were requested by the Pope to send

This is a book on Catholic religious teaching. What can it tell a historian about the reasons for the development of Spanish control of the New World?

Title page of *Doctrina Breve* – the the first printed book in the New World – by Juan de Zumárraga, printed in Mexico in 1544.

'God-fearing men with training, experience and skill to instruct the natives … and imbue them with Christian faith.'

In the development of the Christian Church in the New World, Spanish monarchs were given a unique authority. In 1508, through the *Patronato*, Spanish monarchs had the right to appoint all bishops in the New World. They also had the right to found churches and to tax the Church. However, from 1512 Ferdinand gave the Church in the New World its own income by giving them control over church taxes there.

Much of the missionary work was done by friars. As Henry Kamen states in *Spain 1469–1714*: 'From their arrival in America in 1510, the friars of the Mendicant Orders set the pace and determined the objectives of Spain's religious mission.'

In 1524 Franciscans, under Martin de Valencia, began the mission to Mexico. These were followed by Dominicans two years later. By 1560 they had established 80 churches in New Spain. Missionary work was aided by the Spanish decision to ban traditional customs. These laws helped destroy the fabric of native society.

Missionary work in Peru faced greater difficulties. The Quechua people of the High Andes were more determined to defend their own religious practices. It was not until the 1650s that Christianity made an impact there.

The independent authority and wealth of the missionary church in the New World brought it into conflict with the Spanish settlers. An issue which caused conflict was the treatment of the Indians. An important Church spokesman was the Dominican friar, Batholome de las Casas. In his book *Historia* he put forward the view that Indians had rights and should be treated fairly. He had sufficient influence to persuade the Spanish monarch to allow Indian self-government on the island of Hispaniola in the West Indies. In 1542 de las Casas was able to persuade Charles I to pass the New Laws. These stated that the encomienda system should end; all Indians who were held as slaves should be freed. However, the New Laws caused resentment among Spanish settlers. They even caused a revolt in Peru. Although Charles I and his Court supported the views of de las Casas in the New World, they carried little weight.

1. Explain how the Spanish established their empire in the Americas.

2. What were the major changes made by the Spanish, in the Americas, between 1492 and 1556?

3. How far can Spanish rule in the Americas be regarded as a success?

a) For Spain and the Spanish monarchy?

b) For the native peoples of the Americas?

6.5 To what extent did the government of Spain under Charles I differ from the government of Spain under the Catholic Monarchs?

The death of Ferdinand in 1516 was a turning point in the history of Spain. Through the accident of birth and the untimely death of Ferdinand's children, the crown of Castile and Aragon passed to Charles, son of Philip of Burgundy and Joanna the Mad. For the first time Castile and Aragon were united under one monarch.

In addition to Castile and Aragon, Charles inherited the Netherlands and Franche Comté from his father. By 1519 he was elected Holy Roman Emperor. From 1519 to his abdication in 1556 Spain became part of a large Habsburg empire which spread across Europe (see map).

In 1519 one of Charles' main advisers, Mercurino Gattinara, wrote to him stating: 'you are on the road towards Universal Monarchy and on the point of uniting Christendom under a single shepherd.'

In what ways was the Government of Spain under Charles I similar to the Catholic Monarchs?

There seems to be a considerable degree of continuity in the style of government between 1474 and 1556. Charles inherited the conciliar system of government.

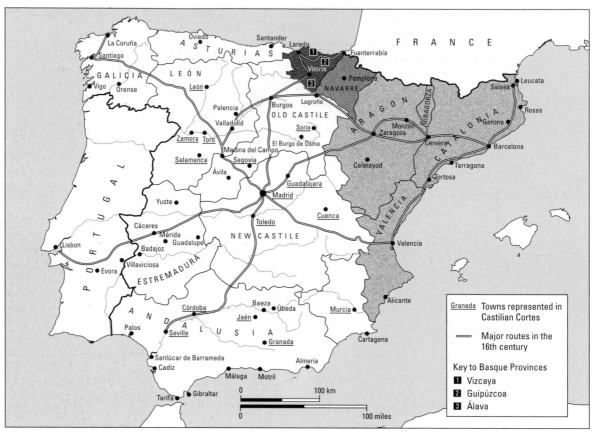

Habsburg Spain in the early 16th century

By 1516 Spain had a variety of councils which advised the monarch.

Conciliar Government under the Catholic Monarchs (1474–1516)

Royal Council of Castile (reorganised 1480)
Royal Council of Aragon (reorganised 1494)
Council of the Inquisition, 1483
Council of the Military Orders, 1495
Council of the Cruzada, 1509

To these councils Charles I added the following:
Council of War, 1517
Council of State, 1522
Council of Finance, 1523
Council of the Indies, 1524
Council of Italy, 1555

The type of council that advised the monarch fell into two categories: advisory and administrative. For example, the Council of War provided Charles with advice on military matters. The Council of State was also advisory but did act as a co-ordinating council dealing with decisions from other councils. The Royal Councils of Castile and Aragon were administrative dealing with the government of the two kingdoms and also acting as a court of law.

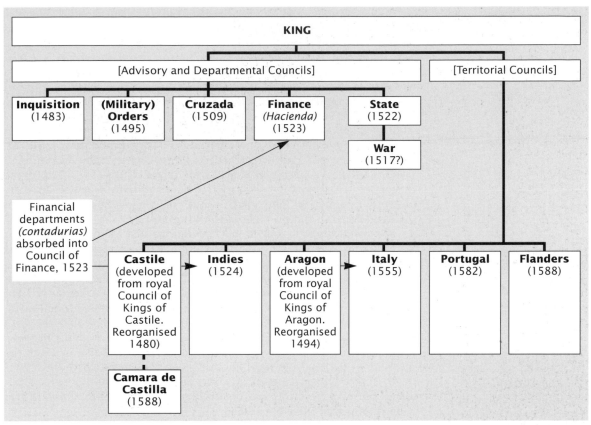

```
                              ┌─────────────────────────────┐
                              │            KING             │
                              └─────────────────────────────┘
                 ┌──────────────────────────────────┐   ┌──────────────────────┐
                 │  [Advisory and Departmental Councils]  │   │  [Territorial Councils] │
                 └──────────────────────────────────┘   └──────────────────────┘
```

Inquisition (1483)	(Military) Orders (1495)	Cruzada (1509)	Finance (Hacienda) (1523)	State (1522)

War (1517?)

Financial departments (*contadurias*) absorbed into Council of Finance, 1523

Castile (developed from royal Council of Kings of Castile. Reorganised 1480)	Indies (1524)	Aragon (developed from royal Council of Kings of Aragon. Reorganised 1494)	Italy (1555)	Portugal (1582)	Flanders (1588)

Camara de Castilla (1588)

Conciliar system

Along with the traditional structure of government Charles continued to staff his councils with *letrados* (lawyers).

Throughout the period 1474 to 1556 government in Spain was firmly centred on the monarch. Councils were established when the need arose. In no sense could the conciliar form of government be regarded as a united, co-ordinated system. To emphasise this, Spain did not possess a fixed capital city in this period. The government existed wherever the monarch decided to hold court.

Also, Charles' empire could not be regarded as a single state. Far from being a 'universal monarchy', it was a *monarquia* (i.e. a collection of territories which regarded Charles as their ruler). Throughout Charles I's rule Castile and Aragon remained separate kingdoms. The only councils that covered the affairs of both kingdoms were the Council of State and the Inquisition. As historian J. H. Elliott notes: 'Charles was, and remained, an old-style ruler who liked to lead his armies in battle and to govern his subjects personally, and there remained to the end of his life an element of the improvising amateur about his manner.'

Apart from conciliar government, there were other similarities between the Catholic Monarchs and Charles I. This was most apparent in local government. Between 1474 and 1556 local government was left firmly in the hands of the aristocracy in both Castile and Aragon.

Although Charles continued with the conciliar system of government, he did extend its role to include new areas. For instance, the Council of State, created in 1522, dealt with the affairs of both Spain and the Holy Roman Empire. Also during his reign the rise to power and influence of a senior administrator took place. From 1527 to the end of his reign this position was occupied by Francisco de los Cobos, a letrado from Andalucia. During his career he was responsible for Castile, the New World and Italy.

In foreign affairs the senior administrator was a Burgundian, Nicholas Perrenot, Lord of Granvelle. However, this did not mean that rivalry and faction did not affect Charles' government. In the 'secret instruction' he sent Philip, in 1543, Charles warned his son about the rivalry at court between de los Cobos and Cardinal Talavera, who led rival factions.

An area of controversy surrounds Charles' relations with the towns of Castile. During the reign of the Catholic Monarchs the support of these towns was so important. Both Isabella and Ferdinand had made considerable efforts to tour their kingdoms to maintain this support. However, at the beginning of his reign, Charles faced major opposition. In 1520–1521, a number of important towns rebelled against Charles' rule. According to historian Perez Zagorin, in *Rebels and Rulers, 1500–1600* (1982), the Revolt of the Communeros was 'the biggest urban rebellion in early modern Europe. Not only that, it was the biggest Spanish revolution between the 16th and the end of the 18th centuries.'

The revolt began in Toledo in 1520 and was led by Juan de Padilla. It spread quickly to Segovia, Salamanca and Valladolid. However, the rebels were defeated by a royal army at the Battle of Villalar in 1521.

The outbreak of revolt can be blamed, in part, on Charles' government of Spain in the first years of his reign. His decision to give senior government posts to Burgundians rather than Castilians caused resentment. However, the causes of the rebellion can be traced back into the 15th century. In late medieval Castile, there had always been hostility between the towns and the nobility. Following the death of Isabella, in 1504, the hostility of the towns to royal control began to develop. With the arrival in 1516 of a foreign king, in the form of Charles, these problems developed into open revolt. It was only with the support of the nobility that Charles was able to restore order.

In what ways was Charles I different from his predecessors in the way he governed Spain?

Charles I by Titian

An absentee king?

Of his 39 years as King of Spain Charles spent 16 years in Spain.

September 1517–May 1520

July 1522–July 1529

April 1533–April 1535

December 1536–Spring 1538

July 1538–November 1539

November 1541–May 1543

At the same time as the Communeros revolt, Aragon also faced political unrest. However, the revolt of the Germanias (1519–1524) was led by town guilds who were resentful of the power of the nobility and the Moriscos who lived on their estates. With the defeat of both revolts, the power of the nobility in both kingdoms was strengthened.

The Communeros Revolt and Charles' responsibilities as ruler in Spain, Germany, Italy and the Netherlands affected his relations with the Cortes. This national institution represented 18 towns in Castile. For the rest of his reign Charles used the Cortes as a way of financing his wars across Europe. In this sense his relationship with the Cortes differed from his predecessors. Although the Cortes of Castile met 15 times during his reign, its role was limited. In 1527 Charles summoned the nobles and clergy to the Cortes at Valladolid. He did so again in 1538. In 1544 the Cortes itself asked to be called only every three years.

An area of government activity that Charles did change was finance. In 1523 he established the Council of Finance. According to Henry Kamen it had two main objectives: to co-ordinate the work of existing finance departments and to act as a treasury for state revenue. Charles realised that to finance his expensive wars against Turks, German Protestants and the French (see Chapter 3) he required large sums of money. To him Castile was to be the main source of revenue. This involved heavy taxation and the use of gold and silver from the New World. As Charles told his brother Ferdinand, in 1540: 'I cannot be sustained except by my realms in Spain.'

From the New World Charles received an average of 220,000 ducats a year from 1534 to 1543. He also raised large sums of money from the sales tax, the *alcabala*, which was granted by the Cortes. Even these large sums were not sufficient to meet the costs of his wars. For example, the campaign against the French at Metz, in 1552, cost two million ducats. To meet these military costs Charles used other methods to acquire money.

Charles was given permission by the Pope to take part of the Spanish Church's income. By 1551 this sum brought Charles 500,000 ducats a year. In addition, he raised money through the *cruzada*, which produced 120,000 ducats a year by 1554. The government also decided to sell large number of bonds (*juros*) from which the buyer received interest. Charles also raised large loans in Antwerp and from the Fugger banking family in Germany.

As the historian John Lynch states, in *Spain under the Habsburgs*, 'Finance was the key to much of Charles' policy and of the history of Spain during his reign.'

The financial demands placed on Spain by Charles were enormous. In 1556, 68% of all state revenue was spent on foreign wars. One year after his abdication, in 1557, his son Philip II was unable to pay his debts. Spain had become bankrupt.

1. Explain the meaning of the term 'monarquia' as it applied to the empire of Charles.

2. In what ways did the government of Spain change between 1474 and 1556?

3. To what extent did the government of Spain under Charles I differ from the government of Spain under the Catholic Monarchs?

6.6 How successful was Spain in foreign affairs under Charles I?

In foreign affairs Charles continued several traditional Spanish policies. He continued the wars against the Moors in North Africa and he continued to defend Spanish interests in Italy.

However, Charles was not merely King of Castile and Aragon. As Holy Roman Emperor he saw himself as defender of western Christendom. This involved conflict with the Turks and German Protestants. As the leading member of the Habsburg family and successor to the rulers of Burgundy, he became involved in a series of wars with Valois France. First against Francis I, then against Henry II, Charles seemed to be almost constantly at war with the French.

For a general coverage of the wars of Charles V see Chapter 9. In this chapter only those aspects of foreign policy that affected traditional Spanish policy will be discussed. However, Charles' ability to defend traditional Spanish interests often conflicted with his role at Holy Roman Emperor and ruler of the Netherlands.

One area where Charles continued the policies of his Spanish predecessors was in North Africa. The *Reconquista* did not end with the capture of Granada in 1492. Ferdinand had taken the crusade against the Moors to the coast of North Africa.

In 1535 Charles organised an expedition against Tunis. Leading a force of 30,000, Charles planned to recapture the city which had fallen to a Turkish fleet under Barbarossa (Khayr al-Din). Although this expedition was successful, a further attack on Algiers, in 1541, failed. When Charles abdicated, in 1556, the hopes of a successful crusade against the Moors had come to nothing. In 1551 Spain lost control of Tripoli, in 1554 it lost control of Penon de Velez and in 1555 it lost Bougie.

However, there were some successes. In 1528 the Genoese admiral, Andrea Doria, became an ally of Charles. For the rest of Charles' reign Doria helped to prevent the Turkish fleet from attacking Spain and its possessions in the western Mediterranean.

Another area of traditional Spanish policy involved conflict with France. In 1521 Charles stopped a French invasion of Navarre. In Italy, by 1556, Charles had kept control of Milan and Naples. However, it took his son, Philip II, to bring the wars with France to an end at Câteau-Cambrésis, in 1559.

According to Martyn Rady, in *The Emperor Charles V* (1988): 'All too often, Charles' failure as a ruler is ascribed to the sheer size of his empire. An alternative explanation might be the unattainable range of obligations he felt bound to discharge.' Indeed, Charles left to his son, Philip II, major foreign policy conflicts with France and the Turks.

1. What were the main problems facing Charles in foreign policy during his reign?

2. In what ways did Charles continue the foreign policy of his Spanish predecessors?

3. How successful was Charles in defending Spanish interests in foreign affairs?

6.7 How far did Spanish society and the economy change between 1450 and 1556?

During the period 1450 to 1556 Spain experienced a number of important economic changes. Firstly, the population increased. In 1500 the population of Castile was some five million although some have placed it as high as eight million. Aragon had a population of approximately one million. According to Henry Kamen the population of Castile rose by 50% between 1530 and 1580. This development was to have important effects on demand and prices.

Over this period Spain became heavily dependent on sheep farming. This activity was encouraged by the policies of the Catholic Monarchs. Wool was exported to the Netherlands, which led to a decline in the textile industry. Sheep farming by the Mesta also had an adverse effect of arable farming. Combined with a rise in population, by the middle of the 16th century Spain was finding it difficult to feed its population.

Finally, the expensive foreign wars of Charles I led to a major increase in taxation. It also meant that the benefits, which could have been gained from acquiring gold and silver from the New World, were wasted. By 1556 Spain had amassed a large debt to foreign bankers. The government had also created a large debt through the sale of bonds (*juros*).

These developments meant that a major problem facing the Spanish economy and society was the rise in prices – the Price Revolution. The causes of price rises (inflation) were many.

- A rise in demand. The rise in population, without a corresponding rise in food production, led to a rise in food prices. For instance, in the southern province of Andalucia wheat prices rose 109% between 1511 and 1559.

- Gold and silver imports from the New World increased the amount of currency in circulation. The increase in the quantity of money led to a rise in prices. This can be explained by the Quantity Theory of Money. According to this theory:

MV = PT

M = the quantity of money in circulation

V = the velocity (or speed) at which the money circulates in the economy

P = the price level

T = the number of transactions the money makes.

It is believed by many economists that V and T tend not to change over a short period of time. Therefore, any increase in the supply of money leads directly to a rise in prices.

- The increasing costs of warfare also caused prices to rise. The wars of Charles I cost huge sums of money.

Inflation had an adverse effect on society. Whilst the prices of essential goods like food and oil were rising by more than 100%, wages for labourers were rising by only 30%–40%. Priests also suffered. They received fixed incomes, which bought less and less as prices rose. Even the nobility suffered. They received part of their rents from their peasants in cash rather than goods.

However, the people who suffered most were the labourers. Many became vagrants (wandering poor). Vagrants created major problems for the maintenance of law and order as they wandered the countryside looking for better paid work.

Not everyone suffered economic hardship in this period. The political stability created by the Catholic Monarchs allowed internal trade to develop. This helped towns to grow in size. During the first half of the 16th century Burgos, a centre of the wool industry in northern Spain, grew in population from 8,000 to 21,000. The development of transatlantic trade to the New World benefited Seville and Cadiz. It also allowed those involved to become rich.

Spain did not see any major developments in industry in this period. The country possessed lead and copper mining, as well as iron mining in the Basque province of Vizcaya. It also had a textile industry based on towns such as Valencia. According to historian A.D. Ortiz, in *The Golden Age of Spain* (1971), a major obstacle to industrial development were town guilds. These guilds opposed technical improvements or the concentration of production into large units.

When Philip II became King of Spain he inherited a large empire without the economic resources to sustain it.

1. What were the main problems affecting the Spanish economy and society between 1450 and 1556?

2. To what extent, by 1556, did Spain have the economy to support a large empire?

Source-based questions: Religion in the reigns of the Catholic Monarchs, 1474–1516

SOURCE A

The Holy Office of the Inquisition, seeing how some Christians are endangered by contact and communication with the Jews, has provided that the Jews be expelled from all our realms and territories, and has persuaded us to give our support and agreement to this, which we now do … We do so despite the great harm to ourselves, seeking and preferring the salvation of souls above our own profit.

From a letter to the Count of Aranda from King Ferdinand, 31 March 1492. Taken from Judios de Toledo ['Jews of Toledo'] *by Pilar Leon Tello.*

SOURCE B

Throughout the 1480s the signs multiplied of the approaching end of the era of cultural co-existence in Spain between Christians, Moors and Jews. Religious considerations were partly responsible … Ferdinand and Isabella … were deeply afflicted by the genuine … fear that Christian souls would be lost for eternity by the … influence of other faiths. It was expressly for this reason that they established the Castilian Inquisition in 1479 and extended it to all their realms over the following years.

From Ferdinand and Isabella *by Felipe Fernandez-Armesto, 1975*

SOURCE C

The problem of the Inquisition frequently discussed … was how Jews should treat the converso fugitives who sought admission to the Jewish fold … What we first gather from these discussions is that the conversos were known to the Jews not as forced converts (i.e. secret Jews) but as real converts and full-fledged Christians … If they had been viewed as forced converts there would have been no problem about accepting them … Since they [the conversos] had been Christians for several generations and behaved as such … there arose the question of their authentic Jewishness; and this moved most rabbis to regard [them] as gentiles i.e. non-Jews.

From The Origins of the Inquisition in 15th Century Spain *by Benjamin Netanyahu, 1995*

1. *Using information from this section explain the meaning of the following terms which are highlighted in the sources.*

(a) *'The Holy Office of the Inquisition' (Source A)*

(b) *'the era of cultural co-existence' (Source B)*

(iii) *'the conversos' (Source C).*

2. *Study Source A.*

How useful is this source to a historian writing about the religious history of Spain in the years 1474 to 1516?

3. *Study Sources A and B.*

How far do these sources agree on the reasons for the persecution of the Jews?

4. *Study Source B and use information contained in this chapter.*

How valid is the historical interpretation offered by Fernandez-Armesto about the origins of the Spanish Inquisition?

5. *Study Sources A, B and C and use information contained in this chapter.*

To what extent was the expulsion of the Jews in 1492 due to purely religious reasons?

7 Renaissance France 1450–1559

7.1 What impact did the reign of Louis XI have on France?

7.2 Why did France intervene in Italy in 1494 and what impact did it have on European affairs?

7.3 How far did the French economy and society change between 1450 and 1559?

7.4 How successful was the foreign policy of Francis I and Henry II?

7.5 Historical interpretation: How powerful was the French monarchy under Francis I and Henry II?

Key Issues

● *How did the government of France change 1450–1559?*

● *How successful was French foreign policy 1450–1559?*

● *To what extent did France experience social and economic change 1450–1559?*

Framework of Events

1453	Hundred Years' War with England comes to an end
1461	Louis XI becomes king
1465	War of the Common Weal (or 'Public Weal')
1477	Charles the Bold of Burgundy killed at Battle of Nancy
1482	Treaty of Arras
1483	Charles VIII becomes king at age of 13
1494	Charles VIII invades Naples. Italian Wars begin
1495	League of Venice against Charles VIII
1500	Treaty of Granada with Ferdinand of Aragon
	Louis XIII invades Milan
1515	Battle of Marignano
	Parlement established at Rouen in Normandy
1516	Concordat of Bologna with Pope
	Peace of Noyon
1517	Francis I calls an Assembly of Towns
1521	First War with Charles V begins
1523	Parlement established at Dijon in Burgundy
1525	Battle of Pavia; Francis I captured
1526	Treaty of Madrid
1527	Assembly of Notables
	Second War with Charles V begins
1529	Peace of Cambrai or Ladies' Peace
1532	Brittany becomes part of France
1534	Day of the Placards
1536	Third War with Charles V begins
1537	Parlement established at Grenoble
1538	Truce of Nice
1540	Rouen parlement suspended
	Gabelle tax extended to Vendée and Guyenne
1542	Fourth War with Charles V begins
	Guyenne rebellion begins
	Francis I reforms financial administration

1544	Loss of Boulogne to England
	Treaty of Crépy
1547	Henry II becomes King
1551	Boulogne returned to France
1552	Fifth war against Charles V; France takes Metz, Verdun and Toul
1555	First Calvinist church opens in Paris
1556	Five Year Truce of Vaucelles
	Charles V, Holy Roman Emperor, abdicates
1557	Henry II breaks truce
	Battle of St Quentin
1558	French take Calais
1559	Treaty of Câteau-Cambrésis; end of Habsburg–Valois Wars
	Henry II dies in a tournament.

Overview

Huguenots: French Protestants. Genevan Calvinists who settled in France were named after Victor Hugues, a burgomaster, and were known as Huguenots.

Fiefs: An area under the control of a local aristocrat.

Duchy: Land ruled by a duke.

THE historian David Potter, in *A History of France 1460–1560* (published in 1995), has subtitled his work 'The emergence of a Nation State'. This suggests that France went through considerable change in this period. In 1450 France was still at war with England in the 100 Years' War; in 1559 France was on the verge of a series of civil wars known as the Wars of Religion. These wars lasted until 1598, although a final peace between the government and the **Huguenots** did not take place until 1629.

In terms of size, France grew from 425,000 square kilometres at the start of Louis XI's reign to 460,00 square kilometres by 1559. Today France is 551,000 square kilometres. However, at the start of the period the kingdom of France lacked unity and effective central control. Brittany and Burgundy were self-governing – outside the control of the French king. In addition, within France there were territories controlled by foreigners: Avignon and Comitat Venaisson were controlled by the Pope; the town of Orange was controlled by the house of Orange-Nassau; and Calais was controlled by England.

Within France itself large areas were controlled by the aristocracy. These **fiefs** owed allegiance firstly to their local lord. The map opposite gives you an idea of how extensive these areas were.

One of the major developments in this period was a growth in the power and influence of the French monarchy. During the reign of Louis XI, the **Duchy** of Burgundy was brought under his control. In addition, the monarchy became more financially independent. Some historical controversy surrounds the reigns of Francis I and Henry II. Historians such as R. J. Knecht regard these reigns as the establishment of 'absolute monarchy' in France. By 1559 France was under the effective control of the monarch.

According to David Potter, the fact that France did not disintegrate during the Wars of Religion was due to the changes made in government before 1560. Other historians disagree. The American historian J. Russell Major believes that the French monarchy before 1559 still had to rule with the consent of the people. He highlights the importance of the *parlements* (see insert on page 148). To Russell Major the French monarchy was not absolute, but consultative.

In foreign affairs, France was almost continuously at war after 1494. The invasion of Italy by Charles VIII began a period of warfare that affected most of

France showing the major fiefs in the late 15th and early 16th centuries

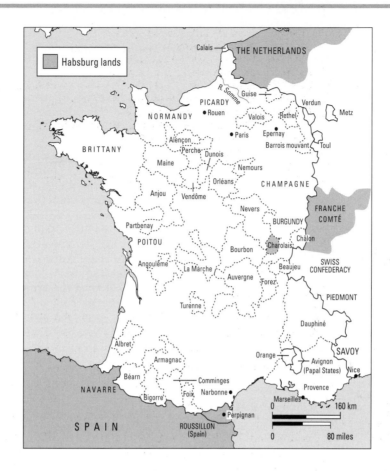

western Europe by 1559. The wars were limited to Italy in the period 1494 to 1516. After 1519 the wars escalated into a conflict between the French House of Valois and the House of Habsburg. This Habsburg–Valois conflict involved France, Spain, the Netherlands, Italy, England, Scotland, Ottoman Turkey and the Holy Roman Empire. By 1559 the French had little to show for this long period of warfare. They had acquired Metz, Toul and Verdun in Lorraine and had taken Calais from England. Hopes of acquiring territory and influence in Italy were unfulfilled. The financial costs of these wars had brought the French monarchy to the verge of bankruptcy.

In social and economic affairs, the French population increased rapidly in this period. This was due to a number of factors, such as the end of the 100 Years' War, the absence of plague and the increase in the birth rate. Combined with the financial costs of war this development led to a general rise in prices (inflation). The period 1530 to 1559 saw a fall in the standard of living across France. However, the major social change was the growth of Protestantism within France. Initially, it took the form of Lutheranism in the 1530s. By the 1540s Calvinism had begun to penetrate France. In 1559 Protestantism had established itself.

In 1559 France faced a major crisis. Henry II's unexpected death at a tournament left the monarchy to Francis II. The monarchy was on the verge of bankruptcy. The economy was in a state of crisis and religious conflict between Catholic and Protestant was coming to a head.

The Government of Renaissance France

The king

The king was the centre of government. He conducted foreign policy, declared war and issued laws. He was advised by the King's Council. However, as the period progressed he had an inner group of advisers (*Conseil étroit*) and the *Conseil secret*.

As the dispenser of law the king was advised by the Grand Council. The king appointed officials to run the administration. The most important were the Constable, the Chancellor and the Admiral of France. The role of the Constable and Admiral were defined by the king. The Chancellor was in charge of the chancery, which had the task of implementing the decisions of the king.

At local level the king appointed provincial governors. These were members of the nobility and were given the task of dealing with local disputes. There were 11 provincial governors in charge of France's border provinces.

Parlements

These were courts of law. There were seven in 1515 and ten by 1547. They had the power to deal with legal cases and had the right to register royal decrees to make them legally binding. The most important was the Parlement of Paris. Its jurisdiction covered almost half of France. The Parlement of Paris contained 60 lay and clerical councillors in 1515, rising to 160 by Henry II's reign.

Parlements in the 16th century

Lit de justice

This was a meeting of a parlement with the King and the king's ministers present. Usually met to force a parlement to register a decree or edict.

Estates General

This was a national assembly of the three estates of France: the Clergy, the Nobility and the Third Estate (usually towns). In this period an Estates General met at Tour in 1484; there was a partial Estates General in 1506; and in 1560 another Estates General was called.

Local government

The basic unit of local government was a bailliage. There were 100 in France. The person in charge (a bailli) had mainly military duties. The bailliage judged local cases and published royal decrees. In January 1552 Henry II added a new layer of administration between a bailliage and a parlement: the présidial. There were 61 of these. Their main role was to bring in more money for the king through the sale of offices.

Pays d'election and Pays d'état

France was divided into two parts. The Pays d'election was an area where the king could raise taxes on his own authority. The Pays d'état, which included Languedoc, Provence, Burgundy and Brittany, was the local assembly had the right to raise taxes.

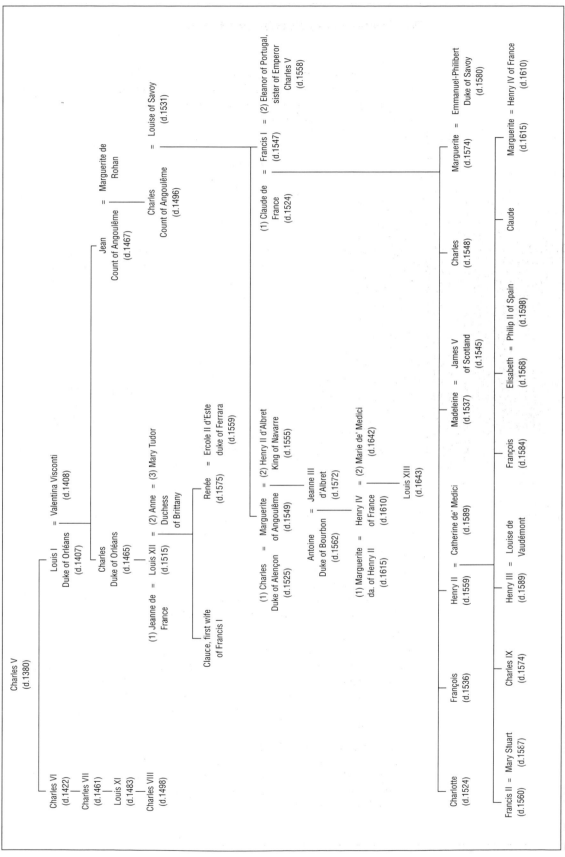

The French House of Valois

<table>
<tr><td colspan="2">The Kings of France 1450–1559</td></tr>
<tr><td>Charles VII</td><td>1422–1461</td></tr>
<tr><td>Louis XI</td><td>1461–1483</td></tr>
<tr><td>Charles VIII</td><td>1483–1498</td></tr>
<tr><td>Louis XII</td><td>1498–1515</td></tr>
<tr><td>Francis I</td><td>1515–1547</td></tr>
<tr><td>Henry II</td><td>1547–1559</td></tr>
</table>

French currency

The main French currency of the period was the livre, sometimes called the livre tournais. It was divided into 20 sols or 240 deniers. In this way it resembled British currency before decimalisation, when one pound was worth 20 shillings or 240 pence.

The most important French coin was the écu. Its value increased in the period from 36 sols in 1498 to 50 sols by 1551.

7.1 What impact did the reign of Louis XI have on France?

Louis XI (1423–1483)

Born at Bourges on 3 July 1423, the elder son of Charles VII and Marie d'Anjou. In his early years he lived in obscurity in the castle of Loches. He was described by his enemies as 'the Universal Spider' because of his cunning and intriguing methods. In 1440 he became involved in a rebellion, the Parguerie, against his father. The rebellion failed. Louis succeeded his father at the age of 38. He defeated the League of the Common Weal in 1465. His position was strengthened with the birth of a son in 1470 and the death of his brother in 1472. Louis XI increased royal territory at the expense of Burgundy in 1477. He left the French monarchy strong with a good financial base.

Louis XI has been described by Daniel Waley, in *Late Medieval Europe* (1964), as 'a hard man and a hard worker; authoritarian, unscrupulous, expecting no scruples in others'. More recently, David Potter in *A History of France 1460–1560* (1995) describes Louis XI as 'one of the most formidable rulers in French history'. During his reign, France continued its recovery from the 100 Years' War which had begun under Charles VII. The power of the French monarchy increased at the expense of the aristocracy. Louis also increased French territory, most notably his acquisition of the Duchy of Burgundy. His reign has been described as establishing 'a new monarchy' in France, making a decisive break with the French monarchy of the Middle Ages.

In what ways did Louis XI affect the working of royal government?

The most important part of royal government was the King's Council (*Conseil du roi*). It contained members of the royal family, leading members of the aristocracy and the holders of the main offices of state, such as the Chancellor of France. During Louis XI's reign, the chancellors were Pierre de Morvilliers (1461–1465), Guillaume Jouvenal des Ursins (1465–1472) and Pierre d'Oriole (1472–1483). The aim of this body was to offer advice to the King. During Louis XI's reign, a total of 462 royal councillors took part in the business of the King's Council. The main reason for appointment to this body was loyalty to Louis XI.

The work of the King's Council was, however, changed during Louis' reign. An Inner Council (*Conseil étroit*) was created, by 1484, containing some 12 royal councillors – to discuss the most important matters. There was even a secret council (*Conseil secret*) of three royal councillors – to discuss the most important and sensitive issues of state. The actual work and administration of these councils was done by the king's secretaries.

Although these bodies aided decision making, the king was the highest judge in France. To assist him in this area was the Great Council. It acted as a high court of law. It could issue decrees (*arrets*) on points of law.

So, although royal administration improved during the reign, France was still not under the direct control of the monarch. Local parlements had the right to register laws. Local aristocrats controlled large areas. Towns were self-governing. The lack of communications also limited the power of the French king, although Louis did create a postal service.

France also lacked a centralised system of collecting taxes. Taxes were collected in local units known as *généralités*. Fortunately for Louis XI, the

The revenue of the French Monarchy

The French Monarchy received money from two sources:

- Ordinary revenue: this came from the King's own lands.

- Extraordinary revenue: this came from taxation.

There were three main types of tax in France during Louis XI's reign:

The taille: a direct tax. The amount was decided by the King's Council. There was also the possibility of an additional taille known as the *crue*, or surtax. It was a tax on land. The Church and the aristocracy were exempt, so were some towns, such as Paris. This tax brought in approximately one third of all revenue.

The Gabelle: a tax on salt. The monarchy had a monopoly on the salt trade from the reign of Charles V (1346–1380). The main area affected by this tax was north and central France.

The Aides: duties on certain goods – a form of Value Added Tax (VAT). Examples of this tax were duties on wine and cattle.

100 Years' War had created conditions for an increase in the monarch's financial power. In 1439 the Estates General gave Charles VII the right to raise a standing army. To finance this army the King was given the power to raise taxes on his own authority. Louis XI used this right to increase his financial independence. Between the start and end of his reign the annual average amount raised in taxation rose from 1.8 million livres to 4.8 million livres.

During Louis' reign relations with the Catholic Church seemed to go through a period of change. In 1461 relations between the monarchy and the Catholic Church were governed by the Pragmatic Sanction of Bourges of 1438. This forbade appeals to Rome and the payment of money to the Pope. At the end of 1461, Louis XI promised the Pope that he would abolish the Pragmatic Sanction. This agreement was even registered with the Parlement of Paris. It was never put into effect. In 1472 Louis made a new **concordat** with Pope Sixtus IV. This allowed a division of authority over the French Catholic Church between King and Pope. However, Louis continued the practice of limited papal control within France.

Concordat: An agreement between the Pope and a ruler about how the Catholic Church should operate within the ruler's lands.

According to historian Stanley Leathes, in *The Cambridge Modern History* (1903), Louis' 'means were various and even inconsistent, but his general policy was clear'. That policy was to increase his own political power at the expense of others.

How did Louis XI deal with the French aristocracy?

The French monarchy faced a challenge to its authority throughout the 15th century, from powerful local rulers. These were members of the aristocracy. As France recovered territory from England during the 100 Years' War, the French king was able to place royal governors in charge of these newly-conquered lands. This occurred in Normandy and Gascony.

For most of the rest of France, the aristocracy had political power. The most extreme cases were Burgundy and Brittany. Both these areas were technically part of France. However, they were ruled as if they were independent states. Within France, the Bourbon family dominated central France north of the river Loire.

For the first half of his reign Louis XI had to deal with threats from the French aristocracy and from within his own family. In 1464–65 this reached its peak with the formation of the League of the Public Weal. This group included John II (Duke of Bourbon), Francis II of Brittany, the Count of Armagnac and Charles, Count of Charolais. The figurehead for this aristocratic conspiracy was Louis' own brother, Charles. Louis was able to defeat this conspiracy for several reasons. Firstly, the conspiracy lacked effective co-ordination. This allowed Louis to defeat his opponents one at a time. He defeated the Duke of Bourbon first, then stopped the Count of Charolais at the Battle of Montlhèry. Secondly, Louis used diplomatic means to buy off his opponents. At the Treaty of Conflans (October 1465), the Duke of Bourbon received control of Languedoc and a gift of 100,000 crowns. The Duke of Burgundy received Boulogne and Guisnes. Louis' brother Charles received Normandy. This treaty seemed to be a victory for Louis' opponents. However, Louis' concessions broke up the League. Quarrels broke out between League members concerning territory. This allowed Louis to recover Normandy in 1466. He also made an alliance with the Earl of Warwick, which lessened the threat of English intervention.

When Philip the Good of Burgundy died in 1467, Louis tried to undermine the rule of the new Burgundian ruler, Charles of Charolais, who became known as Charles the Bold. He attempted to cause an uprising in the Burgundian city of Liège. Unfortunately for Louis, he was held prisoner by Charles at Peronne. He was forced to give up more territory – this included Brie and Champagne – to his own brother Charles.

In the period 1471 to 1476 Louis had to face threats from both Charles the Bold and Edward IV of England. Between 1471 and 1472 Louis was at war with Burgundy. The war involved attempts by Louis to recover towns on the river Somme lost to Burgundy. It ended inconclusively in a truce. In 1475 Edward IV of England attempted to revive his claim to the French throne. He arranged for a joint invasion of France with Charles the Bold. However, in August 1475 Louis signed the Treaty of Pecquigny with Edward. He 'bought off' Edward by promising a marriage between his son Charles and Edward's daughter Elizabeth. He also gave Edward a payment of 75,000 crowns. The marriage never took place but the offer served its purpose of ending English intervention.

The turning point in Louis' reign came in 1477. In a war between Lorraine and Burgundy, Charles the Bold of Burgundy was killed by the Swiss at the Battle of Nancy on 5 January 1477. This allowed Louis to take over the Duchy of Burgundy. By the Treaty of Arras, in 1482, Louis retained control of Burgundy, Boulonnais and Picardy. Also under the treaty Louis arranged the marriage of the **Dauphin** Charles to Margaret, the daughter of Holy Roman Emperor Maximilian and Mary of Burgundy. Margaret's **dowry** included Artois and Franche Comté.

Dauphin: The heir to the throne in France.

Dowry: The money, or wealth, which a father has to give to the husband of his daughter. For a peasant it might amount to a few chickens. For a monarch this might be an entire territory.

Louis' success was also due to a degree of good fortune and ruthlessness. In 1472, his brother Charles had died. In 1481, the last remaining heir to the House of Anjou died leaving Louis in control of the provinces of Anjou and Provence. England became involved in its own internal struggle, known as the War of the Roses. This limited the possibility of English intervention. While Aragon and Castile faced internal problems, Louis was also able to take over Roussillon and Cerdagne in 1462. He also executed aristocrats who threatened his control. In 1475 he executed Saint-Pol and in 1477 Nemours.

According to the historian J. R. Hale, in *Renaissance Europe, 1480–1520* (1971), 'modern "France" [was] governed on lines firmly sketched by Louis XI'. This suggests that Louis XI helped to limit the power of the

1. Draw a spidergram showing the main problems which faced Louis XI during his reign.

2. What do you regard as the most important problem facing Louis XI? Give reasons for your answer.

3. How far did Louis XI increase the power of the French monarchy?

aristocracy, created a more financially independent monarchy and regained territory lost in the 100 Years' War. More recently, Janine Garrisson in *Sixteenth Century France, 1483–1598* (1995) states that 'the way in which Louis XI and his councillors governed in the aftermath of the 100 Years' War provided the model that was to be followed by all his successors, from Charles VIII to Henry II. He sought to concentrate powers in a few hands, to bring all business, however trivial, under the immediate eye of the monarch.'

However, this did not mean that threats to the monarchy from the aristocracy came to an end in 1483. In 1485 Louis, the Duke d'Orléans, with the support of the Duke of Brittany, led a revolt against the Regency government during Charles VIII's minority. What Louis did do was to lay the foundations for an increase in royal power which took place during the reigns of Francis I and Henry II.

7.2 Why did France intervene in Italy in 1494 and what impact did it have on European affairs?

Charles VIII (1470–1498)

Born in Amboise on 30 June 1470, Charles was only 13 when his father, Louis XI, died. His older sister, Anne de Beaujeu, was regent during his minority (1483–1491). She crushed a rebellion of nobles, led by Duke Francis II of Brittany, in 1485. After Francis' death in 1491 Anne of Beaujeu made sure Brittany became attached to France through the marriage of Charles VIII to Anne, daughter of Francis II. Charles was regarded as weak and ineffectual as a ruler. He died at the age of 28.

Why did Charles VIII invade Italy?

If the reign of Louis XI was a turning point in the internal history of the French monarchy, then the reign of Charles VIII (1483–1498) saw a major change in the history of western Europe. The invasion of Italy in 1494 began a series of wars that resulted in a major conflict between the French royal house of Valois and the Habsburgs. These wars were to dominate western European affairs until 1559.

Why did Charles VIII wish to invade Italy? One view put forward by historians such as Janine Garrisson was that Charles VIII had ideas of leading a crusade against Islam. The first part of this plan was to be the conquest of Naples. Charles VIII was not regarded highly by either contemporaries or historians. One contemporary, Gasparo Contarini, described him as 'in body as in mind, he is of no great value'. While Commynes stated that Charles was 'very young, weakly wilful, rarely in the company of wise men [and] endowed with nether money nor sense'. In 'Lectures in European History', written in 1925, J.M. Thompson takes a similar view, by describing Charles VIII as a 'weak fool, full of romantic ideas'.

There is also a view that the idea did not come from Charles VIII but from his adviser, Guillaume Briconnet. He was an ambitious *general des finances* for part of southern France. He had been promised the position of Cardinal of the Catholic Church by the ruler of Milan if the French intervened in Italian affairs.

This view is linked to the fact that the French were invited to participate in a war in Italy by Ludovico Sforza, the Duke of Milan. Sforza needed French help. Once his nephew, Gian Galeazzo, reached adulthood he would become Duke of Milan in Ludovico's place. Galeazzo had the support of King Ferrante I of Naples. So Ludovico wanted the French to remove the threat of Naples. Sforza's invitation can be regarded as the pretext rather than the main reason for French intervention.

However, there were also dynastic reasons. Charles VIII had a claim to the throne of Naples. In 1481 his father, Louis XI, had received from Charles of Maine (a province of France) the right to succeed to the throne of Naples. This claim came at a time when France was in a position to expand. Louis XI had removed the threat of the French

French campaigns in Italy 1494–1516

1494–95 Charles VIII's invasion. Occupation of Naples
Retreat from Naples. Battle of Fournovo (1495) between French and Spanish.
Peace of Vercelli

1499–1500 The Milanese War of Louis XII
Battle of Novara (1500) – French defeat Ludovico Sforza of Milan.
Treaty of Granada (1500): Louis XII and Ferdinand of Aragon agree to divide Naples between them.

1502–1504 The Naples War of Louis XII
Battle of Garigliano (1503): French defeated by Spanish

1507 War against Genoa. French invade and occupy Genoa.

1508–10 War of the League of Cambrai. The League of Cambrai included Pope Julius II, Ferdinand of Aragon, Louis XII, Maximilian the Holy Roman Emperor, the Dukes of Savoy and Ferrara and the Marquis of Mantua against Venice.
Louis XII declares war on Venice (April 1509)
Battle of Agnadello (1509): Venice defeated by French

1512 War of the Holy League
Holy League had been formed in 1511 between Pope Julius II, Venice and Ferdinand of Aragon against France.
Battle of Ravenna (12 April 1512): French defeated

1513 Louis XII's Third Invasion of Italy
Treaty of Mechlin
Battle of Novara (6 June 1513): French defeated by Swiss

1515–1516 Francis I's invasion of Italy
Battle of Marignano (13 September 1515): French defeat Swiss
Concordat of Bologna between Francis I and the Pope (August 1516)
The Peace of Noyon (August 1516): agreement whereby Spain recognised French control of Milan.

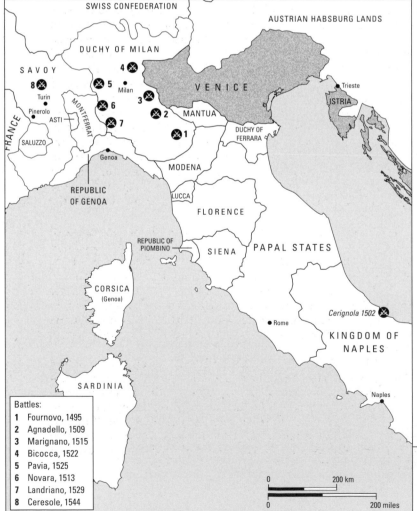

Battles:
1 Fournovo, 1495
2 Agnadello, 1509
3 Marignano, 1515
4 Bicocca, 1522
5 Pavia, 1525
6 Novara, 1513
7 Landriano, 1529
8 Ceresole, 1544

North Italy during the Italian Wars and Habsburg–Valois conflict

Papal States: dominated central Italy and ruled directly by the Pope. Its central location meant that the Pope would be involved in any political problem affecting Italy. Under Pope Julius II the Papacy took an active role in the Italian wars.

Florence: a wealthy Tuscan city state rule by the Medici family. The Medicis had been heavily involved in maintaining peace in Italy through the Italian League since 1455. By the early 1490s Florence was affected by the preachings of Savonarola which disrupted Florentine government until he was executed in 1494.

Genoa: a city state whose wealth was based on trade.

Venice: like Genoa, a city state whose wealth came from trade. Both city states were ruled by a Doge, a monarch who was elected from the wealthy members of each city.

Kingdom of Naples: dominated the southern part of Italy. Ruled by Ferrante I at the beginning of the Italian Wars. Centre of conflict between France and Spain.

Kingdoms of Sicily and Sardinia: both ruled by Spain.

Duchy of Milan: ruled by the Sforza family at the beginning of the Italian Wars. Claimed by Louis XII of France. Became a major source of conflict between France and the Habsburgs under Charles V.

Ferrara: a small state which had the misfortune of being bordered by both the Papal States and Venice.

Other states interested in Italy:
Aragon: controlled Sardinia and Sicily. Possessed a dynastic claim to Naples.
Holy Roman Empire: faced conflict with Venice over Austrian Habsburg lands on the Adriatic.
France: dynastic claims to Milan and Naples.

Which of the battles mentioned were (a) French victories? (b) Habsburg victories?

Louis XII (1462–1515)

Born at Blois on 27 June 1462, son of Charles Duke of Orléans and Mary of Cleves. Louis was forced to marry Joan of France, daughter of Louis XI. In 1488 he led a rebellion against the Regent Anne, which failed. He was imprisoned for three years as a result. Louis took part in the Italian Wars of 1494–95. He married three times. His second wife was Anne of Brittany, the widow of Charles VIII. After her death, in 1514, Louis married Mary Tudor, Henry VIII's sister, three months before his own death.

Francis I (1494–1547)

Born at Cognac on 13 September 1494, son of Charles of Orléans and Louise of Savoy. In 1514 he married Claude of France, the daughter of Louis XII and Anne of Brittany. As a result, Brittany came under his control in 1532. Louis XII died without leaving a son: under **Salic Law** Francis was the senior male heir. In 1529 he married Eleanor of Austria, the sister of Charles V, Holy Roman Emperor. Francis was a great patron of the arts and invited Italian artists such as da Vinci and Cellini to France.

Henry II (1519–1559)

Born in St Germain-en-Laye on 31 March 1519, the second son of Francis I and Claude of France. He became heir to the throne when his elder brother Francis died in 1536. In 1533 Henry married Catherine de' Medici who bore him ten children, three of whom later became kings of France (Francis II, Charles IX and Henry III). He was influenced when king by Anne de Montmorency and, during the latter part of his reign, by the Giuse family. Henry was planning a major persecution of Protestants when he died fighting in a tournament to celebrate the Treaty of Câteau-Cambrésis on 10 July 1559.

Salic Law: The law of succession in France where only males can become monarchs.

aristocracy. In 1488, at the Battle of Saint Aubin-du-Cormier, the Duke of Brittany had been decisively beaten. In 1491, by the Treaty of Sable, France gained direct control of Brittany. France had also made agreements with England, at the Treaty of Etaples in 1492, and with the Catholic Monarchs of Spain with the Treaty of Barcelona (1493). In this latter treaty, France gave up Roussillon and Cerdagne to Aragon. By the Treaty of Senlis, Charles gave Franche Comté and Artois back to Burgundy. As a result, Charles VIII had removed potential threats to France, allowing it to concentrate on Italy.

Finally, Italy held out to Charles VIII the possibility of increasing both his political power and wealth. Italy was the centre of Mediterranean trade. It contained wealthy city states such as Florence, Siena and Venice. By increasing French influence in Italy, Charles might also increase his own personal wealth. As L. W. Cowie states, in *Sixteenth Century Europe* (1977):

> 'The obvious battleground for the French was Italy. It was disunited and defenceless, offered valuable works of art and prosperous cities to loot, could be entered without great difficulty by French forces in possession of the Alps, and offered territory which would strengthen France's position in Europe and provide her with further Mediterranean ports.'

What impact did the French invasion have on Italian and European affairs to 1516?

The Italian Wars involved campaigns by three French kings: Charles VIII, Louis XII and Francis I. The French invasion also ended a period of peace in Italy which had existed since the Peace of Lodi of 1454. From 1494 to 1559 Italy became a major battleground in Europe. Initially, it involved France and the Italian states. French involvement forced both Spain and the Holy Roman Emperor to protect their influence in Italy. The wars became a central feature of the Habsburg–Valois wars that affected western Europe under the French kings Francis I and Henry II.

The French invasion showed the political disunity and military weakness of the Italian states. The French army of 25,000 crossed the Italian peninsula with ease to take control of Naples by the end of February 1495. A major factor in France's success was their military power. No individual Italian state possessed a military force to stop an army of 25,000. Another factor was the unpopularity of some Italian rulers. The French were welcomed into Florence because of the unpopularity of the ruling Medici family at that time.

However, Charles VIII's invasion had the almost immediate effect of creating a coalition of states against France. Only a month after the French entry into Naples, on 22 February 1495, the League of Venice (or Holy League) was formed. It included most Italian states, except Florence, the Pope, Ferdinand of Aragon and Emperor Maximilian of the Holy Roman Empire. Charles VIII was forced to withdraw from Naples. In July 1495 he narrowly avoided a major defeat at the Battle of Fournovo. In the Treaty of Alcala, with Ferdinand of Aragon, he agreed to divide Naples with the Spanish.

The wars of Louis XII between 1500 and 1515 widened the conflict further. Through war and diplomacy Louis attempted to re-establish French influence in Naples and to take over Milan. French intervention also encouraged conflict between Italian states. However, by the time of Louis' death, French claims to Milan and Naples were unfulfilled. It took Francis I to complete Louis XII's aim of taking Milan. His victory over the Swiss at Marignano, in 1515, re-established French power in North Italy.

The Battle of Pavia, 1525 – tapestry by B. van Orley

?

1. Which of the following reasons do you regard as the most important in explaining the French invasion of Italy in 1494?

a) The claim of Charles VIII to the kingdom of Naples

b) The internal stability of France

c) The wealth and disunity of the Italian states.

Give reasons for your answer.

2. Why was France unsuccessful in increasing its influence in Italy during the reigns of Charles VIII and Louis XII?

3. 'The Italian Wars of 1494 to 1516 show that the Italian states were not in control of their own destiny.' Assess the validity of this statement.

Renaissance warfare

The Italian Wars provide an excellent example of the types of land warfare used in early 16th-century Europe. By the time of the Renaissance medieval type warfare was giving way to a new form based on the military formations of Ancient Rome. The most effective unit in medieval warfare had been cavalry (knights in armour). These eventually gave way to infantry.

The bulk of any army was the infantry. These were used in closely formed units on the battlefield. Most rulers relied on professional soldiers (mercenaries) to provide the central force. The Swiss had a reputation of providing the best infantry. They defeated Charles the Bold at the Battle of Nancy in 1477. Their reputation as the best European troops lasted until the Battle of Marignano in 1515. The French were able to supplement their infantry with the raising of French troops. The main weapons of the infantry were the pike and halberd. These were merely long wooden poles with an iron spike or lance at the end. The preferred weapon, however, was the firearm. The arquebus (see page 239) was a forerunner of the musket. It was cumbersome, had a range of around 200 yards (190 metres) and was very unreliable in rain.

A major advance in military technology was the bronze cannon. The use of cannons helps explain the speed and success of the French invasions of 1494 and 1500. However, as the century progressed, better fortifications limited the effects of artillery. It also helps explain the indecisive nature of warfare between Valois France and the Habsburgs.

The traditional part of the army for noblemen had been the cavalry. The nobility usually volunteered for service. In 1498 Louis XII of France created a light cavalry. This force used arquebuses and fought on foot, but used horses for mobility around the battle-field. Cavalry had been defeated decisively by infantry at the Battle of Agincourt in 1415. However, the French cavalry of Francis I decisively defeated the Swiss infantry at the Battle of Marignano in 1515.

The Italian Wars of 1494 to 1516 show how weak the individual Italian states were to foreign intervention. Not only had France occupied Milan and Genoa by 1516, Spain had taken control of Naples. Italian weakness can be demonstrated by the Treaty of Granada, of 1500, where France and Aragon agreed to partition Naples between themselves. The wars opened up old wounds between Italian states. For instance, in 1482 Venice had gone to war with Milan and Naples over Ferrara. The wars saw a reappearance of this rivalry. The insert on French campaigns in Italy (page 154) illustrates how individual Italian states changed sides in this period for their own advantage.

The Italian Wars did demonstrate that French intervention could be opposed if the Italian states worked together. The League of Venice of 1495 forced Charles VIII out of Naples. The Holy League of 1511 forced Louis XII out of Milan by 1513. A major player in organising these alliances was Pope Julius II.

7.3 How far did the French economy and society change between 1450 and 1559?

In what ways did the size and distribution of France's population change between 1450 and 1559?

In the century before 1450 France had suffered the double blow of a major epidemic – the Black Death, which had affected most of Europe after 1349 – and the ravages of war. Any calculation of the French population in this period is likely to be a general estimate. Reliable population data simply does not exist. In 1929 the French historian F. Lot calculated that the French population in 1328 was somewhere around 16 million. This fell dramatically because of the Black Death and the effects of the 100 Years' War. However, historian Pierre Chaunu, writing in 1977, believed the population had recovered by 1500 to 16 million again. E. Le Roy Ladurie believes it had risen to 20 million by 1559.

There are various reasons put forward for this population change. One was the relative absence of plague and epidemics in this period. This is particularly true of the fall in leprosy in the first half of the 16th century. Infant mortality dropped by approximately 30% in the half century after 1450, as a result. Also, although France was at war for much of the period 1450–1559, the vast majority of the fighting took place outside France.

Another reason was a lowering in the age of marriage for women. This led to an increase in the number of children born. The birth rate figure for much of this period was 40 births per thousand. This development, combined with an increase in the number of marriages, led to an increase in population. According to the Burgundian chronicler Jean de Clerq, writing in 1466, 'From Easter until the middle of August there were more marriages in the towns and villages of Artois and Picardy than the older folk could recall ever having seen before, or having heard from their forbears.'

Not only did the French population grow, but its distribution also changed. In 1450, 95% of all French people lived as peasants in villages. Most were engaged in **subsistence agriculture**. During the century after 1450, there was a noticeable migration from the countryside into towns. For instance, Lyons grew from 20,000 in 1450 to 40,000 by 1500, and to 70,000 by 1550. By far the largest French town was Paris with a population of 300,000 by 1560.

Part of the reason for this movement was the poor quality of agricultural land in parts of France. Peasants from the Massif Central area migrated to Languedoc. Those in Brittany migrated to Normandy for similar reasons. Also, many landowners attempted to improve their lands through increasing the size of farms. However, the main cause of migration within France, in particular to towns, was the increase in population.

Subsistence agriculture: This is the production of food solely for those that produce it and not for market.

Did French society become more unified in the period 1450–1559?

In 1450 the kingdom of France was divided by language, law and custom. French, as we know it today, is *langue d'oil*. It was spoken in northern France. In southern France people spoken another language, similar to French, known as *langue d'oc*. Today this language is known as occitan. On the edges of the kingdom, Breton was spoken in Brittany, Flemish in Flanders, Basque in the south west and Provençal in the south east. With the impact of printing and an increase in the education of lay people, French became the language of the ruling classes.

France was also divided by law, customs, weights and measures. Weights and measures differed from region to region, even from town to town. The method of assessing taxes also varied. The direct tax, the taille, was assessed differently in northern and southern France. Each province possessed its own law. In northern France customary law dominated; in southern France it was Roman law.

How did industry and trade develop between 1450 and 1559?

The increase in population and the growth of towns aided the development of the French economy. A feature of the growth in economic prosperity was the increase in the number of fairs and markets in towns. This development was encouraged by kings such as Louis XI who granted permission for them to take place. Markets provided a location for the sale of agricultural produce. Fairs encouraged foreign traders to France to sell their goods. The biggest fair in France by the early 16th century took place in Lyons.

Overseas trade also developed. Following the end of the 100 Years' War, France's Atlantic and Mediterranean ports began to improve their trade links. The most important ports to develop were Marseilles on the Mediterranean and Bordeaux on the Bay of Biscay. The latter grew as a result of the wine trade.

During the period 1450–1559, the French wine industry grew considerably. This was particularly true of the Bordeaux area, which produced claret. Wine was produced not only for home consumption but also for export to countries such as England.

Although the main cloth-producing areas of western Europe were Flanders and Tuscany, France did begin to develop its own industry at this time. It was centred on Languedoc in southern France. An industry where France proved to be an important European leader was printing. France received its first printing press in 1470 at the Sorbonne University in Paris. University towns were the main centres and purchasers of printed books. Initially, books tended to be on religious themes such as the Bible and the 'Imitation of Christ' by Thomas à Kempis. However, these were followed by books on Ancient Roman classics such as Cicero and Ovid. By the early 16th century, printed books in French were beginning to appear. An offshoot of this industry was the development of newsletters. These were important to the major social development in France during the 16th century, the appearance of Protestantism.

Why did Protestantism develop in France?

Christian humanist movement:
The development of new ideas about how the Catholic church should operate in the Renaissance period. Usually associated with critics of the Church such as Erasmus. This movement hoped to reform the Church from within, not create a new Protestant Church.

Protestantism developed in France for a number of reasons. Firstly, it was linked to the **Christian humanist movement** associated with individuals such as Erasmus. Criticism of the Catholic Church, combined with the availability of printed books on religious issues, helped the spread of Protestantism. There seems to be a close correlation between the level of literacy and the growth of Protestantism. This is certainly true of studies of Protestantism in Lyons and Dijon. As historian Robin Briggs states in *Early Modern France* (1977):

> 'By the 1540s the pace of conversions was becoming rapid. By this date Calvin had given Protestantism a form which was well calculated both to win and to hold the loyalty of Frenchmen; his establishment of a base at Geneva gave him the opportunity to train ministers. The French Catholic Church was in no state to take up the challenge, plagued as it was by non-residence and ignorance on the part of its clergy.'

Historians are increasingly coming to link the rise of Protestantism with economic factors. By the 1540s economic prosperity was giving way to economic crisis. Urban workers and craftsmen were facing a fall in their standard of living due to rising prices (inflation). By the 1540s

Protestant groups had been identified in Orléans, Soissons and Rouen. There does seem to be a link between Protestant ideas and urban areas. R. J. Knecht, in *The Rise and Fall of Renaissance France 1483–1610* (1995), points out that 'Calvinism drew its adherents from virtually all strata of society and from a bewildering variety of occupations'.

However, the growth of Protestantism did not go unchecked. On the night of 18 October 1534 Protestant placards (or posters) were put up in many French towns. A placard was even put on the door of Francis I's bedchamber. This event led to the persecution of Protestantism by the authorities. The parlements of France had the responsibility of dealing with this problem.

It is difficult to state how many Protestants there were in France by 1559. The first Calvinist Church in Paris had opened in 1555. However, the growth of Protestantism was sufficiently worrying to act as a factor in ending the Habsburg–Valois Wars. Both Henry II and Philip II wanted peace by 1559 so they could deal with **heresy** in their own lands.

Heresy: The rejection of the doctrines and authority of the Roman Catholic Church.

Conclusion

In 1559 France signed the Treaty of Câteau-Cambrésis which ended over 40 years of warfare with the Habsburgs. This should have been a moment of celebration. But, as Janine Garrisson points out in *A History of Sixteenth Century France* (1995), 'The Treaty demobilised thousands of gentlemen and even more soldiers. More than 40 years of foreign war, of regular pay and frequent plunder, had accustomed gentlemen and commoners alike to a warrior's life. It was hard for them to settle back down to a civilian existence.'

Also by 1559 France had entered upon a period of social and economic crisis. The rise in population and prices led to an increase in poverty and hardship. The number of beggars and vagabonds increased by mid-century. The growth of printing and new religious ideas, combined with these economic changes, led to the growth of Protestantism. Under a strong monarch these social and economic forces were kept in check. As historian R. J. Knecht has noted: 'France in 1559 was a nation in crisis: the economy was showing signs of strain, social tensions were mounting, and religious differences were becoming acute. On top of all this, the death of Henry II created a vacuum at the heart of government which various factions competed to fill.'

1. Draw a spidergram showing the main social and economic changes in France between 1450 and 1559.

2. Why was France on the verge of a major social and economic crisis by 1559?

7.4 How successful was the foreign policy of Francis I and Henry II?

What were the causes of war between the Habsburgs and Valois France?

The central feature of French foreign policy under Francis I and Henry II was the Habsburg–Valois conflict. This involved a series of wars up to the Treaty of Câteau-Cambrésis of 1559.

In some ways the Habsburg–Valois conflict was a continuation of the Italian Wars. Francis I pursued his dynastic claims to both Milan and Naples. As a 'Renaissance Prince' he also wanted the international prestige and glory of being a successful king in battle.

However, this conflict widened with the election in 1519 of Charles I of Spain as Emperor Charles V of the Holy Roman Empire. Charles V ruled a variety of territories. These included Castile and Aragon, the Netherlands, Franche Comté and the Habsburg lands of Austria. If you look at the map on page 162 you will see that Charles' possessions encircled France. From

The Habsburg–Valois Wars

Study the maps on pages 154 and 162 to find the location of the places mentioned below.

The First War: 1521–1526

1521 French attack Spanish Navarre. Habsburgs attack Mézières in France.

1522 Milan revolt against France. French forced from city.

Battle of La Bicocca, near Milan: defeat for France. Habsburgs capture Genoa.

1524 Charles of Bourbon defects to Charles V. He invades France. Siege of Marseilles

Francis I invades Milan

1525 (February) Battle of Pavia: French defeat by Habsburgs. Francis I captured.

1526 Treaty of Madrid: Francis gives Burgundy to Charles, renounces all claims to Italy, promises to marry Charles's sister Eleanor, and to join a crusade against the Turks.

Francis I refuses to honour the treaty.

The Second War: 1527–1529

1526 The League of Cognac against Charles V: contained France, Venice, the Pope, England.

1527 Habsburg troops occupy Florence. Sack of Rome by Habsburg troops

1528 French take Lombardy in Italy, occupy Rome and besiege Naples.

Genoa defects to Charles V. Cuts off French army in south Italy.

1529 Defeat of French at Landriano in North Italy by Habsburgs: Peace of Cambrai (Ladies' Peace). Francis I gives up all lands in Italy. He gives up the border towns of Lille and Tournai in the Netherlands to Charles. He also pays a ransom of 2 million écus which sees the release of his two sons who had been held hostage since 1526 by Charles.

Treaty of Barcelona. Sforza family reinstated as rulers of Milan under Habsburg protection. Pope recognises Charles V as King of Naples and agrees to crown him Holy Roman Emperor. Habsburgs dominate Italy.

The Third War: 1536–1538

1536 French attack Savoy and Piedmont in north Italy.

Charles V invades northern France, Piedmont and Provence in south-east France.

A Spanish army attacks Narbonne in south-west France.

1537 French retake Piedmont.

1538 Truce of Nice, with the Pope acting as peacemaker.

The Fourth War: 1542–1544

1541 French agents assassinated at Casale near Milan.

Fighting near Perpignan, in Roussillon.

1542 French occupy Luxembourg.

1543 French and Ottoman fleets attack Nice. Ottoman fleet 'winter' in Toulon.

1544 French victory at Battle of Ceresole in north Italy. Victory not exploited.

1545 Charles V and Mary of Hungary invade France. They occupy Epernay and Chateau Thierry near Paris. England attacks France and takes Boulogne.

Treaty of Crépy on 18 September. France abandons claims to lands in Italy. Charles abandons claim to Burgundy. War with England continues until 1546.

1547 Francis I dies.

French army sent to Scotland.

Mary Stuart to marry Dauphin.

The Fifth War: 1552–1556

1551 Henry II renews alliance between France and the Turks.

1552 Treaty of Chambord between Henry II and Maurice of Saxony.

French attack Rhineland; take Metz, Verdun and Toul.

1553 French take Vercelli in Italy.

1554 French invade the Netherlands. French take Casale in Italy.

1554–55 Siege of Siena. French troops besieged by Habsburgs.

1556 The five year truce of Vaucelles. French allowed to keep territory in Piedmont and Corsica.

The Sixth War: 1557–1559

1557 French denounce truce, supported by Pope Paul IV.

Spanish invade Papal States.

French army sent to aid Pope.

England joins war against the French.

Battle of St Quentin in northern France. Emmanuel Philibert of Savoy destroys French army.

1558 French take Calais from England.

1559 Treaty of Câteau-Cambrésis ends Habsburg–Valois Wars.

1519 to the mid-17th century, a major aim of French monarchs was to break Habsburg encirclement.

According to David Potter, in *A History of France 1460–1560* (1995), 'the most obvious element of continuity in French policy was the obsession with Italy'. In particular, Francis I was obsessed with Milan. This obsession combined a number of French aims. Its possession would increase Francis' international prestige and it would bring him glory and wealth. It would also break the Habsburg encirclement of France.

On the Habsburg side, Charles wanted to see the return of the Duchy of Burgundy lost to France during the reign of Louis XI. There was also a degree of personal dislike. The most obvious dated from the election of Holy Roman Emperor in 1519. Following his great victory at Marignano, in 1515, Francis I thought he would become the leader of western Christendom through election to the position of Holy Roman Emperor. Having spent 400,000 écus in bribes to the electors of the Emperor, Francis I was very upset when he narrowly lost the election to Charles V. This personal animosity was made worse by the Treaty of Madrid in 1526. Having been captured after the Battle of Pavia (1525), Francis I signed this treaty and then refused to acknowledge it. As a result, Charles V kept Francis I's sons hostage until Francis paid a ransom for their return in 1529. In May 1536 there was even the possibility that King and Emperor would settle their differences by single combat in a duel.

How did the Habsburg–Valois Wars affect Europe?

This Habsburg–Valois conflict was not limited to the Habsburgs and the Valois; the wars also involved Italian states – Savoy and Milan became a major battleground. The wars also involved the Pope, Venice and Siena. In north-western Europe, England and Scotland became involved. On several occasions England became allies of Charles V, as part of Henry VIII's attempt to win back lost territory in France. Although England did gain Tournai and Boulogne for a short period, they ultimately lost their last territory in France with the fall of Calais in 1558. In retaliation for English involvement on the side of Charles V, the French intervened in Scotland in the 1550s.

Throughout the Habsburg–Valois conflict, Charles V was distracted by other problems involving the Turks and German Protestants. In 1529 the Turks laid siege to Vienna. For much of Charles V's reign the Turks were a threat to the Habsburg lands in Austria and in the Mediterranean. In Germany, Charles V faced the Schmalkaldic League of Lutheran princes. The French exploited both of these problems for their own benefit. In the 1530s, Francis I met representatives of the Schmalkaldic League. He even financed their armies. In 1552, Henry II formed an alliance with the Protestant Maurice of Saxony against Charles. In the winter of 1543–44 the Ottoman Mediterranean fleet was allowed to use the French naval base of Toulon. These acts, by Francis I and Henry II, widened the conflict to include most of Europe.

In a broader sense, the Habsburg–Valois Wars aided the increase in political power of the Ottoman Turks. Throughout the first half of the 16th century, Ottoman power grew rapidly in the Balkans and the Mediterranean. On several occasions both the Pope and Charles V called for a crusade of Christian Europe against the Turks. The Habsburg–Valois conflict prevented this crusade from taking place. Even worse, Catholic France allied with the Islamic Ottomans against the Habsburgs. The Wars also aided the growth and consolidation of Protestantism in Germany. French support for the Schmalkaldic League of Protestant princes allowed them to survive Charles V's attacks (see Chapter 5).

Using the information contained in the table on page 160, answer the following questions.

1. Apart from France and Charles V which other states were involved in the Habsburg–Valois conflict?

2. In which part of Europe did most of the fighting take place?

Why did the Habsburg–Valois conflict come to an end in 1559?

The long period of warfare from 1494 came to an end with the Treaty of Câteau-Cambrésis. There seems to be little difference between that treaty and previous attempts to end the Habsburg–Valois wars, such as Madrid in 1526, Cambrai in 1529 and Crépy in 1544. The main difference was that from 1559 to 1598 France became involved in a major political crisis.

However, there were other factors which brought the wars to an end. Both Henry II of France and Philip II of Spain were concerned about the growth of Protestantism in their lands. France was on the eve of a series of Wars of Religion; Philip II faced the growth of Protestantism in the Netherlands.

More important was the issue of financing the wars. In 1557 Philip II had to declare himself bankrupt. Both Francis I and Henry II also had acute financial problems. Conducting war between 1515 and 1559 was an increasingly expensive business. Firstly, a major cost of warfare was payment for mercenary troops. The French used Swiss and German mercenaries. Also, as fortifications became more sophisticated, sieges lasted

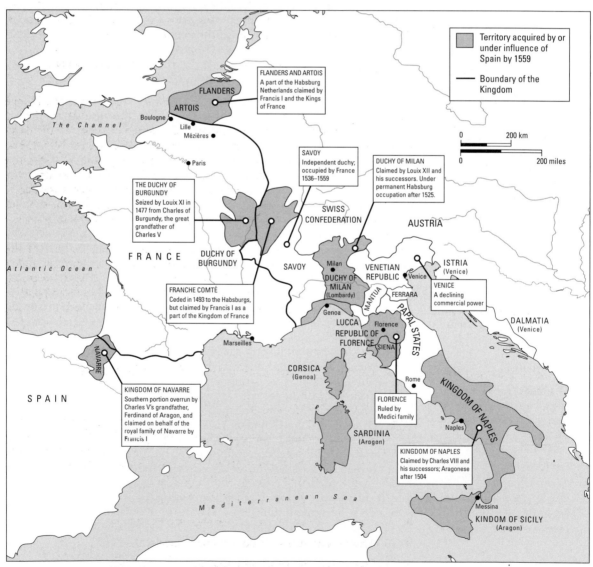

The French kingdom, 1559, showing how it was surrounded by Habsburgs.

longer and therefore became more costly. The latter stages of the Habsburg–Valois wars were characterised by sieges, such as Metz in 1552, St Quentin in 1557 and Calais in 1558.

During Francis I's reign, the financial base of the French monarchy saw little change. The main taxes were still the taille, gabelle and aides. However, the burden of taxation rose.

- The taille: 2.4 million livres in 1515 rose to 9 million livres in 1546 (taking out inflation).

- The gabelle: 400,000 livres c.1515 to 700,000 livres in 1547.

- Aides: 1.2 million livres c.1515 to 2.15 million livres by the end of the reign.

Unfortunately, these rises did not provide sufficient revenue to pay for the costs of war. Francis raised money through selling jobs in the parlements, and seized money from the Catholic Church. In 1543 Francis even placed a tax on walled towns. He also borrowed from bankers and members of the aristocracy. By the time of his death, Francis I owed the bankers of Lyons alone nearly 7 million livres. Henry II continued to borrow heavily. However, defeat at St Quentin ruined his creditors. By the time of Henry II's death, France was on the verge of bankruptcy.

How successful were Francis I and Henry II in their foreign policy?

After nearly constant warfare in Europe between 1515 and 1559, France had little to show for its efforts. In Italy the Habsburgs still dominated Milan and Naples. France kept control of a small number of towns in north-west Italy: Pinerolo, Turin and Saluzzo. The Treaty of Câteau-Cambrésis of 1559 also marks the beginning of a period of European history where Spain was the dominant power. This was to last until the middle of the 17th century. However, France did gain some advantages. On its eastern border it kept Metz, Toul and Verdun. In the north it had recovered Calais. In addition, Philip II gave up all hope of recovering the duchy of Burgundy.

Internally, the wars had placed great strains on the finances of the French monarchy. It also created social problems and tensions which would surface in the form of civil war after 1559. According to historian Janine Garrisson 'the Treaty of Câteau-Cambrésis was a turning point in French history. The year 1559, like 1815 and 1940, was a channel which engulfed "French passions".'

1. What were France's aims in foreign policy between 1515 and 1559?

2. What methods did the French use to achieve their foreign policy objectives?

3. Why did the Habsburg–Valois wars last so long?

4. To what extent was the Treaty of Câteau-Cambrésis a defeat for France?

7.5 How powerful was the French monarchy under Francis I and Henry II?
A CASE STUDY IN HISTORICAL INTERPRETATION

The reigns of Francis I and Henry II have been the subject of debate among historians for much of this century. Traditionally, their reigns have been seen as examples of Renaissance or 'New' monarchy. This differed from medieval monarchy in the following ways.

- The monarchy became financially independent.

- The political power of the aristocracy was reduced.

- Government administration became centralised.

- The use of lawyers in administration.

These changes increased the political power of the monarchy. The main historical questions are to what extent the French monarchy increased its power in this period and did the reigns of Francis I and Henry II create a new type of monarchic government for France?

The main debate on this issue has involved a British and an American historian. In Britain, R. J. Knecht has supported the view that the French monarchy did increase its political power to the point where it could be described as absolutist. In contrast, J. Russell Major believes that the French monarchy possessed many medieval characteristics. He has described it as a 'popular and consultative' type of monarchy. This meant that neither monarchy had the political or military power to rule without consent. His views were contained in two main works: *Representative Institutions in Renaissance France, 1421–1559* (1960) and *Representative Government in Early Modern France* (1980). Why have these historians differed in their views?

The case that France became an absolutist monarchy

The symbolic position of the King of France
According to R. J. Knecht, in *Francis I and Absolute Monarchy* (1969), 'the doctrine of absolute monarchy existed in Renaissance France'. Even before the reign of Francis I, the king of France possessed considerable power. The use of Salic Law helped to ensure that the succession to the throne was not disputed.

This position stands in marked contrast to England where, between 1399 and 1485, four kings were deposed (Richard II, Henry VI, Edward V and Richard III). In addition, at the *sacrée* (the coronation) the king was anointed which gave him special powers – such as the ability to cure **scrofula**. Apart from a priest, the king was the only person to take both bread and wine at Communion during Mass.

Scrofula: An inflammation of the neck caused by tuberculosis of the lymph gland.

The king was seen as the dispenser of justice. This was enhanced by the king's travels around his kingdom fulfilling this role. Through judicial hearings, processions, literature and the construction of large royal chateaux the French monarchy possessed the image of great power. Even the Parlement of Paris admitted that its authority came from the king.

Relations with the Catholic Church
A major argument in favour of an increase in royal power in this period is the Concordat of Bologna of 1516 with Pope Leo X. The Concordat stated that bishops and abbots would be nominated by the King but would be given their spiritual office by the Pope. This ended the French Church's custom of electing bishops and abbots. The Concordat also gave the king of France a tenth of all monies raised for the Pope within France. According to historian Janine Garrisson, 'The Concordat was a crucial document in aligning the Church of France and its enormous landed wealth behind the Crown. From now on, bishops and abbots were the king's men. The French clergy became the king's trump card. What need was there to follow Henry VIII into schism [break with Rome], or to emulate the German princes in raising the banner of the Reformation?'

Finance
France was almost continuously at war during the period 1450–1559. Therefore, finance was extremely important. In *French Renaissance Monarchy: Francis I and Henry II* (1984), R. J. Knecht states that 'by the end of Francis I's reign three objectives of his financial reforms had been achieved: centralisation; uniformity and simplification'.

It seems clear that at the beginning of Francis I's reign little change had been made to the tax system since the end of the 100 Years' War (see insert on French taxation). Four officials, called *Tresoriers de France*, were responsible for ordinary taxation. The collection of extraordinary taxation was handled by four *Generaux des finances*. Each was responsible for an area called a *généralité*. Mainly as a result of the financial demands of war, attempts were made to improve the financial administration in 1515–17, 1522–24 and 1542–44. For instance, in 1523 a new official, the *Tresorier de l'Epargne* (Treasurer of the Central Treasury) was put in overall control of the king's revenues. He owed allegiance directly to the king. In 1524 this new official was aided by the *recever des parties cauelles*. One of his functions was to handle the money raised from the sale of offices (jobs).

In 1542, in the Edict of Cognac, Francis joined the administrations of ordinary and extraordinary revenue. He divided the four généralités into 16 new districts called *recettes-general*. Not only was the financial system altered but also the king had the right to tax without the need for agreement with any consultative body such as an assembly or parlement. France was divided into two areas: the *pays d'élections* and the *pays d'états*. The *pays d'élections* were provinces of France where taxes were set by the King's Council. This covered most of France. The *pays d'états* were provinces where the right to tax was made by local estates. These provinces included Languedoc, Brittany, Burgundy and Provence. However, according to R. J. Knecht, the king could raise a new tax in the *pays d'état* without prior consultation. He states in *The Rise and Fall of Renaissance France* (1996): 'In Languedoc, the towns, clergy and nobility were all taxed regardless of the estates. Only Carcassonne was totally exempt. Francis none the less imposed an infantry tax on them.'

Central and local administration

At the beginning of Francis I's reign, the king had the power to appoint some 4,000 officials to enforce his views throughout France. During the period 1515 to 1559 this number increased rapidly, mainly as a way of raising money because many of these jobs were sold. As Robin Briggs notes in *Early Modern France* (1977), 'the king established a new court or tribunal to exercise judicial or administrative functions in a particular area. Posts in this new institution were then offered for sale, with the attraction of a small salary paid by the Crown. In many ways the system was an ingenious extension of patronage, since the new officials were dependent on the king and his council for support in the exercise of their powers.'

Another example of royal power within France was the position of provincial governor. Although their precise role is difficult to define, they were appointed by the king to settle local disputes. The French historian Bernard Chevalier saw them as part of a process that saw a real increase in royal power during the early 16th century.

The Parlements and the dispensing of justice

According to Claude de Seyssel, in *La Monarchie de France* written in 1515, the greatness of French kings came from their willingness to accept three restraints on their power: religion, justice and the police. A central feature on any debate about the extent of royal power in France must address the relationship between the king and the parlements. The parlements possessed considerable power. They had the right to hear judicial cases and could raise taxes in the *pay d'états* provinces. In relation to the king, they had the authority to register royal decrees. Without their agreement, royal decrees did not have the force of law.

However, R. J. Knecht provides a wide variety of examples to prove that the power of the parlements was limited. The Concordat of 1516 was widely disliked by many groups within France, including the Parlement of Paris. The agreement took away the right to elect bishops and abbots and seemed to increase the power of the Pope within France. The Parlement refused to register the Concordat. Francis I used bullying tactics to force the Parlement to submit, which included the threat of setting up a rival parlement in Poitiers. As a result, the Parlement of Paris accepted the Concordat. In 1540 the Parlement of Rouen faced similar tactics by Francis. The Parlement failed to register 16 sections of the Ordinance of Villers-Cotterets. Francis I forbade the Parlement to go into recess until it registered the Ordinance. Eventually, in September, Francis closed down the parlement. However, it was reopened in 1541.

The king's authority over the parlements was also reflected in his control over provincial estates such as those in the *pays d'états*. After all, the king called them, fixed the date and place of their meeting, appointed the president and determined their agenda.

The fact that neither Francis I nor Henry II called a meeting of the Estates General supports the view that royal power was not limited by the need to consult. This view is enforced by Francis I's use of the *lit de justice*. This was the personal appearance of the king in a parlement to enforce the registration of legislation. As historian Janine Garrisson notes, the *lit de justice* was 'a piece of royal theatre, magnificently staged and crushing to those it was designed to coerce'. An example was the *lit de justice* of 24 July 1527 when the Parlement of Paris was forced to register a law about appeal to the Grand Council.

On one occasion, Francis I called an Assembly of Notables. This was a meeting which was somewhere between a *lit de justice* and an Estates General. It took place in 1527. It was called because Francis I needed money to pay for the release of his two sons held hostage by Charles V since 1526. It was also asked to refuse the Treaty of Madrid. On both issues, the assembly agreed.

The case against the view that Absolute Monarchy was created in France

The parlements and the dispensing of justice

J. Russell Major, in *Representative Institutions in Renaissance France 1421–1559* (1960), states that 'the popular, consultative nature of monarchy continued unmodified for the first third of the period and was only mildly altered thereafter'. This view is supported by the fact that parlements did exist and did possess considerable power. On occasions kings were forced to use intimidation but these were the exception rather than the rule. Far from being an 'absolute monarch', Francis I created three new parlements during his reign: Rouen 1515; Dijon 1523 and Grenoble 1537.

The king also consulted with his subjects on important matters. In 1517 Francis I called an Assembly of Towns and in 1527 an Assembly of Notables. A view on how limited Francis I saw his role was put forward by Louise of Savoy in 1525, during Francis I's imprisonment following the Battle of Pavia. She stated to the Parlement of Paris: 'It is not necessary that he [the king] often use his absolute power, which is reserved for great and urgent affairs.'

The King's power was limited further by the lack of any uniform law within his kingdom. In the north, customary law operated; in the south, Roman law. No attempt was made in this period to centralise the legal system. Instead, the French monarchs were willing to allow the local nobility considerable power in dispensing law in their own areas.

Administration

Although the number of office holders increased in this period, local power was firmly in the hands of the nobility. The historian David Potter

Charles of Bourbon: The clash between Francis I and Charles of Bourbon was similar to the clash between Louis XI and Charles the Bold of Burgundy.

Charles had a large amount of land in central France. He had the power to raise his own taxes and had a large personal army. He held one of the three most important offices of state, Constable of France. In 1521 Charles' wife, Suzanne of Bourbon, died. Her nearest relative was Louise of Savoy, the mother of Francis I, who claimed Bourbon lands.

Charles had his lands confiscated in 1523 because he refused to marry Louise of Savoy. He left France and entered the service of Charles V. Charles of Bourbon made an alliance with Charles V and Henry VIII of England. They planned a joint invasion of France. Charles was to receive Burgundy and lands in Provence. He invaded France on 7 July 1524. He besieged Marseilles but failed to take it. The Bourbon lands first went to Louise of Savoy and, on her death, to Francis I.

believes that the idea that lawyers began to take a major role in French administration at this time is a myth. Apart from the notable exception of **Charles of Bourbon**, the great noble families still retained considerable power. The career of Anne de Montmorency illustrates this point. Anne was a major adviser to Henry II and maintained great power in his own region. [Anne was a male name in France at this time.] As J. Russell Major notes, 'The Valois, like the Tudors, had to rely on the support of their more powerful subjects.'

The failure to achieve greater centralisation is understandable when one considers the size and geography of France and the lack of communications. Also, parts of the French kingdom were not directly under the king's control. This is true of Brittany before 1532 and Navarre for the whole of the period.

The Church

The Concordat of Bologna increased the king's personal control over the French Church. However, it did not stop the growth of Protestantism. It was only with the Affair of the Placards in October 1534 that Francis I took action. However, for most of the period the need to root out heresy and to try religious cases was put into the hands of local parlements. By 1559 Protestantism had grown rapidly in France, thereby undermining the king's authority in religious matters.

Finance

A major feature of a 'New' or Renaissance monarchy is the financial independence of the king. Although both Francis I and Henry II reformed the financial system, they failed to achieved financial independence. The main taxes were still the taille, gabelle and aides by the end

Provinces of France in 1552

of this period. The effects of almost continuous war meant that the monarchy had to borrow heavily from bankers. By the time of Henry II's death, the monarchy faced bankruptcy.

Conclusion

Whether you believe that France in this period became an absolute monarchy depends on your definition of the term 'absolute'. R. J. Knecht believes that 'absolutism existed in theory'. This means that the French king possessed the authority to rule without the need for consultation. In practice, the king did possess considerable power. He had the right to conduct foreign policy and to lead his army in battle. However, after the Battle of Pavia Francis I gave up the latter right. Also, the king had the power to dispense justice for the common good. As one deputy at the Estates General in Orléans, in 1560, remarked, 'justice alone distinguishes kings from tyrants, for both of them have the same power'. In this sense, the king did not possess the authority to do what he liked. From the information contained in this section you will have to decide whether or not French monarchs in this period were tyrants.

1. What are the main areas of disagreement between R. J. Knecht and J. Russell Major about the power of the French monarchy between 1515 and 1559?

2. Why have historians differed in their views about the power of Francis I and Henry II?

Source-based questions: Francis I and absolute monarchy

SOURCE A

Of these bridles by which the absolute power of the king of France is regulated I deem that there are three main ones. The first is religion, the second justice, the third the polity.

As to the first, it is certain that the people of France have always been and still are devout and religious above all other nations. So it is essential that whoever is king make known to the people by example that he is a zealous observant of the Christian faith. If the people had another opinion of him, they would hate him and perhaps obey him but ill. If the king lives in accordance with the Christian religion he can scarcely act tyrannically.

The second bridle is justice, which beyond any doubt is in greater authority in France than in any other country of the world, especially on account of the Parlements, which were institutions chiefly to bridle the absolute power that the kings might want to use.

The third bridle is that of polity, that is to say, the many ordinances, made by the kings of France themselves which tend to the conservation of the realm in general and in detail. These have been kept for such a long time that the princes never undertake to derogate [detract] from them; and if they wanted to do so, their commands would not be obeyed.

From The Monarchy of France
by Claude de Seyssel, 1515

SOURCE B

The king forbids you to meddle in any way in affairs of state or in anything other than justice and commands that each year you shall obtain letters confirming your delegated authority.

He forbids you to judge [religious] matters and declares null and void any attempt by you to contravene this ban. He also cancels all the limitations imposed by you on the power and regency of his mother. He has revoked all that you have attempted in dealing with cases on appeal, appointments etc.

The king forbids the court to apply in future any limitations to his ordinances, edicts and charters. Should members of the court find it necessary in the interest of the king or the state to add or remove something, they will bring this to the king's notice.

The king declares that you have no jurisdiction over the chancellor of France. This belongs to the king alone and no one else.

From an edict by the King defining the power of Parlement, July 1527

SOURCE C

Absolutism in practice has always fallen short of its theoretical completeness and Francis would appear to have been about as absolute as any European monarch of his day could ever hope to be. He repeatedly expressed his determination not to tolerate any 'Venetian Senate' in his kingdom and never showed the slightest inclination to take advice from a circle wider than his own council. The Concordat was imposed upon the Church against its wishes and those of the Parlement and University of Paris. By his use of special judicial commissions the king showed contempt for the normal process of the law. It is difficult to reconcile his treatment of the Constable of Bourbon with respect for the rights of its subjects. Francis I's fiscal exactions won him the international reputation of being a tyrant. His attempt to extend the gabelle to the provinces of the south west in 1542 provoked a serious rebellion which he had to put down by force.

His reign witnessed a considerable expansion of the royal domain, the creation of a more manageable fiscal administration, the establishment of closer links between central government and the provinces.

From Francis I and Absolute Monarchy
by R. J. Knecht, 1969

---

1. Using the information contained in this chapter, explain the meaning of the words and phrase highlighted in the sources:

(a) 'Parlements' (Source A)

(b) 'the Constable of Bourbon' (Source C)

(c) 'the gabelle' (Source C).

2. Study Source A.

What value is this source to a historian writing about the reign of Francis I?

3. Study Sources A, B and C and use information from this chapter.

To what extent was Francis I an absolute monarch?

The Catholic and Counter Reformations

Key Issues

- *Was the Counter Reformation a Catholic revival or a counter-attack on Protestantism?*

- *How important were the reforms of the Roman Catholic Church in this period?*

- *How successful was the Catholic Reform movement in achieving its objectives?*

8.1 What impact did Renaissance ideas have on the Roman Catholic Church?

8.2 How much reform had taken place within the Roman Catholic Church before the Council of Trent?

8.3 Historical interpretation: Why did the Roman Catholic Church begin a major programme of reform at the Council of Trent?

8.4 What was the impact of the Council of Trent on the Catholic Reform movement?

8.5 How important were the Jesuits to the Counter Reformation?

8.6 What other factors led to the success of the Counter Reformation?

8.7 How successful were the Catholic and Counter Reformations?

Framework of Events

1517	The Oratory of Divine Love established
1521	The Theatines established
1522	Adrian VI becomes Pope
1527	Sack of Rome by the troops of Charles V
1529	The Capuchins established
1530	The Barnabites established
1535	The Ursulines established
1536	The Reform Commission set up in Rome
1537	Paul III becomes Pope
1538	The Reform Commission of Cardinals reports
	Cardinal Borromeo appointed Archbishop of Milan
1540	Jesuit Order is recognised
1541	Diet of Regensburg (Ratisbon). Reconciliation with Lutheranism becomes impossible
1542	Inquisition set up in Rome
1545	Council of Trent meets for first time
1551/52	Second meeting of Council of Trent
1555	Paul IV becomes Pope – hostility to reform movement by Pope increases
1559	Index is published for first time
	Peace for Italy at Câteau-Cambrésis
1560	Reform Commission of the Curia set up
1562/63	Final session of Council of Trent
1564	Bull of Pius IV confirms rulings of the Council of Trent
1566	Pius V becomes Pope
1572	Gregory XIII becomes Pope
1585	Sixtus V becomes Pope.

Overview

THE Counter Reformation, also known as the Catholic Reformation, covers a wide period – from 1500 to at least 1660. It involved vast changes within the whole Roman Catholic Church. There is considerable debate among historians as to whether it was simply a reaction to the Reformation process started by Martin Luther, or something quite separate. Roman Catholic historians, such as Philip Hughes, argue that it was not a reaction to Luther, but a process which started during the Renaissance period of the late 15th and early 16th centuries. This predates the assault on the Catholic Church by Martin Luther and Ulrich Zwingli and suggests that the Roman Catholic Church was willing to reform itself without any external pressures from Protestants such as Luther and Jean Calvin. The Renaissance, it is argued, with its re-examination of traditional ideas and beliefs, had a refreshing and reforming impact on the Roman Catholic Church – just as it did on art, architecture and education.

There is a tendency among Catholic historians to see this process of internal change as one which the Roman Catholic Church started by itself, without the efforts of Luther and Calvin. It was not motivated by a fear that Protestantism might become the dominant religion in Europe.

There are many separate factors involved in this process known as both the Catholic Reformation and the Counter Reformation. Which phrase is used depends on the views of the historian using it. Some of the key factors are:

- Reactions by Roman Catholics against the medieval Church and its old-fashioned practices, which seemed very out of place in the Renaissance atmosphere of enquiry and challenge.

- A strong reaction both within the Roman Catholic Church and among its lay supporters against Luther and his new ideas.

- Some men wishing to reconcile Roman Catholicism to Protantism.

- Pressure on the Papacy to reform itself and its Church in Italy both from within the Roman Catholic Church and from outside it, and rid itself of its poor image of corruption and being too involved in Italian politics.

- There were also numerous non religious factors ranging from varying degrees of support from Catholic monarchs to distractions, such as pressure from the Turks in the Mediterranean.

However, once a decision was taken to reform – and it did take a long time to come, given the huge challenge made to the Church by Luther and Zwingli – there was a tremendous drive by the Roman Catholic Church to improve. This took many different forms. The basic theology (religious beliefs) of the Church was re-evaluated and redefined. The role of the Papacy was reconsidered and new religious orders came into being. The way in which the Church educated its members was looked at closely There was a great drive to ensure that there were better quality bishops working in their **dioceses** and paying more attention to the quality of **pastoral care**.

Senior members of the Roman Catholic Church met for three long periods in a great council set up by the Papacy, known as the Council of Trent. They considered

Dioceses: Areas where they were in charge of the priests and the spiritual life of all lay people.

Pastoral care: The way in which the clergy looked after the people in their parish.

all the major issues and challenges which faced the Church and recommended solutions to them. A new vigour came into the Church. Not only did it seek to revive and inspire its members and its priests, but it also hoped to win back those lost to Lutheranism and Calvinism (fully described in Chapter 4). It also hoped to gain fresh converts among peoples in newly-discovered territories such as in Central and Southern America.

Index: A list of books and authors which no Catholic should read.

New practices, such as the **Index**, and new organisations, such as the **Inquisition**, were created. These were designed to enforce uniformity on Catholics. Kings and Queens in other countries were pressured into, and given assistance in, the process of stamping out Protestantism in their territories. One of the most dynamic of new religious orders, the Jesuits, was used in this process. By 1600 the reformed Church had halted the spread of Protestantism, and by 1661 the Roman Catholic Church was firmly re-established in several areas, such as Poland and Bohemia, which had been 'lost' to Protestantism.

Inquisition: Set up in 1542 in Rome, but followed earlier practices, particularly in Spain.

Lutheranism and Calvinism had not been wiped out, but they were being attacked by a re-invigorated Church that was absolutely clear about its aims and purposes. Roman Catholicism had been both reformed and saved. It was to remain a dynamic and vital force in the history of Europe through to the present day.

8.1 What impact did Renaissance ideas have on the Roman Catholic Church?

Just as the Renaissance had inspired many of those who had become Protestants, this new approach to learning, literature and the arts had its impact on the Catholic Church as well. The traditional view of the Counter Reformation, or the Catholic Reformation, is that it is a process that started, possibly in the 1530s, in response to the threat of Lutheranism. However some historians, such as Michael Mullett, see this revival of Roman Catholicism as having older roots. A study of Spain at the end of the 15th and beginning of the 16th centuries (see Chapter 6), under King Ferdinand and Queen Isabella, shows both a reforming process and a new energy appearing in the Roman Catholic Church. The Church was increasingly appointing high-quality bishops and their influence was spreading to local level. Many of the abuses, such as **nepotism** which were traditionally seen to be the main causes of the Reformation in Germany, were being wiped out in countries like Spain years before Luther started his attack on indulgences in 1517.

Nepotism: Someone who has power and authority uses that authority to obtain jobs for members of their family.

Others writers, such as H. O. Evennett, state that the Counter Reformation would have happened any way. It was simply shaped and given an added degree of momentum by the Protestant Reformation and the desire of the Catholic Church to fight it.

Humanity of Christ: Seeing Christ and his message as a caring and forgiving one.

The growing focus in much late medieval religious writing was on the essential **humanity of Christ** (and not on the vengefulness of God). The Dutch priest Gerard Groote founded a new organisation of clergy, the Brethren of the Common Life, in the late 15th century. This organisation was clearly stimulated by the new ideas of the Renaissance. Groote's publication the *Imitation of Christ* placed a focus on prayer, meditation, reading and the **sacraments**. It was to have a real influence on key figures in the Counter Reformation itself, such as the Jesuit leader, Ignatius Loyola. There was a stress in his writings on the individual

Sacaments: A sacrament is an important procedure whereby a member of the Church can receive favour (grace) from God. Roman Catholics believed in 7 sacramants: Baptism; Penance; Confirmation; Communion; Anointing the sick; Holy Orders and Marriage.

**Girolamo Savonarola
(1452–1498)**
A Dominican friar who led a
great campaign to purify the
Roman Church in Northern Italy
in the late 15th century. The
Church ordered his execution
but his ideas of purification
within the Church were to have
an impact on later reformers.

*1. In what ways did the
Renaissance have a
major influence on the
Catholic Reformation?*

*2. What were the
major influences which
encouraged reform
within the Roman
Catholic Church in the
early 16th century?*

person re-evaluating his or her own faith, and placing less emphasis on the old traditional teachings of the Roman Church.

The Renaissance also had its effect on the great Italian priest and radical preacher Girolamo Savonarola. Desiderius Erasmus too, with his attacks against the Papacy and his great scholarly writings (stressed earlier in Chapter 4), had a great influence on hundreds of clergy and laymen, and caused them to rethink their own ideas. There were other leading Roman Catholic figures, such as Gasparo Contarini (1483–1542), who re-evaluated their beliefs and came to similar conclusions to Luther about the way to salvation. Contarini was influenced by his renewed study of the great classical writers.

This list could go on, but it is clear that among a large number of important members of both the clergy and the laity the intellectual challenges posed by the Renaissance made it obvious that their religious ideas and beliefs needed re-evaluation.

It was also becoming less easy to accept that the Catholic Church was the only source of all truth, and that it was always right and should not be criticised. Just as 'youth' always feels the need to challenge what older generations see as the 'lines' to be toed, the young men growing up in an atmosphere of new learning were bound to be influenced by it. Without Luther and his fellow reformers, the changes to come in the Roman Catholic Church in the 16th century would not have been quite so profound, but they would have happened nonetheless.

8.2 How much reform had taken place within the Roman Catholic Church before the Council of Trent?

A simplistic view of the Counter Reformation is that when the Papacy finally realised the error of its ways, it called a council of the Roman Catholic Church to decide on reforms and to plan its counter-attack on Protestantism. This Council met between 1545 and 1563. It made decisions, which were implemented by a self-reformed Papacy. Secular rulers such as Philip II of Spain backed up this reforming Papacy. Philip was to launch a Catholic fleet in 1588 in an attempt to invade and destroy Protestant England. He also ensured that there was a reformed clergy, and did much to try to destroy Protestantism, in his own lands. This reforming movement was helped by a dynamic new order of priests, the Jesuits, who were to spearhead the counter-attack on Luther and Calvin.

There was also a list of banned writings known as the 'Index'. This was designed to prevent young men reading dangerous authors and thinking too much for themselves. Also set up was the Roman Church's 16th-century version of a secret police, the Inquisition, now ready to stamp out any dissent by force.

The historian Owen Chadwick, in his book *The Reformation* (1990), argues that as early as the 1520s several Roman Catholic religious groups had been formed. These groups, influenced by the same ideas as Luther and other reformers, had a deep wish to purify the Church of its abuses and to re-motivate its members. The main groups were the Capuchins, the Oratory of Divine Love, the Ursulines and the Theatines. They have been given a prominence by Catholic historians such as Janelle, arguing the case that the Roman Catholic Church was capable of reforming itself, and was in fact reforming itself, before it was driven by Luther to do it.

Only in Italy do these orders seem to have had much impact, and they may be the only examples of a real desire on the part of the Church to change. These orders were a symbol of change, but there was not much substance to their work. They showed an awareness of a need for changes in belief, as well as dissatisfaction with the leadership and priorities of the Roman Catholic Church.

The key to any reform within the Catholic Church lay with the Papacy. There is little evidence of a wish on the part of the Papacy to either reform itself or the Church it controlled, or to tackle the problem of Luther seriously. Several of the Popes in the first part of the 16th century – such as Julius II (1503–1513) and Leo X (1513–1521) – behaved in an appalling way. They were not only obstacles to reform but also examples of the type of corruption and abuses which triggered much of the Reformation in the first place.

There was only one Pope in the first part of the 16th century who showed any serious desire to reform and that was Adrian VI (1522–1523). As he was Pope for such a short time, he could achieve little. His two successors, Clement VII (1523–1534) and Paul III (1534–1549), were not enthusiastic when it came to reform, being reluctant to start a process which might reduce their power and influence. The first glimmer of hope came in 1537 when Paul III set up a select committee of cardinals to give a report on the state of the Church. This appears to have been an attempt on his part to postpone taking any action rather than doing something positive. It must be remembered that, by this stage, Luther was now fully established in Germany and Protestantism was also a major force in Switzerland. England, too, was in the process of breaking away from Roman control. So it was clearly time to act decisively.

Even though all the Cardinals on the Committee, with one exception, were Italian, their report proved to be a fairly serious attack on the Roman Catholic Church as it then stood. They criticised strongly many aspects of the Church; for instance, the hold that superstition had among Catholics and the poor behaviour of many monks. They criticised indulgences and

The Capuchins

Founded in 1528 by four friends in Italy, the Capuchins placed great emphasis on their poverty and work for the poor. They placed no great store on academic achievement, as other older orders did, and felt that their main work should be in setting an example of a 'good' life. They were quite a contrast with many essentially 'medieval' monks who had, in some cases, placed more emphasis on accumulating great wealth, or in others on extreme asceticism (simple, strict way of life) and had isolated themselves from the community. They grew in numbers, into possibly the hundreds, and spread out across Europe. They were known to have had a beneficial impact on the Roman Catholic Church in what is now Belgium and in preventing the spread of Protestantism there from France and Holland. It could be argued, however, that the influence of a passionately pro-Catholic ruler was perhaps more important in keeping the area free from Protestantism, and that the Capuchins had only a supporting role here.

The Oratory of Divine Love

Founded in 1514, the Oratory was a mixture of both priests and lay people who met regularly to worship. They placed a real emphasis on good and charitable works. They were a good indicator that there were changes afoot in Italy, and that there was a desire among priests and lay people to reform the Church. However, they were so few in number that their influence was limited. There were probably no more than a few dozen directly involved in this group.

The Ursulines

An order of women, founded in 1535. They were not dissimilar to the Capuchins in their methods, and did a fair amount for both charity and education in Northern Italy. Again the numbers were few.

The Theatines

Formed in 1521, again in Italy, the Theatines do not seem to have had much impact as their numbers were small. Some were nobles, which naturally gave it added status, but it never seemed to have got bigger than 30 members.

the immorality in the City of Rome, which seemed to get its lead from the Vatican and the Pope. They also criticised the money-grabbing conduct of some Cardinals and the misuse of papal power for secular ends. There was little debate on matters of actual religious belief and it was clear that some of the views which Luther had were also shared by some of these Cardinals.

Overall, the report of the Select Committee of Cardinals was a pretty alarming document. It ought to have provoked the Pope into drastic action. Some of the ideas produced by the Renaissance, which had influenced both Luther and Calvin, were present among these Cardinals.

However, this reform commission achieved little. There is evidence that there was an awareness among the more perceptive Cardinals of the failings within the Church. There was *no* evidence of a desire on the part of the Papacy either to improve or to take on the major challenge of Luther. It seems fair to say that by the middle of the 16th century little had been done to reform the worst abuses of the Roman Church or to respond to the challenge of Calvin and Luther. The reform committee did reveal that senior figures within the Church were becoming more aware of the abuses and the harm that had been done, and why it had happened. They made a diagnosis and it was now up the Roman Catholic Church to find a cure. They were also aware of the low esteem with which many viewed the Roman Catholic Church. Obviously, with new orders such as the Theatines around, saintly people from within the Church were coming forward to lead it along a purer path. However, although these orders were growing in influence, there were still too few of them. Also, they seem to have had so little support from the Papacy. Their impact was limited.

1. What, by 1540, had been achieved by those who wished to reform the Roman Catholic Church?

2. Why had so little reform taken place within the Roman Catholic Church by 1540?

8.3 Why did the Roman Catholic Church begin a major programme of reform at the Council of Trent?
A CASE STUDY IN HISTORICAL INTERPRETATION

There is considerable dispute among historians as precisely what to call the process of change which took place within the Roman Catholic Church in the second half of the 16th century. Some, such as A. G. Dickens, have called it the 'Counter Reformation' – seeing it as partly an attack on Luther and partly as a reaction to literalism (where the Bible is the basis of all belief). Other historians, such as P. Janelle, prefer to call it the 'Catholic Reformation'. They see it as part of a reform process and religious revival, which had links going back into the medieval period. It was part of a long-evolving process, which owed little to Luther. Others argue strongly that the main impetus for reform came from secular authorities such as Philip II of Spain or his father Charles V, the Holy Roman Emperor in the time of Luther. Others might argue that it was secular rulers such as Francis I of France (1515–1547) who played the most important part in obstructing the progress of the reformers. They were more significant than the Church; for example, when the young Calvin fled persecution in France, this owed more to the King of France than to the Pope.

There is also dispute among historians as to when this Counter Reformation (which is what we will call it from now on) actually started. There is even dispute between historians about when it ended. V. H. H. Green suggests that the most appropriate starting date is 1517, when Luther nailed his theses on the door of the castle church in Wittenberg. He sees it ending in 1650. Green also sees the founding of the Oratory of Divine Love in 1517 as an important factor in the internal reform of the Church. Others, such as H. O. Evennett in *Spirit of the Counter Reformation* (1970), see the Counter Reformation not starting until the 1540s, and carrying on until well into the 17th century.

A. G. Dickens, in *The Counter Reformation* (1969), however, sees the key starting point with Luther and argues the whole process terminated in the 1650s. Some, such as Owen Chadwick in his book *The Reformation*, date the start well into the 1550s, when the Council of Trent looked like having a real impact. They see the process coming to a rapid end around 1600. In a well-argued publication, *The Counter Reformation* (1995), Michael Mullett sees the origins of the Counter Reformation going well back into medieval times. He sees the termination of the Counter Reformation much later on, in the middle of the 17th century. Mullett feels that it is not until the Council of Trent, in 1545, that the reform movement really starts to have an impact, and that it was well into the latter part of the 16th century that the Counter Reformation could be said to have got going. John Bossy, in *Christianity in the West, 1400–1700* (1985), agrees largely with this timescale and places great emphasis on a long period of preparation, which goes back into the 15th century. He sees the high point as between 1550 and 1600, but he also feels that the key process of implementation takes place in the 17th century.

Main causes of the Catholic and Counter Reformations

- Renaissance ideas

- Reaction against medievalism

- Ideas from reformed Church in Spain

- Pressure from secular leaders such as Charles V

- Reaction against Luther

- Desire for a reformed Church – e.g. the Theatines

- The breaking away of countries such as Germany, England and Sweden from Papal control

- Dislike of Papal excesses

- New orders such as the Jesuits

- The ideas of the Reform Commission.

Some Catholic historians, such as Adolf Harnach, argue that 'the Counter Reformation was simply a shadow of the Reformation', a response to a great need. Others see it as a revival, a restoration or, in some cases, a spontaneous improvement. Two key Catholic historians, P. Janelle and Hubert Jedin (in the *Council of Trent*), argue that the Catholic Reformation would have happened at any rate and was only shaped by the Protestant Reformation and the desire of the Catholic Church to fight Protestantism.

1. What are the main areas of dispute between historians over the Counter Reformation?

2. Why has the Counter Reformation been such a controversial topic among historians?

The debate as to whether Luther merely speeded up a process which was already underway will no doubt continue, as will the argument as to when the Counter Reformation started and ended. It seems important for some Catholic historians to maintain that their Church was aware of its failings and was taking on reform before Luther nailed the issue firmly on to the Church's agenda. The Church was not simply reacting rather too late to events. Recent work, such as Mullett's, has the advantage of considerable recent research on the Church in the late 15th and early 16th centuries, which details the growth of reform movements within the Church and the impact of Renaissance scholarship. It is less inclined to take the rather narrow and simple view that the Catholic Church was totally in the wrong until Luther challenged it and then it was forced against its will to react.

8.4 What was the impact of the Council of Trent on the Catholic Reform movement?

Council of the whole Church:
A meeting of all the senior members of the Church. Such a Council could have major decision-making powers, and could possibly be seen as superior to the Pope.

When Martin Luther challenged the power of the Papacy, one of the demands he made was for a general **Council of the whole Church**. In the 15th century there had been a council at Constance between 1414 and 1418. That Council had played a part in solving some of the major issues dividing the Church at the time. Although Councils since had been less successful in dealing with major issues, it was very much a part of Roman Catholic thinking that a council consisting of all the senior clergyman from all parts of the Catholic world would have the ability and the authority to solve the great religious issues of the day.

The Emperor Charles V regularly called for a council to deal with the issue of Luther and Church reform. However, he rarely got much support from the Papacy because popes feared that it would reduce their power. It might also make them more dependent on the secular rulers such as Charles V. No one was entirely sure exactly what power a general council of the Church had. It was feared, particularly by the popes, that secular rulers in both France and Germany might use the Council to impose their own authority over the Church in their own countries. This would also serve to reduce Papal power and, possibly, wealth. Pope Paul III was willing to call a council as he was frightened by the spread of Lutheranism. He was aware that he needed the backing of the Church Council to help impose Roman Catholicism on all secular rulers. (This was very important in Germany where many German princes liked Luther's ideas.)

Throughout the 1530s, Charles V indicated that he would support such a move, but made it clear that he would demand a political price in return. That was supported by the Papacy because of Charles' anti-French policy. The French were hostile to the idea of the Council, as they were keen on the idea of Lutheranism spreading in Germany. This would weaken the power of their great enemy: Emperor Charles V. Therefore secular politics played quite an important part in preventing the calling of a general council. This was in addition to the reluctance of the Papacy to create a forum, which could challenge its secular power and influence. Secular rulers were to be just as important in putting off what was becoming increasingly obvious to all. It was the only way in which the Church might be radically reformed and the threat of Luther ended.

By 1541 circumstances had changed. An attempt to reach agreement with Luther at the Diet of Regensburg had failed. Also, Charles V had failed to defeat Luther's supporters in battle. It now seemed obvious to all that the only possible solution lay in calling a general council.

There was considerable debate about where a council might actually meet. Secular rulers such as Charles V would have preferred it in a territory where they were in direct control and therefore more able to influence it. However, the final decision was that it should be at Trent in northern Italy. This was near Rome, very Roman Catholic, but still an independent territory free from too much influence from either the Pope or from Charles V.

The first session of the Council of Trent met in 1545, with 31 Bishops present. There were many different hopes placed upon those who met at Trent. It was hoped that the split between Luther and the Roman Church would be ended, the Roman Catholic Church would reunite and that the Church would reform itself. Inevitably, the meeting opened with a long debate on the possible agenda, particularly whether institutional reform or doctrinal clarification should come first. In the end, they decided that they should deal with both aspects together.

It was clear from the start there would be complete hostility to

Protestantism and, therefore, any chance of ending the religious breach was very unlikely. The atmosphere was favourable to a counter-attack on Luther. There was never a sign of any serious wish for reconciliation. Those who met at Trent failed to appreciate what Luther was about. The general atmosphere at the Council was hostile to the whole spirit of the Renaissance. Even the works of Erasmus were to be condemned. There was a real determination to reform and improve, but not to compromise on what they felt to be the basic beliefs of the Roman Catholic Church.

Although technically speaking in session for over 18 years, the Council in practice sat for only four and a half years. There were three sessions. The first between 1545 and 1547 took place during the papacy of Paul III, who was never an enthusiastic supporter of reform. The second session took place between 1551 and 1552, during the papacy of Julius III; another Pope who was less than enthusiastic with the whole process. However when Pius IV (1559–1565) was in control, the meetings were particularly productive. Perhaps even more important to the success of the Council was that Pope Pius IV was prepared to accept most of the ideas and recommendations of the Council. He put them into a single document and ensured that they actually happened.

The desire for reform had always been there, but it had taken a huge amount of pressure from not only reforming clergymen, but also from rulers such as Charles V. News which so regularly came into Rome from countries such as England, Sweden and Germany about the disappearance of yet another group of former Roman Catholics into the arms of Protestantism naturally provided an incentive to meet and act. There is some debate about whether, if the Council had met earlier, it could have healed the breach between Luther and the Roman Catholic Church. This might have been possible if there had been an immediate reaction by the Roman Catholic Church to Luther in the early 1520s, followed by radical reform within the Roman Catholic Church. If the nationalistic hopes of secular rulers such as the German princes and the kings of Sweden and Denmark had also been overcome, then perhaps an earlier Council might have worked and prevented a deepening split.

However, by 1530 it is almost certain that the divisions were far too deep. The Roman Catholic Church would never have accepted ideas such as the priesthood of all believers and **justification by faith alone**. It is also very unlikely that Luther or Calvin would have accepted Roman Catholic views on the sacraments (see page 172).

Justification by faith alone: A key Protestant idea on how eternal salvation was attained; only true believers could be 'saved', good works and a pious life did not help.

There is debate among historians about how important the Council of Trent was to the process of reform within the Catholic Church. Some, like Michael Mullett in *The Counter Reformation*, do not give the process of reform much coverage in their studies of the period. Mullett sees other factors, such as a reformed and more dynamic clergy, as more important to the whole process. Others, such as P. Janelle, see the willingness of the Papacy to implement the recommendations of Trent as of greater importance than the Council itself. Hopeful recommendations of reform can be of limited importance unless they were actually carried out.

Some historians, such as Keith Randall in *The Catholic and Counter Reformations* (1990), see the new Order of the Jesuits (see later) as one of the key factors in the success of the Counter Reformation. These were the men who could carry out the attack against Protestantism on the ground and convince people of the virtues of the Roman Catholic Church.

Overall the Council could be seen to have been a success. Once the whole issue of procedure – who should vote and how – and the agenda were sorted out, they got down to work. Although the meetings are spread over many years, the sessions themselves were productive. A great deal was done to clarify the beliefs of the Roman Catholic Church. The

Creed: From the Latin, *Credo*: 'I believe'; simply a statement of beliefs.

Council members agreed on the basic beliefs as early as 1546 and laid them down in a revised **Creed**. This was soon followed by a precise definition of the role of the Bible in Roman Catholic belief. The differences between the Catholic and the newly-emerged Protestant belief were now very clear. It was stated that the Bible was seen as only one of the sources of truth to Catholics. This was in contrast to the Protestants who felt that the Bible was the basis of all belief.

What use the laity could, and should, make of the Bible was also laid down by the Bishops at the Council of Trent. This was done to ensure that the role of the Roman Catholic Church as the main interpreter of the Bible and its message was made clear. Here there was even more of a division between the ideas of Luther and the Roman Catholic Church.

The Council stressed the importance of tradition to the Church and its ancient practices. They tackled the issue of which was the most appropriate edition of the Bible and who could use it. It was agreed that only the Church and its members could interpret the Bible. This meant the breach between Luther and the growing Calvinist movement was now irreparable.

The idea of censorship by the Church was upheld. The Church insisted on the right to decide what Catholics could or could not read. There was a major attack on the idea of justification by faith alone and the part played by **relics** and indulgences was also clarified.

Relics: Such as bits of the true Cross or bones of saints which were supposed to assist in attaining salvation.

Engraving by Schiavonetti, showing a session of the Coucil of Trent. The Council ran for 18 years.

How useful is this engraving to a historian writing about the Council of Trent?

Main Roman Catholic beliefs clarified at Trent

- Main sacraments, e.g. baptism and confirmation, agreed on
- Role of preaching stressed
- Role of priest in interpretation of Bible stressed
- Importance of Mass stated
- Transubstantiation emphasised as a major part of belief
- Real presence of Christ stressed
- Transubstantiation reaffirmed
- Importance of penance repeated
- Ideas on purgatory clarified
- Role of relics and saints in worship clarified.

Simply by clarifying the Roman Catholic beliefs and making a clear statement of what the Church did and did not believe in, the Council took a huge step forward. It enabled the supporters of the Church to have a secure basis of belief from which they could not only try to reconvert Protestants, but also attempt to convert those who belonged to different religious groups in other parts of the world. It also gave to the local priest the means with which to re-evangelise his own flock (congregation).

What was also very important to the Counter Reformation and to the Church was that the power of the Pope was in no way reduced by the Council of Trent. The Papacy's reputation was raised, not lowered. Therefore it was easier for the Papacy to reimpose its authority on the Church and to carry out the positive and beneficial recommendations of Trent. The clarity of thought that emerged from Trent made it easier to reform the Church as a whole, as well as to preach a clear message.

In addition to the clarification of Catholic religious beliefs, the Council of Trent dealt with many other issues. Much of this came through pressure from Spain. It was agreed that the worst excesses of indulgences should go, but they could still remain in a form less open to corruption. There were many debates on the need for a better-educated clergy and the feeling was that a training college for priests (known as a seminary) should be created in all dioceses. The fundamental difference between a priest and the layman was stressed, so that clergy could provide a real lead to a community. The idea of celibacy (not getting married) for the clergy was re-emphasised. It was to remain a requirement for all clergy and nuns.

A priest and a bishop unselfishly serving the community – both trained and educated men whose sole object was to help the community as a whole – was given great emphasis. Not only were they to ensure that their congregations obtained salvation, but they were to help with schools, families and charity. There was to be less emphasis on some of the older and more traditional aspects of the priest's duties, such as chanting masses for the dead and encouraging harsh self-punishment for sins. There was to be more emphasis placed on setting a good example and effective action to assist the community as a whole.

Latin was kept as the language of the church services, but there was to be more of a focus on preaching a clear message in a language the laity understood. Regular contact between a priest and the community was to be maintained, and it was clear that the Council intended preaching to be used in the counter-attack on Lutheranism. There was to be a big, new focus on compassion and caring by the Church and much was done to encourage the pastoral role of the priest.

Another area that the Council considered was the discipline of all its members. Not only was a higher standard expected among parish priests, but also bishops were expected to reside in their dioceses, visit parishes and to lead a more moral life. Having mistresses and getting jobs for relatives was forbidden. This was a more difficult topic for the Council to take on and review, simply because it threatened jobs and comfortable lifestyles. But it did, and did it successfully.

The Popes themselves were not too keen on radical reform, which might affect their own powers of patronage and therefore the very power of the Papacy itself. However, the Papacy came out of Trent in a much stronger position. It had managed to resist all attempts to reduce Papal power, and older ideas that a council might have more authority than the Pope had not reappeared at Trent. The Council of Trent was, in effect, a good alliance between senior clergy and the Popes to achieve real reform.

There had been some discussion during the meetings at Trent about the possibility of reducing Papal power but this had been resisted successfully. However, it was implicit in the findings of Trent that the Papacy was expected to lead the Counter Reformation in all respects, and that included setting a better example than had been the case in the past.

It is not an easy task to assess how important the Council of Trent was. It certainly emphasised the fundamental breach between Luther, Calvin and the Roman Catholic Church. However, it is clear now that the Roman Catholic Church began to regain the initiative in the religious divisions in Europe. There was obviously a better cause to fight for and those who were prepared to take on Protestantism knew that there was a new dynamism behind them. Both Catholic laity and clergy knew exactly where they stood and what they were to fight for. Some see Trent as the central feature in stopping the advance of Protestantism. The central core of the Church was reformed and renewed, and that energy spread out to its grassroots.

It could be argued that institutions such as the Inquisition, and organisations like the Jesuits did more. It is also possible to argue that the support of Kings such as Louis XIII of France and Philip II of Spain was particularly important. Psychologically, Trent was very important; it was felt that a serious 'house cleaning' had taken place. Failings had been identified and remedied. The beliefs of the Church were made clear in no uncertain terms and new men, such as Michele Ghislieri (Grand Inquisitor to both Pope Paul IV and Pope Pius V, and made a saint in 1712), were advanced to key positions. It demonstrated that the Roman Catholic Church was conscious of its past failings and determined to improve on them. It provided an excellent base, from which committed Catholics could move forward. They were secure in the knowledge that they were the defenders of a popular and revived faith.

1. In what ways, and to what extent, did the Council of Trent assist the process of revival within the Roman Catholic Church?

2. How important was the Council of Trent to the Counter Reformation?

8.5 How important were the Jesuits to the Counter Reformation?

The Council of Trent on its own would have achieved little without someone willing to implement the decisions made. Several of the religious orders examined earlier in this chapter played a part in spreading the message of this revived and reformed Church across Europe. However it was one particular group of men, known as the Society of Jesus – perhaps more commonly known as the Jesuits – that played a vital role in taking the ideas agreed at Trent and putting them into

Ignatius Loyola (1491–1556)

Loyola had come from an extremely orthodox Roman Catholic background in Spain. Initially a soldier, but underwent a profound religious change when recovering from his wounds in 1522. After going on a pilgrimage to the Holy Land in 1523, he studied at various universities in Spain and France. In August 1534, he and six friends vowed to convert all Muslims to Christianity. However, war made it impossible to reach Jerusalem. Instead the band of seven went to Rome and pledged their lives in the service of the Pope. They were formally recognised as 'Jesuits' by Pope Paul III in 1540.

Vows: Solemn and binding agreements to give up such things as wealth and marriage and work collectively for the Roman Catholic Church.

practice throughout Europe. These men brought a new fervour and a commitment to the process of reform and renewal within the Roman Catholic Church.

The order was founded by Ignatius Loyola. It is probable that Loyola had not heard of Luther when he became a convert to an extreme form of Roman Catholicism in 1522. His conversion seems to have been the result of his own reading, mainly studying medieval religious works. Loyola was also strongly influenced by the then aggressive Roman Catholicism in Spain. Spain had a long tradition of a crusading spirit, which was trying to drive out or convert all the Jews and Muslims who lived in Spain. As mentioned earlier, a study of Spain in the early years of the 16th century will show that the spirit of the Counter Reformation does predate the arrival of Luther at Wittenberg.

Loyola's experiences of military discipline were to stay with him and affect his organisation. As a result of his conversion, he took himself on a pilgrimage to Jerusalem in 1523. This, and his studies, convinced him of his vocation and in 1534 he founded a group of like-minded individuals, not unlike the Oratory of Divine Love. There the similarity ends, because as a result of the dynamism of Loyola and his colleagues, they were soon to become a major force throughout Europe. It is very unusual for a single individual to have such an impact. Loyola should be seen in the same light as Luther and Calvin. The small group of seven friends who took their **vows** together to work in the world would have been surprised at what their decision led to. They decided not to isolate themselves in monasteries or retire to universities, but to work wherever they had the greatest chance of helping the Roman Catholic Church and ensuring its spread and survival. Initially, the order grew slowly but by 1540 it had expanded to a group of about 60 men and had obtained formal recognition from the Papacy. This was done in order to enhance their status and make it clear that they had official backing for their work.

These men, sometimes known as the 'shock troops of the Counter Reformation', had an enormous impact throughout Europe for the next 150 years. There are many reasons why they proved to be so important.

● First and foremost is the fact that Loyola recruited men of exceptional ability. He trained them with great thoroughness.

● The organisation of this group was outstanding.

● The rules of the Jesuit organisation were clearly laid down in the 'Constitutions', which Loyola had drafted between 1547 and 1551.

● Loyola was intending to recruit only a spiritual élite. He took great care to ensure that only the committed and suitable were chosen.

● The strict entry regulations, plus a severe probationary period, ensured that all candidates were suited to, and trained for, the job in hand. In many cases the Jesuit recruits were only let loose after ten years of intensive training and preparation.

● Loyola ensured they were fully educated and capable of dealing with not only the physical challenges that were to face them, but also the intellectual ones.

● They could take the fight for religious truth into the enemy's camp.

● Loyola demanded complete poverty, complete chastity, complete obedience, as well as complete adherence to his and the Pope's rules from his recruits.

By 1556 membership had grown to 1,000. It was an extremely efficient organisation, targeting its key resource of able men exceptionally well, backed by an able administrative and support system. Loyola knew that good planning and supplies were vital to the success of any military campaign. His bureaucracy never became too dominant. It existed solely to serve the reform of Roman Catholicism, the prevention of the growth of Protestantism, the conversion of as many Protestants back to Roman Catholicism as was possible – as well as missionary work in non-Christian countries.

Pope Paul IV, not always seen as a great friend of the reform of the Roman Catholic Church, gave it vital support in its early years – as he had done with the Theatines. It was under his jurisdiction that the Jesuit influence spread throughout Italy, Poland, Germany and Spain. The Jesuits became known as great educators, particularly in France and Belgium. Jesuit schools soon became well known for the quality of the education they provided in many countries. The Jesuits were particularly concerned to educate the sons of ruling élites. They placed a tremendous focus on bringing lay people into their churches and exposing them to the influence of their usually outstanding preaching. The Jesuits, unlike many of the medieval religious orders, placed little importance on simply saving their own souls. Instead, they placed great stress on saving the souls of others by direct and positive action.

Some proved to be very independently minded. There was little point in employing men of outstanding ability if a central bureaucrat in Rome would dictate all actions. However they were very proud that they always presented an image of unity and commitment to their basic ideals. Loyola was elected leader for life; so there was no dispute about who was the leader. No rivals were tolerated and the need for absolute obedience was always stressed. The Jesuits tried, as far as possible, to keep out of secular politics and did not chase promotion within the Church. This they felt would distract them from their primary objectives.

Just as the Council of Trent was to lay down a clear definition of Roman Catholic beliefs, the Jesuits had a clear programme designed not only for intending Jesuits but also for those who might wish to become part of the spiritual revival of Roman Catholicism. These 'spiritual exercises' were a process through which a committed Catholic could examine his or her own faith (preferably with the help of a Jesuit). It enabled them to clarify their religious thinking along the 'right' lines, and would ensure they remained committed and positive Catholics from then on. The Jesuits took particular care to target this process on men of influence or on young men who might in their time become rulers or leaders of the societies in which they lived.

The Jesuits were to have a huge impact in the second part of the 16th century and beyond. Wherever you look at the progress of the Counter Reformation you see the Jesuits' hard work. For example, in the detailed negotiations in the Council of Trent itself some of the most brilliant religious work was done by Jesuits. The Jesuits helped in the re-conversion back to Roman Catholicism of many people in Poland, Bohemia and parts of Germany. They became confessors and religious advisers to many rulers. They set up seminaries for training priests and colleges for laymen throughout Europe. They whispered in the ear of Catherine de' Medici of France to ensure that she remained firmly on the Roman Catholic path. They sent missions to France, Germany, England, Ireland, Scotland and Scandinavia. It is apparent that few conversions were made in England, but a huge amount of preventive work was done. It is argued that France, parts of Germany and most of what is now Belgium would not have remained Roman Catholic without the efforts of the Jesuits.

'The Dream of Philip II' by El Greco (1578) – this painting shows the king seeing a vision of the holy monogram of Christ, IHS, adored by angels. With Philip are St Paul, the Pope and the ruler of Venice. On the right are the jaws of Hell.

1. In what ways did the Jesuits assist the spread of the Counter Reformation?

2. To what extent can it be argued that the Jesuits were the most important feature of the Counter Reformation?

In southern Germany Jesuits played a vital part in keeping so many key rulers Roman Catholic – such as the ruler of Bavaria. If they had not worked so hard on Ferdinand, the successor to Charles V in Austria, from 1556 to 1564, as well as on his son Maximilian, then the history of religion in central southern Europe would have been very different.

One typical example was the Jesuit, Diego Lainez (who succeeded Loyola as leader) whose activities included ensuring that Catherine de' Medici did not give in too much to the Protestants in the French wars of religion. He then had to prepare a report on Roman Catholic beliefs for the Pope in Rome. He was to lead a mission to several Italian cities to re-invigorate the faithful, and then led a missionary expedition to Africa. Lainez was also to play a key role as a debater and Papal supporter during the Council of Trent. With men as able and as adaptable as that, the Jesuits were bound to make a huge impact.

The superb training of the Jesuits, recruiting men with all types of ability, and the fact that they had a superb *'esprit de corps'* and dynamism, led to success. They brought out the best of old Catholicism. This ranged from the absolute commitment of the Spanish Church to the superb intellectual training that came from the University of Paris. It also contained the high degree of pastoral experience that had been a feature of the best of old Catholicism. The 'spiritual exercises' gave clear and detailed instructions to both priest and layman. The Jesuits were a sophisticated international organisation, which ignored office and status and temptations of the flesh, but were fully prepared to be involved in politics if it would help them to achieve their ends. They gained a reputation for having a ruthless desire to achieve their objectives whatever the cost. In England they earned real hatred, when they came to keep their old faith alive, for attempting to overthrow the lawful monarch – the Protestant Elizabeth. They were also part of the process trying to impose a Catholic Scotswoman, Mary Stuart, on the English throne. The fact that many died for their faith, as several of the Jesuits who came to England did, only increased the respect in which they were held.

When the Council of Trent ordered colleges and seminaries to be set up in all dioceses, it was the Jesuits who put it into practice in many instances. Not only did they run those seminaries, they also expanded into schools and universities – to educate the sons of the rulers. They preached, they wrote, they argued, they taught, and they were sent to travel to the ends of the earth to spread the message. They were the driving forces behind the implementation of the Counter Reformation; it could have remained a rather empty shell without them.

8.6 What other factors led to the success of the Counter Reformation?

There were four other important ingredients, which led to the success of the reformers. The first was the Papacy itself. There were three Popes after Trent (Paul IV, Pius V and Sixtus V) who played a vital role in the implementation of the reforms of the Council. They were examples of the type of Papacy the reformers had hoped would be the leader of a revived Roman Catholic Church. The second was the Index, which was simply a form of censorship to ensure that radical and dangerous ideas did not spread to the faithful. The third was an organisation that was frequently seen with horror – the Inquisition. The fourth was the willingness of the secular rulers to use their power, authority and armies to stamp out Protestantism in their own countries and in others. All four ingredients were to play an important part, with perhaps the rulers being the most important of the four.

The Papacy

Paul IV, pope between 1555 and 1559, was not a great enthusiast for the Council of Trent. However, he had been an enthusiastic supporter of the Inquisition, and had played an important role in setting up the Index. He had also played an important part in ending many of the financial abuses, which had given the Papacy such a bad name.

Pope Pius V (1566–1572) had been an Inquisitor earlier in his career. He played a major role in trying to establish a greater degree of moral behaviour in Rome. He himself led a blameless life and expected a high standard of personal conduct from those who served at the Papal court. Pius V cut back the size of the court and worked hard to remove the aura of corruption and sleaze which had surrounded the Papacy. He was also to play a central role in the implementation of the ideas of the Council of Trent, and he was an enthusiastic supporter of the Jesuits.

The Catholic Church was fortunate in that Pius V was succeeded by two Popes – Gregory XIII (1572–1585) and Sixtus V (1585–1590) – both of the whom shared Pius V's determination to reform the Papal court. They wanted to implement the findings of the Trent, play a smaller part in Italian politics, and show less concern with display and ostentation. They were also willing to do all they could to assist secular rulers, such as the Kings of France, to restore Catholicism to what they felt was its rightful place in Europe and in the minds of the people of Europe.

Following the Council of Trent, the Popes played a less active role in Italian politics. They tried to see their main role as spiritual leaders of the whole Roman Catholic Church.

The Index

Banning books was nothing new to the Roman Catholic Church, and the practice went back centuries. However, the invention of the printing press made the spread of ideas which the Church disapproved of much easier. In the past, most books were written by monks and priests; and most of those who were literate were also clergy, so monitoring the spread of heretical ideas was much easier. The plan to draw up a complete list of all forbidden books seemed to originate from Charles V about 1546, and was originally given to the University of Louvain, which was in one of his territories. The Inquisition, under the orders of the Papacy, extended and took over the responsibility for maintaining and updating the list in 1557. The Council of Trent in 1564 gave the idea official approval. A permanent commission, under the Pope, was set up to examine all works published and to indicate whether they were fit or not for Catholics to read.

Overall, the impact of the Index does not seem to have been that significant. It led to a burning of books in some parts of Italy, but seems to have been largely ignored in France and in Spain. It certainly was not important in preventing the future spread of Protestantism. It is perhaps of more significance as an indicator of the new mood of the Roman Catholic Church, rather than as a preventer of heresy.

The Inquisition

Initially seen as the most repressive and aggressive aspect of the whole of the Counter Reformation movement, the Inquisition has always had a 'bad press' from contemporary Protestants and some later historians, perhaps carried away with the propaganda of the times. This organisation was set up in 1542 by a group who believed that there had been too much conciliation of the Protestants. It was given Papal backing by means of a **Bull**. The Inquisition was given considerable power to start with, and all Catholics were required to accept its authority. For example, it had the power to imprison on suspicion, torture, and confiscate property and execute those it found guilty. The only person capable of pardoning anyone found guilty by the Inquisition was the Pope. Normal legal methods, such as giving the accused the right of a defence for example, did not apply. It was effective inside Italy but, as with the Index, did not really apply outside Italy. Local rulers, such as in France, preferred their own courts to be used in the way that appealed most to them. They had no desire to have another legal system operating in their countries over which they had no control.

In Spain the Inquisition gained a fearsome reputation, dating back to the late 15th century. It was totally dependent on the monarch for its operations and there were several occasions in the later 16th century

Bull: Basically a papal law, which bound all Catholics. The Pope's seal, which was fixed to all documents issued by the Papacy, had a 'bull' on it.

Painting of the Inquisition by Pedro Berruguete (c.1440–1503), court painter to the King of Spain. This illustration shows only the lower half of the work: Paul III's reorganisation of the Inquisition; he used it to great effect against the Protestants of Italy.

where the Inquisition in Spain acted against what the Pope saw were the best interests of the Roman Catholic Church.

Overall, the Inquisition's impact was limited and the repressive agencies operated by the Church were not important to the Counter Reformation process. Dynamic leadership and real evangelism, backed up by powerful secular leaders, were the key to reconversion and prevention of the further spread of Protestantism.

The role of secular rulers

Absolutely vital to the success of the Counter Reformation was the attitude and commitment of the ruler of that country at that time. Looking at the areas which were seen as the 'success stories' of the Counter Reformation – such as Poland, Bohemia, Bavaria and what is now Belgium – a firmly Catholic ruler was the vital factor, even though Jesuits and armies may have helped. England became Roman Catholic again under Mary Tudor, but firmly Protestant under Elizabeth in spite of all the efforts of the Jesuits and the army and navy of Philip II of Spain. France tolerated Protestants when the monarch wished to, and stopped tolerating them when the monarch did not wish to, as was the case under Louis XIII in the 1620s. Spain became the dominant militant arm of aggressive Catholicism as Philip II wished it to happen, and much the same happened in Europe during the Thirty Years' War. The attitude of the secular ruler was always a vital part of the success of the Counter Reformation, just as it was in the initial reformation process itself in countries like Germany and Scandinavia.

1. *Using this chapter and the chapters on France and Spain in the 16th century, explain how important the role of the secular ruler was to the Counter Reformation in those territories.*

2. *'The Index and the Inquisition were only minor parts of the Counter Reformation process.' Do you agree?*

8.7 How successful were the Catholic and Counter Reformations?

It is not easy to lay down the criteria by which the success or failure of this movement can be judged. Certainly the Roman Catholic Church was a fundamentally different and better organisation in 1661 than it had been in 1500. The corruption and immorality that had been the hallmarks of Rome and its Church leaders in the early part of the 16th century, which had so shocked the young Martin Luther, had gone. The hierarchy of the Church were conscious that they had to choose popes of a high calibre who could provide not only the effective leadership but also the excellent example that a revived Roman Catholic Church needed.

With a moral and purposeful leadership, and a clear and understood theology, as well as a reformed city (the Vatican) and clergy, the Catholic Church was in far better health to resist the encroachment of Protestantism. With the dynamic aid of the Jesuits, whose contribution cannot be underestimated, the terror and fear inspired by the Inquisition in some areas, and an effectively enforced Index, the Church was a position not only to ensure that its existing members stayed loyal to the faith, but areas lost to Protestantism might now be reconverted.

Areas which might so easily have been lost to Protestantism, such as what is now Belgium, remain Catholic to this day. In France, Protestantism made serious gains until about 1600. However in the course of the 17th century, enforced by both Cardinal Richelieu and Louis XIV (King of France in the second part of the 17th century), Protestantism almost ceased to exist as a major force. Heroic attempts were made by both spiritual and secular leaders to bring England back to the true faith, but failed. Spain and Italy remained true to the old Church. Scandinavia remained lost, as did much of northern Germany. Much of southern Germany, as well as parts of the Holy Roman Emperor's territories in

1. In what ways could it be argued that the Counter Reformation was unsuccessful?

2. 'Without the Jesuits there would have been no chance of a successful Counter Reformation.' Is this comment fair to other contributors to the process?

eastern Europe, were either retained as Catholic, or won back at a later stage.

The Roman Catholic Church now had a clearly defined theology, a much clearer sense of mission, quality leadership at all levels and a genuine sense of vocation. The corruption and immorality, which had slowly damaged the Papacy, was never to return. The Papacy learned to focus more on its role as spiritual leader and to stay as far as it was possible out of Italian politics. The Church's members now had a more educated clergy, which was more conscious of its pastoral and spiritual role. The Jesuits formed an élite, which ensured that a high-quality Catholic education was available to the sons of rulers and noblemen. The Jesuits also ensured the Roman Catholic Church went on the offensive where possible and also performed high-quality missionary work throughout the world. Overall, it was a huge and profound change.

Source-based questions: The Council of Trent

SOURCE A

It must be known that ever since 1529 ... the Emperor never ceased whenever he saw Pope Clement or Pope Paul ... and at every diet in Germany ... continually to solicit ...the convocation of a general council to provide a remedy for the evils which had arisen in Germany and for the errors which were being propagated in Christendom. As regards Pope Clement ... it was never possible to make him fulfil his commitment. His successor, Pope Paul, declared at the commencement of his pontificate that he promised to announce and convoke the council immediately; ... nevertheless, these demonstrations and first zeal gradually cooled down and, following the steps and example of Pope Clement, he temporised with soft words and always opposed the convocation and meeting of the council.

Autobiography of Charles V, 1556

SOURCE B

Each of us should keep before his eyes the things that are expected of this holy Council ... the uprooting of heresies, the reformation of ecclesiastical discipline and of morals, and lastly external peace of the whole Church. Wrong opinions about faith, *like* brambles and thorns, have sprung up in God's garden entrusted to us. Even if these poisonous weeds have sprung up of themselves, nevertheless, if we have not tilled our field, as we ought ... we are no less to be reckoned their cause than if we ourselves had sowed them ... Let us come to what are called 'abuses': ... we cannot even name any other causes but ourselves.

Address by Cardinal Pole to the Council of Trent, January 1546

SOURCE C

If anyone shall say that the sinner is justified by faith alone ... let him be [condemned] ...

If anyone shall say that children ... are to be re-baptised when they reach years of discretion, or that it is better that the baptism of children is omitted ... let him be [condemned] ....

If anyone shall deny that in the sacrament of the most Holy Eucharist are contained truly, really and substantially the body and blood, together with the soul and divinity, of our Lord Jesus Christ, and consequently the whole Christ, but shall say that he is in it only as a sign or figure or force, let him be [condemned].

The Holy Council ... commands that the use of indulgences ... is to be retained .... In granting them, however, it desires that ... moderation be observed, lest by too great facility, ecclesiastical discipline will be weakened.

Excerpts from the canons of the Council of Trent

---

1. Explain the following in the context of the sources:

(a) 'general council' (Source A)

(b) 'reformation of ecclesiastical discipline' (Source B)

(c) 'justified by faith alone' (Source C).

2. Using Source A and your own knowledge, explain why it took so long to call a general council of the Church.

3. How useful are these sources in explaining the importance of the Council of Trent?

4. Using these sources and your own knowledge, explain how the Counter Reformation achieved the success it did.

Philip II of Spain 1556–1598

9.1 What problems did Philip II inherit from his father Charles I?
9.2 Historical interpretation: To what extent was Philip II an absolute monarch?
9.3 How did the Spanish overseas empire develop in the years 1556 to 1598?
9.4 How successful were Philip II's religious policies?
9.5 What were the social and economic problems that affected Spain during Philip II's reign?
9.6 How successful was Philip II in foreign affairs?

Key Issues

- *How successful was Philip II's foreign policy?*

- *How far did the government of Spain change during Philip II's reign?*

- *To what extent can the reign of Philip II be regarded as a 'Golden Age'?*

Framework of Events

1556	Philip II becomes King of Spain
1558	Mary Tudor dies
1559	Treaty of Câteau-Cambrésis
	Philip arrives in Spain from the Netherlands
1560	Philip marries Elizabeth of Valois
1561	Madrid made capital of Spain
1565	Siege of Malta by Ottoman Turks
1566	Beginning of Dutch Revolt
1568	Don Carlos, Philip's first son, dies
	Morisco Rebellion begins
	Elizabeth I seizes Genoese bullion: major deterioration in Anglo–Spanish relations
1570	Philip marries Anne of Austria
1571	Battle of Lepanto
1573	Vazquez becomes secretary
1578	Murder of Escobedo
	Prince Philip (future Philip III) born
	King Sebastian I of Portugal dies
	Truce with the Ottoman Turks
1579	End of First Ministry
	Perez dismissed
1580	Philip II becomes King of Portugal: Iberian peninsula is united
	Peace Treaty with the Turks
1583	Granvelle replaced by Zúñiga, Idiáquez and Moura
1584	Treaty of Joinville with Catholic League in France
1585	War begins between England and Spain
1587	Mary Stuart is executed in England
1588	The Armada against England
1590–91	Revolt in Aragon
1595	Spain declares war on France
1598	Treaty of Vervins ends war with France
	Philip II dies.

Overview

P
HILIP II was the first ruler to receive the title King of Spain. Like his father, he ruled over a collection of territories that had separate laws and administrations. However, during Philip II's reign the Spanish monarchy became centred on Castile. In 1561 he created a permanent capital at Madrid. His advisers, usually Castilian, bore the main burden of taxation. After 1559, except for a stay in Portugal from 1580 to 1583, Philip spent his reign in Spain.

There is some dispute among historians about whether or not Philip II was an absolute monarch. He certainly had a more direct, active role in government compared with his father. Virtually every matter dealt with by his government had to receive a personal input from Philip II. This development led to delays in decision making as well as over-working the King.

The reign of Philip II has been described as the Golden Age of Spain. In this period Spain played a dominant role in European affairs. It was the most powerful Catholic state. As a result, it played an important part in the Catholic and Counter Reformations (see Chapter 8). Philip II was enthusiastic about implementing the religious changes agreed at the Council of Trent (1545–1563), although he questioned the increase in the authority of the Pope. Using the Index and the Inquisition, Philip II maintained religious conformity in Spain. The one significant religious minority was the **Moriscos**, who although technically Christian, were treated as second-class subjects. The most serious rebellion within Spain during Philip II's reign took place between 1568 and 1570 when the Moriscos of Granada revolted.

Moriscos: People who were once Muslims who had converted to Christianity but still spoke Arabic and who dressed in Muslim/Arab clothes. They were suspected of being secret followers of Islam.

Titian's portrait of Philip sent to England to be shown to Mary Tudor.

In addition to his lands within Europe, Philip was monarch of a large overseas empire mainly in the New World. This provided him with large quantities of gold and silver bullion, which allowed him to finance wars against the Turks, France, England and the Dutch rebels in the Netherlands. However, throughout his reign, Philip suffered from severe financial problems. His military commitments outweighed his ability to finance them. As a result, Philip II was constantly in debt which occasionally resulted in bankruptcy.

While historians may have seen Philip's reign as a 'Golden Age', the seeds of Spain's decline were sown in this period. Not only was the Spanish monarchy in permanent debt, but also Spain was entering a period of economic and social decline by the last decade of Philip's reign.

Although the origins of Spain's decline as a great power may have begun at this time, Spain was still western Europe's greatest power during Philip's reign. This was helped in part by the French Wars of Religion which prevented France from threatening Philip's position. Also, after 1578, the Ottoman Turks became involved in conflict with Persia (Iran) which distracted them from expansion into the central Mediterranean.

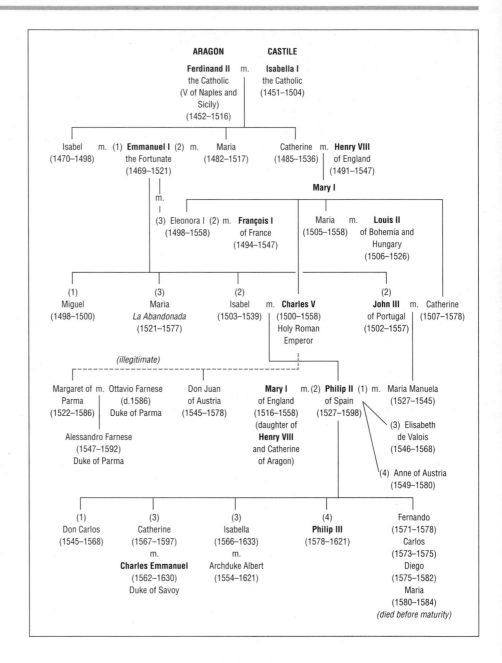

9.1 What problems did Philip II inherit from his father Charles I?

Philip's lands

Abdicate: To resign from the position of monarch.

In October 1555 in Brussels, Charles I of Spain (but known to the rest of Europe as Charles V, the Holy Roman Emperor) announced his decision to **abdicate**. In the months that followed, Charles divided up his lands between his brother Ferdinand and his son Philip. The latter was given the Habsburg lands of Austria and Hungary. In 1558 he was elected Holy Roman Emperor as Ferdinand I.

By February 1556 Philip had become ruler of Castile, Aragon, and the Habsburg lands in Italy (see map). These lands would have made Philip a major figure in Mediterranean affairs. In addition, Philip was given

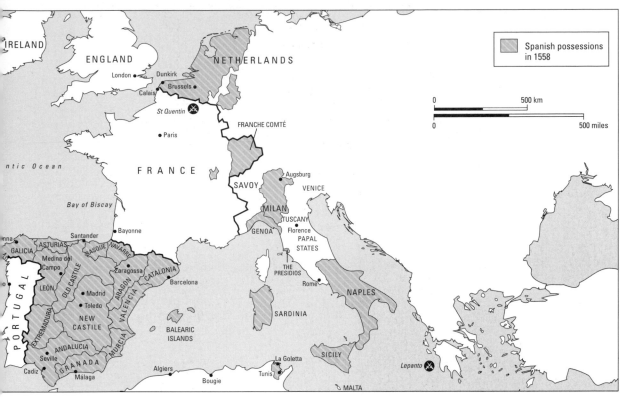

The monarquía of Philip II, 1558

control over Spanish lands in the New World. This gave him considerable wealth. From the 1540s large quantities of gold and silver were transported from the New World to finance Philip's government and foreign policy.

However, Charles also gave his son his Burgundian lands. These included Franche Comté and the Netherlands. The inclusion of these lands meant that Philip's territories virtually surrounded France. This development had two important effects on Philip's reign. Firstly, Philip would be involved in the conflicts between France and the Habsburgs. Secondly, for virtually all his reign Philip would be affected by major problems in the Netherlands. (The Dutch Revolt is covered in Chapter 10.)

It might seem odd that Charles gave the Netherlands and Franche Comté to Philip, rather than Ferdinand. However, at the time of Charles' abdication, Philip was King Consort (the Queen's husband) of England. Therefore, Philip was in an important position to defend the Netherlands against the French.

Philip's empire contained self-governing and separate states, unlike France or England. Each part recognised Philip as their ruler. In this sense, Philip's empire was like his father's. It was a 'monarquía' (see map) – that is, a collection of separate states with the same ruler.

Philip II ruled over 15 million subjects of which eight million lived in Spain and three million in the Netherlands. Around four million lived in the Italian lands (Milan, Naples, Sicily and Sardinia).

According to the historian Henry Kamen, 'by imposing on Spain the Burgundian territories (Franche Comté and the Netherlands), Charles forced it to take on the leadership of an empire which its military nor its economic capacity had earned'. Philip was obliged to build up Spain into a world power almost from scratch.

Philip II at the Battle of St Quentin, 1557, painted by Peter Paul Rubens

Valois France: France under the rule of the House of Valois, the royal family which ruled France until the death of Henry III in 1589.

Status quo: Keeping things unchanged.

War with France

When Philip became King of Spain, in January 1556, the Habsburgs were at war with **Valois France**. These wars had affected western Europe since France's invasion of Italy in 1494. By 1556 both France and Spain were facing serious internal problems. The growth of Protestantism and the financial costs of war affected both states. Therefore, in January 1556 Philip accepted the Truce of Vaucelles with Henry II of France.

By 1557 the French had broken the truce, which led to a resumption of war. In August of that year Philip won a major victory over the French at St Quentin (see photograph), which he did not follow up. By 1559 both France and Spain signed the Treaty of Câteau-Cambrésis. This treaty maintained the *status quo* in western Europe.

In 1558, Mary Tudor died. The new queen, Elizabeth I, had been brought up a Protestant. From 1558 Philip had lost England as an ally in his conflict with France. For the rest of his reign he attempted, by various means, to win England back to the Catholic Church and as Spain's ally.

Finance

According to Geoffrey Woodward, in *Philip II* (1992), Philip II's 'greatest domestic problem in 1556 was financial'. The Habsburg–Valois wars and Charles' wars against the Turks and Protestants of Germany had caused great financial strain on Spain. By the time of his abdication, Spain had become the most important source of revenue for Charles. When Philip II became king he inherited a debt of 36 million ducats (see Chapter 6 for explanation of Spanish currency). So great were the financial problems that Philip declared himself bankrupt in 1557. Later in his reign he suspended interest payments on his debts (1560) and he was bankrupt again in 1575 and 1596.

The threat of Islam

Apart from France, Spain's other major adversary were the Islamic states of the Mediterranean, in particular the Ottoman Empire. Philip II inherited the role of defending Christendom against the advance of the Muslim religion. He also had to defend Spanish territories on the North African coast. For instance, in 1551, Tripoli had fallen to the Turks. According to the historian A.W. Lovett, in *Early Habsburg Spain, 1517–1598* (1986), 'by the time of Charles' abdication the struggle between the Habsburg and Ottoman empire was on the point of entering its decisive phase'.

Throughout his reign, Philip II had to deal with this threat. The problem was made worse by the existence of the Morisco minority within Spain, in particular in Granada.

The growth of Protestantism

One of the reasons for the Treaty of Câteau-Cambrésis was the fear of Protestantism in both France and Philip's lands. By the peace of Augsburg of 1555 Lutheranism was limited to northern Germany and Scandinavia. The new Protestant threat came from Calvinism (see Chapter 4). This

1. *What were the major problems that faced Philip II at the beginning of his reign?*

2. *Which of these problems do you regard as the most serious in 1556 and which do you regard was the most serious in the long term? Give reasons to support your answer.*

Protestant religion was growing rapidly in France and the Netherlands. One of the first public functions Philip attended on his return to Spain from the Netherlands in 1559 was an *auto de fe* (see Chapter 6) in Valladolid. Throughout his reign, Philip defended the Catholic Church from Protestant heresy and the threat of Islam.

The Counter Reformation

Philip II did not only have to face the problems of heresy and Islam. In 1556, the Spanish Church was in urgent need of reform. Many parishes did not have a priest. Although bishops may have been wealthy, many priests lived in poverty. In terms of religious practices there were considerable differences within Spain. The major Papal response to the growth of Protestantism was the Council of Trent. The Council began a major reform of the Catholic Church. Philip II became one of the most enthusiastic supporters of these reforms, which he applied to all his lands.

9.2 To what extent was Philip II an absolute monarch?
A CASE STUDY IN HISTORICAL INTERPRETATION

Since the time of Philip II's reign there has been much debate about how Philip governed his lands. According to historian R. Trevor Davies, in *The Golden Age of Spain* (first published in 1937), 'from his own day ... he has been represented as a gloomy tyrant, and a religious fanatic ever thirsting for fresh victims to torture and to destroy'. This view constituted 'the Black Legend' of Philip II. He was seen by Protestant Europe as their main enemy. His support for the Catholic faith and his opposition to Protestantism and Islam gave the impression of a dictator. Also, to the Dutch he was seen as a foreign tyrant trying to take away their local rights and independence.

How far is this an accurate view of the government of Philip II? Part of the problem for the historian is the fact that Philip II did not leave behind any memoirs, nor did he leave many papers of a personal nature on which we could assess his motives or aims. There is a small amount of correspondence between Philip and his daughters, Isabella and Catherine, where he gives them advice. He also left a political testament to his son, in 1597, about how to govern Spain. Even with these, we are left with many unanswered questions about his approach to government.

The case in favour of the view that Philip II was an absolute monarch

In 1543 when Philip became Regent of Spain, his father gave him instructions on how to govern. One of the most important was to 'depend on no one but yourself'. Philip II believed in the 'Divine Right of Kings'. He believed his authority to govern came to him directly from God, to whom he was answerable. Therefore, when Philip's method of government is compared to his predecessors there is evidence to suggest that he took a more active role in government.

Central control from Madrid
In 1561 Philip made Madrid the permanent capital of his empire. He also insisted on dealing with all the matters that were brought before his government. Throughout his reign, Philip was suspicious of advisers. He always attempted to allow them limited knowledge. In this way he alone had complete knowledge of a subject. This allowed him to keep control. Stories abound of Philip working into the night on a wide variety of issues. The historian John Lynch, in *Spain under the Habsburgs, 1516–1598* (1981), notes that at the time he was planning the Armada against

Corregidores: Royal officials appointed to maintain royal control of towns.

Cortes in Castile: The representaive assembly for the Kingdom of Castile. From 1538, in Castile the Cortes contained representatives from 18 cities and towns. It was usually called by the king to provide him with taxes. In Aragon there were three Cortes: one each for Aragon, Catalonia and Valencia. On occasion all three Aragonese Cortes met as a General Cortes.

Dominions: Areas of land controlled by a ruler.

England, in 1558, Philip was also writing to the Pope about the type of clerical vestment used by priests in Spain. In Castile royal authority was maintained by 66 **corregidores** based in towns.

Unfortunately, this system of governing created problems. Far too often Philip was weighed down with a large volume of state papers to deal with. This led to delays and mistakes. As Henry Kamen notes in his biography *Philip of Spain* (1997), 'surrounded by papers from every corner of the universal monarchy the king inevitably found it impossible to keep all in correct order'.

Decline in the power of the Castilian Cortes

While keeping a strong personal control of the affairs of government, Philip also limited the powers of the **Cortes in Castile**. By the time of Philip's accession it had lost virtually all its privileges. When it was called during Philip's reign its main purpose was to raise extra revenue for the monarchy. In the 1590s Philip also attempted to limit the powers and rights of Aragon, which led to a direct confrontation. Outside Spain, Philip attempted to limit the local independence of the provinces of the Netherlands. His attempts to enforce Habsburg rule led to the Dutch Revolt (see Chapter 10).

Dominance of Castile

In many ways Philip II's government differed markedly from his father's. Philip had established a central base in Spain. Unlike his father, Philip rarely visited his **dominions** outside Spain. Also unlike his father, Philip was a poor linguist. His only working language was Castilian. So, he surrounded himself with Castilian advisers. This helped support the view that he wanted to establish a centralised government based in Castile.

Religious affairs

An area where Philip enjoyed considerable power was in religious affairs. He had inherited many powers over the appointment of bishops within Spain and the New World. As a major religious reformer in his own right, Philip was able to implement those aspects of the Council of Trent he saw fit. Throughout his reign, Philip had difficult relations with many popes. By the time of his death, in 1598, Spain had considerable freedom to organise and run its own religious affairs within the Catholic Church.

It could be argued that Philip had many of the characteristics of an absolute monarch. In *Philip II* (1992) Geoffrey Woodward notes:

> 'In his administration of the Church [Philip] came to control all clerical appointments, disposed of ecclesiastical [church] wealth and mobilised the Inquisition as an instrument of royal authority. In secular affairs, the 1560s saw a reassertion of royal claims to salt deposits, mining rights and customs revenues. Above all, there was an assertion of royal restoration of royal control over military and naval administration.'

The historian John Lynch, in *Spain under the Habsburgs* (1981), states that during the reign of Philip II 'monarchy was absolute. But its absolutism was qualified by conditions, and its powers were less imposing in practice than it was in theory.'

The case against the view that Philip II was an absolute monarch

Continuation of the Conciliar System of Government

Rather than viewing Philip II as an absolute monarch, there is considerable evidence to suggest that he continued the type of government of his predecessors. Philip inherited a system of government based on councils. He proceeded to improve and develop this system. The Council of State remained the main state council, but Philip reorganised and increased the powers of regional council. In all, three new regional councils were created during the reign. Between 1555 and 1559, the affairs of Italy were removed from the Council of Aragon to form a new council. In 1582 a council of Portugal was created, followed by a council of Flanders, in 1588. These all met in Madrid. In this way, all parts of Philip's dominions had an opportunity of dealing directly with him.

To supplement the councils, from 1580 Philip established *juntas* (special committees) to deal with specific problems. Some were temporary, like the one that dealt with the Morisco problem. Others became permanent, such as the junta on Works and Forests. The most important was La Junta de la Noche ('The Committee of the Night') which discussed business on a daily basis. The members of this committee – the most important being Mateo Vazquez – provided an important coordinating role in government.

Rivalry and faction

In both the councils and the juntas Philip relied heavily on *letrados* (trained lawyers). This was a continuation of a practice begun during the reigns of Ferdinand and Isabella.

As with virtually all governments in the 16th century, the government of Philip II was affected by faction disputes and rivalries. Each decade of Philip's rule was affected by this problem. In the 1560s the main factions followed the Duke of Alba and the Prince of Eboli (Ruy Gomez de Silva). By the 1570s rivalry occurred between Alba and Antonio Perez. By the last two decades of the reign faction groups surrounded Idiáquez, Zuñiga, Chinchon and Moura (see next section).

Philip's 'Ministries'

Philip II's style of government involved the use of secretaries. Their position of direct access to the king made them powerful. The 'First Ministry' of Philip's reign lasted from 1556 to 1579. It was dominated by the Duke of Alba and the Eboli faction. In 1579 Antonio Perez (the leader of the Eboli faction following Eboli's death in 1573) was arrested by Philip as a result of the **Perez Affair**. In 1579 a 'Second Ministry' was formed under Antoine Perronet (Cardinal Granvelle). He was the only non-Castilian to hold high office during Philip's reign. Perronet was assisted by Juan de Idiáquez. However, the centre of power in this ministry was in the Junta de la Noche, created in 1585. It consisted of Idiáquez, Moura, Chinchon and Mateo Vazquez as secretary. Juan de Zuñiga y Requesens was a member until his death in November 1586.

Perez Affair: Incident which led to the end of Philip's First Ministry in 1579. Antonio Perez was implicated in the murder of Juan de Escobedo, a supporter of Perez's rival, Don Juan, in 1578. Perez was dismissed from office and replaced by Cardinal Granvelle.

The power of the aristocracy

Another limitation of royal power were the privileges and power of the aristocracy, in particular in Castile. To rule his kingdom Philip needed the support and cooperation of this group. For instance, the Duke of Medina Sidonia controlled large areas of Andalucia and could raise a private army of several thousand men. According to the historian Henry Kamen, in Old Castile the Valescos controlled 258 towns and villages, while the Mendoza Duke of Infantado controlled nearly 800 towns and villages and nominated 500 public officials.

Poor communications and inefficiency

The quality of communications and the level of corruption and inefficiency among government officials also limited royal power. Although Philip was credited with the most efficient postal service in Europe, it still took two weeks for letters to reach Milan or Brussels and two weeks for a reply. As a result, as Henry Kamen states in *Spain 1469–1714* (1991), 'the day-to-day restrictions on royal power are perhaps the clearest evidence that "absolutism", if it existed in peninsular Spain, was more a legal fiction than a political reality'.

The system of justice

However, there is evidence to suggest that Philip did not wish to create an absolute monarchy. In 16th-century Spain there was no tradition of absolute monarchy. This was most clearly seen in the system of justice. To Philip II, the enforcement of laws and justice were some of his most important responsibilities. He inherited a system of hierarchical courts, which he allowed to operate without royal interference. In fact, in Spain, the king could be tried by a normal court. This did not mean that Philip was not capable of executing private justice. The most notable example was the Baron de Montigny, the representative in Spain of the counts of Egmont and Hornes, who were publicly executed in 1570.

Lack of an imperial plan

On a broader scale, there is no evidence that Philip II wanted to create a centralised empire. As Geoffrey Parker noted in *Spain and the Netherlands* (1978) 'it has sometimes been observed with surprise that Philip II, with all his vast dominions, never produced, nor caused to be produced, a "blueprint for empire"'. This view is supported by Henry Kamen in *Philip of Spain* (1997), where he states that 'Philip was not a conscious imperialist. He never held or voiced theories about imperial power or status, and never possessed any recognisable principles of empire.'

All Philip II tried to do was to follow the Instructions of 1543 given by his father: 'he must never recede from one inch of territory, and should maintain integrally the inheritance given by God'.

The Aragon Revolt of 1590–91

To explain the limitation of Philip II's power within Spain, the Aragon Revolt provides a good example. In an attempt to protect Aragon from possible Muslim attack and to prevent the spread of French Protestantism, Philip sent troops into Aragon in 1590. In addition, Antonio Perez, who had been implicated in the murder of Escobedo in 1578, had escaped to Aragon. Philip wanted to have him tried as a heretic by the Inquisition. Perez appealed to the highest judicial officer in Aragon, the Justiciar, for protection.

These incidents led many Aragonese nobles to fear that Philip II wanted to remove the liberties and independence of Aragon. Although Philip II won the right to overrule the Justiciar, he did acknowledge the rights and liberties of Aragon. By the time of his death in 1598, Castile and Aragon were still two separate kingdoms.

Summary

Whether or not you think Philip II was an absolute monarch depends ultimately on your own definition of the term 'absolute'. Philip was absolute in Castile in the sense that he had no superior. He was the source of all authority and made all the appointments and laws.

However, there was a lot of difference between being absolute in theory and absolute in practice. As the historian I. Thompson states, in *War and Government in Habsburg Spain, 1560–1621* (1976), 'absolute monarchy is to be judged not by what it looked like but how it worked'. Perhaps it is against this statement that Philip II's Spain should be viewed.

1. In what ways have historians differed in their views on the issue that Philip II might have been an absolute monarch?

2. Why do you think historians have differed in their views on Philip II as a possible absolute monarch?

3. What evidence is there to suggest that Philip II's Spain could not be regarded as an absolute monarchy?

9.3 How did the Spanish overseas empire develop in the years 1556 to 1598?

Audiencias: A high court of appeal in Castile.

Philip II had inherited from his father a vast set of territories in the Americas. By 1556 Charles had already established Spanish government in the form of **audiencias** (see Chapter 6). From 1524 a Council of the

Indies supervised these territories. However, Philip was aware that Spanish control of these lands was superficial. During his reign, he attempted to increase control over the Americas. He extended the system of government already in existence. Three new audiencias were created: in 1553 in Charcas, in 1563 in Quito and in 1583 in Manila in the Philippine Islands in the western Pacific.

Conquistadores: Individuals who sought to conquer new lands for Spain, such as Hernán Cortés in Mexico.

The **conquistadores** had played such a major role in gaining lands for Spain in the first half of the 16th century. Under Philip II, their activities were controlled more strictly. In 1573 Philip issued a new code of conduct for potential conquistadores. They were warned that 'discoverers by land and sea shall not engage in war or conquest, nor support one Indian faction against another, nor do them any harm, nor take any of their property'.

This policy was influenced by reports of brutality from Catholic missionaries in the Americas. However, other factors played a part. In 1561 a major revolt by Zacateco and Guachichile Indians broke out in northern New Spain (modern-day Colombia and Venezuela). Even civil war between Spanish settlers had occurred, most notably in Peru in the late 1540s.

In governing the Americas Philip was fortunate to have the support of excellent colonial officials. One of the most important was Francisco de Toledo who was Viceroy of Peru from 1569 to 1581. Under his leadership, Peru was brought under effective royal control. He destroyed the last centres of Inca power. In 1572 he executed the last Inca ruler, Topa Amaru. He also began an extensive survey of Peru which allowed him to introduce a **poll tax** on every adult male Indian.

Poll tax: A tax which is placed on individual people, rather than on goods and services.

Perhaps Toledo's greatest achievement was the development of the silver mines at Potosi and Huanacavelica using Indian labour. The silver from Peru became a very important source of income for Philip II (see insert on page 201). The discovery of large quantities of precious metals attracted attention from other European states: Havana in Cuba was attacked in 1555 by the French; during Elizabeth I's reign, English 'sea dogs' attacked Spanish shipping in search of booty (valuables).

To combat these problems, Philip appointed Pedro Menendez de Aviles as Captain-General of the Indies fleet in 1561. Menendez introduced a convoy system to protect Spanish shipping. As Havana was the main meeting point of homeward-bound convoys, he fortified the harbour. This did not stop foreigners taking part in American trade. Henry Kamen quotes a Seville merchant who, in 1578, claimed 'all the trade is in the hands of Flemings, English and French'. Spain's failure to prevent this development had a long-term impact on the economy, which went into decline in the 17th century.

It was also during Philip II's reign that the decrees of the Council of Trent were spread to the New World. These had a significant effect on the operation of the monastic orders, such as Dominicans and Franciscans. These had been so important to the development of Christianity in the first half of the 16th century. Following the Mexican church councils of 1565 and 1585, the power of the monastic orders was reduced.

Instead, the power of the secular clergy (bishops and priests) was increased. This gave Philip greater control over the Catholic Church in the Americas, as all bishops were appointed by royal authority. Unfortunately, this development had an adverse effect on the Indians. The Franciscan attempts to educate the Indians were largely abandoned.

Although Philip II planned to consolidate rather than expand his colonial possessions, two significant developments occurred during his reign. In 1565 an expedition by Miguel Lopez de Legazpi led to the conquest of the Philippine Islands in the western Pacific. This gave the Spanish the opportunity to participate in the spice trade, which was dominated by the Portuguese.

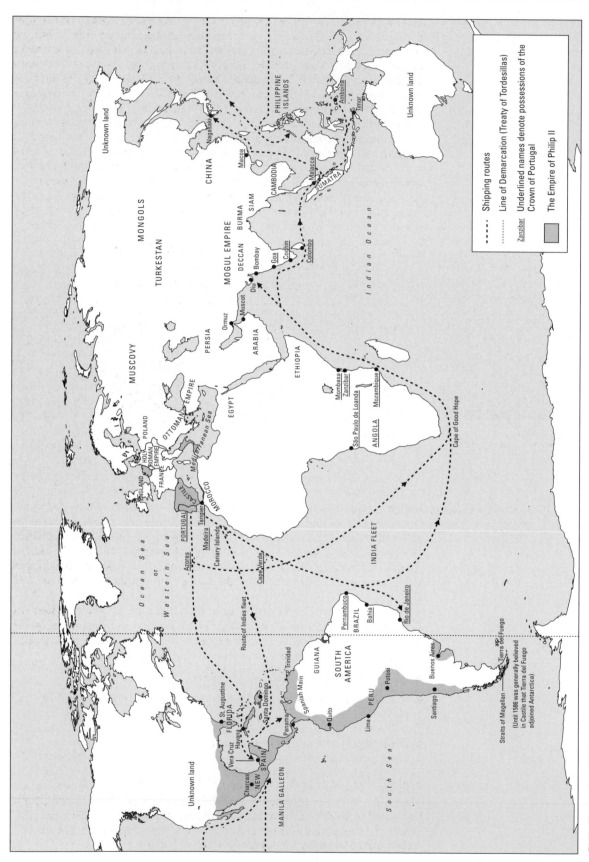

Philip II's empire, 1580

Opposition from the Portuguese was overcome in 1580 when Philip became King of Portugal. In one year Philip's colonial possessions increased considerably. He now controlled Brazil, and Portuguese colonies in Africa, India, China and South East Asia (see map). These allowed him to control trade with China and Japan and the trade in spices. By the time of his death, in 1598, Spain had grown from the position of a major western European power into a world colonial power.

However, the colonial history of Philip's reign cannot always be seen as successful. During his reign the condition of the Indians continued to decline. Outbreaks of smallpox and other European diseases greatly reduced their numbers. In the 1550s, Philip gave the Spanish settlers permission to exploit Indian labour – the *repartimiento* system. It reversed his father's policy on the treatment of Indians. By 1600 this change had resulted in the break up of Indian communities.

1. What were the major changes that affected the Spanish overseas empire during Philip II's reign?

2. How important was the Spanish overseas empire to Philip II?

3. To what extent can Philip's policies towards his overseas empire be regarded as successful?

Imports of gold and silver from the Americas to Spain during the reign of Philip II

Figures given in ducats [1 ducat was worth 375 maravedis].

Period	Total
1556–1560	9,598,798
1561–1565	13,449,043
1566–1570	16,969,459
1571–1575	14,287,931
1576–1580	20,702,329
1581–1585	35,249,534
1586–1590	28,599,157
1591–1595	42,221,835
1596–1600	41,314,201

Silver ducat of King Philip II

9.4 How successful were Philip II's religious policies?

In 1566 Philip II wrote to his ambassador in Rome stating that 'You may assure His Holiness [The Pope] that rather than suffer the least damage to religion and the service of God, I would rather lose all my states and a hundred lives, if I had them; for I do not propose or desire to be a ruler of heretics.'

To many people at the time, and since, this statement summed up Philip's view towards religion. He has been seen as one of the great defenders of the Catholic Church against Protestantism, Islam and Judaism. During his reign four important policies require analysis:

● Philip's reform of the Catholic Church within Spain;

● the use of the Inquisition to keep Spain a purely Catholic country;

● Philip's relations with the Papacy;

● Philip's policy towards the Moriscos.

The reform of the Catholic Church within Spain

Since the reigns of Ferdinand and Isabella, the Catholic Church within Spain had gone through a process of reform. The Catholic Reformation, of which the Counter Reformation was a part, which predated Luther and Calvin. However, by the accession of Philip II, in January 1556, the Catholic

Tridentine liturgy: Religious beliefs of the Catholic Church, which were agreed at the Council of Trent.

Roman Missal: A religious book containing the main prayers and religious services of the Catholic Church.

Church in Spain was still in need of reform. There were many forms of worship. Remoter parts of Castile, such as Galicia, still practised folk religion, which was a mixture of magic and Christianity. Also, large numbers of priests were either illiterate or poorly educated. Many lived in poverty.

The Council of Trent provided the catalyst for change. During the final sessions of the Council, in 1562 and 1563, the Spanish played an active part: Jesuits such as Diego Lainez and Salmeron, Franciscans such as Alfonso de Castro and Dominicans such as Domingo de Soto. The Spanish provided one of the strongest delegations, after the Italians.

However, not all the decisions agreed on at Trent received Spanish approval. Most notable was Spanish reluctance to accept any increase in Papal authority. Nevertheless, Spain accepted the decrees of the Council in July 1554 (only six months after the Pope accepted the Council's findings).

According to Henry Kamen, in *Spain 1469–1714* (1991), 'Trent revolutionised Spanish Catholicism'. This meant that during Philip II's reign the **Tridentine liturgy** was introduced throughout Spain, replacing older prayer books and orders of religious service. By 1571 it was reported back to Rome that all the dioceses of Spain had accepted the new **Roman Missal** and order of religious service. By the end of the reign, all priests had to wear the same distinctive religious dress, preach sermons once a week and encourage the use of the confessional.

Religious conformity was also increased through the strengthening of the power of bishops. In 1572, Philip created a new archdiocese in Burgos, and seven new dioceses in the Kingdom of Aragon. Bishops made sure that the decrees of Trent were implemented. An example of this development is the career of Gaspar de Quiroga who became Archbishop of Toledo and, subsequently, a Cardinal. He developed a strong working relationship with the Jesuits and Augustinian monks who helped him introduce religious changes. These included the development of education and charity for the poor. Most importantly, Quiroga published the *Manual of the Sacraments*, in 1581, which regulated the use of the sacraments in Spain.

Quiroga acted in a firm disciplinary way. He laid down strict codes of conduct for his priests, including the need to record all baptisms, marriages and deaths, and the need to keep religious services separate from social events such as fiestas and bullfights.

In addition to changes in religious service, efforts were made to improve the education of the clergy. This involved establishing seminaries to train and educate priests. By the time of Philip's death, in 1598, 20 new seminaries were created. Surprisingly, Quiroga failed to establish a seminary in his area of jurisdiction, Toledo. In the mid-17th century Spanish bishops were still complaining about the levels of illiteracy among their priests.

According to Dominguez Ortiz, in *The Golden Age of Spain 1516–1659* (1971), the Catholic Church in Philip's reign was 'characterised by a yearning for an intense religious life, purified and disciplined by the hierarchy. From it sprang a militant Catholicism which found its most typical expression in Spain and manifested itself in a variety of fields: teaching, missions for the people, charitable institutions, a flowering of religious art.' Late 16th-century Spain saw the reform of many monastic orders. Perhaps the most notable was the formation of the Discalced (barefooted) Carmelites by St Teresa of Avila in 1562. It also saw the growth of religious literature. Even today works by St Teresa of Avila appear on A-level specifications as examples of Spanish literature.

The implementation of the decrees of the Council of Trent achieved a reconversion of Spain.

The Spanish Inquisition during Philip II's reign

Although the Catholic Church was in urgent need of reform by the accession of Philip II, Spain did not experience a Protestant Reformation which affected areas such as Germany, France and the Netherlands. The reasons for the lack of success of Protestantism can be attributed to the operation of the Holy Office of the Inquisition.

Established during the reigns of Ferdinand and Isabella, the Spanish Inquisition was under strict royal control. To many Protestants the Spanish Inquisition is proof positive that the 'Black Legend of Philip II' was true. To them, the Inquisition was a clear example of Philip II's tyranny. However, from 1562 until the end of Philip II's reign, only six Protestants were burnt at the stake.

The limited impact of Protestantism can be attributed to many factors. One was the degree of censorship. On 7 September 1558 Philip II introduced a censorship law which declared that anyone who imported a book without a royal licence was punishable by death. In addition, an Index of banned books was drawn up. The Index was revised regularly. Between 1583 and 1584 Cardinal Quiroga, who had become Inquisitor-General, greatly enlarged the number of banned books. The list even included books by Thomas More and John Fisher, later to be made saints of the Catholic Church. Their books were banned because of the fear that their views might be misinterpreted.

Not only were certain books banned from Spain, but a block was also put on Spaniards studying abroad. When he returned from the Netherlands, in 1559, Philip II forbade all Spaniards to study at foreign universities, including those in his own dominions such as the University of Louvain in the Netherlands.

The Inquisition also held a series of *autos de fe*, at the beginning of Philip's reign, which virtually destroyed Lutheran ideas within Spain. Under Inquisitor-General Fernando de Valdes, Protestant groups were uncovered in cities such as Valladolid, Seville and the university city of Salamanca. Between 1559 and 1562, six *autos de fe* took place. Philip himself attended the one at Valladolid, in 1559. In total, 77 people were put to death.

It must be remembered that the Spanish Inquisition was not established to deal with the threat of Protestantism. Initially, its main function was to uncover **Conversos** and Moriscos who were still secretly practising Judaism and Islam. Also during Philip's reign, the Inquisition was used to punish Catholics who had committed religious crimes.

According to Henry Kamen, in *Inquisition and Society in Spain in the Sixteenth and Seventeenth Centuries* (1984), over half of those arrested by the Inquisition in Toledo between 1540 and 1614 were Catholics accused of crimes such as **blasphemy** and bigamy.

Perhaps the fearsome reputation of the Spanish Inquisition has been exaggerated. According to Geoffrey Woodward, in *Philip II* (1992), of the 40,000 cases dealt with by the Spanish Inquisition during Philip's reign only 250 were put to death. Others were given varying degrees of punishment. In many ways the Inquisition acted as a deterrent, ensuring that the Spanish kept the Catholic faith. Compared to the numbers killed for religious reasons in France from 1560 to 1598 and in the Netherlands during the Dutch Revolt, Spain escaped remarkably lightly. Also, the Inquisition could be seen as tolerant in other respects. While a witch-burning craze affected many parts of Europe in the late 16th and early 17th centuries (see Chapter 16), the Inquisition did not regard witchcraft as heresy.

Conversos: Jews who had converted to Catholicism in Spain.

Blasphemy: Statements made against the Catholic Church.

Philip II's relations with the Papacy

According to historian John Lynch, in *Philip II and the Papacy*, written in 'The Transactions of the Royal Historical Society' (1961), the monarchy's control over the Church 'was probably more complete in Spain in the 16th

Popes during the reign of Philip II	
1555–1559	Paul IV
1559–1565	Pius IV
1566–1572	Pius V
1572–1585	Gregory XIII
1585–1590	Sixtus V
1590	Urban VII
1590–1591	Gregory XIV
1591–1592	Innocent IX
1592–1605	Clement VIII

century than in any other part of Europe'. The reforms of the Catholic Monarchs and Charles I had secured this enviable position for Philip II.

To Philip II the Pope was both the leader of western Christianity and an Italian prince. As a result, Philip clashed with several popes over issues such as foreign policy. Given Philip's immense political power, successive popes were fearful of his influence over the Catholic Church. One of Philip II's great achievements was to accept the main changes of the Council of Trent, but to question the power of the Pope to intervene in the affairs of the Catholic Church in Spain. This won Philip considerable support across Catholic Europe.

A major area of dispute was money. Philip and his predecessors had received large sums of money from the Spanish Church. These included the royal third of all church tithes collected in Spain, the *subsidio* (an annual payment by the Church of approximately 400,000 ducats) and the *cruzada*. This last payment was granted to Philip's father as a payment for a crusade against the Muslims. It amounted to around 500,000 ducats a year. Although Pius V tried to stop the *cruzada*, in 1566, the same pope granted Philip extra money through the *excusado*, a tax on Spanish church property. By 1571, when Philip was organising the Holy League against the Turks (see section on foreign policy), the Spanish king received what he termed the 'Three Graces', Papal contributions to his revenue. These were the *cruzada*, the *excusado* and the *subsidio*. However, in 1585, Sixtus V was elected Pope. He had a personal dislike of Philip and refused to give Philip any extra money towards the Spanish Armada unless the Armada was successful. Sixtus was on the verge of excommunicating Philip when he died in August 1590.

Another area of dispute was over control of the Society of Jesus (the Jesuits). Relations between Philip and the Jesuits was good, as long as the leader of the Society was Spanish. Then in 1573 the first non-Spaniard, Mercurian, was appointed General of the Order. Philip made efforts to reduce the power of the General. However, by 1593, Pope Clement VIII sided with the then non-Spanish General Aquaviva in opposing Philip's interference.

The main area of conflict between Philip and the Papacy came in foreign policy. Throughout the early 16th century the Papacy tried to maintain its independence from both France and Spain during the Italian Wars (1494–1559). In the second half of the century France was weakened by the Wars of Religion, which allowed Spain to become western Europe's most powerful state. Pius V clashed with Philip on the issue of Elizabeth I's excommunication. When the Pope excommunicated Elizabeth, in 1570, without informing Philip, it thwarted Spanish attempts to bring England back into the Habsburg sphere of influence. Towards the end of his reign, Pope Clement VIII disrupted Philip's plans for intervention in France by allowing Henry IV of France to become Catholic.

On occasion Pope and King did work together. The most notable example was in 1571 with the formation of the Holy League against the Turks. The victory at the Battle of Lepanto led to a period of good relations. Unfortunately, this came to an end when Philip made a truce with the Turks in 1578.

Philip II's policy towards the Moriscos

The most serious rebellion Philip II faced within Spain took place from 1568 to 1570. It involved the Moriscos in Granada. The whole episode was a chapter in Spain's move from a land of religious tolerance (known as the *conviviencia*), which had existed during the Middle Ages, to a land of one religion, by the early 17th century. The Moriscos were the Moorish subjects of the Spanish monarchy who had been forced to convert from Islam to Christianity at the end of the 15th century.

Although Christians they remained a society separate from the rest of Spain. By 1556 some 400,000 out of a population of nine million lived in Castile and Aragon. However, most Moriscos lived in Andalucia, the former state of Granada. There were regarded as second-class subjects of the monarchy. A distinction was made between New and Old Christians in Spain. Old Christians were those who had *limpieza de sangre* ('purity of blood'). That meant they did not have any Jewish or Muslim ancestors. New Christians, the Moriscos and Conversos could not become priests, join the army or have a legal career. There is some dispute about the wealth of the Moriscos. According to L. W. Cowie, in *Sixteenth Century Europe* (1977), 'they were mostly poor and unimportant, and the notion that they were the most industrious part of the population is without foundation'. This view may have been true of the Moriscos living in Aragon and Valencia. However, in Granada, Moriscos were involved in the silk industry.

By the 1560s Moriscos were still a distinctive community in language, customs and the way they dressed. A law of 1526 banning these practices had not been enforced. Not only were the Moriscos a distinctive minority in religious terms, they were also seen as potential supporters of the Turks and the Muslim states of North Africa. With the conflict between Philip II and the Muslim states reaching a new intensity in the 1560s, the Moriscos were seen as agents of a foreign power.

The Morisco revolt in Granada had a number of causes. Between 1560 and 1565 the tax on silk was doubled by the Spanish government. Also, a government commission into the ownership of land confiscated Morisco land – around 100,000 hectares between 1559 and 1568. These events took place when Spain's war with the Muslims became more intense. In 1565 the Turks attacked Malta. In the same year, Muslim forces attacked the coast of Granada and got as far as Orgiva, some 40 kilometres inland.

The catalyst for revolt was both political and economic. On New Year's Day 1567, a royal decree banned the distinctive Morisco dress, and Arabic songs and lierature. In the same year a poor harvest brought economic hardship to Granada. From that time on, the Moriscos of Granada began planning for a revolt which broke out on Christmas Eve 1568, when Spanish troops were moved from Granada to the coast to protect Pain from Muslim attack.

The Morisco Revolt, under the leadership of Fernando de Valor, was the most serious revolt within Spain during the 16th century. The revolt's centre was the Alpujarras region in the Sierra Nevada mountains. It took place when most of the Spanish army was either in the Netherlands or involved in protecting Spain. The Morisco rebels numbered 30,000 by 1569. They were supported by nearly 5,000 Turkish and Berber volunteers from North Africa. The Spanish army, under Don Juan of Austria, was only 20,000 in number. It began a full-scale campaign in 1570.

According to John Lynch, in *Spain under the Habsburgs, 1516–1598* (1981), 'the revolt had lasted two years and strained the resources of the country to the utmost'. However, it could have been much worse. The Moriscos of Aragon and Valencia stayed loyal to the Spanish monarchy and did not take part in the revolt.

By a royal decree of 28 October 1570, the Spanish government decided to deport between 80,000 to 100,000 Moriscos from the Granada area and forced them to resettle in other parts of Spain, such as Extremadura and Castile. In their place about 50,000 Old Christians were given former Morisco lands in the Granada region. In took until 1609, during the reign of Philip III, for all Moriscos to be expelled from Spain.

1. What changes did Philip II make in religious matters within Spain during his reign?

2. What do you think was the most important religious change made during the reign of Philip II? Give reasons for your answer.

3. What do you regard as the most successful of Philip II's religious policies?

Give reasons for your answer.

4. To what extent can you defend the actions of the Catholic Church in Spain?

9.5 What were the social and economic problems that affected Spain during the reign of Philip II?

What financial problems did Philip II face during his reign?

In his Instructions to his son, in 1543, Charles I suggested that Philip 'attend closely to finances and learn to understand the problems involved'. In a sense this was an understatement. Throughout his reign Philip faced severe financial problems. He inherited a large debt which forced him into bankruptcy in 1557.

Philip's own foreign policy proved hugely expensive. For instance, the 'Enterprise of England' (Spanish Armada) cost 10 million ducats. By the year of his death, Spain had a debt of 85 million ducats, the interest payments alone were equivalent to 40% of Philip's annual revenue. In all, Philip went bankrupt four times – in 1557, 1560, 1575 and 1596.

The essence of Philip's financial problems was the fact that his foreign policy commitments could not be met through revenue raised in his own dominions. During his reign he was at war with France from 1556 to 1559 and again in the 1590s. He was at war with England from 1585. He was also intermittently at war with the Turks and the Muslim states of North Africa. Early in the reign, the Netherlands had been an important source of revenue. However, with the outbreak of the Dutch Revolt, this was severely disrupted. By the end of his reign, Philip had spent 80 million ducats trying to put down the revolt. As a result, Philip began to depend more and more on Spain and gold and silver bullion from the New World.

Philip was able to get revenue from three main sources: those he could collect in his own right, those he collected from the Catholic Church and those for which he needed a vote in the Cortes.

The first source included revenue from royal lands and the Military Orders. It also included customs duties. This latter category increased three-fold during his reign, from 56,000 ducats in 1556 to 150,000 in 1598. The most important source of revenue was the Quinta (royal fifth) of all gold and silver bullion imported from the New World. Study the figures on the importation of gold and silver bullion which appear in the section on the Spanish overseas empire (page 198). You will see how this source provided Philip with a large amount of revenue.

The second source was the Catholic Church. These taxes were called the 'Three Graces': the *subsidio*, the *cruzada* and the *excusado*. These brought Philip approximately 1.3 million ducats annually.

A third source of income came from monies granted to Philip by the Cortes. The most important was the *alcabala* (a sales tax similar to VAT) of 10%. At the beginning of the reign, it brought in around one million ducats. This was tripled by the 1570s. However, the Cortes cut the amount to 2.7 million by 1598. Another direct tax was the *servicio*. From 1590 an indirect tax was placed on goods such as wine and vinegar known as the *millones*. From 1596 a new tax was granted, the *sisa*, on basic foodstuffs. Taxes such as the *alcabala*, *millones* and *sisa* fell most heavily on the poor who found it increasingly difficult to pay them.

The sums Philip was able to raise did not meet the expenditures he incurred. Therefore, he had to fill the gap by borrowing money. The two major sources of loans were the Spinoza family in Genoa and the Fugger family in Augsburg. In 1568 a large loan from the Genoese was seized by Elizabeth I while it was being transported to the Netherlands to pay Alba's army.

By the time of his death, Philip II had a debt of 68 million ducats.

However, he had only continued the practice begun by his father and followed by every other monarch in late 16th-century Europe.

Philip II's financial problems

In 1560 and again in 1575 Philip was declared bankrupt.

Figures are in millions of ducats

Year	Income	Debt	Interest payment on debt
1560	3.1	25.5	1.6
1575	5.5	40	2.7
1598	9.7	85.5	4.6

Why did Spain suffer rising prices during Philip's reign?

There is a direct link between Philip's financial problems and the rise in prices in Spain during the second half of the 16th century. The Price Revolution, or inflation, was a Europe-wide phenomenon.

Spain was in part responsible. The large influx of gold and silver bullion into Europe from the Spanish New World greatly increased the circulation of precious metals in Europe. As these precious metals formed the basis of money, it led to a increase in the money supply. With greater supplies of money chasing a limited amount of goods, prices were bound to rise.

However, there were other factors that led to rising prices. From 1530 to 1580 there was a steady rise in population in Castile and Aragon. Unfortunately, agricultural production did not match this rise in population. In addition, from time to time harvests failed leading to an acute shortage of food. Harvest failures occurred throughout the reign but most regularly in the 1590s. The combined effects of these developments meant that demand outstripped supply, thus forcing up prices.

The costs of warfare had an inflationary effect on Spain. Philip's requirement for weapons led to increased demand for imports. For instance, during the Morisco Revolt of 1568–1570 Spain had to import 80% of the weapons.

Rising prices make it difficult to calculate the precise value of money. Therefore, although Philip's revenue and debts rose considerably during his reign some of the rise can be accounted for by the increase in inflation. A social consequences of rising prices was an increase in **vagrancy and brigandage** towards the end of the reign as the poor began to wander the countryside in pursuit of food.

How far did the population structure of Spain change during Philip's reign?

During Philip II's reign there was a steady rise in population. This had begun in the early part of the century and continued until around 1580. From that year on, population growth began to stagnate, leading to a gradual decline of population in the 17th century.

The decline in the birth rate from 1580 onwards seems to have had a number of causes. Many young Spanish men were absent from Spain fighting wars on foreign soil. Also, there seems to be a high incidence of celibacy (decision not to have sexual relations) in Spain. Finally, Spain suffered the effects of famine and plague in the 1590s. This had a devastating effect on parts of the country. In Old Castile alone approximately 600,000 died between 1596 and 1602.

Vagrancy and brigandage: Vagrants were people, of no fixed abode, who wandered the countryside begging or looking for work. Brigands were thieves and bandits who made a living through robbery.

Another development during Philip II's reign was a movement of population from the north towards the south. Associated with this development was the growth of towns. Cities such as Cadiz, Seville and Malaga all grew, no doubt benefiting from increased trade. Cordoba grew from 28,000 in 1530 to 50,000 by 1571.

Population growth in Spain 1530 to 1591

Area	1530	% of total pop.	1591	% of total pop.
Castile	4,400,000	78	6,600,000	81
Aragon	280,000	5	340,000	4
Catalonia	312,000	5.4	373,000	4.5
Valencia	300,000	5.2	400,000	5

How did Spanish trade develop between 1556 and 1598?

1. Why did Philip suffer from major financial problems during his reign?

2. Were Philip II's financial problems the most important reason for the rise in prices between 1556 and 1598? Give reasons for your answer.

3. To what extent did Spain experience social and economic change during Philip II's reign?

Due to poor internal communications and the division of Spain into a number of political units, internal trade was limited during Philip's reign. The most important trading centre was Medina del Campo, in Old Castile. Each year two fairs were held, which attracted trades from all over Spain and beyond.

Traditionally, Spain had been an exporter of raw materials. This continued during the second half of the 16th century. Wool produced by the Mesta was exported through north Spanish ports to northern Europe, in particular the Netherlands. However, the outbreak of the Dutch Revolt severely disrupted this trade. Spain also exported hides and iron from the Basque provinces (see map on page 193). Trade within the Mediterranean was disrupted by the advance of the Turks and the piracy of the Barbary pirates of North Africa.

The major change in the pattern of trade was the development of the trans-atlantic trade with the New World. The most important import was gold and silver bullion. Although a number of towns and cities benefited from the trans-atlantic trade, it was Seville which benefited most. From 1572 Philip II declared that Seville was the only official port allowed to trade with the New World.

Seville in the 16th century – a contemporary woodcut

9.6 How successful was Philip II in foreign affairs?

What were Philip II's aims in foreign policy?

In the past Philip II has received a bad press in foreign policy. 'The Black Legend', put forward by European Protestants, saw Philip as an aggressive Catholic monarch determined to destroy Protestantism. Some historians have regarded Philip II in a similar light. R. Trevor Davies, in *The Golden Age of Spain 1501–1621* (1937), entitled his chapter on Philip's foreign policy as 'Philip II's *Weltpolitik*'. This implied Philip was no different in his policy from the aggressive foreign policy of Germany before the First World War. Davies went on to say that one of Philip's aims was 'the domination of the British Isles and France by means of intervening in their religious struggles'.

Since then, historians have seen Philip in a more favourable light. According to historian Piers Pierson, in *Philip II of Spain* (1975), Philip's policies 'were generally regarded as conservative'. The Venetian ambassador, Michele Suriano reported in 1559 that Philip's aim was 'not to wage war so that he can add to his kingdom, but to wage peace so that he can keep the lands he has'. Henry Kamen, in his biography of Philip (1997), goes further by stating that Philip did not really have a policy at all:

> 'Decision-making in 16th-century government was not what it is today. Modern governments have a "policy" which they attempt to put into effect. At that time governments had no policy. They simply responded to events as the need arose.'

Therefore, Philip should be seen as defensive minded, following his father's Instructions of 1543 that he should not give up one inch of territory. If it is possible to identify aims, Philip's were to defend his inheritance and to defend the Catholic world against both Protestantism and Islam. However, on occasion he could act as an opportunist. The most notable example was his acquisition of the Portuguese throne in 1580.

How successful was Philip's policy towards Islam?

Philip, like his father, saw himself as the defender of the Catholic world against Islam. Among his many royal titles Philip called himself 'king of Jerusalem'. In this sense, Philip's policy can be traced back to the Crusades of the Middle Ages.

Philip also followed the more traditional Spanish policy of controlling the North African coastline, a policy begun under Ferdinand of Aragon. Philip's policy can be divided into two time periods: 1556–1578 and 1578 to the end of his reign. In the first period, Philip attempted to prevent the Turks from dominating the central Mediterranean area. In 1560 he launched an expedition to retake Tripoli. However, the Spanish expedition suffered a disastrous defeat at the hands of Dragut, leader of the Barbary pirates, on the island of Djerba – losing 10,000 men. In 1563, however, Philip was successful in taking Oran.

The major confrontation between Philip and the Ottoman Turks took place in 1570–71. Although the Turks had failed to take Malta, in 1565, they seemed on the verge of dominating the central Mediterranean. Their Muslim allies had taken Tunis and the Turks were about to attack Cyprus. The creation of a Holy League against the Turks was Philip's greatest diplomatic triumph in the Mediterranean area. It comprised Spain, Venice, the Pope, Genoa and the smaller Italian states. According to J. H. Parry, in the *New Cambridge Modern History* Volume IX (1968), 'Philip had little of his father's crusading ardour. For him, the League presented the chance of meeting the Turks for once on equal or superior terms and securing Spanish possession of the central Mediterranean.' In this sense, the Holy League was successful. On 7 October 1571 a Catholic fleet, under the control of Philip's illegitimate half-brother, Don Juan of Austria, inflicted a crushing defeat on the Turkish fleet off the west coast of Greece.

The Battle of Lepanto has been regarded as a turning point in the conflict between Christianity and Islam. However, although Philip achieved his aim, the Turks were far from defeated. They completed their conquest of Cyprus by 1572 and rebuilt their fleet by 1574. Fortunately for Philip, following the death of Sultan Selim II, the Turks were willing to negotiate a truce by 1578. The Turks faced problems on their eastern frontier with Persia (Iran). When the Turks resumed their attacks on Christian Europe, in 1593, it was in Hungary not the Mediterranean.

How did Franco–Spanish relations develop during Philip's reign?

One of the main reasons why Spain was such a dominant western European power during Philip II's reign were the problems facing France. At the beginning of Philip's reign, Spain was engaged in a major conflict with France. Both Valois France and the Habsburgs had been locked in warfare since the outbreak of the Italian Wars in 1494.

For Philip his greatest land victory came within 18 months of his accession, at St Quentin in 1557. By the Treaty of Câteau-Cambrésis, of 1559, France was forced to recognise Spanish dominance in Italy.

What proved to be a mixed blessing for Philip was the outbreak of the French Wars of Religion in 1562. On one hand, the wars of religion neutralised Spain's greatest enemy in western Europe. On the other hand, it created the fear that Protestantism would get a firm foothold in France, from which it could threaten Philip's possessions in the Netherlands, Franche Comté and Spain itself.

The first major crisis facing Philip during the wars of religion came in 1568. In that year his French wife died which cut his links with the French royal family under Catherine de' Medici. This was followed by a French Protestant attack on Spanish Roussillon, at Perpignan in 1571, which was repulsed.

Philip's most important diplomatic involvement in the wars of religion took place in 1584 when he signed the secret Treaty of Joinville with the Catholic League against the French Protestants. From 1584 to 1589 Philip had good relations with the French king, the Catholic Henry III, as well as enjoying the support of the Guise family (which was opposed by Henry III). However, in 1589 Henry III was assassinated which led to the accession of the Protestant Henry of Navarre to the French throne. In 1590, and again in 1592, Spanish armies entered France from the Netherlands in support of the Catholic League. They even occupied Paris. However, in spite of military victories, Philip's intervention in France proved to be a failure. A decisive development was the decision by the Pope, in 1593, to allow Henry of Navarre to become a Catholic. This allowed him to be crowned Henry IV of France. In 1595 Spain declared war on France. Then, in 1596, Philip again became bankrupt, at a time when Henry IV formed alliances with England and the Dutch rebels. In the year of Philip's death, 1598, the Edict of Nantes allowed the religious toleration of French Protestantism. It also saw the Treaty of Vervins between France and Spain. With France in chaos for most of his reign, Philip II had failed to exploit this opportunity for Spain's benefit.

Why did Philip II go to war with England?

When Philip became King of Spain in 1556, he was also King Consort of England. The first two years of his reign formed the highest point of

Habsburg influence in western Europe. The Habsburgs dominated Italy and had France surrounded (see map on page 193).

In 1558, with the accession of Elizabeth I, Philip tried to continue the policy of friendship and alliance with England. He was able to persuade the Pope not to excommunicate Elizabeth even though she had been brought up as a Protestant. Philip even considered the possibility of marriage to keep England within the Habsburg sphere of influence.

The major issue in Anglo–Spanish relations was the Netherlands. For Philip the friendship of England was important in keeping the sea route to the Netherlands open. The alternative route was the so-called 'Spanish Road' overland to the Netherlands from Genoa (see map on page 299). This land route was vulnerable to French attack.

To Elizabeth the Netherlands were important for both economic and military reasons. Antwerp was the main port for the importation of English woollen cloth to Europe. Any disruption of the export of wool would have had a serious effect on the English economy. Elizabeth also feared possible invasion from the Netherlands under Spanish military control. She feared Philip wanted to lead a Catholic crusade to win back England to the Church of Rome.

Relations began to deteriorate from 1568 when Elizabeth seized a shipment of Genoese gold that was en route to the Spanish army in the Netherlands. They were made worse by Catholic conspiracies to replace Elizabeth with Mary Stuart of Scotland.

However, relations reached breaking point in 1584. Philip's treaty with the Catholic League in France and the assassination of William the Silent in Delft, in Holland, forced the English to intervene directly in the Dutch Revolt. The Treaty of Nonsuch (June 1585) with the Dutch rebels was seen by Philip as an attempt by Elizabeth to intervene directly in his own lands.

The war with England was fought mainly at sea and in Ireland. The English navy disrupted Spanish trade with the New World. Spain attempted to aid the Tyrone rebellion in Ireland. Perhaps the most famous episode was the 'Enterprise of England' in 1588. The Spanish Armada has been portrayed as an act of aggression by Philip – an attempt to invade England to return it to Catholicism. However, Philip had hoped to use the Armada as a way to prevent Elizabeth intervening in the Dutch Revolt. He failed. Later, in 1596 and 1597, he sent further Armadas but these were prevented from reaching England because of severe weather.

What was the importance of the acquisition of Portugal on Philip's foreign policy?

The unification of the Iberian peninsula had long been the aim of Christian kings. When Castile was faced with civil war at the beginning of Isabella's reign, in 1469, the King of Portugal had attempted to unite his kingdom with Castile.

By 1578, through marriage (see family tree on page 192), Philip II had a claim on the Portuguese throne. In that year the Portuguese king, along with most of the Portuguese nobility, was killed at the Battle of Alcázarquivir in Morocco. He was succeeded by a 66-year-old great uncle, Henry, who died in 1580.

In acquiring the Portuguese throne, Philip II displayed considerable ingenuity. Within six months of Henry's death, 37,000 Spanish troops invaded and took over Portugal. Philip had already received support for his claim from the Church and nobility in the Portuguese Cortes before the invasion. From 1580 to 1583 Philip resided in Lisbon where he recognised and followed Portuguese customs. In 1581 the Cortes of

Tomar recognised Philip as king; the following year he recognised Portuguese liberties. From 1580, although Philip ruled Portugal, it remained a separate political unit with its own laws.

In 1580 the Iberian peninsula (Spain and Portugal) was united for the first time under one ruler since the days of the Roman Empire. The title of 'King of Portugal' increased Philip's international prestige and gave him a large colonial empire which included Brazil and the Spice Islands. This confirmed Philip II as the most powerful ruler in Europe. It also gave him an ocean-going navy. This allowed him the opportunity to follow a more aggressive foreign policy against England, which resulted in the Armada of 1588.

Summary

A major aspect of Philip II's foreign policy involved his relations with the Netherlands. These are dealt with in detail in the next chapter. By his death, Philip II had failed to crush the Dutch Revolt. England was outside the Spanish sphere of influence and was actively engaged in undermining the Spanish position in the Netherlands. The relations between France and Spain, by 1598, were little different from those agreed at Câteau-Cambrésis in 1559.

Yet most of the territory Philip had inherited from his father was intact. In addition, he had added Portugal and the Portuguese overseas empire, which made Philip II a ruler on the world stage. Also, Philip had to deal with several crises at the same time. For instance, in 1568 he faced a major rebellion at home (the Morisco Revolt), the Dutch Revolt, the threat of the Turks in the Mediterranean and a conflict with England over the Genoese loan. This made it difficult for Philip to use his military resources decisively in one area.

According to Geoffrey Woodward, in *Philip II* (1992), 'Philip's monarquía was far-flung and basically indefensible, only held together by the collective will of Genoese merchants, Flemish bankers, Italian and German soldiers, Portuguese and Italian sailors, American miners and Spanish officials.'

Given these limitations Philip II had been successful in defending his lands. However, he left to his son Philip III a bankrupt state which was living beyond its means.

Source-based questions: the personal rule of Philip II

SOURCE A

Our answer to this is that because of the great and urgent needs and wars we have been unable to avoid the imposed taxes and increases to which you refer in your petition, but when those necessities cease, or we find better means of providing for them, we shall be delighted to relieve these kingdoms. With respect to the salt which you mention in your petition we have annexed to our Crown the saltings* which some knights and other private individuals held.

Moreover, we have imposed a tax on the salt which is imported from Portugal using our right as owner, since salt belongs to our Crown by the laws and ancient rights of these kingdoms.

*Saltings: Places where salt is made from seawater.

From Philip II's reply to a petition from the Castilian Cortes against the introduction of new taxes, 1567.

SOURCE B

Under Philip the monarchy was in transition from personal rule to bureaucracy and royal power was much weaker in practice than it may appear. At the level of executive power, however, there is no doubt that the king was in sole command. All Philip's councils, for example were purely advisory. The king was also permitted absolute rights of life and death over every citizen.

From Spain 1469 to 1714 *by Henry Kamen, second edition, 1991*

SOURCE C

The Council of State, officially the main council, continued to be the main forum in which important Castilian nobles could offer advice to the king, although it seems to have had very little power. The regional councils were more important. They were organised to try to make them more effective.

As Philip rarely attended meetings of the councils himself, he made great use of secretaries. They served as intermediaries between Philip and the councils. The routine business was dealt with by ordinary royal secretaries, one of which was attached to each of the regional councils. But all important papers and requests were dealt with personally by Philip.

From Spain: Rise and Decline, 1474 to 1643 *by Jill Kilsby, 1987*

SOURCE D

Only in Castile was any real attempt made to centralise the administration, and even here, effective control of the towns and countryside fell to the nobility.

The Crown's principal servant in local government was the corregidor. Their main political function was to manage their local [town] council. Most of the local councils resisted the infringement of their customary rights and there was little the corregidores could do to stop them.

From Philip II *by Geoffrey Woodward, 1992*

---

1. Study Sources A and B and use information from this chapter.

Explain the meaning of the following terms which are underlined in the sources.

(a) 'Castilian Cortes' (Source A)

(b) 'Council of State' (Source C).

2. Study Sources A and B and use information from section 2 of this chapter.

How useful are Sources A and B as evidence of Philip II's relationship with the Cortes of Castile?

3. Study Sources A, B, C and D and use information from section 2 of this chapter.

To what extent did Philip II personally rule Spain?

The Dutch Revolt

Key Issues

- Why did the Netherlands seek to overthrow Spanish rule?

- Why was Spain unable to suppress the Dutch revolt?

- Why did the new Dutch state prove to be effective in political and economic affairs?

Framework of Events

1548	'Augsburg Transaction'
1555	Sovereign authority in Netherlands handed over by Charles to his son Philip
1559	Margaret of Parma, half-sister of Philip II, is appointed Regent
1561	Controversial plan for reorganisation of Roman Catholic Church in the Netherlands
1563	Orange and Egmont withdraw from meetings of the Council of State
1564	Philip II blames Granvelle for the failure of church reorganisation. Granvelle is allowed to leave the Netherlands
1565	Segovia Letters
	Bad harvest raises food prices
1566	Outbreak of iconoclasm. Margaret's Accord with nobility and Calvinists. Accord breaks down
1567	Defeat of 'First Revolt'
	Execution of Egmont and Hornes. Alba sets up Council of Troubles
1568	Absent William of Orange is condemned by Council of Troubles
1569	Alba begins the imposition of Tenth Penny
1572	Sea Beggars gain control of towns in Zeeland and Holland
	Resentment at Alba's attempts to renew the Tenth Penny
	William of Orange proclaims himself Stadholder of Holland, Zeeland and Utrecht. Mechelen and Naarden are sacked by Alba
1573	Haarlem falls to Alba's troops; Alba is recalled and replaced by Requesens. Lands around Alkmaar flooded to prevent town's capture

1574	Lands around Leiden flooded to prevent town's capture. Spanish troops vacate South Holland
1575	Philip II declares himself bankrupt. Failure of attempts at Breda to broker a peace
1576	Death of Requesens. 'Spanish Fury'
	Pacification of Ghent. Outbreak of 'Third Revolt'
1577	Don Juan of Austria takes up office as Regent
1578	Holland, Zeeland and Gelderland agree a defence treaty. Protestants gain control of Amsterdam. Duke of Parma is appointed Regent
1579	(6 January) Union of Arras
	(23 January) Union of Utrecht
	Duke of Parma captures Maastricht
1580	Province of Groningen leaves Union of Utrecht and gives allegiance to Philip II. William of Orange is outlawed by Philip II
1581	Act of Abjuration
	William of Orange publishes *Apology*
1583	'French fury'
1584	(10 July) Assassination of William of Orange
	Parma captures Ghent
1585	(17 August) Parma captures Antwerp
	Queen Elizabeth I refuses offer of sovereignty over the Netherlands, but agrees to send troops to Netherlands
1586	Earl of Leicester assumes title of Governor-General
1588	Parma links up with the Spanish Armada
1590	Parma is forced by Philip II to intervene in France, thereby weakening royal forces in Netherlands and giving Maurice of Nassau time to reorganise his army
1592	Death of Parma
1596	Treaty of Greenwich
1598	Beginning of rule of Archdukes in southern Netherlands
1600	Maurice is defeated at Battle of Nieuwpoort
	'Spanish Road' is broken by Henry IV of France
1604	Spínola captures Ostend. England and Spain make peace
1605	Spínola's forces recapture territory in north-east of Netherlands
1606	Spanish army breaks across IJssel line
1607	Armistice (ceasefire)
1609	Truce of Antwerp ('Twelve Years' Truce'). Dutch support for Protestant claimants in Cleves-Jülich dispute
1616	Severe riots in Delft
1617	(January) Start of open quarrel between Maurice and Oldenbarnevelt
	(August) Estates of Holland authorise towns to raise own troops
	(September) Maurice begins counter-attack
1618	National Synod held at Dordrecht
1619	Execution of Oldenbarnevelt
1620	Open hostilities between Spain and United Provinces resume
1621	West India Company is set up
1624	Piet Heyn captures Bahía in Brazil
1625	Breda is captured by Spínola
	Hague Coalition – United Provinces, England, Denmark
1626	Dutch capture Oldenzaal
1628	Heyn captures entire Spanish silver fleet in Matanzas Bay
1629	War of Mantuan Succession
1630	Treaty of Madrid. Capture of Recife by West India Company
1631	Dutch recapture Maastricht
1637	Dutch recapture Breda
1639	Dutch defeat Spanish fleet at Battle of the Downs
1643	Philip IV's offers of peace are rejected
1646	Preliminary peace agreement
1648	Peace formally agreed.

Overview

Netherlands: All 17 provinces which at the time of Charles V's accession owed allegiance to Philip II of Spain. This area comprised (in modern terms) all of the Netherlands, all of Belgium, except for the area around Liège, Luxemburg and parts of what are now north-eastern France.

Union of Utrecht: This was a union of the northern provinces and foreshadowed the future rejection of the authority of the King of Spain.

I N 1555 Charles V (Charles I of Spain) conferred sovereign authority in the **Netherlands** on his son Philip. Charles had made the 17 provinces into a single political unit. At the time this seemed loyal to the sovereign authority of the House of Burgundy, whose head was now Philip II. Within a few years, however, discontent was apparent. By 1566 open rebellion had broken out. Within 13 years the northern provinces of the Netherlands had established the **Union of Utrecht**. They were on the brink of rejecting the authority of Philip II completely. Within two years they had succeeded. Yet by 1584 their rebellion seemed about to be crushed by the might of Spain. The rebel leader, William of Orange, had been assassinated, there was little land left under rebel control, and the reconquest of rebel land, set in motion by the Duke of Parma, seemed unstoppable. In the circumstances, therefore, it seems miraculous that the rebels not only survived, but were also able to set up a prosperous state which combined economic well-being with a flourishing bourgeois culture. In the words of the 19th-century American liberal historian, J. L. Motley, this feat 'must ever be regarded as one of the leading events of modern times'. Certainly, the revolt came to embody some of the most important themes of 16th-century European history:

- centralisation v. provincial estates and local liberties;

- Calvinism v. Roman Catholicism;

- Habsburg v. Valois (since the early years of the 16th century the House of Habsburg, which ruled Spain and the Holy Roman Empire, and the House of Valois, which ruled France, had been in competition for dominance in Europe. The French were, therefore, often prepared to assist the Dutch rebels to overthrow their Spanish overlords.);

- tyranny v. resistance.

10.1 What was the condition of the Netherlands at the start of the reign of Philip II?

Holland: A province in the northwest of the Netherlands. It is not identical to the modern kingdom of the Netherlands.

In 1548 the 'Augsburg Transaction' confirmed that the 17 provinces of the Netherlands had been welded together in a single unit under the control of Charles V, with its capital in Brussels. Nine provinces, mainly in the south, had been inherited by Charles as Duke of Burgundy. Eight provinces, mainly in the north, had been secured by conquest.

Much of the Netherlands was densely populated and prosperous. The western provinces of **Holland**, Zeeland, Hainaut, Flanders and Brabant were heavily urbanised and dependent on trade. Antwerp was the largest town in the Netherlands. It was also the most commercially prosperous town, as well as being one of Europe's key banking centres. Towns in Holland such as Amsterdam and Haarlem were increasing in prosperity and were much involved in trade with the Baltic. On the other hand, formerly important towns such as Ghent and Bruges were beginning to decline. The eastern part of the Netherlands was less densely populated and less urbanised.

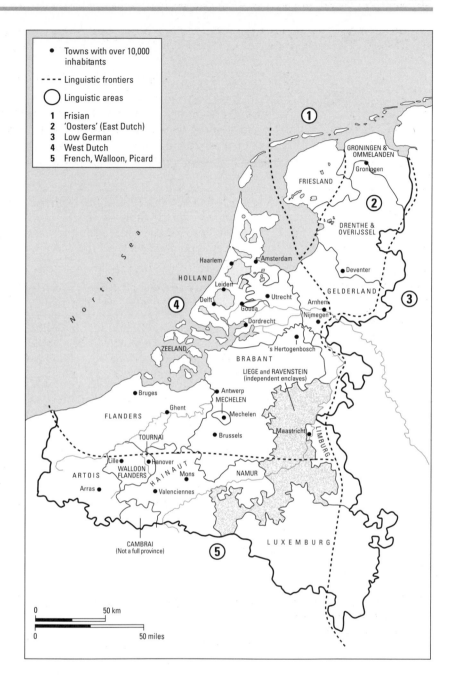

The Habsburg Netherlands in 1549

The Government of the Netherlands

Governor-General

The Governor-General was the person appointed by Philip II to exercise royal authority in the Netherlands on his behalf. In effect, the Governor-General was the king's regent. To assist the Governor-General there were three councils: the Council of State, a gathering mainly of nobles which had responsibility for areas such as internal security; the Council of Finance; and the Privy Council, which had responsibility for justice. In addition, there were law courts in each province, linked to a supreme court based in Mechelen.

Regent: The figure who dominated the government of major towns and who also, therefore, played an important role within the State of their province.

Stadholder

The term 'stadholder' roughly equates with the English 'governor'. The office of Stadholder was in the gift of the sovereign authority. In other words, before the Revolt stadholders were appointed by Charles or Philip and were directly responsible to the monarch. Charles V had divided the northern provinces into three for purposes of the appointment of stadholders, thereby preventing any individual stadholder from becoming too powerful. By 1572 the appointment of William of Orange to the stadholderates in Holland, Zeeland and Utrecht had been illegally taken over by the States, though at this stage they claimed to be acting in the king's name. After the assassination of William of Orange in 1584, the nature of the stadholderate once again became diverse. The States General appointed two stadholders to the provinces other than Holland and Zeeland; in Holland and Zeeland it was to be the right of the provincial states to appoint someone to the post.

States General

Delegations from each of the provincial states met in the States General, which was a parliament representing the whole of the Netherlands.
Because the States General met only once every three years, and because its decisions were required to be unanimous, the States General was an inefficient part of the decision-making process.

---

1   Meetings were held every three years.

2   The most common reason for the summoning of the States General was to discuss tax demands. Meetings were, therefore, usually unpopular with taxpayers.

3   The decisions of the States General were required to be reached unanimously. It was therefore often difficult for decisions to be taken because each provincial delegation was usually bound by instructions from its own states.

States

Each province possessed its own parliament – the States – which represented the clergy, nobility and towns. In addition to their most important role, the protection of local privileges from central authority, the States had several responsibilities:

● They could scrutinise the powers of the agencies of central government in Brussels, insofar as these affected individual provinces.

● They had the power to raise troops.

● They had the right to levy and collect taxes.

The States often had to defend local liberties from what they considered to be the encroachments of central authority.

Town Councils

The urbanised nature of Dutch society gave much power and influence to the larger towns and cities, many of which developed a flourishing **bourgeois** culture. The dominant urban group was the regent élite. No one could be a regent without holding civic office. In practice, this meant that

Bourgeois: In common usage this simply means 'middle class'. More specifically, it refers to the urban middle classes. The Netherlands, whose population was heavily concentrated in towns and cities, had many places where a middle-class urban culture flourished. In such places the townspeople controlled their own councils and guilds and often oversaw a range of charitable organisations. There was a strong sense of identification with the town and an increasing level of patronage of art and education.

most towns were controlled by merchant oligarchies (i.e. closed groups of wealthy merchants). It was often difficult for outsiders, however wealthy, to break into such closed groups. This could lead to tensions, especially when there was generally a growing gap between the regent élites and the cities' active business élites.

Though the 17 provinces were increasingly perceived as a unit, the differences between the provinces remained strong.

- Each province had its own traditions and political culture. This was most strongly entrenched in the States of Holland.

- There were considerable rivalries and tensions between provinces. Holland, for example, consistently believed that its interests were more important than those of other northern provinces.

- The extent to which Habsburg authority was accepted still varied. In Gelderland, especially, Habsburg authority was very fragile.

- Taxation and legal systems varied.

- There were customs barriers at provincial borders.

- The geography of the Netherlands (see map on page 217) often made communication between provinces difficult. The severest limitation on the cohesion of the Habsburg Netherlands was the separateness of north and south dictated by the river.

- There was a range of languages spoken in the Netherlands. French was spoken in the south. It was also the language of the Court at Brussels and the language of the nobility, who tended to regard Dutch as a peasant dialect. Dutch itself had no fewer than five main variants: Frisian was spoken in Friesland; Low German was spoken in a few places in the lower Rhine valley near to the borders with Cleves and Münster.

- There was often tension between the nobility, who were in many cases linked closely to the aristocracies of France and Germany, and the urban élites.

- In the towns there were frequent clashes between regents and **guildsmen** and, in times of poverty, between the élites in general and the urban poor.

- There were considerable rivalries between towns.

Guildsmen: This term described minor businessmen and office holders in the towns. Their political role was less important than that of the regents, to whose position they often aspired.

1. How were the Netherlands governed at the start of Philip II's reign?

2. What were the main strengths and weaknesses of government in the Netherlands at the start of the reign of Philip II?

10.2 What were the long-term and short-term reasons for the outbreak of the revolt?

Long-term reasons for the revolt

Charles closely identified with his Burgundian territories which were, on the whole, governed wisely during his reign. Thus, during the 1540s, the Habsburg régime appeared to be achieving all its strategic, fiscal, administrative and political objectives in the Low Countries.

Nevertheless, there were hints that there might be trouble ahead.

- Charles' birthplace, Ghent, rebelled against his demands for taxation in 1539–40, forcing Charles himself to visit the city to suppress the rebels.

Margaret of Parma (1522–1586)

An illegitimate daughter of Charles V, she married Ottavio Farnese, Duke of Parma, in 1542. She was appointed Regent of the Netherlands in 1559 by her half-brother, Philip II, and held the post until she resigned following Alba's entry into the Netherlands.

William of Orange (1533–1584)

Orange was a member of a noble family which had considerable links with both France and the Holy Roman Empire. Originally a favourite of Charles V, he served Philip II during the early years of his reign. Early signs of a shift in his political position can be seen in his marriage to Anna of Saxony, the daughter of Charles V's enemy, Maurice of Saxony. Like Egmont and Hornes, he quarrelled with Granvelle over the 'new bishoprics' scheme and was removed from his position as Stadholder of Holland and Zeeland. By moving into exile, he avoided the fate which Egmont and Hornes suffered at the hands of Alba and eventually placed himself at the head of the revolt. He was *politique* by nature and was no real revolutionary. However, he convinced himself that Philip II had behaved in a tyrannical manner and had therefore forfeited his right to rule in the Netherlands. His genuinely tolerant views on religious toleration placed him at odds with most of his contemporaries. Orange failed in his principal aim of securing the separation of all 17 provinces from Spanish rule. His assassination in 1584 left the **United Provinces** shorn of leadership at a time when their cause appeared lost.

Count of Egmont (1523–68)

Lamoraal was a distinguished soldier who clashed with Philip II and Granvelle over the new bishoprics scheme. In March 1563, along with Orange and Hornes, he demanded Granvelle's removal from office and withdrew from the Council of State when his demand was rejected. In 1564 he travelled to Spain to secure from Philip a relaxation of the heresy laws and was publicly humiliated on his return to the Netherlands when Philip insisted on the continuation of a policy of repression. Even so, Egmont eventually sided with the authorities during the 'First Revolt'. This, however, was no protection against Alba, who had him arrested on trumped-up charges of treason and executed along with Hornes.

United Provinces: The northern provinces which formed the Union of Utrecht in 1579 and which rejected the authority of Philip II in the Act of Abjuration of 1581.

- There was widespread disaffection at the level of taxes demanded to fight the French during the 1550s, a conflict that many Netherlands taxpayers considered to be of no concern to them. In 1556 the Duke of Savoy wrote to Philip that 'the impression (was) held by the subjects of these provinces that the late wars were fought mainly for Naples, Milan and Navarre, although the Low Countries have borne the principal burden'. Opposition to increased taxation was particularly strong in Philip's own capital, Brussels.

- Heresy had spread quickly from Germany to the Low Countries. It had been suppressed with considerable ruthlessness, about 2,000 heretics being executed in the Netherlands during Charles' reign.

- Many of the more powerful nobility (*grandees*) became increasingly alienated from the government of Philip II. It was alleged, with some justification, that Philip had become over-dependent on Spanish advisers and failed to involve the Netherlands grandees in the business of government.

- Philip's absence from the Netherlands after 1559 made this worse. On his departure Philip appointed his half-sister Margaret of Parma as governess-general. This involved a considerable risk. Philip was fully aware that Margaret was inexperienced in government and would, therefore, be in need of considerable advice. Given Philip's appointment of William of Orange as Stadholder of Holland, Zeeland and Utrecht and the Count of Egmont as Stadholder of Flanders and Artois, it appeared that he was prepared to allow the leading *grandees* their traditional role in government. This was a false impression. He remained in direct contact with Antoine Perrenot (Granvelle), through whom he channelled important business. In the words of Geoffrey Parker, in *The Dutch Revolt*, 'all decisions were being taken in secret by Margaret, Perrenot and the king'. In practice, Philip had set up a structure which was almost bound to lead to a breach

The bishoprics of the Netherlands before (a) and after (b) the introduction of the New Bishoprics in 1559–1570.

between the grandees and the bureaucrats (officials who follow rules and procedures).

- The tension between the grandees and the bureaucrats was made worse by William's marriage in 1561 to Anna of Saxony, daughter of Maurice of Saxony and granddaughter of the Lutheran Landgrave Philip of Hesse. William, in any case, already had links with Lutheran princes. His marriage compounded this sin in the eyes of both Philip and Perrenot. Henceforth, they would each regard him with considerable suspicion.

- There was much fear in the Netherlands that their traditional liberties would be destroyed and that they would be reduced to the status of a Spanish colony. This was reflected, for example, in local resentment of the Spanish bureaucrats whom Philip had left behind in 1559 and in demands for the removal of the garrison of 3,000 Spanish soldiers. Eventually, Philip was forced in 1561 to withdraw them to the Mediterranean after the provincial States refused to fund their upkeep.

It was, therefore, unsurprising that Perrenot wrote to Philip in September 1560, predicting the likelihood of future troubles in the Netherlands. Unfortunately for Perrenot, the troubles came rather more quickly than he had been anticipating. What sparked off the troubles was a scheme to re-organise the administration of the Roman Catholic Church in the Netherlands by providing for 14 new bishoprics.

To Philip the scheme for the new bishoprics seemed perfectly reasonable. It would assist the internal reform of a corrupt and worldly institution, would make easier the Roman Catholic Church's fight against

Episcopal: This term describes the area of jurisdiction of a bishop. Bishopric and diocese are also used.

heresy and it would link the **episcopal** boundaries more closely with political and linguistic boundaries.

Opposition to the scheme

Unfortunately for Philip and Perrenot, the scheme sparked off considerable opposition. Firstly, there was considerable opposition from the merchant élites who dominated Antwerp. They feared that a resident inquisition in the city would be bad for trade. The scheme was opposed by interests within the Church, most notably the abbots of the larger abbeys in Brabant, as it threatened both their own financial position and their status. The towns, especially in the north, thought that the scheme would erode their liberties and privileges.

Also, the scheme was greeted with suspicion by William of Orange who not only feared that the scheme would strengthen royal authority and hence reduce the autonomy of the Netherlands but would also increase the likelihood of religious persecution. Moreover, the grandees, especially Orange and Egmont, were affronted by the secrecy with which the scheme had been planned without consulting members of the Council of State.

These suspicions were reinforced by the way in which Perrenot's position would be enhanced. He was to become a cardinal and **primate** as the first archbishop of Mechelen.

Orange, Egmont and the Count of Hornes had no reservations about whipping up opposition to the scheme. On 29 July 1563 they wrote to Philip II that they would remove themselves from the Council of State unless Granvelle (Perrenot had been given the title of Cardinal Granvelle as part of the reorganisation scheme) was dismissed. The states of Brabant threatened to withhold taxes. This placed Margaret of Parma in a difficult situation. It was clear that the stability of her administration was threatened. She had also come to realise that Granvelle had been critical of her in his correspondence with Philip II. Margaret therefore sought Granvelle's dismissal, justifying the request on the basis that his dismissal was necessary to restore order and good government to the Netherlands. She was successful in her ambition, largely because the Duke of Alba, Granvelle's chief supporter at Court, was temporarily absent and therefore not in a position to defend Granvelle from his enemies. Granvelle therefore left Brussels on 13 March 1564 and never again set foot in the Netherlands.

Primate: This term was used to describe the leading archbishop or bishop within a national church.

Count of Hornes (1524–1568)
Philip de Montmorency, Count of Hornes, was a member of a distinguished Franco-Burgundian noble family. He had been made captain of Philip II's personal bodyguard in 1549 and in 1559 went with him to Spain. Returning to the Netherlands in 1561, he strongly opposed the 'new bishoprics' scheme. When the 'First Revolt' broke out Hornes was in a difficult position, but decided not to take up arms against the king. This did not save him from the vengeance of Alba, who had him executed on a trumped-up charge of treason.

Religion and the outbreak of the First Revolt

Though Granvelle's departure eased the situation, it could not prevent the collapse of the Crown's authority in the Netherlands. Clearly, there were issues at stake which ran much deeper than personal antagonism to Granvelle or opposition to the 'new bishoprics' scheme.

There were, essentially, two connected problems: economic discontent and the growth of heresy. There was a depression in the Flemish textile industry following the transfer of English cloth exports to Germany. The Baltic trade, which was especially important to Amsterdam, had collapsed because of the war between Denmark and Sweden. Then, to top it all, the very bad winter of 1564–65 was followed by a disastrous harvest.

The issues were linked because of the tendency among the authorities to assert that many of those who were discontented primarily for financial reasons were, in fact, heretics who needed to be suppressed. Heresy had been a problem in the Netherlands since the 1520s. Lutheranism had been purged much more effectively by Charles V's authorities in the

Netherlands than it had been in the Holy Roman Empire. Anabaptism (see Chapter 4) was regarded with utter hostility, and suspected Anabaptists were treated with great ferocity.

Calvinism, though from modest beginnings, was to prove a much sterner threat. Even as late as 1561 there were only about 20 Calvinist congregations in the whole of the Netherlands, and public worship only existed in the **Walloon** towns of Valenciennes and Tournai. Nevertheless, adherence to the reformed faith grew swiftly during the 1560s, especially in the south, partly because of the influence of Huguenot refugees from France. As a result, by 1566 about 300 places had Calvinist congregations and the basis of a Calvinist organisational framework was in place.

The grandees had tended to be fairly relaxed about the growth of heresy. Egmont, on his visit to Court in 1565, had advised Philip II to relax his anti-heresy measures. This strategy was twice repudiated by Philip, firstly in an order of 13 May to proceed with the execution of six repentant Anabaptists and then in his **Segovia Letters** of October 1565. Instead, Philip ordered the grandees to enforce the anti-heresy laws rigorously, thereby creating a dilemma for the nobles. Either they could obey their sovereign and enforce the laws, which would be a deviation from the principles which they had been urging, or they could refuse to obey, which could be construed as treason.

Matters were taken out of their hands by more militant nobles. The Segovia Letters sparked off outright revolt by a group of Protestant nobles led by Hendrik van Brederode. On 5 April 1566 Brederode and about 200 other noblemen, who became known as the 'Beggars', presented Margaret of Parma with a denunciation of the Inquisition. They required that the Inquisition be set aside, and issued a scarcely veiled threat to armed rebellion should their demand be rejected. The 'Beggars' were careful not to oppose the authority of the king. Nevertheless, their actions were undoubtedly radical. They had forced themselves into Margaret's presence and she had been obliged to give in to their demands. Royal authority had been critically compromised.

To make matters worse for the Crown, Brederode and the Beggars incited considerable popular support. There was an upsurge in Calvinist activity, particularly in the areas of the Beggars' influence. Preaching in the open air (known as hedge preaching) began in May 1566. By the following month, huge Calvinist gatherings had met in Antwerp, Breda and 's-Hertogenbosch. Within two months most of the Netherlands had been swept up in the fervour of preaching which released an accumulation of tension which had built up over four decades. This fervour was even commemorated in Pieter Bruegel the Elder's painting 'The Sermon of St John the Baptist'.

Neither the government nor the church authorities was able to respond to the challenge posed by the hedge preachers. To make matters even more critical this absence of authority encouraged the outbreak on a huge scale of **iconoclasm** in churches. This had been widely anticipated. In July Calvinist preachers in Kortrijk were 'trying to impress upon their hearers the need to pillage the churches and abolish all images'. Granvelle's associate Viglius made the important link between popular militancy and economic crisis, predicting that 'working folk constrained by hunger' would join in the disturbances. Finally, taking literally the words of the commandment against the worship of graven images, crowds smashed images in a convent at Steenvoorde on 10 August. Over the next few days the iconoclastic fury spread through much of the rest of Flanders and Brabant, where it appears to have been carefully organised, and from there into the northern provinces, which witnessed little opposition. Precisely

Walloon: The term used to describe the French-speaking provinces of the Netherlands; also used to describe a native of those areas.

Segovia Letters: These were letters sent by Philip II from Segovia in Spain. They formally rejected the advice of the Council in Brussels to relax the implementation of the anti-heresy laws and insisted on the continuation of the campaign against heretics. The issue of the letters sparked off an upsurge in militant Protestant activity.

Iconoclasm: The breaking of images. This followed from a literal interpretation of the Second Commandment, which prohibited the worship of graven images. Radical Protestants assumed from this that they had a duty to destroy images which they found in churches.

Fernando Alvarez de Toledo, Duke of Alba (1507–1582)

Alba had enjoyed a long and distinguished military and political career in the service of the Spanish Crown. In 1567 Philip II responded to the outbreak of revolt by sending Alba to the Netherlands as Governor-General and as commander of a large army. Alba's army quickly restored order, but the duke created immense resentment in the Netherlands by his execution of Egmont and Hornes and by the troops' treatment of the towns of Mechelen and Naarden. Alba thus became a frequent target for Dutch and Protestant propaganda. By 1573 even Philip II had become convinced that Alba's policies were counter-productive, and he was replaced by the more moderate Requesens (see page 228).

1. *How important was religion in sparking off the First Revolt?*

2. *Which was more important in sparking off the revolt: popular discontent or the resentment of the nobility? Give reasons for your answer.*

how much adherence there was to Calvinism in the Netherlands at this time is open to some debate. Historian Geoffrey Parker, in particular, is sceptical. Much of the apparently spontaneous iconoclasm was carefully planned, with ample evidence to suggest that itinerant (moving from area to area) iconoclasts were being rewarded for their activities. Many people had become 'spiritually disorientated' and in an atmosphere of poverty and anti-clericalism were willing to join in.

The widespread scale of law-breaking finally alarmed the nobility, apart from the militants surrounding Brederode. Accordingly, an accord (agreement) was reached with Margaret. Persecution would cease if, in return, there were no further threats to Roman Catholic worship and if the iconoclasm ceased. Moreover, Protestantism would be allowed to continue in those areas where it was already established.

Margaret did not see the Accord as a long-term solution. She was trying to re-establish her position by building up support among the Walloon nobility. Meanwhile, she attempted to secure more support from the king by means of the dangerous strategy of exaggerating to him just how serious the position was. To Philip only one solution was feasible; he would have to send an army to the Netherlands to end the problem of heresy once and for all. Ironically, the problems in the Netherlands had actually burnt themselves out even before the army, under the Duke of Alba, arrived in the Netherlands. This happened for a number of reasons:

- The more militant nobles, perceiving that the king might resort to force, backed down.

- Margaret became more assertive. She broke the Accord by restricting the extent of Calvinist worship in towns where it was already established, raised some new troops herself and broke a small Calvinist force in west Flanders, thereby destroying Calvinism as a movement in that area.

- The grandees were unsure how to proceed. William of Orange had discredited himself with Calvinist opinion by siding with Margaret's army at the siege of Osterweel and then left for the safety of Germany. Egmont had also supported Margaret in west Flanders.

It was evident that Calvinist militancy, at least temporarily, had burnt itself out and that most of the nobility were proving loyal. It was clear that matters were returning to something like normal. It was a tragedy, therefore, for the Netherlands that Alba arrived assuming not only that a full-scale rebellion was in progress but also that most Netherlanders were heretics.

10.3 Why did Alba's 'pacification' of the Netherlands fail?

Part of the explanation for this lies in the fact that Alba and Philip had wrongly interpreted the nature of the problem in the Netherlands. Those who either sought the removal of Spanish authority or who were committed heretics were small in number. Alba proceeded on the assumption that the two groups were large in number and therefore needed to be intimidated into submission. A further part of the explanation lies in the fact that Alba's arrival effectively usurped Margaret's authority.

In addition, Alba made a whole series of other errors which were to make matters worse. By demanding the disbanding of Margaret's troops who had successfully restored order in West Flanders, he not only undermined Margaret still further but also alienated those nobles who had commanded the army. Also, Alba's own army was billeted mainly in towns that had hitherto been loyal. Not only were residents forced to accommodate and pay for the army's upkeep, they had to put up with the soldiers' unruly behaviour. The effect was that support for the Crown diminished in areas where this had been previously quite strong.

The Duke of Alba further upset Netherlands opinion by sacking some of Margaret's advisers. He set up the Council of Troubles to investigate cases of treason and heresy. There were over 1,000 executions as a result of the Council's investigations.

Finally, much to Margaret's disgust, the Duke of Alba ordered the arrest and execution of Egmont and Hornes. Public opinion quickly forgot their earlier evasiveness. Instead, Egmont and Hornes were now heroes and martyrs.

Another aspect of Alba's tyranny was that the response of the Council of Troubles anticipated the division between north and south which was to become a central feature of the revolt. To have divided opposition to Spanish rule before 1566 between a militant north and a more passive south would have been futile. In any case, at this stage Calvinism seemed to be more strongly entrenched in the South. This was to be changed by the response of the Council of Troubles, which took far sterner action against

Such allegorical depictions were widely produced in the later 16th century. Why was this? How effectively did they get their message across?

This is an allegorical (narrative represented in symbols) representation of the condition of the Netherlands under the tyranny of Alba. The 17 chained women kneeling before Alba represent the 17 provinces of the Netherlands. To Alba's right stands his ally Cardinal Granvelle. Above him can be seen a devil carrying two papal mitres. The nobility and representatives of the States look on in a worried manner. The central section of the painting depicts the execution of Egmont and Hornes. The extreme left of the picture shows torturing; the extreme right shows a hanging.

alleged traitors and heretics from the north than from the south. Moreover, far more members of the nobility and civic élites from the north than from the south followed Orange into exile. These were to prove the nucleus of those who led the resistance to Spanish rule from 1572 onwards.

Altogether, according to historian Geoffrey Parker, the number of exiles totalled about 60,000. Even this level of emigration could not eradicate Protestantism in the Netherlands. Some congregations continued to worship in secret. Even more Protestants for a time attended Catholic services and therefore conformed outwardly. Even Alba's forces could not maintain complete conformity and levels of attendance at Mass were dropping again by the early 1570s.

Arguably, the two most important reasons for Alba's failure to suppress opposition completely was that anti-Spanish sentiment still had a leader – William of Orange. With the re-imposition of the hated tax, the **Tenth Penny**, the rebels once again had a cause around which most Netherlanders could unite.

Tenth Penny: This was a 10% sales tax which was imposed upon the Netherlands in 1571 by the Duke of Alba. It was resentment at the imposition of this tax which was primarily responsible for the renewed outbreak of rebellion in 1572.

Orange's popularity did, in fact, slump during 1567 and 1568. Radicals like Brederode, who cut the duke from his will, felt that Orange had not been sufficiently supportive of their cause. Once again, however, it was Alba who restored Orange's position. In 1568 the Council of Troubles condemned Orange and ordered the confiscation of all of his property in the Netherlands. With any prospect of reconciling himself to the régime having disappeared, Orange put himself at the head of the revolt, quickly gathering funds and surrounding himself with a large number of exiled noblemen.

In March 1569 Alba summoned the States General in order to secure the funds from taxation to sustain both his standing army and the work of the Council of Troubles. Some of his demands were uncontroversial. This was not, however, the case with the notorious Tenth Penny. The securing of the Tenth Penny was vital for Alba. Not only would it pay the upkeep of the army, which was keeping the Netherlands under its control, it would also mean that the States General and the provincial States would lose their control over the granting of taxation. This would free the Spanish Crown from the limitations which had previously been imposed upon the sovereign power in the Netherlands.

Matters came to a head in July 1571. Alba imposed the Tenth Penny by decree and forced town governments to put the collection of the taxes into effect. This led to acute tensions, particularly in Flanders, Brabant and Holland. The town governments were in a dilemma. They could attempt to evade the taxes, which would have improved their popularity but brought upon them the wrath of Alba, or they could have collected the taxes and risked disorder and riots by the taxpayers. Many of Alba's supporters could see that there would be trouble. His closest supporter among the Netherlands nobility even wrote to Philip to complain that Alba was risking the loyalty of his Netherlands subjects. Alba, always a stubborn man, refused to change his policy or his attitudes. As a result, he sparked off a conflict which was to last until 1648.

1. What actions did Alba take to try to end the revolt in the Netherlands?

2. How justified is the claim that Alba's cruelty made a second revolt inevitable?

10.4 Why, and with what consequences, did the Second Revolt break out in 1572?

The Sea Beggars

The scale of Alba's repression was so great that successful opposition was only likely to spring up from outside the Netherlands. William of Orange had made a couple of minor and unsuccessful military incursions. In

Sea Beggars: The *Watergeuzen* were a band of pirates who could operate legally as privateers because they had been given *letters of marque* (i.e. licences to prey on shipping) by William of Orange. They were a nuisance to Spanish shipping from 1568. They spent the winter of 1571–72 in England before being expelled by Elizabeth I. They returned to the Netherlands and exploited popular discontent against Alba's Tenth Penny by landing at Brielle, a small town in Zeeland. In the process they sparked off a huge popular revolt against Spanish authority.

contrast, it was a sea-borne invasion which was the catalyst of the start of the Second Revolt. The **Sea Beggars**, having spent the winter of 1571–72 in English ports, were expelled by Queen Elizabeth. They solved the problem of where to go by landing on 1 April at the small Zeeland port of Brielle, which had been left without a garrison because Alba needed all his troops to defend the southern border of the Netherlands against a possible French invasion.

At first the Sea Beggars made little progress and were confined to Brielle and the most southerly ports in Zeeland – Flushing, which had expelled its loyalist Walloon garrison, and Veere. At this point the situation was tense. In some cases the loyalist authorities were able to act quickly to prevent potential rebellion. Bossu, the royal Stadholder of Holland, Zeeland and Utrecht, suppressed trouble in Rotterdam.

However, the rebels began to gain the upper hand in May. Count Louis of Nassau, Orange's brother, led a force into Hainaut and captured Mons. Two ports in West Friesland, Enkhuizen and Medemblik, declared their support for the Sea Beggars. In June a rebel force under Count van den Bergh invaded Gelderland, capturing Zutphen and bringing much of Gelderland and Overijssel into revolt. In June and July support for the Sea Beggars spread from West Friesland into North Holland. Most of the towns in North Holland were split between the regents – who tended, albeit without enthusiasm, to retain their support for the government – and the bulk of the business community, who favoured the Sea Beggars. After much hesitation, especially in Haarlem, they sided with the rebels. By the middle of July, with the fall of Haarlem, all of North Holland, except for Amsterdam, was in the hands of the rebels.

The spread of the Second Revolt

It was at this point that revolt became organised. Bossu ordered the towns of Holland to attend an emergency meeting of the States at The Hague. Instead, most of the towns met at Dordrecht on 19 July. At the invitation of William of Orange's secretary, Philip Marnix, the States recognised Orange as the rightful Stadholder, even though he had been dismissed by Philip II and replaced by Bossu. Moreover, they recognised Orange as 'Protector' of the Netherlands as a whole. This was a rejection of Alba's authority. It posed a clear challenge to Philip's sovereign authority, even though William of Orange was still thinking in terms of securing the traditional rights and privileges of the Netherlands (i.e. the autonomous relationship which had existed under the Burgundians and Charles V).

William of Orange was still in a difficult position. His desire to end Spanish military occupation, to promote feelings of religious toleration and to uphold most of the traditional symbols of authority, did not sit easily with the increased political radicalism of many of the towns. Moreover, his own power was limited by the fact that he was not in control of the whole of Holland and Zeeland. Amsterdam, for example, remained in royal hands until 1578. Furthermore, Alba's position recovered in the south, where his sacking of Mechelen induced towns like Leuven and Oudenaarde to surrender, and in the north-east, where the sacking of Zutphen persuaded other rebel-held towns in Gelderland and Overijssel also to surrender.

Alba's failure

William of Orange was, however, able to improve his position. The reasons lie in the way in which the revolt had developed in Holland and Zeeland. Alba was responsible for one massacre too many. On 2 December 1572 his forces virtually wiped out the small town of

Naarden to the east of Amsterdam. This slaughter, however, produced a different response from those of Mechelen and Zutphen. In the rebel towns in Holland and Zeeland, which had risen spontaneously against both church and state, resistance 'stiffened despite the grim prospect'. These towns had already undergone a process of transformation in the direction both of Protestantism and of 'institutional formalisation of the rebellion against the Spanish Crown'. For such towns there could be no turning back. Surrender was not an option. They had to hold out. Their situation generated a revolutionary fervour and determination to fight to the end which did not exist in other parts of the country.

The Duke of Alba tried to reassert his power in Holland by besieging Haarlem. In the end he forced the town to surrender. However, it proved to be an expensive victory. By the time it surrendered, in July 1573, Haarlem had wrought so much damage on Spain's forces and prestige, and given the rest of the rebel towns so long a respite in which to organise their defence, that the entire picture was transformed. Many Spanish resources were tied up in trying to relieve the beleaguered Spanish garrison in Middelburg. Moreover, the Spanish divided their forces by sending some troops north in a strategically pointless attempt to besiege Alkmaar, which failed when the **dikes** were flooded. Meanwhile, the rebels withstood a bitter siege at Leiden. Leiden was strategically crucial. Had it fallen, the rebels would not have been in a position to defend either The Hague or Delft, and the revolt as a whole might have collapsed. The town was finally relieved in September 1574. The dikes had been cut in August, but it was not until the rains of late September that the waters rose sufficiently to drive the Spanish back. Thus was the town, and with it the rebel cause, saved. Calvinists were keen to give the credit for victory to a Protestant God who had intervened to change the weather. Spanish troops were forced to vacate all of South Holland.

Alba's strategy had thus been discredited. His position had also been weakened when the rebels gained naval control of the Zuider Zee in October 1573 to add to their command of the coast from the Scheldt estuary through to Friesland. Philip, realising his deteriorating financial situation, suggested to Alba's successor, Don Luis de Requesens y Zúñiga, that he should look to negotiate a settlement. A formal attempt at producing a settlement took place at Breda in 1575, but Philip was unwilling to concede much. The rebel position was jointly formulated by William of Orange and the States of Holland and Zeeland. They declared that they had no wish to separate themselves from Spanish jurisdiction so long as the king was willing both to permit Protestant worship and to rule in a way which upheld the rights and privileges of the provinces. The States General and provincial States were to be guaranteed a share in government. This was far more than Philip was willing to concede. In effect, prospects for compromise were so remote as to be negligible. William of Orange and the States of Holland formally renounced their allegiance to Philip II and offered sovereignty successively to Elizabeth I and the Duke of Anjou, each of whom was sensible enough to reject the offer.

The revolt, however, was about to take an unexpected turn which left Philip II paralysed for a time. The Spanish Crown declared itself bankrupt. Moreover, Requesens died in March 1576, leaving Philip completely unsure whom to appoint as his successor. Royal authority was once more on the verge of collapse. The situation was made worse when the Spanish troops, who had not been paid following the Crown's bankruptcy, mutinied and went on the rampage. To try to curb the problem the States General, though without the participation of Holland and Zeeland, convened itself, largely on the initiative of the States of Brabant. On 30 October the States General's commissioners agreed an **armistice** with the States of Holland and Zeeland.

Dikes: Much of Holland and Zeeland lay at, or below, sea level. It was necessary to build a complex series of dams (dikes) to prevent towns from being flooded.

Don Luis de Requesens y Zúñiga (1528–1576)
Requesens was a Catalan noble who replaced the Duke of Alba as Governor-General. A more moderate figure than his predecessor, he nevertheless felt under an obligation to follow his predecessor's advice and he, therefore, began as a hard-line ruler. By 1575, however, he was seeking an accommodation with William of Orange. His death in March 1576 weakened Spanish power by leaving authority in Brussels in the hands of a divided Council of State.

Armistice: An agreement between countries who are at war with one another to stop fighting for a time and to discuss ways of making a peaceful settlement.

The two sides would cooperate to drive the mutinous Spaniards out of the country. They would then hold a conference on religion.

At the beginning of November the problem of the mutinous army took a drastic turn for the worse, when it attacked Antwerp and carried on an orgy of rape, pillage and murder. The number of deaths was quickly exaggerated. In some reports as many as 18,000 had perished. This served to reinforce the image of Spanish cruelty which had been so effortlessly developed by Alba and gave credence to those rebels who argued that the problems could never be solved by negotiation. This atmosphere led the moderates on both sides – William of Orange for Holland and Zeeland and the Duke of Aerschot for the States of Brabant – to reach an agreement known as the Pacification of Ghent on 8 November 1576.

1. *What factors enabled the rebel cause to survive between 1572 and 1576?*

2. *To what extent did the Pacification of Ghent represent a victory for the rebel cause?*

3. *Why, nevertheless, might the Spanish have taken some satisfaction from the Pacification of Ghent?*

Terms of the Pacification of Ghent

- All sides united on the need to drive out the Spanish army.

- The authority of the King of Spain continued to be recognised.

- Holland and Zeeland agreed to rejoin the States General.

- The public practice of Protestantism was to be permitted in Holland and Zeeland, though not elsewhere.

- Private Protestant practice would be allowed in all parts of the Netherlands.

- The States General agreed to recognise the validity of Orange's stadholderate.

10.5 Why, and with what consequences to 1579, did the Pacification of Ghent fail?

Union of Arras: This was a union of the southern provinces and was signed on 6 January 1579. It guaranteed the provinces' loyalty to Spain in return for the removal of foreigners from office and of Spanish troops from within the territories of the provinces which had signed the union.

It was undoubtedly the case that many Netherlanders at the time thought that the Pacification would provide the basis for a long-term settlement. However, just over two years later the consensus which had led to the Pacification of Ghent was in ruins and the Netherlands had split itself into two, the Union of Utrecht in the north and the **Union of Arras** in the south.

The Spanish authorities, leaderless and discredited by the sacking of Antwerp, were in no position to prevent the signing of the Pacification. However, it was predictable that they would seek to undermine the Pacification once they had recovered their position.

There was still a willingness among the leadership of the southern provinces to come to an accommodation with the Spanish which would be resisted in Holland and Zeeland. There were increasing tensions within the southern provinces between the Walloon nobility and urban élites, on the one hand, and more radical elements in cities like Antwerp, Brussels and Ghent. Fear of the radicals pushed the élites, however reluctantly, towards an accommodation with the royal authorities. Quite deliberately, no serious attempt had been made to sort out the crucial issue of religion. Any future attempt to solve this problem was likely once again to increase tension.

The aftermath of the Pacification led to a three-way struggle, each of which contributed significantly to the emergence of the two unions.

- William of Orange, the States of Holland and radical opinion throughout the Netherlands wished to assert their independence from Spanish control.

- The new Governor-General, Don Juan of Austria, sought to rebuild royal authority and to minimise the role of the States General. To do this he broke with the States General in July 1577, left Brussels and set up his headquarters in Namur, in the loyalist south-east of the Netherlands, which had kept its distance from the Pacification.

- The States General, dominated by moderate noble opinion, was anxious to use the Pacification as the basis for reaching a long-term settlement with the king. Don Juan's departure from Brussels thrust them much more into the hands of the north, enabling William of Orange to enter Brussels in triumph in September 1577.

The rest of the conflict

The radicalisation of opinion within Holland and Zeeland did much to define the geographical split in the Netherlands in 1579, which was subsequently to determine the shape of the rest of the conflict. The extent of radicalism among the urban artisans (skilled workrs in towns) was increasing. Radicals benefited from being identified with what had become the patriotic and anti-Spanish cause. Moreover, there was a purposeful attempt by the Calvinists within Holland and Zeeland to make substantial conversions. Increasingly, the provinces of Holland and Zeeland were taking on the character of a state-within-a-state. One result of this was that William of Orange, to maintain his position, felt obliged to adopt a more radical position. This led him into increasing conflict with the leaders of the anti-Orange faction in the States General – Aerschot, Bossu and Egmont. What was at stake was control of the northern provinces other than Holland and Zeeland. Increasingly, it was the radicals and supporters of Orange who held the upper hand. The Roman Catholic Church in the north was on the point of collapse, even in an old stronghold like Utrecht.

Amsterdam fell to the radicals in the autumn of 1578. Increasingly, the North, based on the Protestant Union of Holland and Zeeland, was emerging as a coherent state, albeit one with which the other provinces were sometimes reluctant associates. This process was completed by the formation of the Union of Utrecht on 23 January 1579, though its signing had been foreshadowed in July 1578 when the States of Gelderland had put forward a proposal for the union of their province with Holland and Zeeland. It was the Union of Utrecht which created the concept of the 'United Provinces', who were to act as if they were a single province in matters of war and peace. The Union of Utrecht made no pretence of seeking reconciliation with Spain. There was no mention of the king's authority or of any right to continue to practise the Catholic faith, though individual provinces retained jurisdiction over maters of religion.

Even William of Orange was worried about the implications of the Union. He was still hoping to do a deal with the States General to provide for a religiously tolerant union embracing as many provinces as possible. It was only when he realised that this was now an impossibility that he signed the Union of Utrecht on 3 May. He had to accept the logic of an 'uncompromisingly anti-Catholic revolt' based on Holland and with the Dutch Reformed Church as the official church of the union.

At the same time the Spanish position in the south began to revive. In January 1578 they were victorious at Gembloux and in the following month the Spanish captured Leuven. They were now in a position in which they could retake Brussels and thereby regain control over much of the southern Netherlands.

The political centre of the south, the States of Brabant, was also deeply divided, and the States General as an institution in the south was disintegrating. On one side they were faced with a revival of Spanish power; on the other side they were confronted with the increasingly powerful radicalism of the artisans in Ghent and other cities. Faced with the almost equally undesirable alternatives of radicalism and Spanish control, the Walloon nobles, backed by the urban élites, reasserted their Catholicism. On 6 January 1579 the southern provinces formed the Union of Arras. In this they were forced to recognise the authority of the newly-appointed Governor-General, Alessandro Farnese, who was a more politically astute and formidable operator than his mother, Margaret. In return, Farnese agreed to the withdrawal of foreign troops and the recognition of the rights and privileges of the individual provinces. The political power in the south of the States General, however, had come to an end.

? 1. Explain why the Pacification of Ghent failed?

2. In what ways was the Union of Utrecht a forerunner of an independent Dutch state?

10.6 Why did the Spanish recover their position so easily between 1579 and 1584?

Alessandro Farnese, Duke of Parma (1543–1592)
The son of Margaret of Parma, Farnese was a distinguished military commander. He replaced Don Juan as governor of the Netherlands and proceeded to reconquer huge amounts of rebel territory. The scale of his reconquest slowed down from 1588 as he was forced by Philip to give greater priority, firstly, to supplying troops for the Spanish Armada and, secondly, to combating the forces of Henry IV in France. He became increasingly critical of Philip II and, despite his record as a military commander, Philip decided to dismiss him. Farnese died at the Siege of Arras before Philip's order of dismissal could be put into effect.

The open split between the unions of Utrecht and Arras meant that any compromise between them in the short term was impossible. The main beneficiaries of the split in the short term were the Spanish and their allies. The Duke of Parma set out to reconquer the rebellious northern provinces. Almost immediately he enjoyed success, capturing Maastricht in June 1579 and Kortrijk in February 1580. To make matters worse for the rebels, the Union of Utrecht split up. The Count of Renneberg, a Catholic and Stadholder of the north-eastern provinces, decided in March 1580 to break with the Union of Utrecht on religious grounds, inviting Catholics in the north to rise with him against the United Provinces. The province of Groningen retained its position of opposition to the United Provinces, though the extent of popular Protestantism prevented Renneberg's call from having much effect elsewhere. Ultimately, Renneberg's actions, whilst weakening the northern provinces militarily, did make the rebel provinces politically more coherent and certainly increased the 'Protestant' character of the revolt.

The revolt, however, looked as if it might end in the early 1580s. Parma maintained the pace of his reconquest, gradually recapturing those areas of the south which had been under northern control. By 1584 the rebels had been substantially pushed back into their heartlands of Holland and Zeeland. The rebels were in disarray for a number of reasons.

● There was dismay at the speed and extent of Parma's reconquest. The revolt in the south seemed doomed when Parma was able to capture Protestant towns like Dunkirk and Nieuwpoort virtually without firing a shot.

● There were internal disputes over whether or not to offer sovereignty to the Duke of Anjou.

● The performance of the Duke of Anjou and his soldiers, including their rampage in Antwerp, incurred furious opposition amongst the rebels.

● Religious tensions had increased, especially when the fall of Breda was blamed on Catholics who allegedly opened the city's gates to Parma's army.

The Spanish reconquest of the Netherlands, 1577–1589

Areas under States–General control

Neutral areas (Liège and Cambrai)

Areas entirely under Spanish control

• Towns captured by Spain

North Sea

Delfzijl (1580)

Groningen (1580)

Steenwijk (1582)

Coerorden (1592)

Deventer (1587)

Oldenzaal (1580)

's Hertogenbosch (1579)

Zutphen (1583)

Grave (1586)

Nijmegen (1585)

Steenbergen (1582)

Megen (1586)

Geertruidenberg (1589)

Geldern (1587)

ZEALAND

Breda (1586)

Hulst (1593)

Hoogstraten (1583)

Straelen (1579)

Axel (1583)

Geldern (1587)

Venlo (1586)

Wachtendonk (1588)

Antwerp (1585)

Weert (1579)

Sluis (1587)

Harentals (1584)

Nieuwpoort (1583)

Bruges (1584)

Erkelenz (1579)

Dunkirk (1583)

Dendermonde (1584)

Mechelen (1585)

Westerloo (1583)

Gravelines (1578)

Veurne (1583)

Ghent (1584)

Zichem (1579)

Bergues

Aalst (1584)

Vilvoorde (1584)

Diest (1579)

Maastricht (1579)

Oudenaarde (1582)

Leuven (1577)

Ieper (1584)

Ninove (1582)

Brussels (1585)

Tournai (1581)

Nivelles (1580)

L I M B U R G (1578)

ARTOIS (1579)

HAINAUT (1579)

NAMUR (1577)

Kørtrijk (1580)

Diksmuide (1583)

LUXEMBURG (1577)

Ingelmunster (1580)

0   50 km

0   50 miles

1. What factors assisted Spanish recovery between 1579 and 1584?

2. Why did the death of Orange appear to signal the end of the revolt?

William of Orange, acutely depressed, abandoned any pretence at continuing the revolt in the south, left his headquarters at Antwerp and retreated to Delft, thereby signalling that a successful revolt could only be based on Holland and on the suppression of Catholic worship. Even in Holland, his powers were diminishing as the States of Holland consolidated its position as the real source of authority. However much the internal power of Holland had increased, it hardly seemed feasible that it could lead a successful revolt against a resurgent Spain, which was rapidly recapturing the radical towns of Flanders in 1584. It was at this moment of deep despair for the rebels that their leader, William of Orange, fell victim to an assassin's bullet. The end of the revolt could surely not be far away.

10.7 How did a sovereign state of the United Provinces emerge?

During the early years of the revolt William of Orange and most of his fellow rebels were keen to maintain the claim that they were rebelling not against the sovereign authority of King Philip II but simply wished to secure the restoration of the traditional rights and privileges of the provinces. Even when the States of Holland appointed Orange as Stadholder in 1572, he was anxious to maintain at least a pretence of loyalty to the Crown, a position which was confirmed both at Breda in 1575 and at Ghent a year later.

The States of Holland and Zeeland viewed things rather differently. As far as they were concerned, Philip's sovereignty became increasingly meaningless after 1572. The official oaths drawn up for the Pensionary and Delegated Council of Zeeland in 1578 obliged to them to uphold the 'Particular Union' of Holland and Zeeland, but made no reference to the king. Things were different in the other northern provinces. Many officials there had, in fact, been royal appointees who had sworn oaths of allegiance to the king. To renounce such oaths was a momentous and potentially dangerous step.

Nevertheless, by 1581 the notion of Philip's sovereignty had disappeared from the rebellious provinces. This was foreshadowed in the articles (formal agreements) which defined the Union of Utrecht, which contained only one passing reference to the king. However, a number of developments between 1579 and 1581 confirmed the ending of Philip's sovereignty.

- The French Huguenot tract *Vindiciae contra Tyrannos*, which justified resistance to brutal rulers, was published in 1579 and had an immediate impact on radical thinking within Holland and Zeeland.

- William of Orange himself was looking for someone to exercise sovereign authority in the northern Netherlands. This was seen as essential if potentially sympathetic foreign rulers were not to be alienated by any perceived threat to authority. He therefore urged in 1580 that the States General offer sovereignty to the Duke of Anjou, the brother of King Henry III of France. His hope was that this offer would be simultaneously reassuring both to Catholic opinion in the south and to German Lutherans, who were becoming increasingly anxious about the Calvinist rebels in Holland and Zeeland.

- Philip II, against the advice of the Duke of Parma, pushed Orange into a more radical position by declaring him an outlaw in June 1580.

The Act of Abjuration

Act of Abjuration: This was the document in which, in July 1581, the States General formally and finally rejected the authority of Philip II and his heirs to rule over the Netherlands. It further required new oaths of allegiance to be taken by office holders, who were to swear their allegiance to the States General.

In consequence the States General in July 1581 agreed on the **Act of Abjuration**. This formally rejected the authority of Philip II and his heirs, decreed the removal of his portrait from coins and his name from official documents, and required office holders to swear a new oath of allegiance 'to be true and obedient to the States against the king of Spain and his followers'.

The Act of Abjuration did not clarify who was to exercise sovereignty in Philip's place. However, two months later this privilege was conferred on the Duke of Anjou, and on 23 January 1581 he became 'prince and lord of the Netherlands'. This heralded an unhappy period for the rebels. Anjou might have had the royal credentials to persuade conservative opinion to accept him as a ruler. Unfortunately, he was personally unfit to exercise rule, being weak, shallow, vain and unpredictable. He was also unprepared to work within the limitations that the States General had imposed upon his exercise of power. Moreover, his position was opposed within the Netherlands. Holland and Zeeland disliked the fact that the ruler was a Roman Catholic. The States of Brabant refused to grant him any revenue. Anjou considered that he was being treated shabbily, and tried to consolidate his position by seizing Antwerp and other towns. This failed, and the 'French fury', which his troops attempted to impose upon Antwerp, discredited him completely as sovereign, prompting his departure in June 1583.

After Anjou's departure, the issue of sovereignty became more confused. This suited those radicals who were beginning to feel that sovereignty should be vested in the States of Holland. William of Orange, meanwhile, revived the idea (which he had rejected in 1581) that he should be Count of Holland and Zeeland. This caused much controversy, with radicals becoming alarmed at the prospect that Orange might be trying to engineer sovereignty for himself. This particular controversy was ended by Orange's assassination.

That tragedy did not, of course, end debate on the wider sovereignty issue. In any case, this was given greater urgency by the continued deterioration in the rebels' position which seemed to demand a powerful foreign figurehead as sovereign.

It was in these circumstances that King Henry III of France was offered the sovereignty in February 1585, which he declined. In May the same offer was made to Elizabeth I of England who also refused it, although she did agree to offer assistance to the rebels. No further offers of sovereignty were made to foreign rulers or their relatives. In practice, after this time, sovereignty was exercised either by the States of Holland or by Maurice of Nassau or his successors as Stadholder.

1. What was the political significance of the Act of Abjuration?

2. Why did the issue of sovereignty create so many problems for the rebels?

10.8 *The contribution of William of Orange to Dutch success?*
A CASE STUDY IN HISTORICAL INTERPRETATION

Engraving of William of Orange

During his lifetime William of Orange had become known as the father of his people. His sudden and violent death, along with the continued influence of his family in Dutch affairs, ensured that his reputation continued to be respected in the centuries after his death. In the circumstances, it was hardly surprising that in the mid 19th century – a period during which historians often placed considerable emphasis on the stirring deeds of great men – that William's historical reputation was at its height. The person particularly responsible for this was the American historian John Lothrop Motley. In political terms Motley was an American Whig. In other words, he combined his commitment to American liberty with a tendency to identify with the interests of the political élites as well as a suspicious attitude towards Roman Catholicism. Moreover, he drew clear analogies between the growth of a republic founded on liberty in the United Provinces with the later emergence of a similar republic in the United States of America.

It was no surprise that Motley saw William of Orange as his political ideal, a man who combined moderation not only with an apparent zeal for liberty but also with a belief in the virtues of nobility. The history of William and the history of the Netherlands became indistinguishable. 'The history of the rise of the Netherland Republic [was] … at the same time the biography of William the Silent.' Pious, tolerant, morally upstanding and a great military commander, 'the supremacy of his military genius was entirely beyond question'. In Motley's view, had William lived, the seven United Provinces would have become 17. Significantly, Motley ended his three-volume history of *The Rise of the Dutch Republic* (1855) with a graphic description of William's assassination. At this time the fate of the rebels was at their lowest ebb. In the process, therefore, Motley was unable to address the fundamental reasons for the success of the United Provinces in their struggle against Spain.

Dutch contemporaries of Motley were writing in the aftermath of the failure of the reunification of the Netherlands which had been laid down by the Congress of Vienna in 1815. Thus, Robert Fruin, writing in 1871, emphasised those parts of the revolt which stressed the importance of a Dutch national character. The **cosmopolitan** William of Orange became the somewhat unlikely embodiment of those Dutch national virtues.

Cosmopolitan: Travelled or lived in many countries.

Such approaches were explicitly rejected by the Dutch historian Pieter Geyl in *The Revolt of the Netherlands, 1555–1609*, first published in 1932. Geyl was certainly prepared to praise William of Orange's conduct during the revolt. However, he defined his influence much more narrowly than Motley. 'Invaluable had been Orange's services in animating and giving direction to the national feeling.' Moreover, 'his greatness as a leader of the Netherlands people lay precisely in his unsurpassed talent for co-operating with the States assemblies'. On the other hand, William of Orange did not possess the control which Motley had attributed to him. 'The passions of the time had, alas, only too frequently paid little heed to his admonitions', whilst Geyl fully acknowledged the precarious political situation in which the United Provinces found themselves at the time of Orange's assassination. To Geyl, William of Orange was more a product, even a prisoner, of the circumstances of the revolt. This was altogether different than the person single-handedly capable of guiding the Netherlands' destiny, as perceived by Motley.

In contrast, some historians came to idealise William and his personality. Such attitudes were not confined to Dutch historians. The British historian, Veronica Wedgwood, writing during the Second World War, produced an idealised account in her *William the Silent* (1944). In 1946 the British historian George Clark, writing in the aftermath of enemy occupation of the Netherlands, praised William as a symbol of his nation's cause. 'No one who has any faculty for responding to human greatness can doubt that this man was great. He never shrank from responsibility but never magnified his office; he had no equal in constancy or in resource.' Orange's personal qualities were therefore seen as considerable. However, Clark placed considerable emphasis on economic and geographical factors in determining the outcome of the revolt. In the circumstances, William's opportunities to shape and determine the outcome of the revolt were very limited.

In 1971, Helmut Koenigsberger, writing in the *New Cambridge Modern History* series, was prepared to place a greater emphasis on William's role and importance. Though he had failed to preserve the unity of the Netherlands, William had succeeded in keeping alive resistance to Philip II's absolutism and achieved a spirit of cooperation with the States General. This, according to Koenigsberger, was 'a remarkable achievement for a conservative aristocrat turned revolutionary'. William's political understanding and diplomatic skill were unmatched by any of his contemporaries. His achievements and the power of the myth which attached itself to his name after his death enabled the Union of Utrecht to become a viable political structure. Most significantly, Koenigsberger, himself a refugee from political and racial tyranny in the 1930s, stressed that it was always clear that William fought against 'despotic government and religious tyranny'.

More recently, British historian Geoffrey Parker, in *The Dutch Revolt* (1977), though in some respects less sympathetic to the Dutch cause than many other historians, nevertheless accorded a more important role to Orange than had Geyl and Clark. Parker also perceived William of Orange as a more flawed and complex character than had Motley. Parker considers Orange to be 'irreplaceable'. 'Despite all his failures he was the only man who could coax decisions out of the patricians who ruled the Netherlands; although he was a rebel, he was able to secure sympathy and aid from foreign power; for all his mistakes, he commanded the respect and even the love of the population at large.'

This interpretation has some similarities with that produced in 1978 by the Dutch historian Koenrad Swart. Swart acknowledged that circumstances forced William to change direction when necessary. However, Swart went much further in asserting William's qualities. He claims William of Orange was 'one of the most effective statesmen of his time'. Despite numerous defeats and setbacks, he was 'one of those rare individuals of whom it can be said that their actions were decisive at a critical stage of history'. There were two key features to William's achievement in 'effectively organising the resistance of a small, internally divided population': one was securing a broader geographical base for the revolt in 1576 and 1577; the other was laying the foundations between 1572 and 1576 of the strength of Holland and Zeeland, which was the only factor which prevented a complete Spanish reconquest in the years immediately following William's assassination.

In *The Dutch Republic, its Rise, Greatness and Fall* (1995), Jonathan Israel sees William of Orange as a skilful political and military figure who, most of the time, had little option other than react to events which were largely outside his control. Sometimes this involved the employment of different tactics in the north from those which he pursued in the south. In the end, his attempts to maintain the unity of north and south were doomed to be futile.

1. In what ways have historians differed in their views on the contribution of William of Orange to the Dutch Revolt?

2. Explain why historians have differed in their assessments.

10.9 Why did the Dutch emerge triumphant by 1609?

In 1584, at the time of the assassination of William of Orange, the Dutch Republic appeared to be doomed. The rebels had lost their figurehead. Parma's army was on the rampage, capturing Ghent in September 1584, Brussels in March 1585 and, the biggest prize of all, Antwerp in August 1585. In the end, Antwerp fell without a shot being fired, the inhabitants being starved by the effectiveness of the blockade created by Parma's floating bridge of boats across the river Scheldt. It seemed to be only a matter of time before the rebellion collapsed completely. Yet a quarter of a century later the United Provinces were to make a favourable peace settlement with Spain. How did this transformation come about?

At first, there was little sign of transformation, even though the Treaty of Nonsuch in 1585 granted the United Provinces substantial military and financial assistance from Elizabeth I. This amounted to 7,400 troops and £126,000 per annum – about a quarter of the cost of fighting the war. At best, this English assistance might have slowed the speed of the Spanish reconquest. The English force was beset by political problems. Its leader, the Earl of Leicester, annoyed Elizabeth by accepting the title of Governor-General. He also clashed with the Netherlands nobility and with the States of Holland. Moreover, its military effectiveness was limited, handing over Deventer and the forts around Zutphen in February 1587.

The first stage in the republic's revival came as a result of Philip II's decision, against Parma's better judgment, to change his principal strategic objective from the overthrow of the Dutch rebels to the launching of an invasion of England. In order to support this strategy Parma was ordered to place his army at the disposal of the Spanish fleet, thereby immediately reducing the pressure on the rebel army. Once it was clear that the Spanish fleet had been defeated, Parma threw his army into the siege of Bergen-op-Zoom, the only major town in Brabant remaining in rebel hands.

Parma's failure to take Bergen-op-Zoom was his first major setback as a military commander and the first indication that the tide might be about to turn in the rebels' favour. However, the setback was counter-acted a few months later by Parma's capture of Geertruidenberg.

The rebels were assisted shortly afterwards by another strategic decision by Philip II. He ordered Parma to take the bulk of his forces into

The Dutch reconquest
1590–1607

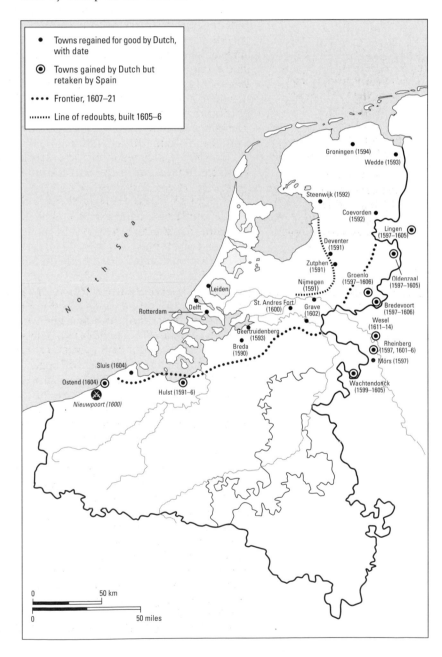

France to try to prevent the new Protestant monarch Henry IV from consolidating his power. In the first instance the rebels were unable to exploit this advantage effectively. The only major success they achieved in 1590 was the recapture of Breda. However, the rebels, with substantial English support, did take a key decision to mount a major campaign to recover the lands in the north-east which had been lost to Parma in the 1580s. This began with the recapture of Deventer and Zutphen, in May and June 1591 respectively.

The Duke of Parma was now in a difficult position. Many of his troops were in France; others had mutinied because of non-payment of wages. He was no longer able to challenge Maurice of Nassau openly on the battlefield. Maurice swiftly benefited from Parma's problems by taking a number of other towns in 1591 and 1592. To make matters worse for the Spanish the relationship between Philip and Parma was crumbling. Philip blamed Parma for the losses which the Spanish were experiencing, even though the defeats were due to events which were outside Parma's control. In Philip's eyes Parma's status was being undermined by his enemies at the Spanish Court. He was openly disregarding Philip's orders and his health was suffering from the strain. In fact, Parma was about to be recalled to Madrid, when he died from wounds sustained at the siege of Arras in 1592. Even though he had by this stage lost his aura of invincibility, his death nevertheless weakened the Spanish cause and, until the emergence of Ambrogio Spínola (see later), dominance on the battlefield was to pass to Maurice of Nassau.

Maurice of Nassau in the ascendant

By the early 1590s Maurice of Nassau's army had five key advantages:

- The rapid improvement in the rebel provinces' financial situation meant that Maurice could put larger armies in the field. This improvement had been brought about by a range of factors:
  - the internal stabilisation of the Republic after 1588
  - the improvement in the strategic situation
  - the reopening of the waterways linking Holland and Germany
  - the influx of capital and skills from Antwerp after 1585
  - the lifting of Philip II's **embargo** on Dutch ships and cargoes in the Iberian peninsula in 1590
  - the Republic's tightening grip on the Scheldt and Ems estuaries and naval blockade of the Flemish coast.

Embargo: Order preventing foreign ships entering or leaving ports.

This enabled Maurice to increase the size of his army from about 20,000 men in 1588, to 32,000 by 1595 and to over 50,000 by 1607.

- At the same time the Spanish financial position was deteriorating with the decline of Antwerp and the continued requirement to fund Spanish military activity in northern France. Discontent in Castile and revolt in Aragon reduced Philip's room for manoeuvre.

- There were fundamental divisions among the Spanish authorities. There was a struggle for power between Parma's successor as military commander, Don Pedro Enriquez Fuentes, and the Count of Mansfelt, who vigorously opposed the use of revenues from the southern Netherlands being used to subsidise the French Catholic League. In the words of Geoffrey Parker, 'each man refused to recognise the other and the Spanish government in Brussels degenerated into almost total anarchy'.

- The Dutch had assistance from the English during the 1590s which was significantly more helpful than the assistance provided by the Earl of Leicester's army in 1586–87. Between 1588 and 1595 Elizabeth I sent 8,000 troops and £750,000 to aid the Dutch rebels, and the force contributed to the rebels' victories at Bergen-op-Zoom, Geertruidenberg and Groningen.

● Maurice reformed the Dutch army by:
  – improving Dutch military tactics
  – making more effective use of his manpower
  – placing greater emphasis on the use of the musket and **arquebus**
  – emphasising the use of the artillery barrage in sieges
  – securing greater standardisation of weapon design
  – improving the training and discipline of his troops
  – and making use of maps and field glasses.
He also placed a greater emphasis on military engineering.

As a result the 1590s saw a steady period of Dutch reconquest (see map on page 237). By 1594, with the capture of Groningen, the rebels occupied most of the land the rebel provinces could lay claim to. They were in control of territory up to the German border in the north-east. Maurice's military record was not impeccable, and he did lose some towns in the east which were difficult to defend. In contrast, however, the rebels' heartland in Holland and Zeeland was virtually impregnable. Their position was bolstered by the Treaty of Greenwich in 1596, in which England and France allied with the United Provinces – recognition of the legitimacy of the rebel cause.

Even so, the United Provinces were to be denied the complete victory which they desired. Jan van Oldenbarnevelt, in particular, wished to secure control of the towns of western Flanders which had at one time been centrally involved in the revolt. He therefore organised an attack on Nieuwpoort which was duly launched in June 1600. From the point of view of the United Provinces this proved to be a disaster. Their forces were repulsed by a numerically larger and more professional army, even though Maurice's military skill was able to limit the scale of the defeat. There were two important political consequences: relationships between Maurice and Oldenbarnevelt were poisoned and the States General had to acknowledge that they would never secure control over the southern provinces.

Equally, the Spanish were coming to the conclusion that they could no longer win back the rebellious provinces. This judgement was reinforced in 1600 when Henry IV of France invaded Savoy. In the process he cut off the 'Spanish Road', the vital supply route which linked Spanish-controlled northern Italy with Franche Comté, Lorraine and the southern Netherlands. Spanish troops repeatedly mutinied in protest at their lack of pay.

In the circumstances, the Spanish did well to consolidate their position after the breaking of the 'Spanish Road'. The person most responsible for this transformation was, improbably, a Genoese banker with no military experience, Ambrogio Spínola. In 1602 he led an army, some raised at his expense, into Flanders which triumphantly recaptured Ostend in September 1604. In the following year he crossed the barrier of the rivers to capture Wachtendonck, Lingen and Oldenzaal. This so alarmed the States General that they erected a chain of wooden fortresses along the banks of the IJssel and Rhine which limited the scope of Spínola's advance.

By this stage both sides had fought each other to a standstill. The Dutch, more vulnerable now that both England and France had made peace with Spain, sought the ending of a conflict which even their economic strength could no longer readily sustain. Oldenbarnevelt had argued in September 1606 that their financial position was weak, and this

---

Arquebus: A portable gun, supported on a tripod by a hook or a forked rest. It was also known as an 'harquebus' (hook-gun).

Jan van Oldenbarnevelt (1547–1619)
A lawyer from Amersfoort in the province of Utrecht, Oldenbarnevelt first came to political notice as Pensionary (town clerk) of Rotterdam and as a member of the States of Holland. He helped to create the Union of Utrecht, negotiated the Treaty of Nonsuch and was elected Advocate of the States of Holland during its dispute with the Earl of Leicester in 1586. Oldenbarnevelt ensured that the States of Holland became the predominant political institution of the new republic, a reflection of Holland's powerful commercial position. His relationship with Maurice of Nassau began to deteriorate in 1604 over Nieuwpoort. They disagreed fundamentally over the truce. Oldenbarnevelt's encouragement of the creation of **waardgelders** in 1616 was seen as treasonable by Maurice, who engineered his downfall and subsequent execution for treason.

Waardgelders: On 4 August 1617 the 'Sharp Resolution' empowered the towns of Holland to raise special troops, the waardgelders, to maintain order. Their creation was perceived by Maurice of Nassau as a threat to his own position. The States General ordered their disbandment. Oldenbarnevelt, on the other hand, claimed that each provincial State had sovereign authority in this area. His assertion of this claim lay at the heart of the accusations of treason laid against him, which resulted in his execution. In the end Maurice was able to secure the end of the waardgelders by threatening the use of force.

position prevailed, despite the scepticism of Maurice and the opposition of the radicals in Holland and Zeeland. The Spanish were in an even worse financial situation. Spínola's vast wealth could not prevent another army mutiny in 1606 for non-payment of wages, which foreshadowed another royal bankruptcy the following year. Both sides were therefore willing to negotiate, and a ceasefire was announced on 29 March 1607. Though Holland and Zeeland rejected the peace terms in August 1608, the formula of a 12-year truce proved acceptable to all and was duly signed on 9 April 1609.

Some issues remained unresolved. The North, for example, was still blockading the mouth of the river Scheldt and the Spanish had not secured any guarantees about toleration of Catholic worship in the north. However, the United Provinces was granted international diplomatic recognition by other states. Its own internal sovereignty was recognised by Spain, if grudgingly and ambiguously. Some Netherlanders remained sceptical about what had been achieved. Oldenbarnevelt, in particular, felt that there had been little glory bought at considerable expense.

1. In what ways were the Dutch responsible for their own success?

2. How far were they dependent on other factors, such as foreign intervention and the weaknesses and mistakes of Spain?

10.10 What problems faced the new Dutch state?

The institutional framework of what was to become the Dutch Republic had begun to develop in 1572. It was more closely defined by the terms of the Union of Utrecht in 1579 and assumed its definitive form by 1609. Most of these institutional trends reinforced the predominance of the province of Holland and tended to increase the resentment of Holland which was often felt elsewhere.

1 The Union of Utrecht had originally assumed that individual provinces would be sovereign, but that they would agree to give up their sovereign rights in the areas of defence, taxation and foreign policy for the greater good of the union. Decisions in the States General were supposed to be taken unanimously, but hardly ever were. Key decisions were increasingly taken by majority vote and the scope of the States General's decisions became much wider. It was to include areas such as the regulation of shipping, administration of the areas captured from Spain, and the regulation of church and colonial affairs.

2 The institutional framework was largely imposed by Holland, which was especially dominant from 1587 to 1609 when the institutional framework of the Republic was being most rapidly developed.

3 It therefore followed that the States of Holland were the most important decision-making body in the United Provinces. Before 1572 the States of Holland, like the other States, was an occasional body with only a limited jurisdiction. Between 1572 and 1576 Orange was at the centre of decision making, but consulted with the States of Holland. After 1576 the States' importance in decision-making processes increased. Its legislative and executive power were increasingly seen as essential to the survival of the Revolt.

4 The States of Holland took on an increasingly urban character. Eighteen towns came to have permanent voting rights in the States of Holland. Moreover, from 1585, except in emergency, the States could only discuss matters which had been circulated beforehand among the authorities of the voting towns. To a great extent this confirmed that the Republic would be essentially an **oligarchy** of the regents. Even so, recognised noblemen were still entitled to attend the States.

Oligarchy: A small group of people who control and run a particular country.

5　Jan van Oldenbarnevelt emerged as the key political figure in the United Provinces and, as Advocate of the States of Holland, he exercised considerable power. Perhaps more than any other person, Oldenbarnevelt laid the foundations of Dutch independence. He did this by ensuring that key military and strategic decisions became vested in the States of Holland, which increased coherence of the United Provinces at the expense of the powers of the individual states.

6　Routine administration in each province was overseen by small, hand-picked standing committees of their States. The States took on a range of key tasks, for example the supervision of flood defences.

7　The office of Stadholder retained importance, and offered scope for the continuation of an aristocratic influence in decision-making processes. After William of Orange's assassination, the practice of having three different stadholders in the north was resumed. Maurice of Nassau was appointed in Holland and Zeeland, though he was not yet old enough to exercise the office in practice. Orange's illegitimate son, Willem Lodewijk Count of Nassau, was appointed in Friesland and later Groningen. The German aristocrat, Count Adolf von Neuenahr, was appointed in Utrecht, Gelderland and Overijssel. After the Earl of Leicester's departure from the Netherlands, it remained unclear whether appointments to the post of stadholder lay with the States General or with the provincial States. In 1595, for example, it was the States General which appointed Willem Lodewijk as Stadholder of Groningen. By 1620, however, it had become the accepted practice for each provincial State to make the appointment. The Stadholder was, in its origins, a non-military office, with responsibilities which related to the political process and to the administration of justice. The Stadholder was entitled to address the States and had a responsibility to resolve conflicts. In practice, of course, the most important responsibility of the Stadholder became military organisation and defence of his province. One feature of this activity was the closeness with which the half-brothers Maurice and Willem Lodewijk co-operated on military matters.

Religion and the emergent Dutch state

The emergent state was still divided on religious matters. This reflected the powerful position which the Calvinists were able to establish from 1572 in Holland and Zeeland, despite their numerical weakness. There were frequent clashes between militant reformist clergy and congregations, on the one hand, and the tolerant urban regents, on the other hand, who were seldom inclined to suppress private Catholic worship.

Militias: Part-time armed forces raised in each State, usually when there was fear of invasion.

The religious situation within the United Provinces remained confused and uncertain throughout the period. In 1572 the regent and noble élites within Holland had, by the standards of the time, a remarkably tolerant attitude towards religious matters. On the other hand, the mood of the **militias** and the people at the time was strongly anti-Catholic, thereby forcing Orange to adopt a more anti-Catholic public attitude than he wanted. This remained the broad situation in Holland and Zeeland throughout the rest of the 1570s. On the other hand, there was little enthusiasm among the people for positively embracing Calvinism. Thus, during the early years of the Republic neither the old Church nor the new commanded the allegiance of most of the people.

However, the reformed religion had two advantages in Holland and Zeeland, the heartlands of the revolt. Its supporters were more numerous, more militant and more committed than those of the Roman Catholic

Church and it was powerful enough to be recognised as the public Church. This meant that it had the backing of provincial and civic authorities under the terms of the Particular Union of Holland and Zeeland in 1575. Moreover, it was effectively organised under the jurisdiction of a national synod, which met every three years, provincial synods and regional classes (gatherings of clergy). The role of the church within each community was governed by the consistory, which comprised both clergy and lay people. Often, consistory members also served as members of town councils. However, the Calvinist Church lacked the power and influence to turn the United Provinces into a theocratic society (ruled by the clergy). This was especially evident in 1586 when most towns in Holland rejected the 'Church order', drawn up by the National Synod supported by the Earl of Leicester, which would have stripped town councils from exercising power in church affairs.

Unfortunately for the militant Calvinists, the population as a whole seemed remarkably unimpressed by the benefits of Calvinism. Thus, in 1587 it was estimated that only 10% of the population of Holland belonged to the Reformed Church. In some towns, such as Delft, Leiden and Dordrecht, the percentage was undoubtedly higher. By 1608 Calvinists comprised about half of the population of Delft. Moreover, though consistory members often served on town councils, they were under-represented among the urban regents.

In practice this meant that they tried to be tolerant when confronted by private worship which was either Roman Catholic or Protestant, but non-Calvinist. Such differences of opinion led to conflict in many towns, most notably Leiden, Gouda and Utrecht. At Utrecht, for example, the guilds and militia in 1586, benefiting from the support of the Earl of Leicester, overthrew and temporarily dissolved the moderate congregation which had included many of the regents. In Amsterdam, the radical town council persecuted Lutherans and **Arminians**. Such tensions would get worse during the 17th century. They would contribute to the greatest domestic crisis faced by the Dutch Republic during the period of the truce.

Disputes had arisen within the Dutch Reformed Church over the controversy between predestination and free will. The Leiden theologian Jacob Hermans, or Jacobus Arminius, challenged Calvinist orthodoxy by asserting not only that Christ had died to save all souls, not merely those of the elect, but also that God allowed a free choice whether or not to accept the divine path to salvation. The debate continued long after Arminius' death in 1609 and was particularly fierce in Holland where the Arminians appealed to the States for support in their **Remonstrance** of 1617. Oldenbarnevelt, the Advocate of the States of Holland, was sympathetic to their point of view because he favoured as wide and inclusive a state church as possible. The opponents of the Arminians replied with a **Counter-Remonstrance** which had the support of the bulk of the clergy in Holland.

What made the opposition of the Counter-Remonstrants more fierce was their belief that the reformed position was under attack, for example in Bohemia and in nearby Cleves-Jülich. In their eyes, Oldenbarnevelt was allying himself with international Catholicism. This gave Oldenbarnevelt's enemies the opportunity to attack him. His two most powerful enemies were the regents of Amsterdam and Maurice of Nassau.

The regents of Amsterdam, who were significantly more Calvinist than their colleagues in other Dutch towns, disliked Oldenbarnevelt's inclusive approach to religion. They felt strongly that he had sabotaged Amsterdam's plans for economic advancement by blocking their scheme for a Dutch West India Company which would undoubtedly have brought about the ending of the truce. Oldenbarnevelt's other opponents did not necessarily wish to see the ending of the truce. However, he had over the

---

Arminians: Followers of the theologian Jacob Hermans (1560–1609), also known as Jacobus Arminius, who rejected Calvinist ideas on predestination, sought revision of the Netherlands Confession which defined church doctrine and tended to assume that the authority of the State was superior to that of the Church. It was followers of Jacobus Arminius who put forward the Remonstrance of July 1610, which sparked off a religious controversy which threatened to tear apart the young state.

Remonstrance: The action of Arminians, led by Oldenbarnevelt, supporters of Arminius who favoured 'liberal' reform of the stricter aspects of Calvinist worship, including the emphasis on the doctrine of predestination.

Counter-Remonstrance: The action of the Calvinists, led by Franciscus Gomarus, who opposed the Arminians and Remonstrants. The support of Maurice of Nassau was crucial to ensuring the Counter-Remonstrant victory during the crisis of 1617–19.

'The Arminian Redoubt at Leiden', 1617–1618

In what respects does this illustration show the political, social and religious tensions in Holland during the crisis of 1617–1619?

years managed to offend many representatives from the States other than Holland and Utrecht, so they were now ranged against them.

Oldenbarnevelt then gave Maurice the excuse to act. There was increasing unrest among sections of Holland's urban population. In order to maintain law and order and defend the position of the States of Holland, Oldenbarnevelt persuaded the States to establish a militia – the *waardgelders*. These were raised in moderate towns sympathetic to Oldenbarnevelt's position: Haarlem, Leiden, Gouda, Rotterdam, Schoonhoven and Utrecht. The resolution establishing the *waardgelders* also declared that army units raised in Holland owed their primary allegiance to the provincial States rather than to the States General. This assertion that sovereignty lay with the individual provinces not only infuriated the Counter-Remonstrants, it was also interpreted by Maurice as an attack on his own authority.

Maurice, who had shown his religious sympathies by attending Counter-Remonstrant services in The Hague, gradually sought to undermine Oldenbarnevelt's position. He sought to build up Counter-Remonstrant strength in the States General which in July 1618 voted to disband the *waardgelders* – a vote of doubtful legality. Maurice then used his authority as Stadholder to disband personally the *waardgelders* in Utrecht. The other towns voluntarily disbanded their *waardgelders* and in August 1618 Maurice, on the authority of the States General, arrested Oldenbarnevelt and his chief supporters and presided over a purge of Oldenbarnevelt's supporters from town councils. In the process the political influence of many of the towns of Holland was significantly reduced and the States of Holland lost its pre-eminence. The Calvinist position was simultaneously reinforced in the National Synod held, significantly, in Counter-Remonstrant territory at Dordrecht. Oldenbarnevelt was convicted of treason on 12 May 1619 and executed the following day. As far as Maurice was concerned, reasons of state required the old man's execution; there is little evidence to support the view that he hoped to spare Oldenbarnevelt provided that he confessed.

1. In what ways was the United Provinces 'a civilised and tolerant state'?

2. Why did the new state experience a crisis between 1617 and 1619?

10.11 What happened to the Spanish Netherlands after 1609?

Government within the Spanish Netherlands was able to recover to some extent from the financial weaknesses and personal rivalries which beset it after the death of the Duke of Parma. In 1595 Philip II appointed a nephew, Archduke Ernest, as governor. Ernest died in 1596 and Philip, uncharacteristically perhaps, lost no time in appointing another nephew, Archduke Albert, to the post. Three years later, Albert's position in the Spanish Netherlands was consolidated by his marriage to Philip III's sister, Isabella. The Spanish Netherlands comprised her dowry. Thereafter, Albert and Isabella, known collectively as the Archdukes, ruled jointly, though they remained dependent on Spanish power to sustain their rule. Their political position was, however, strengthened by the victories enjoyed by Spínola, and their financial position was improved by the Truce, which enabled the army of Flanders to be reduced from 60,000 to 20,000, with a consequent easing of the burden of taxation.

The Archdukes consciously set out to repair relationships with both the nobility and the civic élites and did so with conspicuous success. There were numerous signs of a robust reconstructed political, religious and cultural framework emerging in the south. The philosopher Justus Lipsius produced an influential theoretical justification for the political ordering of the Spanish Netherlands. The population began to increase and rapid agricultural improvement took place. There was a revival of industry, particularly in the Flemish linen industry. Even Antwerp experienced a 'partial but sustained' recovery by developing 'niche markets' in silks, jewellery, tapestries, furniture, religious art and Catholic book production. Ghent and Bruges also experienced some recovery. There was also a considerable revitalisation within the Spanish Netherlands of the Roman Catholic Church. The level of Catholic education was especially intensive, and there was considerable Jesuit activity. There was a huge revival in church building and monasticism. Though the Spanish Netherlands had undoubtedly suffered from the shift of vitality to the North, the impact of this on the South was probably less intense, at least in the first half of the 17th century, than has sometimes been argued. In Geoffrey Parker's judgement, a new 'south Netherlands identity' had been born during the Truce. This embryonic national identity was an 'impressive monument' to the government of the Archdukes.

How successful was the rule of the Archdukes in the Southern Netherlands?

10.12 Why did hostilities resume in 1621?

In general in 1609 there was an acceptance that peace was likely to be financially beneficial to both communities. This was a judgement which was borne out by the increasing prosperity experienced in both North and South during the 12 years of the Truce. Nevertheless, religious divisions in Europe were hardening, and there were elements on both sides who were anxious for conflict to be resumed.

● The fall of Oldenbarnevelt had left power firmly in the hands of Maurice of Nassau and the Counter-Remonstrants, who had been opposed to the Truce.

● There was considerable alarm within the United Provinces at the increase in Habsburg power. Maurice built up the tension between the United Provinces and Spain by encouraging his nephew, Frederick, the Elector of the Palatinate, to take the Bohemian Crown. There was therefore an attempt to build up an anti-Habsburg coalition. After Frederick's flight, first from Bohemia and then from the Palatinate, Maurice did much to aid English intervention to restore Frederick to his electorship.

● Some merchant interests within the United Provinces, particularly those Amsterdam merchants who favoured the founding of a West

India Company, felt that war with Spain would be beneficial to their financial interests.

● There was a strong feeling in Spain that Spanish and Habsburg strategic interests would be best served by a renewal of the conflict. The fall of the Duke of Lerma and his replacement by the Count of Olivares strengthened the position of those who favoured a strong policy.

What Maurice was really seeking during March 1621 was the renewal of the Truce on a similar basis to that of 1609 whilst ensuring that Spain became fully involved in the German conflict. This would have been the best way of guaranteeing the continued security of the United Provinces. In order to guarantee peace he even secretly offered to lift the blocking of the Scheldt. His strategy failed, and in July 1621 the war was resumed on the orders of Philip IV.

> *How justified is the claim that Maurice of Nassau was mainly responsible for the resumption of war in 1621?*

10.13 What, if anything, was changed by war between the United Provinces and Spain 1621–1648?

Ultimately, very little was achieved by either side as a result of the war. Its economic effects on both parts of the Netherlands during the 1620s were harmful. The scale of Spain's wider involvement in the European conflict was such that Spain could never commit its forces fully to the conflict in the Netherlands. There were few significant territorial gains by either side. Indeed, each side eventually concluded that an outright victory on land was unlikely to be achieved.

The war was fought both on land and at sea. The initiative on land was seized by the Spanish when Spínola and his forces captured Breda in June 1625. However, he was unable to build on this victory. Spain's new land route to the Netherlands was blocked when Swiss Protestants gained control of the Valtelline in 1624 and the outbreak of conflict over the Mantuan succession in 1628 further weakened the Spanish effort against the United Provinces. This enabled the Dutch under Maurice's half-brother, Frederick Henry, to launch a counter-attack with the capture of Wesel and 's-Hertogenbosch in 1629 and Maastricht in 1631. For a short time it looked as if the southern Netherlands as a whole might be vulnerable to Dutch attack but, despite the recapture of Breda in 1637, the Dutch made little further progress.

The war was also conducted at sea in the Atlantic and Caribbean. In 1621 the West India Company was finally been established and the States General ensured that it was given naval support. Dutch **privateers**, led by Piet Heyn, captured the Brazilian port of Bahia in 1624. This was quickly lost. However, four years later Heyn captured the entire Spanish silver fleet off Cuba. The financial weakness which this induced was one of the factors which enabled the Dutch to stage the military recovery of 1629. Much more crucial, however, was the victory of the Dutch, under Admiral Tromp, in a set-piece naval battle, the Battle of the Downs. This took place in the English Channel in 1639. Tromp's victory destroyed an armada which had been built up by Olivares and which was carrying large numbers of reinforcements for the army of Flanders.

As early as 1632–33 there had been serious attempts to conclude a peace. By 1641, however, it was even more obvious to the Spanish that they could not overthrow the Dutch Republic. The devastating defeat of their fleet, along with the outbreak of revolts in Catalonia and Portugal, made the case for peace compelling. The Dutch, for their part, were as divided as ever about the wisdom of continuing the conflict. In 1643 Philip IV tried to do a deal with Frederick Henry, offering him recognition

> **Frederick Henry, Prince of Orange (1584–1647)**
> Stadholder of each of the United Provinces, Frederick was the half-brother of Maurice of Nassau. He was both a distinguished soldier and a cautious diplomat. After having steered the United Provinces through the troubled years of the 1620s, he became a generous and sophisticated patron of the arts.

Privateers: Private seamen who were licensed by the State to commit acts of piracy against foreign powers.

of rule over the northern Netherlands, though with Zeeland, 's-Hertogenbosch, the Maas towns and Nijmegen returning to Spain. When Frederick Henry failed to respond positively, Philip then tried to do a deal with the States General. Such behaviour by Philip simply heightened Dutch distrust of his intentions.

However, the negotiations between Spain and the United Provinces became caught up in the diplomatic activities which were bringing to an end the Thirty Years' War. The provincial states debated endlessly during 1644 and 1645 whether they should be directly represented at the peace talks at Münster or whether they should try to conclude a separate deal with Spain. When a decision was finally taken on 28 October 1645 there was no unanimity, Zeeland dissenting from the decision. The talks in Münster dragged on. However, one suggestion there – that the Spanish Netherlands be transferred to French sovereignty – caused sufficient alarm among the Dutch to force them towards an agreement, which was signed in July 1646. Even then, however, there was significant opposition to the peace agreement in Holland, Zeeland, Friesland and Groningen. In the end in October 1646 six provinces voted in the States General for acceptance of the peace settlement. Once again, there was opposition to peace, especially in Zeeland. Eventually, a formal peace treaty was signed at Münster on 30 January 1648 and even Zeeland came reluctantly to accept it. The peace, in any case, was quite favourable to the North. The independence and sovereignty of the United Provinces were confirmed, the river Scheldt remained closed, the Dutch conquests in Flanders and Brabant were confirmed and they also kept their overseas conquests.

1. In what ways did the Dutch threaten the strength of the Spanish overseas empire?

2. Why did it take so long for the two sides to make peace?

10.14 What was the nature of Dutch economy, society and culture during the first half of the 17th century?

For much of the 17th century the Dutch enjoyed a golden age of prosperity and cultural achievement. According to Simon Schama, in *The Embarrassment of Riches*, the Dutch Republic was 'an island of plenty in an ocean of want'. The Dutch, irrespective of their social status, enjoyed higher real incomes, better diets and safer livelihoods than their counterparts anywhere else in Europe.

Economy

The huge economic growth which made this possible can be traced back to the 1590s and continued despite the problems brought about by the resumption of war in 1621. Jonathan Israel argues that there were three phases to the process by which the Dutch achieved economic predominance.

The First Phase (1590–1609)

● Fishing and bulk carrying continued to be important feature of the Dutch economy. 'The high level of urbanisation … of Holland Zeeland on the eve of the Golden Age stemmed largely from the carrying traffic.'

● The Dutch 'rich trades' in high-value commodities, like spices, sugar, silks, dyestuffs, Mediterranean fruit and wine, grew in importance. The responsibility for their development often lay with immigrants who had fled Antwerp and other southern cities to escape religious persecution.

- This domination was crucially aided by the fact that the Dutch once again had access to Spanish and Portuguese ports.

- When the Spanish embargo was reintroduced in 1598 the Dutch had the flair and confidence to invest heavily in new direct traffic to the Indies.

- This investment was matched by the growth in the importance of the Dutch colonies.

The Second Phase (1609–1621)

- Though there was a loss of momentum in colonial developments, Dutch shipping in Europe became even more competitive, both in the Mediterranean and the Baltic. The importance of the fishing industry grew enormously.

- The economy in Zeeland did suffer because of the strength of renewed competition from the South Netherlands.

- There was a further shift in importance from bulk carrying to high-value commerce. Bulk carrying of grain, timber, salt and fish had been dominated by the Dutch since the 15th century. Its importance had been reinforced by the development of the **fluit** which maximised the profitability of low-cost bulk carrying. By the early 17th century, however, the growth in bulk carrying was slowing, and growth in the 'rich trades' became more spectacular. This had several consequences: it substantially increased the wealth of the Dutch middle classes and provided the raw materials and skills which made possible the sophisticated culture of the Dutch Golden Age.

Fluit: A type of boat specially designed for the carriage of bulky low-value goods. Its design was perfected in the 1590s.

The Third Phase (1621–1647)

- Trade in Zeeland recovered as a result of the renewal of the war with Spain.

- There was a further growth in colonial commerce.

- The textile industries in Leiden and Haarlem developed considerably, particularly because of the collapse of the textile industry in Germany.

- Trade with both the Mediterranean and the Baltic suffered during the 1620s. The fluit ports of Hoorn, Enkhuizen and Medemblik never really recovered from this slump.

- There was a significant recovery in trade during the 1630s.

The continued resilience of the Dutch economy did much to ensure its eventual survival in the war against Spain. The herring industry attracted much contemporary comment. Dutch fishermen predominated not only in the North Sea but also off Iceland. An arctic whaling fleet was also built up. However, the relative decline of fishing began in the 1620s, and it is difficult to see how the industry could have sustained the level of profits to make it such a 'gold mine' for the United Provinces. Moreover, Dutch vessels dominated the Baltic trade. Dutch manufacturing became increasingly important. Dutch shipbuilding was both more technologically advanced and financially more profitable than that of its rivals. Textile manufacture became increasingly important. Agriculture remained profitable. The rapid growth of Dutch towns actually made agriculture both more profitable and more intensive.

The devastation wrought by the Thirty Years' War on German agriculture increased the demand for Dutch products. The pressure on land ensured that land reclamation schemes were successfully undertaken, thereby significantly boosting agricultural production. The economic recovery of the 1630s fuelled a capitalist obsession with speculation in tulip bulbs. Unfortunately for many speculators, the tulip-mania collapsed spectacularly in 1637, leaving many bankrupt.

Society

Dutch society during the first half of the 17th century was predominantly urban. Outside the eastern part of the country many towns grew rapidly. The most spectacular growth was in Amsterdam, Leiden and Rotterdam, all of which more than doubled their populations between 1600 and 1647. Much of this increase was due to **immigration**, not only from the South but also from parts of Germany. After 1590 the major motive for such immigration was employment. Wages were higher and jobs were more plentiful.

> **Immigration**: The movement of people into a country in order to live and work there.

The towns were dominated by the merchant élites. Often members of this group were richer than the traditionally dominant regents and had made substantial fortunes from the 'rich trades'. The vast majority of the highest taxed citizens of Amsterdam in 1631 came from this category. Many of them sprang from immigrant stock. The Golden Age also saw the emergence of skilled craftsmen associated with the 'rich trades', often again springing from immigrant stock. These included tapestry weavers in Delft and diamond cutters in Amsterdam. Tile works were set up in cities such as Delft and Haarlem. Within this bourgeois culture, the practice of art was increasingly seen as a means of improving both wealth and social position.

> **Real wages**: What can be bought with money wages taking into account inflation (see page 56).

Real wages rose throughout much of the first half of the 17th century, except during the depressed 1620s. Though life for the unskilled and semi-skilled was never easy, there were good prospects for the highly trained to gain wealth, thereby ensuring that standards of living for many were considerably higher in the United Provinces than elsewhere in northern Europe. For those who lacked the skills, contacts or luck to exploit the opportunities to get rich, the Dutch developed systems of poor relief, mainly organised by town governments.

> **Bourgeoisie**: The urban middle classes. Often the term is used to classify the wealthier members of the middle classes, for example bankers and merchants.

During the Golden Age the **bourgeoisie** (upper middle classes) and their values dominated Dutch society. Increasingly this society became more 'open', especially once the passions raised by the Remonstrant controversy had died down, and religious toleration became more marked. The extent of toleration was extremely wide by contemporary standards and developed especially quickly in view of the religious tensions which had been so evident up to 1618. There was an intense debate over toleration during the later 1620s. Frederick Henry, who succeeded Maurice as Stadholder in 1625, was more inclined towards toleration, believing that a broad-minded attitude towards Catholicism might encourage the ending of the conflict against Spain. The authorities proved to be especially tolerant towards

Catholic practice in the towns of Holland and Utrecht. A separate Remonstrant Church emerged in the 1620s, though some Remonstrants eventually joined the Lutheran faith and a separate congregation of liberal Remonstrants, the Collegiants, began to emerge in the late 1620s.

There had been Jewish settlers in the Netherlands since the 1570s. Temporary synagogues (Jewish places of worship) had been established in Rotterdam and Haarlem, but had been suppressed. The legal philosopher Hugo Grotius published a pamphlet in 1614 arguing for limited toleration of the Jews. In 1616 a rabbi (Jewish priest) reported that Jews were able to 'live peaceably' in Amsterdam, and within a few years members of the Jewish community were being portrayed by the Dutch artist Rembrandt in the same way as other members of the bourgeoisie.

Culture and intellectual life

The spirit of political and religious toleration contributed to an intellectual openness which was without parallel in Europe. The roots of this openness could be found in the late 16th century. When the revolt was at its height the writer Dirk Volckertsz Coornhert (1522–1590) rejected dogmatic theology and advocated toleration. The philosopher Justus Lipsius tried to resolve the ethical dilemmas brought about by the political situation in which Netherlanders found themselves. The leading Dutch intellectuals of the late 16th century tended to support the Orangist political position. This was particularly evident in the career of Simon Stevin, mathematician and military engineer, who was himself a refugee from the South. Stevin became closely associated with the University of Leiden, which had been founded as the North's first university in 1575 and which developed a reputation as an open and tolerant institution of international renown. This was particularly evident in medicine and the sciences, but also in philology, for which the university authorities head-hunted the French scholar, Joseph Justus Scaliger.

By the end of the 16th century Dutch culture and intellectual life was clearly aspiring to the remarkable standards which it would achieve during the Golden Age. The principles of moderation and limited tolerance were, perhaps, most developed in the work of Hugo Grotius, who pioneered the principles on which international law would be formulated. The culture of toleration offered a safe haven within the United Provinces to scholars from other countries; the most important of whom was the French mathematician and philosopher, René Descartes, who was resident in Holland from 1629 to 1648.

The early 17th century saw the emergence of Dutch vernacular literature with writers like Pieter Cornelisz Hooft and Joost van der Vondel. More significant, perhaps, was the development of science and engineering, which was only to peak in the second half of the 17th century with the work of Christian Huygens.

Art

The great flowering of Dutch art began in the 1590s. According to historian Jonathan Israel this was a period in which artistic achievement and innovation in art proceeded on a scale and with an intensity which has no parallel in any other time, or place, in history.

Architecture flourished in the building boom which lasted from the late 1580s to 1621. Three major churches designed by Henrik de Keyser (1565–1621) were built in Amsterdam. However, most of the major new buildings were secular. These included East India House (1606), Exchange (1608–11) and Haarlem Gate (1615–18) in Amsterdam, the Prinsenhof and Old Men's Home in Haarlem and the town hall in Leiden.

The pace of urban building slackened after 1621, though in the 1630s and 1640s Frederick Henry emerged as a patron of architecture, especially in The Hague.

However, the most important expression of Dutch culture lay in painting. Though the greatest period for Dutch painting was the 1650s and 1660s, there was much outstanding work produced during the first half of the 17th century. This was essentially an expression of bourgeois culture. The finest examples of Dutch bourgeois art were militia portraits and group portraits. The most famous militia portrait was Rembrandt's 'The Company of Captain Frans Banning Cocg' (perhaps better known as 'The Night Watch') of 1642. The Haarlem painter Frans Hals painted several group portraits, including 'The Banquet of the Officers of the St George Militia' and 'Regents of the Hospital of St Elizabeth'. Such portraits were commissioned to be hung in public places and demonstrated the collective self-confidence of the bourgeois élites. Rembrandt and Hals, in particular, were in demand as portrait painters, the former being especially innovative in portraying Jewish sitters from among the Amsterdam bourgeoisie. A variety of landscape painting was also to be found. Romanticised Italianate landscapes were popular with Utrecht artists such as Hendrik ter Brugghen, Gerrit van Honthorst and Dirk von Baburen. Such a style was more likely to flourish within the religious culture of Utrecht, which was more tolerant towards Catholicism than many of the towns of Holland and Zeeland. More realistic approaches were associated with Haarlem painters such as Esaias van der Velde, who specialised in landscapes, and Hendrik Cornelisz Vroom, who specialised in seascapes. In the next generation the landscape tradition was continued by van der Velde's pupils: Jan van Goyen and Salomon van Ruysdael.

Townscapes of the sort associated with Jan Vermeer and Pieter de Hoogh and the low-life **genre** paintings of Jan Steen were largely a product of the 1650s and 1660s. Most Dutch artists concentrated on their own specialities. Emanuel de Witte and Pieter Saenredam, for example, specialised in painting church interiors. The major exception to this generalisation was the greatest figure of the Golden Age, Rembrandt. As well as producing official commissions for the Stadholder Frederick Henry and for civic groups, Rembrandt produced numerous portraits and painted many landscapes as well as mythological and biblical scenes.

Genre: French word meaning type, or kind – applied to art, it means a style of painting.

1. What were the sources of Dutch economic strength in the first half of the 17th century?

2. Analyse the social and cultural consequences of Dutch economic growth?

Source-based questions: the sovereignty of the United Provinces

SOURCE A

They [the States of Holland] shall discuss and ordain the best and most suitable means of restoring and re-establishing in their old form and full vigour all the old privileges, rights and usages of the towns, which may have been suppressed and taken away by Alba's tyranny … . His Grace [i.e. Orange] has no other purpose than to see that, under the lawful and worthy government of the King of Spain …, the power, authority and prestige of the States may be restored to their former state, in accordance with the privileges and rights which the king has sworn to maintain in those countries. And without the States, [Orange] shall not endeavour to do or command anything that concerns the provinces or that may be harmful to them. … [Orange] binds himself to undertake or command nothing without the advice or consent of the States or at least the majority of them.

Proposal by William of Orange to the States of Holland, 1572

SOURCE B

And should it be that we, our heirs or successors, should by our own action or that of others violate [the privileges of the States General] in whole or in part, in whatsoever manner, we consent and concede to our aforesaid [subjects] that they need not do us, our heirs or successors any services, nor be obedient to them in any other things we might need or which we might request of them, until such time as we shall have corrected the mistaken course hitherto pursued toward them, and have completely abandoned and reversed it.

Oath of Installation, drawn up by the States General and agreed by the Duke of Anjou, 19 September 1580

SOURCE C

Let all men know that, in consideration of the matters considered above and under pressure of utmost necessity … we have declared and declare hereby by a common accord, decision and consent the King of Spain, … forfeit of his lordship, principality, jurisdiction and inheritance of these countries, and that we have determined not to recognise him hereafter in any matter concerning the principality, suremacy, jurisdiction or domain of these Low Countries, nor to use or permit others to use his name as Sovereign Lord over them after this time.

Act of Abjuration drawn up by the States General, 26 July 1581

SOURCE D

His Excellency [Leicester] … shall be commissioned Governor and Captain-General of the … United Provinces … . [Leicester] shall have full power and absolute command in the matter of war … . [Leicester] shall have full and absolute power in the aforesaid Provinces and associated regions, in the matter of civil government and justice, such as the Governors-General of the Netherlands have in all times legally possessed, and particularly in the time of Charles V of beloved memory… . [Leicester] shall be empowered to summon the States General of the said provinces at any time and place within the said provinces.

The States General bestowing titles and honours on the Earl of Leicester, February 1586

---

1. Study Source A.

Explain the reference to 'restoring and re-establishing in their old form and full vigour all the old privileges, rights and usages of the towns'.

2. How might Source A be used to justify the claim that 'in 1572 Orange's aim was simply to restore the position of the Netherlands to that which had applied during the reign of Charles V'?

3. How useful is Source D as evidence of the political status of the States General in 1586?

4. Using all of the sources and the information contained in this chapter, consider the judgement that the emergence of the United Provinces as a sovereign state was a confused and contradictory process.

The French Wars of Religion and the reign of Henry IV 1559–1610

Key Issues

● *What were the causes of the French Wars of Religion?*

● *Why did the French Wars of Religion last so long?*

● *How important was the reign of Henry IV to the recovery of the French monarchy?*

Framework of Events

1541	Calvinism established at Geneva
1545–63	The Council of Trent reforms Catholicism
1555	Calvinist ministry begins in France
1559	Execution of Anne de Bourg
	Treaty of Câteau-Cambrésis
	Death of Henry II: Francis II becomes king, aged 15
	Domination of Court and government by Guise faction
1560	Assembly of Notables
	The 'Tumult' of Amboise
	Estates General meets for first time since 1484
	Francis II dies of ear abscess; Charles IX becomes king, aged 9 and a half; Catherine de' Medici becomes regent
1561	Colloquy of Poissy
1562	Edict of January
	Massacre at Vassy
	First war begins
1563	Peace of Amboise ends first war. Charles IX reaches age of majority
1564–66	Charles IX's royal tour of France with Catherine de' Medici
1565	Catherine meets Duke of Alba at Bayonne
1567	The Surprise of Meaux. Second civil war begins
1568	Peace of Longjumeau ends second war
	Third war begins
1569	Battle of Jarnac and Moncontour. Death of Louis, Prince of Condé
	Coligny becomes Huguenot leader
1570	Peace of St Germain ends third civil war
1572	St Bartholomew's Day Massacre
	Fourth civil war begins
1573	Siege of La Rochelle
1574	Charles IX dies of tuberculosis; Henry III becomes king, aged 22
1575	Escape of Duke of Alençon, Henry III's brother, starts fifth civil war
1576	Peace of Monsieur ends fifth war
1577	Sixth civil war begins; ends with the Peace of Bergerac

1579	Peasant revolts in Dauphiné and Provence
1580	Seventh civil war begins; ends with Peace of Fleix
1584	Death of Duke of Anjou. The Huguenot, Henry of Navarre, heir apparent
	Catholic League revived
	Treaty of Joinville between Philip II and the Catholic League
	War of the Three Henries (Henry III, Henry of Guise and Henry of Navarre) begins
1585	Treaty of Nemours between Henry III and Catholic League
1588	Day of the barricades. Henry III ejected from Paris
	Henry III orders assassination of leaders of Guise faction
1589	(January) Catherine de' Medici dies
	(August) Henry III assassinated; Henry of Navarre becomes Henry IV
1590	Siege of Paris by Henry IV. Ended by Duke of Parma
1592	Siege of Rouen by Henry IV
1593	Henry IV converts to the Catholic religion
1595	Henry IV declares war on Spain
1598	Edict of Nantes ends Wars of Religion
	Peace of Vervins ends war with Spain
	Maximilian de Béthune takes over French finances
1600–1601	War over Saluzzo
1604	Paulette tax introduced
1606	Béthune becomes Duke of Sully
1609	Cleves-Jülich dispute begins
1610	Henry IV assassinated; Louis XIII becomes king with Marie de' Medici as regent.

Overview

I N the 40 years after 1550, France experienced a period of great internal instability. A series of civil wars, known as the Wars of Religion, divided the kingdom. Depending on which book you read, there were eight or nine wars of religion. All of these wars could be regarded as one conflict separated by short periods of peace. Although these were civil wars, the conflict did lead to foreign intervention. England was the first to try to take advantage of French division. In 1562 the English briefly captured Le Havre. Later in the conflict Protestant princes from Germany, Dutch rebels and the Spanish all became involved.

There is some dispute among historians about the causes of the conflict. Some have highlighted the importance of religion. Others highlight the importance of aristocratic faction. To them the wars were caused by a lack of a strong monarch. Francis II, Charles IX and Henry III were all weak and incapable in their own way. Faced with a political vacuum at the top, leading aristocratic families fought each other for control of a weak monarchy. In this sense the Wars of Religion seem similar to the Wars of the Roses in 15th-century England.

Henry III (1551–1589)
Last member of the House of Valois to rule France. Born in Fountainbleau on 19 September 1551, the third son of Henry II and Catherine de' Medici. Left France in 1573 to accept the throne of Poland but returned the following year to become king on the death of Charles IX. He was a moderate trying to compromise between Huguenot and Catholic. Faced hostility of Catholic League after 1584 when Henry of Navarre became heir. Ejected from Paris by Catholic League in 1588; he retaliated by assassinating Henry of Guise and Louis, Cardinal of Lorraine. Assassinated himself in August 1589 by a Catholic fanatic.

Rival groups in the French Wars of Religion

1   **The Valois Family**
    Kings of France:
    Francis II (1559–1560)
    Charles IX (1560–1574)
    Henry III (1574–1589)

- Catherine de' Medici, mother of all the above and Regent 1560–1563.

- Francis, Duke of Alençon and Anjou, Catherine's youngest son, dies in 1584.

2   **The Guise**
    Power base was eastern France and linked with the House of Lorraine.

- Francis, Duke of Guise; soldier, assassinated in 1563 during the first war

- Charles, Cardinal of Lorraine, family statesmen; died 1575

- Henry, Duke of Guise, assassinated on orders of Henry III, 1588

- Charles, Duke of Mayenne, succeeded Henry as leader of the Catholic League. Fought Henry IV in 1590s.

3   **The Bourbons**
    Power base in southern France and Picardy. Princes of the blood and heirs to the throne if the Valois unable to produce a male heir.

- Anthony of Navarre, killed in first war, 1562.

- Louis, Prince of Condé, Anthony's brother, leader of the Huguenots. Killed at Battle of Jarnac, 1569. Succeeded by Henry, Prince of Condé, who died in 1588.

- Henry of Navarre, succeeded to the throne as Henry IV in 1589.

4   **The Montmorency** (divided on religion)
    Power base in north and central France

- The Constable of France, Anne de Montmorency. Devout catholic but disliked the Guise faction. Killed at Battle of St Denis in second war in 1567.

- The Châtillon faction were Huguenots. The most important was Gaspard de Coligny, Admiral of France. Became leader of Huguenots on Condé's death in 1569. Murdered in St Bartholomew's Day massacres, 1572.

5   **The Politiques**
    Moderate Catholics who wanted peace and reconciliation. Initially associated with Catherine de' Medici and the chancellor, Michel de l'Hôpital. Later associated with the Duke of Alençon.

6   **The Catholic League or Holy Union**
    Extreme Catholic organisation. Began in opposition to Peace of Monsieur in 1576. Revived in 1584 when the Huguenot, Henry of Navarre became heir to the throne. Subsidised by Philip II in Treaty of Joinville. Led by Henry of Guise until his assassination in 1588. Opposed both Henry III and Henry IV. Power of the League declined after Henry IV converted to the Catholic Religion in 1593.

7   **The United Provinces of the Midi**
    Huguenot organisation created after the St Bartholomew's Day massacres of 1572. Aimed to create a state within a state to protect Huguenots. Similar in structure to the Dutch United Provinces. Political power was given to a Protestant Estates General rather than the monarch. Protectors of the United Provinces were the Prince of Condé, then Henry de Montmorency-Damville (a Catholic) and then Henry of Navarre.

The wars lasted for so long because of a number of factors. The characters and age of the French kings were important, so was the nature of conflict. Huguenots fought the reformed Catholicism that emerged following the Council of Trent (1545–1563). Extreme Catholics attempted to annihilate the Huguenots (French Protestants). Finally, foreign intervention prevented the French from solving their internal problems alone.

In attempting to resolve the internal conflicts, Catherine de' Medici is an important and controversial figure. Her aim was to protect the French monarchy. This involved her in trying to reconcile religious differences. However, there is some dispute about whether she changed this policy in the St Bartholomew's Day massacres of 1572. From 1560 to the 1580s Catherine de' Medici tried to influence the course of events, with varying degrees of success.

The civil wars were brought to a conclusion by Henry IV. From 1589 to 1598 he was able to end religious conflict and foreign intervention. He achieved the former by converting to the Catholic religion. He achieved the latter by making peace with Spain.

From 1598 to Henry IV's assassination in 1610 France went through a period of political and economic recovery. With his chief financial adviser, the Duke of Sully, Henry IV was able to reform royal finances. Henry's foreign policy also helped to re-establish France as a major western European power.

Henry IV (1553–1610)		
First Bourbon king of France. Born in Pau, on 14 December 1553, son of Anthony of Bourbon and Jeanne d'Albret of Navarre.	Brought up as a Huguenot. When Anthony died in 1562, Henry became King of Navarre. Escaped murder in the St Bartholomew's Day massacres because of his	marriage to Maguerite of Valois. Became heir to throne on the death of Francis, Duke of Anjou in 1584. Became king on death of Henry III in 1589.

11.1 What were the causes of the Wars of Religion?

The weakness of the French monarchy

The untimely death of Henry II at a tournament in July 1559 created a crisis for the French monarchy. He was succeeded by his 15-year-old son, Francis. According to royal custom, Francis II was old enough to rule at that age. However, he was a weak, sickly individual.

Francis II reigned until December 1560 when he died of an ear abscess. He was followed by an even younger monarch, his younger brother Charles IX. He was nine and half years old. On this occasion his mother, Catherine de' Medici, ruled as **Regent**. Therefore, in the critical years of 1559 to 1562, when the first civil war began, the monarchy was weak and inexperienced. This created a political vacuum at the top of the French political system.

Regent: In this instance, a person who is given royal authority on behalf of another. It usually applies when a monarch is a minor (under age). Not the same as the Regents referred to in the previous chapter.

The problem for the monarchy was made worse by a lack of money. The Habsburg–Valois Wars had left the French monarchy bankrupt. In 1559 the French monarchy owed 40 million livres of which 12 million livres was to be paid to bankers straight away. This lack of finance meant that the monarchy had difficulty keeping a large army. Most of its best troops were mercenaries. It also meant that it did not possess money to reward members of the nobility and thereby gain their loyalty. In December 1560 the Estates General was called for the first time since 1484. It was asked to provide money to help pay off the Monarchy's debt. It refused to do so.

Aristocratic faction and clientage

In the political vacuum that followed Henry II's death, the Guise family took over control of the French court and government. Within days of his death Francis, Duke of Guise had taken over the position of Grand Master from Anne de Montmorency [Anne was a male name at this time]. During Henry II's reign, the Guise faction was one of the powerful aristocratic groups in France. The control over both king and the government by the Guise faction was resented by other aristocratic groups. The Montmorency faction had been influential under Henry II. Now they were deprived of influence at the centre of French government. The Bourbons were another important faction. They had recovered from the treason of Charles of Bourbon in 1523–24 (see Chapter 7) to be an important political force. However, the two leading members of the faction were French Protestants (Huguenots). They were Anthony of Navarre and Louis, Prince of Condé. Although Protestant, there were princes of the blood. If the Valois family failed to produce a male heir, the Bourbon family would succeed to the throne of France.

Although both the Bourbon and Montmorency factions had lost influence at court, they still possessed considerable regional power. Anne de Montmorency remained Constable of France (in charge of the army) and Governor of Languedoc. The basis of their regional and political power was *clientage*. This meant they had the loyalty and allegiance of other noble families in a particular region. They also controlled villages and towns. Finally, they had the wealth to create their own private armies. During the Wars of Religion the conflict between these factions meant that aristocratic groups left or were forced from Court to be replaced by another.

Economic crisis

By 1559 France was facing a series of economic crises. Firstly, the failure of the harvest in 1557 had resulted in widespread famine. Secondly, the 1530s to 1550s had seen a general rise in prices. This had led to a rise in the cost of living which badly affected craft workers in towns. Thirdly, the Habsburg–Valois Wars had led to a steep rise in taxation, in particular the taille (see Chapter 7) which further reduced the standard of living.

The end of wars also meant that thousands of troops, who had been fighting, returned to France. These soldiers returned to a country deep in economic crisis. With no real chance of civilian employment, they were only too willing and able to become involved in warfare.

An important aspect of the economic crisis was the position of the nobility. A traditional view, held by historians such as L. Romier (in 1922), believed the joint effects of inflation and the end of warfare had led to a decline in economic standing of the nobility. More recently, historical research has suggested the opposite. The historian J. B. Wood, in *The Nobility of the Election [district] of Bayeaux, 1463–1666* (published in 1980), has noted that the nobility in Normandy, in many cases, became richer. This view is supported by R. J. Knecht, in *The French Wars of Religion 1559–1598* (1989), when he states:

> 'there were undoubtedly some impoverished noblemen in mid-16th-century France. But there was no economic collapse of the nobility as a whole. Recent research has demonstrated that in Beauce, Normandy, Béarn and Auvergne the nobility grew richer.'

One area where the economic crisis did affect the nobility was pensions. In 1560 the Guise faction, in an attempt to cut the financial costs of government, cut the number and value of pensions of nobles who had fought in the Habsburg–Valois Wars. This had the effect of forcing many nobles into the anti-Guise camp.

The growth of Protestantism

According to the American historian Mack Holt, in *The French Wars of Religion 1562–1629* (1995), 'the French Wars of Religion were fought primarily over the issue of religion as defined in contemporary terms: as a body of believers rather than the more modern definition of a body of beliefs'. Protestantism in the form of Calvinism spread rapidly in France in the 1550s and 1560s. The main Protestant areas, known as the

'Huguenot crescent', spread across France from the south-west in Gascony, through Languedoc to Dauphiné and Provence (see map on page 266). According to Holt, around 10% of the French population (some 1.8 million) had become Protestant by the 1560s.

The growth of Calvinism was due to a variety of factors. One reason was the weakness of the French Catholic Church. Absenteeism, corruption and the ignorance of the ordinary clergy had created a situation in which a new version of Christianity would be attractive.

A traditional view, associated with the German sociologist Max Weber at the beginning of the 20th century, was the belief that the reformation was a social as well as religious movement. It was associated with the urban craft workers. Calvinism, with its emphasis on self-reliance and hard work, was more attractive than Catholicism.

More recently, historians have put forward the view that Calvinism had wider appeal. R.J. Knecht, in *The Rise and Fall of Renaissance France* (1996), states: 'The Calvinist movement was drawn from rich and poor.' Holt believes a wide variety of local factors helped Calvinism develop. One common factor was its attraction to the literate classes, both noble and craft worker. It also attracted a disproportionate number of women and the young.

The Protestant cause was also aided by persecution by the state. In 1559 Anne de Bourg, a Calvinist member of the Paris Parlement, was imprisoned and put to death for insulting Henry II.

The rapid growth in Calvinism took place between 1559 and 1562 when, according to R.J. Knecht, 'the political situation blurred the lines of authority to such an extent that it could develop without undue harassment. It was at this time that it gained large number of aristocratic converts.'

The monarchy attempted to prevent religious conflict by calling a national council of the French Church. In began in July 1561 at Poissy. The aim was to try to find a compromise between the Catholic Church and French Calvinism. The main feature of this attempt was a religious discussion between Catholic and Calvinist representatives, known as the Colloquy of Poissy. This began on 9 September 1561. Unfortunately, the main Calvinist representative, Théodore de Bèze, took an uncompromising stand. In addition, in January 1562, the Monarchy issued the Edict of St Germain, which allowed Huguenots to hold their meetings throughout France, except inside walled towns.

The result of these royal attempts to bring compromise between Catholic and Huguenot failed. It enraged Catholics. According to the historian D. Nugent, the Colloquy of Poissy was a turning point. Its failure made religious conflict almost inevitable.

The organisation of French Calvinism

The Calvinist Church was organised from 'the bottom up'. This was the opposite to the Catholic Church, which was hierarchical. Its organisation was extremely good for establishing and running the Calvinist Church.

Each local church had its own 'consistory'. This was a committee of the minister (religious leader) and the elders (senior lay members). The consistories of a number of churches were grouped into a 'colloquy'. This body administered a region.

At provincial level there was a 'synod', which was made up of representatives from the colloquys. At national level there was the national synod. Between the first national synod and 1600 there were 11 meetings of the national synod.

Calvinist Church organisation was used as an effective way of raising an army during the Wars of Religion. Each consistory was expected to provide a captain, each colloquy a colonel and each provincial synod a general.

The move to war: the 'Tumult' of Amboise, March 1560

This was an attempt by Huguenot noblemen to kidnap King Francis II. The aim was to free the monarchy from the influence of the Guise faction. It combined a religious and aristocratic element. The main plotter was Jean du Barry, seigneur (member of the nobility) of La Renaudie. He was supported by Louis, Prince of Condé – a leading member of the Bourbon faction. The plot was badly organised and uncovered with relative ease. The rebels were captured at Amboise by royal troops under the control of Francis, Duke of Guise. Several hundred Huguenots were executed as traitors.

The event helped to harden attitudes between the Guises and their opponents. The Guises believed there was a Huguenot conspiracy to overthrow the monarchy. The Bourbons and Huguenots believed that the Guise could only be removed by force.

The immediate cause of the first civil war: the massacre at Vassy

The Duke of Guise's troops opened fire on a Huguenot religious meeting inside the town of Vassy. The meeting was illegal under the terms of the Edict of St Germain of January 1562.

Historians differ on the number of dead. Janine Garrisson states 23, R. J. Knecht 30, Martyn Rady 74. The effect was to spark off the first civil war. On one side were the Guise faction – known as the Triumvirate. On the other side were the Prince of Condé and the Châtillon family of the Bourbon faction.

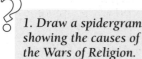

1. Draw a spidergram showing the causes of the Wars of Religion.

2. Why did opposition to the French monarchy develop between 1559 and 1562?

3. What do you regard as the most important cause of the Wars? Give reasons for your answer.

? Source-based questions: The Massacre at Vassy, 1 March 1562

SOURCE A

According to one version, [the Duke of] Guise, on learning that some 500 Calvinists were worshipping close by, decided to remonstrate with them. Some Calvinists barricaded the entrance to the barn, others climbed scaffolding over the porch and started pelting the duke and his men with stones. Some noblemen were struck, including Guise. Furious, they opened fire on the Calvinists with arquebuses. The massacre left about 30 dead and more than a hundred injured.

Exactly what happened at Vassy will never be known. There was wrong on both sides. Under the Edict of January, the Protestants were forbidden to hold services within walled towns. On the other hand, Guise was not supposed to interfere with a private service. The Calvinists were at fault in throwing stones at him and his men, an action hardly consistent with etiquette [rules of polite behaviour]; but Guise overreacted criminally by opening fire on them. Under the most recent edict, the worst punishment prescribed for a religious dissenter was exile, not death.

From The Rise and Fall of Renaissance France 1483–1610 *by R. J. Knecht (1996)*

SOURCE B

Welcomed by the Catholics of the Court and the capital, the news of Vassy encouraged Guise to attempt a further coup with the assistance of Montmorency. The royal family was at Fountainbleau on 27 March 1562 when the Duke of Guise arrived with a troop of horse and urged the Regent to return to Paris under their escort with the King and the Court. Guise knew quite well as Condé that possession of the king's person was worth 'half of France', and both men were ready to use force to legitimise their faction with that person. Guise's coup forced Condé to go on the offensive, justifying his recourse to arms in the Declaration of 8 April 1562, whose stated aims were the liberation of the King and the Regent from Guise captivity and the enforcement of the Edict of January. But Condé and his noble Protestant followers had in fact been preparing for war since the fiasco at Amboise.

From A History of Sixteenth Century France 1483–1598 *by Janine Garrisson (1995)*

Source-based question: The Massacre at Vassy, 1 March 1562

SOURCE C

Only after receiving two formal letters of jussion (royal commands to the court to register legislation without further delay) did the Parlement of Paris reluctantly register 'the Edict of January' on 6 March 1562. Even then, they did so with explicit amendment that they were doing so against their will and only on the king's command. But they already knew it would be impossible to enforce, as the Catholic reaction to the edict had already erupted in violence. Just a few days earlier, on 1 March, Catherine's edict that was supposed to bring peace ultimately led to civil war she had so desperately wanted to avoid. The first shots were fired by troops of the Duke of Guise, as he encountered a group of unarmed Protestants worshipping inside the town of Vassy. The resulting 'massacre', as the Huguenots would henceforth call it, marked the beginning of three generations of armed struggle over the issue of religion.

From The French Wars of Religion 1562 to 1629
by Mack Holt (1995)

1. Using information from the Sources and this chapter, explain the meaning of the terms and phrases highlighted in the sources as they applied to the outbreak of civil war in France in 1562.

(a) 'Edict of January' (Sources A and C)

(b) 'the Regent' (Source B)

(c) 'The fiasco at Amboise' (Source B).

2. Study Sources B and C. How far do these sources differ in their explanation of why the first civil war took place?

3. Study Sources A, B and C and use information contained in this section.

How important was religious conflict between Catholic and Huguenot in causing the First War of Religion?

11.2 What role did Catherine de' Medici play during the Wars of Religion?

Catherine de' Medici – painting by François Clouet

Of all the individuals involved in the Wars of Religion Catherine de' Medici is one of the most controversial. In the past she has been seen as scheming and devious. Until the untimely death of her husband she had been a dutiful wife producing ten children. At the age of 40, and without any previous governmental experience, Catherine was faced with a serious political, religious and economic crisis. Throughout her remaining years she had to look after the affairs of her four sons in an era of civil war.

Catherine de' Medici's aims

Catherine's main aim from 1559 to her death in 1589 was to maintain the independence of the French monarchy. In a letter to her daughter, Elizabeth, who was married to Philip II of Spain, she declared that her main aim was 'to serve God and maintain her authority', not for herself but in order to preserve the kingdom.

In her attempt to achieve her aim Catherine faced major problems. Her first two sons were weak. Francis II was poorly in both health and mind. Charles IX was a minor when he became king. Even her third son, Henry III, who was 22 when he became king in 1574, proved to be a failure as monarch. Her fourth son, the Duke of Alençon, was a troublemaker who

Francis, Duke of Alençon and Duke of Anjou (1555–1584)

The youngest son of Henry II and Catherine de' Medici. Although a Catholic, he sided with the Huguenots in the fifth civil war (1574–76). He became Duke of Anjou in 1576. Seen as a leading politique, but really a plotter against his elder brother Henry III. Involved in marriage negotiations with Elizabeth I in 1578. Led an unsuccessful military expedition to help the Dutch in the Netherlands in 1583.

Michel de l'Hôpital (1503–1572)

Born in 1503 in the Auvergne, the son of a doctor and a friend of Charles of Bourbon. He left France after the trail of Bourbon. Michel studied law in Padua, Italy, before becoming councillor-clerk of the Parlement of Paris in 1537. He was sent as an ambassador to the clergy at Bologna for the opening session of the Council of Trent in 1545. In March 1560 he became Chancellor of France. The post was the most important in France, after the monarch. Michel was a major influence over domestic affairs until 1568. He was a moderate Catholic who wanted to give Huguenots rights. It was on his initiative that the Estates General was called at Orléans in 1560. He was also responsible, along with Catherine de' Medici, for calling the Colloquy of Poissy in 1561. In 1562 he signed the Edict of January, giving Huguenots full freedom of conscience and limited freedom of worship. This policy of compromise was followed with the Edicts of Amboise and Longjumeau.

plotted against his own brother, Henry, and threatened the monarchy through association with Dutch rebels.

To make matters worse, Catherine de' Medici had to operate without money. The monarchy had amassed massive debts by 1559. At the Estates General in 1560 her chancellor, Michel de l'Hôpital, announced debts of 43 million livres. Any attempt to restore the monarchy through the splendour of Court life or the creation of a large army were severely limited by this problem.

The crisis of monarchy occurred in a period of religious and social conflict where aristocratic groups vied with one another to control the monarch.

How successful was Catherine de' Medici in increasing the independence and authority of the French monarchy?

Catherine was not in a position to prevent the domination of the Guise faction at Court at the beginning of the reign of Francis II. Her main aim in the years after 1559 was to bring reconciliation between the factions in France. In this purpose she was ably assisted by Michel de l'Hôpital. Unfortunately, the dominance of the Guise faction aroused hostility from other aristocratic groups and the Huguenots who feared persecution. However, Catherine was extremely shrewd. When Francis II called an Assembly of Notables to meet at Fountainbleau in August 1560, Catherine used the occasion to outmanoeuvre the Guise faction. Supported by Montmorency and the Châtillon group, she was able to get the assembly to relax the heresy laws against Huguenots.

In December 1560 Catherine de' Medici was quick to get the Estates General to accept her as regent when Charles IX became king at the age of nine and a half. It was during Charles IX's reign (1560–1574) that Catherine was able to exercise her greatest influence. The fact that religious civil war broke out in 1562 is an example that Catherine's policies failed. The attempt at religious compromise at the Colloquy of Poissy came to nothing.

To increase the authority and prestige of the monarchy, Catherine used a number of devices. In August 1563 she declared that Charles IX had reached the age of majority at a *lit de justice* (see Chapter 7) at Rouen. He could now rule in his own right. Catherine also embarked on a great royal tour of France with Charles IX. Between 1564 and 1566 they spent two years crossing France. This great royal procession involved the entire Court. Around 20,000 people were involved in the tour. The aim of the royal tour was to increase contact between the French monarchy and the people of France. The intent was to increase royal popularity.

Catherine also attempted to increase the monarchy's prestige and position through the use of marriage alliances. She attempted to arrange a marriage between her sons, the Duke of Anjou (in 1570–71) and the Duke of Alençon (1578), and Elizabeth I of England. Her daughter Elizabeth was already married to Philip II of Spain and in 1572 she arranged for another daughter, Maguerite, to marry the Huguenot leader, Henry of Navarre.

In her bid to make the monarchy more independent, Catherine had a strong element of luck. Many of the main protagonists who had caused the outbreak of civil war in 1562 had died during the first three wars (1562–1570). In October 1562, Anthony of Navarre was killed. In December, Marshal St André was killed at the Battle of Dreaux. In February 1563, Francis, Duke of Guise was assassinated. During the Second War, in 1567, Anne de Montmorency died. In the third war, Louis, Prince of Condé was killed at the Battle of Jarnac in 1569.

However, Catherine did make tactical errors. On the great royal tour she arranged to meet her daughter Elizabeth at Bayonne in 1565. Unfortunately, the Duke of Alba was part of Elizabeth's party. This meeting created great suspicion among the Huguenots. They believed Catherine was plotting with Philip II against European Protestantism. In 1567, Alba led a large Spanish army along the 'Spanish Road' to the Netherlands (see map on page 299). The aim was to put down the Dutch Revolt. However, no one in France, including Catherine, was aware of his true intentions. Fearing Spanish intervention, a group of Huguenots attempted to kidnap Charles IX at the Surprise of Meaux (26 September 1567). This led directly to the third War of Religion.

Catherine has also been implicated in the decisions that led to the St Bartholomew's Day massacres in August 1572. This is dealt with at greater length in the next section. Suffice it to say, Catherine's actions in August 1572 were motivated by a fear of Spanish intervention which could have occurred if Admiral Coligny had led a military expedition to the Netherlands.

Once Charles IX died, Catherine's influence declined. However, it did not stop her from declaring herself as Regent until Henry III had time to return from Poland where he had been elected king the year before. Unfortunately, she was not in a position to influence Henry III who was an independent-minded but lazy monarch. Catherine could not prevent Henry III assassinating the two leading members of the Guise family in 1588.

Catherine also had little influence over her other son, the Duke of Alençon. It was his personal ambition to increase his political influence that led to the fifth war of religion in 1574. He continued to cause trouble until his death, as Duke of Anjou, in 1584.

In her last years Catherine continued to prevent conflict. Once the Duke of Anjou was dead, Henry of Navarre (a Huguenot) became heir to the throne. Catherine attempted to get him to become a Catholic.

Unfortunately for the historian there is a dearth of evidence on Catherine. This has, in part, led to the differing interpretations of her role in the Wars of Religion. Historians such as Nicola Sutherland, in *Catherine de' Medici and the Ancien Regime* (1966) see her as a moderating influence, a person who tried to bring compromise between the warring factions. More recently, R. J. Knecht, in *Catherine de' Medici* (1998), believes that much of Catherine's reputation depends on her role in the St Bartholomew's Day massacres.

1. What were the main problems facing Catherine de' Medici after 1559?

2. What did Catherine do to increase the independence and authority of the French monarchy?

3. How successful was Catherine de' Medici in achieving her aims?

11.3 *The St Bartholomew's Day massacres, 1572*
A CASE STUDY IN HISTORICAL INTERPRETATION

In 1572 four inter-related incidents occurred, following the royal wedding of Maguerite of Valois (Catherine de' Medici's daughter), to Henry of Navarre, member of the Bourbon faction and a Huguenot leader.

● On 22 August a Catholic named Maurevert attempted to assassinate Admiral Coligny, leader of the Huguenots in Paris.

● In the early hours of the morning of 24 August, St Bartholomew's Day, several dozen Huguenot leaders were murdered in Paris.

● Beginning on 24 August, and lasting three days, there was a wave of popular killings of Huguenots by the Paris mob.

● From August to October massacres of Huguenots took place in other towns, such as Toulouse, Bordeaux, Lyons, Bourges, Rouen and Orléans.

The accounts of the numbers killed range from 2,000 to 100,000. However, a more accurate estimate is that around 2,000 were killed in Paris and a further 3,000 in the provinces.

A number of questions have arisen as a result of these events.

● Who ordered the assassination of Admiral Coligny?

● Who ordered the massacre of the Huguenot leaders?

● Were the massacres planned or spontaneous?

The background to the massacres

At the end of the Third War, in 1570, permanent peace seemed to be a distinct possibility. The Guise family had fallen from favour at Court. They were replaced by more moderate Catholics who were willing to find a compromise. The Huguenots were in a strong military and political position as a result of the Edict of St Germain, which ended the war. They had control of four fortified towns: La Rochelle, La Charité, Cognac and Montauban. They also had legal safeguards that would enforce this edict.

In addition, Catherine de' Medici had hoped that marriage alliances involving her children would support her move for peace. She planned a marriage between Maguerite de Valois and the Huguenot leader Henry of Navarre. She also planned that the Duke of Anjou (the future Henry III) would marry Elizabeth I of England. Unfortunately, this latter marriage plan collapsed.

By 1572 hopes for peace were declining rapidly. In 1571 the Catholic fleet, under Don Juan of Austria, had defeated the Turks at the Battle of Lepanto (see page 50). It confirmed to many Huguenots the potential threat of a resurgent Catholicism across western Europe, led by Philip II of Spain. The main area of concern was the Netherlands and the Dutch Revolt. In April 1572, the 'Sea Beggars' took control of Brill, thereby gaining control of Holland. These developments led to a demand within France to intervene on behalf of the rebels in the Netherlands to forestall a Spanish Catholic intervention in France. The main supporter of this proposal was Admiral Gaspard de Coligny, leader of the Huguenots. Catherine was faced with the prospect of another civil war or a major war against Spain, western Europe greatest Catholic power.

By 1572, relations between Catholics and Huguenots in France had also deteriorated. In an article in the *American Historical Review* in 1985, entitled 'Prologue to a Massacre: Popular Unrest in Paris 1557 to 1572', Barbara Diefendorf has noted that massacres had already occurred. For instance, in Rouen, on a Sunday in March 1571 (during Lent), over 40 Huguenots had been massacred after they had refused to kneel in front of the **Host** during a Catholic procession.

Finally, personal resentment created tension. Not only had the Guise faction fallen from favour at Court, but also Coligny was readmitted to the King's Council in September 1571. He also received a large pension. The Guise faction hated Coligny for two reasons: firstly, because he was a Huguenot; secondly, because he was implicated in the assassination of Francis, Duke of Guise in February 1563.

Who ordered the assassination attempt on Coligny?

Initially it would seem that the Guise faction was responsible. Maurevert, the assassin, fired the shot that wounded Coligny from a house owned by the Guise faction. On 23 August, the following day, a judicial inquiry revealed the involvement of Henry, Duke of Guise. However, the issue of foreign policy might suggest that the Guise faction did not act alone.

Gaspard de Coligny (1519–1572)

Admiral of France and leader of the Huguenots after Louis, Prince of Condé's death in 1569. He advocated military intervention on behalf of the Dutch rebels against Spain. The attempted assassination against Coligny sparked off the St Bartholomew's Day massacres.

Host: Catholics believe that a bread wafer, known as 'the Host', represents the body of Christ.

Coligny was the main supporter of intervention in the Netherlands. Catherine de' Medici viewed such intervention with alarm. In May 1572 Louis of Nassau led a Huguenot army into the Netherlands and captured the Catholic towns of Mons and Valenciennes. This development could force a Spanish Catholic invasion of France.

Matters came to a head with the Genlis affair. In July 1572 a Huguenot named Genlis, leading a Huguenot force, was defeated by the Spanish near Mons. This forced Coligny to support the idea of immediate armed intervention. This whole issue split the Court and King's Council.

Circumstantial evidence would suggest that Catherine and Charles IX worked with Henry of Guise to assassinate Coligny. Ever since the Surprise of Meaux in 1567, Catherine had become concerned about a Huguenot takeover. This was her opportunity.

An alternative view is put forward by historian Nicola Sutherland in *The Massacre of St Bartholomew and the European Conflict 1559–1572* (1973). She believes that such action by Catherine was illogical because she had always attempted to reconcile the Catholics and Huguenots. This is reinforced because the event took place shortly after the marriage of one of her daughters to a Huguenot.

Who ordered the massacre of the Huguenot leaders?

Evidence would suggest that the assassination attempt on Coligny was the attempt to kill one man, not the prelude to more general murder. However, by the morning of 24 August 1572 several dozen Huguenots were murdered in a co-ordinated act, including Coligny.

On Saturday 23 August a meeting of the King's Council took place to discuss the attack on Coligny. According to Mack Holt, in *The French Wars of Religion 1562–1629* (1995), the Council feared Huguenot reprisals and decided on a pre-emptive strike. The major factor in this decision was the existence of a Huguenot force of 4,000 just outside Paris under the

St Bartholomew's Day massacres, Paris, 1572 – painting by François Dubois

1. What evidence exists to suggest that Catherine de' Medici was involved in:

a) the attempted assassination of Coligny on 22 August?

b) the murder of the Huguenot leaders on 24 August?

2. Why have historians differed in their views on the role of Catherine de' Medici in the events of 22–26 August 1572?

3. 'The involvement of Catherine de' Medici in the massacres of St Bartholomew's Day is purely circumstantial.' Assess the validity of this statement.

command of Teligny, Coligny's brother-in-law. As both Catherine de' Medici and Charles IX were present at the Council meeting they must bear responsibility for these murders which involved the King's Swiss Guards. Between the massacres and his own death, in 1574, Charles IX supported these murders by stating that he had punished Huguenot conspirators with a lawful exercise of royal justice.

Were the massacres of 24 August spontaneous or planned?

The evidence which survives from the massacres, which affected Paris for three days, suggests spontaneity. The Paris militia and Catholic mobs ran amok, murdering men, women and children. Several of the victims were mutilated and burnt. This suggests that the mobs were murdering heretics. There is plenty of evidence to suggest that many of the mobs believed they were fulfilling the will of God in removing heresy.

However, there had been serious tension between Catholic and Protestant since the Edict of St Germain. The existence of thousands of Huguenots in Paris attending the royal wedding brought tensions to a height. Any action that occurred which inflamed Catholic–Huguenot rivalry could have sparked off a massacre. The King's Council decision of 23 August to make a pre-emptive strike against the Huguenot leadership helped cause the Paris massacre.

Paris was joined by other provincial towns in the murdering of Huguenots. The main cause of these massacres seems to be the built-up resentment of Catholics against Huguenots. However, the Paris massacre must have acted as an example.

11.4 How far did the Wars of Religion change between 1562 and 1598?

Foreign intervention

A feature that affected the wars throughout was foreign intervention. This development was inevitable. Firstly, the internal instability of France was seen as an opportunity to gain territory or influence. In 1562 the English used the opportunity of the first war to regain Calais. They attacked and captured Le Havre. Unfortunately, the strategy backfired. The expedition united the two opposing French sides, who together were able to expel the English.

Secondly, the French civil wars must be seen as part of a wider religious conflict involving western and central Europe. John Casimir of the Palatinate (in the Holy Roman Empire), a Calvinist, intervened on a number of occasions: in 1567, 1576 and 1587. Although defeated by the Guise-led army in 1587, the presence of Protestant German mercenaries in 1576 forced Henry III to accept the Peace of Monsieur. In the third war in December 1568, William of Orange and his brother Louis of Nassau attempted to aid the Huguenots by attacking northern France from the Netherlands. In June 1569 the Duke of Zweibrucken led an army of German mercenaries across France from Germany to relieve a Catholic attack on La Rochelle.

The most important intervention was by Spain from 1584. In that year Philip II signed the Treaty of Joinville with the Catholic League and offered financial support against Henry III and Henry of Navarre. In 1590 a Spanish army intervened on behalf of the Catholic League to raise Henry IV's siege of Paris. English troops also became involved and fought for Henry IV in Brittany. From 1595 to 1598 Spain and Henry IV were officially at war.

France 1562–1598

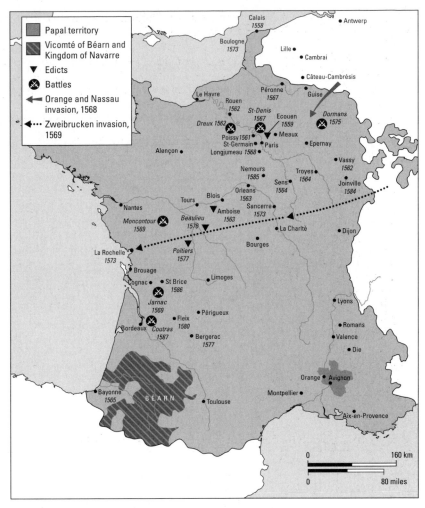

Although foreign involvement was a common feature throughout the wars, the level of foreign intervention increased greatly with Spanish involvement after 1584.

The impact of the St Bartholomew's Day massacres

The events of 1572 were a turning point in the Wars of Religion.

● The peak of popularity for French Calvinism was 1572. After that date, it went into decline.

● After 1572 the Huguenots became openly hostile to the French monarchy. In the first three wars they had been opposed to royal policies. After 1572 they became opposed to the French monarchy itself. In southern France the United Provinces of the Midi was formed. This was a Huguenot state within a state. It was similar in organisation to the rebel provinces of the Netherlands.

● New political theories of resistance to royal power developed after 1572. On the Huguenot side, a number of books and pamphlets were produced which questioned the right of the French monarchy to rule. In 1573 Francois Hotman produced 'Franco-Gallia' and Théodore de Bèze produced 'The right of magistrates over their subjects'. Bèze argued that the purpose of any state was the welfare of its subjects. As a result, political power came from the people. After the massacres, the

French monarchy had given up the right of allegiance of its Huguenot subjects.

Henry III and the growth of Catholic Opposition

In 1584 The Holy Union or Catholic League was revived (it had initially been formed in 1576). It had reformed as a result of the death of the Duke of Anjou. His death meant that a Huguenot, Henry of Navarre, was heir apparent. Although formed to stop a Huguenot becoming king, the League increasingly began to oppose Henry III. They felt that Henry was too accommodating towards the Huguenots. Also Henry III's private life, in particular his homosexuality, appalled Catholics.

Under the leadership of the Guise, the Catholic League began to oppose the King. By 1588 Henry III was forced to leave Paris on 12 May by the League. This was the lowest point in the whole period of warfare for the French monarchy. In July 1588 Henry was forced to accept the Edict of Union which repeated the Treaty of Nemours of 1586. Henry accepted the League's demands that he should fight heresy and recognise the Cardinal of Bourbon (a Catholic), not Henry of Navarre, as his heir. In retaliation, he had the leaders of the Guise faction assassinated. In the following year, a Catholic fanatic, Jacques Clement, assassinated Henry III on 1 August 1589. From that date until 1593, when Henry of Navarre (now Henry IV) converted to the Catholic religion, the war was a straightforward religious conflict.

Principal areas controlled by Huguenots and Catholics during the Wars of Religion

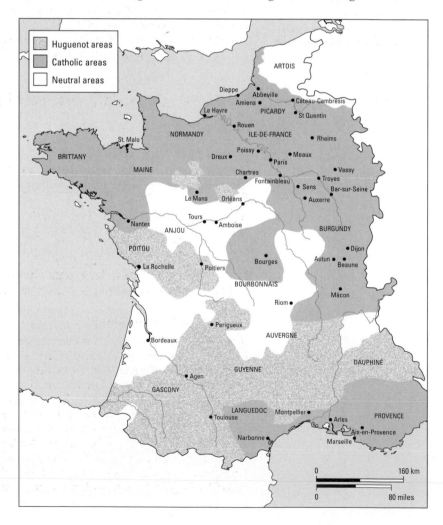

Social effects of the wars

The Wars of Religion were not continuous. They were several periods of peace. Also, the wars did not affect every region of France in the same way. However, during the wars there were two waves of peasant revolts. The first took place in 1579, the second in 1593–94.

The causes of the first peasant revolts were a mixture of the decline in royal authority, a rising population and the economic impact of nearly 15 years of warfare. It affected south-east France. In 1593–94 peasants began to band together to prevent the pillaging of both the armies of Henry IV and the Catholic League. In south-west France the peasants, calling themselves 'Latecomers' [*Tard-Avises*], made demands that included lowering taxes. In May 1594 as many as 20,000 peasants assembled near Bergerac, in Perigord, to put forward their grievances. These peasant uprisings helped to convince Henry IV that an end to the civil wars was important to prevent major social upheaval.

The position of the French monarchy

As the wars progressed, the position of the French monarchy declined. The first three wars (1562–1570) were mainly about royal policy. After 1572 both Huguenots and extreme Catholics began to question the authority of the monarchy itself. In addition, the monarchy was financially impoverished throughout the period. Inheriting a debt of 40 million livres in 1559, matters simply got worse. This prevented the monarchy developing an effective and independent military force to impose its authority. Therefore, it had to rely on alliances with the different faction groups within France.

1. Why did the French Wars of Religion begin in 1562?

2. In what ways did the Wars of Religion affect France?

3. In what ways did the nature of the wars change between 1562 and 1598?

4. Using information from sections 11.1 to 11.4, explain why the French Wars of Religion lasted so long.

11.5 How successful was Henry IV as king between 1589 and 1610?

At the beginning of his reign Henry IV faced a number of problems.

● The Wars of Religion

● The conflict between the Bourbons and the Guises

● The need to restore royal authority

● The need to restore royal finances

● The need to prevent foreign intervention, in particular from Spain.

Henry IV was fortunate in dealing with these problems. Because most of his opponents were dead, he was the undisputed leader of the Huguenots. In 1590 the Cardinal of Bourbon died leaving no real Catholic leader.

Ending the Wars of Religion

In the period 1589 to 1598 Henry IV proved to be an effective military leader. He was able to defeat the armies of the Catholic League. He was also able to avoid major confrontation with the Spanish until after 1595, when he had sufficient military strength.

In 1593 Henry IV made the momentous decision to convert to Catholicism. This act split the Catholic community and removed the main reason why Catholics opposed his rule as monarch.

By 1598 he was able to buy off the leaders of the Catholic League with bribes of four million livres. He was also able to end the conflict between Huguenots and Catholics with the Edict of Nantes. Although the Edict created a Huguenot 'state within a state', it did bring an end to the wars for the time being. They were to erupt again during the 1620s, during the reign of Louis XIII.

Edict of Nantes, 13 April 1598

● Huguenots allowed full liberty of worship in all places outside Paris where their faith was already established.

● Huguenots given similar rights as Catholics.

● Over 100 fortified towns, including La Rochelle, Montauban and Montpellier, given to Huguenots for eight years.

● Provincial synods of Huguenots could meet freely.

● Groups set up in each parlement of France, comprising equal numbers of Catholics and Huguenots, with the intention of dealing with any breaches in the Edict.

Henry IV also made peace with Spain at Vervins. The international boundaries of France were to be those of the Treaty of Câteau-Cambrésis.

Restoration of royal finances and improving the economy

This was one of Henry IV's major achievements. He was ably assisted by his main financial adviser Maximilian de Béthune, who was made Duke of Sully in 1606.

When Henry IV became king, the monarchy had a debt of 200,000 million livres. Crown income was around 30 million livres. Henry spent the first six years of his reign going from one financial crisis to another, his troops remaining unpaid for long periods.

In an attempt to find a solution to the crisis, Henry called an Assembly of Notables in 1596. They agreed to a 5% sales tax on all transactions – the *pancarte*. Collection began only in 1601, and due to considerable resistance from many towns was discontinued in 1602.

Sully was appointed in 1598 and was able to transform this appalling state of finance to a position of solvency by 1610. In that year the monarchy had a surplus of 15 million livres. Sully achieved this by the following means:

● He declared France bankrupt and the creditors received only a part payment of the debts they were owed. This included foreign states such as England and the United Provinces.

● He shifted the balance of paying taxes from the towns and peasants to the more privileged. For instance, he increased the salt tax, the gabelle, which was paid by both nobles and the Third Estate.

● He introduced a new tax called the *Paulette* or *Droit annuel* in 1604. This was a voluntary tax paid by office holders, in return for a guarantee that they could sell their offices to whoever they wished. The tax was equivalent to 1/60th of its annual value. The Paulette brought in 2 million livres a year, 10% of all revenue.

● Attempts were made to stop the outflow of bullion to other countries by setting up royal factories to produce luxury goods (e.g. Gobelins and Savonnerie de Chaillot).

● A new system of book-keeping was introduced which enabled a close watch to be kept on how the money was spent as a bid to cut down on waste.

Paulette: A tax introduced in France by the Crown in 1604. All office holders had to pay one-sixtieth of the annual value of the office, in return for which it became saleable and hereditary. It was named after its first collector, Paulet.

- Sully reduced the powers of parlements over taxation. For instance, in 1603 he created eight new *elections* (districts for collecting taxes) in Guyenne. By 1610 the *élus* (the Monarchy's chief financial representatives in each election) were functioning in the provinces of Bresse, Bugey and Guyenne.

- Commissions for commerce were established in 1602, restoring silk weaving in Tours and Lyons. Linen production in Picardy and Brittany was also developed.

- Some 5.5 million livres were spent on bridge and road construction between 1605 and 1610 to improve internal communications.

- As superintendent of fortification Sully improved France's frontier defences. In 1604 he set up a network of officials responsible for each frontier province. They had the task of introducing bastions into town wall defences.

Henry IV's foreign policy

Cutting the Spanish Road
Like other French monarchs before him, Henry IV was concerned about the Habsburg Spanish encirclement of France. In the War of Saluzzo, 1600–1601, the French invaded Savoy in a dispute about the territory of Saluzzo. The war involved Spain on the side of Savoy. In the Treaty of Lyons in 1601 the French received Bresse, Bugey, Valromey and Gex. They had closed most of the Spanish Road. At one point it was reduced to a single bridge across the river Rhone.

Subsidising Spain's enemies
Instead of fighting, Henry IV gave money to Spain's enemies. Between 1605 and 1607 he gave the United Provinces two million livres per year. He also gave money to Geneva and to some German Protestant princes.

The prevention of war
Between 1601 and 1609 Henry IV attempted to prevent the outbreak of religious war in Europe which might adversely affect France. He intervened to end a dispute between England and the Papacy in 1606 to 1609. However, his greatest achievement was the Truce of Antwerp of 1609 between Spain and the United Provinces.

The Cleves-Jülich Dispute 1609–1610
Following the death of the Duke of Cleves-Jülich on 25 March 1609, a war developed between German Protestant princes and the Catholic Habsburgs over who should rule the territory. Henry IV was willing to intervene on behalf of the Protestants, but on the way to war he was assassinated by a Catholic fanatic, Francois Revaillac, on 14 May 1610. (See pages 353–4 for more detail on the Cleves–Jülich Dispute.)

1. How was Henry IV able to bring an end to the Wars of Religion?

2. What methods did Sully use to improve French finances and the economy?

3. How successful was Henry IV in bringing about the recovery of France?

The rise of Sweden in the 16th and early 17th centuries

Key Issues

● *How did Sweden grow as an independent power in the 16th century?*

● *What impact did Gustavus Adolphus have on Sweden in the early 17th century?*

● *What was the impact of Sweden on European history in the 16th and early 17th centuries?*

12.1 How important was the 16th century to the development of Sweden as a major power in both the Baltic and in northern Europe?

12.2 Why was Gustavus Adolphus able to make Sweden into a major European power?

12.3 How successful was Gustavus Adolphus' foreign policy before 1630?

12.4 Historical interpretation: Why did Gustavus Adolphus intervene in Germany in 1630?

12.5 What were the results of Gustavus Adolphus' intervention in Germany?

12.6 Gustavus Adolphus: an overall assessment

Framework of Events

1397	The Union of Kalmar
1522/23	Sweden becomes an independent power
1527	The Reformation is accepted in Sweden
1560	The death of Gustav Vasa
1594	Birth of Gustavus Adolphus
1599–1604	Civil War in Sweden
1604–11	Reign of Charles IX
1605–10	Series of defeats of Sweden by Poland
1611	Gustavus Adolphus inherits the throne of Sweden
	Charter of Nyköping
1612	Oxenstierna becomes Chancellor of Sweden (until 1654)
1613	War with Denmark finally ends; Peace of Knared
1617	Peace of Stolbova
1621–25	Polish war
1626	Battle of Wallhof. Defeat of Poles. Gain of Livonia. Battle of Lütter
1627	Wallenstein on the Baltic
1629	Edict of Restitution. First negotiations with Richelieu
1630	Gustavus Adolphus lands at Stralsund on north German coast
1631	Treaty with France
	Gustavus wins Battle of Breitenfeld
1632	Battle of Lützen. Death of Gustavus Adolphus
	Regency of Christina and Oxenstierna
1633	League of Heilbronn formed
1634	Battle of Nördlingen
	Form of Government
1638	Treaty with France
1643	Swedish invasion of Denmark
1648	Treaty of Westphalia.

Overview

I T is not usual for most standard histories of Europe to spend a lot of time dealing with the smaller nations, which ring the shores of the Baltic. The nations there tend to be small in population and limited in resources. Generally, they have had a limited impact on the rest of European history. The focus of such histories invariably tends to be on the 'great' powers such as France and the Habsburg nations. They only look at the history of the smaller nations when they intrude on the activities of the 'great' powers. Sweden is a remarkably interesting example of how a nation, limited in resources and population, can rise from comparative obscurity to play a vital role in the whole evolution of European history. Much of the reason for this remarkable breakthrough lies with the work of a single individual, King Gustavus Adolphus. He is an example of how much impact an individual can have on the course of history if he seizes opportunities and makes maximum use of the resources available with the skills at his disposal.

Sweden gradually evolved into a nation state over several decades in the 16th century, much of it under the control of a single, cautious King, Gustav Vasa. The resources of the nation were used in a remarkable way by one of Vasa's descendants, Gustavus Adolphus, who ruled between 1611 and 1632. In the course of that reign he not only altered the course of his country's history, but also radically influenced the direction of the history of Europe and the Reformation. If he had not died in battle at a comparatively young age (38), and had survived for another year or two, he might have overthrown the Habsburgs in Austria, altering the whole balance of power in Europe. For a period of about three years Gustavus Adolphus decisively altered the course of the Thirty Years' War in Germany. He played a vital role in the Habsburg–Bourbon conflicts, and helped to secure the survival of Protestantism in Northern Europe. He completely reformed his own state in a decade and a half and rewrote the rules by which war was conducted. His country increased hugely in size and gained an empire along the southern shores of the Baltic. For a while Gustavus Adolphus was also the master of much of Germany. It was a quite remarkable achievement.

Gustav Vasa (1523–1560)
He liberated his country from Danish rule (1520–1523) and put down local uprisings of nobles and peasants. By 1544 he was secure enough to make his title hereditary. His grandson was Gustavus Adolphus.

Gustavus Adolphus (1594–1632)
A noted warrior king, he waged successful wars against Russia (1613–1617) and Poland (1621–1629). This, combined with Danish defeat in the second phase of the Thirty Years' War, made Sweden the dominant power in the Baltic. Swedish power was reinforced by its participation in the Thirty Years' War. Bolstered by French money, Gustavus invaded northern Germany to protect the Protestant cause and to restrict the power and influence of the Holy Roman Empire and Wallenstein in the north. He came near to succeeding, where Christian IV of Denmark had failed. Gustavus took his army – the most efficient in Europe since its nucleus was conscript instead of mercenary – into Germany in 1630. He succeeded, with his brilliant victory at the Battle of Breitenfeld, in becoming the acknowledged leader of the Protestant cause. Sweden's dominance, however, lasted less than three years. After a victory at the Battle of Breitenfeld in 1631, Gustavus won the Battle of Lützen the following year, but was killed during the fighting. Although his forces were victorious, Gustavus was irreplaceable.

12.1 How important was the 16th century to the development of Sweden as a major power in both the Baltic and in northern Europe?

To explain fully how Sweden managed to burst on to the European 'scene' in 1630 and alter the whole course of the Thirty Years' War, it is necessary to look back into the 16th century. For several centuries before then the Danes had ruled Sweden. This had been established in what was known as the Union of Kalmar of 1397. This meant that most of what are now Denmark, Norway and Sweden were under one Danish ruler. This colonial rule was imposed by force and was deeply resented by those who lived in what is now Sweden. Although there were no great racial or religious differences between Danes and Swedes then, there were differences in culture, language and tradition that went back centuries. The Swedes resented what they saw as alien rule, particularly as the Danes considered their own interests first and foremost and were not seen to consider the interests of other areas.

However, in 1523 the Union of Kalmar broke down. The Swedes revolted and broke away, led by Gustav Vasa. This was a nationalistic revolt against hated absentee rulers. Vasa was successful, and ruled Sweden until 1560, having had both the time and the skill to set up a new ruling dynasty. He had sufficient time as ruler to ensure the establishment of his family as the ruling family of Sweden, and the Danes were not strong enough to re-establish their rule.

The Swedes were hated by the Danes, who resented the breakaway nation. They had limited resources at that time, and a population in the early 16th century of just over a million. The fledgling Sweden was surrounded by other hostile powers, such as Poland and Russia, that were also keen to expand into the Baltic area. Sweden also had long borders with Denmark, which were very difficult to defend. Sweden had further problems with access to the lucrative Baltic trade. Survival was in itself a major feat for the growing nation, desperate to strengthen its poor geographical position (see map).

Sweden was hemmed in and had no outlet to the North Sea or the Atlantic. Denmark controlled the vital outlet, known as the Sound. Gustav Vasa succeeded in not only enabling Sweden to survive as an independent nation, but setting it on the path to Baltic domination.

Infrastructure: Essential needs to run a country with, such as roads.

With limited resources in terms of **infrastructure**, population and skills, Vasa had to exploit what natural resources Sweden had, mainly iron ore and timber. He was able to rely on the help of many of the north German shipping ports, such as Lübeck, which had both the goods-carrying capacity and the desire to break the Danish control of the Sound and Baltic trade. Vasa consolidated his power internally in order to ensure that there was the basis of a national administrative system.

Gustav Vasa played an important part in ensuring the supremacy of Lutheranism in Sweden, which helped to ensure social stability as well. With a single religion it was a great asset that Sweden was not divided over religion as countries such as France were to be. Vasa established a system for the assessment and collection of taxation, which ensured a regular income for the monarchy. This enabled him to pay for both an administrative and judicial system, and lay the basis for an army and a navy. Vasa also played a role in developing the mineral resources of Sweden, which led to a need to expand trade abroad and develop markets for the iron and copper of Sweden. It also produced a valuable and regular income. In providing 37 years of comparative stability Gustav Vasa established a dynasty with secure foundations.

Vasa was an astute politician who was quite prepared to negotiate, in his early years, with the Danes in order to buy time. He was able to work

The Baltic region at the start of the 17th century, showing major products

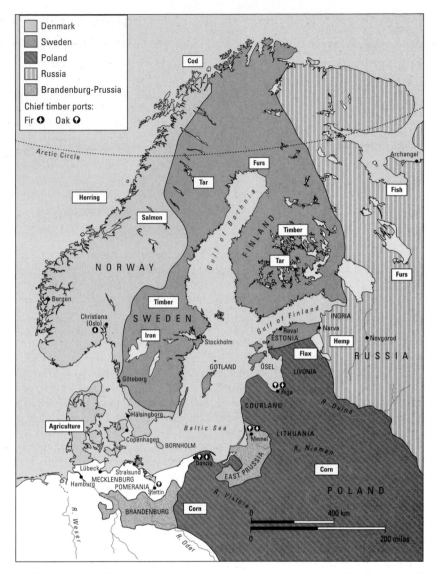

Riksdag: A representative assembly/parliament which had members from the middle classes in it.

Rad: The Council of State; a mix of Upper Chamber and Cabinet, which was dominated by the nobility.

well with the **Riksdag** to ensure that he got support against both external and internal enemies. This ability to carry with him the most important elements in Swedish society was important. It was also the key to the domestic success of his successor, Gustavus Adolphus.

Gustav Vasa was able to get the **Rad** to accept royal authority. He ensured that the Riksdag were also loyal by making sure they knew what he was intending to do and that he was identifying his interests with theirs. He had an advantage in that he was one of the few survivors of a Danish massacre of most of what was the then Swedish nobility. Therefore, there were not too many rivals to his claim to be the rightful Swedish King.

Vasa managed the transition from Catholicism to Lutheranism particularly well. This added to his power and wealth because he took over the Church's resources. Lutheran ideas of subordination of the Church to the State had a great appeal to him, particularly as the Church had been untaxed in the past and owned about a quarter of the land in Sweden, compared with the royal family's 5%. When the Church was effectively nationalised, Gustav made sure that many noble families got former church and monastic land. This ensured their loyalty to the new faith. The ability of the Church to influence a nation through its preaching and

Gustav Vasa's triumphal entry into Uppsala, Sweden, in 1523. This fresco was painted in 1837.

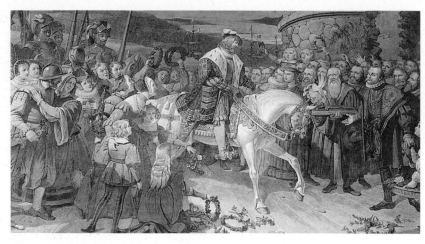

through education was not lost on Vasa, and he wanted it as a loyal subordinate. There is a similarity between him and the first two Tudor monarchs in England, Henry VII and Henry VIII, in the way in which they established the monarchy and dealt with the Church.

As Andrina Stiles points out, in *Sweden and the Baltic 1532–1571* (1992), Gustav was not a pleasant character. He was capable of brutality, violence and ruthlessness. However, he was a crafty politician, skilled and hardworking with great drive and ambition. He saw the potential of Sweden and was determined to show the way to achieving a greater role for it in the Baltic. He also developed the monarchy into a powerful and centralising force.

His successors, Eric XIV (1560–1568) and John III (1568–1592), were less dominating figures. However, they played a role in ensuring that the basic ideas of Gustav Vasa continued to be imposed. Some growth took place in the economy and some territorial expansion into what is now Estonia (see map on page 273). This gave Sweden the port of Reval on the East Baltic coast, which was important for the future. It also gave Sweden a potentially strong enemy in the form of Poland. Growth in terms of national and royal strength was erratic, but there.

It was after the death of John III, in 1592, that Sweden entered a period of difficulty. The King who inherited the throne, Sigismund, was a Roman Catholic. There followed a long and difficult period of civil war. Sigismund was deposed between 1599 and 1600. Not only was he a Roman Catholic, which caused bitter resentment in Sweden, but Sigismund was also King of Poland. He had firm ideas on ruling completely on his own, which did not go down well in the Riksdag. His successor was the less than competent Charles IX (father of Gustavus Adolphus).

Not only was the quality of kingship poor under both Sigismund and Charles, but Sweden was involved in a long struggle for survival against the combined forces of Russia, Poland and Denmark. By 1611, when Gustavus Adolphus came to the throne, the very existence of Sweden was in doubt. Charles IX had been put on the throne, with a great deal of support from some noble families as well as the Riksdag, and this inevitably weakened the position of the monarchy. **Usurpers** tend to owe favours to those who help them usurp, and the helpers tend to want the favours repaid. Charles had also quite unnecessarily provoked a war with Poland that he could not afford. As a result, the Swedish forces were defeated twice: in 1605 at the Battle of Kirkholm, and again in 1610. Charles IX had managed to get involved in further disastrous war with Denmark in the closing months of his life, and was in the process of being defeated there when he died. The great legacy of Gustav Vasa in the first part of the 16th century was squandered in a few years.

Usurpers: Monarchs who have a poor claim to the throne but threaten to seize the throne illegally.

1. What were the main strengths and weaknesses of Sweden during the period 1500–1611?

2. How important was Gustav Vasa to the development of Sweden in the 16th century?

12.2 Why was Gustavus Adolphus able to make Sweden into a major European power?

It is difficult to know where to start in describing the range and depth of the problems facing the young king (he was only 17). Gustavus had inherited a terrible legacy from his father. Sweden was a country that seemed to have few resources to enable it to stand up to its enemies. It had a population of not much more than a million scattered over a large area. There were few large towns and no wealthy merchant middle class to build up a flourishing system of commerce. There was poor quality soil. What is more, there was a real chance of invasion from Russia, Poland and Denmark, all eyeing Sweden as a potential colony with some attractive mineral resources and useful coastline. A look at the map on page 273 will show how easy it was for Denmark and others to invade.

Gustavus' father, Charles IX, had chosen to abandon the usual policy of ruling with at least a degree of consultation with the Rad and Riksdag. Instead he had resorted to terror, violating the tradition of decades. This had alienated the nobility and much of the peasantry. Even the normally loyal Church was upset at Charles IX's management of them. The country was, to all intents and purposes, bankrupt. It was an exceptionally grim picture, which offered little hope for the future. Survival seemed unlikely, let alone growth internally or externally.

There were, however, some natural advantages for the monarchy within Sweden. There was the potential for a royal income. It tended to come in 'kind' – goods as opposed to cash: iron, copper, animal pelts and timber – but these could be sold for cash or traded abroad.

The country was also largely self-sufficient for food. The degree of national unity and sense of nationalism, which had been built up by Gustav Vasa, was still there. There was still a broad acceptance by the Swedish people that the monarchy should have authority. Trade flowed fairly freely. The Church, although irritated by the treatment it had received from the Catholic Sigismund and the incompetent Charles, was basically loyal. The country was uniformly Protestant. There was the possibility of regular royal revenue and a sensible administrative and communication system had been built up, which was there to be exploited. Given a strong leader who could fight as well as administer, and who was also a competent politician and diplomat, there was a chance for progress.

Also encouraging was the growing tendency of Denmark to look to play a part in European politics, where it was very much a minnow among whales. Denmark looking south would give Sweden a useful breathing space. The distinctly unstable base on which the Russian monarchy (known as Tsars) was built meant that it was a force that could only mount an intermittent challenge to Sweden. Poland also looked a dangerous enemy, but it had an incompetent King (the expelled Sigismund) and a highly politicised nobility with every intention of increasing their own power at the expense of the monarch. Poland also suffered from bitter internal religious disputes between Catholic and Protestant. It also had difficult frontiers to defend against all those who had designs on Polish territory. These were the rays of light coming through what was otherwise a very dark picture for Gustavus Adolphus.

Although only a young man, Gustavus managed to take on a series of domestic problems with remarkable speed and ability. He had been educated well – about the only legacy of any quality that his father had left him. He was a talented linguist and had a good theoretical instruction in topics ranging from war to mathematics. Gustavus had travelled widely in Sweden and knew his country well. He had been on the Council of State (the Rad) since the age of 10. He was at least familiar with the problems

---

Axel Oxenstierna (1583–1654)
Oxenstierna was an able and successful diplomat and administrator, who had demonstrated his skills in peace negotiations with Denmark, Russia and Poland. He was appointed Chancellor of Sweden in 1612 by Gustavus Adolphus. After the death of Gustavus, he was granted full powers by the Swedish parliament to administer the German lands which were then occupied by the Swedish army. Oxenstierna was largely responsible for the formation of the League of Heilbronn. He was able to secure substantial financial aid from the French to enable Sweden to continue its military presence in Germany.

---

facing Sweden and the way in which it had been governed. He had a considerable sense of service and duty. Gustavus could be highly original in matters ranging from the tactics of warfare to administration. He also had the ability to spot talent and to use it well.

Gustavus Adolphus was also conscious of his own weaknesses – like Louis XIII of France. He had the intelligence to appoint a Chief Minister who could compensate for his own weaknesses, such as his impulsiveness. One of his first acts was to elevate Axel Oxenstierna to Chief Minister, or Chancellor. Oxenstierna was from a noble background, so there was none of the bitterness about using the lowborn that was to cause so many problems to Cardinal Mazarin in France (see Chapter 14) and encourage faction fighting at the French Court. The Swedish nobility liked to have noble ministers. Gustavus was good at using other key nobles in positions most suited to their ability. Just as there was a partnership between King and Oxenstierna, there was a partnership between nobles and monarch which avoided the weakening disputes which many other countries were to have. Much the same applied to Gustavus' relationship with the Riksdag. He would take them into his confidence and listen and consult before he made major moves. He understood instinctively what important Swedes would, and would not, accept.

The nobility

Gustavus Adolphus' first major task was to pacify the nobility alienated by the inconsistent treatment they had received from Charles IX. There was, potentially, a constitutional crisis brewing. The way Gustavus dealt with it, along with Oxenstierna, is indicative of the strength of the partnership and the qualities of the two men. He accepted a document at the end of 1611, when he was new to the throne. This was not dissimilar to the Magna Carta in England, and was known as the Charter of Nyköping. It passed into law early in 1612. In it, the king agreed to obey the Constitution, accepted the rule of law and promised to use his nobility to help him govern. Oxenstierna drafted the document, but Gustavus played the vital role in convincing a potentially dangerous nobility of his sincerity and willingness to work within its framework. It represented a reconciliation between monarch and noble. It began a partnership which was to bring internal peace to Sweden, and terror to north Germany. Gustavus' tact and diplomacy, as well as his good sense, ensured that the strength of his monarchy was not weakened but strengthened.

Gustavus' main domestic reforms

The system of government set up his able predecessor, Gustav Vasa, was a totally personal one. It depended on the quality of the monarch and his ability to do business. Such a system broke down under the incompetent rule of his three successors. Gustavus Adolphus was determined not to return to a medieval system, which would not give him the opportunity to make Sweden into a modern state.

There were several reform ideas present in the Charter of Nyköping, one of which was to give nobles key jobs. There were to be no **sinecures**, along the lines of the French office holders. These nobles could become salaried officers of state, working for a system of delegated royal authority. This established procedures of decision-making and centralised administration which could run the country if the king was ill, was a minor, or was abroad.

The judicial system was not so much overhauled, as created. This was done in the Judicature Ordinance of 1614. With a central Court of Justice and laws which were well publicised, by the late 1620s there had emerged a proper legal profession and legal structure in Sweden. In a time when

Sinecures: Jobs that involved pay but no work.

there was not much literacy, little in the way of an educated middle class and poor communications over a large territory, this was a huge achievement. The Swedish educational system was very weak, and it took time to produce an educated class that could provide suitable candidates for both a civil service and a legal system.

A central bureaucracy was created with clear lines of communication and a known authority at the top. For the first time a central **Treasury** was created in Stockholm (it no longer moved in a large box with the monarch). It had proper records, **audit powers** and the capacity to plan for the future. In 1618 the Exchequer Ordinance was issued formally, creating this new system. In 1623 a national accounting system was created.

The key to the whole administrative system was the Chancery, the centre of Government. This was not dissimilar to the Privy Council that Thomas Cromwell created in England in the 1530s. It a type of Cabinet where policy could be both made and co-ordinated. It had its own proper War Office, known as the College of War, which had executive powers delegated to it in order to enable it to maintain an army and a navy. A system of local government was also created to ensure that information and decisions could go up and down, from capital to locality, and taxes and recruits could be assessed and raised. This local government reform helped to maintain law and order in the localities. The complete system of government in Sweden was totally overhauled by the middle 1620s. It was a remarkable achievement given the young age of the new monarch and the legacy of his father. It is a demonstration of Gustavus' talent. It also showed the effectiveness of the partnership he had developed with Oxenstierna, the nobles and people of Sweden.

Educational reforms

With a growing demand for educated personnel able to staff this growing bureaucracy, Gustavus created a new type of school known as the gymnasium. This taught a modern syllabus consisting of history, law, politics, mathematics and science. The clergy, who had run education badly, were replaced as the educators of the future leaders of Sweden. Gustavus expanded the only university, at Uppsala, and created a new one at Dorpat. He pillaged the libraries of Germany to equip them properly. He took care not to upset the Protestant clergy, and reassured them with his Statute of Orebro in 1617. This was a hostile anti-Catholic statement which made it clear that Gustavus and Sweden would remain Protestant.

In 1620 Gustavus married Maria Eleonora, the daughter of the Protestant Elector of the north German state of Brandenburg, to show his commitment to Protestantism. The fear of Swedes that he might go the way of his Catholic predecessor Sigismund was gone.

Finance

To finance his highly expensive foreign policy Gustavus tackled the whole issue of royal income with remarkable ability and imagination. War (and he was to be at war for most of his reign) was always seen as the quickest way to bankrupt a country and a monarchy. Any student of French, Spanish or English history in the 16th and 17th centuries will see what harm war can do to a nation's finances. Rather than pay for war using the normal methods of high taxation, sale of offices, borrowing or the sale of assets, Gustavus Adolphus adopted a new approach. Although in the early 1620s he had to raise taxes slightly, he managed to finance most of his expensive wars by other means. On the odd occasion when he **farmed out** the collection of taxes in the French way, its profiteering and exploitation

Treasury: Both a storehouse for royal money and a place of record.

Audit powers: The ability to check that all the civil servants were being honest.

Farmed out: The right of collection of future taxes was sold to the highest bidder.

led to unpopularity, so Gustavus quickly dropped it. He did sell come crown lands, but not on the scale that monarchs like Henry VIII and Elizabeth I of England had to do to wage their wars. Gustavus' main work was to ensure that all paid what they owed, and that there were no exceptions to paying taxes – like the nobility in France.

In addition, Gustavus ensured that skilled men were not taken from the vital manufactories of iron and copper, so the hard currency they earned was continually increased. He made sure that tolls were paid when he gained control of ports and river mouths on the Southern Baltic coast. In addition to his French subsidy, he ruthlessly exploited his position as master of north Germany to raise cash from German towns. In 1632 he received more from Nuremberg than from the large subsidies he was given by Cardinal Richelieu of France (see Chapter 14). Swedish taxpayers were in the remarkable situation in 1633 of paying less in taxation than they had three years earlier. This was in spite of the fact that a huge Swedish army was being deployed in Germany. Gustavus almost made war into a paying business by the time he died.

In order to develop royal income further, Gustavus Adolphus did what he could to exploit the natural resources of Sweden, as well as to loot Germany. Possession of several north German ports, as well as part of the coast of what is now Poland, led to an ability to collect customs (taxes on imports and exports). Gustavus did all he could to bring in foreign technical experts to develop his iron and copper industries. The war in Germany played a part in damaging one of his key commercial competitors in that area.

Adolphus brought in Louis de Geer, a Dutch gun-maker, to build up a Swedish artillery industry, the products of which were to cause havoc on the battlefields of Europe later. Shipping and commercial development was encouraged, and the growth of the port of Göteborg is an example of his official encouragement. Behind the military development lay important industrial and commercial development, and Gustavus realised the vital link between the two. Like other great commanders, he knew that supply is the key to victory.

The army

Vital to Gustavus' later achievements was the Swedish army. Previously based on little more than **feudal levies**, there was no tradition of military quality; nor was there an administrative base from which a proper army could be organised and directed. With the founding of his 'College' of War, similar to a modern Department of Defence, Gustavus created an administrative centre, which had full power to raise and organise an army. It could operate while he was abroad and not in a position to direct it personally. The College ensured that his army and navy were paid and supplied. Although it had a shortage of educated and skilled men, like much of the Swedish government at the time, it worked particularly well when compared with many other European nations. It maintained not only a large Swedish army in Germany for more than 15 years, but also paid and organised a large number of mercenaries.

Gustavus' army was one of his greatest achievements. Sweden had no real record of military achievement and Gustavus inherited an inefficient conscription system producing poor-quality infantry. The nobility were unwilling to provide much in the way of cavalry (troops on horses). Survival, let alone any territorial expansion, was unlikely and the few fighting tactics that had been tried in earlier wars were primarily defensive. Gustavus decided to create a national conscript army. He rejected initially the mercenary route used by so many other countries.

Feudal levies: A system whereby each landowner had to provide a certain amount of soldiers in time of war.

It was cheaper to run an army this way and easier to maintain morale when soldiers were convinced they were fighting a patriotic war.

Gustavus paid his soldiers on time, and fed and equipped them well. He created manageable fighting units, equipped with quality **pikes** and muskets. Gustavus ensured that attention was paid to practical details, such as proper clothing, footwear and the supplies necessary to keep an army on the march and ready to fight. He paid a lot of attention to developing artillery. He played a vital role in developing a new type of light gun, which could be moved around the battlefield to provide both mobile and highly concentrated firepower. It was these light artillery pieces that were to play such an important part in breaking up the mass infantry assaults of the Imperial troops in the Thirty Years' War in Germany.

Gustavus was always willing to learn from allies and opponents. For example, how not to manage infantry from the Spanish tercio (see Chapter 3) and how to train men in battlefield conditions from the experienced fighter, Maurice of Nassau. He rethought infantry tactics, using smaller and more mobile columns and lines of infantry. He was also highly successful in using all three fighting arms – cavalry, infantry and artillery – well together. His own management skills on the battlefield were exceptional and he had the right mixture of forethought and boldness.

Gustavus had far too few men in Sweden for his imperial ambitions, and inevitably had to rely on mercenaries in the end, but the core of his army remained Swedish. It was a disciplined and loyal force when compared with all the other armies of Europe at the time. Starting with about 18,000 men in 1621, the army rose to nearly 150,000 men by 1632 – a remarkable achievement given its high quality. That army was to alter the whole balance of power in Europe. The improvements were based on administrative reforms to start with, and once that organisational core was there, the rest could follow.

The navy

Gustavus had commanded ships at sea while very young, and was aware of the importance of naval supremacy in the Baltic for Sweden's survival, let alone expansion. Several earlier defeats by the Danes at sea made him aware of the importance of seapower for both attack and defence. **Blockade** from the sea was a vital weapon of Baltic war in the past, and Gustavus was determined to use it for Sweden's benefit. To do this he had to have a large navy. With a growing trade abroad vital to income and expansion, it needed protection from predators. Ships were built and well administered, and in Klas Fleming he chose a naval leader well. By 1630 Gustavus had assembled a fleet of 100 ships and 15,000 sailors. The historian Michael Roberts points out that Gustavus moved his army across the Baltic in 1630, leaving from seven different Swedish ports and all landed safely together on the German shore. It was one of the most remarkable feats of planning and organisation in the whole of the Thirty Years' War.

In 1644, during the reign of his young daughter, that navy was to destroy the Danish fleet, until then the naval masters of the Baltic.

Oxenstierna

All this was not just the achievement of Gustavus alone. He and his Chancellor Axel Oxenstierna operated as a partnership, and Oxenstierna continued his work after Gustavus' tragic death. The cautious Oxenstierna perfectly compensated for the impulsive and impetuous Gustavus. He proved to be an excellent administrator, able not only to manage the detail of individual departments, but also to assist with broad policy whilst

1. How successfully did Gustavus transform Sweden and its government in the years to 1630?

2. What were the principal methods by which Gustavus modernised the Swedish State?

co-ordinating the work of several departments and managing the country while his master was abroad. Oxenstierna did much of the drafting of the vital Charters and Ordinances, as well as the crucial negotiations with, and management of, the Rad and Riksdag. The way in which Oxenstierna ensured the loyalty of the Swedish people and communicated to them the wishes and aspirations of his master was exceptional. Like Richelieu and Louis XIII it is difficult to analyse the relationship between the two men clearly. However, it is fair to say that without Oxenstierna and his administrative ability and skill in translating his master's wishes into reality, Sweden's history in the 17th century might well merit nothing more than a footnote in a book such as this, and not a major chapter. Jill Lisk, in *Struggle for Supremacy in the Baltic* (1966), maintains that by 1625 Gustavus and Oxenstierna had created one of the best-administered states in Europe and it would be difficult to find a country better led.

12.3 How successful was Gustavus Adolphus' foreign policy before 1630?

There is some debate as to just how weak Sweden's international situation was when Gustavus came to the throne. Denmark was still harbouring real hopes of regaining its former colony. Poland under Sigismund still retained a claim to the throne of Sweden. Both were more powerful nations with the means of implementing those ambitions. Russia, too, had Baltic ambitions and Sweden had a long frontier with Russia. However, the ambitions of Denmark in Europe, the incompetence of the Polish King and the current weakness of the Tsar of Russia may have made Gustavus' position stronger than it seemed. The fact that it was unlikely for any of his three main threats to co-operate may also have helped to strengthen his position and encourage his imperial ambitions.

Denmark and Poland

Gustavus Adolphus' first decision was to make the Peace of Knared with Denmark in 1613. While the Danes renounced claims to the Swedish throne and territory, they still left a major part of what is now Sweden in Danish hands. The Treaty originally left the vital port of Alvsborg in Danish hands, but Gustavus was able to buy it from the Danes at a high cost.

An alliance with the Dutch followed soon after. The Dutch were a great goods-carrying nation and this treaty was necessary if Gustavus was to get a good export business for his iron and copper. Similar deals followed with the **Hanse ports** in 1614.

Hanse ports: The large commercial centres on the southern shores of the Baltic.

This stabilised the situation to the South so that Sweden could concentrate on the long struggle with Poland and Russia to the East. Gustavus waged war with Poland, fighting on the eastern Baltic shore, capturing Riga in 1621. This gave him a major base and fort on the southern Baltic coast. Gradually, Sweden was becoming a major Baltic power. Gustavus was always prepared to compromise with Sigismund of Poland, if Sigismund was prepared to give up his claim to the Swedish throne. However Sigismund would not, so the war dragged on. Gustavus would have preferred to concentrate on building up Sweden's strength in the period around 1620 rather than fight the Poles. There were occasional truces with Poland, such as in 1622, but they were short-lived. Sigismund had had two Habsburg wives, was a great supporter of the Counter Reformation and had a great weakness for plotting to overthrow Gustavus' Sweden.

Gustavus' primary aim was security. He was determined not to tolerate the Polish threat. By 1626 he had expanded out of the Riga base and had taken most of Livonia. Military success followed for Gustavus in 1626 when he defeated a Polish army and took the important port of Reval. The fact that the Turks were attacking the Poles to the South was also a great asset for Gustavus. Sigismund was locked in fairly permanent conflict with Russia. However, his success came to an abrupt halt in 1629, when a Polish army backed by experienced Imperial forces (soldiers fighting for the Habsburg Emperor), pushed back a Swedish army under Gustavus, near the river Vistula. Apparently Gustavus was nearly killed as a result of his usual rash behaviour on the battlefield. However, in the ensuing peace Sweden did particularly well as a result of clever French mediation. In the Truce of Altmark (1629) Gustavus was given important Prussian **tolls**, which produced a lot of cash for Sweden. He also obtained confirmation of Sweden's gains on the north German coast in Prussia. War was beginning to pay real dividends in terms of cash, territory and status. With Livonia as well now a Swedish territory, Gustavus was well on the way to becoming a 'European' power.

Tolls: Charges on ships and goods going through a port.

War with Russia ended with the Peace of Stolbova in 1617. This was a major success for Gustavus in that what is now Estonia and Finland remained securely in the hands of Sweden. There was no further major risk from that quarter again, and Gustavus was now able to concentrate his attention on the South.

Gustavus' relationship with Denmark had always been difficult. They were 'old enemies' but Gustavus was sympathetic towards Christian of Denmark's attempt to become the champion of the Protestant cause in Europe in the Thirty Years' War. Gustavus had his own problems in the east with Poland. He asked for assistance from the Danes or the Protestant Princes of North Germany in the early 1620s, but the price he named was too high, in terms of cash and rewards from them. This was probably intentional. Adolphus had little time for many of the Protestant German princes, seeing them as uncommitted to anything except their own self-interest, and easy prey for the Imperial forces leading the Counter Reformation. He felt they had little interest in Protestantism.

The new balance of power in the Baltic

With the destruction of the Danish army at Lutter in 1626, and the arrival in the Baltic region by 1628 of the Imperial general Albrecht von Wallenstein, the balance of power in Europe and in the Baltic changed abruptly. A new and terrifying threat for Sweden came close to home. With the Count of Olivares, the principal Minister of the King of Spain, plotting a Baltic empire, and two imperial armies under Generals Tilly and Wallenstein ravaging territories close to home, Gustavus had justified grounds for fear. Wallenstein being named the 'General of the Baltic Sea' and starting to build a navy at Wismar naturally confirmed his worst suspicions. Gustavus made a defensive treaty with the Danes in 1628 and pondered the future.

By 1629 Gustavus had totally transformed Sweden. It was now not only a major power in the Baltic but had also transformed itself internally. It was now a well-run state which made excellent use of its resources.

1. What were the main reasons for Swedish expansion by 1630?

2. How successfully had Gustavus changed the international status of Sweden in the years to 1630?

12.3 Why did Gustavus Adolphus intervene in Germany in 1630?
A CASE STUDY IN HISTORICAL INTERPRETATION

There is an important debate among historians on this issue. Some of it is fairly academic, as Gustavus Adolphus was already in possession of parts of what is now North Germany or Poland as a result of his Polish wars. His military intervention further to the south and west could be seen just

Edict of Restitution of 1629: Act which ordered that land taken from the Catholic Church since the Peace of Augsburg in 1555 had to be given back.

as an extension of this. However, Gustavus viewed his gains from Poland as part of another conflict, and his decision to intervene in Germany, which grew gradually between 1628 and 1630, must be seen in another context. Contemporaries felt that his decision was religious. Gustavus feared that Protestantism was about to be wiped out. It could have been, given the success of the Catholic or Counter Reformation in Bohemia and elsewhere. The **Edict of Restitution of 1629** and the arrival of the Imperial Roman Catholic forces on the Baltic coast, would have confirmed his view that a major intervention was necessary to save Protestantism.

Some Swedish historians, such as Ingvar Anderssen in *History of Sweden*, see Gustavus' aims as primarily defensive. His main aim was to defend Sweden from the Imperialist ambitions of Albrecht von Wallenstein. Wallenstein's proclaiming himself as 'General of the Baltic Sea' and starting to build a navy in the Baltic naturally provoked Gustavus into a defensive reaction. There was a strong case for Gustavus attacking this Imperialist enemy on foreign soil to prevent an invasion of Sweden.

A third reason, suggested by historian Michael Roberts, for Gustavus' invasion of Germany was simply imperialism. Adolphus desired not only to extend Sweden to its 'natural' (limited only by geographical factors, such as the sea or a major river) frontiers, but also to dominate the Baltic and possibly the north German coast and its **hinterland** as well.

Hinterland: The area behind a coast which is linked to it economically.

To a certain extent the conflict could be seen as a natural extension of Gustavus' own character. He enjoyed war and he was a good leader. He felt it was an essential part of the monarch's role and he was anxious to take on the most formidable enemies he could find in order to test himself and his troops.

The process of direct Swedish involvement in north Germany came about gradually. With the destruction of the Danish army at Lütter in 1626, Imperial (and Roman Catholic) forces moved north. Gustavus knew that any alliance with the Danes could lead to fighting in Germany, as the Danes could not resist alone the advance of the Imperial forces. As a result of this Imperial advance, by the end of 1628, Gustavus had got the backing of the Swedish Diet for a full invasion of Germany.

In late 1628, Achim von Arnim, one of the Imperial generals, seized the island of Danhold, just off the strategically key area of Stralsund (see map on page 273). Gustavus ordered Swedish soldiers to come to the aid of the Danish soldiers there and then took over from the Danes to keep Stralsund out of Catholic hands. A quick glance at the map on page 273 will reveal why Gustavus could not tolerate the takeover of Stralsund by Imperial forces, particularly with his commercial ambitions. Both Oxenstierna and Gustavus were motivated primarily by the needs of Sweden's security at this stage. While the more cautious Oxenstierna favoured placing the whole of Swedish military resources on the defence of Stralsund, the more aggressive Gustavus felt the best method of defence was to attack south. The fact that Stralsund by the end of 1629 had been integrated into Sweden ought to be noted as well. Gustavus clearly was coming to stay in north Germany and expand his territorial holdings along the southern shores of the Baltic.

However, events beyond the control of Gustavus then began to push him closer to a vital decision. The Emperor issued the Edict of Restitution in 1629. This again inspired the north German princes to look for leadership to defend their possessions, as many had a lot of former Church property in their own possession. Also the Danes, with whom he had an alliance, did a deal with the Emperor behind Gustavus' back. Gustavus was not invited to the Danish/Imperial talks, but he still made it clear to both the Danes and the Emperor what he expected Sweden to gain as part of any peace settlement affecting the Baltic regions. The terms Gustavus demanded for peace in the Baltic are revealing about his motives for being in north Germany. He wanted Imperial troops out of that area, no Imperial fortifications on the Baltic Coast, and no Imperial army or navy in the Baltic region. He wanted the Danes to regain their lost territory to prevent further Imperial and Catholic encroachments near the Baltic. He would be prepared to leave Stralsund when, and if, he felt secure. Security seems to have been the main motive for any Swedish involvement in Germany at this stage.

The Danes made peace with the Emperor at Lübeck in 1629, without consulting Gustavus. They also failed to meet what he saw as the essential terms for security in the Baltic. De Charnace, a French envoy sent by Cardinal Richelieu, helped Gustavus to make a deal with the Poles at Altmark in 1629 to end the conflict between Sweden and Poland. Cardinal Richelieu was looking for someone prepared to lead north Germany and its Protestants against the Habsburgs so that the French could take Habsburg territory in Italy. Richelieu and de Charnace saw Gustavus Adolphus as an ally whom they could easily manage. They offered him a supportive treaty and a subsidy of 300,000 riksdalers (Swedish currency) if Gustavus was prepared to intervene with his army in north Germany. This offer was turned down in 1629, as Gustavus wanted freedom of action and had no intention of being a hired help to a wily French cardinal pursuing his own agenda elsewhere.

Whether Gustavus was tempted by the possibility of invading his old and badly weakened enemy, Denmark, or was waiting for a more 'just' cause, is arguable. Certainly most of the key Protestant leaders of Germany, such as John George of Saxony, were hostile to the idea of a Swedish offer of 'support'. The idea of a Protestant crusader may have had propaganda appeal, but it is unlikely to have been a major factor in Gustavus' mind. The time was right to invade, if he was ever going to. The Imperial army was not well paid and General Wallenstein was detested by many for his ambitions. Russia was weak and divided, deep in its 'Time of Troubles', and Poland was attacking Russia for its own reasons. There was chaos in Germany, and France and Spain were in conflict in Italy.

In 1630 Gustavus took the decision to intervene in a major way in Germany, with the defence of Sweden and its interests in the forefront of his mind. Personal and imperial ambitions were also important to him. The historian Michael Roberts, in his study of Gustavus, makes it very clear that these were his priorities. However, Roberts does indicate that Imperial ambitions may have come more into the picture once his initially successful defensive operation was over. With a unified country behind him, popular support and a growing sense of Swedish nationalism, the time was right to copy what most of his neighbours were trying to do. Denmark, Poland and Russia were all trying to expand their territories – and into Sweden as well. Wallenstein was doing much the same further south, so why not follow suit?

Jill Lisk, in *The Struggle for Supremacy in the Baltic* (1966), also debates the issue at length, and perhaps spends more time than other historians looking at the religious aspects of Adolphus' invasion of Germany. She feels that at times the role of a Protestant hero was one motive that appealed to Gustavus. Lisk argues that Gustavus put Sweden first, but claims that Protestantism came a closer second than other historians concede. She feels that there was more of an aggressive aspect to his ideas than the security-based arguments put forward by Michael Roberts.

Andrina Stiles, in *Sweden and the Baltic* (1992), follows much the same line of thought, but places more emphasis on the pragmatic aspects of Gustavus' character. She quotes Oxenstierna writing that to 'disrupt the plans of the enemy, whose proceedings and intentions with regard to the

1. **What different interpretations have been put forward by historians to explain why Gustavus decided to intervene in Germany in 1630? In your answer consider the views of (a) Michael Roberts, (b) Jill Lisk, and (c) Andrina Stiles.**

2. **What do you regard as the most convincing reason for Gustavus Adolphus' intervention in Germany in 1630? Give reasons to support your answer.**

Baltic are well known, His majesty intended therefore to ensure the safety of his kingdom in the Baltic and to liberate the oppressed lands', but 'it was no part of his first intention to push on as far as he did'. Stiles argues that security was always the key motive in Gustavus' mind. Territory on the north German coast, acting as a buffer if need be, and a permanent empire there if he failed to get an effective league of Protestant princes, was what Gustavus Adolphus wanted. Andrina Stiles sees Gustavus' dislike of the German princes for their failure to support him in his attempt to help them or act in a unified way as an important factor in his later actions. She does not feel that his motives were particularly religious or economic, unlike Roberts who places more stress on the latter. Roberts also places stress on Gustavus' timing. He argues that another reason for Gustavus' intervention in Germany was because the Emperor had decided to sack the ambitious General Wallenstein, and many of Wallenstein's soldiers had left to fight against the French in Italy.

Certainly in Gustavus' discussions with the north German princes he made it clear that if a leader of sufficient calibre emerged to defend North Germany and Protestantism from attack, then he might feel secure and withdraw his troops. How genuine this was is debatable. It may well have been designed to ease their obvious fears that the imperialist Wallenstein was going to be replaced by another aggressive and 'colonially' minded master, Gustavus of Sweden.

12.5 What were the results of Gustavus Adolphus' intervention in Germany?

From the military point of view, Gustavus was very successful in 1630. He cleared East Pomerania and Mecklenburg of Imperial troops and managed to feed and pay his soldiers by his conquests. He had some support from the German princes who saw Gustavus as a useful tool for persuading the Emperor to respect their territory and their religion. So successful was the Swedish army that in January 1631, while wintering in Germany, Gustavus was able to negotiate excellent terms with Richelieu at the Treaty of Barwalde. He managed to obtain from the French a huge subsidy of 400,000 riksdalers a year; in return he agreed to keep a Swedish army in Germany for five years. This would help to tie down Habsburg forces so that Richelieu could follow his Italian ambitions and possibly reduce the threat of Habsburg encirclement and invasion of France. As Richelieu was a cardinal in the Roman Catholic Church, Gustavus agreed to accept tolerance of Roman Catholicism in any territories he might occupy. Being paid to mount an aggressive war was an appealing idea to Gustavus. Although he did not see himself in the 'mercenary' position in his relationship with Richelieu and the French, Richelieu certainly did.

Encouraged with this deal with the French, Gustavus became increasingly ambitious. He was anxious to help the Protestant city of Magdeburg that was under siege from the Emperor's Catholic forces. Gustavus decided to invade the central part of Germany. He had promised to help save Magdeburg, but he failed. He almost certainly had too few troops to achieve this objective. The horror in Germany at the sack of Magdeburg, where almost 20,000 Protestants were slaughtered, coupled with the loss of face that Gustavus inevitably suffered, encouraged him to take more direct action.

After a brilliant defensive action at the Battle of Werben, against the Catholic forces of the Emperor in the early spring of 1631, Gustavus joined up with several German princes. These included John George of Saxony, who normally would have nothing to do with foreigners. With these combined forces he destroyed General Tilly's Catholic and Imperial army at the Battle of Breitenfeld near Leipzig in 1631. Gustavus demonstrated to the rest of Europe the brilliance of his new military tactics. Although General Tilly and his troops managed to drive away the Saxon soldiers in the early stage of the battle, Gustavus was able to inflict a devastating blow on the Imperial army by the end. Tilly lost 20,000 of his 35,000 men in one afternoon. He was opposed by a Swedish army of only 24,000 men. Gustavus lost only 2,000 men. The whole balance of power in Europe changed abruptly.

Gustavus then made a bad tactical error in not destroying Tilly's forces totally and leaving the general time to regroup his forces. He was to regret this decision later. Gustavus then moved further south with his army, towards the Rhine. He took Frankfurt in November 1631, and then moved to Mainz to winter with his army. As always he made the Germans pay and feed his troops.

Gustavus' plans

It was in this period, between the fighting campaigns of 1631 and 1632, that Gustavus drew up the Document, which at times helps and at other times hinders the attempt by historians to work out his motives. This is the '*Norma Futurum Actionum*', a series of ideas justifying his actions and indicating future plans. Gustavus wrote of his wish to destroy the Habsburg grip over Germany. He also wrote of a new Protestant Union and of a Swedish-controlled Federation hostile to both Catholicism and the Habsburgs. Religion did not seem to play a major part in his thinking in this Document. This adds to the idea that the 'religious' phase of the Thirty Years' War was definitely over by the time that Gustavus arrived in Germany and made his deal with Richelieu.

Gustavus therefore had to decide what to do and where to go. He now had a major problem in that there was no natural barrier behind which Sweden, the Baltic and Protestantism could shelter – unlike the Rhine between Germany and France, or the Pyrenees between France and Spain. He was, in effect, the master of half of Germany. Many Germans were viewing his residence with some hostility, particularly when he was expecting them to pay for the privilege of having him as their defender and to have their libraries looted to equip his new university. As Oxenstierna said in 1632, 'Gustavus Adolphus intended to safeguard his Kingdom and the Baltic Sea and to liberate the oppressed lands; and then after to proceed as things might fall out: to begin with he did not intend to go as far as he did.'

Gustavus was clearly searching for a security solution, and he wished to keep the South Baltic shore for a start. How to protect that territory was also a major concern for him. He hoped to get some form of working agreement with the German princes, but he failed there, as they simply did not wish to replace the Emperor with another overlord. Ideas of a type of Swedish protectorate over north Germany were also mentioned; as were ideas for some form of permanent league of Protestant leaders in north Germany, with Swedish presence in it. Having mentioned a huge range of ideas in order to get some sort of statement of intent out to both his allies, potential allies and his enemies, Gustavus set out in the spring of 1632 towards Vienna and the heart of the Roman Catholic Empire. He had a huge group of six armies and over 100,000 men with him.

Just as he made a bad error in leaving the remnants of Tilly's army in being after the Battle of Breitenfeld the previous year, Gustavus Adolphus made another serious error in leaving the Imperial general Pappenheim in the rear of his advance in the Lower Saxon circle. Again Gustavus made the conquered German territories pay for the privilege of having his army cross their lands, which did not do a great deal to encourage a strong alliance with the German princes and their peoples.

The march across central Germany came to an abrupt end for Gustavus in November 1632 at the Battle of Lützen, where Gustavus was killed leading his troops. His soldiers, now led by the German, Bernard of Saxe Weimar, managed to turn this potential disaster into a military victory. Again serious damage was done to the Imperial forces, and a major Protestant army was left in being in Germany.

1. What message is this painting trying to give of Gustavus Adolphus?

2. What value is this painting of the battle to a historian writing about Gustavus Adolphus?

Gustavus Adolphus leading a cavalry charge at the Battle of Lützen, 1632.

Life after Gustavus' death

The Emperor breathed a huge sigh of relief, as the most formidable of his enemies was now dead. However, the Swedish army was to remain in Germany until 1648, and his mission was continued by Oxenstierna and Gustavus' daughter, Christina. Richelieu, too, may not have been unhappy at the death of one who he had hoped would be a protégé, but had turned out to be too dominant a partner. Richelieu was now able to direct events more to his own satisfaction.

The Thirty Years' War straggled on in Germany, with Sweden taking less of a direct role in the overall course of the war. Instead Sweden descended to the level of a hired mercenary force. Control of Sweden passed to Oxenstierna, as Gustavus left the six-year-old Christina on the throne. Even though the military tide at times went against Sweden on the battlefield, as it simply lacked the resources to take on the imperialists single handedly, Gustavus' aims were eventually fulfilled.

There were to be defeats, such as at Nördlingen in 1634, when the Swedish army was badly defeated by the Cardinal-Infante Ferdinand of Spain. However, at the Peace of Prague in 1635, which turned out to be a failed attempt to resolve the whole conflict in Europe, it was confirmed that Protestantism was secure in Europe. It was agreed then that Sweden would retain Pomerania and Wismar, and the French subsidy would continue.

Swedish territorial gains by 1648

Sweden and the Baltic were saved, and the Habsburg and Catholic threats were driven off. The direction of the anti-Hapsburg conflict passed more directly into the hands of the French. Some success did follow on the battlefield, with a major military defeat of the Imperial armies at the second Battle of Breitenfeld in 1643. This time the Swedes were not to play such a leading role, but an important one none the less. Swedish military power and presence was an important factor in providing the will to continue the war to the bitter end for several of the Protestant and anti-Hapsburg forces.

Sweden defeated the Danes again in 1645, and this decisively confirmed Sweden as the major Baltic power. It was a largely Swedish army that was in the process of besieging Prague when the Thirty Years' War ground to an end in 1648. The bulk of Gustavus' objectives were undoubtedly achieved. There was to be no Spanish or Habsburg Baltic Empire and Sweden had for the first time in its history played a vital role in Europe. Gustavus Adolphus had gained status for his country and the right for a seat for Sweden at the peacemaking, alongside the other major European powers.

Whether Sweden actually gained from Gustavus' intervention is debatable. Certainly it expanded in territory and gained huge prestige, but the graveyards of Germany were full of Swedish, as well as German, soldiers. Although the cost of the war was not as devastating for Sweden as it was for countries such as Saxony or France, it was still high. It placed a strain on the people and on the Swedish economy. What has to be considered is whether or not Gustavus really acted in the best interests of Sweden. It could be argued that he overextended Sweden's limited strength and resources and committed it to mainland Europe where it had no real interests.

Gustavus' quarrels with both Poland and Denmark were to continue after his death. It could be argued that he might have been much better off simply ending those disputes in a permanent way with two close neighbours. However, Gustavus had created a modern state from a backward one, and that achievement alone was remarkable.

Adolphus would have been pleased with the Treaty of Westphalia in 1648, which finally brought to a close the German aspects of the Thirty Years' War (the war between France and Spain was to drag on until 1659), where Sweden's north German possession was confirmed (see map on page 287). In addition, Sweden gained the status of a major north German power with a vote in the Imperial Diet. Western Pomerania, Stettin, Wismar, Rügen, Bremen and Verden all passed into Swedish hands. The mouths of the great north German rivers the Oder, the Elbe and the Weser were now in Swedish hands. How essential they were to the real interests of Sweden can be debated. They may well have been the cause of future problems once Prussia and other kingdoms started to grow and begin to resent the presence of an alien nation in Germany. Sweden may have been better off defending itself from its own original shores, and this may well have placed less of a strain on its resources. Some of Gustavus' gains had come through the weakness of others, and once they were stronger then Sweden found itself out of its depth. However, he had intervened at a decisive moment in the Thirty Years' War, defeated the awesome forces of the Habsburgs and ensured the survival of Protestantism in Germany. The effect of Breitenfeld and Lützen was enormous, just as were the effects of Gustavus' and Oxenstierna's work on Swedish domestic history.

> ? 1. How important was Gustavus Adolphus' role in the Thirty Years' War in Germany?
>
> 2. Did Sweden gain more than it lost from its involvement in the Thirty Years' War?

12.6 Gustavus Adolphus: an overall assessment

Gustavus Adolphus' reign in Sweden is a remarkable example of what one individual can achieve given determination and ability. If he is to be judged on what he achieved in Sweden alone, then Gustavus Adolphus was outstanding. He created a modern nation state from what had been a poor backwater. Not only did he expand his country into the immediately neighbouring areas, such as Denmark, Finland and Russia, but also he started to create a major empire on the other side of the Baltic. He took on much larger and more powerful neighbours to do that.

In addition to his expansion in the Baltic region, Gustavus transformed his country. He created a new administrative and legal system, as well as a modern educational system. He spotted what might be the vital natural resources of his nation and utilised them commercially. He managed huge changes in his country with the consent and active support of the ruling élites – you will be hard-pressed to find any other European ruler in the 17th century who achieved that. There was no civil war. Gustavus managed to create an internal infrastructure that could support a new and effective army and navy. These great changes alone guarantee him a place in any European history textbook.

To add to all that, he invaded Germany. Not only did he transfer a large army successfully across the Baltic, but also he rewrote the rules of war. He managed to defeat the best that Europe could put against him, with their larger armies and greater experience. He altered the balance of power in Europe completely and changed the course of the Catholic or Counter Reformation. It must also be remembered that Gustavus Adolphus had already taken on the great powers of Denmark, Poland and Russia, and the growth of his Baltic Empire demonstrates his success there. At the same time, while other countries bankrupted themselves as a result of being involved in war, Sweden made a profit out of it.

It would be difficult to fault Gustavus' performance in Sweden itself, and he was a remarkable general. The main criticism that can be directed against him is his impetuosity. He was aware of that failing and in his appointment of Axel Oxenstierna he brought in the cautious approach that he needed to compensate for his own failings. Oxenstierna was not present when Gustavus made his fatal mistake at Nördlingen. Gustavus' greatest error was perhaps to fail to set himself clear enough targets in Germany. He seemed unsure as to what he was trying to achieve when he invaded and he was drawn deeper and deeper into Germany and its politics. Ultimately, Sweden did not have the resources to compete against major powers for a long period of time.

It could be argued that Gustavus was simply lucky in his timing – the Swedish people were looking for positive leadership and his neighbours and enemies were weak, divided and exhausted by constant warfare. Any competent ruler could have done what he did; he was just filling a vacuum. The evidence here suggests otherwise.

Using information obtained in this chapter, explain why Gustavus Adolphus made such an important impact on the history of Sweden and Europe.

Source-based questions: Gustavus Adolphus in Germany

SOURCE A

Between Their Most Serene Majesties the Kings of Sweden and France there shall be an alliance for the defence of the friends of each and both of them, for the safeguarding of the Baltic and Oceanic Seas, the liberty of commerce, and the restitution of the oppressed States of the Holy Roman Empire; and also in order to ensure that the fortress and defence-works which have been constructed, in the ports and on the shores of the Baltic and Oceanic Seas, and in the Grisons*, be demolished and reduced to the state in which they were immediately before this present German war. And because up to the present the enemy has refused to give a just reparation for the injuries he has caused, and has hitherto rejected all appeals, [the allies] take up arms to vindicate the cause of their common friends. To that end the King of Sweden … will at his own expense bring to and maintain in Germany 30,000 foot and 6000 heavy-armed cavalry. The King of France will contribute 400,000 Imperial Thaler, that is, a million *livres*, every year, which will be paid and accounted for without fail to the agents of the King of Sweden deputed for that purpose, either at Paris or Amsterdam, as the King of Sweden may find the more convenient; whereof one half to be paid on 15 May, and the other on 15 November each year. The raising of soldiers and sailors, the sale of ships and materials of war, are to be free as between the territories of the allies, but are to be refused to enemies. If God should be pleased to grant successes to the King of Sweden, he is in matters of religion to treat territories occupied by or ceded [given over] to him according to the laws and customs of the Empire; and in places where the exercise of the Roman Catholic religion exists, it shall remain undisturbed. Any other States or Princes, as well within Germany as without, who may wish to accede to this league, shall be admitted to it … With the Duke of Bavaria and the Catholic League friendship, or at least neutrality, is to be preserved, provided that they on their side observe it. And if, by the grace of God, an opportunity to treat for peace should present itself, the negotiations shall be conducted jointly by the allies, and neither will without the other initiate or conclude a peace, this alliance shall last for five years … ; if a sure peace is not obtained within that time, it may be further extended by agreement of the allies.

From the Treaty of Barwalde, January 1631

*Grisons: Passes in the Alps, which was vital to the Habsburgs for transferring troops from Spain into central Europe.

SOURCE B

Swedish state income and expenditure in 1633

Income [In riksdaler]	1633
Sweden and Finland	
'Ordinary' revenue	1,229,920
'Extraordinary' revenue	573,872
Customs and excise	22,040
Loans	59,384
French subsidies	400,000
Estonia, Livonia, Ingria	
Ship tolls and customs	125,299
Other income	238,937
Prussian ship tolls	*614,000*
Total	**3,263,452**

Expenditure	
Sweden and Finland	
Court expenses	15,753
Salaries of council of state	55,752
Judicial salaries	5,223
Chancery and foreign affairs	1,351
Exchequer and financial administration	358,524
Army and army administration	84,202
Navy and naval administration	96,769
Local government	107,123
Debts paid	350,882
Other expenses	304,462
Deductions from revenue	753,789
Total expenditure	**2,134,830**
Total income	**3,263,452**
Surplus	1,128,622

1. Explain the meaning of the following terms, which are highlighted in the sources, as they applied to the reign of Gustavus Adolphus.

(a) 'Holy Roman Empire' (Source A)

(b) 'Ships tolls and customs' (Source B).

2. Study Source A and use your own knowledge. Does Source A fully explain the reasons why Gustavus invaded Germany?

3. What information can you use from Source B to show that Gustavus was a successful ruler of Sweden?

4. 'Gustavus only waged war in order to make money.'

On the evidence of the two sources and using your own knowledge, assess the validity of this statement.

The decline of Spain? 1598–1659

Key Issues

● *How far did the government of Spain change under Philip III and Philip IV?*

● *How successful was Spanish foreign policy between 1598 and 1659?*

● *To what extent did Spain experience social and economic change in the years 1598–1659?*

13.1 How did Philip III's government differ from government under Philip II?

13.2 What impact did the Duke of Lerma have on Spanish foreign policy?

13.3 In what ways did Spain experience social and economic change between 1598 and 1659?

13.4 How far did foreign policy change under Olivares?

13.5 How successful was the Count-Duke Olivares in domestic policy?

13.6 Historical interpretation: The decline of Spain – an assessment

Framework of Events

1598	Philip III becomes king
1599	Duke of Lerma becomes the 'King's favourite' (*valido*)
1604	Treaty of London ends war with England
1607	Spain becomes bankrupt; Crown debts are suspended
1609	Treaty of Antwerp brings 12-year truce with the United Provinces
	Moriscos expelled from Spain
1615	Franco–Spanish marriage treaties
1618	Lerma is forced to resign
	Thirty Years' War begins
1621	Philip IV becomes king
1622	Olivares becomes chief minister (*valido*)
1624	Valtelline War with France begins
1626	Union of Arms is decreed. Treaty of Monzon ends Valtelline War
1627	Spain becomes bankrupt; Crown suspends payment on debt
1628	Piet Heyn captures Spanish silver fleet in Matanzas Bay
	Mantuan Succession crisis
	Debasement of currency
1631	Treaty of Cherasco ends War of the Mantuan Succession
1634	Battle of Nördlingen
1635	Franco–Spanish War begins
	Debasement of the currency
1639	Sea Battle of the Downs. Admiral von Tromp defeats Spanish fleet off Kent
1640	Revolt in Catalonia; revolt in Portugal
1643	Olivares falls from power
	French defeat Spanish Army off Flanders at Rocroi
1647	Luis de Haro becomes king's favourite
1648	Treaty of Münster; Dutch gain complete independence from Spain
	Peace of Westphalia ends Thirty Years' War
1652	Catalonia returns to Spain
1659	Treaty of the Pyrenees ends Franco–Spanish War.

Overview

THE period of Spanish history from the death of Philip II to the middle of the 17th century has been seen as a period of decline. During that period, Spain was replaced as western Europe's most powerful state by France. There has been considerable discussion about why Spain declined in power and when this process actually began.

During the reign of Philip III (1598–1621), Spain was still a major power. By the time of Philip III's death, Spain was in a more powerful position than in 1598. Part of this success must be attributed to the Duke of Lerma who was Philip III's chief minister until 1618. The Duke of Lerma realised that Spain's limited financial resources could not meet its military commitments. As a result, he sought peace with the Dutch and with England. He also kept on good terms with France. However, Spain's increased stature in foreign affairs after 1610 was aided by the assassination of Henry IV of France, in 1610. Henry IV was succeeded by a child, Louis XIII.

Some of the blame for the decline in Spain's military position must be attributed to Count-Duke Olivares. He was Philip IV's chief minister from 1622 to 1643. During his period in power there was a renewal of war with the Dutch, involvement in the Thirty Years' War in Germany and war with France after 1635. All these commitments placed great financial strains on Spain. They helped to spark off revolts in Catalonia and Portugal in 1640. In 1648 Spain recognised the independence of the United Provinces. By 1659 France was fast becoming western Europe's most powerful state.

Bullion shipments: There were two silver shipments a year from the Americas – the Terra Firma Fleet sailed from south America, the other sailed from Mexico.

The one recurring problem faced by Spanish rulers throughout this period was the problem of finance. Philip II had left a large debt. No Spanish ruler was able to raise sufficient revenue to meet the costs of war and government. Most of the financial burden fell on Castile. In addition, **bullion shipments** from the Americas began to decline in the 17th century, most notably from 1639. The Spanish Government tried various methods to acquire revenue: *juros* were sold (see Chapter 6); loans were raised from foreign bankers; and the silver content of coinage was reduced in a process called 'debasing the coinage'. However, expenditure was always greater than revenue. Part of the cause lay outside the control of the government. Spain's population began to decline from the 1580s. This was

Epidemics: Occurrences of a disease that affect a very large number of people living in an area and which spread quickly to other people. Can result in many deaths.

due in part to **epidemics**. In addition, Spanish industry suffered a decline. Important sources of wealth, such as the northern Netherlands, were lost because of the Dutch Revolt. By the 1650s the economic base on which the Spanish monarchy depended was smaller than in 1598.

Count-Duke Olivares (1581–1645)
Born Gaspar de Guzman in Rome, Italy, the son of the Spanish ambassador to the Pope. In 1607 he succeeded his father as Count Olivares. Eight years later he entered the service of Philip III. In 1622, following the death of de Zúdies, he became Philip IV's chief minister. In 1625 he was made Duke de Sanlucar la major. From that time until his death he was known as Count-Duke Olivares. He tried to revive Spain's finances by spreading the costs of government to all parts of Philip IV's lands. The Union of Arms unfortunately caused resentment and helped lead to the revolts of 1640.

Conciliar system of government: The system of government in operation in Spain from the time of the Catholic Monarchs. It involved the establishment of councils for specific purposes (e.g. war), the Inquisition and specific regions (e.g. Flanders, Italy, the Indies). These councils had the power to advise the monarch.

During this period the nature of government changed. The personal government of Philip II was replaced by government through a chief minister. This individual was termed the 'king's favourite' or *valido*. Under Philip III the main *valido* was the Duke of Lerma. Under Philip IV it was Count-Duke Olivares. The *validos* still used the **conciliar system of government** which existed under Charles I and Philip II. However, they added a system of committees. This improved the operation of government (see diagram).

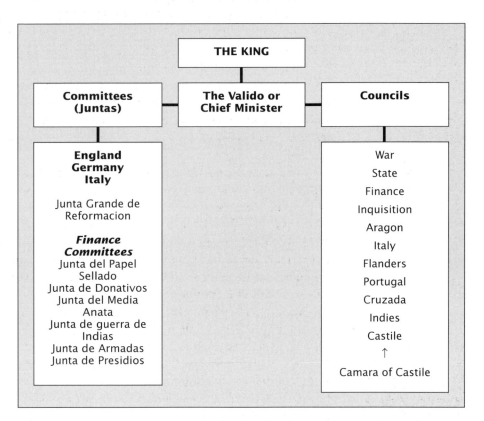

Spanish Government under Philip III and Philip IV

13.1 How did Philip III's government differ from government under Philip II?

During the reign of Philip III (1598–1621) the government of Spain changed considerably. The new king was very different from his father. In fact, Philip II had a low opinion of his son's ability to rule. He stated that 'God who has given me so many kingdoms, had denied me a son capable of ruling them'. There is some truth in Philip II's view. Unlike his father, Philip III did not take such a direct and active role in the government of Spain. He also allowed the Spanish aristocracy more influence in decision making.

The most important feature of this development was Philip III's decision to delegate power to one person. This individual took on the role of a chief minister ('King's favourite', *valido*). Another change that took place after 1598 was the decision by Philip III to tour extensively through Spain. Philip II had spent much of his reign locked away in the Escorial Palace (near Madrid) dealing with affairs of state.

What impact did the Duke of Lerma have on the government of Spain?

Lerma, Duke of (1553–1625)

Francisco Gomez de Sandoval y Rojas became the Marquis of Denia, then the Duke of Lerma in 1599. He was appointed a court official under Philip II and became chief minister (*valido*) under Philip III. Lerma followed a peacemaking foreign policy, negotiating peace with the Dutch and England. He used his position as chief minister to accumulate titles and jobs for himself and his friends. His period in office was noted for its corruption and waste of royal finances. In 1618 his downfall was organised by his son, the Duke of Uceda. Shortly before his fall from power, he was made a cardinal by the Pope.

From the beginning of the reign until 1618, the Duke of Lerma was the royal favourite. In 1612 Philip III issued a decree which stated that Lerma had full power to make decisions on the king's behalf. As an individual he offered a new departure in government. He was from Valencia rather than Castile. He was also an aristocrat rather than a *letrado* (lawyer). Under his leadership, the conciliar system of Philip II was remodelled.

The Duke of Lerma bypassed the conciliar system by creating a number of committees which dealt with special or urgent problems (see diagram on page 293). In 1600 the Junta de guerra de Indias was created. It dealt with military affairs. Later other committees was added, such as the Junta de hacienda which dealt with financial matters. The Junta de Inglaterra (England), the Junta de Alemania (Germany) and Junta de Italia (Italy) dealt with specific areas of foreign policy. According to historian John Lynch, in *Spain under the Habsburgs, 1598–1700* (1969), this was 'a realistic development, sponsored by the administration itself, in response to the growing burden of work'.

This does not mean the conciliar system failed to function. In fact the opposite occurred. Both the Council of State and Council of War met regularly. The regional councils also continued to function. These included the Councils of Castile, Flanders, Aragon, and the Indies. In the 17th century personal rule by the king was replaced by rule by council. The historian Henry Kamen states, in *Spain 1469–1714* (1991): 'for the rest of the Habsburg regime in Spain power rested with the councils'.

However, the secretaries who ran these committees during Philip II's reign lost influence to the Duke of Lerma. This meant that Lerma was in charge of a patronage system that allowed him to amass a great deal of wealth for himself and his supporters. Two individuals who benefited under this system were Rodrigo Calderon and Don Pedro Franqueza. Philip III's reign saw a decisive shift in power away from the *letrados* in favour of the aristocracy.

Another development worth consideration was a revival in the power of the Cortes (government), in particular in Castile. This was due to the king's need for taxation, which the Cortes had the power to grant.

Why were the Moriscos expelled between 1609 and 1614?

One of the most important decisions taken by Philip III's government was the decision to expel the Morisco population. According to Henry Kamen, in *Spain 1469–1714*, this action was 'one of the most ill-considered policy acts of the century, carried out against the views of a large body of informed opinion in Spain, denounced by foreigners and very quickly regretted on all sides'.

Following the Morisco Rebellion in Granada, in 1568–1570, the government considered the idea of removing the Moriscos from Spain. They were regarded as possible supporters of the Turks and the Islamic states of north Africa.

There are several reasons why the Moriscos were expelled at this time. It was no coincidence that the expulsion from Castile took place at the same time as the Treaty of Antwerp (early April 1609). This created a 12-year truce in the war between Spain and the Dutch. The decision to expel had already been taken by the Council of State, on 30 January 1608.

The Treaty of Antwerp was unpopular in Spain. It occurred at a time of economic hardship. As a result, the decision to expel can be seen as an attempt to gain popularity. This explanation goes some way to explaining

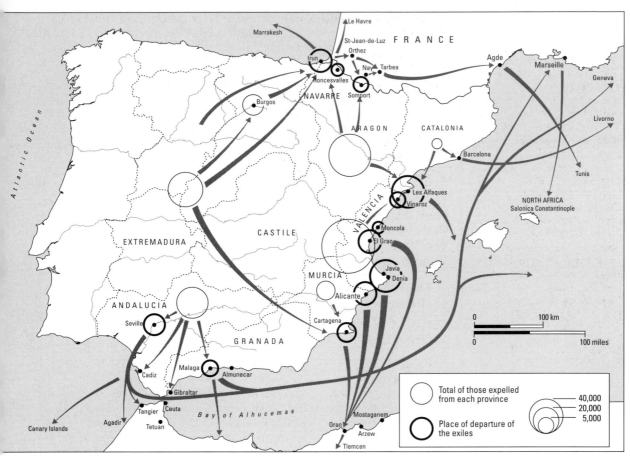

The expulsion of the Moriscos

Regional distribution of Moriscos in 1609	
Valencia	117,000
Aragon	61,000
Castile	45,000
Andalucia	30,000
Murcia	14,000
Catalonia	4,000
Granada	2,000

Lerma's own change in opinion – before 1608 he had been opposed to the idea of expulsion.

Another factor was more long term. Even after the failure of the Granada Morisco rebellion, the Moriscos remained a separate community within Spain. By 1609 attempts to assimilate them into the wider Christian community had failed. In addition, it was feared that Moriscos might join forces with French Protestants to undermine rule in Aragon. As a result, the Archbishop of Valencia, Juan de Ribera, urged Lerma to expel the Moriscos.

However, the element of personal greed was also a factor. The Duke of Lerma wanted to give the lands of the expelled Moriscos in Valencia to the nobility. In all nearly 300,000 Moriscos were expelled. The hardest-hit area was Valencia where the Moricos made up a third of the population.

There is some controversy over the impact of the expulsion. In 1633 a royal confessor wrote, 'it is a very short time ago since the Moriscos were expelled – an action which did such harm to these kingdoms that it is a good idea to have them back again'.

Although comprising 4% of the total population of Spain, the expulsion had a severe effect on some areas – such as Valencia (see insert). Contrary to one of the motives for expulsion, the Valencian nobility made a considerable financial loss due to a fall in rents.

How did the Duke of Lerma deal with Spain's financial problems?

During Philip II's, Spain faced major financial problems. The expenditure required to maintain Philip II's foreign policy commitments outstripped his ability to finance them. On four occasions Philip II could not meet his debt repayments: in 1557, 1560, 1575 and 1598. He left Philip III a debt of 68 million ducats. According to historian Graham Darby, in *Spain in the Seventeenth Century* (1994), Philip III's expenditure was between 8 and 10 million ducats per year. This can de divided into the following.

- The army of Flanders cost approximately 4 million ducats a year up to the Treaty of Antwerp of 1609.

- The army of Milan was funded mainly by Philip III's Italian lands.

- The Spanish navy cost around 1 to 1.5 million ducats a year.

- Philip III's court expenditure was some 1.5 million ducats per year.

The revenue to pay for this expenditure came primarily from gold and silver imported from the Americas, and from taxation in Castile. Unfortunately for Philip III the amount of money acquired from the New World declined during his reign, compared to the reign of Philip II.

The value of gold and silver bullion imported from the New World

Figures in millions of ducats. Philip III acquired one-fifth (the Quinta tax) on all imports.

Years	Value
1596–1600	41,300,000
1601–1605	29,200,000
1606–1610	37,600,000
1611–1615	29,400,000
1616–1620	36,100,000

---

1. *Using the information above, calculate how much revenue differed from expenditure during the reign of Philip III.*

2. *How far do you think Philip III's financial problems were inherited from his father, Philip II?*

Apart from the Quinta, Philip II received revenue from the taxes established under Philip II (see Chapter 6):

- The *alcabala* raised approximately 3 million ducats per year.

- *Millones* raised around 2.5 million ducats per year.

- The *servicio* raised about 500,000 ducats per year.

- The Three Graces from the Catholic Church (*cruzada*, *subsidio* and *excusado*) raised a further 1.5 million ducats per year.

What measures did Philip III's government take?

To deal with his financial problems, Philip III's government took a number of different measures.

- The Duke of Lerma debased the currency. This meant that the silver content of coins was reduced. In addition, the vellon became a standard coin in Castile. Initially, it had some silver but later became a completely copper coin. The aim of this was to provide a profit for the Crown. It led to a fall in the value of currency, leading directly to a rise in prices (inflation). In 1608 Philip promised the Castilian Cortes that he would not issue vellon coins for 20 years. However, in 1617 he again issued these coins, when faced with mounting debts. Philip III may have produced a profit in the short term; in the long term, he increased Spain's financial problems.

1. What do you regard as the main problem the Duke of Lerma had to face in domestic affairs?

Give reasons for your answer.

2. How far did Philip III's government differ from government under Philip II?

- The Duke of Lerma continued the policy of issuing state bonds called *juros*. These were purchased by individuals who, in return, received an annual payment from the government. In 1598 the 'juro' debt stood at approximately 85 million ducats, of which 4.5 million ducats had to be paid annually to juro holders. The juro debt increased during Philip III's reign to around 5 million per year by 1621.

- A third policy, which was forced on the government, was to stop paying interests on debts or annual payments on juros. This was a form of state bankruptcy. It occurred in 1607.

The financial problems continued under Philip II's successor, Philip IV. The financial burdens of Spain have been cited as an example of Spain's decline as a great power.

13.2 What impact did the Duke of Lerma have on Spanish foreign policy?

Ambrogio (or Ambrosio) Spínola (1569–1630)
A Genoese banker with neither military experience nor training, Spínola emerged unexpectedly as the key Spanish commander during the later stages of the Dutch Revolt. He took over command in 1603 at the siege of Ostend, in return for lending the Archdukes the money to continue. He then successfully led an army across the 'great rivers barrier' in 1605. His victories helped to persuade the Netherlanders of the advantage of a truce. The resumption of war in 1621 once more enabled Spínola to emerge as a military commander.

When historians write about the decline of Spain many see the beginning of this process in 1598 with the death of Philip II. However, during the reign of Philip III Spain reached the status of Europe's dominant power. In the *New Cambridge Modern History* Volume IV (1970), the historian Hugh Trevor-Roper stated: 'in the decade after 1610 Philip III seemed "monarch of the world", more powerful in peace than his father had been in war'. Henry Kamen, in *Spain 1469–1714* (1991), supports that view. He states that Spain had 'created an apparently durable chain of alliances that raised Spanish influence to the highest point it ever achieved in Europe'. How far are these assessments accurate?

The Duke of Lerma has received a 'bad press' from historians concerning his domestic policy. However, in foreign affairs he followed a policy which was realistic when considering Spain's financial difficulties. During his period in office Spain made peace with both England and the Dutch. In his attempt to increase Spanish influence, Lerma was aided by able diplomats such as Gondomar in England and Baltasar de' Zúñiga in Vienna.

In 1604 the Treaty of London brought peace with England. Unfortunately, Spanish intervention in the Tyrone Rebellion in Ireland had ended in failure in 1601. Peace with England allowed Spain to concentrate their military forces on the Dutch Revolt. Initially they had some success. In 1604 General Spínola captured Ostend. However, in 1606 the Spanish army of Flanders mutinied over lack of pay.

By 1609 a 12-year truce was signed at the Treaty of Antwerp. The treaty accepted Dutch independence and made no reference for the Dutch rebels to withdraw from Spanish territory overseas. Many at the time saw the treaty as a humiliation for Spain. However, peace with the Dutch allowed the Duke of Lerma to deal with the Turkish threat in the Mediterranean. In 1609 a Turkish fleet was destroyed off Tunis.

A turning point in Spanish foreign policy came in 1610 with the assassination of the French king, Henry IV. For the rest of Philip III's reign France was under a regency during the minority of the new king, Louis XIII. This allowed Spain to dominate the affairs of western Europe. Between 1611 and 1615, Lerma was able to improve relations with France. A treaty between the countries was signed in 1612, followed in 1615 by a marriage alliance when Louis XIII of France married Philip III's daughter, Anne of Austria.

Between 1614 and 1615 war broke out in north Italy between Savoy and Spain. Charles Emmanuel of Savoy was defeated by the Army of Milan at Vercelli. The peace preserved Spanish power in north Italy.

Ambrogio Spínola receives the Surrender of Breda in 1625 – detail from a painting by Diego Rodriguez de Silva y Velásquez (c.1635).

By the time of his fall from power, in 1618, Lerma had greatly eased Spain's military commitments. His foreign policy had increased Spanish influence to a new height in European affairs. However, he was fortunate that, following Henry IV's death, France no longer appeared as a threat to Spanish interests.

How did the Duke of Lerma's fall affect Spanish foreign policy?

According to historian John Lynch, in *Spain under the Habsburgs 1598–1700* (1969), Lerma's 'unbridled greed, unscrupulous use of patronage and the scandalous behaviour of some of his clients outraged public opinion'. Lerma was also blamed for the poor economic condition of Spain and the financial difficulties facing the government. In the end, he lost power because of a court intrigue against him started by his own son, the Duke of Uceda. His departure led to a new, more aggressive phase in foreign policy.

The principal influence of Spanish foreign policy between 1618 and 1621 was Baltasar de' Zúñiga. Under his influence, Spain became involved in the early stages of the Thirty Years' War. In 1619 Spain sent troops to aid the Austrian Habsburgs against rebellion in Bohemia (see Chapter 15).

A major concern of the Spanish in the reigns of Philip II, III and IV was the need to protect the overland route linking Genoa with the Netherlands. Known as the Spanish Road, this was the principal route for reinforcing the Army of Flanders. In 1620 General Spínola occupied the Palatinate, a territory on the west bank of the river Rhine. This intervention made sure that the Spanish Road was secure.

By 1621 the Spanish position in Europe seemed strong. In that year the 12-year truce with the Dutch expired. Although Spain and the Dutch had been at peace in Europe since 1609, Dutch traders had established themselves in the East Indies, west Africa and Brazil. To safeguard Spanish trade and to protect Spain's international reputation, the Council of State decided to resume the war with the Dutch by the summer of 1621. The war was declared by Philip IV, as Philip III had died on 21 March 1621.

1. In what ways was foreign policy under the Duke of Lerma different from foreign policy during the last years of the reign of Philip II?

2. How successful was the Duke of Lerma's foreign policy?

3. How far did foreign policy change between 1618 and 1621?

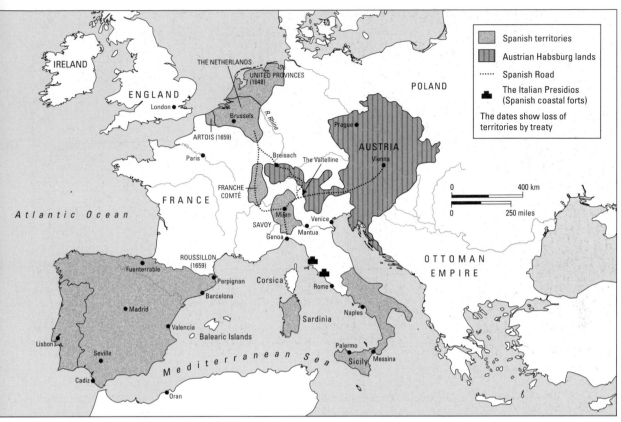

The Spanish monarchy in Europe in the 17th century

13.3 In what ways did Spain experience social and economic change between 1598 and 1659?

Why did the population of Spain decline between 1598 and 1659?

During the period 1530 to 1580 the population of Spain increased to around 8.5 million. After that date, population declined steadily to reach 7 million by 1700. The population declined for a number of reasons. Firstly, the expulsion of the Moriscos between 1609 and 1614 saw a net loss of some 275,000. However, a major cause was an increase in the mortality rate. This was caused by the outbreak of epidemics in 1596–1602 and again from 1647–1652. Over one-tenth of the population lost their lives in these outbreaks. The loss of population was not uniform across the country. Valencia and Catalonia saw the lowest fall in population; Castile and Extremadura saw the biggest loss.

Another cause of the rise in the death rate in Spain was war. From 1635 to 1659 Spain was involved in a major war with France. In addition, revolts broke out in Catalonia and Portugal in 1640, which also increased the loss of life.

This loss of population has been seen as a cause of the decline of Spain. In a sense, it was. The loss of population reduced the amount of taxation from the *alcabala*, *millones* and *servicio*. It also saw a fall in the amount of rent received by aristocratic landowners.

In the *New Cambridge Modern History* (1970), historian J.H. Elliott gives an example of the effects of population decline on one Castilian village, Villatoro. As a result of an epidemic, its population was reduced

The population decline of certain Castilian towns, 1580–1650 (in households)

Town	1587–1594	1601–1611	1640–1650
Avila	2,826	–	1,123
Burgos	2,247	1,528	800
Cadiz	900	400	–
Cuenca	3,095	–	800
León	1,086	–	600
Medina del Campo	2,760	–	650
Palencia	2,561	1,143	800
Salamanca	4,953	–	2,965
Segovia	5,600	3,100	1,625
Talavera de la Reina	2,035	1,804	1,512
Toledo	10,933	–	5,000
Valladolid	8,112	6,000	3,000

from 300 to 80. However, the Council of Finance reduced its tax burden by only 15,000 maravedis, to 135,000 maravedis per year. If this example is typical, then the Castilian peasantry suffered an ever-increasing tax burden as a result of population decline.

Did Spanish agriculture and industry change in this period?

A criticism has been made of the role of the Mesta and Spain's agricultural problems. The influence of this organisation is seen as ensuring the dominance of sheep farming in Castile at the expense of growing crops, in particular grain. However, the main problem facing agriculture was a decline in population. As the century progressed, more and more Castilian villages were deserted. In 1609 the Duke of Lerma attempted to deal with the problem. He encouraged absentee landlords to return to their estates in the hope that this would ease the problem. The measure proved ineffectual.

The result of these developments, according to John Lynch in *Spain under the Habsburgs 1598–1700* (1969), was the continuance of 'periodic subsistence crisis and [the need] to depend on the import of foreign grain'.

Spanish industry also faced serious problems. Virtually every part of Spanish industry went into decline in the first half of the 17th century. The once-powerful textile industry suffered from the loss of foreign markets. This led to unemployment. Similar problems faced the mining and shipbuilding industries.

According to American historian Earl Hamilton, writing in 1938 in the *Economic History Review*, the economic decline of the first half of the 17th century led directly to the decline of Spain as a great power. An assessment of the idea that Spain declined in the period 1598 to 1648 is covered in the last section in this chapter.

1. In what ways did Spanish society and the economy change between 1598 and 1659?

2. To what extent did the social and economic changes of this period lead to the decline of Spain?

13.4 How did foreign policy change under Olivares?

According to historian John Lynch, in *The Hispanic World in Crisis and Change 1598–1700* (1992), Count-Duke Olivares followed a traditional form of Spanish foreign policy, albeit with more aggression. He quotes a paper written by Olivares to Philip IV on 21 November 1621 on this matter. Olivares stated: 'Almost all the kings and princes of Europe are jealous of your greatness. You are the main support and defence of the Catholic religion; for this reason you have renewed the war with the Dutch and with other enemies of the Church who are their allies; and your principal obligation is to defend yourself and attack them.'

In guiding Spanish foreign policy, Olivares faced several problems.

● The renewal of war in the Netherlands against the Dutch.

● The global conflict against the Dutch in the Atlantic and in the Americas.

● The need to safeguard the overland route from Genoa to Flanders (the Spanish Road).

● The need to protect Spanish possessions and influence in Italy.

● The need to support the Austrian Habsburgs in the Thirty Years' War.

● The renewal of conflict with France in 1624–26, 1628–31 and 1635–59.

● The renewal of conflict with England in 1625.

The foreign policy of Olivares can be divided into two periods. From 1621 to 1626 he had considerable success. After that date, the foreign policy problems of Spain increased. A turning point came in 1635 with the entry of France into the Thirty Years' War. By the time of Olivares' fall from power, in 1643, Spain was facing a crisis in foreign policy.

Why were the years 1621–1626 a period of success for Spain?

In dealing with the threat to the Spanish Road, Spanish troops had occupied the Valtelline, an area inhabited by Catholics but ruled by Protestants (known as the Grisons). The Spanish faced the threat of French intervention between 1624 and 1626. However, the Treaty of Monzon with France, in 1626, recognised Spanish control of this vital area.

The resumption of war with the Dutch rebels led to a series of Spanish victories. Under the leadership of General Ambrogio Spínola, the Army of Flanders was able to win back lost territory. This culminated in the capture of Breda, after a siege, in June 1625.

The conflict with the Dutch was not confined to Europe. In South America the Dutch had captured the important port of Bahía, in Brazil, in 1624. A year later the Spanish retook the town. They also defeated a Dutch attempt to take the island of Puerto Rico in the Caribbean.

England, who had been an ally of the Dutch up to 1604, reopened conflict with Spain in 1625 when the Duke of Buckingham launched an attempt to capture the naval base of Cadiz. Again the Spanish were successful. A peace treaty was signed in 1630 ending the conflict.

Finally, Olivares and the Austrian Habsburgs launched an ambitious plan to control the Baltic area, thereby denying the Dutch an important trade route. A Spanish naval force under Toledo and Santa Cruz planned to join the Austrian Emperor's army led by generals Wallenstein and Tilly to take control of north Germany.

The historian Henry Kamen has described 1625 as a *wunderjahr* ('wonder year') for Spain. The following year, King Philip IV addressed the Castilian Cortes stating: 'our prestige has been immensely improved. We have had all Europe against us, but we have not been defeat, nor have our allies lost, whilst our enemies have sued [asked] me for peace.'

Why did Spain's fortunes change in foreign affairs after 1626?

Spain's change of fortunes in foreign affairs coincided with a financial and economic crisis. Spain failed to pay its debts in 1627. Olivares even offered to resign from his position in October 1627. This was refused by Philip IV.

A major problem faced by Spain was the untimely death of the Duke of Mantua, in north Italy. His death led to a war about who should replace him. Lasting from 1628 to 1631, the War of the Mantuan Succession took place against France for control of this important north Italian state. The war proved costly for Spain both in terms of finance and prestige. It cost 10 million ducats. By 1631 Spain had lost support of both the Austrian Habsburg Emperor and of Savoy. Olivares was forced to make an unfavourable peace at Cherasco. This treaty allowed France to keep the strategically important town of Pinerolo, in north Italy. More significantly, the new Duke of Mantua was the French nominee – the Duke of Nevers.

In the Holy Roman Empire, Olivares' Baltic plans were left in disarray. In 1631 the Protestant kingdom of Sweden entered the Thirty Years' War. Under the leadership of King Gustavus Adolphus, the Swedes were able to expel Imperial troops from north Germany.

Following the great successes of 1621 to 1625, Olivares had placed himself in a position to negotiate a peace with the Dutch rebels. However, Olivares' desire to defeat the Dutch proved to be very costly. In 1628 the Dutchman Piet Heyn captured the Spanish silver fleet at Matanzas Bay, Cuba.

The years after 1626 were not all lacking in success. In 1633–34 Spanish and Imperial fortunes in Germany changed dramatically. In September 1634 a combined army of Spanish and Imperial troops, under Philip IV's brother the Cardinal-Infante Ferdinand, inflicted a crushing defeat on the Swedes at the Battle of Nördlingen. However, this victory, and the seizure of Trier by Spain, had the effect of forcing France into war with Spain in 1635.

Between 1635 and his fall from power in 1643, Olivares faced increasing problems in foreign affairs. These problems were made worse by an inability to raise sufficient money to meet all of Spain's military commitments. The war with France showed the changing fortunes of the two states. In 1635 France could raise the equivalent of 14 million ducats to fund its armed forces. In contrast Spain could raise only 8 million ducats.

The war with both France and the Dutch produced some victories for Spain. In 1636, the Cardinal-Infante Ferdinand, in command of the Army of Flanders, led a diversionary attack on France which got within 80 miles of Paris at Corbie. This forced a French army under the Duke of Condé to leave Franche Comté. However, in 1638–39 the Spanish suffered major defeats. In 1638 the French captured Breisach, cutting off the 'Spanish Road'. In 1639 a Spanish fleet was destroyed by the Dutch Admiral von Tromp off the Kent coast, in the Battle of the Downs. Another armada to Brazil was also defeated. The strains of war and the financial cost of maintaining armies in the field led to the outbreak of rebellion in Catalonia and Portugal in 1640.

By 18 May 1641, Olivares reported to the Council of State: 'The present situation threatens, unless something is done quickly to finish altogether with your Majesty's Monarchy, leaving us not even one corner of territory.'

When Olivares fell from power, following a court intrigue led by

Philip IV's wife, Spain had experienced a recovery in its military fortunes. However, the heavy financial costs of war had driven parts of the Iberian peninsula into rebellion.

Also shortly after Olivares' departure, the Army of Flanders suffered a crushing defeat by the French, at Rocroi. This was the first time in over a century that a Spanish army was defeated in the field.

How did Spanish foreign policy develop between 1643 and 1659?

The period 1643–1659 was one of further defeat and crisis for Spain. Following the defeat at Rocroi, the French general Condé captured Dunkirk in 1646. In the following year, revolts broke out in Sicily and Naples.

At the Peace of Westphalia, in 1648, which ended the Thirty Years' War, Spain finally acknowledged the independence of the United Provinces in the Treaty of Münster. Then, in 1659, peace was made with France in the Treaty of the Pyrenees.

Spain was forced to hand over the provinces to Roussillon and Cerdagne, which were part of Catalonia. In Flanders the Spanish gave up to the French most of Artois. Dunkirk was given to the English Republic. This treaty has been seen as a turning point in European history. Before that date, the dominant western European power was Spain. After 1659, France under Louis XIV took over that position. According to Graham Darby, in *Spain in the Seventeenth Century* (1994): 'The Peace of the Pyrenees was a peace of equals'.

In 1659 the armies of Flanders and Milan were still formidable forces. Spain still dominated Italy and possessed the largest overseas empire of any European state.

1. What were the main problems facing Count-Duke Olivares in his conduct of Spanish foreign policy?

2. To what extent can Olivares be regarded as a failure in foreign policy?

3. How far was Spanish foreign policy under Olivares different from foreign policy under the Duke of Lerma?

13.5 How successful was the Count-Duke Olivares in domestic policy?

Just as Philip II became closely associated with the Duke of Lerma, so Philip IV's favourite (*valido*) was the Count-Duke Olivares, until 1643. Philip IV (who reigned 1621–1665) has been the subject of differing interpretations by historians. Martin Hume, in *The Court of Philip IV* (published in 1906), claimed that the relationship between the King and Olivares as 'a king to whom pleasure was a business, and a minister to whom business alone was pleasure'.

This view was supported by the German historian Ludwig Pfandl, in 1927, who described the king as 'a Hercules in pleasure and impotent in government'. More recently, a new interpretation has developed. The Spanish historian Jose Alcala-Zamora stated, in 1975: 'Philip IV always intervened in, and informed himself of, and decided upon affairs of government. At least during the first 20 years of his reign, his industriousness yielded nothing to that of his grandfather [Philip II], and on many occasions exceeded it.' Therefore, when studying the history of Spain between 1621 and 1643 it should be noted that Philip IV and Olivares worked closely together. Any change in the organisation of government was not merely the work or views of Olivares alone.

What changes did Olivares make to the organisation of government?

In the period from the fall of the Duke of Lerma, in 1618, to the rise of Olivares to the position of *valido* in 1621–22, Spanish government was dominated by two figures: the Duke of Uceda and Baltasar de' Zúñiga. Their dominance coincided with a major change in Spanish foreign policy.

By 1622 Philip IV had given Olivares complete control over government and patronage. Unlike the Duke of Lerma, Olivares was more interested in government than using patronage to enrich himself. In fact, Olivares disliked the task of handing out offices. In 1626 he wrote privately to Philip IV requesting the king to take over this task.

Olivares developed the governmental changes begun under Philip III. The creation of committees was continued and developed. New committees (*juntas*) included the *junta de armadas* dealing with naval affairs and the *junta de presidios*, dealing with frontier garrisons. Olivares was accused of bypassing the councils that existed. This was partly due to the fact that he was junior in rank to many of the council members. As a result, if he was to control government he had to operate outside the conciliar system. However, the committees were seen by him as an efficient way of dealing with specific tasks.

Like previous chief ministers and monarchs, Olivares' main aim in government was to conserve Spain's position and reputation as a 'great power'. In this sense domestic policy was subordinate to foreign affairs. An important area of government linked to this issue was finance. New committees established by Olivares in this area included the *junta de media anata*; the *junta del papel sellado* and the *junta de donativos* which dealt with special sources of revenue not already dealt with by the Council of Finance.

To improve the operation of government Olivares also created the *Junta Grande del Reformacion*, in August 1622. This committee had the task of improving the operation of government through removal of corruption. The committee made several recommendations, such as the abolition of some government posts and the end of emigration.

Unfortunately for Olivares his suggested reforms faced stiff opposition from the Castilian Cortes in 1624. Reforms such as closing brothels (houses of prostitutes) and financial reforms were defeated. The fact that the Castilian Cortes was summoned by Philip IV for 30 out the 44 years of his reign shows how desperately the monarchy needed new taxes. It also reflects that as a result of this development the Cortes was able to exercise more power and influence.

How did Olivares try to improve Spain's financial position?

In his reform programme Olivares made many suggestions to improve Spain's financial position. He recommended the abolition of the *millones* and *alcabala* taxes and their replacement with one new tax. He also suggested the creation of one national bank. Most controversially, he suggested that the financial burden of providing Spain with armed forces should be spread throughout Philip IV's empire. This Union of Arms would ease the financial burden on Castile.

On 26 July 1626, Philip IV declared the implementation of the Union of Arms. The plan was to raise an army of reservists of 140,000 men paid for by all Philip's provinces (see insert).

Although a good idea in theory, the Union of Arms faced opposition outside Castile. The Cortes in Catalonia, Valencia and Aragon pleaded poverty which forced Philip IV to lower their quota of troops. Flanders refused to comply until 1627 and then only suggested raising 12,000 troops. What made matters worse was the outbreak of the War of the Mantuan Succession (1628–1631) which required considerable expenditure rather than extra troops. Unfortunately for Olivares his planned Union of Arms failed to spread the financial burdens of empire. Castile still provided the most finance.

In other areas, Olivares tried to improve the financial position. He tried to cut rising prices (inflation) by withdrawing the copper-based vellon

The Union of Arms

The amount of men each province was expected to contribute.

Castile	**44,000**
Catalonia	16,000
Naples	16,000
Portugal	16,000
Flanders	12,000
Aragon	10,000
Milan	8,000
Sicily	6,000
Valencia	6,000
Other lands	6,000

coins in 1626. However, he was forced to reintroduce the vellon because of falling silver imports from the Americas. In 1628 he had to reduce the value of Spain's currency by half. This process was known as 'debasing the currency'. Today it would be called the devaluation of a currency. This was followed by a further debasement in March 1636.

Olivares also tried to raise money through loans and by placing taxes on a wide variety of goods, such as playing cards and salt. Perhaps one of his successes was to persuade Philip IV to reduce the costs and expenses of his court. Certainly, Olivares was willing to take desperate measures. In 1627 he suspended the payment of debt to the people from whom Spain had borrowed money (creditors).

By the time of his fall from power in 1643, Olivares had attempted to reform Spain's finances. By a series of policies – including defaulting on debts, debasement of the currency and introducing new taxes – he was able to prevent a financial collapse. Unfortunately, he created serious problems for his successors. As the historian John Lynch notes, in *Spain under the Habsburgs 1598–1700*, Olivares' 'vision of a greater Spain was too ambitious for the period of recession in which he lived, and he himself had no talent for political manoeuvre and compromise'.

This problem was shown most clearly in 1640 with the revolt of Catalonia and Portugal.

Why did Catalonia and Portugal revolt in 1640?

The greatest catastrophe to affect Olivares' rule in Spain was the outbreak of rebellion in Catalonia and Portugal. These developments are a turning point in the history of Spain as western Europe's greatest power. The rebellion in Catalonia led to the occupation of that kingdom by France from 1641 to 1652. The rebellion in Portugal eventually led to the separation of Portugal, and its overseas empire, from Spain. Why was Spain brought to the verge of disintegration by the 1640s?

Catalonia

In the first weeks of May 1640 there was a revolt in Catalonia. What made the revolt so serious was that it took place during the war with France (1635–59) in a strategically important region for Spain. Initially, the revolt was against the presence of a royal army which was defending the kingdom against possible French invasion. In fact, the origins of the Catalan revolt were more deep-seated.

Olivares has been criticised for provoking a revolt by sending a royal army to Catalonia. Perez Zagorin, in *Rebels and Rulers 1500–1660* (1982), states that in 1640 'Olivares was resolved more than ever to reduce the province's [Catalonia] independence'. However, John Lynch puts forward a different view. In *The Hispanic World in Crisis and Change 1598–1700* (1992), he claims that it was not Olivares' 'intention to put an army into Catalonia, in order deliberately to provoke a rebellion, the crushing of which would then be a pretext to abolish Catalan liberties'.

Instead Olivares had planned to involve Catalonia more in the defence and financing of the war against France which had begun in 1635. The attempt to implement the Union of Arms was the principal cause of the revolt. The attempt to raise armies within Catalonia and the demand that the province finance these troops were seen by the Catalans as an infringement of their rights (*fueros*). For instance, in January 1640, the Catalan *audiencia* had declared that housing troops in Catalonia was illegal. Olivares' decision to ignore this judgement increased suspicion of his possible motives.

The revolt also had a strong social and economic element. It coincided with a period of food shortage. Rebels attacked the wealthy. In many ways

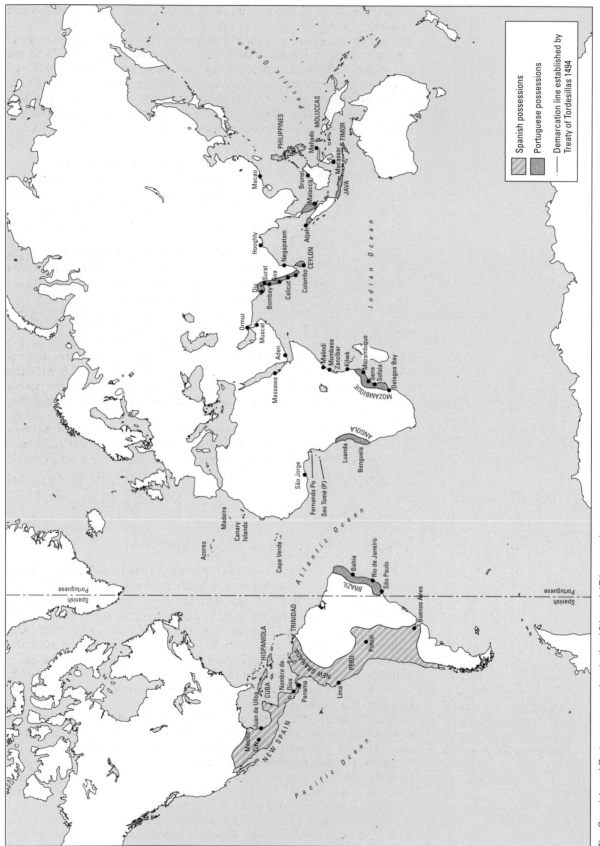

The Spanish and Portuguese empires in the 16th and 17th centuries

it was a rebellion of landless peasants against landowners in defence of Catalan rights.

However, Olivares' uncompromising attitude, combined with a belief that the Catalans would help in the defence of Spain, backfired. By September 1640 representatives of the Catalan rebels had approached Louis XIII of France for protection. A formal defence agreement was made with France in October. From 1641 to 1652 Catalonia was occupied by a French army. When Catalonia returned to Spanish control, Philip IV promised to recognise Catalan self-government.

Portugal

Although Catalonia occupied a strategically important part of the Franco–Spanish frontier in time of war, Portugal was a more important part of Philip IV's empire. Not only was Portugal larger, with a bigger population, it also contained a large part of Philip IV's overseas empire. It included Brazil, Angola, Mozambique and trading posts in India, the East Indies, China and Japan.

In some ways the revolts in Catalonia and Portugal had similar origins. The attempt to increase Portugal's taxes, as part of the Union of Arms, had led to violent protests between 1628–30. These increased demands took place at a time when revenue from Portugal's colonies was in decline.

The Catalan revolt in May 1640 acted as a catalyst for the Portuguese revolt in December. In that month John, Duke of Braganza declared himself John IV of Portugal. However, the Portuguese revolt had deeper origins. Unlike Catalonia, Portugal had a more recent experience of independence. In did not become part of Philip II's empire until 1580. After that date it retained its own laws, language and colonies. Any attempt by Olivares to reduce Portuguese self-government was bound to create deep resentment.

Unfortunately for Olivares, the Portuguese revolt took place at a time when Spanish forces were employed elsewhere. The Spanish army was involved in fighting France and in trying to put down the Catalan revolt. The Spanish navy had been badly beaten by the Dutch in 1639 at the Battle of the Downs. By the time an army could be sent to Portugal, in 1659, it was too late. Portuguese independence was formally recognised in 1668.

Why did Olivares fall from power in 1643?

According to John Lynch, in *The Hispanic World in Crisis and Change 1598–1700*: 'the revolts of Catalonia and Portugal reduced the Count-Duke's policy to dust'. There was even a plot by the Duke of Medina-Sidonia for Andalucia to **secede** from Spain in 1641. However, the revolts occurred at a time of major economic difficulty for Spain. Transatlantic shipments of silver dropped dramatically after 1638. By 1640 the Spanish government's finances were in chaos. In addition, Spain was fighting a major European war against both France and the Dutch. The combination of all these problems led to Olivares' fall. On 17 January 1643 Olivares asked Philip IV's permission to resign.

According to Graham Darby, in *Spain in the Seventeenth Century*: 'there is no doubt that Olivares was a failure, and he failed on a monumental scale. The very thing he sought to prevent, the collapse of Spanish hegemony [power] he actually brought about.'

Secede: To formally end membership of the group to which a country belongs, and to form a separate country.

1. What were the main changes Olivares made to Spanish government and finance?

2. Why do you think Olivares faced major problems in trying to implement his reforms?

3. Who do you think was a more effective *valido (favourite)* – the *Duke of Lerma or the Count-Duke Olivares* – in domestic affairs? Give reasons for your answer.

13.6 *The decline of Spain: an assessment*
A CASE STUDY IN HISTORICAL INTERPRETATION

A traditional view has been the belief that from the time of Ferdinand and Isabella to the early 17th century Spain experienced a 'golden age'. Several texts on Spain have used the term as their title. In 1937 R. Trevor Davies entitled his history of Spain from 1500 to 1621 *The Golden Century of Spain*. In 1971 Dominguez Ortiz wrote a text entitled *The Golden Age of Spain 1516–1659*.

These interpretations suggest that Spanish power reached its height during the 16th and early 17th centuries. After that period, Spain declined in power. Even contemporaries took this view. In 1600 Martin Gonzalez de Cellorigo stated that Spain had become 'a republic of the bewitched, living outside the natural order of things'. He looked back to the reigns of the Catholic Kings as a period of greatness. More recently, several books have referred to the issue of decline. The *New Cambridge Modern History* Volume IV, which covers 1608–09 to 1648 is entitled the 'Decline of Spain and the Thirty Years' War' (1970). Part of the problem in assessing the decline of Spain, as the terminal dates of the books above suggest, is to find a common sets of dates for Spain's 'golden age' and its subsequent decline.

The decline took many forms. One view is that Spain's decline was part of a wider crisis that affected all western Europe. Theories about a general crisis of the 17th century put forward the view that all Europe faced economic decline, social disorder and war.

There is also the view that Spain's decline was due to its religious policies. The abandonment of the *conviviencia* and the expulsion of the Jews and Moriscos created a state that went into economic decline. At the beginning of the 20th century, the German sociologist Max Weber published *The Protestant Ethic and the Spirit of Capitalism*. This put forward the view that economic development became associated with the Protestant religion. This helps to explain why Protestant states such as Holland and England improved their economic position at the expense of Catholic states like Spain and Portugal.

According to the American historian Earl J. Hamilton, in 'The Decline of Spain', which appeared in the *Economic History Review* in 1938, Spain experienced economic decline which, in turn, saw the decline of Spain as a major power. He mentions a number of factors.

- The fall in population numbers in Spain during the period after 1580.

- Inflation and currency problems.

- The financial burdens of Empire which fell heavily on Castile.

- The loss of the northern Netherlands.

- The failure of the Castilian economy to develop to meet the growing financial needs of Empire.

- The decline in silver and gold imports from the Americas by the early 17th century.

The combined effects of these developments ultimately led to the military and political decline of Spain by the 1650s.

An interesting twist on the economic causes of Spain's decline was made by Henry Kamen in 'The Decline of Spain – A Historical Myth?' in *Past and Present* (1978). He put forward the view that Spain did not decline economically in the 17th century because it had never been in a position to provide the economic basis for a large empire. In *Spain 1469–1714* (1992), Henry

Kamen states: 'The Spanish universal monarchy had come into existence through inheritance rather than conquest, and Spain's limited resources had never been capable of an active imperial programme.'

Although Spain never possessed economic resources for the defence of such a large empire there was a degree of financial mismanagement which assisted decline. The use of *juros* and the debasement of the Spanish coinage both created major economic problems.

In *The Rise and Fall of the Great Powers* (1988) Paul Kennedy has pointed to the issue of relative decline. Although Spain continued to maintain large armed forces in the 17th century its position in Europe was affected by the recovery of France and the rise of the United Provinces. For the period 1559 to 1629 France had been adversely affected by the Wars of Religion. Under Cardinal Richelieu France had recovered. The foundations of Louis XIV's state had been laid by the 1650s. In addition, the United Provinces rose to prominence as a major trading power during the 17th century.

The relative decline of Spain can be seen in military power. In 'The Military Revolution 1560–1660 – A Myth?' in *Spain and the Netherlands* (1978), Geoffrey Parker produced the following table:

Increase in military manpower 1470–1710

Date	Spain	United Provinces	France	England	Sweden
1470s	20,000		40,000	25,000	
1550s	150,000		50,000	20,000	
1590s	200,000	20,000	80,000	30,000	15,000
1630s	300,000	50,000	150,000		45,000
1650s	100,000		100,000	70,000	70,000
1670s	70,000	110,000	120,000		63,000
1700s	50,000	100,000	400,000	87,000	100,000

---

1. Why have historians disagreed about the decline of Spain?

2. How far were economic reasons important in the 'Decline of Spain'?

3. To what extent can the following individuals be held responsible for Spain's decline as a major military and political power in Europe?

(a) Philip III

(b) Philip IV

(c) The Count-Duke Olivares.

These figures do not include the Ottoman Empire, which was a formidable opponent of Spain. Therefore, these figures suggest that from the mid 17th century Spain was no longer in a position to be regarded as Europe's greatest military power. From the 1660s France became western Europe's most formidable military power. By 1670 Spain had entered a period of military and political decline from which she did not recover.

The role of individuals played a part in the decline of Spain. After the long rule of Philip II, Spain was ruled by monarchs of lesser quality, Philip III and Philip IV. On a number of occasions after 1621 Philip IV had the opportunity to make peace with the Dutch. However, he refused. Philip IV wanted a return of the 'rebel provinces' and would settle for nothing else. This prolonged the Thirty Years' War until the Spanish had to accept the independence of the United Provinces in 1648. The actions of individuals such as Philip IV and Olivares forced Spain to fight too many enemies at once. This over-extended Spain's limited financial resources, thereby accelerating the country's economic decline.

Source-based question: The financial problems of Spain

SOURCE A

The income and expenditure of the Spanish Monarchy 1621–1640

Income	%
Granted by the Castilian Cortes	38.0
Granted by the Aragon Cortes	1.1
The Three Graces	15.6
Bullion from the Americas (1621–39)	9.5
Sale of *Juros*	9.0
Debasing the coinage	7.5
Sale of government posts	3.5
Salt tax	2.9
Media Anata (tax on government salaries)	1.3
Others	11.6

Total income: **237.3 million ducats**

Expenditure	%
Debt repayments on loans	70.4
Mediterranean fleet	5.3
Atlantic Fleet	4.5
Forts and garrisons	3.7
Army within Spain	3.2
Royal household	5.0
Administration	2.5
Others	5.4

Total expenditure: **249.8 million ducats**

Adapted from Spain 1469–1714 *by Henry Kamen (2nd edition, 1991)*

SOURCE B

The kingdoms of Aragon, Valencia and Catalonia contribute nothing to Your Majesty's expenses beyond their own frontiers, and money even has to be sent to them from Castile to pay their garrisons. Would Your Majesty please consider the possibility of discussing with the Council of Aragon whether those kingdoms could themselves undertake the provision of the money required for paying troops garrisoned in them. Everything is met out of the resources of Castile and out of what comes from the Indies, and literally nothing is contributed by Aragon, Valencia, Catalonia, Portugal and Navarre. As a result, Castile's revenues are pledged to the hilt, and it finds itself in such a state that one cannot see how it can possibly go on paying such vast sums.

An extract from a Council of Finance document, 2 December 1618

SOURCE C

The most important thing Your Majesty's Monarchy is for you to become King of Spain: by this I mean, Sir, that Your Majesty should not be content with being King of Portugal, of Aragon, of Valencia and Count of Barcelona, but should secretly plan and work to reduce these kingdoms of which Spain is composed to the style and laws of Castile, with no difference whatsoever. And if Your Majesty achieves this, you will be the most powerful prince in the world.

From a secret instruction to King Philip IV from Olivares, 25 December 1624

1. Using information in this chapter, explain the meaning of the following terms which are highlighted in the extracts above as they applied to Spain in the years 1598 to 1659:

(a) 'The Three Graces' (Source A)

(b) 'Debasing the coinage' (Source A).

2. Study Sources B and C.

Of what value are these sources to a historian writing about the history of Spain between 1598 and 1659?

3. Study Sources A, B and C.

To what extent does the information contained in Source A support the views put forward in Sources B and C about the financial burden placed on Castile?

4. Study all the sources and use information from this chapter.

How far were the financial problems of the Spanish monarchy in the period 1621–1659 caused by military commitments abroad?

14 The development of France during the reign of Louis XIII and the minority of Louis XIV 1610–1661

Key Issues

- *What benefits did France gain from the dominance of Cardinals Richelieu and Mazarin?*

- *What was the importance of this period to the evolution of absolutism in France?*

- *How important a role did France play in the history of Europe in this period?*

Framework of Events

1610	Death of Henry IV; accession of Louis XIII
1614	Estates General meets; Regency ends
1616	Rebellion of Condé and the Huguenots
	Richelieu becomes Secretary of State
1617	Concini Plot
1618	Thirty Years' War breaks out in Europe
1619	Banishment of Richelieu from Court
1621	Death of Luynes
1622	Peace of Montpellier. Richelieu made a cardinal
1624	Richelieu made First Minister
1625	Huguenot revolt starts in La Rochelle
1626	Treaty of Monzon; Chalais Conspiracy; Assembly of Notables
1627	Death of Duke of Mantua
1628	Surrender of La Rochelle
1629	Treaty of Alès. Edict of Restitution. Code Michaud
1630	Day of Dupes. Capture of Savoy
1631	Treaty of Cherasco. Chambre d'Arsenal
1632	Death of Gustavus Adolphus of Sweden
1634	Battle of Nördlingen
1635	Capture of Trier
1636	Year of Corbie
1638	Birth of Louis XIV. Gaston no longer heir to throne
	Treaty of Hamburg
1639	Revolt of the Nu-Pieds
1641	Cinq Mars rebellion
1642	Death of Richelieu
1643	Death of Louis XIII
	Battle of Rocroi

1648	Battle of Lens. Peace at Westphalia. The First Fronde
1649	Peace of Reuil
1651	Exile of Mazarin. The Second Fronde
1653	Collapse of Third Fronde. Alliance with England
1659	Peace of Pyrenees with Spain
1660	Death of Mazarin.

Overview

THE period between 1610 and 1661 is traditionally seen as one of vital development for France. It had taken on the armed might of both Spain and the Habsburg Austrian Empire and helped to defeat both. France was now *the* major European power. The focus for European events moved decisively away from Madrid or Vienna to Paris. French armies, or those of their allies, had defeated the best that Spain and Austria could offer. The Habsburg Catholic dream of destroying both France and Protestantism had gone by 1661. Ironically Catholic France, led by two Roman Catholic cardinals, had played a huge role in ensuring the survival of Protestantism in Europe. France made many internal changes in this period as well. The Huguenots (French Protestants), who had been given considerable power in the Peace of Nantes in the reign of Henry IV, were to have their military and political power broken by Richelieu (First Minster 1624–1642). Richelieu also tried to curb the power of a backward and frequently rebellious nobility, but with only partial success. He did what he could to destroy any institution or group of people, which stood in the way of the power of the monarch, and an important stage in the development of an absolute monarchy in France occurred in this period.

The changes were sharply focused in this period, almost exclusively on the power and prestige of France and its monarchy, and vital areas of France were neglected. An outdated financial system was worked to death, which cost the monarchy dearly later. Little attention was paid to commerce, the colonies or agriculture. Again, this was to have a damaging effect on the development of France. It was also to prevent monarchs and ministers achieving their objectives.

14.1 What was the importance of the Regency period to the history of France?

Traditionally, the years 1610–1624 are seen as an interlude between the strong and effective monarchy of Henry IV and the 'rule' of the equally powerful and assertive Cardinal Richelieu, First Minister of France between 1624 and 1642. The image given of this period is one of both political and social disorder. The ruler of France at this time was Marie de' Medici, the Italian widow of Henry IV – a not very intelligent or balanced woman. After the assumption of authority by the young Louis XIII (aged 8) in 1610, there was a period of plots and counter-plots, rebellions and factional rivalries, not dissimilar to the years before Henry IV restored order in France.

The period (1610–24) reveals both the strengths and weaknesses of the French monarchy and society. It demonstrates that without an able and dominating personality at the top, France would remain a weak country.

There would be serious social divisions and the country would be unable to make full use of its potential. It would be split by noble faction fighting, led by a nobility which retained a right of rebellion when they saw fit. There might also be serious religious divisions.

Perhaps the key lesson learned by the young King Louis XIII in this period was the need for an able man with a commitment to the development of the power of the French monarchy. This man could compensate for his own weaknesses and ensure not only the survival of the French monarchy, but also its development along the autocratic (firm rule by a single figure) lines that Henry IV was establishing in his reign. The period demonstrates that although the French and their nobles were instinctively monarchists, they all tended to have a different view of what the monarchy should, and should not, be allowed to do. They wanted it run on their terms, for their own ends. Both King and future minister learned a lot in these turbulent years. They saw how quickly France could slide back into the anarchic days of the Wars of Religion (see Chapter 11). They learned which potentially disruptive forces needed managing most. This would ensure the stability and resurgence of France and its monarchy.

How important was the work of Marie de' Medici as Regent?

Although the young king, Louis XIII, formally took over when the Regency ended in 1614, his mother Marie was the dominant influence at Court until 1617. She was seen as an unintelligent intriguer in a Court dominated by great nobles, in much the fashion of the earlier times of Catherine de' Medici. Some historians, such as G.R. Treasure, in his biography of Richelieu, see Marie as 'ineffectual'. The historian Robin Briggs, in *Early Modern France* (1977), describes Marie de' Medici as 'stupid' and dependent on 'luck'. More recently, Y-M. Berce, a French historian, in *The Birth of Absolutism: France 1598–1661* (1996), is more complimentary about her. He points out that there were some achievements in her tenure of office and that she could have handed over a worse legacy to her son when he dispensed rather brutally with her loyal and adequate services.

A painting of Marie de' Medici by Sir Anthony van Dyke

Marie soon dispensed with the services of the Duke of Sully, the key minister of Henry IV. However, she kept on several other ministers, such as the Duke of Villeroi (who was mainly concerned with foreign affairs) and the Chancellor Brulart de Sillery (who had a vital administrative and co-ordinating role). This ensured that there was both continuity and stability at Court and in the administration of the country. It ought to be remembered that Henry IV, at the time of his death, was about to embark on a war on account of his passion for a 15-year-old girl called Catherine. He had married the girl to the Duke of Condé on the grounds of his suspected homosexuality. Henry had the idea that a homosexual would not therefore object to her having an affair with the King. Catherine was perhaps more of a force for stability than she has been given credit for.

Marie de' Medici was also important in ending any chance of war with the Habsburgs over Cleves-Jülich (a fairly minor dispute over the religious leadership of a small area of Germany, started in 1609). An expensive war was the last thing that France needed, even though Sully had supposedly left a surplus in the Treasury. Marie also played a role in the negotiations that preceded the marriages of the young King Louis XIII to the Spanish princess Anne, and her own daughter Elizabeth to the future King of Spain, Philip IV. Given the highly complex and extraordinarily tense state of Europe in the build-up to the Thirty Years' War, Marie could certainly have done a lot worse. The Treaty of Fontainbleau of 1612, which dealt with these royal marriages, also contained a defensive alliance with Spain, with guarantees of peace between the two countries for the following 10 years. Declarations like these were not uncommon, but France could manage well without a war at the time. As a caretaker, Marie de' Medici had some merits.

The period of her Regency has been called the 'years of drift', but peace is not necessarily bad. Marie was also willing to continue to implement the terms of the Edict of Nantes, which gave tolerance and security to the Huguenots. This was a wise and sensible policy designed to keep the peace between Catholic and Protestant in France.

How successfully did Marie deal with the French nobility?

Marie de' Medici has been strongly criticised in this respect. However, given the problems that her husband, Henry IV, her son, Louis XIII and her grandson, Louis XIV, had with the nobility, it is hardly surprising she also had difficulties with the nobles. Certainly there was no change in attitude on the part of the great noblemen, such as the dukes of Condé and Guise, who felt that no law applied to them. They regularly behaved in a way that would be seen as treason in other countries, such as England. It took the savagery of the French Wars of Religion, and the determined work of three extremely able men – Richelieu, Mazarin and Louis XIV – in the course of the 17th century to contain the social, economic and political power of the French aristocracy. So it is not right to criticise Marie too seriously on this front.

Manipulation and backstairs negotiations came naturally to her, and it was through intrigue, bribes and pensions that she kept the nobility quiet in the early years of Louis XIII's reign. The Duke of Condé led a revolt in 1614, but it was Marie who played an important part in suppressing it. She also reconciled Condé with the King. Condé had no desire to replace the King. It seemed his revolt was more to do with being left out of power. He also resented the arrival at Court of the Queen's favourite, Carlo Concini, and his influence over the Court and the country. What worried the defenders of royal power was not only that Condé had been able to raise a large number of supporters in his attack on the Monarchy, but also that Huguenots in some areas supported him. Concerns about the pro-Spanish, and therefore supposedly pro-Catholic, policy of the recent royal marriages worried many Huguenots, who joined up with Condé in protest. The spectre of religious war was raised again, and a young cleric called Armand Richelieu, who had just started to work for Marie, noted it well.

Marie was not able to break noble power – that took decades – but she was at least able to contain it with some success.

How did Marie deal with the Estates General in 1614?

The Estates General was the nearest the French had to a representative assembly. It was rarely called and had only advisory powers. There were elements of representation in this body. It had met four times since 1560, and that was unusually frequent. The Estates General was a consultative body and the main reason for its summoning was to gain support for the monarchy after the revolts of Condé and Frederick Bouillon (the Huguenot leader). There were three chambers, or Houses, in the Estates General: Noble, Clergy and Commons. What made it difficult for the Estates General to achieve change was the rivalry between the nobility, the clergy and the

---

Henry of Bourbon, Prince of Condé (1588–1646)
Closely related to the King (cousin), he had a claim to the throne if Louis XIII died. Son of Louis de Bourbon; father of Louis II. Henry led a revolt in 1614, but was later reconciled with the King.

Commons. They were all aware how great a problem the assassination of Henry IV had created and they wanted a return to political stability. Only a strong monarchy could provide it.

The potential for serious difficulty for the Monarchy was there, but Marie de' Medici was in her element in the intrigues which surrounded the meetings of the Estates. She was aided by a talented young bishop called Richelieu who proved to be an excellent source of information and advice on how to manage the situation. He was able to play on the social divisions between the three Chambers.

All the Estates were critical of the financial demands of the government and the burden of taxation, but with their separate agendas and demands, Marie was able to divide and rule. The nobles wanted to end the sale of **offices** and the *Paulette* (tax on hereditary purchase of offices). They felt that selling offices for life was creating a semi-noble class, which might start to rival their noble class. The Third Estate, the Commons, attacked the huge pensions which were being paid by Marie to the higher nobility. These pensions naturally came out of the taxes paid by the middle class. For example, the Prince of Condé had been given 4 million livres at the beginning of the reign as a bribe to satisfy his ambitions and greed. Repaying his rebellion with a huge pension naturally appalled the middle class.

Offices: It was common in France to sell jobs, such as tax collectors, to the highest bidder.

King Louis XIII was forced to agree to reforms in response to the demands made on him by the Estates. However, he was able to use the conservative Parlement of Paris (a legal body made up of lawyers, which was required to agree to such legislation) to prevent anything happening later, by getting it to refuse to agree to the reforms.

Another example of Marie's management of the Estates was the conflict between the French clergy (those who wanted French influence to dominate the Catholic Church in France) and the Pope. It indicates her ability to contain a difficult situation. This issue was to cause serious problems later in the century.

The Estates could have resulted in a serious loss of power by the Monarchy, and Marie played an important part in preventing this. She realised that direct confrontation would not succeed, so she relied instead on playing one group off against another. She managed to neutralise the various groups whose demands might have reduced the power of the monarchy.

A portrait of Louis XIII by Justus von Egmont

Why did Marie de' Medici fall from power by 1624?

The internal history of France in the seven years before 1624 is complex. It demonstrates how quickly France could lapse into internal conflict without a strong monarch. Marie had gained confidence from her management of the Estates General and had started to get rid of the services of those who had served her husband well. She promoted the husband of her Italian friend, Carlo Concini, to a senior position at Court. An era of favouritism began. Many would tolerate Marie's power and influence while she behaved rationally. They would not tolerate the rule of a vain Italian man whose sole concern was money. The Prince of Condé and the royal falconer, Charles d'Albert Luynes, plotted together. This led to the public murder of Concini in 1617, and the execution of his wife. Marie was banished to Blois and a young bishop, Armand Richelieu, whom she had promoted to a high position had to depart hurriedly from Court as well. The era of nobles squabbling over who should control the King had begun again.

Louis XIII certainly gained in popularity from the death of Concini, but with the departure of Marie from Court there was an absence of leadership at the top in France. Louis XIII was still very young and although not without some sense, he knew he was not a policy maker. He had no vision of what France might achieve, nor did he have the management skills needed to run a country which was still split religiously and dominated by a powerful nobility. If there was leadership between 1617 and 1621 it came from Luynes, and his period of office was marked by serious internal strife.

War in Europe broke out in 1618, and it had worrying religious and strategic overtones for France. It raised the tension in France, as many Catholics wanted the French monarchy to follow a pro-Catholic policy to help defeat Protestantism in Europe. The cautious Villeroi, who had a role in the making of foreign policy, died in 1617. However, the government was still led by the Chancellor Sillery, who did what he could to put into practice the reforms recommended by the Estates General. These were attempts to make the system of taxation fairer and easier to collect. Sillery skilfully managed the **Assembly of the Notables** in 1617. This led to the abolition of the *Paulette*. The Parlement of Paris was a conservative body resistant to change. They were determined to resist an attack on what they saw as their privileges. They were to prevent any serious reform. An opportunity to start to reform the outdated taxation system of France was lost.

Another serious noble rebellion broke out in 1620, with Condé again playing a dominant part. What his motives were is uncertain. He seemed to have no wish to dominate at Court, as he was neither a courtier nor an administrator. Condé seemed only to want to make his presence felt. He was a traditional 'overmighty subject' with wealth and power, always reluctant to accept any form of control – royal or otherwise. The incompetence of Luynes in both dealing with Condé and a separate Huguenot revolt, which had broken out in Béarn, was very obvious. When he died in 1621 Luynes was not replaced as leading minister. Up to 1621 the Huguenots were peaceful and loyal citizens and had been provoked into unnecessary conflict by incompetence at Court. The Huguenots needed reassurance that their right to worship and to take precautions for their defence were secure. Incompetence at Court prevented this. What further worried the Huguenots was the rise of a group at Court which was pro-Catholic and opposed to the whole idea behind the Edict of Nantes.

Direction at Court after the death of Luynes came as much from Marie de' Medici as from anyone. She was back in favour with her son. The young clergyman who was friendly with her, Richelieu, had effected the reconciliation. By 1622 Marie had restored order, and made peace with the Huguenots at Montpellier. The Huguenots then had to accept a reduction in the fortresses they controlled. They suffered a real blow to their power and defensive ability.

The period 1617–1622 had seen a serious blow to the monarchy in France. The country seemed to have descended into faction fighting and internal religious conflict again. The Crown had become a pawn of a selfish nobility. The religious issue had not gone away and the financial concerns raised by both the Estates General and the Assembly of the Notables had simply been shelved. The Thirty Years' War had started in Europe which worried both Catholic and Protestant Frenchmen. Other Frenchmen such as Richelieu with an eye to the map of Europe could see a serious growth in the power of their old rivals, the Habsburgs, both in the Low Countries and in Germany. There was a further crisis growing in the Valtelline (see map on page 320). This route was the passage for Spanish troops into Germany and up to the Low Countries. It was important that France intervened in order to protect itself. The nearest Louis XIII had to a first minister, at that point in time, Charles Marquis de la Vieuville, mismanaged the negotiations with the Spanish so badly over the Valtelline that France appeared publicly

Assembly of the Notables: A semi-representative body, which tended to represent the higher nobility more than anyone else.

humiliated. The mismanagement of the marriage between Charles of England and a French princess also demonstrated Vieuville's incompetence. Although the marriage took place, there was endless argument over the dowry.

Louis XIII was out of his depth. All he had to assist him was his difficult mother, the ageing Sillery, and nobles like the Prince of Condé who seemed to have no skills other than fighting. Louis XIII realised there was a serious gap in the policy-making processes at Court which needed filling.

Overmighty nobles with a taste for rebellion, growing religious tension between Catholic and Protestant, and the growth of Spanish and Austrian Habsburg power in Europe were leading to a sense of crisis in France. Although no longer a minor, Louis XIII did not appear capable of decisive action and seemed to be dominated by his mother. Major Court appointments were going to those who did not appear competent. Both the Estates General and the Assembly of Notables had made it clear that there was a need for social and economic reform, but nothing was being done about that either.

1. Explain the reasons for the growth in instability in France after the death of Henry IV.

2. How effective was Marie de' Medici as Regent?

14.2 Why did Richelieu become the First Minister and how was he able to establish himself in power?

There are several reasons why Richelieu became First Minister (chief minister) in 1624. His father having served Henry III as a minister. His father's intention had been for the young Richelieu to adopt the conventional noble career of soldiering, but when the 'family' bishopric of Luçon became vacant in 1607, he got it with the backing of Henry IV. Unlike some of those who gained promotion in the Church because of their family connections rather than their beliefs and suitability, Richelieu proved to be an able bishop. He was one of those who ensured that the revived and reformed Catholicism of the Council of Trent was implemented in his diocese. He rapidly gained a reputation as an able and sincere reformer. Richelieu was ambitious and tried to gain further office at Court on the death of Henry IV. He hoped that his Catholic background might now carry more weight than at the Court of the 'politique' and formerly Protestant, Henry IV.

'Politique': Name given to those who did not take the division between Catholic and Protestant too seriously.

Richelieu first came to official notice during the complex politics surrounding the meeting of the Estates General in 1614. He managed to ingratiate himself well with both Marie de' Medici and Carlo Concini, then the dominant figures at Court. He was seen as an important defender of the Church and a noted praiser of Marie. He demonstrated his political and negotiating skills in discussions in 1616 to end the dispute between Condé, Marie and the young King. Mainly by ingratiating himself with Marie, Richelieu gained the promotion he longed for in 1616, as Secretary of State. He had responsibility for war and foreign affairs.

Armand Jean du Plessis Richelieu (1585–1642)
The third son of minor noble, he became Bishop of Luçon (which was in the family gift) at the age of 22. In 1614, while giving an address in the Estates General, he caught the attention of Marie de' Medici (the Regent) who gave him a minor post in the royal council. Richelieu became a cardinal in 1622, retaining his position in the royal council. Then, from 1624 until his death, he was the First Minister in France (*principal ministre*). He was responsible for administering the Crown's domestic affairs and assisting Louis XII in his foreign policy. Liked to think of himself as indispensable.

It is easy to criticise Richelieu for what can be seen as an attempt to grovel his way into power, but it must have taken skill on his part to rise in an atmosphere of intrigue and plot. Marie, for all her failings, spotted the obvious talent of Richelieu and supported his rise.

Richelieu had a chance to demonstrate his skill briefly in raising and administrating royal armies against noble troublemakers in 1617. However, he was abruptly and rudely dismissed when Concini fell from power. He was fortunate not to be torn apart by the mob which was engaged in tearing the corpse of Concini to pieces in the streets of Paris. Politics was a dangerous game in early 17th-century France. Richelieu learned a lot in his first period at Court.

Richelieu went into internal exile with Marie at Blois, but took care to correspond with Luynes, the latest royal favourite. In spite of a further banishment in 1619 to Avignon, Richelieu still managed to keep his name in the minds of those who mattered. Again it was his skill as a negotiator that brought him back to royal attention in 1621. He was Marie's representative in the complex negotiations that led to the reconciliation between the King and his mother, which subsequently led to her return to Court. Richelieu returned to Court as well, as part of the agreement. When Cardinal de Retz died in 1622, Richelieu's reward was the dead Cardinal's rank at the personal request of the King to the Pope.

Richelieu was not personally close to the King until 1624. As the inability of Vieuville to provide leadership and policies was becoming more and more apparent, notice of this was encouraged by a sophisticated propaganda campaign secretly inspired by Richelieu himself. As a result, Richelieu came back on the Council. The King rapidly accepted him as his leading minister. The fact that both the major court factions of *devots* and **Gallicans** supported and respected Richelieu is a tribute to the cardinal's ability to appear as all things to all men.

The key reasons for Richelieu becoming First Minister were as follows.

Devots: People who were actively Catholic and in favour of Papal power.

Gallicans: Those who favoured the policy of France controlling its own Church.

- He was able and it showed.

- He was a competent administrator, as had been shown in his work in Luçon and at Court earlier.

- He was an extremely skilled player in the art of court politics.

- He was not only a man of ideas, but also a man of action.

- He had confidence in himself and in his own ideas.

- He was a clever manipulator of both men and opinion.

- He had an excellent working knowledge of the machinery of 17th-century French politics.

- He had an excellent understanding of the psychology and motivation of his enemies and friends, his inferiors and, most importantly, his superiors.

- He had identified himself to the King – who had dismissed him scornfully a few years earlier – as very different from the incompetent or greedy courtier solely out for fame and fortune (such as Concini, Luynes or Vieuville).

- Richelieu's understanding of the young King and his mother were excellent. He had the ability to be friendly with them both at different times.

- He knew what was worrying the monarch in 1624 and convinced the King that he was the man to ease those worries.

- Richelieu was able to convince the King that he was the man who had the vision and the administrative skills to overcome the problems facing France in the 1620s.

- His loyalty to the monarchy and his desire to strengthen it was made very clear. He knew just how to calm the fears and suspicion of the King.

Once in power Richelieu then had to ensure that he stayed there, while at the same time dealing with the large range of political, religious, social, economic and international problems that faced France.

Louis XIII was no fool in the sense that he knew he was out of his depth. Many of the obvious solutions to his and France's problems were becoming apparent in the 14 years between the death of his father and the arrival of Richelieu as chief minister. However, Louis lacked the confidence in his own ability to implement the necessary policies. He realised that, however much he personally disliked Richelieu, they actually shared similar ambitions for both the monarchy and France. He knew that Richelieu had the political skills to carry them out. Richelieu was not a threat. In fact, he had become a necessity.

> **1. Explain the reasons why Richelieu became First Minister in 1624.**
>
> **2. To what extent did Richelieu become chief minister through his own skill?**

14.3 *What were the aims of French foreign policy to 1631 and to what extent were they successful?*
A CASE STUDY IN HISTORICAL INTERPRETATION

One of the reasons behind the appointment of Cardinal Richelieu was the inability of his predecessors to manage the foreign policy of France effectively. There had been dissatisfaction over the English marriage, which had not brought benefits to Catholics in England as hoped. This had also led to a row over the dowry. There was real concern over the growth of Spanish power. By 1624, Spanish and Austrian Habsburg power was increasing throughout Europe. Protestant forces had been defeated in Bohemia by 1621 by the Austrian Habsburgs. This did not formally affect Catholic France but it did cause concern as it led to a further growth of Habsburg power. The rivalry between France and the Habsburgs was centuries old. Not only was Spain becoming more of a force in Italy, but by 1624 it was clearly on the ascendant in the Netherlands with General Spínola pressing back the Protestant Dutch. The Habsburg ring seemed to be tightening. With the growth of Habsburg power, it was inevitable that France should feel threatened (see map on page 320).

Richelieu's international aims have been the subject of many debates. They can be described as being to raise the status of France in Europe and to end Habsburg supremacy. Historians like Robin Briggs, in *Early Modern France* (1977), argue that Richelieu was motivated primarily by 'outright hostility to Spain'. He saw the conflict as part of a long-established rivalry that went back centuries. The marriage between the sister of Louis XIII and the heir to the English throne, as well as the alliance with the Protestant Dutch, were all part of this anti-Spanish feeling of Richelieu. The same applies to Richelieu's intervention in the Valtelline. Briggs does admit that 'Richelieu's intentions at times remain surprisingly obscure' and that he could be simply 'opportunistic' (taking advantage of whatever opportunity presents itself and not working to a specific long-term plan).

The historian W. E. Brown, in *The First Bourbon Century in France* (1971), argues that Richelieu's anti-Spanish views can be overestimated. Richelieu correctly guessed that the unity of the Habsburgs was neither strong nor to be feared. Brown maintains that much of Richelieu's foreign policy is simple aggression and that he was anxious to take over territories that belonged to other countries. Ultimately, Richelieu wanted the ascendancy of France in Europe.

Y-M Berce, a leading French historian, maintains in *The Birth of Absolutism: France 1598–1661* (1996) that much of the anti-Spanish feeling which dominated French foreign policy in the period came from Louis XIII, rather than Richelieu. Louis and Richelieu shared the fear that Spain was out for world domination. Berce quotes Richelieu as saying 'our overriding objective must always remain to impede the progress of Spain'. He suggests that Richelieu was more defensive in approach than his master. Richelieu was more interested in gaining the balance of power in Europe, with no one power dominating, but if he could make France into a great influence then he would take whatever opportunity came along.

Historian R. Wilkinson, in *France and the Cardinals* (1995), states it more simply. Maintaining that Richelieu simply wanted to cut the Habsburgs down to size, and ensure France's 'security', he writes that 'Richelieu's so-called foreign policy was therefore in practice just a war policy'.

The major biographer of Richelieu in English (published in 1991), R. J. Knecht, is probably the least assertive about Richelieu's aims. He maintains that 'Richelieu's foreign policy motives are an open book'. At times Knecht stresses Richelieu's fear of Habsburg encirclement portrays his policy as primarily defensive. At other times he feels Richelieu was exaggerating the possible threat from Spain in order to rally support for a more aggressive foreign policy which he really believed in. Ultimately, Knecht describes Richelieu's work as being with 'careful limited objectives pursued with a steady eye to what was essential'. Richelieu was never keen

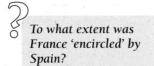

To what extent was France 'encircled' by Spain?

France's position in Europe, 1610

to be a leader of the Counter Reformation in Europe. He was criticised for that by many in France who would have preferred a more aggressively Catholic policy. Richelieu had been a good supporter of the Counter or Catholic Reformation when Bishop of Luçon, but he placed the prestige of France and the destruction of Habsburg power above religious interests. There was also an element of a personal quarrel between Richelieu and Count-Duke Olivares, the chief minister of Philip of Spain.

How did Richelieu deal with the Valtelline issue?

Richelieu's first real task in foreign policy was to deal with the issue of the Valtelline. This was the key route known as the 'Spanish Road'. By this route the Spanish could keep up their attempt to destroy the Dutch rebels. With limited command of the sea route up the Channel, this had become a vital route for Spanish control. Naturally the French were worried by a further growth in Spanish power to the north. If Spain were to recapture Holland, with its huge resources of both shipping and colonies, it would be a devastating blow to French prestige and power. The opportunity of threatening Spanish communications was too important to lose. With growing Spanish power in northern Italy as well, where they were trying to build up a power base, Richelieu felt they had to be stopped.

Grisons: Those who lived in the higher parts of the vital passes and valleys in the Valtelline area.

The political situation in the Valtelline area was complex. A group known as the **Grisons** were mainly Protestant. They were the dominant political force and the landowners. Those who lived in the lower valleys were Roman Catholics. In the 1620s the 'valley' Catholics had revolted and expelled their Protestant masters, the Grisons, with the aid of Spain and Milan. Milan and its surrounding area had come under Spanish control. Naturally once in possession the Spanish had stayed there, wishing to keep control of such a vital route for their troops. However, they had handed over peacekeeping duties to the more neutral Papal troops.

Richelieu started trying to get rid of the Papal troops in 1624, seeing them as agents of the Spanish. He was initially successful, replacing the Papal troops with French ones. Things looked even more promising when he allied with the ambitious and pro-French Duke of Piedmont and Savoy. But when the Duke tried to increase his territory by taking Genoa, he was badly beaten. At the Treaty of Monzon in 1626, Richelieu had to accept a return to the situation at the start in both the Valtelline and in northern Italy. His first step in foreign affairs had achieved little.

Although Richelieu's propaganda machine hailed it all as a victory, in fact he had not done well. Richelieu was furious because he had had to weaken his forces by having to return to deal with the Huguenots in France who were in rebellion. The passes remained open to Spain and the Spanish troops, who were to prove so vital in the defeat of the Swedish army at Nördlingen (see Chapter 15), passed through the Valtelline. The possible allies of France in Italy, such as Venice and Savoy, were not impressed by this poor demonstration of French power, nor were the Dutch who might well be useful in a conflict with Spain. Another factor that also partially saved Richelieu was that Olivares did not want a war with France at that stage. However, a clear signal had been sent to Europe and the Habsburgs that France was back in the game.

How effectively did Richelieu deal with the Mantuan Succession Crisis of 1628–1631?

Richelieu's second major involvement in foreign policy followed soon after, and it was again in the same part of the world. In 1627 the Duke of Mantua died leaving no obvious heir. The strategic importance of the area is obvious (see map on page 324). A base in Mantua would enable the French to threaten Spanish communications in the areas and expand their own influence in the rich lands of northern Italy. What made the area even more important was the fact that there were vital forts at Mantua and Casale. The latter was close to Milan and was a key element in Spanish dominance in northern Italy. There were two possible claimants to the throne: the first was the French Duke of Nevers, backed by France and by the Pope.

Richelieu showed strong diplomatic skills, particularly when backed by the talents of the monk Père Joseph, one of his key agents. Joseph was important in winning over the Pope. The Spanish also had a candidate, their supporter in Italy, Charles Emmanuel of Savoy.

The French claimant started by seizing the territory with French backing. Even though badly distracted by plots, Huguenots and severe money shortages, Richelieu had to intervene. Many of the *devots* were not happy with such an apparently anti-Catholic policy. They saw the Spanish leading the Counter Reformation in Europe, so this policy caused divisions at home. The King was made to choose between war and peace, and choose the former. It was not an easy step to take, as by 1629 the Spanish and Imperial forces seemed to be on the rise. They had destroyed the Protestant forces led by the Danes and were now expanding into the Baltic, as well as on the Rhine.

At the instigation of Richelieu, open war between France and Spain broke out. By 1629 Richelieu and Louis XIII had put a full army of 35,000 men into northern Italy to stop the Spanish taking the fortress of Casale and dominating the entire area. The French had to retreat back over the Alps in a hurry in 1630 when a Spanish army, under General Spínola, arrived. The conflict continued with major French successes in taking the vital forts of Pinerolo and Saluzzo. They also defeated a combined Piedmontese and Savoyard army at Avigliano in 1630. But Mantua itself was captured and looted by the Spanish, and it looked as if the tide was about to turn in favour of Spain.

However fortune favoured the French as both the Spanish claimant and their key general, Spínola, died. The Swedish King, Gustavus Adolphus, landed a Protestant army on the north German shores of the Baltic and this distracted the Habsburgs. With the French army close to exhaustion, both sides were keen on a settlement. An able Papal agent, Jules Mazarin, negotiated a treaty between France and Spain. This led to a peace being signed at Cherasco in 1631 with the French gaining the fortress of Pinerolo.

Gains had been made in Italy, French prestige had started to rise in Europe and Spanish power and ambitions had been curtailed in northern Italy. Also, a French supporter was now in place in an important strategic area. As far as Spain was concerned, the Mantuan affair was a sideshow. It was much more concerned with Holland and central and northern Europe at the time. There may have been some slight territorial and strategic gain for France, but more worrying was that Spain and Austria were now both working more closely together, and their combined powers were awesome.

Summary

The affairs in the Valtelline and Mantua were part of an important learning process for Richelieu and Louis XIII. Although neither affair was very successful, at least there was no humiliation for France. The need for a powerful army was made very obvious. France was definitely not ready for a major confrontation with the mighty Habsburgs. However, a statement of intent had been made.

1. What were Richelieu's aims in foreign policy up to 1631?

2. What did France gain and what did it lose by Richelieu's foreign policy before 1631?

3. Why have historians disagreed over the aims of Richelieu's foreign policy before 1631?

14.4 Did Richelieu's later foreign policy achieve its objectives?

Père Joseph (1577–1638)
Religious name of François Joseph le Clerc du Tremblay, a Capuchin monk. He came from an aristocratic background. Joseph was a personal friend of Cardinal Richelieu. He was strongly anti-Habsburg as they would not back his idea of a crusade against the Turks. Richelieu used him as a negotiator in foreign policy and listened to him, unwisely, on economic matters. Richelieu probably intended him as his successor. Père Joseph's nickname was *L'Eminence Grise* (the 'Grey Eminence') in reference to his grey habit (monk's outfit).

Richelieu's diplomatic offensive against the Habsburgs started in 1630. At the Imperial Diet at Regensburg in 1630, the Emperor intended to get the German electors to elect his son as King of the Romans, making his succession as Emperor almost inevitable. However with the Battle of Lütter in 1626 (where the Protestant Danes were defeated by Catholic forces) and the 1629 Edict of Restitution in the background, the sophisticated diplomacy of Père Joseph prevented that. Père Joseph managed to persuade the German princes that France might be a suitable protector of their interests.

The arrival on the north German coast in 1630 of Gustavus Adolphus was an important defining moment for Richelieu and France. It was a complex situation in that, while Richelieu was delighted to see an ally against the growing Habsburg encirclement threat, it was difficult for Catholic France to work with him too openly, as Gustavus' aims were so obviously Protestant.

Gustavus' real aims in invading Germany are discussed in Chapter 12. An alliance with the Swedish King had mixed blessings. For a start, Richelieu knew that there was a fairly powerful group in France who wished to see Catholicism supreme in Europe and who felt that support for the Habsburg policy of exterminating Protestantism in Europe was a proper course for France. Helping Protestant Sweden gain German Protestant allies and smash the militant forces of the Counter Reformation was not supposed to be the task of a French Roman Catholic Cardinal.

Richelieu's conscience could be eased by the fact that Olivares, the Spanish First Minister, had supported French Protestants against Louis XIII in earlier years, so this might be seen as fair retaliation. Also, Richelieu tended to get on well with the anti-Habsburg Pope, Urban VIII, so he could be seen as having some 'divine' backing.

Richelieu's agent, Baron de Charnace, negotiated an agreement with Gustavus Adolphus. It seemed to be a contradictory policy he was pursuing. His overall aim, if he had one, was preventing Habsburg supremacy in Europe; as a result he could not be too choosy over his allies. Richelieu would have preferred Roman Catholic Bavaria as an ally against the Habsburgs, but he had to make do with Gustavus Adolphus who was anxious to put the Elector Frederick back on the Palatinate throne. (Maximilian of Bavaria had received this as the price for his support at the Battle of the White Mountain in 1620.) One of the major causes of the Thirty Years' War was when Bohemian subjects of the Habsburg Emperor revolted against his rule, and asked the Protestant ruler of part of Germany, the Elector of Palatine, to rule over them.

There was also a Franco–Bavarian alliance in 1631, which is a good illustration of Richelieu's thinking at the time. The two countries agreed not to aid the enemies of each other. In return for Richelieu agreeing to support Maximilian's attempt to obtain more voting rights for imperial elections, Maximilian agreed not to assist the Habsburgs against France. French diplomacy was becoming complex, as well as contradictory.

How did the Treaty of Barwalde alter the balance of power in Europe?

The Treaty of Barwalde in 1631 between France and the Swedes changed the balance of power in Europe. The Baltic was now secure for the Swedes, and Richelieu now had an ally operating with a large army in his Habsburg enemy's rear. However, Gustavus was not a reliable ally. There is no sign of any grand plan on Richelieu's part here. His main ambitions lay in northern Italy at the time. To see Richelieu's agreement with Gustavus as part of a carefully planned strategy would be completely mistaken; it was a rushed gamble by a desperate man who had given little thought to the implications of this decision. There were parts of it he would live to regret, particularly when Gustavus started getting imperial ambitions of his own in Germany. It actually worked, but not in the way Richelieu intended. In fact, he was deeply relieved when Gustavus was killed at Lützen in 1632 and Sweden became more of a manageable ally. A Swedish Protestant triumph was not part of Richelieu's plans. His motives bebame clear when Père Joseph was sent to negotiate with Albrecht von Wallenstein and Bavaria against Gustavus early in 1632.

The Battle of Breitenfeld in 1631, when a Swedish army destroyed a Catholic and Imperial army, terrified Richelieu. If anyone was going to be the champion of German princes against the Emperor then Richelieu wanted it to be himself.

Richelieu was getting progressively more aggressive and sure of himself.

A map of France in the 17th century

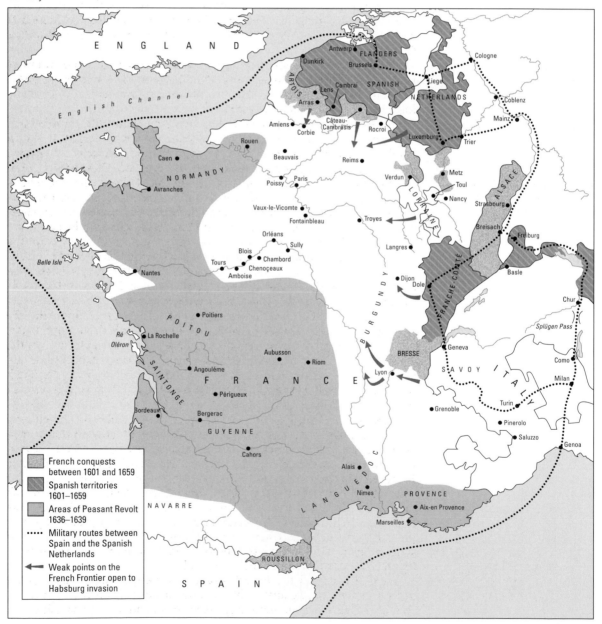

Lorraine was taken by his forces in 1631 and a year later he joined with the Swedes in occupying Trier (see map opposite). Negotiations were opened with the Protestant Dutch in 1634, leading to a treaty of alliance in 1635. Another treaty followed with the Protestant League of Heilbronn (a group of German princes committed to defeating the Emperor and preserving Protestantism). It was a long and hard struggle. With the Swedish army beaten at Nördlingen in 1634 and Gustavus killed earlier at the Battle of Lützen, it was necessary for France to take on the leadership of the anti-Habsburg coalition and abandon what pretence there was of it being a war of religion. Germany now became a battlefield between France and its Habsburg enemies. It would have suited Richelieu's anti-Habsburg ambitions if Gustavus had lived a little longer and had finally reached Vienna and destroyed the Emperor at home, but he had served his purpose.

The Battle of Nördlingen has been called a 'disaster' for Richelieu's policy, but it certainly meant that if he wished to defeat the Habsburgs he could not sit on the sidelines and get someone else to do the work. For the first time under Richelieu, France had no serious allies and few friends. It had to take on the full force of Spain and its Empire, as well as the German emperor, on its own.

It became a **war of attrition**. There were both disasters and triumphs for France, which continued until after the death of Richelieu in 1642. They were not finally resolved until peace was made in 1659 by Richelieu's **protégé**, Cardinal Mazarin.

France was always chronically short of money with which to develop a large army and there were always nobles and even members of the Royal family who did not see working with the Habsburgs to further their own dynastic ambitions, or put down Richelieu, as treason. The Spanish could still mount a powerful army and in the **Cardinal Infanta** they had a first-rate general, as Nördlingen showed. In the course of 1635 and 1636 the French suffered many defeats: in the Netherlands they were driven back, and the gains they had made earlier in Alsace and Trier were lost as well.

The year 1636 produced a real crisis when a Spanish army from the Netherlands got within 80 miles of Paris. If it had not been for Louis XIII keeping his nerve, then the panic-stricken Richelieu might have been driven out of Paris. It was the long supply lines and Spain's difficulty in finding both the men and the money to pay for a war that saved France, not Richelieu's leadership. Given the number and range of allies, and the population and resources of France, Richelieu should have done better but he was not a great wartime administrator. Some naval victories in the Channel, under the unlikely leadership of Archbishop Sourdis, helped weaken Spain, but the Spanish remained powerful. A further Spanish invasion from the south in 1637, across the Pyrenees, was driven off with difficulty.

It was a major struggle on Richelieu's part to keep an over-ambitious war going. With the war costing more each year, and with government income falling but the cost of collecting it rising, more offices were sold and the currency was devalued. Keeping six armies, which Richelieu did, was bleeding France dry. What is more, by 1638 none of the armies had been successful. The only glimmer of hope lay outside France, with the Grisons making life difficult for the Spanish trying to move troops into northern Europe. The loss of the Spanish fleet in 1639 and the revolt of Catalonia (a major Spanish province) and Portugal (then a Spanish possession) in 1640 did a lot to weaken Spain. Certainly, these internal factors did more to harm Spanish fighting capacity than the French army did.

What also helped the French cause was the growing Dutch military success against the Spanish. This tied down more Spanish troops there. The Dutch also became more aggressive at sea, attacking Spanish ships.

War of attrition: Process whereby one side simply tries to grind down and exhaust the other first.

Protégé: One who has had their career advanced by someone in power.

Cardinal Infanta: Leading member of the Spanish royal family; also a cardinal in the Roman Catholic Church.

A new Swedish army was organised by Axel Oxenstierna, the Swedish Chancellor, and that helped to weaken Spain. Also, the Protestant forces in Germany were being well led by a competent Protestant general, Bernard of Saxe Weimar. The Habsburgs started to do badly in the Thirty Years' War in northern Europe by 1640. The poor quality of Imperial generals after the deaths of Spínola, Wallenstein and the Cardinal Infanta also proved to be helpful to Richelieu's cause.

Quite what Richelieu was trying to achieve by 1640 is unclear. Possibly he was simply out to defeat the Habsburgs. Another possibility could be an ambition to expand to the 'natural' frontiers of France or even to the Rhine. There is also debate as to whether his motivation was essentially aggressive or defensive. It seems that he had limited territorial and anti-Habsburg objectives. He was prepared to use diplomacy and other people, such as Gustavus Adolphus, to achieve his objectives. Richelieu would only get involved when absolutely necessary.

By 1640 an exhausted Spain offered peace, but Richelieu declined. In fact, he became an obstacle to peace in Europe. He did not want to keep up alliances with Protestant powers and he hated the damage to the economy of France that war was causing, but he was determined to destroy the enemy and undermine the chance of Habsburg supremacy. He wanted to ensure that its power was destroyed forever.

There were French gains in Arras and Picardy in 1640–44. Peace with Lorraine was achieved, as well as partial integration. The real military triumph came after Richelieu's death when the Prince of Condé's son finally defeated the Spanish at the **Battle of Rocroi** in 1643. This was the first major defeat of the Spanish army for many decades. The war was to drag on until 1659, at a huge cost to France.

Battle of Rocroi: In May 1643 a strong Spanish army crossed from Germany, through the Ardennes mountains, into northern France. The Duc d'Enghein commanded the French army. They destroyed the Spanish army. There were 8,000 dead Spanish soldiers and 7,000 captured.

1. In what ways did Richelieu's foreign policy after 1631 differ from his earlier policy?

2. 'Wasteful and it achieved nothing for France'. Discuss this view of Richelieu's foreign policy from 1624 to 1642.

What had been gained by the time of Richelieu's death?

By the time of Richelieu's death in 1642 France had been seriously weakened economically and the First Minister had placed it under huge strain, which was to explode within a few years. France had certainly gained respect as a major European power. There were territorial gains in Artois and the slow grinding down of Spain and Austria had started. Richelieu had got a small toehold in Italy and some territory around Roussilion. It was perhaps a poor legacy to leave to his successor, Cardinal Mazarin.

14.5 What were the strengths and weaknesses of Richelieu's domestic policies?

Why were the Huguenots seen as a problem?

Many Frenchmen saw the Edict of Nantes of 1598, which had brought the French Wars of Religion to an end, as more of a truce than an end to a long conflict. No European society was yet mature enough to cope with tolerating such religious divisions in one community. England was perhaps exceptional in having a monarch like Elizabeth who had no wish 'to open windows into men's souls', but she was exceptional. Besides, anti-Catholicism was still a feature of English society well into the 19th century.

Richelieu inherited a problem with the Huguenots and it was clear that he was expected to deal with it. The Huguenots were particularly strong in certain areas of France. As recent research suggests, they formed about 5%–6% of the population at the time (earlier estimates had placed it as low as 3% or as high as 10%). The Huguenots had both noble support and were strong in heavily commercial areas. The Edict of Nantes had made them into a privileged group and many Catholics resented this. Richelieu himself did not believe in enforced conversion of Protestants to Catholicism, but as a bishop he had been involved in a fair amount of persuasion to convert, and with some success. He was prepared to tolerate those Protestants who obeyed the law and the authority of the Crown, which was unusual. This tolerance was to gain him criticism later from more ardent Catholics. There were plenty of Huguenots who saw a limited future for themselves in France.

Louis XIII was keen to eliminate the Huguenots. He had been furious at the willingness of the Huguenots to involve themselves in the revolts against royal authority in Béarn and Navarre in 1620. Louis XIII had played a personal role in the suppression of those revolts. The ability of the Huguenots to arm themselves quickly and to rally noble support was worrying, and the strength of the 200 or so fortified areas granted to them by the Edict of Nantes made the suppression of this revolt extremely difficult. The fact that the Huguenots tended to look to republican Geneva for support did not go down well with a monarch with hopes of 'divine' rule. The republicanism of the Calvinist Dutch (identical to the Huguenots) naturally led to unfortunate comparisons. The existence of the Huguenots and the rights granted to them went against the theory of monarchy then present in France. It also went against the accepted principle of *cuius regio eius religio* then prevalent in much of Europe, where it was felt vital for the stability and security of the state that the people and the monarch should worship in the same way. This principle, established in Germany at the Peace of Augsburg in 1555, tried to bring the first set of European religious wars to an end.

Cuius regio eius religio: Latin expression that suggests that the religion of the ruler should be the religion of the population he or she rules.

Some success in repressing the Huguenots as a major military force had been achieved in 1621–22. Several Huguenot fortified towns lost their right to have fortifications. However, there were times when the King was personally humiliated by the failings of his own troops against the Huguenots. The king's favourite, Luynes, actually died while organising a siege against a fortified Huguenot town, Montauban. A peace with the Huguenots was agreed at Montpellier in 1622; while the Edict of Nantes was confirmed, some Huguenot garrisons agreed to be cut. Louis XIII and many at Court saw the Montpellier agreement as little more than a truce, and were obviously determined not to tolerate such a potentially disruptive force within the kingdom. In fact, the majority of the Huguenots recognised that their future was probably limited, given the growth of the Jesuits in France and the rise of Cardinals like Richelieu to power. They were keen to compromise as much as possible. It was the action of a few 'hotheads' that led to the conflict that broke out at La Rochelle.

The La Rochelle Huguenot Revolt, 1625

The possible defeat of Protestantism in Europe naturally worried the Huguenots in the 1620s and made them more militant. This was a major issue by the time Richelieu came to power in 1624. In many respects he was not the originator of policy. Richelieu inherited a firmly anti-Huguenot policy. There was a strong *devot* party in France, which acted as a pressure group to ensure that a Catholic policy was carried out, both in domestic and foreign policy. They were unhappy with Richelieu's dislike for the Catholic Habsburgs and later tendency to ally with Protestant powers.

By 1625 La Rochelle, one of the great Huguenot strongholds, was in open revolt. It remained so until 1628. The Huguenots were prepared to gain foreign support, mainly from their fellow Protestants in England. However, the combination of limited resources of both James and Charles of England, the lack of any strong naval or army support from a weak England and the remarkable incompetence as a military commander of the Duke of Buckingham, led to that support achieving little. English support did, however, reinforce the view of Richelieu and his master, as well as many other French Catholics, that the Huguenots could not remain in the privileged state left to them by the Edict of Nantes. This applied especially to them living in towns they fortified.

Whereas Richelieu was more content to see the Huguenots as a political problem because they had revolted, others saw them as a threat to the dominance of Roman Catholicism in France. Richelieu was also furious with the impetuous Huguenots of La Rochelle, because he had to divert a large amount of his limited military resources to deal with this internal threat. He had wished to use those forces to prevent the growth of Habsburg power. The last thing he wanted to do was fight his own countrymen. There was agreement in most of France and within the Court in Paris that the Huguenots had to be broken as a possible threat, and their willingness to look to England or Spain for support merely added to this.

Richelieu personally supervised the long siege of La Rochelle. In 1625 he led a three-pronged attack on the town from land and sea. He also enforced a rigid blockade to prevent any food or support getting in. His commitment and presence managing the siege were vital to its success. Military historians pay tribute to Richelieu's skill and dogged resistance. His final victory at La Rochelle was important in gaining the confidence of the King and his own position was certainly more secure as a result of carrying out the King's wishes.

What information does this engraving contain about warfare in the early 17th century?

Engraving showing the siege of La Rochelle in 1628

By 1628 Richelieu had won and the fortifications were destroyed. He was lenient with the rebels, and he had no wish to destroy a potentially profitable seaport. There was some savagery, as is inevitable in civil wars, but Richelieu insisted that the rebels at La Rochelle were treated with respect. The usual rules of allowing the sacking and looting of a town that had resisted a siege and ignored offers of surrender were not put into practice. Richelieu realised it would only have produced a backlash.

Over the next 12 months or so, military force was used to destroy the Huguenot power bases in the rest of France. One of their main leaders, Rohan (Sully's son-in-law) was defeated at Privas in 1629, and the Treaty of Alès was made with the Huguenots. The religious tolerance of the Edict of Nantes was confirmed, but the political and military privileges were removed. The fear of a state within a state was no longer there, and an intelligent peace ensured the loyalty of a small, but economically significant, part of the population. It was a major move towards political and economic unity in France. The legal and religious privileges of the Huguenots remained, and their rights to retain their churches and synods were also left alone. Richelieu was enough of a realist to attain not only what was needed but also what was possible. He needed Protestant allies in Europe against the Habsburgs, and gaining a reputation as a butcher of Protestants was not going to help this. It was a major step towards **absolutism** in France. It increased Richelieu's reputation as a leader and an organiser, and it removed a barrier to the further growth of royal power. Missionary work to convert the Huguenots to Catholicism met with some success. They remained loyal, and Richelieu was to develop a liking for Rohan as a military leader. He later used him effectively in the wars against Spain.

Absolutism: Political system in which one ruler or leader has complete power and authority over the country.

How did Richelieu deal with the nobility and the royal family?

The conventional view of the years when Richelieu dominated France – between 1624 and 1642 – is that he was constantly bothered by a large number of serious plots against both himself and the degree of absolutism that he was trying to impose on France in the King's name. The aims of these plots were partly to remove Richelieu from Court, and partly to have him replaced at the centre of power by whoever was doing the plotting. Another aim of the plots was to prevent the growth of centralised royal power so that the nobles, who had tasted a degree of freedom during the Wars of Religion, could behave as they wished. Many of the nobility wished to maintain a right to rebel. Although they were not opposed to a monarchy, the monarchy they wished to see would tolerate any behaviour by the nobility that liked to see itself above the law in all respects. An outsider might well see this type of noble behaviour as treason, but it was not viewed as such in France. It has already been seen in the case of Rohan, the Huguenot leader who was defeated in 1629. He had returned to a state of comparative loyalty, and fought with great vigour for France.

During the Wars of Religion neither side had felt any shame about getting support from foreign powers, be it England or Spain, in order to wage war in France against the lawful monarch with whom they happened to disagree. Certainly, in Louis XIII's reign there were plenty of examples of treasonable rebellion led by relatives of the King. They ranged from his own mother to his younger brother, Gaston. They were never seriously out to replace the King. Their aim seems to have been to make their presence felt and assert their rights. The main aim of most of the noble rebels was personal ambition and greed. They were upset by the fact that the King took advice from Richelieu and not them. The fact that they might have little advice to give and no desire to stay at Court and administer France seems irrelevant. The lack of any unity or clear policies on their part indicates that they were not the threat to royal absolutism or to Richelieu that has sometimes been made out.

Certainly the more traditional English biographers of Richelieu, such as R. J. Knecht and G. R. Treasure, place a lot of stress on the noble plots against Richelieu and the closeness to destruction he came with some of them. Stress has also been placed on the skill with which Richelieu defeated these threats to himself and royal power, and how fortunate he was in having a master, Louis XIII, so willing to back him against all comers. More general surveys of the period in English, such as Robin Briggs' *Early Modern France* and R. Wilkinson's *France and the Cardinals* (1995) tend to echo this. However, recent French writing, such as Y-M Berce's *The Birth of Absolutism: France 1598–1661* and A. Jouanna's *The Right to Revolt* go in a different direction, indicating that the plots were not a serious threat to Richelieu or the rise of absolutism. French studies of Richelieu tend not to spend much time on them.

Richelieu's intention was to increase royal power at the expense of the nobility's freedom of action. This was naturally disliked. Richelieu's ability to place his own relatives and friends in positions of power and wealth also caused much resentment. The nobles wanted that right. It was mainly an 'in' versus the 'outs' quarrel; it should not be seen as the same as a quarrel between two parties with differing policies and beliefs. At times, some of Richelieu's noble opponents used his anti-Catholic and anti-Habsburg policy as a slogan against him. If they had stuck with it consistently they might have had some success, but in many cases there was little in their work that was anything more than naked ambition.

Richelieu was completely loyal to the French Monarchy and his master, Louis XIII. He expected the same from all others. This was a new idea in 17th-century France. If people behaved correctly and along these lines, they were rewarded.

How serious was the Chalais Conspiracy of 1626?

The first serious attack on Richelieu, in 1626, was known as the Chalais Conspiracy. It was not dissimilar to several that followed. A key player was Louis' younger brother, Gaston d'Orléans, who was the heir apparent. Gaston was erratic, impulsive and self-centred. He had a limited capacity for intrigue and a constant feeling that his views should be taken seriously, when in fact he had nothing of value to offer and no vision at all for France. He was simply waiting for his brother to die. Louis never trusted him, and Gaston's ability to betray anyone at any time did not endear him to many. It also made it easier for Richelieu to manage him.

In 1626 Gaston was unhappy as an attempt was being made to wed him to women he did not wish to marry. As Louis XIII still had no son and heir (the future Louis XIV was not born until 1638), the marriage of the heir apparent was of great importance. A small group around Gaston started plotting to remove Richelieu. It included other great nobles who were related to the King, such as the Prince of Condé, the Duke of Conti and Madame de Chevreuse, the widow of Luynes and the lover of a young nobleman, Henri de Talleyrand (the Marquis de Chalais).

The nobility was essentially a class that did little serious work; some had little else to do but plot. There were also no open channels of opposition. It was not seen as politically correct either to manage one's estates or to get involved in commerce. Quite what the Marquis de Chalais and his fellow conspirators hoped to achieve is not clear. It has been suggested that they wished to put Gaston on the throne, but there is little hard evidence of this. Certainly replacing Richelieu and possibly killing him in the same way that Concini was killed was on their agenda. There seems to have been no desire

Gaston d'Orléans (1608–1660)

Idle and weak character. Always a focus for rebellions, although not usually willing to attack his older brother directly. Involved in the Chalais Conspiracy and other plots. Went into exile between 1631 and 1634. Invaded France against his brother in 1632. Gaston played a more sensible and supportive role during the early reign of his nephew, Louis XIV.

to change any policy or implement one of their own. Richelieu knew of the plot, through his sophisticated spy network. Chalais was arrested and soon revealed all the various ideas of the plotters. He was executed in a way designed to cause maximum pain and act as a deterrent. Louis XIII willingly backed Richelieu in the use of barbaric methods as he wished to show that he had full confidence in his minister. Other minor plotters were exiled. It did not seem to act as much of a deterrent, however.

What was the importance of the Duelling Episode of 1627?

Duelling: Fighting, to the death if need be, between two nobles over some dispute – often trivial.

The Chalais Conspiracy was followed by what was seen, both at the time and since, as a further attempt by Richelieu to turn the French nobility into more useful citizens. **Duelling** was not uncommon among nobles. Not only did it lead to the deaths of many possible future leaders, it also resulted in major family vendettas (feuds) which could cause a serious breakdown of law and order. Richelieu banned it in 1627. A group of young noblemen, led by François de Montmorency Bouteville, challenged this edict by having a duel directly under Richelieu's window. Richelieu reacted to the challenge by persuading the King to enforce the law. He warned the King that unless the law was properly enforced it would soon be mocked by all. Montmorency was executed in spite of protest by his fellow nobles, and Richelieu's reputation as a ruthless killer grew. This was an important demonstration by the King of his support for Richelieu. It was also an important statement that Richelieu and Louis XIII were serious in their attempt to impose royal authority and reduce the feeling by many of the nobility that they were above the law.

To what extent was 'The Day of Dupes' a major plot?

The second major plot against Richelieu, in 1630, was known as the Day of Dupes. There was the usual serious range of conspirators, including Marie de' Medici (the Queen Mother), who was furious with Richelieu. She felt very bitter against her own protégé, Richelieu. She felt he had pushed her away from the centre of power at Court, which she considered to be her rightful place. Another early conspirator was Cardinal Berulle, a staunch Catholic and leading Churchman, who had also played a significant role in helping Richelieu into power. Berulle had become alarmed with the anti-Habsburg and anti-Catholic direction of Richelieu's foreign policy and his apparently soft line on the Huguenots. Berulle conveniently died in 1629, but he did represent a few leading Frenchmen who disliked the direction of Richelieu's foreign policy. With no outlet for loyal opposition in the way it was actually possible on the floor of the House of Commons in England, little was left but plotting and intrigue. The great councils of state were the means through which royal policy was transmitted, not debated.

The key figure in the plot was Louis de Marillac, Keeper of the Seals (a major post in the French government) and a major figure in the royal administration. An ambitious man who was also a keen administrative reformer, Marillac neither cared for Richelieu personally, nor did he like the direction in which Richelieu's policies were going. Marillac felt that they were costing huge sums of money, which led to an increasing tax burden on the peasantry and raised the likelihood of local revolt. He also backed several of the potentially anti-noble plans which had come out of the Assembly of Notables in 1627. These included the destruction of all noble fortifications, except those near the frontiers of France, and the abolition of the hereditary offices of Constable and Admiral (commander in chief of the Army and head of the Navy respectively). These offices were usually held by noblemen regardless of their administrative capacity. To

Richelieu this was a price that had to be paid if France and its monarch were to gain their rightful place. Marillac wanted a Spanish alliance, as Spain was a Catholic country – not a war with Spain.

This plot was unusual in that, although it had the usual array of royal conspirators, such as Marie and Gaston, and possibly there were links to Queen Anne herself, there were serious policy issues at stake. There was the element of a 'progressive' Party about them. With the King favouring the Devot group and showing some concern about the effects of high taxation on his subjects, this was a more serious threat than most. It was hoped that the King might waver in his support for Richelieu.

On the famous 'Day of Dupes', in 1630, when Marie hoped to deceive the King into getting rid of Richelieu, she herself was deceived. With the King seriously ill, and the Court divided over the issues raised at Regensburg (whether the Emperor should be allowed to nominate his own son as heir to the Imperial throne), there was an attempted takeover of power at Court. It seemed likely that Richelieu's days in power were numbered.

Marie and Marillac tried to displace and exile Richelieu. But once the King recovered his health, Marie was promptly banned from Court and never returned. Gaston fled to Lorraine, then a semi-independent state on the borders of France under its own duke, and Marillac was executed in the usual way. Richelieu came closest here to losing his position, but his situation was never at risk again.

A further plot followed in 1632, led by the Duc de Montmorency, head of one of the greatest noble families in France. He was also Governor of the province of Languedoc and Admiral of France. Montmorency was backed by angry Huguenots and a bored nobility resentful of the growing authority of Paris. With Richelieu anxious to impose more and higher taxes to fund his imperial ambitions, Montmorency was asked to lead a rebellion of the disaffected. He had been a loyal servant of the Crown in the past, both under Henry IV and Louis XIII, and had not long returned from military service in Italy. Personal anger came into it as he had been sacked from the post of Admiral, which had gone to a Richelieu supporter. Montmorency had hoped to get the post of Constable instead. Although the peasantry of the area would not back him directly, they were prepared to take up arms to protest about taxes, which made the revolt look worse than it actually was. From the view of the Court it looked like a concerted effort by many hostile groups, particularly as the first move was the invasion of France by Gaston from the north. However, with such differing and conflicting aims, the plotters were never able to act together. General Schomberg easily broke the revolt at Castelnaudary. Even though he was a duke, Montmorency was executed. The plot was more of a gesture of defiance against the Court and its hopes of raising more money and power by introducing more officials into local areas who answered to Paris. In addition to the reasons given above, it was a centralisation versus localism conflict. It never seriously threatened Richelieu, his master or his policies. Gaston, as usual in the background, added little. He was reconciled yet again with his brother in 1634. Marie never returned to favour.

The Bourbon and the Cinq Mars Plots

There were two more plots along similar lines. The first came in 1641, when a prominent noble, Louis de Bourbon, led an invasion to overthrow Richelieu. He was helped by the Duke of Lorraine and the Cardinal Infanta of Spain (always anxious to stir up trouble in France). The aim of this revolt was to get the 'relief of the people and the defence of liberty'. Bourbon's manifesto personally attacked Richelieu for usurping power. He was clearly bitterly opposed to Richelieu's centralisation programme. Bourbon actually managed to defeat the royal forces at the Battle of La Marfee in 1641.

Louis de Bourbon, Count of Soissons (1604–1641)
The man who recaptured Corbie after the terrible disaster of 1636 and who detested Richelieu, fled to Lorraine in 1641, the bolthole for most dissidents.

Frondes: A fronde was a sling used by children to throw mud. In 1648 the term was applied to two anti-government movements in France: the *Fronde parlementaire* (1648–49) and the *Fronde des princes* (1649–53). The first centred upon attempts by the Parlement of Paris to remove Mazarin and the Regent from power; the second was a reaction to the government by royal princes and members of the nobility.

1. What were the main problems Richelieu faced in domestic affairs?

2. Which do you regard as the more successful: Richelieu's handling of the Huguenots or his handling of the nobility? Give reasons for your answer.

Perhaps one of the most likely chances of destroying Richelieu was there. Tragically for the rebels and fortunately for Richelieu, Bourbon died by accident – rumour has it he lifted the visor of his helmet using a loaded pistol and shot himself. Again the willingness of the rebels to associate with the enemies of France, committing what others might well see as high treason, should be noted. The nobles felt it was their right to rebel and not inappropriate in the circumstances to utilise the enemies of their country to further their own ends. It is little wonder that Richelieu saw them as a barrier to the modernisation of France and the authority of the French monarch.

The final plot came in 1641. This was known as the Cinq Mars Plot, and it had all the usual ingredients. Marie de' Medici was involved; there was correspondence with the enemy, Spain, and a young and impulsive 'fall guy', Henri, Marquis de Cinq Mars. He was friendly with the King, but that did not spare the usual horrible death. Gaston – again the stirrer – survived, even though he was no longer the heir to the throne. The main tip-off came from Anne of Austria, perhaps slighted by the degree of affection the King had shown towards Cinq Mars or possibly terrified that she might be deprived of access to her sons if the plot was discovered.

The **Frondes** demonstrated that Richelieu failed with the nobility. He lacked any clear plan to utilise their strengths or deprive them of the power to disrupt France. Richelieu was a nobleman himself and that may have made it difficult for him. He failed to find a way to harness the nobility's aspirations. They remained a parasitic class. Louis XIV was to remove their power in the next reign but perhaps it was the executioners of the French Revolution and the guillotine in the following century who finally produced a solution to the problem of the French nobility.

14.6 How able an administrator was Richelieu?

Whereas you can see that Richelieu's foreign policy was no great success in his own lifetime, at least he started France on the route to becoming the dominant force in Europe. He laid the base for the successes which Louis XIV was to achieve in the second part of the 17th century. While we might now question whether this was much to the advantage of the average French man and woman in 17th-century France, at least France's profile was raised.

In domestic matters, the record is not even as strong as that. It is argued that Richelieu's main contribution was to move the Monarchy towards absolutism, but the reaction, which was to follow soon after his death, destroyed the monarchy. It has also been argued that Louis XIV achieved his absolutism to a certain extent by learning much from Richelieu's mistakes. One of those was not having a first minister.

There is a strong case for arguing that Richelieu did considerable damage to France and its people. This is partly because of the poor quality of his administration of France domestically and partly by his rigid subordination of the needs of the people to his international ambitions for France.

Y-M Berce, in *The Birth of Absolutism: France 1598–1661*, refers to the taxation policy which occurred during Richelieu's tenure of power as 'fiscal terrorism'. That description is not inappropriate. Richelieu was simply not interested in any aspect of it, provided it produced enough to fund the monarchy in the state which he thought was appropriate and paid for the ambitious foreign policy he felt was necessary. Richelieu has been seen as a founder of absolutism in France with his reduction of noble, Huguenot and Parlement power. It could be added that in relying on a system that was inefficient, corrupt and obviously unjust to fund it all, he was fatally weakening the structure on which the monarchy was built. Just as financial strength was fundamental to the rise of Gustavus Adolphus of Sweden and financial weakness was crucial to the fall of the Stuarts in England and Scotland, money was a deep-rooted problem for the Bourbon monarchy. Richelieu did it no service by ignoring the demerits of the system and the crying need for reform, and squeezing it until the bitter response to the pressure he put on it almost destroyed the monarchy he was trying to promote.

Richelieu inherited an out-of-date system of raising and assessing taxation. He passed it on to his successor in a worse condition. The main source of crown income was the taille (see Chapter 7). There was also the Gabelle, a type of indirect tax. As with the taille, there were a huge number of exemptions from this tax on salt.

The Gabelle produced as much as 13 million livres in a good year like 1640, but frequently cost more to collect than it brought in. Various royal officials collected these taxes; again the power and role of such officials varied from area to area. In theory, the process was simple. With a theoretical income of about 108 million livres, there should have been more than enough to fund the monarchy and its ambitions. In practice, it was not as simple as that. Income rarely reached a third of the possible 108 million livres and the whole process caused unpopularity. In fact, it regularly provoked open revolt. With many of the officials who were supposed to collect the taxes having purchased their office (right to collect taxes), they were more concerned with getting a cash return on their investment than in sending large sums off to Paris. The right to collect taxes was regularly auctioned off to the highest bidder, which again led to a determination to collect on the investment. Offices were sold, which led to a devaluation of the status of the office. Frequently, more and more offices with the responsibility for the collection of taxes or administering justice were sold, which led to duplication and inefficiency. Interest payments of sums loaned to the government were bought and sold. With the value of these declining, the credit of the government declined and borrowing became more and more expensive.

Rentes: Investments in government stocks.

By 1640 the actual cost to the state of these *rentes* and office holders has been estimated at nearly 50 million livres, getting on for half of the possible income for the Crown. At times it amounted to more than the actual income to the monarchy. The quality of several of the main administrators, like Claude de Bullion (Finance Minister), was appallingly low. Richelieu seemed uninterested in the lack of income and in the damage that was being done to the monarchy and to the kingdom. The price that was being paid for short-term cash gains was very high. As the historian R.J. Knecht writes in his biography of Richelieu: 'Bullion created the worst of both worlds, an illogical and unpopular system that worked to the advantage of a few and the expense of many without any real gain to the Crown.' With all three of the worst (and there were many) revolts against the Crown – in 1626 in Quercy, in 1636–37 known as the revolt of the Croquants, and in 1639 the revolt of the Nu-Pieds – anger at the oppressive taxation system was among the main grievances of the rebels. Another cause was a desire to protect the privileges of those that had purchased their offices and saw their investment being devalued by the sale of even more offices to do the same thing.

Richelieu weakened the monarchy and he weakened the ability of France to achieve the objectives he set out for it by maintaining a weak system and managing it badly. The endless sales of offices, which caused confusion and further reduced the number of those who actually paid tax, put more incompetents into the administration and therefore lowered the status of the monarchy – which he was supposed to be advancing.

There was no sign of any serious planning or foresight on his part. Richelieu inherited a system which was on the brink of bankruptcy and passed it on in an even weaker state. He may have felt himself a prisoner of the system. It can be argued that others of great quality, like Jean-Baptiste Colbert in the reign of Louis XIV, failed as well. However, if Richelieu had tackled it with the same determination and cunning he used in dealing with the Huguenots or the Habsburgs, he may well have left the French monarchy a great deal more powerful.

In 1639 it was estimated that the cost of collecting the actual income of 32 million livres was 47 million livres in total – and that was in a year when devaluation of the currency and the sale of yet more offices was resorted to to keep the armies paid. Compulsory billeting of soldiers on civilians was regularly resorted to, and attracted more unpopularity. It was frequently reckoned in some of the border regions that French soldiers were worse looters than the invading Spanish. Attempts to ban the sale of offices were too easily given up as the desire for office and status was insatiable. So Richelieu simply raised the *Paulette* and made money out of it. It has been suggested that there might have been an ulterior motive here as devalued and duplicated offices posed less of a threat to a monarchy wishing for more power. Richelieu had obviously made a great deal of money out of office himself. He was not a good example, however worthy the causes (such as patronage of the arts) he might find to spend it on.

> **?**
> **1. What were the main reasons for financial difficulties in France while Richelieu was First Minister?**
>
> **2. To what extent can it are argued that Richelieu weakened the French monarchy?**

14.7 How much did Richelieu contribute to the growth of absolutism in France?

The creation of the post of intendant

Much has been written about Richelieu's importance to the growth of absolutism in France. He was to play an important part in the rise of an all-powerful monarchy, which ended many of the old feudal privileges that lay with both nobles and towns, and the separate areas of France. The way in which he managed, or failed to manage, the nobles and the Huguenots are used to illustrate how he was trying to break down barriers to royal power. Certainly he failed to gain the financial self-sufficiency that would have been a vital part of such an attempt. In addition, his work with **intendants** and parlements needs to be looked at as well.

One way in which Richelieu tried to bypass the existing administrative system, with its hereditary officials concerned with protecting their privileges and incomes, was to develop the office of the *intendant*. These were not new officials, but the way in which Richelieu used, and hoped to develop, their powers was. He was looking for a royal servant with only one loyalty, to the monarch and to France. Richelieu wanted no loyalty to a caste or to an area, as was the case with so many of the nobility. Nor did he want officials who were primarily interested in preserving their office and its income. The sheer incompetence of so many officials who could not be removed encouraged Richelieu to bypass the existing channels of collecting and assessing taxation, by simply imposing another group of officials on top. These were paid a fixed annual salary and were not from the locality in which they served. There was therefore less risk that they would start to sympathise with the locals and be less obedient to central government. They were moved regularly from area to area. They were easily removed, and they were encouraged to develop their own police forces to protect themselves and to make the collection of taxation easier. They had important administrative, as well as judicial, roles. The *intendants* also had responsibility for maintaining law and order in an area. They could raise troops and **billet** them. The *intendants* also acted as sources of information about the behaviour and loyalty of the local population.

Intendants: The idea of a royal official directly responsible for an area to the crown was not new; Henry IV certainly had ideas of developing a loyal agent in the localities. The *intendants* were roving inspectors acting for the central government; under Richelieu, they became more settled and their powers were extended. Among their new duties was the supervision of tax collectors.

Billet: Order local people to feed, clothe and house troops, usually at their own expense.

The main motive for using *intendants* was to raise money for war. They were not intended to become alternative sources of power. They proved such useful agents that they soon became permanent features of French government. The hostility they aroused became apparent in the Frondes, when they had to be removed to pacify the nobles, office holders and municipalities whose jurisdiction they were supposed to have upset. Once royal authority was re-established at the centre, the *intendants* soon followed out to the localities.

Part of the aim behind developing the *intendants* was to break down the self-interest of regions. It was also intended to remove some of the powers of noble governors, who did rebel and took their regions with them into rebellion. This was demonstrated both in the Huguenot troubles of the early 1620s and in the later noble conspiracies. The Code Michaud (a reform programme of the late 1620s) stressed the need for such royal agents in the interest of efficiency. The drafters of the Code were no lovers of Richelieu but men who wanted sense to prevail in the ancient and inefficient administration of France. So Richelieu was not a great innovator himself, he simply took the ideas of others and put them into practice.

In addition, Richelieu also took care to replace Governors and Lieutenant Governors (royal officials in charge of regions) with loyal supporters. By 1634, 12 of the 16 had been replaced. Often these men were only too pleased to have the backing of the *intendants* in the implementation of their duties of taxing, raising troops and maintaining order.

Richelieu's management of the parlements

Whereas the *intendants* were simply intended to supplement and not supplant the existing bureaucracy, another part of the so-called growth of absolutism was Richelieu's management of the various Parlements. These were medieval creations, made up mainly of lawyers, and their purpose was essentially legalistic. They were very different from the developing English Parliament, which was demanding much greater influence on policy and legislation. They were much nearer the 'talkshops' that the name suggests. The parlements were law courts with the role of registering royal edicts, and they had a mild right of protest about royal wishes. They should not be compared to the elective, representative and policy-making English Parliament. They did have a right of remonstrance (protest), and they could be critical of any policies which might affect the status, income or interests of the middle-class lawyers who made up their membership. They also had a record of defending Gallican liberties. The parlements were not a problem under Henry IV, but some of the parlements did make a bid for greater powers to defend the right of subjects. Their hostility to favourites like Concini and Luynes was strong.

It is easy to see why Richelieu would see them as a narrow and selfish group determined to protect their own privileges at the expense of the Crown. One implication of their ideas was that the king might be *under* the law – a concept that Richelieu would not tolerate. These courts covered about one-third of France. They could be over-ruled by a *lit de justice* (a royal order to be quiet). Richelieu did not like the parlements' bureaucratic and judicial resistance to change. He personally supervised the registration of royal edicts (simply statements of the royal will), which were in fact the way in which law was made in France. The members of parlements resented his autocratic treatment of them. They also resented his successful attempts to turn the parlements of one type, known as the *pays d'état*, where they had greater autonomy, into another type, known as the *pays d'élection* (although no election was involved) where the custom was greater obedience to royal wishes.

The parlements also hated the special legal commissions which

Jansenists: Religious dissenters who, although Roman Catholic, had very different ideas on how eternal salvation was attained.

Richelieu set up to deal with the Montmorency and Cinq Mars affairs, and the Chambre d'Arsenal created in 1631 to deal with political offenders and others like the **Jansenists** and the Nu-Pieds (see page 335). They felt he was taking on legal powers which were rightfully theirs. His decision to cut their powers, and the lowering of some of their political ambitions, also irritated them. Richelieu did not have a plan to turn France into an absolutist state. He just wanted the government to operate more efficiently. Between 1635 and 1640 he was quite prepared to imprison or exile key members who opposed him over the creation of new offices. Richelieu was the main force behind a *lit de justice* in 1642, which specifically ordered parlements to confine themselves to legal matters.

At times concessions to parlement could be made by the King, who was as intolerant as Richelieu to any attempts at independence by these courts. He knew they represented a significant and powerful class of people in France who a king would like to see both as loyal supporters and taxpayers. However, the overall impact of this treatment of the parlements was one of resentment and the monarchy paid a high price for this during the later Frondes.

Richelieu's relationship with Louis XIV

The main reason why Richelieu got into power and stayed there was because the King, Louis XIII, wanted him. Few ministers serving any monarch can have been so disliked and detested as Richelieu was and few can have had to overcome more attempts to deprive him of power. Certainly Richelieu built up an extensive power base, gained huge patronage powers, and ensured that it was his followers that got as many key offices as possible. He always waged an impressive propaganda campaign, being one of the first to realise the power of the press in influencing public opinion.

Louis XIII was able in some ways, articulate and well trained. He was also impulsive, secretive and could be cruel. However, he was able to recognise his own weaknesses. He may have disliked Richelieu personally, and at times they did not get on at all well. None the less, he had learned from his experience with Luynes that working with people you liked could prevent you from getting what you wanted. Louis XIII realised early on that Richelieu had considerable ability, as well as power (in fact, he was at times frightened by that ability). He also realised that Richelieu was actually more concerned to use that power for ends that Louis approved of, such as strengthening the monarchy and France. Louis XIII realised that Richelieu did not care for the sort of personal power so apparent in people like Concini or Condé. He saw that Richelieu was a loyalist through and through. Although he might like to acquire wealth (Richelieu certainly did that and looked after his family as well), the man's heart was in the right place. There was a selflessness about Richelieu that Louis XIII had the sense to see and use.

Richelieu managed the King well, as Robin Briggs states in *Early Modern France* (1977), 'Louis wanted to be ruled, yet chafed when he was'. Richelieu took care to keep the King informed and always tried to offer him a choice. Both men ultimately wanted the same thing most of all, and that was what kept the relationship going.

Conseil d'État: Meeting of all the main office holders in France. It was a large and unwieldy group of men.

Richelieu used the old Councils effectively, relegating the older units such as the *Conseil d'État* to administrative matters. Other bodies, such as the *Conseil d'en Haut* (smaller in number and therefore more easy to dominate), were used for policy making as Richelieu had more control over the individuals on them. Cardinal Richelieu was a good manipulator of what was there, rather than a reformer like Thomas Cromwell in England. The *Conseil d'en Haut* frequently contained able men by 1640, such as Sublet de Noyers at the War Department and Claude Bouthillier at Finance who had replaced one of Richelieu's most disastrous appointments, Claude de Bullion. Again the focus of Richelieu's efforts was on making do with what was there and subordinating all to his foreign policy ambitions.

The expansion of the army and navy

Under Richelieu the French army grew in size, rising from approximately 30,000 in the early 1620s to about 200,000 by 1640. He created the office of military *intendant*, and the loyal Noyers ran the administrative side of the army with some competence between 1636 and 1645. The army proved to a huge drain on the nation's resources and billeting was a major cause of social and economic unrest. The recruiting and management of the army remained feudal (in the sense that landowners were expected to produce soldiers in times of war) and inefficient, but the work of Noyers paid off by the early 1640s with its focus on basics – pay, equipment and provisions. New talent was encouraged; one being the future administrator and general, Michel Le Tellier. This investment finally paid off at Rocroi in 1643 when the Spanish army was defeated. R. J. Knecht claims in his biography *Richelieu* (1991) that one of the biggest criticisms of Richelieu is that he failed to tackle the huge problems created by the demands of a significantly larger army. Instead he relied on limited expedients to raise, feed and pay his troops.

Richelieu also tried to expand the Navy significantly. There was considerable growth, but he was starting from a very low base. He put himself in overall charge in 1626, when he abolished the post of Admiral. Richelieu still tended to rely on hiring ships from the Dutch when he needed a large fleet. Sully had created a galley fleet in the Mediterranean. Richelieu was not interested in the Mediterranean. Instead he tried to develop ports and docks on the Atlantic Coast. By his death, an Atlantic fleet was slowly emerging. It was neglected by Mazarin, and soon vanished. Part of Richelieu's reasons for encouraging naval growth was to develop **colonies**. There were a small number of French colonies in both the West Indies and in Canada. However, social attitudes in France were hostile to commercial growth; it was simply not fashionable to make money and invest in new enterprises. Nobles did not feel it was the proper way to spend time. Richelieu also felt he could achieve real progress simply by legislating from Paris, but this was to lead to problems as circumstances in the unexplored regions of Canada were beyond his range of knowledge.

Richelieu: a final assessment

When Richelieu died in 1642 there was lots of joy at his death. Few were loathed as much as he was, by so many. He died a very rich man and it is interesting to debate how far money was the motive for his work. Certainly, he proved not always to be a strong administrator although he was a clever politician. For him to rise as high as he did, and to remain there for so long, is a great tribute to his political skills.

- He was certainly a great French nationalist and did more than any other to build up France in the early 17th century. He set an example that was to be followed by Louis XIV in the second half of the century.

- He was also a great strategist and had a vision of the sort of role which France could play in Europe and how it could dominate Europe.

- He built up the French State and it can be seen as the forerunner of the modern state.

- He was a superb propagandist, and knew how to market an idea and how to put down opponents.

- He was the dominant force in France at a vital moment.

Colonies: Countries controlled by a more powerful country, which uses the colony's resources in order to increase its own power or wealth.

1. How did Richelieu attempt to increase royal power in France?

2. How successful was Richelieu in making the French monarchy absolute?

- He changed the country's priorities and returned France to its old expansionist days.

- He centralised power and expanded the state at the expense of good government and care of the people.

- He centralised power, which upset the localities.

- He was tough and intelligent, and identified himself with the state.

- He dominated the impulsive king.

- He failed overall as an administrator, but managed to reform the army, navy and the Church.

- Religious divisions remained, and the nobles and parlements fought back in Frondes within a few years of his death.

It could be argued that most of his work was immediately undone. A strong case could be made for saying that his only real achievement was staying in power for 18 years.

How great was Richelieu's contribution to the development of the French State, in domestic and foreign affairs, to 1642?

14.8 How did Mazarin come to succeed Richelieu as First Minister of France?

Anne of Austria (1601–1666)
Married Louis XIII when she was 14. They disliked each other so had as little contact with each other as possible. Although dismissed by some historians, such as Robin Briggs, as 'unintelligent and lazy', Anne's reputation has changed in recent years and she is seen by others such as Y-M Berce as 'a strong minded women willing to take advice and decisions'.

Louis XIII died soon after Richelieu, in 1643, leaving a four-year-old boy as his heir. Louis XIII detested his wife and his will specified that a council containing such unlikely royal supporters as Condé and Gaston should govern France until the young Louis was of age. Louis XIII wanted no repetition of the events of the period of his own minority. There had been a regency with his mother tending to govern using favourites. However, he was clearly missing the advice of Richelieu, as it was unlikely that such a council would have brought stability to France. Queen Anne soon persuaded the Parlement of Paris to overturn the will. Advised by Cardinal Mazarin, she assumed control of France. What was to follow

A painting of Cardinal Mazarin by Philippe de Champaigne

Jesuits: Catholic order of priests founded by St Ignatius Loyola (see page 182) in 1534 to fight against the Reformation. From 1540 the Jesuit Order came under the direction of the Pope. Jesuits were intelligent, well-educated priests. Their religious education lasted seven years.

may well not have been in the interests of France and the French people, but it was certainly in line with the policies of Louis XIII and Richelieu. The war with Spain was to continue to its bitter end and the Crown of France tried to continue with its centralisation and absolutist policies.

To a large extent Jules Mazarin had been groomed to succeed Richelieu. Trained by **Jesuits**, he had risen in the Papal diplomatic service. By 1640 he was working full time for Richelieu, who had been impressed by his ability and skill as a negotiator during the Treaty of Cherasco in 1631. Mazarin's work in tipping off the Court about the Cinq Mars plot may well have endeared him there, but he seems also to have played a part in preventing Anne and Gaston being banished for their involvement in plots. This proved to be useful later and demonstrated his skill at backing all sides at the same time.

Mazarin was made a cardinal in 1642 and joined the Council early in 1643. He had wisely judged the future by keeping on excellent terms with Anne, the wife of Louis XIII, and had taken the precaution of becoming godfather to Louis XIV. Like his supporter Richelieu, he had risen partly on the skirts of a woman. Anne had a shrewd idea of what was good for the French monarchy. She was equally keen to defend the interests of France against her own Habsburg family and to secure the throne of France for her son. She knew enough about Gaston and Condé to wish to avoid the faction fighting that would inevitably follow their 'rule' in France.

France was ruled from 1643 to 1661 by a partnership between Anne and Mazarin to start with, followed by the arrival of the young Louis in the early 1650s. They were tempestuous years.

The foreign policy of Mazarin

Mazarin's aim seems to have been to complete the work begun by Richelieu and Louis XIII. In spite of the need in France for peace and the terrible internal struggles called the Frondes, Mazarin insisted on keeping the war with Spain going to the bitter end. He personally directed policy and played a key role in negotiating the various peace treaties involving France. He was more directly responsible for the strategy and the execution of military and diplomatic policy than Richelieu ever was.

The war in Italy kept going until the late 1640s. It was never totally successful but played a part in grinding down the power of Habsburg Spain. Mazarin was fortunate in that the quality of French generalship rose, as did the fighting ability of its troops. The work of the military intendants paid off. The Prince of Condé and Marshal Henri de Turenne were first-rate generals, as the victories of Rocroi and Lens in 1643 and 1648 demonstrate. Spain's reputation as a military power declined.

Mazarin was a skilful negotiator. He was heavily involved from 1643 to 1648. He negotiated an agreement with the Danes in 1645 to get favourable treatment in Baltic trade through the Sound (the entrance to the Baltic which the Danes controlled). In another agreement with Sweden, in 1644, he persuaded the Swedes to keep on fighting in Germany largely for French benefit. They also agreed not to make peace separately. He even managed to keep the Dutch in the war against Spain for longer than he had initially thought possible. This was not an easy task for a Roman Catholic Cardinal.

In the Treaty of Westphalia of 1648, France made the sort of gains that Richelieu had been striving for over 15 years. It gained rights in Alsace, and the key town of Strasbourg. Forts at Breisach and Sundgau and 10 separate cites such as Colmar, as well as the future great forts of Metz, Toul and Verdun, were also gained. Key gains were therefore made to the north and east. Not only were there territorial gains, but French influence moved decisively into what is now Belgium and to the Rhine as a result of these gains.

France's northern frontier was moved further away from Paris. The likelihood of another Corbie was diminishing.

Mazarin was also anxious for France to be seen as the protector of German liberties against a powerful Holy Roman Emperor. This would help tilt the balance of power in favour of France. The war with Spain was to continue for another 11 years after Westphalia. It was sheer exhaustion that ground down the Spanish. Mazarin was quite prepared to ally with a Protestant country like England to achieve his anti-Habsburg objectives. It was at the Battle of the Dunes in 1658, where the Englishman Oliver Cromwell's Ironsides destroyed the Spanish field army near Dunkirk. As a result, the last major army that the Spanish could put into the field was lost. It was also Mazarin's clever threat of a marriage alliance of the young French king to an Italian princess from Savoy that finally convinced the Spanish that there was no future in continuing the war.

At the Peace of the Pyrenees in 1659, further forts in the Netherlands were gained, such as Gravelines. On the other hand, Spain regained some of its losses near the Pyrenees. France also gained Artois and Roussillon. Whether the huge loss of life and staggering cost to France was worth it to defeat the power of the House of Habsburg is debatable. Certainly Habsburg Imperialism had ended and the likelihood of encirclement by Spain was gone. However, the repression of the French people and the burden of taxation were a high price to pay. It was not so much the strength of France that had defeated Spain. It was internal problems facing Spain and a conflict with the Dutch and the English that had finally forced Spain to negotiate. France was simply the less weak of the two powers in the end. The marriage of the young King Louis to the daughter of the King of Spain was agreed – a marriage that was to have a big influence on the future history of both France and Europe. Mazarin promised not to aid Portuguese rebels, which eased Spanish sensitivity on this matter. He also made sure that there would be no claim to the throne of Spain from France. He did his best to ensure that the peace would last in the sense that he did not impose humiliating terms on Spain which they would revoke when they felt stronger. France's ambitions lay in the north and in the west, and he did not want an angry Spain to the south.

1. How far was Mazarin able to achieve the foreign policy aims of Richelieu?

2. How successful was Mazarin as a negotiator in 1659?

14.9 Why did the Frondes break out in France and to what extent was Mazarin responsible ?

Although the period 1643–1661 was vital for the development of France as a major power in Europe, there were also developments of great importance at home. These were a series of internal struggles, which together are known as 'the Frondes'.

This series of damaging internal disturbances were a reaction by the French people – noble, middle class and peasant – against the internal and external policies of Richelieu and Louis XIII. There had been revolts, rebellions and plots against Richelieu, but what was to follow under Mazarin between 1648 and 1653 was on a much grander scale. It came close to destroying both France and its monarchy.

The main cause was money. An attempt to raise more to wage war by taxing towns which were normally exempt from tax, failed in 1644. It only appeared to cause unnecessary concern amongst reasonably loyal people. The only alternative – making peace was not on Mazarin's agenda – was to increase the *taille*. Mazarin cared as little for the provinces and rural France as Richelieu did. In order to get cash he increased the farming of taxes on a large scale and added greater ruthlessness to what

Cabal des Importants: Plot in 1643 led by the Duc de Beaufort and other more minor aristocrats. Mazarin's spies and informers warned him of it in time. Beaufort was imprisoned.

Richelieu had done before. Mazarin was a foreigner and did not have the basic knowledge of rural France, which Richelieu had gained as a bishop. However, he had a good eye for talent and recruited many able men; several, like Michel Le Tellier and Abel Servien, came from comparatively humble backgrounds and had risen up the ranks of the *intendants*. The Crown had enough problems in rising money to run the country in peace-time, and it simply could not cope with constant war.

It had been hoped that a change of monarch and first minister might mean an end to the war and lower taxes. Now resentment of the rule of a woman, aided by an Italian, grew. Cardinal Mazarin managed to deal with noble plots, such as the *Cabal des Importants*, in 1643 in the same repressive way as Richelieu. He insisted on continuing with his war. The final straw for many came in late 1647 and early 1648: deeply involved in the negotiations surrounding the Peace of Westphalia, and desperately short of money, Mazarin tried to compel the Parlement of Paris to accept new taxes. In spite of a *lit de justice*, which demanded obedience, the Parlement of Paris still opposed. This was tantamount to revolution, and was a signal to the rest of France. The fact that the country was at a critical stage of the war is indicative of both the provincialism and selfishness of many of the wealthy 'rebels'.

With the old argument that it was evil ministers imposing changes on the young king, and that Parlement was a defender of liberty against oppression, sympathy for Parlement was immediately widespread across France. Middle-class office holders rallied against what they saw as an attack on their traditional privileges. Parlement, aided by another of the old medieval courts known as the Chambre Saint Louis, drew up a list of articles by 1648 – 27 in all – which, if allowed to stand, would represent an end to the absolutism of the French monarchy.

Their demands ranged from points such as the end of *intendants*, the *taille*, tax farmers and imprisonment without trial, to the suggestion that there should be no taxation without consent. The court accepted these (certainly temporarily in the eyes of Mazarin and Anne) and there was an outburst of great joy coupled with a remarkable outburst of propaganda against Mazarin. An attempt by Mazarin to end the Fronde of the Parlement failed. He not only misunderstood it and underestimated it, but also probably made matters worse. The arrest of the leaders after the agreement to accept the 27 articles had to be countermanded because of Paris rioting, and the demands had to be publicly confirmed by the monarchy in a humiliating way. Radical action by Mazarin had only served to drive many moderates towards the radicals. Mazarin's show of wealth did not help either. The attempts of Richelieu to distance the monarchy from the faction fighting of old had gone.

With a 'peace' negotiated with the Frondeurs at Reuil in 1649, the court had to give in to the Parlement. The whole system of government in France was now under direct attack. The lack of real noble support for the Parlementaires and the absence of much opposition in the demands of the *taille* (which of course did not fall on rich lawyers) should have indicated to Mazarin that there was scope for dividing and ruling. There was no concern shown for the plight of the common people of France by the Frondeurs of Paris.

This did not end the troubles. Condé was dissatisfied, feeling that he should be the dominant figure at Court and not some Italian priest. He became a focus for rebellion. Billeting was reaching huge proportions in the frontier areas as well as nearer Paris and was causing great resentment. Soaring prices and outbreaks of the plague also raised tension and fear. Many nobles joined the Fronde in 1649 and 1650. The attempted arrest of Condé only led to tension growing even higher. The result was Gaston taking control of the council in 1651, a mass uprising through France and the exile of Mazarin and the summoning of the Estates General. France was plummeting into the chaos known as the second Fronde. The situation was made even more chaotic as Condé hated Gaston, and the feeling was mutual. They had no agreed objectives at all.

However, all was not totally lost. Several important figures, such as the soldiers Hugues de Lionne and Abel Servien, remained loyal to Anne against Condé, Gaston and the Frondeurs. Condé and Gaston were only interested in increasing their own personal wealth and power. They were not interested in the aspirations of minor nobles or narrow lawyers in the provinces. All of this indicated that the Court was not faced with a united front against them. There were further complications when the Parlement of Paris made some strongly anti-clerical statements which offended Condé's relative and fellow plotter, Cardinal Gondi.

With the Estates General due to meet in 1651, many grievances were debated first, similar to those of the Parlement of Paris. Billeting, no new offices and regular meetings of the Estates General were high on the agendas of the future members of the Estates General. In the end it did not meet, and in 1652 Mazarin arrived back at Court with 6,000 German mercenaries. The civil war entered a new phase, almost a Mazarin versus Condé fight. Condé was a great general who felt he had been forced into revolt to defend his 'rights' and 'liberties' against the usurping Mazarin. The conflict swung each way, with Mazarin having to retreat into exile again in 1652, but returning victorious in 1653. With the young King Louis having been declared of age as early as 1651, clearly Mazarin could claim to have right on his side.

The Frondes failed to destroy Mazarin or to humble the monarchy for several reasons. Perhaps most importantly Queen Anne supported Mazarin. She felt, correctly, that he was the only way to ensure a powerful throne for her son. In the end the Frondes had no leader and were bitterly divided with fundamentally different aspirations. Gaston of Orléans was weak; Condé was impulsive and selfish, and ultimately had no desire to lead anything. Condé knew what he disliked and had no idea of what he wished to achieve. The peasants and the urban poor who formed much of the assault forces of the Frondes had no love for tax-exempt lawyers who dominated the Parlement, and many nobles had little time for middle-class officials who they despised socially.

Several provincial governors in key areas remained loyal to the Monarch. Richelieu had not put in his followers in such posts for no reason, and several localities split into savage local wars more concerned with local issues. Merchants quarrelled with office holders in ports. The horror which spread across Europe after the execution of Charles of England worried many men who were basically royalist (but anti Mazarin and taxation). This led them into thinking about the possible consequence of a rebellious course of action. In a sense the message of Richelieu was not totally lost on all men and many were convinced that absolutism was the best form of government for France. By 1654, with the young Louis XIV crowned, the *intendants* were back, and a new finance minister, Nicholas Fouquet, was back trying to raise money for the war.

Little had changed. There were the usual revolts in 1656 and 1657 in the provinces against high taxation, which were repressed with a force that Richelieu would have admired. Anne had played a clever waiting game and she must get much of the credit for the defeat of the Frondeurs. Apart from a deep impression on the young Louis, the Frondes appeared to have achieved little. Perhaps they demonstrated the futility of rebellion. They seem negative and futile; a rash protest against forces over which they seemed to have no control. Some have seen them as a failed revolution, but they had no revolutionary aims. The tactlessness of Mazarin regularly made things worse. In some ways the Crown benefited as even moderate reformers were now discredited. As Robin Briggs states in *Early Modern France*: 'What started as a criticism of some abuses of royal power ended by making the king a real enemy of any checks on his power.'

The achievements of Mazarin: an assessment

Perhaps Mazarin's greatest achievement was to survive the Frondes, ensuring that the Monarchy did as well. Although he must take some of the blame for both causing and worsening them, when Louis XIV was old enough to assert himself he found it quite easy to progress and achieve the sort of power and authority of which Richelieu can only have dreamed. Spain was finally defeated, and Habsburg power effectively ended in both central Europe and Italy. France was now in a position to dominate Europe and it was to do so for the next century and a half. Whether by propping up an inefficient and ageing regime Mazarin actually benefited the people of France is debatable, but he certainly helped France on the path to European dominance.

1. What were the causes of the Frondes?

2. Explain why the Frondes were defeated.

3. Did Mazarin do more for France and the development of absolutism than Richelieu did? Give reasons for your answer.

Source-based questions: The foreign policy of Richelieu and Mazarin

SOURCE A

France's only thought must be to strengthen herself and to open doors so that she may enter the states of all her neighbours to protect them from Spain's oppression when the opportunities to do so arise … We must look to the fortification of Metz and advance as far as Strasbourg if this is possible, to acquire an entry to Germany. This must be done in the fullness of time, with great discretion and by unobtrusive secret negotiation.

Richelieu, writing in 1629

It is more difficult to recognise the illness than to cure it, all the more so because of the very violence of the illness. Moreover, in this case the old maxim of meeting force with force cannot apply, since to do so would put France and Christendom in extreme danger, for reasons which are well known to men of sound judgement and who can apply in matters of statesmanship the same care as doctors who avoid drastic purges during prolonged fevers. The chief difficulty lies in the contradiction presented by the disease, for we are torn between fear of the House of Austria and fear of the Protestants. The perfect answer would be to reduce both to such a point that they are no longer to be feared, and it is to this end that efforts must be directed. But at the same time care must be taken to ensure that if the means used do not attain this end, the perfect answer, they should at least serve to ward off the worst effects and provide breathing space in which to muster one's forces and turn events to account without danger … As to the Spaniard and the Swede, we must above all take care that in bringing down one we do not raise the other to such a point that he is more to be feared than the former. We must also act with such caution that instead of setting one against the other, we do not become involved in war with one of them. Such a step would allow the other to increase in such strength that even if the king were victorious he would lose more from the easy manner in which the other became more powerful than he would gain from his own victory … To carry out this difficult operation, in which the issues are so delicate, we must combine industry with force, and diplomacy with arms.

Richelieu, writing in 1631

Source-based questions: The foreign policy of Richelieu and Mazarin

SOURCE B

The French Ambassador confessed to me that they, the French, had a profound apprehension of the power of the Austrian dynasty, seeing Spain and the Empire acting in conjunction. I replied that of course the princes of the House of Habsburg worked closely together, being cousins and friends, but neither had nurtured designs against the interests of France. The proper fear that France should have was of the Church's enemies, which threatened all three crowns, which should therefore unite and not destroy each other.

The Austrian negotiator at the Peace of Westphalia, writing to the Emperor, 1648

SOURCE C

In the space of two years [1641–42] the Kingdom of France had been swollen by the conquest of two vital territories, Artois and Roussillon, which had pushed out the frontiers to the North and the South. The acquisition of rich countryside and wealthy cities was an obvious economic advantage, by the strategic advantages were of more immediate concern to governments of that period. Ten years of fiscal terrorism and political tyranny under Louis XIII and Richelieu had borne their fruit

From The Birth of Absolutism: France 1598–1661, *by Y-M Berce (1996)*

1. With reference to the Sources, and the information contained in the chapter, explain the meaning of the terms highlighted in the context of French foreign policy in this period.

(a) 'Fear of the House of Austria and fear of the Protestants' (Source A)

(b) 'fiscal terrorism' (Source C)

(c) 'political tyranny' (Source C).

2. Study Sources A and B. How useful are these sources as evidence of the problems facing Richelieu in carrying out his foreign policy?

3. Study Sources A–C. Do these sources explain fully the aims of French foreign policy between 1624 and 1648? Give reasons for your answer.

4. Study all the sources and use the information contained in the chapter.

To what extent could it be argued that France gained more than in lost in is foreign policy under Richelieu and Mazarin?

The Thirty Years' War

Key Issues

● *Why did the Thirty Years' War last so long?*

● *To what extent was the Thirty Years' War fought over religious issues?*

● *How great was the impact of the Thirty Years' War on the Holy Roman Empire?*

15.1 What happened to Germany in the aftermath of the Peace of Augsburg of 1555?

15.2 How did a crisis in Bohemia spark off a European war?

15.3 Why, and with what consequences, was there a reaction against the Habsburg triumph?

15.4 Why did the first battle of Breitenfeld not lead to a complete triumph by the Protestant forces?

15.5 Why, and with what consequences, did the French become directly involved?

15.6 What was the significance of the Peace of Westphalia for the Holy Roman Empire and for Europe?

15.7 Historical interpretation: What was the nature of the Thirty Years' War and how extensive was its impact?

Framework of Events

1558	Ferdinand I is elected Holy Roman Emperor
1562	Frederick, Elector Palatine, converted to Calvinism
1564	Death of Ferdinand I; succeeded by Maximilian II
1576	Death of Maximilian II; succeeded by Rudolf II
1577	Lutheran doctrine is redefined
1583	Archbishop-Elector of Cologne deprived of his archbishopric
	Duke of Bavaria gains control of the Roman Catholic Church in Bavaria
1593	Resumption of war between Holy Roman Empire and Turks; Turks invade Hungary
1606	War against Turks comes to an end
1607	Donauwörth Incident
1608	Creation of the Protestant (or Evangelical) Union
1609	Cleves-Jülich crisis; Bohemian 'Letter of Majesty'; creation of Catholic League
1610	Frederick V becomes Elector Palatine
1612	Death of Rudolf II; succeeded by Matthias
1614	Treaty of Xanten
1615	End of Turkish attacks on Austria
1617	Ferdinand of Styria is king-designate of Bohemia and Hungary
1618	Defenestration of Prague sparks off Thirty Years' War
1619	Death of Matthias; succeeded by Ferdinand of Styria
	Deposition of Ferdinand and election of Frederick, Elector Palatine
1620	Mühlhausen Guarantee. Treaty of Ulm. Battle of White Mountain
1621	Frederick is outlawed; allies with Dutch Republic
1622	Jülich is captured by Spanish army commanded by Spínola
1623	Palatinate is transferred to Maximilian of Bavaria
1625	Sweden invades Prussia. Wallenstein raises new Imperial army
1626	Danes defeated by Catholic League at Battle of Lütter-am-Barenberg
1627	Rapid Imperial advances in north Germany
1628	Upper Palatinate is annexed by Bavaria. War of the Mantuan Succession
1629	Edict of Restitution. Peace of Lübeck

1630	Dismissal of Wallenstein. Peace of Regensburg. Swedes invade Germany
1631	Treaty of Barwalde. Sack of Magdeburg. First battle of Breitenfeld. Recall of Wallenstein
1632	Wallenstein captures Leipzig. Battle of Lützen and death of Gustavus Adolphus
1633	Formation of League of Heilbronn
1634	Death of Wallenstein. First battle of Nördlingen
1635	Peace of Prague between Emperor and Saxony France declares war on Spain
1637	Death of Ferdinand II; succeeded by Ferdinand III
1640	Diet of Regensburg
1642	Second battle of Breitenfeld
1643	Beginning of Westphalian peace negotiations
1648	Peace of Westphalia.

Overview

BY the time of the Peace of Westphalia in 1648, the Holy Roman Empire was in many respects different from that which had emerged at the time of the Peace of Augsburg in 1555. That settlement, which had held up with increasing uncertainty for over 60 years, was destroyed by the complex events of the Thirty Years' War. Many of the changes that resulted were momentous. German historian Volker Gerhardt has identified a number of ways in which Europe was altered fundamentally. These included the following.

● Rise of the State, including increased absolutism within many German states

● Shaping of modern diplomacy

● Ending of religious wars

● Need to consider public opinion when determining policy

● Need to limit military violence

● Stimulation of notions of religious toleration.

In the words of Theodore K. Rabb, the ending of the war represented 'one of the decisive moments of Western history'.

The process by which this came about is extremely complex. In order to simplify matters, historians have come to divide the war into four distinct phases.

1 The Bohemian-Palatinate phase (1618–1624), which saw the outbreak of conflict in Bohemia, the crushing of the Bohemian revolt and the destruction of the Rhineland Palatinate as a Protestant power.

2 The Danish phase (1624–1629), which saw the first significant foreign intervention, as a minor Protestant power sought unsuccessfully to reverse the political and religious changes which had been brought about up to 1624.

3 The Swedish phase (1630–1635), which saw the Protestant Swedes, financially supported by Catholic France, invade and occupy large areas of Germany until they were defeated at the Battle of Nördlingen. This part of the war was brought to an end by the Peace of Prague.

4 The French phase (1635–1648), which saw open intervention by the French who were alarmed at the implications for their own security by the rise in Habsburg power. The war had now become a much wider international conflict in which religious and German issues had become of secondary importance.

This classification is an over-simplification. It fails, for example, to take into account some of the wider conflicts with which the war came to be linked.

● Between 1621 and 1648 the war between the United Provinces and Spain was resumed (see Chapter 13). In the minds of many of its participants, this war was closely linked with developments in the Thirty Years' War.

● Poland was involved in a war against both Sweden and Russia at the same time that Sweden was involved in the Thirty Years' War. Clearly, the effectiveness of Sweden's participation in Germany was affected by its strategic objectives in Poland.

● There was a series of wars in northern Italy, the most significant of which was the War of the Mantuan Succession (1628–1631), which also involved Spanish, Imperial and French interests.

● For a time Transylvanian forces, under Bethlen Gábor, sought to exploit Imperial weakness to re-assert **Magyar** independence in Hungary.

Magyar: This term denotes ethnic Hungarians.

Not only were the events of the war complex, they were also seen by many commentators as meaningless. The war did bring about long-term settlement of certain key issues which were 'solid and lasting achievements'. For example, the Thirty Years' War settled German affairs to such an extent that neither religion nor Habsburg Imperialism ever brought about another major conflict there.

It also confirmed the rights, virtually amounting to sovereignty, of the German princes. In the process the powers and influence of representative institutions in many German states were reduced. The princes could determine matters of common interest without the interference of the Emperor.

Within their own territories the Austrian Habsburgs could develop a coherent state which was to form the nucleus for the future Austro-Hungarian Empire.

Such developments could not have been foreseen in 1618. Undoubtedly, one of the reasons why the consequences of the Thirty Years' War were so momentous was the fact that it lasted so long. This also raises the issue of why it took so long for the war to be resolved. There are several inter-connected points that help to explain this.

Bethlen Gábor (1580–1629)
A Protestant Magyar noble and prince of Transylvania, Bethlen led several successful campaigns against the Emperor Ferdinand II – on one occasion reaching the gates of Vienna. His financial weaknesses prevented him from sustaining his campaign against the Emperor, and this made it easier for Ferdinand to enhance his power during the 1620s.

● The whole basis by which international relations were conducted was being challenged. It was not always the case that the religious and strategic interests of participating states coincided. This was most obviously the case with France, but the Emperors also often sought alliances with more moderate Lutheran rulers. In such circumstances, it was difficult for anything other than fragile and short-lived peace to be made.

● Historian Geoffrey Parker, in *The Thirty Years' War* (1997) argues that 'the general crisis of the 17th century' made confrontations between governments

1. In what ways was the Thirty Years' War a series of short, inter-connected conflicts?

2. What was the significance in European history of the Thirty Years' War?

more likely and more difficult to resolve, though he has admitted that this, in itself, does not explain how the war lasted for 30 years.

● Governments, whilst often skilled at raising armies, were less effective when it came to paying them. Consequently, armies could not be organised to achieve rapid and decisive victories.

● Neither side was strong enough to secure complete victory. The Swedes, for example, could not bring about the complete defeat of the Imperialists after Breitenfeld, Wittstock or Jankov. The Imperialists, similarly, could not gain complete victory after Lütter-am-Barenberg or Nördlingen. This led to 'a state of military and political paralysis'. In any case, it was impossible for commanders to maintain a strategic grasp on all theatres of war simultaneously.

Such factors contributed to the prolonging of a war that had an immense significance both for the course of European history and for the emergence of a more distinctive national consciousness within Germany.

15.1 What happened to Germany in the aftermath of the Peace of Augsburg of 1555?

After the troubled years of Reformation and civil war (see Chapters 4 and 8, Germany experienced a period of relative peace and stability in the years following the Peace of Augsburg. This was at a time when other parts of Europe were affected by warfare on a huge scale. There were several reasons for this.

● The Emperor Ferdinand I had a far better grasp of the political situation within Germany than his late brother, Charles V. He was also much less heavy-handed in his approach to the Lutheran princes.

● Habsburg resources had, in any case, been exhausted by the warfare that preceded the Peace of Augsburg.

● According to historian Michael Hughes, in *Early Modern Germany, 1477–1806* (published in 1992), both Catholics and Lutherans were keen to solve religious disputes by compromise in the years after 1555.

● No single leader of anti-Habsburg opinion emerged from among the German princes.

● Though a loyal Catholic, Ferdinand I was prepared to pressurise the Pope into introducing reforms, like permitting clerical marriage and communion in both kinds in order to build bridges between Catholicism and Lutheranism.

Maximilian II (1527–1576)
He succeeded his father Ferdinand I as Holy Roman Emperor in 1564. Like his father he adopted a moderate approach in religious matters, reasoning that this was the best way of keeping the Empire together.

On the other hand, Ferdinand did set off the process by which the Roman Catholic Church in Germany reformed itself. It made itself a more formidable opponent of Protestantism, and won back territory that had earlier been lost to the Lutherans. Thus, the Habsburg territories in Austria and Bohemia became centres of the Catholic or Counter Reformation. Church discipline, religious education and the quality of training for priests were all improved, and Ferdinand encouraged the Jesuits to set up a network of colleges in Austria, Bohemia and Moravia. Under the leadership of Peter Canisius, these were to play a crucial role in the Catholic Reformation within the Holy Roman Empire (see Chapter 8).

Nevertheless, the reigns of Ferdinand I (1558–1564) and Maximilian II

Rudolf II (1552–1612)

The son of Maximilian II, whom he succeeded in 1576, Rudolf presided over a culturally brilliant Court in Prague which excelled both in painting and in science. However, his ability to rule was marred by bouts of insanity. This weakened his power, and he was forced to give ground not only to his brother, Matthias, in Hungary and Bohemia but also to Maximilian of Bavaria in the conduct of the Empire.

John Casimir (1543–1592)

The younger son of Frederick III, Elector Palatine, John Casimir administered the Palatinate during the minority of his nephew, Frederick IV. During this period, the Palatinate Court at Heidelberg emerged as one of the key centres of Calvinism, which also flourished at the university there.

(1564–1576) were both characterised by civil and religious peace and stability. This situation began to change with the accession of Rudolf II to the imperial crown in 1576. Rudolf was a keen patron of both art and science. The astronomers Johannes Kepler and Tycho Brahe both benefited from Rudolf's patronage, and turned his capital, Prague, into a major cultural centre. On the other hand, he was an odd character whose lack of leadership skills was to contribute to the growing crisis within the Empire which was to explode in the Bohemian crisis of 1618.

Germany in the last quarter of the 16th century was characterised increasingly by the emergence of two politically and culturally contrasting groups of states divided by religion. Catholic Germany became increasingly confident and hard line, as the Jesuits became established in many centres. In contrast, German Protestantism became increasingly divided. Lutheranism was split, though there was an attempt to re-impose unity with a redefinition of faith produced by a conference at Bergen in 1577. Moreover, Calvinism, which had not been recognised at the Peace of Augsburg, began to make inroads. Frederick III, Elector Palatine, had converted to Calvinism in 1562. Several other states followed, including Cleves, Nassau and Hesse-Cassel – in all cases as the result of decisions taken by their leaders.

The agreement implied by the Peace of Augsburg broke down from the late 1570s. One reason for this was the pressure which Lutheran princes in the north placed on the ecclesiastical states within their territories. Increasingly, the Reichstag, the Imperial defence circles and the *Reichskammergericht* became paralysed by religious squabbles (see figure).

Moreover, the Calvinist-ruled Palatinate began to emerge as a new focus for anti-Habsburg opinion. Both the Regent John Casimir (1583–1592) and its dominant political figure from 1592, Prince Christian von Anhalt-Bernburg, adopted a hard-line Calvinist approach in their attitudes to the

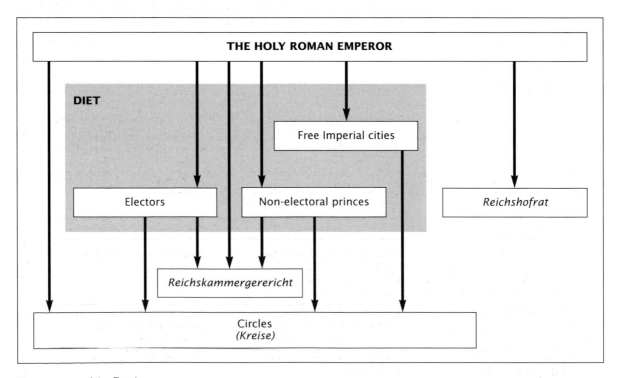

The structure of the Empire

Christian von Anhalt-Bernburg (1568–1630)

A Calvinist convert, from 1595 he served Frederick IV and Frederick V as governor of the Upper Palatinate. In that role he became the instigator and chief organiser of the Protestant Union. He saw the Palatinate as the centre of a group of Calvinist states, including the United Provinces, which could threaten Habsburg dominance. His vision was destroyed by the defeat at White Mountain in 1620, and he was forced into exile.

Habsburgs. Thus, the Palatinate organised opposition to taxes levied to pay for war against the Turks from 1592, deliberately obstructed Habsburg interests in the Reichstag, encouraged the settlement of Calvinist refugees and developed close links with the emerging Protestant power of the United Provinces. The Elector's university at Heidelberg quickly became one of the main intellectual centres for the advancement of the Protestant cause.

In addition to the growing religious tensions, Germany and the Empire were beset by a number of other problems. Southern Germany was destabilised by the increasing assertiveness of the Wittelsbach dukes of Bavaria. The economic and social position of Germany was deteriorating. Agriculture was weakened by the 'Little Ice Age' and food shortages resulted. The mining industry was weakened by foreign competition. There was an increase in crime. There were widespread peasant revolts, as well as significant outbursts of persecution of witches and anti-Semitism.

Political and religious tensions were to come to a head in two crises: the Donauwörth Incident and the Cleves-Jülich Affair.

The Donauwörth Incident

Donauwörth was a free city situated on the borders of Catholic Bavaria and the Calvinist Upper Palatinate, an area of Germany where the political and religious situation was especially tense. Theoretically, it was one of those free cities where both Lutheranism and Catholicism were officially tolerated. However, the bulk of the population was Lutheran and becoming increasingly intolerant towards any substantial expressions of Catholic practice.

Thus, on St Mark's Day in April 1606, when the Catholic clergy in the town attempted to hold a public procession, they were beaten up and their relics were confiscated. The following year, Rudolf II agreed to send a commissioner to try to ensure that the Catholics could enjoy their procession unmolested. This ploy failed miserably, and the priests and their supporters were besieged by a Lutheran mob whose behaviour went

The main religious differences

Roman Catholicism	Lutheranism	Calvinism
Accepted religious authority of Pope.	(Usually) accepted authority in religious matters of secular ruler.	In matters of authority placed stress on Bible, but ruler was still in control in some German states, e.g. Palatinate.
Hierarchy of cardinals, archbishops and bishops.	(Usually) accepted the structure of superintendents laid down in Saxony in 1527.	Self-governing, organised into synods.
Believed in seven sacraments.	Believed in two sacraments.	Believed in two sacraments.
Belief in transubstantiation, i.e. that in the Eucharist the wafer and wine are transformed into the body and blood of Christ.	Belief in the *real* presence, i.e. that in the Eucharist Christ is present within the bread and wine.	Belief in *spiritual* presence in the Eucharist.
Greater stress on sacraments and ritual than on preaching and scripture.	Emphasis on preaching and scripture, though sacraments were still seen as important.	Much greater emphasis on preaching and scripture than on the sacraments.
Strong emphasis on the free will of the individual to achieve salvation through works.	Emphasis on justification by faith alone.	Emphasis on predestination.

Germany before the Thirty Years' War

Legend:

- ── Boundary of the Holy Roman Empire
- ····· Boundary showing Habsburg Dominions 1616
- ⚲ Members of the Erbverein 1609
- Members of the Neuburg Alliance 1605–8
- ☀ Urban disturbances in Germany 1600–18
- ▢ Treaty locations
- ✚ Members of the Catholic League 1612

1 Cologne
2 Trier
3 Strasbourg
4 Mainz
5 Fulda
6 Würzburg
7 Bamberg
8 Constance
9 Ellwangen
10 Augsburg
11 Bavaria
12 Eichstätt

Members of the Protestant Union 1612

1 Cleves
2 Jülich
3 Berg
4 Mark
5 Ravensburg
6 Hesse-Kassel
7 Bayreuth
8 Anhalt
9 Brandenburg
10 Lower Palatinate
11 Baden
12 Württemberg
13 Ansbach
14 Upper Palatinate
15 Neuburg

unpunished by the town magistrates. The Emperor's authority had been openly slighted. Rudolf was so powerless that he was forced to ask his Catholic enemy, Maximilian of Bavaria, to restore order. This was technically illegal, since Donauwörth was situated in the Swabian rather than the Bavarian circle of defence, but Rudolf could hardly expect the Swabian leader, the Lutheran Duke of Württemberg, to do his bidding. As a result, Maximilian marched into the town on 17 December 1607 to restore Catholic worship. To make matters worse for the local Lutherans, the Emperor granted the city to Maximilian, who immediately banned Lutheran worship there in accordance with the *cuius regio eius religio* principle of the Peace of Augsburg (see page 327).

Maximilian's occupation of the city had immediate repercussions. The Emperor, anxious to acquire money to pay for the debts incurred during the recent Turkish War, had called an Imperial Diet which was to meet at nearby Regensburg. To achieve his financial aims, Rudolf needed the support of the moderate Lutheran princes. Instead, Maximilian's actions drove the moderate Lutherans to join with the Calvinist hard-liners whom they had previously distrusted. To make matters worse, the Catholic princes, who were in a majority in their College (i.e. house) of the Reichstag, called for the restoration of all church lands which had been secularised by Protestant princes since 1552. This led the delegation from the Palatinate to walk out of the Diet. They were followed by a number of other delegations, both Calvinist and Lutheran.

A few days later, six leading Protestant princes signed an alliance that became known as the **Protestant Union**. This alliance quickly developed formal links with both the United Provinces and England.

A year later, after Catholic defeat in the Cleves-Jülich affair (see next section), Maximilian of Bavaria responded by setting up and financing a **Catholic League**, which enjoyed informal links with the Spanish Crowns. Thus were drawn the battle lines which would be laid across Germany in the 1620s. In the words of historian Simon Adams, it seemed 'a source of wonderment' that war did not break out immediately, but was delayed for a decade.

The Cleves-Jülich Affair, 1609

Cleves-Jülich was a strategically important state in the north-west of Germany which controlled the lower Rhine. The crisis was sparked off by the death without an heir of its ruler, Duke John William, on 25 March 1609. John William, a Catholic, had tolerated Protestant practice in his religiously divided territories. (The population of Jülich was predominantly Catholic; that of Cleves, Ravensburg and Mark was overwhelmingly Protestant.) The two principal claimants to the duchy, the Elector of Brandenburg and the Duke of Pfalz-Neuburg, were both Lutherans. The duchess and Jülich Estates (representative assemblies) were determined to prevent a Protestant succession. The Dutch House of Orange and their Palatinate relatives were equally determined to prevent the duchy from remaining in Catholic hands.

Within a few days of the duke's death, Rudolf II authorised the duchess to act as regent until he had resolved the question of the succession. After Donauwörth, however, neither the Elector of Brandenburg nor the Duke of Pfalz-Neuburg felt that the Emperor could be trusted. In June 1609, therefore, they announced that they would seek independent arbitration of the dispute and would in the meantime rule jointly, thereby clearly repudiating the authority of the Emperor. To uphold his authority and the regency of the duchess, the Emperor sent his cousin, Archduke Leopold, to command the garrison at Jülich, but he was quickly blockaded by an

---

Protestant (or Evangelical) Union: This was an organisation of Protestant states formed in 1608 to defend the interests of the reformed religions within the Empire. The Union came increasingly under the control of Frederick, the Elector Palatine, and his militant minister, Christian von Anhalt-Bernburg. It became more and more confrontational in its relationships with the Habsburgs.

Catholic League: This was set up in 1609 as an organisation of Catholic states within the Empire. It brought together Bavaria and the surrounding ecclesiastical states, such as the bishoprics of Bamberg and Würzburg. Its dominant figure was Maximilian of Bavaria, the most powerful Catholic ruler within the Empire apart from the Emperor himself. It did try to keep its distance from the Emperor and established its own armed forces on the outbreak of war, under the command of General Tilly.

Maximilian of Bavaria (1573–1651)

The most powerful non-Habsburg Catholic prince within the Empire, Maximilian succeeded his father as duke of Bavaria in 1597. A member of the Wittelsbach family, and hence traditionally suspicious of Habsburg ambitions, Maximilian played a significant role in the building up of the tensions which led to the outbreak of the Thirty Years' War. He exceeded his authority in occupying Donauwörth in 1607 and was seen as a threat to the Upper Palatinate. In 1609 he headed the newly formed Catholic League, which linked Bavaria with the leading ecclesiastical territories of central and southern Germany. In 1614 he married off his sister to the heir to the Duchy of Pfalz-Neuburg, one of the contestants in the Cleves-Jülich dispute, who had converted to Catholicism. This assured him of Maximilian's support. After the outbreak of the war, his forces occupied the Palatinate, and in 1623 he was rewarded with an electorship. His relationship with the Emperor, however, was never close. For example, he opposed the Edict of Restitution and led those who supported Wallenstein's dismissal in 1630, and in 1631 joined France in a defensive alliance, a clearly anti-Imperial move. His ambitions and abilities as a ruler turned out to be counter-productive, as Bavaria was overrun by the Swedes and later by the French. Maximilian was, for a time, exiled from his own capital of Munich.

army raised by the two claimants. At this stage, neither side wanted war. Rudolf was still suffering from severe financial difficulties and the claimants were nervous about starting a war against Imperial authority. On the other hand, the Protestant Union feared the possible consequences of Catholic aggression and could perfectly well see the strategic importance of the duchy. The Union's trump card was to secure the support of the former Calvinist, King Henry IV of France. Despite his growing suspicion of international Protestantism, Henry IV was persuaded by Christian von Anhalt-Bernburg to send troops to Jülich and to agree to diversionary campaigns in the Netherlands and northern Italy. According to historian Geoffrey Parker this promise 'transformed the Cleves-Jülich affair from an Imperial to an international crisis'.

What motivated Henry IV's intervention has been much debated. Geoffrey Parker has suggested that he intervened in order to prevent a wider European war, gambling that Spain would not want to endanger the newly negotiated Twelve Years' Truce in the Netherlands by becoming involved. In any case, Henry's assassination on 14 May 1610 brought an end to wider ambitions. An international army forced Archduke Leopold's surrender.

Though this represented a substantial defeat for the Imperial and Habsburg cause, it did not resolve the issue of who was to be the new ruler of Cleves-Jülich. The Elector of Brandenburg and the Duke of Pfalz-Neuburg became suspicious of each other's intentions. Brandenburg, who had become a Calvinist convert, tied himself closely to the cause of the Protestant Union. He also supported Anhalt-Bernburg's attempts to create an international Protestant alliance which had been cemented by the marriage of the new elector, Frederick V, to Elizabeth, daughter of James I of England. On the other hand, not only had Pfalz-Neuburg become increasingly alienated from his Palatinate relatives, but also his son converted to Catholicism in order to marry the sister of Maximilian of Bavaria. Once again, it seemed that Cleves-Jülich might spark off an international conflict, especially when 15,000 troops from the Spanish Netherlands entered the area to secure Pfalz-Neuburg's control. However, each side again pulled back from the brink, and the Treaty of Xanten in 1614 conveniently divided the duchy between the two claimants.

According to Michael Hughes, in *Early Modern Germany, 1477–1806* (1992), the two crises in Cleves-Jülich 'illustrate very well the basic cause of the Thirty Years' War, mutual fear and misunderstanding, not religious polarisation'. Each side feared that the other was about to launch a great strike, which would need to be met by a defensive, pre-emptive strike. 'In the final crisis which precipitated the war, each side believed it was acting defensively.'

1. In what ways do the Donauwörth and Cleves-Jülich incidents demonstrate increasing political and religious tensions within the Holy Roman Empire?

2. To what extent do the two incidents mentioned above demonstrate that the Habsburgs were 'spoiling for a fight' with the Protestant Union?

15.2 How did a crisis in Bohemia crisis spark off a European war?

Christian von Anhalt-Bernburg and other key figures in the Protestant Union were convinced that the Habsburgs would be prepared to use Spanish troops within the Holy Roman Empire. It was therefore essential for them to find a non-Habsburg alternative to succeed the Emperor Matthias. Anhalt-Bernburg might originally have hoped to see Frederick V elected, but there could never be a majority among the electors for that. He seriously considered supporting Maximilian of Bavaria for the post. Maximilian, though leader of the Catholic League, had certainly inherited the anti-Habsburg tradition of the ruling Wittelsbach house in Bavaria. However, he had reservations about appearing to advance the interests of international Protestantism.

Once his negotiations with Maximilian had failed, Anhalt-Bernburg sought instead to work through Protestant noble sympathisers among the Estates of Austria and Bohemia, as a means of destabilising Habsburg power. There was ample evidence of anti-Habsburg feeling, directed in particular against Ferdinand of Styria, who saw himself as the heir to the childless Matthias. Ferdinand had alarmed Protestant opinion on account of his vigorous encouragement of the Jesuits in areas under his control. In Bohemia, in particular, there was resentment that the Letter of Majesty of 1609, granting religious toleration, had been infringed in two towns. Furthermore, during the winter of 1617–18 there were further attacks on Protestant privileges, including the regency government's refusal to admit non-Catholics to public office. Relationships between Ferdinand and the Bohemian nobility, who had elected him to the Bohemian throne, quickly became poisoned.

Such measures suggested that an all-out attack on Protestantism was about to take place in Bohemia. This led to a meeting of a Protestant **Defensors** in Prague on 5 March 1618. They petitioned the Emperor to redress the injuries done by his regents. Predictably, the Emperor refused. However, he did declare the meeting of the Defensors to be illegal, which was certainly not the case. This simply reinforced the Protestant belief that the authorities were attempting to crush their religion. The Defensors, led by Count Thurn, reconvened on 21 May. Two days later, having been called upon to disperse, they invaded the royal palace and demonstrated their rejection of Ferdinand and the Habsburgs by throwing two regency officials out of the window: this incident became known as the 'defenestration of Prague'. On 25 May the Defensors set up a provisional government, gave them authority to raise an army to drive out of Bohemia garrisons loyal to the Emperor and sought support from the other Habsburg provinces.

What complicated matters still further was the death of the Emperor Matthias on 20 March 1619. The Estates of Upper and Lower Austria and the provinces of Silesia, Lusatia and Moravia refused to accept Ferdinand as their ruler. A rebel army was quickly built up. On 26 August the Bohemian Diet, seeking a Protestant ruler, elected Frederick V, the Elector Palatine. Frederick accepted the post against the advice not only of other members of the Protestant Union but also of his father-in-law, James I of England. However, he was merely a puppet of the Bohemian nobility who were facing up to a full-scale confrontation with Ferdinand, whose election as emperor had been unopposed. Frederick's election was also an affront to Habsburg honour. As the Count of Solms-Brauenfels, a Palatinate noble, noted in a letter to his ruler which the latter characteristically ignored:

> 'If it is true that the Bohemians are about to depose Ferdinand and elect another king, let everyone prepare for a war lasting 20, 30 or 40 years. The Spaniards and the House of Austria will deploy all their worldly goods to recover Bohemia; indeed the Spaniards would rather lose the Netherlands than allow their House to lose control of Bohemia so disgracefully and so outrageously.'

The Spanish reaction bore out these comments. The Spanish Ambassador in Vienna, Count Oñate, advised that sending a substantial Spanish army to Bohemia was the only way that the country could be saved from the Protestants. He was supported in Madrid by Baltasar de' Zúñiga. Their combined pressure overcame the reluctance of the Duke of Lerma. Firstly, the Emperor was given substantial financial support. Secondly, 7,000 veterans of the Spanish Army of Flanders were marched off in the direction of Vienna in May 1619. The Imperial cause was further reinforced when the Catholic League, under Maximilian of Bavaria, was reactivated. Both sides had victories in the summer of 1619. Spanish and Imperial forces defeated the

Defensors: This was the name given to those Bohemian nobles who saw their task as upholding the Bohemian constitution of 1609, in particular the Letter of Majesty which granted a measure of religious freedom to Bohemians. It was their belief that Ferdinand of Styria intended to enforce Catholicism within Bohemia, which sparked off the crisis of 1618, thus beginning the Thirty Years' War.

Legend:

- Boundary of the Holy Roman Empire
- Lower Saxon Circle
- Spanish Road
- Christian IV's campaign 1625–6
- Economic blockade of Dutch Republic
- Treaty locations
- Catholic victory
- Catholic defeat
- Sieges
- Major places affected by Edict of Restitution
- Meetings of Electoral College
- Areas ceded by Ferdinand II to Bavaria and Saxony 1621
- Areas ceded by Ferdinand II to Transylvania 1621–9

The War, 1618–1629

Bohemians at the Battle of Záblatí. The Habsburgs suffered reverses against the Transylvanian army of Bethlen Gábor, which at one stage threatened Vienna. However, at the Treaty of Munich on 8 October 1619, the Spanish committed themselves to even heavier support of the Imperial cause. In March 1620 it was decided that an army of 20,000, under the command of Ambrogio Spínola, would leave the Spanish Netherlands to attack the Palatinate. As Geoffrey Parker wrote, in *The Thirty Years' War*: 'a crucial step in turning "the revolt of Bohemia" into "the Thirty Years' War" had been taken'.

This weakened the strategic position of the Bohemians whose cause further suffered when Bethlen Gábor was forced by lack of money to return to Transylvania. Moreover, the Protestant Union, Emperor Frederick and the Bohemian nobility lacked international support. Financial support from the United Provinces was virtually non-existent, and James I openly dissociated himself from his son-in-law's activities. By November 1619 most members of the Protestant Union had also distanced themselves from Frederick's position. To make matters worse for the rebels, the French arranged a treaty at Ulm in July 1620 between the forces of the Protestant Union and the Catholic League; in practice, this handed an advantage to the Emperor because the League's forces were then free to reinforce the Emperor directly. Thus, the forces of the Emperor came to outnumber those of the rebels. This had two consequences.

● In August 1620 General Spínola and his army invaded and occupied Frederick's own territory, the Palatinate (see map on page 356).

● On 8 November Imperial forces met the Bohemian rebels just outside Prague at the Battle of Bílá Hora (White Mountain). Within an hour, the rebels had been routed.

These victories had several results. Firstly, Frederick and his supporters were driven from Bohemia. Frederick could not return to the Palatinate, which was under Spanish occupation, and was forced to flee to the safe keeping of his Dutch relatives. Secondly, there was widespread popular approval of Frederick's expulsion, in view of the harsh attitude to the Bohemian peasantry adopted by his aristocratic supporters.

Also, the Imperialists reasserted their political and religious authority in Bohemia, Silesia, Lusatia and Moravia. This was done with some harshness. Rebels were executed, sometimes without trial, their property was confiscated and to pay for the conflict the Emperor debased the Bohemian currency. The Letter of Majesty was set aside. In 1628 the Emperor issued a decree expelling all Protestants from Bohemia. Ferdinand changed the constitutional position of his territories. He detached his hereditary lands – Austria, Bohemia and Moravia – from the Holy Roman Empire and created a common system of administration for them. The Emperor enforced linguistic and religious unity and terminated the independence of the States. In the process, Ferdinand set in motion a period which Czech nationalists came to regard as the 'dark ages'.

Finally, the armies of the Empire, the Catholic League and the Spanish Army of Flanders had, at least temporarily, established themselves as predominant in Europe, much to the alarm of Protestant opinion.

1. What issues were at stake within the Bohemian conflict?

2. Why was the Bohemian conflict transformed into a major European war?

15.3 Why, and with what consequences, was there a reaction against the Habsburg triumph?

The Danish intervention, 1625–1629

The extent of the Habsburg triumph worried the major Protestant powers of Europe.

● King Christian IV of Denmark feared a resurgence of Habsburg power within Germany.

● The Dutch feared that the revival of Habsburg power, particularly their control of the Palatinate, would make it more difficult for them to defend themselves against the Spanish onslaught which they were anticipating once the Twelve Years' Truce expired in 1621.

The main focus of warfare during the early 1620s was to be the Rhineland. The Dutch employed the mercenary leader, Ernst von Mansfeld, to harry the Spanish as much as possible in the Rhineland, which he did with little success. Christian IV also intervened, motivated partly by fear of the Habsburgs but also by the hope of gaining territory in the north of Germany which he intended to use to counteract Swedish influence in the Baltic. This strategy proved disastrous, the Danes being decisively defeated by the army of the Catholic League under the Comte de Tilly at the Battle of Lütter-am-Barenberg in August 1626. It looked as if the Protestant cause was doomed. However, the Imperialists were unable to force a complete victory, largely because of the failure of Albrecht von Wallenstein's imaginative but expensive Baltic strategy. (Despite a series of victories, he failed to create an Imperial fleet, and proved unable to take both the strategically significant port of Stralsund and the Danish islands.) Nevertheless, the Treaty of Lübeck (1629), which ended Danish participation in the war, was both politically and financially humiliating for Christian IV. It reinforced the prevailing sense of Protestant gloom.

What was also apparent was that the war had become something much larger than a conflict caused by the personal ambitions and stupidity of Frederick. The Habsburgs had made it clear that they intended to exploit their successes to the full.

The Edict of Restitution, 1629

Though the anti-Imperial position seemed unpromising in 1629, there were some signs that their cause might experience a revival.

Since 1628 the Emperor had been involved in the War of the Mantuan Succession in which he opposed the appointment of a French noble, the Duke of Nevers, to the Duchy of Mantua in northern Italy. This had two major implications. It caused divisions on the Imperial side, because of links between Nevers and Wallenstein, and the antagonism that the war generated increased the possibilities of a French intervention in the war in Germany.

There was widespread opposition within the Imperial Court and among the Catholic princes to Wallenstein's strategic plans. A group of princes, led by Maximilian of Bavaria, was able to outmanoeuvre the Emperor and secure Wallenstein's dismissal in 1630.

However, the most important contribution that the Emperor made, unwittingly, to his enemies' cause was the Edict of Restitution issued in 1629. The edict ordered that all Church property, secularised since 1555, should be restored to the Roman Catholic Church. This was greeted with hostility on all sides.

Protestant princes – even those who had hitherto remained neutral in the conflict, like John George of Saxony – were horrified. They began to become even more fearful for the future of their faith.

Jean, Comte de Tilly (1559–1632)
A native of the Spanish Netherlands, Tilly had a long and successful military career before he was invited to command the armies of the Catholic League in 1618. During the early stages of the Thirty Years' War, he was extremely successful. In 1630 he replaced Wallenstein, whom he detested, as commander of the forces of the Holy Roman Empire. In 1631, his forces captured and sacked the city of Magdeburg. However, in the same year his fortunes took a turn for the worse when he was defeated by the Swedes at Breitenfeld. In the following year he was defeated and killed by the Swedes at the Battle of Lech.

Albrecht von Wallenstein (1583–1634)
A native of Bohemia, Wallenstein had prospered through the acquisition of lands forfeited by the Bohemian rebels after the Battle of White Mountain. In 1624 he was created Duke of Friedland in recognition of his services against Bethlen Gábor. In 1626 he defeated Mansfeld at the Battle of Dessau, and in 1627–28 he drove the Danes out of north Germany, though he failed to capture the port of Stralsund, which prevented the completion of his conquest of the north. Wallenstein had alienated the Catholic princes of the Empire. Led by Maximilian of Bavaria, they pressed for his dismissal, but was recalled following the death of Tilly in 1632. A good organiser and charismatic leader, he drove the Swedes out of Bohemia, but was defeated by them at the Battle of Lützen. He then began to over-reach his authority, and the Emperor, deciding that Wallenstein could no longer be trusted, had him assassinated.

'The Swedish Hercules' – a print dating from 1631

What message is conveyed by this illustration of the King of Sweden?

Some Catholic princes were fearful that the implementation of the edict would make the Habsburgs even more unpopular.

To make matters worse for the Emperor, the French were trying to undermine Habsburg dominance. Thus, at the Diet of Regensburg, the French were already making secret deals with Maximilian and other Catholic princes. They were soon to make a deal with the Swedes.

The Swedish intervention, 1630

The involvement of Sweden considerably widened the scope of the war. The Swedish army, under King Gustavus Adolphus, had landed in Germany in July 1630. At first Gustavus claimed that his campaign was 'in no way directed against his Imperial Majesty … but only and solely for defence against the disturbers of the public peace, both ecclesiastical and secular'. Even this comment was ambiguous, since it could certainly be interpreted that the Emperor was one of the 'disturbers' he had most clearly in mind. (That ambiguity is still reflected in historians' views of Swedish intervention, which is either 'defensive' or 'selfish'.) Moreover,

'General Tilly joins the Jesuits in the spinning room', 1632. This print shows the elderly general spinning cloth with a group of Jesuits and monks.

1. What message is the print trying to convey?

2. How successful is it in conveying its message?

The War in the 1630s

Sweden could quite reasonably see itself as a potential target of Wallenstein's Baltic strategy. By 1630 much of the Baltic coast was, from a Swedish perspective, in potentially hostile hands. Jutland had been occupied, Wallenstein had been installed as Duke of Mecklenburg and Pomerania had been forced to allow Imperial garrisons. Moreover, Wallenstein had loaned 12,000 troops to the King of Poland, the Emperor's brother-in-law, to aid his conflict against the Swedes.

However, it would have been difficult financially for Sweden to intervene had not the promise of French assistance been forthcoming. The French had become increasingly alarmed by the increase in Habsburg power, and had tried to limit this either by getting Maximilian to break with the Emperor or by persuading the King of Denmark to continue with the struggle. They had been successful in securing neither of these objectives. However, they were able to persuade the Swedes to make a peace settlement with the Poles and to take up arms in Germany instead.

At first the Swedes made little progress in Germany. They acquired few allies, even among Protestant princes, most of whom felt that the Swedish invasion should be used simply as a bargaining counter to put pressure on the Emperor. However, the situation was transformed by two factors.

● The Treaty of Barwalde (23 January 1631), which improved the Swedes' financial position by giving them a considerable French subsidy.

● The destruction of the Lutheran city of Magdeburg by Tilly's forces (20 May 1631) immediately forced the Elector of Brandenburg to join the Swedes.

Gustavus Adolphus and his forces then made rapid progress through Germany. Crucially, however, it was the aggression of Tilly, whose forces entered Saxony on 4 September 1631, which boosted the forces of Sweden and Brandenburg by forcing the Elector of Saxony, John George, into reluctant alliance with them. This gave them an army of approximately 40,000 men, comfortably outnumbering the forces of Tilly. The two forces met at Breitenfeld, near Leipzig, on 11 September. After early success against the untried Saxon forces, Tilly was eventually defeated by the superior discipline and tactical skill of the Swedish army. Tilly's army lost about 20,000 men and Gustavus Adolphus also gained control of Tilly's artillery and treasury.

Breitenfeld was the first strategically significant Protestant victory of the entire war, and Gustavus worked quickly to build on his success. The Saxon army occupied Silesia and Bohemia, and in November Prague once again came under Protestant control. The Swedes, meanwhile, moved westwards, capturing in the process a large area of Catholic territory, including the bishoprics of Würzburg, Bamberg and Mainz. Within a few months, the situation had been transformed. Most of the Empire north of a line from Mannheim to Prague lay in the hands of Sweden and its allies.

1. What were the motives for the intervention of Christian IV of Denmark and Gustavus Adolphus of Sweden in the Thirty Years' War?

2. Why was the Swedish intervention more successful than that of the Danes?

15.4 Why did the first battle of Breitenfeld not lead to a complete triumph by the Protestant forces?

The rapidity and scale of Sweden's success created immediate problems for their French backers. Cardinal Richelieu might have been happy to see the Habsburgs weakened on a grand scale. It was quite another matter, however, to see Catholic German territories being subjected to Swedish control or threat. Nevertheless, there was little at this stage that the French could do, except offer military protection to the Archbishop of Trier. In particular, there was little the French could do to assist the greatest of the non-Habsburg Catholic powers in the Empire, Maximilian of Bavaria. Maximilian was panic-stricken. It seemed obvious to most observers that the future of Europe would be decided in the new campaigning season of 1632; it was equally obvious to Maximilian that much of the campaigning would take place in Bavaria, which he regarded as being unable to defend itself from an attack from the north. Maximilian was forced to beg the Emperor to raise a new army under the command of his arch-enemy Wallenstein, whom Maximilian had been largely responsible for forcing out of command only a year earlier.

Wallenstein had been expecting a recall, and he was ready once again to put together a large army – at a price: there should be regular subsidies for his troops paid for by the Emperor and by Spain, he should be fully compensated for the loss of Mecklenburg, and he should be free to negotiate a separate peace between the Emperor and any individual German prince.

Gustavus Adolphus, by this stage, had broadened the modest war aims which he had defined on first invading German territory. He had come up with a scheme which attacked the basis of the Empire. He sought the creation of a league of German princes under Swedish protection. Meanwhile, Axel Oxenstierna set about creating an efficient administrative structure in those territories which were under Swedish occupation.

The 1632 campaign began in March when Tilly was able to expel the Swedish garrisons from Bamberg. In retaliation, Gustavus attacked Bavaria, which was virtually defenceless because Wallenstein had decided to concentrate his forces in Bohemia to drive the Saxons from there. Tilly was killed and his army was routed. There was nothing to stop the plundering of the duchy. Some towns, realising that resistance was hopeless, surrendered to the invaders. Gustavus and Frederick, the Elector Palatine, were able to enter Munich unopposed on 17 May.

Even with the expulsion of the Saxons from Bohemia, the Catholic cause now seemed very weak. Wallenstein was besieged in his heavily-fortified position, Alte Veste, near Nuremberg. Despite the strength of the Swedish bombardment, Wallenstein hung out, and the Swedes retreated to the north-west. This gave Wallenstein the opportunity to move north-east to attack his enemies at their weakest point, Saxony. This strategy proved successful, and Wallenstein was able to enter Leipzig in triumph on 1 November 1632.

Having secured a great triumph, Wallenstein then made a crucial error. Assuming that campaigning for the year was over, he ordered his army to disperse to its winter quarters on 14 November. The Swedes, however, had not finished and two days later they caught up with the remains of Wallenstein's army at Lützen.

The two sides were evenly matched, and the battle was a long and bloody affair. The Swedes were victorious when Wallenstein decided he had sustained too many losses to continue the battle and retreated into Bohemia. The Swedish victory, however, had come at a price: their inspirational leader, Gustavus Adolphus, was fatally wounded. On the other hand, Wallenstein's retreat meant that Protestant forces were able to regain control of Saxony.

The campaign of 1632 had not resolved the situation. On the Protestant side, Bohemia had been lost, and morale undoubtedly suffered as a result of the death of Gustavus Adolphus. However, most of the territories which had been acquired in the previous year were still in Protestant hands. On the Catholic side, much of Bavaria had been devastated.

The traumatic events of 1632 were followed by stalemate in 1633. At first the main armies barely participated in any fighting. The Swedish regent, Oxenstierna, was anxious, mainly on financial grounds, to make peace with the Emperor if Sweden were to secure two fundamental items: creation of a strong Protestant Union to guarantee Swedish security and possession of Pomerania in satisfaction of Sweden's war expenses. The

League of Heilbronn: A group of Protestant states, put together by the Swedish chancellor Oxenstierna, who were prepared to ally themselves with the Swedish occupation of much of the Empire.

former was achieved, up to a point, with the creation of the **League of Heilbronn**. However, this was not as all-embracing as Oxenstierna had hoped as neither Saxony nor Brandenburg, both suspicious of Swedish ambitions, was willing to join. By the autumn of 1633 the latter was threatened as Wallenstein moved north, defeated a Swedish force at Steinau in Silesia and headed towards Pomerania.

The death of Wallenstein

Political developments during the winter of 1633–34 were very complex. There remains much uncertainty as to what precisely Albrecht von Wallenstein was engaged in at this time. He had certainly irritated the Emperor by his unwillingness during 1633 to attack the Swedes head on. His personal conduct was also becoming bizarre. What made things worse, from the Emperor's point of view, was that Wallenstein was entering independently into peace negotiations with his opponents. He was entitled by the terms of the Göllersdorf Agreement to discuss peace terms with Saxony. He was not, however, entitled to discuss terms with Sweden and France.

Wallenstein might have been trying to drive a wedge between his opponents. The Emperor, however, was justified in suspecting Wallenstein of engaging in treasonable conduct, especially as he had exacted an oath of personal loyalty from his senior officers. Whatever the truth of the matter, the Emperor had had enough of his brilliant, though wayward, general. He resolved to be rid of him once and for all. Moreover, he had a further compelling reason for ridding himself of Wallenstein. Philip IV of Spain had at last committed himself to offering substantial military support to Ferdinand. However, it was made clear that this army would not fight under Wallenstein's command. Lacking the political confidence to sack Wallenstein a second time, Ferdinand decided to have the general murdered. Thus, in circumstances that remain obscure, Wallenstein and four of his associates were assassinated on the night of 25 February 1634.

Protestant deadlock

Internal divisions on the Protestant side prevented them from exploiting the temporary weakness on the Catholic side following the Emperor's murder of Wallenstein. The main reason for this was the intense jealousy of Sweden that persisted among some of the Protestant princes in Germany. This came to a head in April 1634 when the Elector of Brandenburg refused to join the League of Heilbronn unless the Swedes gave up their claim to Pomerania, which they were unwilling to do. As a result, there was a crucial division in Protestant strategic objectives during the campaigning season of 1634. On the one hand, Saxony and Brandenburg pushed into Silesia with the ultimate intention of recapturing Bohemia for the Protestant side.

On the other hand, Sweden and its allies from the League of Heilbronn pushed into Bavaria. As a result of this split, neither Protestant force was able to achieve its strategic objectives. The Saxons and Brandenburgers retreated from their position near Prague. The Swedes and the League of Heilbronn met the Imperial forces, now crucially reinforced by Spanish troops, just outside the Protestant city of Nördlingen. The result was a crushing Imperial victory. The Swedish general, Gustav Horn, was captured and his army was forced to retreat north of the river Main, leaving the members of the League of Heilbronn vulnerable to Imperial counter-attack.

1. Why was the Emperor able to recover from defeat at the first battle of Breitenfeld?

2. Can the Emperor's conduct in ordering the assassination of Wallenstein be justified? Give reasons for your answer.

15.5 Why, and with what consequences, did the French become directly involved?

The situation was now delicately poised. There was little inclination on the Imperial side to gloat over their triumph since it was by now an open secret that direct French intervention was likely. In order to cope with the problems posed by a French attack, Ferdinand therefore sought to break the already fragile Protestant alliance by making a separate peace with the Electors of Saxony and Brandenburg. Negotiations began in the autumn of 1634 and eventually the Peace of Prague was signed on 30 May 1635. This was especially significant in that it marked the end of the war as a predominantly religious struggle within the Empire. Instead, it was to become a much wider international and dynastic conflict, in which much of the fighting took place outside Germany and Bohemia.

- Moderate forces within the Empire now predominated. They recognised that the security of the Imperial position depended on securing long-term peace with a significant number of Lutheran states.

- The Emperor made peace with Saxony, Brandenburg and some smaller Protestant states whose armies were incorporated within the Imperial forces.

- Protestant and Catholic territories were to remain in possession of lands held on 12 November 1626. All territories taken since 1630 were to be restored to their owners.

- The Elector of Saxony was to have Lusatia and the Elector of Brandenburg Pomerania.

- The Peace significantly weakened the Swedish position within Germany, as many of the smaller states broke their links with the Swedes and hurried to make peace with the Empire. The Swedes were even forced, as a result, to abandon Bremen and Verden to their Danish rivals.

The imminence of the Peace of Prague forced France's hands. The French, with some justification, were convinced that the Spanish intended to invade French territory. The temptation to bring the fight to Habsburg territory was therefore a strong one. Moreover, the Swedish defeat at Nördlingen, the collapse of the League of Heilbronn and the imminence of the Peace of Prague forced direct French intervention in order to prevent a complete collapse of Swedish power. In all of this their main target was not so much the Emperor as the King of Spain; the French believing that, if Spain could be weakened, the Emperor would not care to continue the international conflict.

Even so, the decision to intervene directly was a difficult one for Louis XIII of France and Cardinal Richelieu to make. The prospect of direct intervention in a foreign war, with the intention of apparently aiding Protestant states, had alarmed Catholic opinion in France. For a long time the French had preferred to act indirectly. They did this in several ways.

- They offered financial support to the Swedes to support their invasion of the Empire.

- They also offered financial support to the Dutch in their conflict with Spain.

- They invaded Habsburg client territories in Mantua, Savoy and Lorraine and occupied strategically sensitive areas in Alsace.

It was fortunate for the French that the Spanish played into their hands by invading the lands of the Archbishop of Trier, who was under French protection, and arresting the archbishop on 26 March 1635. It was clear that Louis XIII and Richelieu could not ignore such an attack on French honour. On 19 May the French declared war on Spain.

The situation in 1635 has been aptly summarised by Geoffrey Parker, in *The Thirty Years' War*:

'These were momentous events, whose consequences were to be felt for years. The elector of Trier was to be kept in prison until 1645; the war between France and the Empire was to last until 1648, the war between France and Spain until 1659. These conflicts merged with the others already afoot – in the Netherlands and in the Empire – until a genuinely European conflict was being fought. And the strain of war on so many fronts at once was to bring most of the states involved to the brink of peace and dissolution.'

Neither side could really afford a full-scale conflict. Both the French and the Spanish, however, were prepared to risk domestic problems in pursuit of their strategic objectives – breaking Habsburg encirclement in the case of the French and upholding Habsburg dynastic interests in the case of Spain. In 1636 the Spanish launched a three-pronged attack on France which reached to within 25 miles of Paris. The anti-Habsburg side received a considerable boost when the Swedes defeated the forces of the Empire and Saxony at the Battle of Wittstock. Moreover, the Spanish lost to the French at Leucate in Catalonia and to the Dutch at Breda. The army of the League of Heilbronn, entirely paid for by the French, tied down the Imperial army in Alsace.

By 1638 all sides in the conflict wished to see peace restored. However, their commitment to peace was superficial. As long as the war continued and each temporarily gained the upper hand, the negotiating position was changed and, thus, the fighting continued. In 1638 peace talks, at Compiègne between the French and Spanish and in Hamburg among the German states, foundered. The French gained the upper hand in 1639 when their German client forces (an army entirely financed by the French), under Bernard of Saxe-Weimar, captured the strategically significant town of Breisach. In the same year, their Dutch allies destroyed the Spanish navy in the Battle of the Downs off the Kent coast of England, and the Swedes, helped by a further French subsidy, were able once again to attempt an invasion of Bohemia.

The scale of Imperial defeats and what Geoffrey Parker calls 'the widespread destruction and demoralisation of Germany' prompted the new Emperor, Ferdinand III, to propose the meeting of an Imperial Diet for the first time since 1613. In September 1640 this duly met at Regensburg and began once again the search for a settlement within Germany. After the disasters of 1639, the Emperor was forced to accept the abrogation (cancellation) of the Edict of Restitution. Despite the condemnation of the Papacy, church property which was in secular hands on 1 January 1627 would remain so.

Developments were slow and were dramatically overtaken by the separate peace negotiated between Brandenburg and Sweden in July 1641, which further weakened the Emperor's position. This enabled the Swedes to advance once again through Saxony, Silesia and then Moravia in 1642. Though the Swedes were unable to keep their position in Moravia, they were able to achieve another stunning victory at Breitenfeld against the Imperialists and their Saxon allies in November. A month later, Leipzig surrendered. To make matters worse for the Emperor, he also lost the support of Maximilian of Bavaria. Maximilian had never been devoted to the Habsburg cause and, along with the Electors of Cologne and Mainz, he held separate peace talks with the French. The final nail in the Imperial coffin was the defeat by the French, in 1643 at Rocroi in the Ardennes, of the Spanish army. Henceforth, there could be no chance of invasion of France from the Spanish Netherlands.

1. In what circumstances did the French intervene directly in the war in 1635?

2. What motivated the French to intervene directly in the war?

3. Why did it take the French so long to overcome the resistance of the Habsburgs and their allies?

4. To what extent does French intervention suggest that the war was no longer mainly about religion?

15.6 What was the significance of the Peace of Westphalia for the Holy Roman Empire and for Europe?

By 1643 all sides were anxious for peace. In January representatives of many of the German princes met in Frankfurt in an attempt to resolve the remaining German issues and to determine how to negotiate with the foreign powers most effectively. Meanwhile, representatives of the foreign Catholic powers gathered at Münster, while Sweden and its allies gathered at Osnabrück. For a time matters were deadlocked as the Emperor, temporarily strengthened because Sweden had gone to war with Denmark, refused to recognise the separate voting rights of the German princes within the peacemaking process. It was not until August 1645 that such rights were conceded by the Emperor, a clear triumph for the principle of princely particularism (see Chapter 5 for definition).

Despite the peace process, fighting continued. An Imperial army, sent to aid Denmark against the Swedes in 1644, was destroyed by starvation,

The War in the 1640s

despite never fighting a battle. In 1645 the Swedes achieved a great triumph against the Imperial army at Jankov, forcing the Emperor to flee and opening up the prospect of a Swedish capture of Vienna and Prague. The Bavarians, having bravely resisted superior French forces for over two years, were eventually defeated at the second battle of Nördlingen. This forced Maximilian to make his own separate ceasefire with France at Ulm in 1647.

However, the French decided to increase their demands, thereby forcing Maximilian into reluctant alliance with the Emperor. Once again, the Imperial and Bavarian army was heavily defeated, this time at Zusmarshausen. This time, though, the French could not continue to exert a high price for peace. The outbreak of the revolt known as the 'Fronde' forced the French to seek a settlement as soon as possible. They were therefore willing to moderate their demands.

The Swedes, meanwhile, had once again invaded Bohemia. But having failed to secure toleration for Protestants in Bohemia they retired from the fray, having received a substantial pay-off. The Emperor, with the Swedes on the brink of taking Prague, was happy to accept peace, even though he knew that he would be leaving his Spanish relatives in the lurch. The Spanish, meanwhile, carried on their war with France for another 11 years. Hostilities between Sweden and Poland also continued. For the rest of continental Europe, however, the peace agreement was signed on 24 October 1648.

The Peace of Westphalia proved to be a significant, and in some respects long-lasting, peace settlement. For several generations it was widely assumed to be the basis of order and stability in Europe.

Key aspects of the Peace of Westphalia

- The sovereignty and independence of each state of the Holy Roman Empire were recognised, thereby rendering the Emperor virtually powerless.

- Sweden was confirmed in possession of western Pomerania, thereby enhancing its control of the Baltic and ensuring that Denmark was a long-term sufferer from the peace settlement. Sweden's possession of Bremen and Verden was confirmed.

- Brandenburg, having lost western Pomerania to the Swedes, was compensated with several ecclesiastical territories, including Magdeburg and Halberstadt. Its possession of Mark and Cleves was confirmed.

- Saxony's possession of Lusatia was confirmed.

- The Lower Palatinate was restored to Karl Ludwig, eldest son of Frederick V.

- Bavarian possession of the Upper Palatinate was confirmed.

- France made several territorial gains, including the bishoprics of Metz, Toul and Verdun and substantial territory in Alsace.

- Spain was forced to recognise the independence of the United Provinces.

Who benefited most?

The country that benefited most from the Peace of Westphalia was France. It was able to make significant territorial gains in the east. Sweden also benefited territorially. The United Provinces benefited from the decline in Spain's international might to confirm permanently their independent status. Some Protestant territories, such as the Rhineland Palatinate and Saxony, did better territorially than their performance during the war might seem to warrant. The traditional role of the Holy Roman Empire was virtually eradicated. Moreover, some territories, such as parts of Alsace, were removed from the Empire. Nevertheless, despite the catalogue of military disasters that had afflicted the Empire in the later stages of the wars, the outcome of the Peace of Westphalia was not a complete disaster for the Emperor. If anything, it ensured that the Emperor could consolidate his power as ruler of the Habsburg lands, and certainly foreshadowed the later expansion of the Habsburg monarchy.

In the end the treaties of Münster and Osnabrück, in the words of Michael Hughes in *Early Modern Germany, 1477–1806* (1992), 'contained nothing startlingly new'. Instead, they confirmed trends that had been evident for several centuries. In particular, they sanctioned the rights and particularism of individual states against the Emperor.

'The Great European War-Ballet' (1647–48). This print shows the European rulers who were represented in the Westphalian peace process. Various groups dance hand in hand. The group on the right features the youthful Louis XIV of France in the company of the King of Portugal, the Prince of Orange and the Swedish General Torstensson. They are matched by the Emperor and three of his allies. They are dancing next to the tomb of Frederick, the Elector Palatine, whilst the body of Gustavus Adolphus lies on the floor. Various rulers look on, including the Ottoman Emperor (extreme right). In the foreground the Swiss cantons and Saxony are trying to pick up as many pieces as they can. The angels are scattering olive branches and apples of discord.

15.7 *What was the nature of the Thirty Years' War and how extensive was its impact?*
A CASE STUDY IN HISTORICAL INTERPRETATION

One of the most enduring debates among historians concerns the nature and extent of the impact of the Thirty Years' War. Traditionally, the war was seen as having certain key features.

- It was a distinctively German conflict that was fought predominantly and more or less continuously in Germany.

- The central issues were the relationship between the Emperor and the princes and the continued religious divisions within the Empire.

- Its effects were catastrophic for the German people and were politically and economically disastrous.

The Thirty Years' War: a German conflict?

In the 19th century – an age of growing German nationalism – the 'national' character of the Thirty Years' War was much emphasised. This was part of a process by which German national identity was recovered by historians. It also served as a warning of what could happen to a divided Germany surrounded by powerful enemies. Gustav Freytag, for example, writing in the late 1850s in *Pictures of German Life,* saw the condition of Germany immediately before the war as 'inwardly diseased'. By the end of the war 'there was little remaining of the great nation'. Even a left-wing historian like Franz Mehring, writing in 1894, claimed that 'never has a great civilised nation had to endure comparable destruction'. This perception was shared by the British historian, Veronica Wedgwood, who argued in *The Thirty Years' War* in 1938 that 'the geography and politics of Germany alone give the key to the problem'. Such an interpretation was challenged in 1939 by the French historian, Georges Pagès, who in *The Thirty Years' War* saw the war as a European conflict largely controlled by the French. Given the time of writing, this might have represented wishful thinking.

The view was further challenged in 1947 in an article by S. H. Steinberg entitled 'The Thirty Years' War: a new interpretation'. The writer attacked the claim that Germany was central to the Thirty Years' War. At this point, it is worth pointing out that Steinberg was a Jewish historian of German birth who had come to Britain as a political refugee from Nazism. Steinberg argued that the war was essentially international in its character, that it was merely one of a wider series of conflicts over domination in Europe and that it was 'not primarily German'.

The centrality of the 'German' character of the conflict has also been challenged by historians who came to their research either from other national perspectives or who studied predominantly non-German sources. Thus the Czech historian, J. V. Polišenský, argued in 'The Thirty Years' War' (1954) that 'Czech historians are also unsatisfied that a war which started with a coup in Prague … and ended with the fighting on the Old Bridge in Prague … has much specifically German about it'. Instead, he argued that it was part of a wider European conflict which had implications for states as widely separated as the United Provinces and Muscovy. To develop this point, Polišenský, spent much of his career exploring non-German aspects of the war and published extensively on Dutch, Swedish and Danish participation.

The Emperors, the princes and religion

The view that the war was fundamentally about the relationship between the Emperor and princes, and about the clash between old and new faiths, was confidently asserted during the mid-19th century by Gustav Freytag in *Pictures of German Life*.

Freytag saw the interests of the Habsburgs and the German nation as being fundamentally opposed. His sympathies lay entirely with the latter. Freytag's views, however subconsciously, clearly reflect the *kleindeutsch* (i.e. anti-Austrian and anti-Habsburg) views of Bismarck and the dominant Prussian political figures of his own time. Moreover, the German people were 'divided into countless territories under weak princes' and as a result they became involved in too many 'trifling disputes'.

Veronica Wedgwood, in *The Thirty Years' War*, also saw the role of the Habsburgs as being central. It was not just their dynastic strength that was crucial; it was also their absolutism and their devotion to the Catholic Church. Moreover, 'empty as was the Imperial title in 1618, the dynasty had not abandoned the hope of restoring to it the reality of power'. To Veronica Wedgwood it was a matter of regret that 'no statesman of genius within Germany' emerged to put a stop to the war and, hence, curb the dynastic ambitions of the Habsburgs. This demonstrates her conservative view about the extent to which individuals might alter the course of history.

Dynasticism: This was the belief that the interests of one's own family were paramount.

There is ample evidence drawn from across the period to suggest that Habsburg **dynasticism** and power was important. This includes the willingness of the Spanish Habsburgs to support their cousins at crucial times in the conflict and the impact of the Edict of Restitution in 1629, which worried even Catholic princes. On the other hand, the Peace of Prague, negotiated shortly after the Emperor had won a stunning victory at the Battle of Nördlingen, suggested that he was capable of being pragmatic. Ferdinand II chose that time to withdraw the Edict of Restitution and build bridges with the more moderate Protestant princes.

The evidence regarding religion is also not always clear cut. Most historians writing in the 19th-century German national tradition were Protestant, and this is reflected in their interpretations of the religious aspects of the war. Thus, Gustav Droysen wrote in his biography *Gustav Adolf* in 1870 of the 'vigorous restoration of Papist teachings which had aroused the indignation of all Protestants'. The Czech historian Anton Gindely, writing in his *History of the Thirty Years' War* in 1882 when Czech national feelings within the Austro-Hungarian Empire were increasing rapidly, blamed religion for the conflict. However, he considered Catholics and Protestants 'equally guilty' for the conflict.

The religious motives of participants in the wars were stressed by a range of historians. In 1890, for example, the English historian C.R.L. Fletcher in his *Gustavus Adolphus* saw his subject as a 'Christian gentleman' and 'champion of Protestantism' – a suitable role model for those who were being trained at the time to govern the British Empire.

The German Marxist historian Franz Mehring, writing in 1894, whilst acknowledging the importance of religious motivation, asserted that the primary motive of the major participants was economic. When princes asserted their religious principles, they were often mainly concerned about church lands. Writing in a more secular age, Steinberg argued in 'The Thirty Years' War: a new interpretation' that 'the conception of the Thirty Years' War as a "war of religion" has been abandoned to a large extent since it has been recognised that religious divisions coincided largely with political, constitutional and economic ones'. Religious enthusiasms were useful as a means of stirring the masses. However, 'rational considerations of political and economic gains determined the policies of the cabinets'.

More recently, Geoffrey Parker in *The Thirty Years' War* has sought to re-establish the importance of religion as a motive of the participants in the war. Those German princes who actually took up arms 'were strongly influenced by confessional considerations'. Their religious sincerity was 'beyond doubt', and 'as long as these men and their German supporters predominated, so too did the issue of religion'. It should, however, be noted that Lutheran Saxony in 1619, and again in 1635, decided to support the Emperor. Thus, they placed a higher priority on maintaining the unity of the Empire than on the furtherance of the Protestant cause. However, the religious character of the war receded. Both moderate Lutherans and non-German participants emphasised 'reasons of state' to explain their involvement.

The effects of the Thirty Years' War

There has been little agreement among historians regarding the effects of the Thirty Years' War. In the mid-19th century historians regarded the effects of the war as appalling. Freytag, in *Pictures of German Life*, wrote of 'annihilation' and described a 'country which had become a great charnel house [vault for the bones of the dead]'. Not only had the war brought death on a huge scale to Germany, it had also resulted in great economic decline. This view was reinforced by another German nationalist historian, Karl Theodor von Inama-Sternegg. Such views struck a chord with German public opinion at a time of rising nationalism since they implied that foreigners, taking advantage of Germany's disunity, had destroyed Germany's society and economy. These arguments were based on a narrow range of sources, some of them dubious, and depended on generalising on the basis of a small part of the country. The two sources which most influenced this group of nationalist historians were a literary source (first published in 1669), *Simplicissimus* by Christopher von Grimmelshausen, and the works of Samuel von Pufendorf (court historian to the Elector of Brandenburg and, therefore, the representative of one of the key participants in the conflict).

Ironically, the first real attack on this interpretation also came from a German nationalist source, Eberhard Gothein. He considered that the war had been blamed for a decline which had begun long before and which had been largely brought about by political confusion and division. His moral was quite clear: only a united Germany could guarantee economic prosperity. Such arguments were bolstered by the work of historians who did detailed work on particular localities. The arguments continued for half a century. A majority of local studies argued that the impact of the war had indeed been disastrous, though a significant minority held that fundamental decline in their areas had set in before the war started. By 1938 Veronica Wedgwood, in *The Thirty Years' War*, was arguing that the effects of the war on German history had been 'greatly and even damagingly exaggerated' and 'were neither so general, so prolonged nor so disastrous as they have been popularly presented'. However, her position was contradictory since she also argued that the war was 'morally subversive, economically destructive, socially degrading, confused in its causes, devious in its course, (and) futile in its results'. It was, in short, 'the outstanding example in European history of meaningless conflict'.

It was S. H. Steinberg in 'The Thirty Years' War: a new interpretation' who argued most forcefully for the limited nature of the effects of the war. Those who had argued differently had accepted too willingly the Brandenburg version of the war, which was concerned with the defence of the Protestant religion and German liberties against Habsburg interference and foreign aggression. Whilst such interpretations had reflected the dominant values of Bismarck's Germany, they could no longer be sustained in the aftermath of the Second World War. Earlier historians, Steinberg argued, had based their arguments too much on the special pleading of those who had been particularly badly affected. Moreover, 'all of the campaigns of the period 1609–1648 were of short duration and the armies themselves of a very small size'. Most of Germany, apart from a few strategically sensitive places, was unaffected. 'The majority of towns never saw an enemy inside their walls.'

More recently, historians like Christopher Friedrichs in *The Thirty Years' War* (1997; edited by Geoffrey Parker) and Heiner Haan have argued that the German experience needs to be placed in a wider European context. Much of Europe was experiencing economic decline after the boom years of the 16th century. Germany was no exception. Thus, the argument that the economy had declined before the war began has gained ground in recent years.

Conclusions

It is possible to arrive at some tentative conclusions, though the varied and incomplete nature of the evidence means that these are never likely to become definitive.

- The population seems to have fallen by about 15%–20%. (Some earlier estimates suggested that the war had been responsible for the deaths of half of all Germans at the time.)
- Within this overall pattern there were considerable regional variations. The worst-hit areas – according to Friedrichs in *The Thirty Years' War* (edited by Geoffrey Parker) – Mecklenburg, Pomerania and

> *Callot's prints were reproduced in a large number of impressions during the period. Why do you think they were so popular?*

'The Hanging Tree' from a series of prints entitled 'The Miseries of War' by Jacques Callot, a printmaker from the Duchy of Lorraine, which was invaded by the French army in 1633. It was in that year that Callot's first set of engravings on the miseries of war were published in Paris.

His prints were not intended to depict specific events, but the series very graphically details the horrors that can happen when military discipline is lost, as often happened during the Thirty Years' War.

Württemberg, *did* lose over half of their population.

- Villages were worse hit than walled towns and cities. The reason why the sack of Magdeburg created such a shock was because it was an exception to this general rule.

- There were a large number of deaths in battle, especially at the first battles of Breitenfeld and Nördlingen and at Wittstock.

- Deaths due to direct military action were only a small part of the picture. Many more people were killed by epidemic disease or by war-related food shortages.

- Almost every section of German society experienced economic decline during the war years.

- Many towns and cities were deeply in debt, often because of payments made to armies to spare themselves from pillage. (The debt of Nuremberg, for example, had grown fourfold between 1618 and 1648.)

- Rural areas often experienced massive, but often temporary, reductions in agricultural output.

- In eastern Germany many vacated holdings returned to their landlords, thereby contributing to the collapse of an independent peasantry and to the rise of large-scale estate farming.

This had led Friedrichs to conclude, in *The Thirty Years' War*, 'that the short-term economic and demographic catastrophe which made such an impression on contemporaries seems exaggerated when placed in the context of Germany's overall development between about 1550 and 1700'. He does acknowledge that this would have been little consolation to those who had suffered directly because 'they had to live with the uncertainties and horrors of the longest, most expensive and most brutal war that had yet been fought on German soil'. Friedrichs concluded that 'those Germans who survived the war to its end knew that it had been an unprecedented catastrophe for the German people and they knew, better than their children and better even than some modern-day historians, why the making of peace and the departure of the last Swedish soldiers provided an occasion for hymns of praise and sermons of thanksgivings all over Germany'.

Moreover, Professor Rabb has placed these events in a wider context by arguing that the reason the war created images of horror was 'its unarguable pre-eminence as the most bloody and anarchic set of events that the Continent had ever witnessed'. Until the French Revolution 'it was thought of as the grim standard, never exceeded, for human depravity'.

1. To what extent have historians disagreed over the issues at stake in the Thirty Years' War?

2. Why have historians disagreed about the effects of the Thirty Years' War?

Source-based questions: The impact of the Thirty Years' War

SOURCE A

The whole bishopric ... is freely yielded up to His Majesty [Gustavus Adolphus].

This week the ... boors [i.e. an insulting way of describing the Catholic peasants] did overcome and surprise 50 Swedish soldiers. ... These boors, when they had mastered them, did cut off their ears and noses, chopped off their hands and feet, and put out their eyes and so left them. ...

As soon as the King of Sweden was advertised [informed] of the cruel insolencies of these boors, he was much displeased, and so much the more because he saw that his soldiers would not put it up but presently cried revenge and burnt their villages, insomuch that in one day there were seen 200 several fires blazing at once.

From 'The Continuation of our Weekly News', London, 6 June 1632

SOURCE B

On 30 September [1633] another troop of one thousand Imperial Spanish cavalry passed through. Although as new recruits they understood no military discipline, they did understand blackmail and robbery, whereat the inhabitants once more left house and home and fled into the woods. ...

On 1 October we once again heard the fearful news that the Swedes had broken in and were plundering and laying waste to the village inn. At Inning they stole four horses. Afterwards the rumour went around that the thieves were Imperial troops.

On 13 October during the first service after reconstruction of Erling village church the alarm was raised several times. ...But only five cavalrymen appeared, asking for fodder.

From Diary of the Thirty Years' War by Maurus Friesenegger, monk of Andechs, Bavaria, 1633

SOURCE C

Since the enemy was also active in these parts and pillaging the whole neighbourhood, and since we were nearly encircled, we decided to make an attempt to ask the victor for mercy. But to our further consternation we had to flee once again into the hills where no one could readily follow us. From there we wandered around, divided into smaller bands, and on 15 September [1634] alone with my nephew and son I hid in the deep Lauterbach valley near the stream in a barn on the fields. ...

We were called back in a letter from our friends, since everything, as far as the times allowed, was back in order, which accorded with the enemy's own best interest.

From A Swabian Clergyman in the Thirty Years' War by Johann Valentin Andreä. (The author was a Lutheran church superintendent.)

SOURCE D

Nor were the wars of the 17th century any more physically destructive or morally degrading in their effects than other wars before or since. Owing to lack of money and difficulties of supply, all the campaigns were of short duration. The armies involved were comparatively small. ... As in every such war the open country and its inhabitants suffered most; the majority of the fortified towns never saw an enemy within their walls. The fable of wholesale ruin must therefore be replaced by the less spectacular recognition that between 1600 and 1650 there took place in Germany a redistribution of populations and fortunes, which benefited some regions, places and persons and harmed others.

From The Thirty Years War and the Conflict for European Hegemony by S. H. Steinberg (1966)

---

1. Study Source A.

How useful is Source A to a historian as evidence about the Swedish campaign in Bavaria in 1632?

2. Study Source B.

On what grounds might Source B be regarded as particularly reliable evidence about the indiscipline of the Imperial troops?

3. Study Sources B, C and D.

How might Sources B and C be used to support Steinberg's argument in Source D that the impact of the war on Germany was limited?

**4. Using all of the sources and the information contained in this chapter, explain why the Thirty Years' War could not be brought to a conclusion during the period 1632–1634.*

16

Social and economic history c.1450–1661

Key Issues

- *In what respects and to what extent did Europe experience economic change during the period c.1450–c.1661?*

- *How much did European society change during the period c.1450–c.1661?*

- *Why did Europe experience an upsurge in the prosecution of witches during the 16th and early 17th centuries?*

16.1 What happened to the population of Europe in this period?

16.2 Why did towns increase in economic importance?

16.3 How did the condition of the peasantry change during the period c.1450–c.1661?

16.4 Why, and to what extent, was there a 'price revolution' during the period c.1450– c.1661?

16.5 What were the major changes in trade and industry?

16.6 Why did witch-hunting become a prominent feature of society during the late 16th and early 17th centuries?

16.7 Historical interpretation: What was the historical basis of witchcraft?

Overview

THE two centuries from 1450 to 1650 witnessed many significant economic and social changes. This period marked the final disappearance of the feudal system from western Europe, though a version of feudalism remained strong in eastern Europe. It also witnessed the emergence of an urban bourgeoisie (as yet, outside the Netherlands, they exercised relatively little political power).

On the other hand, some members of the bourgeoisie were able to make considerable amounts of money from exploiting the emerging capitalist system, as systems of banking, currency exchange and insurance became more sophisticated. The greater sophistication of the capitalist system helped to accelerate changes in the pattern of international trade. With the decline of the Venetian spice trade and the opening up of new trade routes as a result of voyages of exploration, the centre of European trade moved from the Mediterranean to the Atlantic.

By the end of the period the two most important European trading centres were London and Amsterdam. Their growth reflected the development of a recognisably 'modern' form of capitalism within the English and Dutch economies.

Though the financial position of many people improved during this period, there were losers as well as winners. Though the growth in the European population increased the demand for industrial products, it also generated huge inflationary pressures. Food prices rose alarmingly, significantly increasing the financial pressures on the more vulnerable sections of society. The period certainly witnessed an increase in levels of poverty.

The quality of life was threatened in other ways as well. The growth in religious tensions brought about by the Reformation created wars of religion. The level of casualties in the Thirty Years' War, for example, was unprecedented. Many other lives were destroyed by the harsh punishments imposed upon those deemed guilty of witchcraft.

16.1 What happened to the population of Europe in this period?

Numbers

It is very difficult to estimate what happened to the population of Europe in the 200 years after 1450. Outside the city states of northern Italy, systematic counting of the population was unknown. Estimating the size of the population from sources such as parish registers, and military and taxation records can be misleading.

Population estimates, however, have been worked out by J. De Vries in his *European Urbanisation, 1500–1800* (1984), but the figures need to be used with caution.

Population estimates (millions)

	1500	1550	1600	1650
Scandinavia	1.5	1.5	2.0	2.6
England and Wales	2.6	3.2	4.4	5.6
Low Countries	2.35	2.9	3.1	3.9
Germany	12.0	14.0	16.0	12.0
France	16.4	19.0	19.0	20.0
Italy	10.5	11.4	13.1	11.3
Spain	6.8	7.4	8.1	7.1
Austria and Bohemia	3.5	3.6	4.3	4.1
Total for western Europe	61.6	70.2	78.0	74.6

What these raw figures conceal is the reality of life during this period.

● Life expectancy was low throughout Europe. Towards the end of the 17th century the life expectancy among Parisians at birth was only 23 years.

● Levels of infant mortality were high. In France it was estimated that 25% of infants failed to survive the first year of life, and almost half of the children born during the early-modern period failed to reach the age of 10.

● Mortality rates among adults remained high. This meant that marriages were often short-lived. Re-marriage was common.

● Birth rates were high, approximately three times the modern equivalent.

● Illegitimacy rates fluctuated enormously; levels of premarital conception were usually high.

● The density of population fluctuated enormously; the Netherlands and certain Italian city states were the most densely populated areas.

Much of the increase in the population during the 16th century simply represented a recovery to the levels before the Black Death (1346–49), which had been responsible for wiping out about a third of the population. Though nothing as lethal as the Black Death was to recur in the 200 years after 1450, it was still possible for localised plagues to wreak havoc. For example, over half of the population of Milan died in an outbreak of plague in 1630, and 60% of the population of Genoa perished in 1656–57.

Distribution

Outside the Low Countries and northern Italy, the population was overwhelmingly rural. Henry Kamen, for example, has suggested in his *European Society, 1500–1700* (1984) that in 1600 less than 5% of the population of western and central Europe lived in cities with populations of over 20,000 and only a further 20% lived in small towns.

Even so, the population of many cities increased enormously. According to Henry Kamen's figures Lyons in France, for example, quadrupled its population between 1450 and 1550, and the populations of both Antwerp and Seville doubled in size during the first two-thirds of the 16th century. In 1500 only four European cities had over 100,000 inhabitants; by 1600 that number had increased to 12.

Such increases were also matched by the growth in population that took place in many rural areas in the 16th century. Several explanations can be put forward to explain this growth. There was a decrease in the frequency of serious epidemic disease and fewer destructive wars. Population growth did sometimes have unfortunate consequences. It could drive down the level of wages, create land shortages and contribute to subsistence crises (see next section).

The expansion in population seems to have slowed down by the 1580s. The level of epidemic disease rose alarmingly in Mediterranean Europe (i.e. countries with borders on the Mediterranean). Further north the degree of warfare increased substantially, which certainly contributed to the increasing incidence of subsistence crises.

Subsistence crises

Subsistence crises – when bad harvests meant that food supplies were insufficient to provide even the most basic of diets for the poor – happened frequently during the early modern period. Between 1521 and 1663, for example, the area around Paris suffered 13 subsistence crises. The incidence of crises in north-western Europe grew in the second half of the 16th century. One factor that might well have contributed to this increase was climatic change. A 'little ice age' reduced growing seasons, thereby contributing to the bad harvests which pushed up the price of basic foodstuffs. The 1590s seem to have been particularly badly affected. In areas as far apart as the north of England (Newcastle upon Tyne and Cumberland) and Provence (Aix-en-Provence) in France, there was evidence of starvation in 1597. In 1637 it was claimed that famine in the Franche Comté had led to **cannibalism**.

Even when subsistence crises were not in evidence, standards of living for the poor tended to decline during the second half of the 16th century. Grain prices grew sixfold between 1480 and 1600. Wage rates could not keep up with this pressure and, according to historian Richard Bonney, this led to a 'progressive deterioration in the quality of the diet'.

Cannibalism: Eating the flesh of living things of the same type, e.g. humans eating other humans.

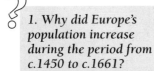

1. Why did Europe's population increase during the period from c.1450 to c.1661?

2. What were the social and economic consequences of the increase in population?

'Peasant Wedding Feast' by
Pieter Bruegel the Elder, 1568

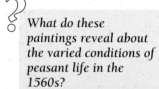

*What do these
paintings reveal about
the varied conditions of
peasant life in the
1560s?*

'Census at Bethlehem' by Pieter Bruegel the Elder, c.1566

16.2 Why did towns increase in economic importance?

Only a small minority of the European population lived in towns. By 1650, only about 10% of the population lived in towns with populations of over 10,000. Most of the towns were themselves small. In 1500, for example, only Paris, Milan, Venice, Naples and Constantinople had over 100,000 inhabitants. By 1650 a further six cities – London, Rome, Palermo, Lisbon, Amsterdam and Madrid – had attained populations of 100,000. Most towns, therefore, even in highly urbanised areas, like parts of Italy and the Low Countries, were quite small.

Towns were often insanitary places with high death rates. Their populations were especially vulnerable both to subsistence crises and to epidemic disease. They were often dependent on immigration to maintain the size of their populations. Immigrants, however, were usually plentiful. They were not only attracted by economic factors such as job opportunities. In some cases, the appeal of towns could be religious or political. Strasbourg, in particular, as a self-governing Protestant city within the Holy Roman Empire, attracted many religious exiles. The growth of Amsterdam, at the expense of Antwerp, was fuelled by the wholesale emigration of Calvinist refugees from the latter city. The establishment of the Spanish Royal Court at Madrid and at the nearby Escorial Palace led to the rapid growth of Madrid at the expense of other towns in Castile, such as Valladolid and Toledo.

Though the 16th and 17th centuries were a period of slow but steady urban growth in western Europe, towns in eastern Europe seem to have been in decline. Richard Bonney in *The European Dynastic States, 1494–1660* (1991), has estimated that only 2% of the population of Muscovy were urban dwellers. Moreover, Muscovite towns were too small to exercise any real economic influence over their hinterlands. Poland, in contrast, had a large number of small towns with populations of under 10,000. Often such towns were controlled by the nobility and were unable to exercise the independent civic life associated with many towns in Italy and the Netherlands.

Many towns were politically dominated by oligarchies. The best example of such domination by a few people was Venice. Despite concentrating political power in very few hands, the Venetian system did appear to guarantee relative political stability. Its constitution remained in force, largely unchanged, until the Venetian Republic was killed off by Napoleon in 1797. Similar closed oligarchies dominated many towns in the Netherlands, such as Gouda. It seems evident that in many towns, like Nördlingen in the Holy Roman Empire, wealth and power became more concentrated during the 16th and first half of the 17th centuries. However, this was not always the case, as is demonstrated by the example of Leiden in the Netherlands, where the increase in wealth was enjoyed by a far higher proportion of the population.

Towns often witnessed the scene of great political disorder, though this was usually short-lived. Among the largest cities there were food riots at Lyons in 1529, Naples in 1585 and Palermo in 1647. Some towns experienced violence against outsiders: there were anti-Jewish riots at Frankfurt-am-Main in 1614 and anti-Algerian riots in Marseilles in 1620. Tax riots, for example at La Rochelle in 1542 and Bordeaux in 1548, were common. In Ghent in 1539 the citizens rose against Charles V, partly because of taxation and partly in defence of their civic privileges which were being eroded by the Emperor. Defence of civic privileges was also at the heart of the Revolt of the Communeros in Castile in 1520–21. Religious radicalism prompted disorder in Ghent in 1578.

1. What factors assisted the growth of towns in Europe during the period c.1450–c.1661?

2. Why did towns sometimes experience political and social instability during the period c.1450–c.1661?

16.3 How did the condition of the peasantry change during the period c.1450–c.1661?

Serfdom: State or condition of being a peasant (i.e. a slave having to work for someone with little or no pay). Serfs were not able by law to move from their land or to inherit property.

In most parts of Europe, outside the Low Countries, most people lived in the countryside. In Europe west of the river Elbe this meant that most country dwellers were either free peasants, who worked on land which they leased from landowners, or landless labourers. In eastern Europe, on the other hand, **serfdom** still existed and was in fact consolidated during the 16th and 17th centuries.

It is impossible to generalise confidently about the position of the peasantry in western Europe. Conditions of tenure and standards of living varied enormously. The peasantry in Spain seem to have suffered from high levels of rent and taxation, a situation which contributed to the steady depopulation of the countryside, the growth of towns and emigration to the New World. From a strong position at the start of the 16th century, peasant conditions appear to have become more unfavourable in France, where the situation was often made worse by the frequency of civil wars and political instability. The situation was made worse in those areas where peasant holdings were divided at death among the heirs, thereby leading to the creation of too many uneconomic holdings that were unable to sustain a peasant lifestyle. Thus, many peasants were reduced from proprietor status to that of labourers. This was an especially grim fate because the period witnessed a fall in real wages for the labouring poor.

In eastern Europe the increasing scope of serfdom seems to have been largely a product of two factors: the relative shortage of labour and the extent of the political power of the nobility. In Prussia, between 1526 and 1633 the law was tightened no fewer than five times in order to limit the rights of peasants to move from their land or to inherit property. Laws were passed in 1556 and 1608 to tie the peasants more closely to their estates in Hungary. Estates became increasingly dependent on the labour services of the peasantry. Consequently, a free peasantry virtually disappeared. For example, in Bohemia in 1654 it was estimated that only about 500 peasants enjoyed free status. The reduction in peasant status was most marked in Muscovy. The other side of the coin was the increasing size of noble estates, which further consolidated the political power of the nobility.

Noble rank in most European countries conferred privileges as well as power. Most nobles on the European continent were exempt from direct taxation. In Poland from 1496 and in Hungary from 1514 landownership was restricted to the nobility. In western Europe, despite their privileges, the nobility did come under financial pressure. In Castile, for example, noble incomes seem to have kept pace with inflation through most of the 16th century. In the 17th century this ceased increasingly to be the case. The problem was made worse because many nobles were unable to sell land because of the existence of the practice of **entail**. Because of their inability to realise the value of some of their assets, they were forced into borrowing increasing sums of money. In France, where the practice of entail was much rarer, many estates became increasingly fragmented and unprofitable. Marriage to rich heiresses, sometimes from backgrounds in trade, was often necessary to maintain a family's fortunes. The aspiration to acquire a landed estate was often highly developed among the urban bourgeoisie. Many Paris city councillors, for example, were able to acquire noble status through the acquisition of land. Many coal-owning families from Newcastle upon Tyne in England were able to acquire landed estates in the surrounding counties.

Entail: A legal process by which a landowner or landholder attempted to ensure that a property could not be disposed of or divided by his descendants.

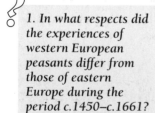

1. In what respects did the experiences of western European peasants differ from those of eastern Europe during the period c.1450–c.1661?

2. Why did a free peasantry virtually disappear in eastern Europe during the period c.1450–c.1661?

16.4 Why, and to what extent, was there a 'price revolution' during the period c.1450–c.1661?

Though it is difficult to generalise with confidence about European price levels, it is clear that the 16th and 17th centuries did experience substantial amounts of price inflation. It has been asserted, for example, that there was more than a fivefold increase in food prices in England in the 170 years after 1450. The increase in France at the same time was more than sevenfold. Even within the same country price inflation could be variable. For example, throughout the 16th century there were variations in wheat prices in Paris, compared with Lyon.

In general, though harvest failures could bring about sudden increases, it appears that there was a rapid inflation during the first half of the 16th century, followed by a more steady price rise. Though the price of manufactured goods rose more slowly than that of food, the impact of the price rise was catastrophic for many wage-earners, wages having risen much more slowly than prices. On the other hand, price inflation, by reducing the long-term cost of borrowing, did encourage a growth in capital investment.

There is little agreement among historians as to the reasons for rising prices.

- The American historian Earl J. Hamilton saw the primary cause of inflation as arising from the increased supply of money brought about by the Spanish import of precious metals from their Latin American colonies. (This relationship had first been noticed by Martin de Azpílcueta Navarro of the University of Salamanca in 1556.) Hamilton's arguments have since been criticised by other historians. They argue, for example, that Hamilton under-estimated the importance of the existing silver production within Europe, that there were technical flaws in his calculations and that there was no necessary correlation between the period of greatest imports and the period of most steeply rising prices.

- The policy of debasement of the coinage, frequently resorted to by French and English monarchs, for example, undoubtedly stimulated inflationary pressures in those countries.

- The increasing population created problems for the food supply. It was impossible within the agrarian conditions of the 16th and 17th centuries to increase the supply of food in proportion to the increasing size of the population. This created inflationary pressure on food prices. This pressure was at its worst at times of bad harvests.

- Contemporary writers often laid the blame for rising prices on the greed of producers, merchants and landlords.

1. Why did the period from c.1450 to c.1661 experience so much inflation?

2. What were the social and economic consequences of inflation during the period c.1450–c.1661?

16.5 What were the major changes in trade and industry?

International trade

At the start of the 16th century the two most important trading areas of Europe were the Low Countries and northern Italy. Both areas were renowned as centres of textile manufacturing. Such manufacturing included the substantial production of woollen cloth. Each area, however, also specialised in the production of high value-added luxury products: Florence and other cities in northern Italy specialised in the production of silk products, Flanders was a centre of tapestry-weaving and metal-working, and Venice dominated the spice trade.

Following the voyages of exploration, patterns of trade began to change. Venice lost its monopoly of the spice trade, and the Portuguese opened up trading contacts in Asia. The centre of European trade gradually moved from the Mediterranean to the Atlantic. By the 17th century England and the United Provinces had become the dominant trading nations.

Industry

During the 15th and early 16th centuries the economic importance of industry was still limited. Few organisations employed large numbers of workers. There were some exceptions to this. The largest of all employers in Europe was the Arsenale, the shipbuilding yard in Venice that employed over 2,000 by the mid-1550s. At the same time the Tolfa alum mines near Rome employed over 700. The Grand Lease coalmines near Newcastle upon Tyne employed over 500 people by the early years of the 17th century. Most organisations were much smaller. Even the new tech-nology of printing offered less employment. The great Antwerp printing house of Plantin employed about 160 workers. Most printing operations were much smaller.

The organisation of industry changed during the period. In the late 15th century medieval craft guilds still enjoyed considerable prominence. In attempting to protect the incomes of their members, the guilds were, in practice, anti-capitalist. For larger-scale enterprises to thrive, the power of the guilds needed to be broken. Often this took place by means of employers setting up their enterprises outside the jurisdiction of town corporations and, therefore, outside the control of the guilds. This process was at its most intense in England, where manufacturing showed itself more flexible to the needs of the market than was often the case elsewhere, thereby helping to establish the basis for future economic dominance.

The emergence of international capitalism

The 16th and early 17th centuries witnessed the growth of an increasingly sophisticated economic system. This was dominated by the great banking dynasties of Augsburg, Genoa, Florence, Lucca and Antwerp. During the first half of the 16th century the dominant figures on the international financial stage were the Fuggers of Augsburg. Their original dominance grew out of their control of the Habsburg mining interests in the Austrian Tyrol and Hungary, originally secured in return for financing the wars of the future Emperor Maximilian in 1491. Banking, however, tended to be a fairly insecure activity, especially during the 16th century. Most banking operations were small and were extremely vulnerable to changes in the political and financial situation.

In order for international trade to flourish it was essential to develop bills of exchange which made it unnecessary to transport huge amounts of coinage from one place to another. The commercial organisation of these tended to be dominated either by exiled Italian bankers or by the Fuggers. There were several financial centres that developed to facilitate the exchange of such bills. The French Crown sought to profit from such business by encouraging the development of the fairs at Lyons. However, a rival set of 'Besançon' fairs were set up under Spanish auspices. Originally held in the Spanish-controlled region of Franche Comté, they were even-tually based in Piacenza in Italy, a city under the control of the dukes of Parma. These fairs supplemented the development of Antwerp, which for

1. In what respects were the patterns of trade and industry different c.1661 from what they had been c.1450?

2. Examine the principal characteristics of European capitalism by the middle of the 17th century?

much of the 16th century was the centre of sophisticated financial operations in Europe and where the first recognisable stock exchange originated. Arguably for the first time, huge fortunes could be made from speculative investment.

Although Antwerp's predominance declined following the financial crash of the 1550s, it nevertheless remained a city where substantial profits could be made in a variety of activities: including printing, textile manufacturing and metal-working, as well as financial services.

16.6 Why did witch-hunting become a prominent feature of society during the late 16th and early 17th centuries?

What factors promoted the emergence of witch-hunting in the late 15th century?

Though belief in the supposed reality of witches had existed for centuries in European popular culture, it was not until the early 15th century that the concept of witchcraft as a crime emerged on a significant scale. By that time the idea had taken hold that the individual, through unnatural sexual intercourse with the Devil, could acquire magic powers. Through the exercise of those powers the witch could engage in *maleficium*, the harming of one's neighbours or their property. By condoning and encouraging this belief, the educated élites could translate the popular belief in witches into serious criminal activity. The first significant persecution, motivated by religious reasons, was directed at the Waldensian heretics who lived in a remote Alpine region between Italy and France.

Official attitudes to witches, which were already hardening, were reinforced by two crucial developments in the 1480s.

● In 1484 Pope Innocent VIII issued a bull encouraging the pursuit of witches within the Holy Roman Empire.

● In 1486 two Dominican friars, Jacobus Sprenger and Heinrich Kramer, who had earlier drafted the papal bull, published a handbook for detecting witches, the *Malleus Maleficarum* ('The Hammer of Witches'), which was subsequently republished on numerous occasions.

The *Malleus Maleficarum* was important for two main reasons.

● It gave potential prosecutors clear guidance on how to investigate and prosecute witches, including arrangements for the use of torture.

● It established a range of characteristics that could demonstrate criminal activity. Female witches were likely to be more common than males because of the insatiable desire of women to seek sexual relationships with the Devil. The extent of the power of witches was established.

The powers of witches

1   To change human beings into the shapes of beasts.

2   To enter human bodies.

3   To inflict disease.

4   To kill children or offer them up to the Devil.

5   To injure animals.

6   To produce stormy weather in order to destroy crops or inflict personal injury.

Legal practice tended to make a distinction between two types of witchcraft.

● The widespread popular view that sorcery could be used as a means of attacking the community in general or those against whom a suspect might bear grudges in particular, for which convictions might be secured on the evidence of neighbours.

● Pacts with the Devil, which required a confession to secure proof and which, therefore, encouraged the use of torture.

Inquisitorial system: This was a process of investigation into witches – the adoption of which was likely, in most circumstances, to increase the chances of prosecution and conviction: by reducing the rights of the accused, by allowing judges to act on their own initiative, and by removing any punishment from an accuser who pressed false charges.

Brian Levack, in *The Witch-Hunt in Early Modern Europe* (1985), argues that legal developments during the period actually encouraged the process of witchcraft persecution. Firstly, the **inquisitorial system** of criminal procedure, which was widely adopted in continental Europe, made it easier for cases to be prosecuted. It was easier to secure conviction when courts had the right to use torture, which seems to have been used extensively in the Holy Roman Empire and in Scotland. The level of persecution was less marked in England, where common law procedures did not permit the use of torture except in treason cases.

Secondly, secular courts operating a local or regional jurisdiction – for example, in parts of the Holy Roman Empire and in Lorraine – tended to secure a higher number of convictions and executions than, say, courts, in England, which were operating within a national legal system. In France, the Parlement of Paris was less severe in its attitude to witches than were the provincial parlements.

1. What were the characteristics of the two main types of witchcraft?

2. What were the legal reasons for the emergence of witchcraft prosecution?

Why did the persecution of witches grow in importance?

It is impossible to state accurately the total number of witchcraft persecutions and executions. Nevertheless, it is clear that some estimates have been grossly exaggerated. Recent estimates have suggested that the total number of prosecutions for witchcraft during the 16th and 17th centuries was in the region of 111,000, about half of which took place within the Holy Roman Empire. The historian Brian Levack has suggested that the number of executions was in the region of 60,000; Robin Briggs, in *Witches and Neighbours* (1996) suggests that 'sober research' can only justify an estimate of 40,000 deaths.

A number of points have been put forward to explain the growth of persecution. However, none of these provides an adequate explanation. For each of the explanations, there are circumstances that prove exceptions to the rule. For example, changes in legal procedure help to explain the growth of persecution. Here the evidence is not absolutely conclusive. Those parts of the Holy Roman Empire, for example, which applied the

Imperial Code of Justice strictly, prosecuted far fewer witches than those which did not.

The religious changes and tensions of the period obviously played a part. Martin Luther and Jean Calvin, as well as militant Catholic reformers such as Peter Canisius, emphasised fear of the Devil in their writings. Keith Thomas argues, in *Religion and the Decline of Magic* (1971), that the campaigns of reformers against magic and medieval superstitious practices reinforced a witch-hunting mentality. Emphasis on literal interpretations of the Bible reinforced the message that 'thou shalt not suffer a witch to live' (Exodus 22:18). Certainly, witch-hunting seems to have been most intense in areas that contained large religious minorities or which adjoined neighbouring states dominated by another faith. This has led E. W. Monter to argue that prosecution of witches was an alternative to the prosecution of heretics. This was especially the case in western parts of the Holy Roman Empire.

Further backing to the witch-hunting cause was offered by writers as varied and as influential as Jean Bodin in his *Démonomanie des Sorciers* (1580) and King James VI of Scotland in his *Daemonologie* (1597).

Witch-hunting seems, on the whole, to have been more pronounced in Catholic than in Protestant societies. On the other hand, strongly Catholic societies like Spain and Italy were relatively free from witch-hunting. The best example of this concerns the attitude of the Inquisitor Alonso de Salazar, who investigated an outbreak of witch-hunting in the Spanish Basque country. In contrast to his counterparts over the French border, Salazar became convinced that the hysteria set off by witch-hunting produced false confessions. This led him to conclude that the concept of witchcraft was in itself non-existent. In the process, he brought to an end the Spanish Inquisition's connections with the persecution of witches; the Inquisition subsequently intervened with local jurisdictions in Spain to bring persecution to an end.

Attempts have been made to link witch-hunting with the Thirty Years' War. Persecutions, however, tended to take place in areas which had barely been touched by the conflict. Moreover, witch-hunting ceased once those areas became involved, for example, Lorraine and the Franche Comté.

The second half of the 16th century certainly witnessed a substantial increase in witch-hunting. In the 1580s it was especially bad in Switzerland and the Netherlands. It quickly died out in the Netherlands, which developed a tolerant and rational political culture. Dutch Calvinism began to perceive the Devil as a spiritual rather than a physical concept. Once this view was widely held among the political élites, witchcraft persecutions based on notions of diabolism (dealing with the Devil) died away.

By the end of the 16th century the centre of witch-hunting activity had moved to the Holy Roman Empire. There were 133 executions in one day in Quedlinburg (Germany) in 1589. There were also large-scale persecutions in the archbishopric of Trier in the later 1580s and 1590s, which can be clearly linked to the extreme attitude of the archbishop and his advisers. As Robin Briggs points out in *Witches and Neighbours*, 'their determination to stamp out witchcraft was so intense that judges and clerics who questioned the conduct of the persecution were themselves tortured into admissions of guilt and executed'. A similar situation occurred in the bishoprics of Bamberg and Würzburg in south-western Germany between 1627 and 1631. These German panics, in which the number of persecutions built until doubts set in, leading to the sudden collapse of the whole process, were not necessarily typical of the whole witch craze, but they were arguably the most extreme examples of witch-hunting. The authorities, in Robin Briggs's words, were 'carried away by the crazed logic of denunciations extracted by torture'.

1. What factors promoted the emergence of witchcraft as a frequently prosecuted crime?

2. In which areas, and when, was witch-hunting most popular?

Who were the witches?

1   Except in Russia, most accused witches were female. Of those accused in Scotland, for example, 86% were female. In south-western Germany the figure was 82%. Only Russia seems to have had a majority of male witches.

  ● Women were perceived to be morally and intellectually weaker than men and were therefore more likely to give in to the temptations of the Devil.

  ● Women were perceived as more sexually indulgent than men. According to the *Malleus,* 'all witchcraft comes from carnal lust, which is in women insatiable'. This, according to some educated opinion, was bound to lead to sexual pacts between the Devil and witches.

  ● Some customary female roles, such as cooks, healers and midwives, gave women the opportunity to practise harmful magic.

  ● In male-dominated society, women had much more difficulty in defending their interests than did men.

2   Many of those accused were relatively elderly by the standards of the time. Thus, 87% of accused witches in Essex whose ages were known were over 50. The figure in Geneva was 75%. Brian Levack has put forward a number of tentative explanations of this.

  ● Older women had often been the objects of mounting suspicion over the years.

  ● 'Wise women' and folk healers were usually elderly.

  ● Older people showing signs of senility could be more prone to anti-social behaviour which created hostility among neighbours.

  ● Older people were often perceived as being more likely to resort to sorcery.

  ● Older women, especially widows, were often seen as sexually predatory. Quite why the Devil should have been so attracted sexually to the elderly was never satisfactorily explained. However, widows and spinsters seem to have been particularly vulnerable to accusations.

3   The greater likelihood of accused witches being elderly did not mean that the young escaped completely. In Würzburg in Germany, for example, more than 25% of the executed witches between 1627 and 1629 were children.

4   Most accused witches came from the poorer sections of society. Often they were living on the margins of subsistence at a time when living standards among the rural poor were declining. Occasionally, relatively wealthy people were accused in the later stages of large-scale hunts.

5   Witches often had reputations for religious and moral deviance. Essentially, they were outcasts within their own society. Such attitudes were heavily criticised by the Elizabethan writer Reginald Scot, who denied the validity of the concept of witchcraft. Witches were 'commonly old, lame, blear-eyed, pale, foul and full of wrinkles … lean and deformed, showing melancholy in their faces to the horror of all that see them'. Witches, therefore, were used as scapegoats by their own communities.

1. What were the main variations in the pattern of persecution of witches?

2. Why were women more frequently the target of witchcraft persecution than men?

Why did witch-hunting subside?

After about 1650 European witch-hunting declined significantly. Witch-hunting still occurred in Scotland, Scandinavia, Poland and Russia, and there was a major witch-hunt in the colony of Massachusetts in 1692. Although popular witch beliefs survived for long afterwards, the level of prosecution declined significantly.

The most important factor in the decline of witch-hunting was the change in the mental outlook of most educated Europeans. Their more rational approach accepted that there could be natural explanations for misfortune, which need not necessarily have been caused by individuals in league with the Devil.

Also, the educated élites became less tolerant towards the superstitious beliefs of the lower orders.

Finally, judicial (legal) procedures began to change. Torture became less acceptable and the demand for more solid evidence made it more difficult to secure convictions.

16 .7 *What was the historical basis of witchcraft?*
A CASE STUDY IN HISTORICAL INTERPRETATION

Cults: Religious groups which worship a particular rituals, especially those whose beliefs and behaviour are considered strange, unnatural or harmful.

Sabbat: Special application of 'sabbath' – a midnight meeting of witches, deomns or sorcerers, presided over by the Devil, supposed to have been held annually as an orgy.

Anthropology: Scientific study of people, society and culture.

Historical explanations of the character of witchcraft have varied enormously. Some of them have had so little basis in historical reality that they have been described as 'hopelessly wrong' by one of the most recent historians of witchcraft, Robin Briggs in *Witches and Neighbours* (1996).

The French historian, Jules Michelet, writing in 1862, saw witchcraft as a politically subversive movement associated with **cults** of fertility. His views were dismissed by James Sharpe as 'the product of the romantic imagination of an ageing radical'. Michelet's views were reinforced by Murray, in *The Witch-Cult in Western Europe* (1921), and by her article in *Encyclopaedia Britannica*, for many years the most influential works on witchcraft. She argued that witches were worshippers, in opposition to Christianity, of the ancient pagan cult of the goddess Diana and that the witches' **sabbat** was a traditional fertility rite. Murray was one of the first writers to try to apply insights derived from **anthropology** to the study of witchcraft. Unfortunately, her sources were unsound and her weak theories were exposed by Norman Cohn in *Europe's Inner Demons*.

In the 1950s and 1960s attitudes to early-modern witchcraft were shaped by two historical developments: the Nazi extermination of Jews and the persecution of American left-wingers by Senator Joseph McCarthy and his associates. Witches were seen as scapegoats, though the extent and consistency with which they were scapegoated never approached that which applied to European Jews from 1941 to 1945.

More recently, historians have returned to anthropology to provide insights into the mental world of witches. Anthropological approaches were used by Keith Thomas in *Religion and the Decline of Magic* (1971) and by Alan Macfarlane in *Witchcraft in Tudor and Stuart England* (1970). Christina Larner's *Enemies of God: the Witch-Hunt in Scotland* (1981) moved towards a political interpretation of witchcraft, placing emphasis on the role of James VI and the Calvinist Church in promoting a culture of persecution. The recent growth in feminist perspectives in historical writing has been applied to witchcraft. Feminist writers have tried to explain why the majority of victims were female. Often, their explanations are over-simplified, though this is not the case of the Australian historian Lyndal Roper in *Oedipus and the Devil: Witchcraft, Sexuality and Religion in Early Modern Europe* (1994). She has subtly linked psychological and feminist perspectives. Individuals borrowed the images of witchcraft to express their own psychic conflicts. In *Witches and Neighbours* (1996), Robin Briggs has sought to revise some of the most commonly-held assumptions about the persecution of witches in the 16th and 17th centuries.

- Most witch persecutions arose from below.

- The range of victims was wider than the stereotype of the feeble, poor and elderly woman.

- Cunning folk, wise women and midwives were only rarely accused of being witches.

- Witch-hunting was, in reality, fairly rare. Religious warfare was responsible for far more deaths.

- Witch beliefs were essential to contemporary society. Men and women had a fear of evil magic and 'projected' the evil in their community on to more marginal members of the village community.

- There were few differences between the English and continental experience of witchcraft.

1. *Why have historians and other writers disagreed so frequently about the nature of witchcraft in the 16th and 17th centuries?*

2. *In what ways have traditional views about witch-hunting been revised by recent research?*

Source-based questions: the behaviour of witches

SOURCE A

When she had gotten these sheep, she desired to have one Andrew Byles to her husband, which was a man of some wealth, and the cat did promise that she should, but that she must first consent that this Andrew should abuse her, and so she did. And after, when this Andrew had thus abused her, he would not marry her, whereupon she willed Satan to waste his goods, which he forthwith did; and yet not being contented with this, she willed him to touch his body, whereof he died.

*From the confession of Elizabeth Francis,
Essex, 1566*

SOURCE B

And further, … the witch waxeth odious and tedious to her neighbours, and they again are despised and despited of her, so as sometimes she curseth one, and sometimes another, and that from the master of the house, his wife, children, cattle etc. to the little pig that lieth in the sty. Thus in process of time they have all displeased her, and she hath wished evil luck unto them all, perhaps with curses … Doubtless at length some of her neighbours die or fall sick, or some of their children are visited with diseases that vex them strangely …, which by ignorant parents are supposed to be the vengeance of witches … The witch, seeing things sometimes come to pass according to her wishes …, being called before a Justice, by due examination of the circumstances is driven to see her … desires and her neighbours' … losses to concur …; and so confesseth that she, as a goddess, hath brought such things to pass.

From The Discoverie of Witchcraft
by Reginald Scot, 1584

SOURCE C

[Jehennon Colin] came to beg alms …, but the witness, who was busy around her children and animals, replied that two of her daughters had been there just before, and that since she was not among the richer people she did not have the means to give so many alms. When Jehennon heard these words she went away very quickly. The witness, seeing her depart in this way, remembered the evil rumours and reputation she had of being a witch and, fearing some misfortune, took a bowl of milk and a piece of bread, with which she went out immediately, calling her several times to give her alms. But she turned a deaf ear, pretending not to hear, while the neighbouring women called out to the witness that she heard perfectly well but had no intention of responding, which was the reasons she was in great fear that some evil might befall her. [She lost a calf on the following day and her small son died some time later.]

*From a witness statement of Jehennon Gaultrin,
Lorraine, 1594*

SOURCE D

I am a witch. Ten years ago … I was … walking alone through the woods all dreaming and thoughtful that I had been so long a childless widow, and that my relatives discouraged me from remarrying, which I would have liked to do. When I arrived at the place of the round oak in the middle of the woods I was astonished and very frightened by the sight of a great black man who appeared to me. At first he said to me 'Poor woman, you are very thoughtful', and although I quickly recommended myself to St Nicolas he then suddenly threw me down, had intercourse with me, and at the same time pinched me roughly on the forehead. After this he said, 'You are mine. Have no regret; I will make you a lady and give you great wealth.' I knew in the same hour it was the evil spirit, but could not retract because he had instantly made me renounce God.

*From the interrogation of Catherine la Rondelette,
Lorraine, 1608*

---

1. Study Source B.

What does Source B reveal about the reasons for Scot's scepticism concerning the existence of witches?

2. Study Sources B and C.

How useful are these sources to a historian writing about social relationships among the poor in the late 16th century?

3. Study Sources A, C and D.

With reference to these sources, and to the information contained within this chapter, examine and explain the varying motives of three women accused of witchcraft?

4. Study all four sources and use information contained within this chapter. 'It is a mistake to see the persecution of witches as essentially directed and managed from below.'

How convincing is this claim?

Further Reading

**CHAPTER 2   The Renaissance and voyages of
discovery**

Texts designed for AS and A2 Level students

Renaissance Italy by Robert Hole (Hodder and
Stoughton, Access to History series, 1998)

The Renaissance by Alison Brown (Longman, Seminar
Studies in History series, 1988)

More advanced reading

Patronage in Renaissance Italy by Mary Hollingsworth
(John Murray, 1994)

The Renaissance by Peter Burke (Macmillan, 2nd edition,
1997)

The Art of the Renaissance by Peter and Linda Murray
(Thames and Hudson, 1963)

Art and Society in Italy, 1350–1500 by Evelyn Welch
(Oxford University Press, 1997)

Renaissance by George Holmes (Phoenix Illustrated,
1998)

A Concise Encyclopaedia of the Italian Renaissance edited
by Sir John Hale (Thames and Hudson, 1981)

CHAPTER 3   The Ottoman Empire

Texts designed for AS and A2 Level students

The Ottoman Empire 1450–1700 by Andrina Stiles
(Hodder and Stoughton, Access to History series,
1989)

The Ottoman Empire 1566–1617 by V. J. Parry
(Cambridge University Press, New Cambridge
Modern History series, 1968)

The Ottoman Empire 1520–1566 by V. J. Parry
(Cambridge University Press, New Cambridge
Modern History series, 1962)

Europe in the 16th Century by H. Koenigsberger and G.
Mosse (Longman, 1968)

More advanced reading

The Ottoman Empire 1300–1600 by Halil Inalcik
(Weidenfeld and Nicolson, 1973)

CHAPTER 4   The Reformation

Texts designed for AS and A2 Level students

Luther and the German Reformation, 1517–1555 by Keith
Randell (Hodder and Stoughton, Access to History
series, 1989)

John Calvin and the Later Reformation by Keith Randell
(Hodder and Stoughton, Access to History series,
1990)

Luther by Michael Mullett (Routledge, Lancaster
Pamphlets, 1986)

Calvin by Michael Mullett (Routledge, Lancaster
Pamphlets, 1989)

The German Reformation by Andrew Johnston
(Longman, Seminar Studies in History series, 1994)

More advanced reading

The German Reformation by R. W. Scribner (Macmillan,
1986)

Religious Thought in the Reformation by B. Reardon
(Longman, 1995)

**CHAPTER 5   The Holy Roman Empire under
Maximilian I and Charles V, 1493–1556**

Texts designed for AS and A2 Level students

The Emperor Charles V by Martyn Rady (Longman,
Seminar Studies in History series, 1988)

*Charles V: Ruler, Dynast and Defender of the Faith,
1500–58* by Stewart MacDonald (Hodder and
Stoughton, Access to History series, 1992)

The Renaissance Monarchies, 1469–1558 by Catherine
Mulgan (Cambridge University Press, Perspectives in
History series, 1998)

More advanced reading

Early Modern Germany, 1477–1806 by Michael Hughes
(Macmillan, 1992)

Reformation Europe, 1517–59 by Geoffrey Elton
(Fontana, 1963)

Charles V: Elected Emperor and Hereditary Ruler by
M. Fernández Alvarez (Thames and Hudson, 1975)

Article

'The Emperors Charles V and Ferdinand I' by Martyn
Rady in *History Sixth* (March 1991)

CHAPTER 6   Spain 1450–1566

Texts designed for AS and A2 Level students

Spain: Rise and Decline 1474–1643 by J. Kilsby (Hodder
and Stoughton, Access to History series, 1987)

Government and Society in Late Medieval Spain by Glyn
Redworth (Historical Association, New Perspectives
in History No. 31, 1993)

The Monarchies of Ferdinand and Isabella by J. Edwards
(Historical Association, New Perspectives in History
No. 36, 1996)

Spain in the Reigns of Isabella and Ferdinand, 1474–1516
by Geoffrey Woodward (Hodder and Stoughton,
Access to History series, 1997)

The Emperor Charles V by Martyn Rady (Longman,
Seminar Studies in History series, 1988)

More advanced reading

Golden Age Spain by Henry Kamen (Macmillan, 1988)

Spain 1469–1714: A society in conflict by Henry Kamen
(Longman, 2nd edition, 1991)

Spain under the Habsburgs Volume 1: Empire and
Absolutism 1516–1598 by John Lynch (Basil
Blackwell, 2nd edition, 1981)

Rebels and Rulers 1500–1600 by Perez Zagorin
(Cambridge University Press, 1982)

The Spanish Kingdoms Volume II (1410–1516) by
J. N. Hillgarth (Oxford University Press, 1978)

Imperial Spain 1469–1716 by J. H. Elliott (Arnold, 1963)
Ferdinand and Isabella by Felipe Fernandez-Armesto (1975)
The Golden Age of Spain 1516–1569 by Dominguez Ortiz (Weidenfeld and Nicolson, 1971)

Articles
'Isabella and Ferdinand of Spain A Reassessment' by Geoffrey Woodward in *History Review* No. 32, December 1998

CHAPTER 7   Renaissance France 1450–1559

Texts designed for AS and A2 Level students
France: Renaissance, Religion and Recovery 1494–1610 by Martyn Rady (Hodder and Stoughton, 1990)
French Renaissance Monarchy: Francis I and Henry II by R. J. Knecht (Longman, 1994)

More advanced reading
A History of France 1460–1560 by David Potter (Macmillan, 1995)
A History of Sixteenth Century France 1483–1598 by Janine Garrison (Macmillan, 1995)
The Rise and Fall of Renaissance France 1494–1610 by R. J. Knecht (Fontana, 1996)
Renaissance Warrior and Patron: The Reign of Francis I by R. J. Knecht (Cambridge University Press, 1994)
The Making of French Absolutism by D. Parker (Arnold, 1983)
Representative Government in Early Modern France by J. R. Major (Yale University Press, 1980)

CHAPTER 8   The Catholic or Counter Reformation

Texts designed for AS and A2 Level students
The Counter Reformation by Michael Mullett (Routledge, Lancaster Pamphlets, 1995)
The Catholic and Counter Reformation by Keith Randall (Hodder and Stoughton, Access to History Series, 1990)

More advanced reading
The Counter Reformation by A. G. Dickens (Thames and Hudson, 1969)
The Counter Reformation by P. Janelle (Collier Macmillan, 1971)

CHAPTER 9   Philip II of Spain 1556–1598

Texts designed for AS and A2 Level students
Spain: Rise and Decline 1474–1643 by Jill Kilsby (Hodder and Stoughton, Access to History series, 1987)
Philip II by Geoffrey Woodward (Longman, Seminar Studies in History series, 1992)
Habsburg and Bourbon Europe: 1470–1720 by Roger Lockyer (Longman, 1974)

More advanced reading
Philip of Spain by Henry Kamen (Yale University Press, 1997)
Early Habsburg Spain: 1517–1598 by A. W. Lovett (Oxford University Press, 1986)
Spain under the Habsburgs Volume I by John Lynch (Oxford University Press, 2nd edition, 1981)

Spain 1469–1714 by Henry Kamen (Longman, 2nd edition, 1991)
Philip II of Spain by Piers Pierson (Thames and Hudon, 1975)
The Golden Age of Spain 1516–1659 by Dominguez Ortiz (Weidenfeld, 1971)

CHAPTER 10   The Dutch Revolt

Texts designed for AS and A2 Level students
The Netherlands: Revolt and Independence by Marty Rady (Hodder and Stoughton, Access to History series, 1987)
The Dutch Revolt, 1559–1648 by Peter Limm (Longman, Seminar Studies in History series, 1989)

More advanced reading
The Dutch Revolt by Geoffrey Parker (Penguin, 1977)
'William the Silent and the Revolt of the Netherlands' by Koenrad Swart (Historical Association pamphlet, 1978)
The Dutch Republic: its Rise, Greatness and Fall, 1477–1806 by Jonathan Israel (Oxford University Press, 1995)

CHAPTER 11   The French Wars of Religion and the reign of Henry IV (1559–1610)

Texts designed for AS and A2 Level students
France: Renaissance, Religion and Recovery 1494–1610 by Martyn Rady (Hodder and Stoughton, Access to History series, 1990)
The French Wars of Religion 1559–1598 by R. J. Knecht (Longman, Seminar Study in History series, 1989)
'Catherine de' Medici and the Ancien Regime' by N. Sutherland (Historical Association pamphlet, 1966)

More advanced reading
The French Wars of Religion 1562 to 1629 by Mack Holt (Cambridge University Press, 1995)
A History of Sixteenth Century France 1483–1598 by Janine Garrisson (Macmillan, 1995)
Catherine de' Medici by R. J. Knecht (Longman, 1998)
The Rise and Fall of Renaissance France 1483–1610 by R. J. Knecht (Fontana, 1996)
Myths about the St Bartholomew's Day Massacre by R. M. Kingdom (Yale University Press, 1988)

CHAPTER 12   The rise of Sweden in the 16th and early 17th centuries

Texts designed for AS and A2 Level students
Sweden and the Baltic, 1523–1721 by Andrina Stiles (Hodder and Stoughton, Access to History series, 1992)
The Struggle for Supremacy in the Baltic by Jill Lisk (University of London Press, 1966)

More advanced reading
Gustavus Adolphus and the Rise of Sweden by Michael Roberts (English University Press, 1973)
The Swedish Imperial Experience by Michael Roberts (Cambridge University Press, 1973)

CHAPTER 13   The decline of Spain? 1598–1659

Texts designed for AS and A2 Level students

Spain Rise and Decline: 1474–1643 by Jill Kilsby (Hodder and Stoughton, Access to History series, 1987)

Spain in the 17th Century by Graham Darby (Longman, Seminar Studies in History series, 1994)

Articles

'Early Modern Spain: The Difficulties of Empire' by Henry Kamen in *History Sixth* (2), 1998

'The Decline of Spain' by Geoffrey Parker in *History Today*, April 1984

'Philip IV and the Decline of Spain' by R. A Stradling in *History Today*, March 1981

More advanced reading

Spain 1469–1714 by Henry Kamen (Longman, 2nd edition, 1991)

The Hispanic World in Crisis and Change 1598–1700 by John Lynch (Blackwell, 1992)

Philip IV and the Government of Spain by R. A. Stradling (Cambridge University Press, 1988)

Spain and its World, 1500–1700 by J. H. Elliott (Yale University Press, 1986)

CHAPTER 14 France 1610–1661

Texts designed for AS and A2 Level students

The First Bourbon Century in France by W. E. Brown (University of London Press, 1971)

Early Modern France by Robin Briggs (Oxford University Press, 1977)

France and the Cardinals by R. Wilkinson (Hodder and Stoughton, Access to History series, 1995)

More advanced reading

The Birth of Absolutism: France 1598–1661 by Y-M Berce (Macmillan, European Studies series, 1996)

Cardinal Richelieu by J. Bergin (Yale University Press, 1985)

Mazarin by G. R. Treasure (Routledge, 1995)

Richelieu by R. J. Knecht (Longman, 1991)

CHAPTER 15   The Thirty Years' War

Texts designed for AS and A2 Level students

The Thirty Years War by Stephen J. Lee (Routledge, Lancaster Pamphlet, 1991)

The Thirty Years War by Peter Limm (Longman, Seminar Studies in History series, 1984)

More advanced reading

Europe in Crisis, 1598–1648 by Geoffrey Parker (Fontana, 1979)

The Thirty Years' War edited by Geoffrey Parker (Routledge, 2nd edition, 1997)

Early Modern Germany, 1477–1806 by Michael Hughes (Macmillan, 1992)

CHAPTER 16   Social and economic history

Texts designed for AS and A2 Level students

Years of renewal: European History 1470–1600 edited by John Letherington (Hodder and Stoughton, 1988)

More advanced reading

The European Dynastic States, 1494–1660 by Richard Bonney (Oxford University Press, 1991)

European Society, 1500–1700 by Henry Kamen (Hutchinson, 1984)

Witchcraft and Magic in 16th and 17th Century Europe by Geoffrey Scarre (Macmillan, 1987)

The Witch Hunt in Early Modern Europe by Brian Levack (Longman, 1985)

Witches and Neighbours by Robin Briggs (HarperCollins, 1996)

Index